LEGAL NEGOTIATIONS

Getting Maximum Results

Mark K. Schoenfield
Partner Torshen, Schoenfield & Spreyer, Ltd., Chicago
Member of the Illinois Bar

Rick M. Schoenfield
Partner Ettinger & Schoenfield, Ltd., Chicago
Member of the Illinois Bar

SHEPARD'S/McGRAW-HILL, INC.
P.O. Box 1235
Colorado Springs, Colorado 80901

McGraw-Hill Information Services Company
New York • St. Louis • San Francisco • Auckland • Bogotá
Caracas • Colorado Springs • Hamburg • Lisbon • London
Madrid • Mexico • Milan • Montreal • New Delhi • Oklahoma City
Panama • Paris • San Juan • São Paulo • Singapore • Sydney
Tokyo • Toronto

1234567890 SHCU 897654321098

Library of Congress Cataloging-in-Publication Data
Schoenfield, Mark K.
    Legal negotiations : getting maximum results / Mark K.
  Schoenfield, Rick M. Schoenfield.
        p.   cm.
    Bibliography: p.
    Includes index.
    ISBN 0-07-049304-9
    1. Practice of law—United States.   2. Attorney and client—United
  States.   3. Negotiation.   I. Schoenfield, Rick M.   II. Title.
  KF300.S36   1988
  349.73'023—dc19
  [347.30023]   88-37958
                                                                    CIP

ISBN 0-07-049304-9

The sponsoring editor for this book was Mary Kay LaRue and the legal editor
was Susan Wessel.

To Barbara, Laura, and Jeffrey, for their fairness in negotiating and, most of all, for their love.

MKS

To Bobbi.

RMS

And to our parents.

MKS & RMS

Acknowledgments

Mark K. Schoenfield acknowledges the influence of the following persons on his thoughts about negotiation: Jerry Torshen, Jim Seckinger, Lou Cohn, Melissa Nelken, Rick Green, Jack Heinz, Andy Gordon, Jon Waltz, the late Bob Childress, and those lawyers, business professionals, and executives who have been teaching team members and participants at the many negotiation programs taught by him.

Rick M. Schoenfield acknowledges learning from working with Joe Ettinger, and from the following present and past members of Northwestern's clinical teaching program: Tom Geraghty, Diane Geraghty, Steve Lubet, and Mark Schoenfield.

Preface

While negotiations vary widely, attorneys consistently confront problems and issues concerning negotiating methods and techniques. Whether novice or experienced, the lawyer must grapple with a series of questions that determine whether optimal results will be achieved. For example, he or she must determine how best to:

Maintain credibility

Persuade

Decide whether to confront or cooperate

Obtain information and reduce uncertainty

Plan creatively, efficiently, and effectively

Properly identify client goals

Counsel the client to create understanding

Obtain clear authority from a satisfied client

Use and respond to emotional appeals or pressures

Choose and implement strategies and tactics from a wide range of available alternatives, rather than from only a few used from habit or lack of knowledge

Understand the dynamics of the process

Push for optimal results, and yet close deals and settlements beneficially

Structure and draft agreements to achieve client goals and protect or improve gains made during the negotiation

Having knowledge to answer these questions properly leads to increased effectiveness and improved negotiation outcomes. Lack of this knowledge not only decreases the negotiator's effectiveness, but also adds to the difficulty, tension, stress, and uncertainty inherent in negotiations.

Legal Negotiations: Getting Maximum Results is designed to present comprehensive, readily usable approaches to all aspects of negotiating, and to improve negotiating skills of both novice and highly experienced negotiators. The materials are not aimed merely at separating the forest from the trees, but rather at identifying methods for prevailing in an array of forests and rocky terrain, and anticipating and avoiding pitfalls. It is a book for lawyers, although most of the material is equally applicable to business professionals and entrepreneurs, as well as other professionals who negotiate.

Legal Negotiations begins with an introduction and orientation to the dynamics of the negotiation process and basic guidelines for negotiating effectively. Chapter 2 explains how to identify and define client goals. The third chapter details the nine key strategies and countermeasures. In the next four chapters, 52 useful tactics are examined, as well as tactical countermeasures. Chapters 8 and 9 contain structured steps for proper planning, an often overlooked, yet critical, factor. Techniques for persuasive communication and eliciting information are explored in Chapter 10. The next chapter explains methods for drafting agreements, and practical ethical considerations are reviewed in Chapter 12. After each chapter, a summary and review assists the reader in integrating the material. In addition, a detailed Appendix provides a working guide for use in actual negotiations.

Using these methods, lawyers and other negotiators can improve their skills, understanding, power, control, and results.

All entities and persons in the examples are fictitious, and do not depict any living or deceased person, or any entity.

Contents

The Optimal Approach to Negotiating

1

§1.01 Introduction

Most lawyers recognize the importance of negotiations in their lives. They spend a substantial part of their professional time negotiating. In addition, like everyone else, they also negotiate in their personal lives.[1] An attorney's real effectiveness as a professional is heavily influenced by his or her negotiating skill, or lack of it. How he or she is perceived by clients and other lawyers is greatly affected by this skill or the lack of it. Most matters, whether they are transactional or adversarial, are resolved by negotiation.[2] However, few lawyers (or nonlawyers, for that matter) fully understand the art and science of negotiation.[3]

---

[1] Menkel-Meadow, *Legal Negotiation: A Study of Strategies in Search of a Theory*, 4 Am B Found Res J 905, 908 (1983). H. Cohen, You Can Negotiate Anything 15-16 (1982).

[2] S. Goldberg, E. Green & F. Sander, Dispute Resolution 19 (1985) [hereinafter Goldberg]; H. Cohen, *supra* note 1; Menkel-Meadow, *supra* note 1.

[3] In studying negotiations in the context of social psychology, it has been suggested that pertinent topics from social psychology include utility theory, social judgment theory, influence theory, social facilitation theory, coalition theory, and the relative effects of the person and the situation, and that significant variables affecting a negotiation can include the objectives, incentives, strategies, tactics, role reversal, conference size, complexity of the issues, accountability to the negotiators' constituencies, and stresses and

Virtually everyone, though, recognizes the uncertainty that is present in negotiations. Uncertainty and lack of control are the two key factors which often can make negotiating a difficult, frustrating, anxiety-filled, and stressful endeavor. The lawyer may be uncertain about questions such as:

1. What does the client really want to achieve?
2. What is it realistically possible to achieve?
3. What does the other party really want?
4. What is the other negotiator really seeking?
5. What are the best means to influence the other party and its negotiator?

The uncertainty and lack of control are compounded by the many factors that can lead to negotiations which fail to achieve their objectives. These include:[4]

1. Lack of a sufficient understanding of the negotiating process
2. Inadequate prenegotiation information gathering
3. Improper analysis and planning
4. Ineffective communication
5. Lack of knowledge about and ability to use a broad range of strategies and tactics
6. Becoming lost if a lack of movement or a deadlock occurs
7. Inadvertently being placed in a position or placing another in a position where compromise is impossible without a loss of face
8. Parties allowing emotions to govern decisions due to a failure to counsel properly
9. Differing opinions by the parties, due to their possessing different information to the disadvantage of both
10. Unrealistic client expectations
11. Habitually negotiating with only one style
12. Linking multiple matters together
13. Having bottom line positions that do not overlap to form an area of potential agreement, or have very little overlap, because of miscalculations of benefits, detriments, and risks

The goals of the authors are to assist negotiators in:

1. Reducing their levels of uncertainty, stress, and anxiety
2. Increasing their degree of control and efficiency

---

tensions involved in the negotiation. D. Druckman, Negotiations: Social-Psychological Perspectives 20 (1977).

[4] Goldberg, *supra* note 2, at 88.

3. Improving and maximizing their negotiating results

These goals can be achieved through a readily implemented negotiation approach to improve perceptions, analysis, and communications abilities, while providing a flexible system for choosing from a full spectrum of strategies and tactics. These strategies and tactics encompass a wide variety of techniques and methods, including the use of power, competitiveness, persuasion, bargaining, cooperation, problem solving, and combinations, so that counsel can effectively adapt to any situation and achieve the optimal results possible in terms of the client's goals and the realities of the situation.[5] This will benefit anyone who negotiates serious matters. "Knowledge plus skills plus self esteem equals competence."[6]

Of course, all of the problems in negotiations cannot be totally eliminated. Any such promise would be false. But the problems can be significantly curtailed and performance can be markedly improved through an increased understanding of the negotiation process and of the best means by which the negotiator can influence outcomes. This understanding will be presented in a form which then can be successfully and practically implemented. The starting point for this increased understanding and the ability to implement it successfully is the consideration of the very process of negotiation. This is a basic premise for optimal negotiating.

§1.02 Negotiation as a Process

Negotiation is a process through which parties determine whether an acceptable agreement can be reached. It is far more than just a series of offers and counteroffers. It is not merely a choice between being competitive or cooperative. Rather, negotiation is the process through which information is exchanged, evaluated, and used as the basis for decisions about whether to agree at a given point or at all.

Effective negotiation entails the controlled gathering and exchange of a wide variety of information to assess the parties and the potential for agreement. This information includes the parties':

1. Positions
2. Needs
3. Interests
4. Goals

To the extent that a negotiator's personal position can influence the process, the information also includes the personal interests, needs, and goals of the negotiator.

---

[5] See Menkel-Meadow, *supra* note 1, regarding the general approaches to the study of negotiation.

[6] T. Warschaw, Winning By Negotiation 18 (McGraw-Hill, Inc 1980).

Information must be obtained effectively and efficiently, as well as disclosed selectively and persuasively. By doing so, counsel's effect on the process is maximized. Disclosures may be verbal or nonverbal, through word or by action. There are many strategies and tactics that can be used to gather and convey facts, arguments, offers, and positions. By systematically planning and analyzing that information to understand the needs, interests, and goals of the parties and their negotiators, counsel can determine the best means to advise his or her own client and to motivate the other party to move in the desired direction. With authorization from the client after proper counseling, counsel can choose from a wide range of strategies and tactics to fit the situation and the participants and thereby maximizes the odds of achieving optimal results.

Negotiation is a highly dynamic process. The parties and their negotiators begin the process by separately assessing their needs, interests, and goals in order to determine their positions. They take into account any relevant market factors for monetary and other terms. During their interaction in negotiating, however, those assessments can and usually do change. The parties receive new information. One party makes the first offer, and tentative conclusions are confirmed or contradicted. Usually there is a series of offers and counteroffers. Decisions must be made to remain with or to alter positions and plans. The parties convey messages through oral and written communications. There is acceptance and rejection. All of this provides information to be evaluated and properly categorized. Some unknowns are always present, although astute negotiators have techniques to minimize the unknowns and the degree of uncertainty. It is this dynamic, shifting nature of negotiation that in large part makes it difficult and complex.

Negotiations involve not only substantive matters, but also the method of negotiation,[7] so there will also be communication about procedure. By viewing negotiations as a process of controlled information exchanges, a negotiator can become more effective. Failures to gather, disclose, withhold, and fully consider information will be minimized. Instead, the negotiator will focus on and use opportunities to create better results.

§1.03   The Effective Negotiator

Negotiation is necessarily an interpersonal process.[8] The most effective negotiators tend to have certain types of skills and abilities that lead to achieving optimal results. These are listed below in the order that they emerge in the process of negotiating.

1.   Being in control of one's self
2.   The ability to elicit the client's needs, interests, and goals
3.   Properly counseling the client regarding the situational realities

---

[7] R. Fisher & W. Ury, Getting to Yes, Negotiating Agreement Without Giving In 10 (1981); H. Cohen, You Can Negotiate Anything 154 (1982).

[8] G. Bellow & B. Moulton, The Lawyering Process 443-44 (1978).

4. Obtaining clear authority from the client

5. Understanding and being able to utilize the full range of effective strategies and tactics

6. Planning efficiently

7. Being credible

8. Perceptively analyzing the other party and its negotiator

9. Being able to tolerate conflict and ambiguity[9]

10. Knowing or learning the relevant market factors

11. Disclosing information selectively and persuasively

12. Obtaining necessary information

13. Listening and perceiving the real information being conveyed

14. Making changes in strategy, tactics, or counseling of the client regarding terms, as becomes appropriate during the negotiation

15. Being both patient and relentless

16. Knowing when and how either to close the negotiation with an agreement, or to terminate it because a desirable agreement cannot be reached[10]

One view of the characteristics of an effective negotiator in order of their importance can be seen below. The rating was done through a survey of senior lending officers.[11]

1. Preparation and planning skill

2. Knowledge of subject matter being negotiated

3. Ability to think clearly and rapidly under pressure and uncertainty

4. Ability to express thoughts verbally

5. Listening skill

6. Judgment and general intelligence

7. Integrity

8. Ability to persuade others

9. Patience

10. Decisiveness

---

[9] C. Karrass, Give & Take: The Complete Guide to Negotiating Strategies and Tactics 87 (1974).

[10] Some efforts have been made in the field of social psychology to study the effects of various personality characteristics on negotiating behavior. These personality characteristics include anxiety, authoritarianism, cognitive complexity, tendency toward conciliation, dogmatism, risk avoidance, self-esteem, and suspiciousness. Hermann & Kogan, *Effects Of Negotiators' Personalities On Negotiating Behavior,* in D. Druckman, Negotiations: Social-Psychological Perspectives (1977).

[11] H. Raiffa, The Art and Science of Negotiation 119 (1982).

11. Ability to earn respect and confidence of opponent

12. General problem solving and analytic skills

13. Self-control, especially of emotions and their visibility

14. Insight into other's feelings

15. Persistence and determination

16. Ability to perceive and exploit available power to achieve objective

17. Insight into hidden needs and reactions of own and opponent's organization

18. Ability to lead and control members of own team or group.[12]

Methods to achieve these characteristics of an effective negotiator, or to improve in these areas, will be covered in the sections that follow. These will explore and explain how to enhance one's skills and performance.

§1.04   The Role of the Client

Counsel and client should form a team.[13] The client makes the ultimate decision about those terms which must be minimally met in order to make an agreement worthwhile. Those necessary terms constitute the bottom line which counsel must achieve, and the outer limits of counsel's negotiating authority. These limits must be clearly understood by both the attorney and the client. To the extent that the attorney has special knowledge or particular insights, counsel should advise the client regarding the appropriate bottom line position. The final decision, however, must be that of the client.

In general, the choice of strategy and tactics is that of the lawyer. As a professional negotiator, and the person directly involved in the negotiation, the lawyer generally is the most knowledgeable about the negotiation and has the best feel for the negotiating situation. This places the attorney in the best position to make the necessary strategic and tactical decisions.

There are, however, certain situations in which the client should have significant input or should make strategic or tactical decisions. These exceptions exist whenever:

1. The choice of a strategy or of a tactic may itself directly impact on the business or personal life of the client, apart from the ultimate resolution of the negotiation

2. The client is a sophisticated negotiator and is directly involved in the negotiation process[14]

---

[12] *Id.*

[13] The literature on legal negotiations has been criticized for underemphasizing the significance of the role of the client. Menkel-Meadow, *Legal Negotiation: A Study of Strategies in Search of a Theory,* 4 Am B Found Res J 905, 930 (1983).

[14] The client may or may not be sophisticated in other ways. Other forms of sophistication must not be confused with sophistication with respect to negotiations.

By establishing a team approach, the negotiator can utilize his or her training and skills while maximizing the client's satisfaction with the negotiating process. The client is able to make informed decisions and to feel important and involved. The client's role will be examined further in the chapters on goals and planning.[15]

§1.05 Conflict: Negotiators Who Love It or Hate It Too Much

Negotiations inevitably involve a degree of conflict. The degree of conflict is determined by a combination of:

1. The extent of the differences between the parties' positions; and

2. The personalities and the personal styles of the negotiators

Of all of the flaws that any negotiator may have, the single most devastating one is to be averse to conflict. While conflict can be less than pleasant, some negotiators are so intensely averse to it that it clouds their judgment and seriously lowers their level of performance.

Those who are so averse to conflict become uncomfortable with and, consciously or unconsciously, fear negotiations and concede, rather than stand up to conflict. People fear negotiation who identify it with "strife, conflict, anxiety, the possibility of losing, pressure, being dominated, and being coerced."[16] They identify it with negatives, rather than with the positive possibilities it presents.

To ameliorate being averse to conflict, the first step is self-realization and acknowledgment. One must recognize the problem. Step two is an improved understanding of the negotiation process, and of all of the tools which a negotiator can use to deal with conflict. These tools are planning, strategy, tactics, and communication skills. The third step is a determined implementation of this increased knowledge.[17]

A different flaw is presented by those who seem to thrive on conflict. These people seek out or create conflict for reasons known only to them. These negotiators can undermine their own efforts, since creating unnecessary conflict can be seriously counterproductive.

Those who seem to thrive on conflict should strive to modify their behavior as well, so that they restrict their desire for conflict to those situations in which it is required or appropriate, such as where intimidation or the exercise of

---

[15] *See* **chs 2, 8, & 9.**

[16] T. Warschaw, Winning By Negotiation 2 (McGraw-Hill, Inc 1980).

[17] If these three steps are not successful, the attorney may have such a deeply rooted emotional problem with conflict that some form of therapy will be necessary to deal with the problem. Often, however, these three steps will provide the key to unlock the counsel's true negotiating potential.

power best achieves the client's goals. They should follow the same three steps as those recommended for persons who are averse to conflict.[18]

Effective negotiators fit into neither of the above categories. Rather, they are willing to avoid, create, minimize, or maximize conflict where appropriate, and they have the skill to do it. For them, decisions regarding conflict are based solely on the long-run and short-run effects these decisions will have on the ultimate goal of the negotiation.

§1.06   The Optimal Approach

Creating a system that is applicable to and which can be utilized in any negotiation requires both structure and flexibility. The chapters that follow provide an opportunity for learning this system, with its full range of options, through a step-by-step procedure.

Chapter 2 concerns the client's goal(s). Since those goals form the basis of the negotiation, they are the natural starting point. The analysis of clients' goals and how they form the basis for effective negotiation leads directly to the analysis of potential strategies, presented in Chapter 3. A strategy establishes the negotiator's general approach in the negotiation. The discussion of strategy is followed by four chapters regarding tactics. While strategy concerns broad decisions, tactics are the various maneuvers through which the negotiator implements the strategy of choice. A wide and varied range of tactics is presented, because each works well in some negotiations or parts of negotiations, and poorly at other times. While most negotiators have a few strategies and tactics that they are aware of and feel comfortable using, the most effective negotiators tend to employ the complete spectrum of strategies and tactics over the course of various negotiations.

Chapters 8 and 9 concern planning the negotiation. Planning encompasses a blending together of the analysis of goals, strategies, and tactics.

Communications skills are essential in negotiating optimal results. After the discussion on planning, Chapter 10 will explore the skills involved in both the disclosure of information and the receiving of information.

Next, drafting techniques and methods are analyzed. Aside from the ever-narrowing situations in which oral agreements are utilized, a lack of drafting skills can lose earlier hard-won negotiating gains.

Finally, Chapter 12 will consider various ethical considerations and problems in the field of negotiation. Negotiators are expected to be honest in their factual statements, yet they are expected to puff and to conceal some of their knowledge.[19] The tension between these requirements gives rise to ethical issues that are implicit in the negotiating process.

These negotiation methods, techniques, and insights can improve one's negotiating arsenal by providing a more complete command of the many ways

---

[18] These steps will often be helpful. If they are not and a desire for conflict interferes with the use of appropriate negotiation methods, an emotional problem may exist which requires some form of therapy.

[19] W. Fallon, AMA Management Handbook 5-48 (1983).

to control and affect the negotiating process. The technical, multi-layered nature of the material is deliberate. Simplistic views of negotiations, even if correct on occasion, can have only limited effectiveness. Given the wide range of situations, needs, interests, goals, and possibilities that are faced by professional negotiators, such simplistic views often will be inapplicable, inaccurate, and ineffective. Truly enhanced negotiating performance flows from understanding the numerous complexities that can arise, and the various means to deal with them.

§1.07 Summary and Review

I. Negotiation is a dynamic process of exchanging information to decide whether to agree and, if so, the optimal terms for agreement

II. Counsel should form a team with the client

III. The client is the ultimate decision maker on whether to agree to proposed terms

IV. The lawyer counsels the client and chooses the strategies and tactics except when a strategy or tactic itself will directly impact the client's life or when the client is himself or herself a sophisticated negotiator actively involved in the negotiation process

V. Effective negotiators are neither averse to conflict nor do they thrive on it

VI. Effective negotiators avoid, create, minimize, or maximize conflict as appropriate to achieve the client's goals in both the long run and the short run

Client Goals

2

§2.01 Introduction

Before selecting one or more strategies and tactics, the nature of the client's goal or, more usually, goals, must be analyzed. The nature of a client's goal can influence that choice, since some strategies and tactics are more appropriate and useful for certain goals than for other goals.[1] This chapter will explore various methods to analyze and to classify client goals. In the next chapter, various strategies and their relationship to client goals will be explained. Chapters 4, 5, 6, and 7 then will discuss tactics, including the relationship of tactics to the various strategies dictated by the client's goals.

The client's goals are those tangibles or intangibles which the client must achieve, as well as those which, though not essential, the client wishes to achieve. Thus, the two primary categories of client goals are *essential* goals and *desired* goals. It is important to separate client goals into these categories, since

---

[1] Menkel-Meadow, *Legal Negotiation: A Study of Strategies in Search of a Theory*, 4 Am B Found Res J 905, 922-23 (1983). Menkel-Meadow states that: "In my view, studies of negotiation should begin with assessments of purpose and goals, because the lawyer's and client's goals and purposes in particular kinds of cases may greatly affect the way in which the negotiation is conducted in terms of options, solutions, and behaviors." *Id* 923.

essential goals are "deal killers" unless they are achieved, while *desired* goals determine how good a deal is, as well as, at times, which party's offer should be accepted.

Client goals may appear to be objective or subjective. The personal worth of the goal to the client, however, always has a degree of subjectivity based on the client's "values, needs, feelings, and experiences."[2] For this reason, the lawyer may need to explore, with the client, the value placed on the goal. If the subjective and objective values greatly differ, the goal's value to the rest of the world or to certain others may be compared to the value initially placed on it by the client. In this way, the client's final decision on value is made after receiving full information.

The initial client interview should include eliciting the client's goals.[3] If the attorney is the client's regular counsel, or if the attorney has handled similar matters for that client in the past, the attorney may already be familiar with certain aspects of the client's goals. Even so, counsel should confirm his or her understanding of those goals with the client to ensure that the goals have not changed. With clients who are well known to counsel, a very informal confirmation through casual conversation can be appropriate. For less well-known clients, a more exacting confirmation is useful to guard against misinterpretation.

The only exception to the requirement that client goals be confirmed each time would be a series of transactions or matters that are part of an overall or similar group occurring at approximately the same time, although perhaps involving multiple other parties. Even so, the best practice is to explicitly ask the client if the same goals apply to each transaction or matter in the apparent group.

Client goals encompass a wide range of both tangible and intangible desires.[4] Examples include:

Obtaining a particular piece of property

Selling a particular piece of property

Receiving the highest possible price

Paying the lowest possible price

Maintaining a business or personal relationship

Improving a relationship

---

[2] R. Lewicki & J. Litterer, Negotiation 9 (1985).

[3] M. Schoenfield & B. Pearlman Schoenfield, Interviewing and Counseling xxi (1981); D. Binder & S. Price, Legal Interviewing and Counseling: A Client-Centered Approach (1977); T. Shaffer, Legal Interviewing and Counseling (1976).

[4] The client's goal(s) may be affected by the client's psychological motives, including rationalization, projection, displacement (taking out emotions directed towards one person on another person), repression, reaction-formation (unconsciously repressing a feeling and then acting in a manner that is the opposite of the repressed drive), self-image, and role playing. G. Nierenberg, The Art of Negotiating: Psychological Strategies for Gaining Advantageous Bargains 37 (1968).

Developing a relationship with a new customer or supplier

Gaining respect from others

Avoiding the loss of another's respect

Causing someone else to lose the respect of others

Taking a supplier or customer away from a competitor in order to hurt the competitor

Preventing a strike

Punishing an opponent

Structuring a settlement for greater total dollars to the plaintiff with fewer immediate dollars from the defendant

Gaining vindication

Forming a business entity to engage in a new venture for a mutual gain

Obtaining financing

Restructuring financing

Receiving favorable publicity

Avoiding unfavorable publicity

Causing unfavorable publicity for another

Obtaining more favorable publicity than another

Resolving a dispute

Receiving tax benefits without expenses for the other party

A list of all client goals would be virtually endless. These particular examples were chosen to indicate the wide variety of client goals, and will be used to illustrate and to explain the categories of client goals used in the analysis which follows. Although some client goals have certain similarities, important distinctions exist between categories of goals which in turn affect the negotiator's choice of strategy and tactics.

Even within the limited number of client goals contained in the examples, patterns begin to emerge that lead to certain categories. In order to be in a position to decide which strategies and tactics may be the most useful for a particular negotiation, the negotiator first must classify client goals into one or more of six categories. These are:

1.   Aggressive client goals (**§2.02**)

2.   Competitive client goals (**§2.03**)

3.   Cooperative client goals (**§2.04**)

4.   Self-centered client goals (**§2.05**)

5.   Defensive client goals (**§2.06**)

6.   Combinations of client goals (**§2.07**)[5]

§2.02   Aggressive Client Goals

Aggressive client goals are those which seek to undermine, deprive, damage, or otherwise injure a rival or an opponent.[6] The client's focus is *not* on the client's own result, but rather it is on the effect on the targeted party. Aggressive client goals may even result in an economic loss for the client, at least in the short run. In such instances, however, the damage to the other party provides the desired gain. The motivation may be revenge for past deeds, including prior negotiations, or may reflect what the client perceives to be its long-term interests.

The client goals listed in the above examples included several illustrating aggressive client goals. They are:

Taking a customer or supplier away from a competitor in order to hurt the competitor

Causing someone else to lose the respect of others, resulting in a business loss, personal unhappiness, or both

Precipitating unfavorable publicity for another, leading to a loss of customers for a business or votes for a candidate

Punishing an opponent, such as bringing suit, in part, to teach the other party that adverse actions will result in costly and time-consuming consequences

The client's targeting of an aggressive goal may be logical in a business sense of economic cost-benefit analysis. It also may be a deeply emotional decision due to anger or hurt feelings. Provided that it is made as a fully informed choice, an attorney should respect an economically unwise but emotionally satisfying client goal. However, legal counseling may be necessary to ensure that the client's choice is an informed one.

If the client's decision is an intensely emotional one, the client may or may not be able or willing to discuss the true reasons for the decision, especially if it is relatively soon after whatever event precipitated the client to seek counsel in order to achieve the emotional goal. The emotional factor may still be too high and intense. When the client is unable or unwilling to discuss his or her

---

[5] Maximizing the other's results has also been suggested as a possible, although less common, client goal. McClintock, *Social Motivation in Settings of Outcome Interdependence*, in D. Druckman, Negotiations: Social-Psychological Perspectives 57 (1977). Druckman and McClintock refer to this as altruism. Using game theory, they also suggest the motivational categories of cooperation (maximizing joint results), individualism (maximizing one's own results), competition (maximizing the difference between one's own results and another's results), and aggression (minimizing the other's results).

[6] In game theory, aggression is viewed as seeking to minimize the other's results. McClintock, *Social Motivation in Settings of Outcome Interdependence*, in D. Druckman, Negotiations: Social-Psychological Perspectives 57 (1977).

true feelings and reasons, the client may instead present apparently logical reasons which, in reality, are rationalizations to justify the desired course of action. In addition, the client may not be able to really hear and absorb the advice offered.

Over time, however, such a client may become more willing to recognize and to discuss the real motivation or to listen to advice that places the matter in perspective. In addition, the anger or hurt may lessen as time passes, so that the client is no longer as strongly committed to pursuing the matter in as aggressive a fashion. Thus, it is especially important for lawyers to occasionally, indirectly or directly, probe clients in this situation, to determine whether their willingness to discuss their motivation or their ability to discuss acceptable solutions has changed.

In the end, the informed decision of the client to choose between objective and subjective factors governs, regardless of whether the client continues to favor the emotionally based decision. After all, it is the client's life, and not that of the lawyer.

These guidelines for counseling clients have been presented in the context of emotional client goals because that type of goal tends to involve highly charged emotions more than other goals. However, the same guidelines apply to any client goal when it is a product of intense and perhaps blinding emotional reactions.

§2.03   Competitive Client Goals

A competitive client goal is one in which the client seeks to gain more from the negotiation than the other party receives.[7] In fact, the client hopes to obtain as large a comparative advantage as possible.[8] Thus, there is a direct negative correlation between competitive parties' achieving their goals.[9] More to one party means less to the other, and each party seeks to attain as much as possible. Examples of competitive client goals are:

> Receiving the highest possible price
>
> Paying the lowest possible price
>
> Getting a better public image than another person or entity

A competitive goal almost always results whenever one party is to pay money to another. From the payor's perspective, paying less is better, since each dollar paid is a loss to the payor if the item could have been obtained for a lower

---

[7] These goals have also been termed "distributive." H. Raiffa, The Art and Science of Negotiation 33 (1982).

[8] This may result either from maximizing one's own relative edge, or by minimizing the other party's relatively advantageous outcome. McClintock, *Social Motivation in Settings of Outcome Interdependence,* in D. Druckman, Negotiations: Social-Psychological Perspectives 57 (1977).

[9] R. Lewicki & J. Litterer, Negotiation 24 (1985).

sum. The payee, of course, has the opposite point of view. More dollars received means a better bargain.

Such situations involve what may be categorized as a "limited pie." There are a set number of dollars potentially involved. The parties actions will not change that outer limit. For example, suppose that a diamond is the item being negotiated. The buyer wishes to purchase the diamond and is willing to pay up to $60,000.

Figure 2-1

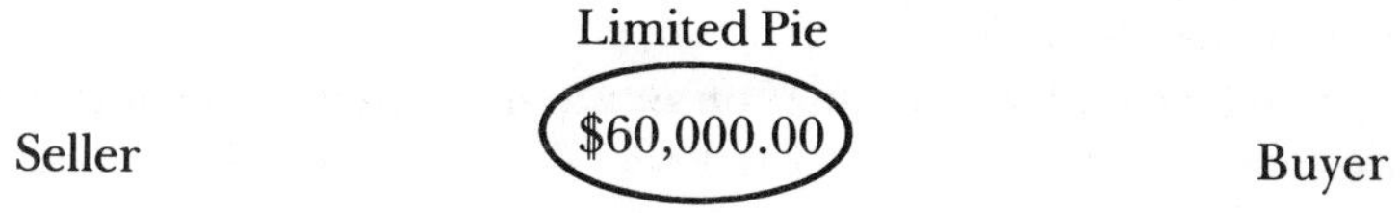

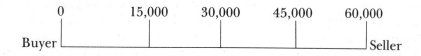

Limited Pie

Seller $60,000.00   Buyer

The limited pie consists of $60,000. If the diamond can be purchased for $40,000 instead of $60,000, the buyer is at a competitive advantage. Each dollar more to one party means one less dollar to the other party as they have to share the limited pie.[10] Bargaining under these circumstances is sometimes depicted linearly, with each side trying to move the other towards its end.[11]

Figure 2-2

```
        0        15,000    30,000    45,000    60,000
Buyer  |_____|_____|_____|_____| Seller
```

In terms of game theory, this limited pie, win/loss type of situation is a zero-sum game.[12] A gain to one party creates a direct and proportional loss to the other. Thus, the situation is, by its very nature, a competitive one.

A competitive situation can also occur due to tax consequences. In the sale of a business, the allocation of assets between "goodwill" and items that are subject to depreciation can constitute a win/lose issue for the buyer and sell-

---

[10] Karrass, *The Negotiating Game,* in G. Bellow & B. Moulton, The Lawyering Process 445 (1978).

[11] Menkel-Meadow, *Legal Negotiation: A Study of Strategies in Search of a Theory,* 4 Am B Found Res J 905, 920 (discussing G. Bellow & B. Moulton, The Lawyering Process 58 (1978)).

[12] Menkel-Meadow, *Toward Another View of Legal Negotiation: The Structure of Problem Solving,* 31 UCLA L Rev 754 (1984); H. Raiffa, The Art and Science of Negotiation (1982).

er.[13] In business transactions, matrimonial cases, and other matters, tax effects can be the pivotal factor in recognizing intrinsically competitive client goals and evaluating the economics of various potential and actual offers and demands.

Fundamental approaches for competitive goals include:[14]

1. Pushing hard to press the other party as close as possible to its bottom line, such as by using extreme positions and very small concessions

2. Persuading the other party that the best resolution that it can achieve is less favorable than it anticipated, but that a settlement still can be at or above its bottom line so that the party should agree

3. Persuading the other party to alter its bottom line by influencing its objective or subjective valuation of the items at issue or of the costs of those items

4. Considering reevaluation and shifting one's own bottom line if the other party's bottom line would otherwise preclude an agreement

Negotiators may define a situation as involving competitive client goals in another way. The magnitude of the differences between the parties, in and of itself, can lead to the conclusion that the negotiation is a competitive one. In 25 studies of bargaining behavior, 21 of the studies found that the greater the conflict that the parties perceived, the more likely negotiators were to act competitively.[15] That is, they reacted to large differences between parties' positions as necessarily arising because of limited pie, win/lose, zero-sum game factors. This reaction to such large differences may or may not be correct. A careful analysis is essential to determine whether the negotiation really involves a competitive client goal, an aggressive goal, one of the other three discussed below, or some combination of goals.

Whether the situation is exclusively competitive, or only competitive to a degree, depends on the overall context. The critical distinctions and factors will be explored in the next four sections concerning cooperative goals, self-centered goals, defensive goals, and combinations of goals that can interact with each other in a given negotiation.[16]

§2.04   Cooperative Client Goals

Cooperative client goals are goals which are achieved through an agreement that leads to mutual gain and for which the other party's concurrence is needed.[17] The essential factor for a cooperative goal is the absence of a correspond-

---

[13] Frisch, Jr. & Rosenzweig, *Representing the Seller of a Small Business*, in Attorney's Guide to Negotiation 4-15 (1979).

[14] R. Lewicki & J. Litterer, *supra* note 9, at 80, 82 & 86.

[15] *Id* 133.

[16] *See* §§2.04-2.07.

[17] Cooperative goals should maximize the parties' mutual results. McClintock, *Social Motivation in Settings of Outcome Interdependence*, in D. Druckman, Negotiations: Social-Psychological Perspectives 57 (1977).

ing cost or loss for the other party when one party achieves its goal. There is a positive correlation between each party's achieving of its goals.[18]

Examples of cooperative goals are:

Formation of a joint venture, partnership, or corporation to engage in a business venture and to achieve a mutual profit

Tax benefits arising from structuring a transaction or settlement so that both parties gain through either a direct split of the tax benefit or a cash payment to one and the direct tax benefit to the other

A structured settlement through which the plaintiff receives a greater number of total dollars spread out over time, while the defendant pays less money in the present than would otherwise be required[19]

Achieving increased respect from others through the blending of both parties' strengths into a unified entity or program

Two important aspects for recognizing, considering, and effectuating cooperative client goals are the size of the "pie" and the nature of the parties' relationship. In the earlier example of a competitive goal, a diamond was to be purchased for a price potentially as high as $60,000.[20] The pie was assumed to be a limited one, in which the dollars gained or saved by one party resulted in a directly corresponding loss or cost to the other party. Now, assume that the parties could structure the transaction so that each party would achieve a tax advantage of $5,000 regardless of the negotiated price of the diamond. A cooperative goal then emerges, that of achieving a tax advantage for both the seller and the purchaser.

Figure 2-3

Limited Pie
(Competitive)

$60,000.00

Expanded Pie
(Cooperative)

$70,000.00

Thus, the pie has been increased from $60,000 to $70,000 without cost to either party.

Note that $10,000 of the pie is not subject to negotiation. Each party can achieve only a $5,000 tax gain. Neither party can obtain any tax gain without the cooperation of the other party in structuring the transaction. Neither party gains its monetary tax benefit if the other fails to also obtain a tax benefit. It

---

[18] R. Lewicki & J. Litterer, Negotiation 24 (1985).

[19] For a detailed discussion of structured settlements, see §7.03.

[20] See Fig 2-1.

is therefore clearly advantageous to both parties to cooperate in order to expand the pie.

The nature of the relationship between the parties can differ even though cooperative goals are involved. The sale of an item with tax advantages to both parties involves a cooperative goal, but it may be a single interaction that is the parties' only contact with each other. That type of cooperative goal is a short-term one. In contrast, a joint venture to engage in a business together and to achieve a mutual profit involves a continuing interaction between the parties. This type of cooperative goal has a long-term purpose. As discussed in the chapters on strategy and tactics, whether a cooperative goal is for the short run or for the long run can influence the choice of strategy and tactics.

Those cooperative goals which lead to a relatively long-term relationship, such as a joint venture or partnership, may require the client to demonstrate a willingness to make a real effort to reach an agreement. This can prove to the other party that the deal itself is viable, because the client is willing to act affirmatively in the spirit of cooperation to make it succeed. Such a demonstration of a cooperative spirit may be almost as important as the tangible, defined roles and potential benefits in making the proposed deal an attractive proposal, by enhancing the likelihood that the expected roles and benefits will in fact occur.

Often, whether or not cooperative client goals can be achieved depends on the goals of the other party. Prenegotiation information gathering[21] or obtaining information during the negotiation[22] regarding the other party's goals, needs, and interests is essential for determining whether it is feasible to achieve cooperative goals.[23]

§2.05   Self-Centered Client Goals

Self-centered client goals are those that depend solely on what the client achieves, regardless of what the other party receives.[24] Thus, this type of goal is neither inherently antagonistic nor helpful to the other party to the negotiation. For a client with a truly self-centered goal, the results for the other party are simply a neutral byproduct of attaining the client's goal. This type of goal does not necessarily require any particular cooperation from the other party, other than the creation of the agreement itself.[25]

Examples of self-centered client goals can be:

> Obtaining a particular property
>
> Selling a specific property

---

[21] See §§4.06 & 8.03.

[22] See §§4.04, 4.07, & 4.08.

[23] See §§8.03 and 4.04-4.08 concerning gathering and obtaining information.

[24] This has been referred to as "individualism." McClintock, *Social Motivation in Settings of Outcome Interdependence,* in D. Druckman, Negotiations: Social-Psychological Perspectives 57 (1977).

[25] See §2.04 regarding cooperative goals.

Improving a business or personal relationship

Gaining respect from others

Developing a relationship with a new customer or supplier

Gaining vindication

Obtaining financing

Receiving favorable publicity

Receiving tax benefits without cost to the other party

Obtaining a position within an organization that can lead to important contacts that may be personally beneficial in the future

Resolving a dispute

Making a loan

Of course, depending on the circumstances and on the client's motivation, many of the examples set forth above could also involve competitive, cooperative, aggressive, or defensive goals, or a combination of goals. Indeed, in most, if not virtually all, situations, the client is likely to have more than one goal.[26]

§2.06   Defensive Client Goals

Defensive client goals are those in which the client seeks to avoid a particular outcome. The avoidance aspect distinguishes defensive client goals from self-centered ones, which focus on attaining something.

Examples of defensive client goals are:

Avoiding a loss of respect

Preventing a strike

Avoiding the loss of a good customer or supplier

Restructuring financing to prevent an imminent foreclosure

Maintaining a business or personal relationship

The last example provides an opportunity to illustrate the difference between defensive, self-centered, and aggressive client goals, as well as the way that different goals sometimes can result in the same action. In a collective bargaining negotiation, a transportation firm can seek to have its employees make prompt deliveries in order to maintain its business volume. This is a self-centered goal. If the same action to maintain volume is intended to avoid a loss of customers, the goal is a defensive one. To the extent that the same activity is designed to lure new customers away from competitors in order to weaken the competition, the goal is an aggressive one.

---

[26] See §2.07 regarding combinations of goals.

§2.07   Combinations of Client Goals

In some instances, a client will have a single goal. The goal of a plaintiff in a personal injury suit typically is a competitive one: obtaining the maximum possible dollar recovery from the defendant. Correspondingly, the defendant's insurer simply may have the competitive goal of paying as little as possible after as much delay as is practical. Those two factors ultimately are weighed in light of the present dollar value of the settlement under consideration. Similarly, a property owner's sole goal may be to sell the property if a certain minimum or higher price can be attained. Unless it can be attained, the owner will not sell. Of course, a prospective buyer may have the single, corresponding goal of purchasing if a certain maximum price or a lower price can be obtained.

More often, however, clients have more than one goal for the negotiation.

Example 2-1

Personal injury plaintiff Hill is not just seeking the competitive goal of maximizing his dollar recovery. That goal exists along with other goals, such as:

Gaining the respect of others through a sufficiently high recovery (a self-centered goal)

Avoiding the loss of the respect of family and friends by avoiding a low recovery (a defensive goal)

Punishing the defendant and/or its insurer by maximizing their total expenses of settlement, attorney's fees, and litigation costs (an aggressive goal)[27]

Gaining the respect of others by forcing the defendant and/or its insurer to expend a sufficiently high total amount on the settlement, attorney's fees, and litigation costs (a self-centered goal)[28]

Furthermore, with counseling, this same plaintiff may add the goal of increasing the economic value of the defendant's offer by structuring the

---

[27] For example, some personal injury plaintiffs are more amenable to accepting a relatively low settlement offer if they consider that the defendant or its insurer has had to spend a substantial amount of resources to defend the suit, and therefore is not disposing of the plaintiff's claim as cheaply as it might seem. This type of situation may arise in any type of case in which the client's interests are emotional as well as economic. The client needs to feel an importance and self worth or that the other side is being punished through the cost to the other party. If these needs lead to one of the client's goals, it may be essential, in counseling the client about a reasonable settlement offer that the client is reluctant to accept, to explicitly explain the opponent's costs to the client. Often this may occur when, because of liability problems, a relatively low settlement offer is a reasonable offer.

[28] A self-centered goal may lead a client to react in the same way towards a proposed settlement and may necessitate the same sort of counseling as an aggressive goal when these goals reflect emotional needs. For instance, compare this example of a self-centered goal with the preceding example of an aggressive goal.

settlement without increasing the cost to the defendant.[29] That cooperative goal can help to attain the otherwise competitive goal of maximizing
the total dollar recovery.

Example 2-2

Forming a partnership involves a cooperative goal. It also may involve
competitive goals concerning the prospective partners' respective shares.
In addition, to the extent that each party has different personal cash flow
needs which do not conflict, self-centered goals can come into play. The
cash flow goals are self-centered as long as each partner's needs can be
met without affecting the cash flow goal of the other parties.

Example 2-3

Collective bargaining negotiations can present conflicts between different
types of goals. The economic and noneconomic issues frequently include
both distributive bargaining over competitive goals such as wages
and integrative bargaining[30] on cooperative goals to solve mutual problems.[31] On occasion, if an effort is made to "bust the union," the negotiation also will involve management's aggressive and the union's defensive
goals.

These examples illustrate the interplay between various goals, and the manner in which different goals sometimes can lead to the same actions and results
as well as different ones. In fact, many self-centered, aggressive, defensive, and
cooperative client goals have an intrinsically related competitive goal. Those
seeking to sell or to purchase a piece of property (self-centered) almost always
want to do so at the most favorable possible price and terms (competitive).
The wholesaler using price discounts to lure new customers away from competitors (aggressive), or to prevent its own customers from switching to a competitor (defensive), still wants to do so using the lowest customer discount
(competitive) that will accomplish that objective. An investor entering into a
restaurant franchising partnership with an experienced restaurateur (cooperative) normally seeks a reasonable return on its investment (self-centered). This
usually means seeking as favorable a partnership structure as possible (competitive) without jeopardizing the cooperative and self-centered goals of forming
a partnership with the right knowledgeable and trustworthy operating partner
that will generate the desired return on the investment.

On the other hand, multiple goals also may conflict. In the first of the situations in the prior paragraph, the seller of property has the typical competitive

---

[29] *See* **§7.03.**

[30] Distributive bargaining refers to win/lose, limited pie negotiation over how finite
resources will be divided. Integrative bargaining involves goals that can be integrated
for mutual gain.

[31] Mandle, *Collective Bargaining Negotiation,* in Attorney's Guide to Negotiation 14-2
(1979).

goal of maximizing the sale price. That seller, however, also may have the self-centered goal of just wanting to be rid of the property because it no longer meets the seller's needs for size, prestige, and income. Those two goals, the competitive one of price maximization and the self-centered goal of accomplishing a sale, can conflict. The seller then must determine at what point the sale price is sufficient, although not necessarily maximized, because of the goal to sell a property which no longer fulfills the seller's needs. The number of goals can increase through subsequent events.

Example 2-4

> While in the process of selling their home, the Brons purchase a replacement. They now add the defensive goal of avoiding the dual expense of paying for and maintaining both properties. Achieving that defensive goal by obtaining a sale of the first property then conflicts with the original goal of maximizing the sale price, because the available offers are for lesser amounts than expected. This requires a prioritization or compromise between the two goals.

Identification and categorization of client goals with precision is essential, so that counsel properly can choose among potential strategies and tactics. It also is important to prioritize multiple goals, especially those that conflict, since one cannot always achieve all goals. The client, after appropriate counseling, must determine the priorities for the goals.[32]

A conflict between client goals sometimes can be avoided. The following example demonstrates the many client goals that can come into play, as well as how a conflict between goals can be resolved.

Example 2-5

> The property to be sold is a business that includes an industrial building. In this transaction, the seller desires to sell the business in order to:
>
> Be rid of the building (self-centered)
>
> Have increased liquid assets (self-centered)
>
> Avoid further losses, since the business was operating at a deficit (defensive)
>
> Maximize the sale price and thereby maximize net profits (competitive)
>
> Structure the sale itself to minimize taxes without cost to the purchaser (self-centered)
>
> Distribute profit-sharing benefits to minimize the taxes of the employees and of the owner (both self-centered and altruistic with respect to the employees and self-centered with respect to the owner)

---

[32] *See* M. Schoenfield & B. Pearlman Schoenfield, Interviewing and Counseling (1981).

Obtain promises of continued employment for long-time, valued employees with whom personal relationships had developed, thereby both maintaining the quality of those relationships (self-centered) as well as avoiding a loss of respect (defensive), and eliminating the need for severance pay (self-centered)

Since certain of those goals could only be accomplished with the support and agreement of the purchaser, and because the purchaser received the corresponding benefit of valuable, experienced employees, a cooperative goal also existed.

If the seller had been forced to negotiate severance pay with those long-term employees, the seller might have had a competitive goal to minimize that pay, or at least a self-centered goal of keeping that expense below the level which the owner felt comfortable in paying. This would have conflicted with his self-centered goal of maintaining the personal relationships with the employees and his defensive goal of avoiding a loss of respect. The conflict was avoided, however, by the cooperative negotiation for continued employment by the purchaser of the business.

Conflicting client goals can be generated by situations that involve strong, antagonistic feelings towards the other party such as divorce, defamation, and partnership breakups. The client may seek to maximize the monetary recovery, while, at the same time, gain vindication, punish the other party, and increase the other party's respect for or fear of the client without regard to the legal expense. At least, this can be the initial posture of the client. Obviously, the goal which seeks maximum monetary recovery conflicts with the goals that disregard legal expenses, to the extent that the client really wants to resolve the matter by attaining the greatest possible net economic benefits.[33] This conflict not only affects the determination of a bottom line position acceptable to the client and the choices of strategy and tactics, but it also affects the timing of serious negotiations. The latter is affected because the priority between the conflicting goals can change over time. The client may have higher monetary goals and more regard for expense after fighting with the other party sufficiently either to achieve the goals of vindication, punishment, respect, and fear, or to release enough emotion through that fighting so that those goals lose their earlier priority.

Unfortunately for the lawyer, it is not unusual for such clients to switch attorneys when the emotional goals lose their priority, so that the client can blame the first lawyer for not reaching a settlement or for high expenses, even though all of that was caused by the client's initial priority for emotional rather than monetary goals. Clearly, this suggests the need for early and continuing client counseling to attempt to avoid such a situation.

---

[33] Compare the effect of this type of emotional involvement with the type illustrated earlier in this section.

Conflicting goals also can arise where the party is not monolithic, but rather has internal conflicts and bargaining.[34] In such instances, the attorney may hear different goals expressed by different members of the client entity. In addition, counsel may hear shifting goals expressed due to internal negotiations within the client if it is an entity. In such cases, active counseling with the ultimate decision maker is essential to avoid misunderstandings with the client and misdirected efforts.

§2.08   Conclusion

There are six categories of client goals:

1. Aggressive
2. Competitive
3. Cooperative
4. Self-Centered
5. Defensive
6. Combinations

As the examples illustrate, it is usually overly simplistic to refer to a client as having only a competitive, or a cooperative, or any other single goal. In almost all instances, the client will have a number of goals. There are very few real-life purely competitive or purely cooperative negotiations.[35]

Cooperative, aggressive, self-centered, and defensive goals often have a corresponding competitive goal. Furthermore, in an important sense, whenever the client seeks to maximize its net profits through negotiation, a self-centered goal exists. That goal may be sought to be achieved through the use of either competitive or cooperative subgoals. In some negotiations, both competitive and cooperative goals will exist that lead to the self-centered goal of maximized net profits.

At times, the client's goals will conflict, although sometimes that conflict can be avoided. If the client's goals initially appear to conflict, the lawyer must determine whether the conflict can be eliminated by legal counseling to ascertain whether the conflict is real or merely due to:

1. Confusion on the part of the client
2. A lack of clarification from the client

---

[34] H. Raiffa, The Art and Science of Negotiation 12 (1982).

[35] After teaching one seminar, author Mark K. Schoenfield received the following anonymous written comment: "You are wrong about there rarely being purely cooperative or purely competitive negotiations. Before we were married, my wife and I had a purely cooperative relationship. Since our marriage, it has been a purely competitive one. I am sure there are many examples of purely cooperative and purely competitive negotiations." This dissenting view is cited for the reader's own evaluation.

Where the goals conflict, they must be balanced and prioritized in order to determine the least favorable result that the client finds acceptable as opposed to not reaching an agreement at all. That will constitute the client's bottom line position.

The nature of the client's goals is essential in determining the client's bottom line position and the lawyer's authority in the negotiation.[36] The client's goals also affect the choice of strategy and tactics.[37]

Before determining bottom line authority, strategy, and tactics, the client goals must be examined as guideposts in negotiating. Goals can be general or specific. To the extent necessary, however, the goals must be translated into concrete points. These points should be capable of being:

1. Accepted in a negotiation
2. Drafted into specific terms within an agreement
3. Legally enforced, unless all that the client desires, or all that is possible, is a statement of principle or intent which is not or may not be enforceable in court due to its generality

If the goals as stated by the client cannot be used for these purposes, the attorney must counsel the client to clarify the goals.

Client goals are especially important in a different way with respect to the tactics of obtaining and disclosing information.[38] At times, discovering the true nature of the other party's goals can provide a significant advantage for the negotiator.[39] On the other hand, at times, the selective disclosure of your client's true goals can be essential to move the other party forward so that an agreement can be reached.[40]

The client's goals define the purpose of the negotiation. That purpose, as perceived by the attorney, may affect not only the choice of strategies and tactics, but also the attitude and behavior of the negotiator.[41] A cooperative negotiation requires a cooperative attitude, while an aggressive one may require a professionally adversarial, although not necessarily unpleasant, tone.[42]

By understanding the impact of the client's goals on the negotiating process, as well as understanding the specific goals of the client and of the other party in the particular negotiation, the lawyer can negotiate more efficiently and

---

[36] *See* §§8.04 & 9.03.

[37] *See* chs 3-7 & 9.05.

[38] *See* ch 4.

[39] *See* ch 8.

[40] *See* §§3.08 & 5.06.

[41] Menkel-Meadow, *Toward Another View of Legal Negotiation: The Structure of Problem Solving,* 31 UCLA L Rev 754, 760 (1984).

[42] See §5.14 regarding tone.

effectively.[43] Therefore, it is necessary both to understand the client's goals and to provide advice, if necessary, regarding those or other possible goals. To be able to do so may require early, continuing, and effective client interviewing and counseling.[44] This may well be a prerequisite to effectively conducting the negotiation.[45]

As a negotiation progresses, goals may change. The negotiation itself may influence the client's goals. New facts can emerge. Resistance by the other party can lead to reevaluation of one's position. External factors may also affect the client's goals. Financial considerations may shift, policies may be altered, or alternative opportunities may present themselves.

Due to the potential for changes in a client's goals, counsel may need to check with the client periodically to ascertain whether the goals have remained the same. To the extent that counsel receives new information which the client is not aware of and which could alter the client's goals, further client counseling is essential.[46] Just as negotiation is a process that requires continual vigilance, the attorney-client relationship is a process which requires similar vigilance.

In negotiation, the attorney must separate his or her own professional goals of aiding the client from the client's goals. The goals of a lawyer are to help the client to:

1.   Achieve the client's goals unless barred by ethical prohibitions[47]

2.   Modify those goals if appropriate through proper, realistic counseling[48]

The lawyer must retain a professional objectivity to negotiate effectively. Accordingly, counsel should not have his or her perceptions or analysis skewed by the client's goals or feelings. Only by maintaining objectivity with a dedication to the client's interests can the attorney's effectiveness be maximized.

Translating client goals into concrete items subject to negotiation is essential. Whether a goal is even achievable may not be apparent until the lawyer and the client struggle to decide on the precise terms to be sought. "It is a good rule . . . not to decide on what needs to be done until it is clear how it is going to be done and whether it can be done successfully."[49]

---

[43] Menkel-Meadow has suggested that "what must be antecedent to any negotiation behavior . . . (is) a conception of negotiation goals." Menkel-Meadow, *supra* note 41, at 758.

[44] *See* M. Schoenfield & B. Pearlman Schoenfield, Interviewing and Counseling (1981) [hereinafter Schoenfield].

[45] Menkel-Meadow, *Legal Negotiation: A Study of Strategies in Search of a Theory,* 4 Am B Found Res J 905 (1983). Menkel-Meadow suggests that law schools "therefore include client counseling and interviewing as an integral part of any negotiation course." *Id* 933.

[46] *See* **ch 2.**

[47] *See* **ch 12.**

[48] *See* Schoenfield, *supra* note 44.

[49] Draper, *American Hubris: From Truman to the Persian Gulf,* (Book Review) The New York Review of Books, July 16, 1987 at 47.

§2.09 Summary and Review

   I. Client Goals
- A. Tangible or intangible
- B. Objective and subjective value
- C. Can shift or modify over time
- D. Affect choice of strategy and tactics, as well as tone
- E. Important in determining the client's bottom line

  II. Aggressive Client Goals
- A. Seek to undermine, deprive, damage, or otherwise injure a rival or opponent
- B. May be an emotional choice and objectively illogical, but also can be objectively logical under an economic cost-benefit analysis

 III. Competitive Client Goals
- A. Seek to gain more than the other party
- B. Win/Lose

 IV. Cooperative Client Goals
- A. Agreement leads to mutual gain *rather* than a loss for one party corresponding to a gain for the other party
- B. Growing "pie," not a limited pie

  V. Self-Centered Client Goals
- A. Client has an objective to achieve, regardless of what the other party receives

 VI. Defensive Client Goals
- A. Seek to avoid a particular outcome

VII. Combinations of Client Goals
- A. Multiple client goals are usually present
- B. May lead to conflicting client goals
- C. Can require establishing priorities for goals
- D. Sometimes conflicts between goals can be eliminated

Strategy

3

§3.01 Introduction

Strategy is the overall concept for negotiation chosen by the negotiator. It may involve making concessions, trading concessions, refusing to make concessions, or other methods of negotiating. The most useful strategies will be outlined in the following sections of this chapter.[1]

---

[1] Not all negotiating behavior that occurs will fall into the strategies that are described in this chapter. In large part, that is because, unfortunately, many negotiations are conducted either without any clear-cut conception of strategy or with an ineffective strategy.

Before describing and explaining these strategies, tactics should be distinguished from strategies. A strategy provides the overall approach used throughout the negotiation, unless replaced by a different strategy. It is a long-run plan for the entire negotiation or for a particular issue within the negotiation. In contrast, a tactic is a particular maneuver used at a specific time during the negotiation for a more limited role. Tactics are used to implement a strategy in the particular context of the specific negotiation.

Strategies are chosen for use in a particular negotiation in order to achieve the client's goals.[2] The nature of those goals will affect which strategy or strategies are chosen, as discussed in the sections concerning the specific strategies.

The choice of strategy also may be affected by a large number of factors which include whether:[3]

A transaction or a dispute is involved

There is more than one issue involved

New issues can be injected into the negotiation

The parties' interests are short-term or long-term

The parties' relationship is long-term, or limited to one negotiation, or somewhere in between

The negotiators' relationship is long-term, or limited to one negotiation, or somewhere in between those two categories

The parties' interests are economic, noneconomic, or both

The parties value the negotiable items in the same way

The parties are negotiating voluntarily or not voluntarily

The negotiations are being conducted privately or publicly

The negotiations are or may be the subject of publicity

The client is an individual, a group of individuals, a company, a union, or some other type of organization

What is at stake has great or little value to the parties

One party stands to gain or to lose the most

The negotiation is a routine matter (for example, plea bargaining a minor misdemeanor or traffic offense for someone with a clean record), or is not so routine

The parties' actual and perceived power in terms of the facts, the law, economic resources, morality, etc. is equal or unequal

The negotiating is being conducted face-to-face, or by phone, or in writing, or through a combination of these means

---

[2] G. Nierenberg, The Art of Negotiation: Psychological Strategies for Gaining Advantageous Bargains 108 (1968). Nierenberg describes this in terms of satisfying the client's "needs."

[3] Menkel-Meadow, *Legal Negotiation: A Study of Strategies in Search of a Theory,* 4 Am B Found Res J 905, 927-28 (1983).

There are viable alternatives (such as a trial, no sale, etc.) available, as well as the degree to which those alternatives are acceptable

In addition, the choice of strategy also is affected by the negotiating approach, personal characteristics, and psychological orientation of the other negotiator.

§3.02   Personal Credibility

Before focusing on specific strategies, the issue of personal credibility must be examined. One commentator has stated that there is "no substitute" for "integrity."[4] Another has called it "one of the most important aspects of successful negotiating."[5]

Imagine a negotiation in which one negotiator did not believe anything said by the other negotiator—not the demands, professed reasons, promises, threats, or anything else. Obviously, one would neither want to nor be able to reach an agreement if the other negotiator was not believed at all. Such negotiations might sound like this:

Example 3-1

"I will not make any concessions."

"Oh yes you will."

"Here is a guaranteed appraisal for $45,000.00."

"It is not genuine."

"Let's exchange financial statements to decide on a fair percentage division of the profits for a partnership combining our two businesses."

"Your financial statement is so highly exaggerated that it's a fraud."

This example is plainly exaggerated to the point of absurdity in its premise that nothing said by one negotiator is believed by the other. However, it illustrates a fundamental point about strategy. No matter which strategy is chosen, it cannot effectively influence the other negotiator's behavior and decisions unless he or she believes the strategy. Otherwise, it will be discounted and disregarded by the other negotiator. A crucial component of creating a believable strategy is the personal credibility of the negotiator. That credibility must be established and maintained.[6]

---

[4] C. Karrass, Give & Take: The Complete Guide to Negotiating Strategies and Tactics 89 (1974).

[5] Mandle, *Collective Bargaining Negotiation*, in Attorney's Guide to Negotiation 14-16 (1979).

[6] Rifkin, *Negotiating Patents, Trade Secrets and Know-How Licenses*, in Attorney's Guide to Negotiation 15-19 (1979).

Personal credibility tends to be attributed to negotiators who exhibit certain characteristics. A credible negotiator tends to be comfortable and confident, without being brash or arrogant. This demonstrates a realistic sense of strength without being offensive, and without appearing to have such falsely high expectations that the negotiation is unlikely to be productive.

A credible negotiator also tends to be prepared, organized, and business-like, without being stuffy.[7] Candor needs to be projected and, in litigation, so does a willingness to proceed to trial.[8] This tends to force the other negotiator to respect the positions that one takes and to act in a serious manner, rather than engaging in gamesmanship. It also tends to make the other negotiator more forthright. Having authority and acknowledging that fact also are helpful, although not essential,[9] factors.

Part of being prepared, of course, is being knowledgeable about the matter being negotiated. No negotiator, though, can be expected always to know everything. The negotiator should know at least those things that a very good and well-prepared lawyer ought to know in a given situation. Within these limits, however, it will not diminish and may even enhance one's credibility to candidly admit when something is not known. Such enhanced credibility can occur, for example, when one then proceeds to obtain the necessary information.

Most importantly, the credible negotiator behaves honestly.[10] One cannot be believable unless one is perceived as honest. This does not mean disclosing information, except when such disclosure is appropriate.[11] It does mean not engaging in lies. As negotiations usually cannot involve total openness and candor, lies must be distinguished from accepted practices such as trying to mislead the other party regarding one's bottom line.[12] The atmosphere of the

---

[7] Williams, *Negotiation: Legal Negotiation and Settlement,* in S. Goldberg, E. Green & F. Sander, Dispute Resolution 54-55 (1985). Williams reported on the results of a survey of attorneys regarding the behavior of effective negotiators. The results found that being realistic, rational, analytical, knowledgeable on the facts and on the law, and legally astute were among the traits of lawyers who were deemed to be effective negotiators. *Id* 54-55.

[8] Sandels, *Negotiation in Business Litigation,* in Attorney's Guide to Negotiation 11-17 (1979).

[9] M. Zimmerman, How to Do Business with the Japanese 99 (1985).

[10] Williams, *supra* note 7. The same survey of lawyers, discussed in note 7, found that the traits of an effective negotiator included being ethical, trustworthy, and honest. *Id* 54. This was true regardless of whether the negotiating style was considered to be competitive or cooperative, although that did affect the importance attributed to these traits. *Id.* For negotiators who were viewed as being cooperative, being honest was considered to be the most important trait, with ethics ranked third, and trustworthiness ranked sixth. *Id.* If this is correct, it would seem that one cannot negotiate in a cooperative manner unless one has personal credibility. For negotiators who were viewed as competitive, honesty, ethics, and trustworthiness were rated as eleventh, fifteenth, and twentieth in priority, respectively. *Id.*

[11] See **§4.02** on the disclosure of information.

[12] White, *Negotiation: Machiavelli and the Bar: Ethical Limitations on Lying in Negotiation,* in

negotiation should be one of trust,[13] with careful listening[14] so as not to mislead oneself about the words being spoken.

To be perceived as credible, negotiators must avoid the appearance of attempting to deceive others. They must keep their word and be able to deliver on promises. When they indicate that they do not have specific authority on a given point, but believe that the client will follow their recommendation, they usually must be correct.

One important method to establish credibility is to always follow through and keep one's word, regardless of whether it is a promise or a threat. When actions, which were forecast, in fact occur, the other negotiator learns to listen carefully to counsel and to respect counsel's words. Especially in repeated negotiations with the same attorney or law firm, counsel must be concerned with his or her long-run reputation, including that for "toughness."[15]

Both negotiators and parties tend to trust the other side when the other side is perceived as:[16]

1. Being similar to the negotiator and/or party

2. Having a positive attitude towards the negotiator or the client

3. Depending on and needing the party

4. Acting in a cooperative and trusting manner

5. Making concessions or working towards a joint solution of the issues

6. Beginning with statements and actions that are cooperative, open, and nonthreatening

Since the "other side" consists of both the other negotiator and the other party, the perception of one of them can overcome or negate the perception of the other. The analysis becomes even more complex when the party, the negotiator, or both, consists of multiple individuals or entities, each of which contributes or detracts from creating or maintaining a sense of trust.

Statements of requirements may have to be cushioned so as to avoid making trust a personal issue between the negotiators.

Example 3-2

"Given the past problems between our clients on whether one agreed to something and then reneged, or changed its position, we'll need to have the offer in writing this time with all of the terms set forth. This has

---

S. Goldberg, E. Green & F. Sander, Dispute Resolution 67 (1985). See **ch 12** regarding ethics.

[13] M. Zimmerman, *supra* note 9, at 97.

[14] *See* **§4.04.**

[15] H. Raiffa, The Art and Science of Negotiation 13 (1982).

[16] R. Lewicki & J. Litterer, Negotiation 112 (1985).

nothing to do with you personally. But, we will all be better off by avoiding any further problems this way."

Example 3-3

"I am certainly willing to accept your word. But, in order to prevent personal issues of trust from arising during negotiations, I always insist that such representations be in writing. It also avoids any questions if either of us were to be hit by a car or some similar event were to happen."

Allies can be useful in creating trust.[17] A third party who is respected by the other party or its negotiator can serve, in effect, as a reference to establish credibility.

At times, a negotiator has to devise actions in order to create a sense of trust.

Example 3-4

With a client who was a service provider, the negotiator initially needed to offer to make most of a contract contingent on a new customer's satisfaction, although still requiring payment for services actually rendered. This allowed the negotiator to develop sufficient trust to obtain a large contract with that customer.

Example 3-5

A condominium association sued a contractor who was making repairs to a building that adjoined the condominium. The suit was to prevent trespass and damage to the condominium building. The dispute arose, in part, because the contractor had failed to sufficiently secure large plastic sheets that were being used to protect some areas while painting nearby portions of the building. At night, these plastic sheets blew noisily around in the wind thereby disrupting the sleep of the condominium association's residents.

Both to prevent the problem from recurring and to create a sense of trust and goodwill, the contractor initially offered to remove the plastic sheets at the end of each working day. The trust and goodwill that were created benefited the contractor in later negotiating the more complex and significant issues. Of course, once the parties agreed that the plastic would be removed each afternoon before the workers left, the contractor then had to ensure that this was done. Otherwise, he would have destroyed all confidence and trust, and he would have had to reopen the negotiation in a far more difficult position than he was in originally.

Negotiators also can increase their credibility by getting the other party to identify with them.[18] Sometimes, identification can come from behaving in a

---

[17] See §6.05 regarding allies.

[18] H. Cohen, You Can Negotiate Anything (1982). Cohen refers to this as "the power of identification." Id 75-79.

reasonable, professional manner.[19] Perhaps since such behavior is to be expected, however, other behavior may be even more important in achieving identification. This behavior involves demonstrating empathy and understanding. Being empathic and understanding towards the needs of the other side is likely to generate identification.[20]

Similarly, if one explains and expresses his or her client's needs in such a way that the other negotiator or the other party feels empathy, that too is likely to create identification. The empathy itself, of course, can be a valuable influence as well.

Generating identification by conveying and creating empathy and understanding is most likely to occur by:[21]

1. Focusing on the parties' real interests, not the positions that they are taking

2. Considering those interests in terms of some objective criteria

Identification also can operate in reverse, thereby causing a loss of personal credibility.[22] For instance, a negotiator may display a total lack of concern for the legitimate needs of the other party. That lack of concern can be perceived by the other side as a lack of basic fairness on the part of the negotiator. If so, there will be a negative identification and a loss of personal credibility, since someone who is not fair is less likely to be believed.[23] It has been aptly observed that: "More often than people care to admit, identification (whether with or against) plays a significant role in negotiations and decision making. That's why behaving decently and trying to help others is the equivalent of having a canteen of water in the Gobi Desert."[24]

Another method of enhancing credibility relates to the fascination which many people have for those viewed as celebrities or insiders. People often want to see and to meet celebrities and insiders. There also may be identification with the celebrity or insider. For the negotiator, personal knowledge of or association with powerful or celebrity figures can transform the negotiator into an actual or quasi-insider or celebrity. This may create the perception that the negotiator is more interesting and more rewarding to deal with than those without such status. Some people believe that those with such personal knowledge

---

[19] *Id* 76. *See also* Menkel-Meadow, *Legal Negotiation: A Study of Strategies in Search of a Theory,* 4 Am B Found Res J 905, 927-28 (1983).

[20] H. Cohen, *supra* note 18, at 76.

[21] Focusing on the parties' interests, not on their positions, and using objective standards to resolve disagreements are two of the four basic points of the negotiating method that has been named "principled negotiation" or "negotiation on the merits." R. Fisher & W. Ury, Getting to Yes, Negotiating Agreement Without Giving In (1981). [Hereinafter Fisher.] The other two basic points in this method are to separate the people from the problem and to generate a variety of options before deciding how to proceed. *Id.*

[22] H. Cohen, *supra* note 18, at 77.

[23] *Id* 77.

[24] *Id* 79.

or relationships also are more credible. In dealing with those people, the negotiator's credibility will be enhanced by the status attributed from the connection with powerful or celebrity figures.

On the other hand, if talk of relationships with powerful persons, celebrities, or insiders is seen as mere boasting or as an unsuccessful attempt to intimidate, the results will be counterproductive. Indeed, it may even unintentionally inject an extraneous power struggle into the negotiation, as the person without such status seeks to prove that he or she is neither impressed nor intimidated, and that he or she must be treated as an equal.

Just as other work on the matter at hand and preparation for negotiating begins before the actual negotiation, so does establishing one's personal credibility. There often is contact between the negotiators prior to actually negotiating, and that is the time to begin building trust and establishing credibility.[25] This can be done through the negotiator's general behavior, or through a specific action, as in Example 3-5 about the contractor. Indeed, it may be easier to establish trust during this time.[26] Of course, the concern and the need for personal credibility continue throughout the negotiating process.

Even in large metropolitan areas with many lawyers, reputations tend to develop and become known, since lawyers often practice in particular areas of the law. A lack of credibility can be a devastating handicap. The worst type of credibility problem is a reputation for lacking honesty. "It's often said that dishonesty in the short-run is a poor policy because a tarnished reputation hurts in the long-run."[27]

Credibility can be even more important when negotiating in some other cultures. For instance, the Japanese traditionally have been more concerned with integrity and trust for long-term relationships.[28]

In establishing or maintaining credibility, it may be necessary to separate one's self from those who are not credible to the other party or its negotiator. If the client or associates are not trusted by the other side, there are two approaches which can be taken. Preferably, the other side can be persuaded that its perception is erroneous. That, however, may be a difficult or an impossible task. Second, as either an alternative or a fall back position, one can acknowledge the other side's perception without agreeing with it. At the same time one must then establish or maintain one's own credibility, clearly delineating one's own reputation as a matter that is separate and apart from those who are distrusted.

Some negotiators use a "trust me" approach as a tactic to foreclose demands for specific information or representations. Unless counsel believes that such trust is completely warranted under the circumstances, the "trust me" approach should be rejected and countered, although care should be exercised that this is not insulting and does not create unnecessary antagonism. Countermeasures to the "trust me" approach include:

---

[25] Raiffa, *supra* note 15, at 163-66.

[26] *Id* 165-66.

[27] *Id* 345.

[28] M. Zimmerman, *supra* note 9, at 91-92.

1. Reference to the need for a complete written agreement without separate oral portions, regardless of the source

2. Citing a need to probe the source of the lawyer's information, and not personal veracity

3. Pointing out that, if one or both attorneys are not available at some later time, there may be confusion or disagreement

4. Custom and practice, with the corresponding need to require certain measures because anything less may constitute malpractice

5. The client's suspicions or requirements, and not any personal feelings on the part of counsel

§3.03   No Concessions

The first strategy to be examined is that of making no concessions at all. This is considered first because it is the strategy which takes the toughest stance, in that no compromises will be made from the position that is initially taken in the negotiation. When a no concessions strategy is adopted, the negotiation becomes a unilateral process. Once the client's position is announced, the only possible agreement has been unilaterally defined by that party. The negotiation still may involve a discussion or debate about whether there should be an agreement on those terms, and perhaps a test of whether there will truly be no concessions. If this strategy really is being implemented, though, no other terms will be considered by that side unless those terms involve some restructuring without any concessions.

The no concessions strategy is most useful when the party employing it has so much more power than the other party that it can dictate very favorable terms. Such a disparity in power may be due to some adverse consequences which the powerful party can cause to be inflicted on the other side. It also can flow from the weaker party's extreme need for whatever the powerful party has to offer. Regardless of the source of power, the key to implementation is to have so much more power than the other side that it is forced to accept the terms that are "offered" without the possibility of any concessions, even though those terms are highly favorable to the powerful party.

The no concessions strategy sometimes is called "Bulwareism."[29] This name comes from General Bulware who was the chief operating officer of General Electric at a time when the labor movement was extremely weak in comparison to General Electric.[30] Labor's weakness at that time included an inability to mount an effective strike. Bulwareism consisted of demanding that the employees agree to certain terms and conditions without a discussion of any potential concessions by the company.

This "take it or leave it" strategy was successful for a number of years while the disparity of power between General Electric and the unions forced the

---

[29] Note, *An Analysis of Settlement*, 22 Stan L Rev 67 (1969), in G. Bellow & B. Moulton, The Lawyering Process 523 (1978).

[30] *Id* 524.

employees to accede to what, from their point of view, were extremely poor terms. The employees yielded to the company's terms, because refusing to do so would have resulted in their discharge, new workers being hired in their place, and the likelihood that they would not be able to find other employment, or at least employment with wages that were comparable despite General Electric's poor terms.

The no concessions strategy worked well for G.E. over a period of approximately 20 years due to these historical factors. Then it resulted in a very costly strike.[31] Despite that eventual strike, the many years that it was effective would seem to qualify it as a long-term success for G.E.

As G.E.'s history suggests, the no concessions strategy may work for a period of time, and then no longer be effective due to changing needs and strengths. Trade negotiations with the Japanese provide another example of this. In the 1970s, Western negotiators dealing with the Japanese often could obtain fast results with a take it or leave it approach.[32] More recently, it has been said that a no concessions strategy for such negotiations may have become viable "only in the case of really outstanding technology that the Japanese have no hope of duplicating."[33] Today, one would have to check current market conditions to determine whether that quote remains factually accurate. Regardless of whether conditions have changed, it serves to illustrate that historical patterns can emerge in which particular strategies or tactics are generally effective or ineffective.

A no concessions strategy sometimes can be successfully utilized by an apparently weak party, who can inflict devastating consequences, such as by implementing the strategy with the threat of bankruptcy. A credible threat of bankruptcy can transform an apparently weak party into a very powerful party through the adverse consequences it can create. This occurs when:

1. If the unilaterally set terms are not accepted, the clearly most advantageous choice for the client is bankruptcy; and

2. The other party will receive far less in a bankruptcy proceeding than what the offered terms provide

In this way, the unilateral terms still provide enough for the other party, so that there is sufficient incentive for it to accept the offer. Under such circumstances, the threat of bankruptcy creates extremely strong leverage for acceptance of the terms being offered pursuant to the strategy of no concessions.

Another circumstance in which this strategy can be highly effective is when the party employing it is confident that someone else will accept the terms being offered even if the other party in the present negotiation rejects them. This requires at least a very high level of confidence. When such confidence exists and is justified, then the response of the other party in the negotiation

---

[31] C. Karrass, Give & Take: The Complete Guide to Negotiating Strategies and Tactics 218 (1974).

[32] M. Zimmerman, How to Do Business with the Japanese 114 (1985).

[33] Id.

becomes almost irrelevant. If it accepts the offer, then the client's goal has been attained. If it rejects the offer, though, the rejection really does not matter, since the client can obtain the same benefits through an agreement with someone else.

Time also can be a factor that leads to the adoption of a no concessions strategy. This can occur in two ways.

1.   Cost efficiency: The amount involved may be too small to justify expending much time negotiating. Doing so just may not be cost efficient.

2.   Available time: The amount of time available to negotiate may be too short for an elaborate negotiation.

In either of these circumstances, a strategy of no concessions should be considered. However, other strategies should also be evaluated.

A different circumstance leading to the choice of the no concessions strategy arises when the same terms must be available to everyone for marketing reasons. In this situation, the party employing the no concessions strategy must be consistent with various third parties. Such consistency is needed to avoid setting a precedent that will cause either:

1.   An abandonment of its no concessions, set terms policy

2.   Hostility from others who were told that the terms were not negotiable or that they were receiving terms as favorable as anyone else would receive

The most common example of this type of situation is a price which is set so that it is "competitive" in the market place, but which is non-negotiable.

Non-negotiable terms may encompass the entire transaction, or be limited to a specified portion of the transaction. In the latter situation, the total negotiation includes both negotiable and non-negotiable terms.

A different form of the no concessions strategy is the use of bids or written proposals as the simultaneous starting and ending points for the negotiation. In effect, the party establishing the bidding procedure is stating: "Give me your best offer on a take it or leave it basis, when it will be compared to your competitors' best offers." A variation of this procedure involves some negotiation with the best bidder, either by design or by necessity, because certain terms were not covered by the bid.

Choosing a bid procedure forces the other party to make the first and, usually, the only offer. It normally forces the bidder to make a reasonable offer because of the competition that will submit other bids. However, the integrity of the bid process can depend on the existence of viable competitors, fairly drawn requirements and specifications that do not unfairly favor one competitor, and the absence of illegal horizontal price fixing.

On the other hand, a bidding procedure can eliminate the flexibility that is needed in many negotiations by all of the parties. Its use also may be limited by custom. For instance, it is difficult to imagine a group of attorneys competing for a client by submitting sealed, written bids as if they were contractors seeking a construction contract.[34]

The danger of a no concessions strategy is that it can prevent an agreement on terms which, although less favorable, are still acceptable to the client. People generally expect a negotiation to involve some concessions.[35] The no concessions strategy can offend them, make them feel as though an attempt is being made to coerce them, or simply may not be believed. If those are the reactions that are induced, the negotiation may not progress unless the negotiator either has sufficient power to force an agreement, or switches strategies and begins making concessions. A strategy shift away from no concessions can make counsel look as though he or she was ineffectively bluffing, which is a position that should be avoided.[36]

Counsel should be careful to avoid inadvertently creating a foolish bluff by a rash or miscalculated use of the no concessions strategy.[37] To avoid embarrassment, if the other party refuses to acquiesce to a no concessions strategy, counsel must be prepared either to:

1. Terminate the negotiation

2. Extricate oneself out of the apparent corner gracefully through an effective, face-saving maneuver[38]

To minimize the danger of an adverse reaction to the no concessions strategy, an especially sensitive and careful evaluation must precede its use.[39] Counsel must determine whether it is likely to be viable or too risky in view of the potential counterproductive effects.

To further reduce the risk of a negative reaction to the no concessions strategy, it may be important to act in a nonaggressive manner, without appearing either apologetic or defensive.[40] It may also be helpful to phrase the demand in terms of the reasons that the client is not in a position to offer anything

---

[34] Some clients, however, now demand written budgets and cost quotations for legal projects. This may be a move towards a quasi-bidding procedure.

[35] *See* Davis, *Settlement Negotiations: Strategy and Tactics,* 21 Trial 82, 83 (1985); Nolan, *Settlement Negotiations,* 11 Litigation 17, 19 (1985). Indeed, in the context of personal injury cases, Nolan suggests that the defendant will automatically assume that the plaintiff's initial demand is at least twice as much as the plaintiff is willing to accept and that the plaintiff will never believe that the defense attorney is really initially offering all of the money that the defendant or the insurer has authorized. While one may consider that opinion to be too generalized or too extreme, it illustrates why a no concessions approach may be inconsistent with the other side's expectations.

[36] See **§5.13** regarding bluffing.

[37] *Id.*

[38] See **§5.19** regarding face-saving.

[39] *See* **§8.07.**

[40] Tedeschi & Bonoma, *Measures or Last Resort: Coercion and Aggression in Bargaining,* in D. Druckman, Negotiations: Social-Psychological Perspectives (1977). H. Cohen, You Can Negotiate Anything 43 (1982).

else and by explaining how the demand is fair.[41] A nonaggressive demeanor and the use of objective fairness criteria to justify the ultimatum may reduce the often antagonistic nature of a no concessions position. This can allow the other side to respond affirmatively without losing face.[42]

While the no concessions strategy is often thought of as being harsh or one-sided, it need not be so limited. For example, an offer under the no concessions strategy could be structured using the win/win tactic, so that the offer presented is very positive and appealing to the other side.[43]

Countermeasures to combat a no concessions strategy include the following:[44]

1. Appeal to a higher level of authority to change the party's position
2. Ignore it and proceed as if concessions are possible
3. Present cost savings or win/win measures that justify a concession
4. As a seller, offer less, such as fewer services, thereby effectively increasing the price
5. As a buyer, demand more, thereby, in effect, reducing the price
6. Terminate the negotiating session

Other types of restructured proposals or new information also can be utilized as countermeasures, so that the negotiating situation which the no concessions strategy addressed no longer exists. The most useful tactics in this regard are:

7.   Information disclosure[45]
8.   Fact creation[46]
9.   Win/win proposals[47]
10. Inserting new issues[48]
11. Deadlock[49]
12. Surprise[50]
13. Litigation[51]

---

[41] H. Cohen, *supra* note 40, at 43-44.

[42] *See* **§5.19;** Brown, *Face-Saving and Face-Restoration in Negotiation,* in D. Druckman, Negotiations: Social-Psychological Perspectives (1977); Fisher, *supra* note 21.

[43] See **§5.06** concerning win/win proposals.

[44] C. Karrass, *supra* note 31, at 219-20.

[45] *See* **§4.02.**

[46] *See* **§4.03.**

[47] *See* **§5.06.**

[48] *See* **§5.20.**

[49] *See* **§5.23.**

[50] *See* **§5.28.**

[51] *See* **§7.02.**

With respect to client goals, the no concessions strategy should be considered for goals that are aggressive, competitive, or self-centered, provided that the other conditions conducive to an effective no concessions approach are present. These goals do not involve the type of interactive spirit as cooperative goals, or the strong need to reach an agreement often found with defensive goals. Thus, the no concessions approach is inappropriate for defensive goals and rarely, if ever, useful for cooperative goals. By comparison, if the goal is to aggressively demonstrate power as a precedent for anticipated future situations, and sufficient power is possessed to make the no concessions strategy work, then it will be the best approach to achieve that goal.

§3.04   No Further Concessions

Sometimes, the parties are close to reaching an overall agreement or resolving an issue. One party may be able to achieve an agreement on its terms at that point by switching to a strategy of no further concessions, thereby forcing the other party to make the last concession. Counsel must judge whether such a shift in strategy is likely to be successful or to jeopardize the entire matter.

In discussing this strategy, it is assumed that the party choosing it is doing so not because it has reached its bottom line limit of authority, but because it believes that it can force the other side to accept its terms. That is an entirely different situation than when a party, which has reached its bottom line, refuses to yield anything further because it believes that no agreement would be preferable to further concessions.

While the no concessions strategy is implemented at the outset of the negotiation, the no further concessions strategy is implemented after some concessions have been made. Except for that distinction concerning the timing of the strategy, the considerations discussed with respect to the no concessions strategy also are applicable to the no further concessions strategy.[52]

The timing of when to refuse to make any, or any further, concessions is very significant. As noted above, one of the problems involved with doing so at the very beginning of the negotiation is that people generally expect some give and take in a negotiation, and they are liable to react negatively if there is none. That risk is greater in the no concessions strategy than in the no further concessions strategy, since one or more concessions previously will have been made.[53]

The countermeasures to this strategy are the same as those for its parent, the no concessions strategy. These countermeasures include appealing to a higher level of authority to change the party's position, ignoring it and proceeding as if concessions are possible, presenting cost saving measures that justify a concession, offering less or more to effectively alter the price, terminating

---

[52] *See* **§3.03.**

[53] Cohen has suggested that an ultimatum should be used only at the end, never at the start, of a negotiation. H. Cohen, You Can Negotiate Anything 43 (1982).

the negotiating session, information disclosure, fact creation, win/win proposals, inserting new issues, deadlock, surprise, and litigation.[54]

§3.05   Making Only Deadlock-Breaking Concessions

On a scale with a reluctance to make concessions as a measure of toughness, the strategy of making a concession only to break a deadlock is the next toughest strategy, after no and no further concessions. This strategy constitutes a form of brinkmanship. Issues are pushed to the point of a deadlock, which occurs when the other party is actually or virtually ready to cease negotiating because of a material impasse.

This strategy generates an atmosphere of tension and difficulty. In response to it, the other party may cease negotiating for a number of reasons. The other side may come to believe that a satisfactory agreement cannot be reached due to the intransigent attitude that is being displayed. It also may become too tired of or too offended by the strategy to proceed with further negotiations despite a last minute concession to attempt to revive the negotiation.

Therefore, the decision to use the deadlock-breaking concessions only strategy should be made with the same high degree of caution used to decide on the no concessions strategies.[55] Moreover, for the same reasons, effectuating this strategy may necessitate utilizing the same sensitive methods described for making those strategies more palatable to the other side.[56]

Accordingly, a strategy of compromising only to break a deadlock tends to have potential viability for aggressive, competitive, or self-centered goals. In contrast, cooperative goals require a more open, less tense process aimed at obtaining mutual benefits. This strategy also generally is inappropriate for defensive goals in light of the high need to reach an agreement that usually is involved with defensive goals. Under such circumstances, employing a strategy of conceding only to break a deadlock normally is far too risky.

§3.06   High, Realistic Expectations with Small, Systematic Concessions (HRESSC)

Successful strategy generally involves: "[E]xtreme initial offers, well above (or below) one's resistance point, making concessions few, small, reciprocal, and each one rationalized, explained, justified on some basis other than mere pursuit of agreement."[57]

HRESSC refers to the strategy of combining high, realistic expectations with small, systematic concessions. Thus, the strategy combines a planned approach to both the objectives of the negotiation and the compromises that may be

---

[54] See §3.03 regarding the countermeasures to the no concessions strategy.

[55] *See* §§3.03 & 3.04.

[56] *See id.*

[57] M. Saks & R. Hastie, Social Psychology in Court 124 (1978).

employed to reach those objectives. As a general rule, it is the strategy which achieves the best results. That does *not* mean that HRESSC always is the best strategy. It may or it may not be depending on the particular situation. Overall, however, it is the most useful strategy.

The HRESSC strategy requires assessing the objective value of the subject matter in the negotiation. This is necessary in order to properly formulate high, but realistic expectations. The assessment may be of the value of a case in litigation or of the assets that are available in a transaction.

High realistic expectations mean that the negotiator has neither undervalued the client's position, thereby losing a feasible opportunity, nor overvalued it so unrealistically high that any chance for a good, but unspectacular, agreement is blocked. By avoiding those pitfalls, the opening position is established sufficiently high that it encompasses any real opportunity to make a highly favorable settlement. However, the opening position is not set so high that the other negotiator feels that an agreement will be impossible. If the opening position is miscalculated so that it reflects a high but unrealistic expectation, counsel may be placed in the unfortunate position of attempting to gracefully make a large concession and essentially restart the HRESSC strategy. The concept of choosing the right opening position is examined in further detail in the chapter on planning.[58]

With respect to possible concessions, the HRESSC strategy has three components. These are (1) the size of the concessions, (2) the use of "concessions" which involve no cost to the client whenever possible, and (3) the advance planning of concessions.

As its name indicates, the strategy involves making small compromises. A small concession is a relative concept. A $500 negotiation may involve $25 to $50 concessions. For a $10,000 negotiation, $250 to $500 concessions are relatively small. In contrast, for a $10 million negotiation, a $500 concession would be laughable. There, a relatively small concession could range from $25,000 to $500,000.

What is relatively small is dependent on two factors. First, it must be considered in light of the range or difference of dollars (or other things) that exists in between the opening positions of the parties. Second, this relativity must be evaluated in terms of the aggregate amount involved in the negotiation itself. That aspect of the evaluation normally involves both objective and subjective considerations of what the case or the transactional matter is worth.

Although the foregoing discussion used dollars to illustrate the concept, this strategy can be utilized for nonmonetary as well as monetary negotiations. When money is not directly involved, often the subjective evaluation of the relative size of the concession becomes increasingly important because adequate objective measurements either do not exist or are more open to question and disagreement.

Small concessions are important because they tend to prevent missed opportunities to reach an optimal settlement. An optimal settlement is the most favor-

---

[58] *See* §9.02.

able point at which an agreement can be formulated with the other party and the other negotiator at the present time. If large concessions are made, it often is difficult to know whether the agreement could have been reached at some point in between the last offer that was rejected and the large concession which finally led to the resolution of the negotiation. With small concessions, relatively little has been relinquished in that last concession before the agreement was reached. Giving a large last concession, however, creates the distinct possibility that a great deal more was given away than was necessary, simply due to the size of the concession. Similarly, multiple concessions should not be made so rapidly that they in fact become a large concession. Speed also is a relative term. If the negotiator receives desired reciprocal concessions, then speed is less significant, since each concession stands independently. However, when concessions are made fairly quickly without receiving desired concessions in return, small concessions can become a large concession as a negotiating reality.

Small concessions also may reduce the other party's expectations.[59] They may create or reinforce the appearance that the negotiator is not willing to agree to substantial concessions, since he or she is making only small concessions.

Often, negotiators make only small concessions as they near the boundaries of their authority, after having made very large concessions earlier. Although this can be appropriate, it is a mistake to just follow a pattern of reducing the size of concessions as one nears the limits of one's authority. To do so makes the negotiation far too predictable.

Small concessions are an integral part of the HRESSC strategy. With other strategies, larger concessions can be used where small concessions are inappropriate or clearly useless. Note, however, that the use of small concessions also is a tactic which can be utilized for other strategies.[60]

Whenever possible, as part of its systematic concessions, the HRESSC strategy seeks to employ concessions which apparently concede something, but, in fact, relinquish nothing or little of value from the client's perspective. Like small concessions, such systematic no or low cost concessions are used to avoid missing opportunities for an optimal settlement.

The term "systematic" describes the procedure followed by the negotiator, who systematically exhausts a series of "concessions" at the same cost level to the client before moving to concessions at the next greater cost level. The alternative "concessions" at the same cost level constitute the system:

Figure 3-1

Cost Level	Cost To Client	Concession	Concession	Concession
1	$10,000	A	B	C
2	$20,000	D	E	F

---

[59] *See* Hammer & Yukel, *The Effectiveness of Different Offer Strategies in Bargaining,* in D. Druckman, Negotiations: Social-Psychological Perspectives (1977).

[60] See §5.09 regarding bargaining.

To make systematic concessions, the negotiator first plans alternative concessions at the same cost level. (Concessions A, B, and C at Level 1, and D, E, and F at Level 2.) In this negotiation, concession A is offered first. If rejected, then concession B followed by C are tried. Only after all alternative concessions A, B, and C at Level 1 are tried unsuccessfully does the negotiator move to offering any Level 2 concessions. The Level 2 D, E, and F concessions are systematically explored one at a time to determine whether any of those concessions will bring about an agreement before the negotiator offers concessions from the next higher cost level.

Example 3-6

Assume that a seller can provide daily delivery service at no greater an incremental cost than delivery within 48 hours would entail. The seller can initially offer to make deliveries within 48 hours, then make a concession to guarantee deliveries within 24 hours, and finally offer daily delivery. These concessions are systematic in that each one can be used to require a reciprocal concession from the buyer, yet neither of the delivery concessions cost the seller anything.

Systematic concessions can also involve changes in the amount to be paid which do not involve any material cost to the party making the payment. No "material cost" is involved when the cost differential is too insignificant in context to be considered at all important.

Such a change in payment might involve moving from a lump sum payment to payment over time as the following example illustrates.

Example 3-7

A buyer first offers to pay $25,000 to the seller. Several concessions and 45 minutes later, the buyer increases the offer to $42,000. The seller rejects that offer and makes a counterproposal of $50,000. The buyer reasonably estimates that it can use the $42,000 that it previously offered to generate payments totaling $50,000 if the payments are made over a two-year period of time. Accordingly, the buyer concedes and accepts the $50,000 price on the condition that the payments can be spread out over a two-year payment period.[61] Assuming that the price concession with payments over time still has greater value to the seller than the immediate payment of $42,000, the buyer has proposed a concession at no cost to itself which has enough value to the other party to obtain a satisfactory agreement.

---

[61] This is also a conditional proposal, since the amount is conditional on its being paid in installments. See §5.11 regarding the tactic of conditional proposals.

The other part of the systematic concessions concept is that, in advance of the negotiation, the negotiator plans the compromises that will or that might be offered at various potential points in the negotiation. Both the concessions themselves and the timing or circumstances under which they will be offered are anticipated. While this approach is not independent of the actions of the other party, neither does it merely react to those actions. Rather, it provides flexibility to take the initiative or react depending on the actions which actually occur during the negotiation. The advance planning is likely to help to maximize one's results, and to minimize pressure to merely respond to the other negotiator's tactics, arguments, or offers instead of affirmatively moving in the direction of one's own choice.

The HRESSC strategy is very useful for competitive, aggressive, self-centered, or defensive goals. It also can be used when the major client goal is a cooperative one, to the extent that some competitive elements exist within that cooperative goal as well. Its general utility is due to the fact that HRESSC is a method that allows one to carefully probe and test the other party's reactions, in order to determine the optimal settlement point.

Countermeasures include the use of an HRESSC strategy in response, with positions that counteract or overcome the other party's HRESSC strategy. Other countermeasures include the no concessions, no further concessions, deadlock-breaking only concessions, and problem solving strategies.

§3.07   Concede First

As its name implies, the concede first strategy consists of making the first concession. Making the first concession may disarm the other party, reduce tension, create goodwill, and generate an atmosphere of movement and compromise. In addition, making the first concession allows one to demand a reciprocal concession in the spirit of fair play, either at that time or subsequently, and the early first concession can lead the other negotiator to reciprocate.[62]

Example 3-8

After making the first concession, a negotiator tells the other negotiator:

"You know, you really cannot expect us to concede anything else. We made an important concession at the outset of this meeting. You still have not given us anything significant enough to match that concession. At this point, you are ahead, and it isn't fair to expect more from us. We are willing to be flexible, but only if you demonstrate flexibility as well."[63]

The name "concede first" might be construed to imply that this strategy is limited to the opening stages of the negotiation. However, this strategy also

---

[62] W. Coffin, The Negotiator: A Manual For Winners 33 (1973).

[63] This example also demonstrates the use of a fairness argument. See §5.10 concerning discussion.

can be effectively utilized at the opening stage of negotiating a particular issue within the overall negotiation. Due to its inherently limited nature, though, it must be used in conjunction with one or more other strategies.

If the concede first strategy is adopted, the concession must have some value to the party that is receiving it. From the perspective of the party that is making the initial concession, it must not have so much value that it seriously undermines that party's subsequent bargaining position. Although the initial concession must cause the recipient to feel as though it has received something worthwhile, too large an initial concession can remove an important bargaining chip from the giver's arsenal, thereby adversely affecting the giver's ability to maneuver during the remainder of the negotiation.

It can be difficult and sometimes impossible to successfully withdraw a concession without sabotaging the entire negotiation. To many negotiators, once concessions are given, they are "immutable" and are not to be altered.[64] Therefore, this first concession must be planned and structured so that it will not be necessary to attempt to withdraw it later, even if the other side subsequently refuses to make a reciprocal concession.

Furthermore, the concede first strategy, particularly if the first concession is too large, can have seriously detrimental, unintended effects for the conceding party. It can backfire. The recipient may perceive this first concession as a sign of weakness, since it comes at the outset of the entire negotiation or of that portion focused on a specific issue. Such a perception can lead the other party to raise its expectations of what it can obtain, and to consequently harden its position. Therefore, caution should be exercised before deciding to implement a concede first strategy.

The danger that this strategy may backfire can be tempered by the mode of presentation. Not only the timing and the size of the initial concession, but also the manner in which it is made can affect how the other party perceives and reacts to it. Certainly, the party giving the concession should exercise every effort to appear confident and to avoid the appearance of weakness. Accompanying the concession with an explicit explanation for it is an additional method of minimizing the possibility that the concession will be misunderstood.[65]

The corollary to this principle is that the concede first strategy should not be chosen if one is operating from a position of weakness. Doing so only will increase the other side's knowledge or perception of that weakness. Furthermore, the strategy relinquishes a bargaining chip that a weak party cannot afford to give away without at least obtaining a specific, agreed, reciprocal concession in return.[66]

The key questions in making this choice of strategy decision are whether, in the specific negotiating situation and given the particular other negotiator and other party, the concede first strategy will:

---

[64] *See* M. Zimmerman, How to Do Business with the Japanese 99 (1985).

[65] The use of reasons and rationales is explored in **§5.10** on discussion.

[66] Demanding specific, reciprocal concessions is a form of bargaining. See **§5.05** regarding reciprocity.

1.   Reduce tension, create an atmosphere conducive to reaching an agreement, and be likely to allow one to demand a reciprocal concession; *OR,*

2.   Cause the other party to infer that it is in a position to increase or harden its demands or its aspirations.

Regardless of whether the other party's inference is correct or erroneous, such an inference is, of course, totally counterproductive for the party making the concession. Once made, the inference becomes the reality for the other party, and can be extremely difficult to change.

It is necessary to focus on the specific other negotiator and the actual other party, because the effect of the concede first strategy, whether positive or negative, is so dependent on their perception of it. If they are taking a hard, competitive approach, then the concession is likely to be seen as a sign of weakness, and it will have negative results.[67] Early signs of such an attitude on the part of the other side include their taking an extreme initial position, such as a tough or ridiculous opening demand, or their use of high pressure, emotional tactics such as acting outraged or angry.[68] Those types of conduct should be viewed as warning signs not to employ the concede first strategy.

The concede first strategy is used far less often than the HRESSC or problem solving strategies.[69] It can be used to effectively achieve competitive, cooperative, self-centered, or defensive client goals, depending on the specific context of the negotiation. Rarely if ever can it be utilized for aggressive client goals where the other party to the negotiation is a target to be injured by the aggression. If, however, the target of the aggressive goal is a third party and the other party in the negotiation is the means to achieve that goal, then the strategy can be useful.

Example 3-9

A manufacturer seeks to sell to a retailer that is currently purchasing from the manufacturer's competitor. If the manufacturer achieves that goal, its sales will reduce or replace the retailer's purchases from the manufacturer's competitor. Part of the manufacturer's motive is, in fact, to undermine its competitor. Thus, it has an aggressive goal whose target is the competitor. With regard to the retailer, the manufacturer has a competitive goal in that it wants to achieve the highest possible price and profits for its goods, while achieving agreement with certain price/cost limitations. It also may have a cooperative goal if factors exist that allow it to structure incentives such as volume discounts to produce greater profits for both the manufacturer and the retailer. Under these circumstances, the retailer is the means to carry out the aggressive goal against the competitor, and a concede first strategy might be appropriate depending on the exact circumstances.

---

[67] H. Cohen, You Can Negotiate Anything 121 (1982).

[68] *Id.*

[69] The problem solving strategy is examined next in **§3.08.**

The opening concession under this strategy can assume a multitude of forms. In sales agreements, it may involve a purchaser's right to cancel the contract after an initial period if the purchaser is dissatisfied with the goods or services that are being provided. In real estate transactions, the concession could be a provision allowing cancellation of the contract within a specified number of days if the buyer has the property inspected by a contractor, architect, or engineer, and then is not satisfied with the property. Such a concession encourages the purchaser to enter into a tentative agreement, since the purchaser will obtain the property if the inspection is satisfactory, while avoiding the cost of the inspection until it is known that a desirable deal can be made. A variation of this approach is the option to purchase, under which the seller receives a specified payment even if the purchaser decides not to proceed after the inspection. This can be useful when the inspection will take a significant amount of time because it includes certain types of testing, and the seller is unwilling or reluctant to take the property off of the market for more than a brief period without receiving some compensation.

The concede first strategy also can be used in those rare circumstances when any real negotiation may lead the other party to discover information that will harm the client more than the concession being given.

Example 3-10

An opportunity exists to negotiate an issue of tax liability with the I.R.S. There is a significant danger, however, that to do so will lead the I.R.S. to discover other, more costly issues. Accordingly, the decision is made to concede first, seeking a quick resolution before the other issues are uncovered.[70]

Other examples of possible first concessions include renewal privileges, small discounts from the normal rate, and incentive payments for above average performance.[71] The variety of appropriate, initial concessions for the concede first strategy is limited only by situational realities and creativity.

A danger of the concede first strategy is that the concession will be accepted by one who refuses to acknowledge that reciprocity is appropriate or required, and who thereby simply retains the concession without later making one in return. Accordingly, a refusal to reciprocate is a countermeasure to the concede first strategy when it can be done without adversely affecting the ultimate outcome of the negotiation.

No countermeasure should be employed when the concede first strategy allows the other party to create movement in a desired direction with follow-up bargaining. Then, the concede first strategy should not be resisted by the other party, but rather used to pursue its own ends.

---

[70] *See* Wise, *Negotiations with the Internal Revenue*, in Attorney's Guide to Negotiation 2-14, 2-15 (1979).

[71] The latter has become commonplace for professional athletes, although it is often a bargained-for concession, rather than an opening concession by management, because of its value.

§3.08   Problem Solving

Problem solving is the second most generally useful strategy after HRESSC.[72] It is conceptually quite different than the previously discussed strategies of no concessions, no further concessions, deadlock-breaking concessions only, HRESSC, and concede first.[73] Those all center on concessions, i.e., relinquishing or refusing to relinquish something of value.[74]

Unlike concession based strategies, problem solving focuses on initially creating a procedural agreement that the negotiators will work together to discover and identify the problems that are preventing an agreement, and to determine whether the parties share common interests in resolving those problems.[75] Common interests are those which both parties have, apart from their individual needs. The parties' separate needs often are disclosed in the process of establishing the boundaries of the common interests, and the extent to which the needs of one do not conflict with the needs of the other.

Next, the negotiators discuss the matter to make those determinations. Assuming that they successfully identify the problems and that they also agree on common interests shared by the parties for the resolution of those agreed on, identified problems, the negotiators then proceed to the last, but most crucial step in the problem solving process. They strive together to discover fair, mutually beneficial solutions which resolve the previously identified problems in light of the shared, previously agreed upon interests. In this way, problem solving is used to create an agreement that is satisfactory to both parties because it resolves jointly defined problems through mutually identified common interests while meeting each of their essential needs. For this reason, when problem solving is successful, both sides feel that they have won. To summarize, the operative steps are:

1.   A procedural agreement to use problem solving

---

[72] The authors recognize that this is the subject of an ongoing debate in the literature on negotiations. *See* Menkel-Meadow, *Legal Negotiation: A Study of Strategies in Search of a Theory*, Am B Found Res J 905 (1983); Fisher, *supra* note 21; Pruitt & Lewis, *The Psychology of Integrative Bargaining*, in D. Druckman, Negotiations: Social-Psychological Perspectives (1977).

[73] The problem solving approach has also been labeled "collaborative bargaining," "integrative bargaining," "principled negotiation or negotiation on the merits," "cooperative bargaining," and "solution devising." *See generally,* Menkel-Meadow *supra* note 72 and H. Cohen, You Can Negotiate Anything (1982); Pruitt & Lewis, *supra* note 72 (integrative bargaining); H. Raiffa, The Art and Science of Negotiation (1982) (integrative bargaining); Fisher, *supra* note 21 (principled negotiation or negotiation on the merits); G. Williams, Legal Negotiation and Settlement (1983) (cooperative bargaining); W. Zartman & M. Berman, The Practical Negotiator (1982) (solution devising).

[74] These types of strategies have been variously referred to by such labels as positional, competitive, compromise, distributive, or adversarial bargaining. *See* Pruitt & Lewis, *supra* note 72; Menkel-Meadow, *supra* note 72; S. Goldberg, E. Green & F. Sander, Dispute Resolution (1985) [hereinafter Goldberg]; G. Nierenberg, The Art of Negotiation: Psychological Strategies for Gaining Advantageous Bargains (1968).

[75] *See* Fisher, *supra* note 21; H. Cohen, *supra* note 73, at chs 8 & 9.

2.   Identification of the problems preventing agreement

3.   Determination of any common interests and limiting separate needs

4.   Discussion to discover fair, mutually beneficial solutions

Problem solving is described by some, using game theory terminology, as a win/win strategy.[76] For our purposes, though, the phrase "win/win" will be used to describe a tactic employed as a unilateral endeavor by a single negotiator.[77] In contrast, the phrase "problem solving" is used for a strategy that is a joint endeavor of the negotiators. The situation is considered from a mutual problem solving point of view, and each negotiator must take into account the desires not only of his or her own client, but also those of the other party.[78]

Example 3-11

A manufacturer and a dealer were engaged in a dispute about service, in an area covered only by generalized contractual terms which were arguably susceptible to varying interpretations. To avoid future questions concerning the requirements, the parties agreed that the manufacturer could terminate the dealer if certain specified acts occurred.[79] The manufacturer also retained the right to terminate under other general provisions of the original agreement.

In order for problem solving to be a useful strategy, certain conditions must exist. First, the parties, or the negotiators, or both, must want and agree to work together to identify the problems preventing an agreement and to formulate a mutually advantageous solution. Second, the parties must have a mutual interest in solving the particular problems in the same ways, so that everyone is operating together in good faith. Third, the negotiators must identify the same problems and agree on how to define them. Fourth, the problems cannot be solved simply by one side yielding, but rather by creating a previously unconsidered, mutually beneficial solution.

The first three conditions may exist in a particular situation, or they may require development through effort, persuasion, negotiation, and sensitivity to the other party's real needs. The last point probably is the most important, since the problem solving strategy can be successful only when the other party's real needs can be satisfactorily met through an agreement that also will satisfy the client's goals.[80]

Needs or interests provide the motivation for a party to seek something in the negotiation. Objectives are those items which the party articulates as what

---

[76] *See* H. Cohen, *supra* note 73, at chs 8 & 9.

[77] *See* **§5.06.**

[78] R. Lewicki & J. Litterer, Negotiation 26 (1985) [hereinafter Lewicki].

[79] *See* R. Givens, Advocacy: The Art of Pleading a Cause 48-49 (Shepard's/McGraw-Hill, Inc 1985 Supp 1986).

[80] H. Cohen, *supra* note 73. Cohen summarizes this point by stating that: "Successful collaborative negotiation lies in finding out what the other side really wants and showing them a way to get it, while you get what you want." *Id* 161.

it desires to meet its needs or interests. Since objectives are not needs or interests and even may exaggerate or mislead as to the real need, parties engaged in problem solving must move beyond previously stated objectives to discuss needs and interests. In this way, the negotiators seek to discover the means to achieve common interests and nonconflicting separate interests, without violating essential conflicting interests.

Counsel must recognize that the clients on both sides may place different values on the matters that can be conceded, so that the possibility of an agreement is increased by trading concessions across issues. This reflects the problem solving focus on the basic point of determining the needs both of one's own client and of the other party.[81] In this sense "problem solving begins by attempting to determine the actual needs of particular clients."[82]

Being sensitive to the other side's needs and interests involves both reality and perception. One should be empathetic so as to be able to discover those real needs and interests.[83] This becomes particularly significant to the extent that the other party's real underlying needs and interests are distinct from its expressed positions.[84] Thus, in problem solving, one must focus on interests and needs, not negotiating positions.[85]

One's demeanor also should be cooperative and empathetic so as to help build the trust that is needed to cooperatively solve problems in good faith.[86] This may be necessary to defuse an initial competitive, emotional, or antagonistic attitude of the other party or of the other negotiator.[87] Any such attitudinal problems with the people involved in the negotiation must not be confused with the substantive problems at issue, but must be handled on a separate

---

[81] Menkel-Meadow, *Toward Another View of Legal Negotiation: The Structure of Problem Solving*, 31 UCLA L Rev 754, 795 (1984). Menkel-Meadow discusses "problem solving" as a matter of orientation, as distinct from strategy. "Unfortunately, some of this new literature tends to confuse collaborative negotiation styles or strategies with what must be antecedent to any negotiation behavior—a conception of negotiation goals." *Id* 758.

Although problem solving is used here to name a strategy because it is descriptive of that strategy, this is more of a difference in semantics, than of substance. Menkel-Meadow's appropriate concern for an orientation that is attuned to the client's goals is encompassed by the considerations expressed not only in this section, but also with respect to client goals and planning. *See* **chs 2 & 8.**

[82] Menkel-Meadow, *supra* note 81, at 801. *See* **ch 2.**

[83] H. Cohen, *supra* note 73, at 149-205; Fisher, *supra* note 72, at 24.

[84] Just as one's own client may have psychological motives that need to be recognized and which may affect the negotiation, the other party is equally liable to have various psychological needs that affect it. *See* **ch 2.** Fisher, *supra* note 21; H. Cohen, *supra* note 73.

[85] Fisher, *supra* note 21; H. Cohen, *supra* note 73, at chs 8 & 9; G. Nierenberg, *supra* note 74. This is one of the four cornerstones of Fisher and Ury's "principled negotiation" approach.

[86] H. Cohen, *supra* note 73, at chs 8 & 9 (1982); Fisher, *supra* note 72. See **§3.02** regarding the negotiator's credibility.

[87] *See* R. Givens, *supra* note 79.

level.[88] A cooperative, empathetic demeanor also can be important because the other party's real psychological needs may include the manner in which the negotiation is conducted.[89]

One method for engaging the other negotiator in a problem solving effort is to raise the problem in the form of a question or a request for suggestions. The question or request may be either direct or implicit.

Example 3-12

"I saw a hole in our draft at this point regarding how to cover your purchaser's ability to pay if she is sued for medical malpractice, especially if there are future problems with tail-end coverage, or changes in her practice. I really don't know how to cover this. We could have an escrow, but that may not be a good idea."

Problem solving often requires a degree of creativity with respect to both the way in which the problem is perceived and in creating mutually beneficial solutions. Often, the negotiation must be reexamined to find the real issue causing the impasse, rather than to continue discussing the issues as they have been previously articulated. Patience and perseverance may be needed, since the problem solving process may be slow.[90]

The definition of the problem is important. It should be as simple and direct as possible, in order to facilitate focusing in a specific direction when seeking solutions. To the extent possible, the definition also should depersonalize the problem.[91] This can alleviate the danger that the negotiators or the parties will be too judgmental, or take matters too personally.[92] Once the problem is defined, unless an acceptable solution can be presented in the initial discussion that follows, a solution may be uncovered by identifying each obstacle impeding settlement as exactly as possible.

Focusing on avoiding mutually adverse or potentially undesirable outside forces can be a means of establishing a mutual interest. Such outside forces may be:

1.   Government action

2.   A jury or a judge deciding the facts at trial so that one side wins totally while the other side loses totally

3.   A competitor gaining an advantage

4.   The expiration of a financing commitment

---

[88] This is another of the four basic elements of Fisher & Ury's "principled negotiation" approach. *See* Fisher, *supra* note 21.

[89] H. Cohen, *supra* note 73, at chs 8 & 9; Fisher, *supra* note 21.

[90] Pruitt & Lewis, *supra* note 72.

[91] Lewicki, *supra* note 78, at 116; Fisher, *supra* note 21.

[92] Lewicki, *supra* note 78, at 116; Fisher, *supra* note 21.

Problem solving can involve devising some means to broaden the pie so that it is no longer the same fixed amount which must be divided, and so that a zero-sum, win/lose game is converted to a win/win or positive sum game.[93] Although unlike the strategies previously discussed, because the problem solving strategy is not focused on concessions, creating a solution still may involve trading concessions. Typically, however, this would consist of exchanging concessions on issues that have differing value to the parties, so that both sides feel that they are gaining something and not merely compromising what they are willing to accept as in a strictly monetary negotiation.[94] Such an exchange is greatly facilitated whenever one or both of the concessions can be given at no cost to the party providing it.[95] At other times, however, a competitive element within an issue will necessitate some competitive bargaining.

Both to expand the pie and to find concessions that the parties value differently, it may be useful to consider the distribution of resources in terms of:[96]

What will be distributed

When it will be distributed

By whom it will be distributed

How it will be distributed

How much will be distributed

This can be true not only in the context of negotiating a transaction, but also in the context of litigation.

Problem solving attempts may benefit from generating a variety of options before reaching a decision on a course of action.[97] This process is aided by raising suggestions instead of fixed solutions. The suggestions are made with an acknowledgment, or in an atmosphere indicating, that someone else later may devise a better suggestion. Of course, consistent with the strategy's philosophy, these suggested options should be devised with a view towards mutual gain.[98] Either brainstorming, perhaps with the other side, or obtaining different perspectives from different experts or other sources, may be helpful.[99] Brainstorming, for problem solving or otherwise, is a process which requires that the participants:[100]

---

[93] Menkel-Meadow, *supra* note 81, at 809; Pruitt & Lewis, *supra* note 72.

[94] Pruitt & Lewis, *supra* note 72. Pruitt and Lewis refer to this as "logrolling." *Id* 163-64. They also suggest a third method of creating a solution, that of alternating turns. However, that seems unlikely to be applicable to many legal negotiations.

[95] See §§5.06 and 5.08 regarding no cost and relatively low cost concessions.

[96] Menkel-Meadow, *supra* note 81, at 810.

[97] Fisher, *supra* note 21. This is another of the four bases of Fisher and Ury's "principled negotiating" approach.

[98] *Id.*

[99] *Id* 58-72.

[100] T. Warschaw, Winning By Negotiation 138 (McGraw-Hill, Inc 1980).

1. Speak spontaneously, thinking out loud as long as it is relevant and constructive

2. Refrain from evaluating or criticizing the statements of others

3. Be willing to repeat one's ideas if others want to hear them again

4. Build on the suggestions of others by adding to or modifying them

5. Persist in the effort even if there is a prolonged silence

Seeking to focus on principles which can then provide a guide for the specifics of an agreement also may be beneficial. It is not easy to agree that a specific, concrete resolution is fair. Useful principles to follow to determine fairness are needed, and these can be difficult to derive. To be utilized, the principles need to constitute objective criteria for evaluating a resolution of the issues.[101]

When the solution to the problem involves agreement on a standard or a formula that will be used to ultimately resolve the issue, the standard or formula should entail criteria as specific as possible. This helps to avert future disagreement in determining the specific resolution dictated by the controlling standard or formula. For example, deciding that a matter should be resolved on the basis of constitutional due process is of little assistance when the real disagreement concerns the application of due process to the particular facts.

In seeking solutions, one can look to precedent and community practice.[102] On the other hand, the problem solving negotiator should be wary of allowing precedent or community practice to repress creativity and innovation. This is particularly true where precedent and community practice were themselves the product of a prior negotiation which the client was not a party to, and the results of which neither fully solve the problem in question nor totally satisfy the client's goals. Thus, depending on the particular circumstances, precedent and common practices should not be automatically accepted, but instead should be treated as starting points for thought, since they merely resulted from prior negotiation.[103]

§3.09   Examples of Problem Solving

The following examples illustrate productive problem solving efforts. They also demonstrate the necessity of an atmosphere dominated by cooperation, rather than by competition.

Example 3-13

Two businessmen plan to launch a new venture as equal owners. The two are quite enthusiastic about this apparently lucrative opportunity. After having agreed on what they had considered the "major" issues, they stall on how to value their respective interests in the event of a future

---

[101] Fisher, *supra* note 21, at 84.

[102] *Id.*

[103] H. Cohen, *supra* note 73, at 58-59.

disagreement leading one to buy out the other. However, they do agree that they are firmly committed to proceeding with the deal, and that a way to determine the value of their shares in the event of a buy out is essential. One then suggests that, if they cannot agree on the value in the event such a management deadlock arises, each party should have the right to offer the entire business for sale to an outsider. The party which procures an acceptable offer from an outsider then would have to allow the other party an opportunity to "match" the outsider's offer by paying an amount equal to one-half of it for the first party's one-half interest. If the offer was not so matched, the business would be sold to the outsider, and the proceeds would be split equally between the two owners. They agree that this method avoids the undervaluing that could arise from trying to sell a one-half interest with potential deadlock, or from a statutorily forced dissolution sale.

Example 3-14

The seller and the purchaser of commercial real estate property have agreed on the price of the property and on other economic terms. The seller occupies a portion of the location, and it will be moving out. The purchaser needs to have its own store in the property by a certain date, so that it is extremely important that the seller vacate the premises on time. The seller assures the purchaser that it will move out on time, explains the economic reasons which strongly motivate it to do so, but it also explains the circumstances which constrain any earlier move. The buyer remains quite concerned about the timing of the move, and is reluctant to proceed. The seller then offers to add a draconian penalty clause for any late move except due to acts of God, feeling absolutely confident that the penalty clause will never be invoked. The purchaser now is satisfied and signs the contract. This method of assuaging the buyer's fears does not involve any time or expense to the seller, which has its own independent reasons necessitating that it move out by the required date in any event.

Example 3-15

The purchaser of goods is unwilling to enter into a long-term agreement without significantly higher discounts than those available under potential short-term arrangements. The magnitude of the requested discounts far exceeds those which the seller is willing to consider. The parties argue back and forth about the general advantages and disadvantages of a long-term contract, as well as about the price trends each of them foresees over the long-run period of time. Unable to find a common figure or a mathematical formula, an impasse develops. They decide to try to explore their feelings about and methods for deciding the appropriate discount. During the ensuing discussion, the seller learns that the buyer's real concern is that she does not want to have some competitor later receive a lower price through a more favorable discount. This is not a meaningful concern for the seller in light of the other advantages provided by a long-term contract. Thus, the seller does not object to adjusting the discount in the future should such a situation ever arise. Accordingly, the seller solves the problem by offering the purchaser a "most favored nation" clause, under which the buyer is entitled to receive discount terms as favorable as those given to any other buyer in the future during the term of the contract.

Example 3-16

The founder and sole shareholder of a manufacturing company is ready to retire. His four grown children are the key employees, and they decide to formulate a proposal to purchase the business. They agree on a number of essential terms. Two sons, though, want a clause which guarantees employment for all of them unless the business is sold to an outsider. The other two, a son and a daughter, assert that such an arrangement would be unworkable. After much discussion, they agree on how to define the real problem. That problem is the relationship of total compensation, employment, and ownership. Each of them now receives approximately equal compensation as an employee, and each would invest an equal amount towards the purchase of the business. If, after the purchase, however, any of them were to be terminated as an employee by the others, that person's compensation would be zero if no dividends were declared, and it would be considerably less even with the highest foreseeable dividends. The four then are able to agree that the corporation should purchase the stock of any shareholder who is terminated as an employee. The next problem is to devise a method for the valuation of the stock. The group is unable to agree on either a set amount or on a mathematical formula. They all agree, though, that their goal is to set a fair price for the stock considering certain factors about the business. After further discussion, they agree that in the event that such a situation arises, if they cannot agree on a price for the stock at that time, the issue will be submitted to binding arbitration.

In all of the foregoing examples, the right conditions existed for the application of a problem solving strategy. In each of the illustrations, the four necessary conditions for the use of the problem solving strategy were present.

1. Mutual desire and agreement of the parties (negotiators) to engage in problem solving
2. Parties mutually interested in solving the problems in the same way, so they operated in good faith
3. Parties (negotiators) jointly identify and agree on the problems
4. A win/win situation is possible

If the appropriate conditions do not exist, counsel cannot productively engage in problem solving.

Example 3-17

The parties have been unable to agree on the amount which would settle a pending suit based on breach of contract claims. The negotiators are the lawyers for the plaintiff (P) and the defendant (D).

P: We basically agree that a breach took place, but we can't seem to agree on the amount for settlement. That's the problem.

D: That is the problem. You want too much to settle this case.

P: Oh, no. You just aren't willing to pay enough.

This is *not* an example of a problem solving strategy despite having the negotiators agree on a defined "problem." There is no attempt to identify common interests or to work together to formulate a mutually beneficial solution under which both parties "win" by having their vital interests protected. That type of approach could lead directly to an agreed settlement figure, or to a formula or method through which an agreeable settlement amount could be determined. Instead, there is a fight either to just pay more or to pay less, so that only one party will benefit (i.e. win) at the expense of the other party.

A different issue arises when one party is not interested in proceeding in good faith because it really defines the problem differently than the way it is discussed in the negotiation. That party views its interests as antagonistic, rather than mutual, and proceeds accordingly rather than in a truly cooperative manner.

Example 3-18

The CEO of a company calls in his purchasing and transportation managers. He informs them that cuts are being made in the company, and that their departments have some overlapping functions. The CEO then directs that each determine how to eliminate any overlap within his or her own department and how to implement a personnel reduction of at least 20 per cent. The two managers negotiate with the CEO in a cooperative, problem solving way regarding the required reduction. The CEO relents to the extent that the minimum reduction in force will be 15 per cent. The two managers then agree to cooperate with each other, and to meet again with the CEO in two weeks.

Two weeks pass. At the meeting, the transportation manager presents a plan for his department that follows the original, cooperative, problem solving approach. He proposes eliminating 17 per cent of his department's employees. The purchasing manager, however, views the situation differently. She sees it as a competitive one in which her power and responsibilities are threatened. From her perspective, this is an issue of protecting her turf and intracorporate empire building. She devised quite a different proposal. Her recommendation is accompanied by a detailed cost-benefit analysis. She proposes that, because of economic efficiencies, her department only be cut 5 per cent, while the transportation department be cut by 30 per cent.

This illustrates the dangers and the problems that can arise when needs and interests clash rather than coincide, but problem solving is attempted anyway. It also reflects the potential danger of being the one to rely on problem solving if the other party will not participate in good faith.

The problem solving strategy is most often associated with cooperative client goals, since both involve situations in which resolving the problem creates a mutually beneficial, win/win outcome.[104] Similarly, just as cooperative client goals are associated with continuing, trusting, mutually beneficial relationships between the parties, so is the use of problem solving.[105]

To the extent that only a strictly competitive goal is at issue, problem solving often does not provide a useful approach, since a competitive goal seeks only to take as much as possible from the other party and does not seek a win/win outcome.[106] This assumes, though, that the negotiation is truly a zero-sum game with only a competitive issue. Typically in such instances the issue is the payment of money, which the parties value in the same way.[107]

A competitive goal, however, can have problem solving aspects. While acquisitions and mergers generally involve competitive goals, problem solving sometimes can be necessary because of uncertainty about the future of the newly structured entity. The negotiation may require a sharing of otherwise confidential information, with payment based entirely, or in part, on contingencies.[108]

Aggressive, self-centered, defensive, or competitive client goals may allow for the use of the problem solving strategy, however, to the extent that a cooperative element also exists.[109] Thus, the same breach of contract case in Example 3-17 above could be appropriate for problem solving if the parties and their negotiators were willing to work together to achieve goals that they had in addition to their competitive goal of wanting the most favorable (highest or lowest) settlement amount possible for their side. The dialogue between the attorneys in the breach of contract case could proceed as follows.

Example 3-19

P: You won't pay as much as our case is worth, given the evidence which we both have seen in discovery.

D: We've narrowed the difference a great deal. Both parties will benefit by saving considerable expense if we can resolve this without another year of discovery and a trial. This is an especially critical time to make

---

[104] Menkel-Meadow, *Toward Another View of Legal Negotiation: The Structure of Problem Solving*, 31 UCLA L Rev 754, 775-78 (1984).

[105] H. Cohen, *supra* note 73, at 197.

[106] *Id.*

[107] *Id.*

[108] H. Raiffa, The Art and Science of Negotiation 91 (1982). This situation also is an example of selective information disclosure. *See* **§4.02.**

[109] See **§3.16** regarding combining strategies.

the effort to resolve this, since we are about to start the experts' phase, and that will be expensive for both of us.

P: I can agree with that.

D: As I see it, we each have a really strong opinion on the value of the case, and the problem is that we can't find a way to resolve the difference that remains.

P: I'll agree with that as well. Where are you headed, since you obviously have something in mind?

D: If that's the problem and we agree that both parties would benefit from a prompt resolution without further expense, could we consider either of two solutions? First, do we agree that we have an honest difference of opinion based on each of our experiences with these matters?

P: That's fair.

D: Then we should split the difference, since, while either of us may be right, it's equally likely that the right number lies in between each of our figures.[110]

P: Before I consider that, what is your other proposal?

D: We could do an abbreviated form of alternative dispute resolution just on the remaining difference. I suggest either traditional binding arbitration or a mini-trial. Each of our two present positions would form the outer parameters for any decision. That way, any decision will resolve this at your figure, my figure, or somewhere in between.[111]

In Example 3-19, both parties had the defensive goal of wanting to avoid substantial, unnecessary litigation expenses. The attitude of the attorneys was partially cooperative, rather than strictly competitive.

Another way that the discussion in the breach of contract case could proceed is:

Example 3-20

P: You won't pay as much as this case is worth. Let's get serious, settle this, get a check, and I'll dismiss the thing.

D: That's out of the question at the numbers that you're talking about.

P: What's the real problem? Do we disagree that much on the amount?

D: It's less a disagreement on the amount than the economic realities. The numbers that you're talking about present a serious, if not impossible cash flow issue for my client. The amount is somewhat too high as well, but cash flow is the major problem.

P: I can work with you on that. Of course, if we accommodate your client with some sort of reasonable time payment plan, there will have to be an interest factor.

---

[110] See §5.16 regarding the tactic of splitting the difference.
[111] See §6.07 regarding alternative dispute resolution.

Here again, there was a consideration of more than just the narrow issue of the amount of money to be paid. Linear thinking about the amount was expanded to allow for new possibilities. Furthermore, a concomitant degree of cooperation was present. Needs and interests were disclosed by introducing the cash flow problem and the payment plan issue. The parties' goals, although still competitive, also became self-centered. Each began to see a way to maximize its own results without having to be entirely competitive, since the disclosed needs and interests did not conflict in part.

Problem solving also can play a role in aggressive goals, at least if the aggression is directed towards a third party, not towards the other party in the negotiation.

Example 3-21

P: You won't pay as much as this case is worth.

D: We think that the trial could go either way and that your demand is too high.

P: It's true that no one can be sure of what will happen at trial. Perhaps there is another way to accommodate my client that would allow me to settle for a smaller amount.

D: What do you have in mind?

P: Well, your contract for raw materials with our competitor X Corp is about to expire. If you contracted with us instead of with them, on the right terms, of course, we could come down significantly on a settlement figure in this case.

D: Let's discuss some specifics.

Here, the plaintiff's attorney saw an opportunity to achieve an aggressive goal, cutting into the business of the client's competitor. At the same time, the defense attorney recognized a self-centered or perhaps defensive opportunity to minimize settlement costs.

The primary countermeasures to problem solving are:

1.   Refusing to engage in it
2.   Focusing secretly on win/lose solutions while articulating them with credible rationales as mutually beneficial, win/win resolutions.

§3.10   Goals Other than to Reach an Agreement

Normally, the parties negotiate in a genuine attempt to reach an agreement, thereby making a contract, resolving a dispute, creating a partnership, etc. At times, however, a party may negotiate with a purpose in mind other than seeking to reach an agreement, at least at that time. These extraneous purposes, detailed in the sections that follow, lead to negotiations which are disingenuous,[112] distorted, or an exercise in gamesmanship. This may occur either initially or throughout the negotiation.

This strategy can be used to attain any type of client goal. If used with a cooperative goal, however, great care must be taken to avoid poisoning the relationship between the parties. Especially in an otherwise cooperative negotiation, the negotiating for purposes other than to reach an agreement strategy, if discovered by the other side, may lead to the party using this strategy being perceived as disingenuous, overly manipulative, or in other highly unfavorable ways. Once that perception occurs, it may well make further negotiations either extremely difficult or impossible.

§3.11   —Delay

One potential purpose of negotiating, other than to seek an agreement, is to delay. The effort to create a delay may be in order to allow other events to develop or to avoid the consequences that will follow a breakdown in the negotiation. With this in mind, one party may try to cause a delay by engaging in the negotiation process without any genuine intention of moving forward and without making a good faith effort to reach an agreement at that time or at any time.

Example 3-22: Allowing Other Events to Develop

An investor was negotiating the formation of a limited partnership. In reality, however, the investor wanted to stall any decision concerning whether to proceed with a new partnership until reports arrived regarding an alternative investment opportunity. The investor knew that he was financially incapable of investing in both of the potential opportunities. By appearing to negotiate, the investor hoped to prevent the potential partner from seeking to replace him with other investors until he could decide which of the two investment opportunities was preferable.

Example 3-23: Avoiding the Consequences of a Breakdown in the Negotiation

The management negotiating team believed that the union would strike, rather than accept the company's best authorized offer. The management negotiating team also believed that after several weeks of a strike the union would soften its position. The company's business was such that it experienced significant seasonal sales fluctuations. In addition, management feared that certain extremists in the union would engage in sabotage if the company attempted to speed up production and to stockpile goods in anticipation of a strike. Weighing these factors, the management negotiating team adopted a strategy for delay. Accordingly, it proceeded

---

[112] See **§12.02** regarding ABA ethical prohibitions on negotiating only to delay or burden another party.

to negotiate in a manner which confused and prolonged the process into a slower sales period.

Example 3-24: Avoiding the Consequences of a Breakdown in Negotiations

In this case, the chances of the defendant's being held liable were quite high. The defendant feared that the jury would return a significantly high damages award. The prejudgment interest rate was well below the rate being earned by the defendant through the investment of the funds that would have to be used to pay a judgment. Accordingly, delay was a profitable endeavor. In addition, the defendant was a closely held corporation. The owner-operator of the defendant corporation wanted to continue her salary as long as possible, since she could not be held to be personally liable. However, the feared adverse judgment would force the company into bankruptcy. For this reason as well, the defendant wished to delay a resolution of the suit for as long as possible. One of the means that was chosen to accomplish the delay was to engage in extremely slow moving negotiations without any genuine intention of resolving the suit.

Delay can create costs. For instance, environmentalists may discourage a developer through protracted litigation.[113] This also is an example of delay as a form of fact creation.[114] An actual or a potential delay in itself can create negotiating leverage against one who will be adversely affected by a delay. At some point, the party using the strategy of negotiating for delay may create sufficient leverage in this manner that it can switch to a different strategy, but begin from a stronger position.

§3.12   —Discovery

A negotiator who is genuinely seeking agreement may disclose information for a variety of reasons, including:

1. To persuade the other negotiator
2. To assist the other negotiator in persuading the ultimate decision maker for the other side
3. To persuade the other side's real decision maker regardless of the opinion of the other negotiator

Often this information would not be disclosed if the negotiator knew that the other party was seeking information for its own sake and was not really interested in formulating an agreement. However, another extraneous purpose of a negotiation can be the discovery of information for purposes other than to try to reach agreement.

---

[113] H. Raiffa, The Art and Science of Negotiation 13 (1982).
[114] See §4.03.

Except to a significant extent in litigation, discovery in negotiations functions any way that the parties decide it should function. At least for civil litigation, very liberal rules for formal discovery now govern in most jurisdictions.[115] In contrast, other types of proceedings permit only limited or no formal discovery depending on the type of proceeding and the jurisdiction. Such proceedings commonly include felony cases, misdemeanor cases, quasi-criminal cases, and administrative hearings.[116] Of course, for nonlitigation matters, as well as cases in the prelitigation stage, formal discovery does not exist.

Even when liberal, formal discovery rules are applicable, though, those rules exclude certain areas from inquiry. For instance, even the most liberal discovery rules provides protection for the attorney's work product.[117] Similarly, all discovery rules shield privileged communications from disclosure.[118] Thus, engaging in informal discovery can be both valuable and necessary.

Negotiation can constitute an effective means for conducting informal discovery. The other attorney, or the other party, may be encouraged to talk about facts, legal theories, its strategy, or other information during an apparent discussion of the strengths and weaknesses of each party's position or through similar ploys.

It should be noted that eliciting such information is both proper and a valuable technique in bona fide[119] negotiations. Similarly, providing the selective disclosure of information is an appropriate and worthwhile technique in a bona fide negotiation.[120]

Counsel must be on guard, however, against the other side's attempts to obtain facts, legal theories, strategies, or other information under the guise of negotiation. It is often unclear whether the other side is genuinely trying to reach an agreement or is pretending to negotiate just to obtain informal discovery. Under such circumstances, caution and strict adherence to the principles of selective disclosure should be followed.[121]

Example 3-25

The client is arrested at a demonstration and charged with the misdemeanor of disorderly conduct. He is a student with no prior record. The state's key witness is a police officer. There is no formal discovery allowed

---

[115] See, for example, Fed R Civ P 26-37.

[116] See Fed R Crim P 16 for an example of limited discovery.

[117] The concept and parameters of work product that is protected from discovery differs in certain instances between the federal courts and the state court systems.

[118] Although the existence and the scope of the privilege may vary from jurisdiction to jurisdiction, such privileges as the attorney-client privilege are standard throughout the nation. Privileged attorney-client matters basically consist of oral communications between the attorney and the client during which no third party is present, or of written communications of which no copy is transmitted to a third party.

[119] See §§4.07 and 4.08 regarding obtaining information through bargaining and through discussion.

[120] *See* §4.02.

[121] See §4.02 regarding making only deliberate disclosures in the negotiation process.

because it is a misdemeanor charge. The police report is either unavailable or so brief that it does not provide any meaningful information concerning the testimony to be expected from the officer. In addition, defense counsel does not believe that the officer will talk to her so that she can uncover the officer's version of the facts. The prosecutor approaches the defense attorney and offers to plea bargain the case for a form of probation. The defense attorney has no intention of recommending this offer, because she believes that she has a good chance of prevailing at a trial on the merits since the complaint is void due to a jurisdictional defect, and there is virtually no likelihood that a more severe penalty would be imposed even after a trial and a finding of guilty. The defense attorney also knows these additional facts: (a) the client will follow her recommendation; (b) the prosecutor will not agree to dismiss the case without the consent of the complainant; and (c) such consent will not be forthcoming because there is ill will between the complainant and the client. In other words, the defense attorney knows that negotiating will not produce an agreement. Nevertheless, the defense attorney (D) commences an apparent negotiation with the prosecutor (P), seeking to learn the arresting officer's story and thereby gain an advantage at trial:

D: Look, the kid is 20 years old and has never been in trouble before. Why bother to prosecute a disorderly charge. Just arresting him was enough.

P: That's why we're offering expungable probation. Besides, we've got a complainant to deal with.

D: That's all true, but it was a legitimate demonstration and the kid didn't even do anything disorderly. (With mild indignation) I can't understand how the officer could have arrested him in the first place.

In response to this ploy, the prosecutor gives a short summary of the alleged facts that led up to the arrest. The defense attorney asks questions about details that the prosecutor cannot answer, acts confused about the sequence of events, and continues to insist that she cannot have a client plead guilty when she cannot even understand the basis of the arrest.

P: (In exasperation at the stubbornness and apparent lack of understanding on the part of the defense lawyer): Just a minute. Let's get the officer over here and let him explain it to you. Officer, would you come over here and explain why you arrested the defendant?

By employing this discovery strategy, defense counsel succeeded in learning valuable information prior to trial that otherwise would have been inaccessible.

§3.13 —Influencing the Client

The strategy of acting for a purpose other than seeking an agreement also encompasses actions that really are aimed at influencing the negotiator's own client. The actions may be done to impress the client or to ventilate the client's own feelings which the client wants to have expressed in the negotiation. Such posturing includes justifications of the client's position, statements with inflammatory rhetoric, the use of personal characterizations, debate, and taking extreme positions.

Labor negotiations often commence with the union's representative haranguing management for perceived wrongs which may or may not even be susceptible to direct negotiation. An example of the latter would be complaints about management's general attitude. In many instances, the purpose of that behavior is not to influence or to inform management of the union's grievances. Rather, it is to impress the union's own constituency, its membership, with the union negotiator's understanding of the membership's feelings, and with the willingness to express those feelings in a powerful, highly assertive or aggressive manner. This can enhance the negotiator's credibility with the membership, thereby creating a greater degree of influence for the negotiator when issues or tentative agreements later are submitted for a decision. Such enhanced credibility can be a crucial factor in obtaining approval of provisions that would be unacceptable to a membership which was dubious about its own negotiator. Similarly, if the membership is angry or frustrated, a vivid expression of those feelings at the outset of the negotiation can defuse those feelings. That diffusion of emotion can make it easier to have a more reasonable internal discussion within the membership group than could otherwise occur.

The same pattern and phenomenon can apply to business or to other clients and their counsel. For this reason, the presence or absence of clients at the negotiation is an important consideration. Their presence may impede the negotiation process by causing counsel to act differently in order to influence or to impress the client.[122] There are times, however, when a strategy to influence one's own client is appropriate and perhaps even necessary in order to ultimately be able to obtain authorization for a reasonable settlement proposal.

A critical caveat exists. Engaging in this strategy, even if it successfully impresses the client, is not in the client's best interests if it leads to a failure of the negotiation process. Such failure can occur if counsel's antics in impressing his or her own client so offend or frustrate the other negotiator that the process is irreconcilably sabotaged.

§3.14 —Influencing Third Parties

Besides seeking to influence one's own client, the negotiator may endeavor to influence third parties, either instead of or in addition to the client. One type of setting in which this occurs is a business, labor, or governmental negotiation in which the parties want either to use or to avoid public pressure. The

---

[122] *See* §6.02.

strategy then is developed by focusing on influencing the public's perception of both the negotiation and of the parties themselves. Rather than acting to directly attempt to resolve the subject of the negotiation, actions are devised that are aimed at creating a public image.

For example, one's client could be portrayed as acting responsibly, fairly, and in the public interest. At the same time, the appearance is created that the other side is irresponsible, unfair, and without regard for the public's interest.

The ultimate objective of this strategy is to build public pressure to eventually obtain a favorable agreement in the negotiation, or to use the public images created for other purposes, or both. Note that the appearance can and should be based on real facts persuasively presented. Often, however, because the parties' perceptions of the facts are polarized, whether the portrayal is honest or dishonest is subject to serious and heated debate.

Other third parties also can be the objects of this strategy. A variety of reasons exist for such targeting. Family members, business associates, and friends may be targeted in order to bring their influence to bear on the client, or on the other party. The other party's clients, customers, referral sources, and suppliers could be the targets in order to cause economic injury to or apply pressure on the other party. Care must be taken, in such instances, to avoid actions which could be the basis of economic interference with a contractual relationship or other tort action.

Sometimes, this strategy actually consists of threatening to employ it, rather than actually implementing it. The decision to employ or to threaten is dependent on a number of factors. These factors include the severity of the threatened consequences and the other party's potential reaction to the threat. Furthermore, counsel must evaluate whether carrying out the threat will cause continuing pressure on the other party or instead create an adverse consequence to the other party that a subsequently negotiated agreement will not cure. If the latter is true, then, although the threat may lead to an immediate concession in the negotiation, once it is carried out, its usefulness for the negotiation is ended. It even may make a negotiated agreement more difficult to reach by creating a revenge motivation for the other party. For instance, powerfully adverse publicity that a negotiated settlement will not ameliorate falls into this category.

Example 3-26

The plaintiff, a consulting firm, sues a former client for failing to pay for services that the plaintiff provided. The former client, now the defendant, threatens to make public statements that the quality of the plaintiff's services was abysmal, so that many of the plaintiff's present and potential clients hear of the defendant's criticisms. Depending on the circumstances, the defendant may be able to carry this threat out gradually, thereby giving the plaintiff time to concede and avoid further harm to its reputation. The defendant's concept is to pressure the plaintiff into a settlement that is more favorable to the defendant in order to avoid unfavorable publicity. It may do so, or it simply may anger the plaintiff into taking a harder line, depending on two factors. The first is whether the plaintiff is actually likely to suffer adverse economic consequences if it does not settle, and the defendant proceeds with its threat to make highly critical statements about the plaintiff's services. Second, and inter-related, is the plaintiff willing to accept whatever risk of adverse business consequences may exist rather than agree to otherwise unacceptable set-tlement terms? The latter factor can be affected by whether the plaintiff believes that it can successfully threaten a business defamation claim or some other action which will deter the defendant from proceeding with its own threat of adverse publicity.

Example 3-27

A doctor in a small town is sued for malpractice because he left a surgical sponge in a patient during an operation. Although the doctor clearly breached his duty to the patient, there is a serious question as to whether the complications that the patient suffered were proximately caused by the sponge, or whether they occurred for entirely different reasons. The doctor's insurance policy allows the doctor to veto any settlement. Despite the fact that the insurance company is prepared to make a nego-tiable settlement offer, the doctor refuses to authorize any settlement. In an effort to break this deadlock, the plaintiff's attorney (P) has the fol-lowing conversation with the defense attorney (D):

P: You know, this case should really settle, but you aren't even willing to negotiate.

D: The company is willing to negotiate, but the doctor is refusing to settle, and under the policy, he has that right.

P: How can he take that position after he leaves a sponge in his patient?

D: All that I can say is that he doesn't feel the suit is justified, because the sponge didn't cause any harm.

P: The causation issue is triable from either side, but, if I were your client, I would be worried about something else. He is in a small town, and if this case goes to trial, it's going to get a lot of publicity. If I were he, I wouldn't want to see a headline that said: "Local Surgeon Leaves Sponge In Patient: In Trial For Malpractice," even if he later prevails. That's not going to do much for his practice. In fact, he ought to be a lot more worried about that than about settling. Why don't you talk to him about that?

The above example reflects the type of situation in which the threat of public-ity may result in concessions. On the other hand, once the unfavorable publicity actually occurs, the subject of it, such as the doctor in the example, may feel that there is no longer anything to be gained by negotiating.

§3.15 Moving for Closure

The move for closure strategy consists of acting to close the deal and to create a firm agreement. It follows the use of other strategies which have brought the negotiation to a point at which it is preferable to:

1. *Gain Certainty:* Have a firm agreement on the offered terms rather than

2. *Risk Loss Of:* To continue to negotiate and risk losing the agreement

In most, if not all, negotiations, the risk of losing an available deal is a real one. People can change their minds from meeting to meeting.[123] Cash flow needs or cash flow capabilities, competition from other potential parties to the deal, alternative transactions, the perceived desirability of the proposed terms, and a variety of other factors can change over time. Prior evaluations may be altered indirectly by fluctuating emotional and psychological feelings or beliefs. The basic fact often is that the agreement which can be made today may not be available tomorrow.

Of course, the risk of losing an available agreement need not be considered until an offer is made which is above the receiving party's bottom line. In other words, the offered agreement must be one that, either before the negotiation began or at some point during the negotiation, the party determined was better than not making any agreement at all.[124]

The closure strategy requires deciding the issue of whether to accept the offer at present, or to continue to negotiate with the hope that an even better agreement can be achieved. This issue requires weighing:

1. *Value:* The value of the agreement that is presently available

2. *Risk:* The risk that the offer will be withdrawn while even better terms are sought

3. *Potential:* Any better terms that are realistically judged to be potentially available

4. *Odds:* The chance of achieving those potentially better terms[125]

One must consider whether the higher the value that is deemed to be potentially available, in context, means a lowering of the chances that it will be attained.

---

[123] W. Coffin, The Negotiator: A Manual For Winners 37 (1973).

[124] This point is referred to in the literature in a number of ways, including the "best alternative to a negotiated settlement (BATNA)." Fisher, *supra* note 21, at 104. It is also sometimes referred to as the settlement point or the settlement limit. See also §§8.07, 8.08, and 9.03 regarding assessing strengths, weaknesses, and interests, estimating the other party's bottom line, and setting one's own bottom line.

[125] If the rather subjective calculations of the value available now (VAN), the risk that it will be lost (RVAN), the value available potentially (VAP), and the chance that the value available potentially will be obtained (CVAP) all were to be expressed mathematically, the formula would be: VAN / RVAN versus VAP / CVAP.

Counsel should be very cautious about risking the loss of an agreement whose terms the client has authorized the attorney to accept. At best, the lawyer will be blamed by the client if an acceptable deal is lost because the counsel pushed too hard for an even better, but unattainable, deal. In a worst case scenario, a malpractice claim could be made if the lawyer's actions were unreasonable.[126] Either way, client dissatisfaction is the natural and inevitable consequence, and this is certainly undesirable from counsel's perspective. Therefore, before deciding to risk the loss of an agreement that is acceptable to the client, the attorney should discuss the risk and the potential benefits of continuing to negotiate in a detailed, direct communication with the client, so that the ultimate decision is that of the client. This process of decision making is ethically mandated, since decisions about whether to agree at a given level must be made by the client.

Insurance companies can face a special risk in unreasonably refusing to settle within the policy limits, because they can be monetarily responsible for a verdict in excess of the policy limits in many jurisdictions if their refusal to settle was unreasonable.[127] Defense counsel may share in that risk if there is improper negotiation and a negligent failure to close at an authorized level. A malpractice theory may be used by the insurer against the defense attorney who fails to settle a case by refusing a demand that is within the lawyer's settlement authority, where later there is an adverse verdict in excess of the rejected demand.[128]

The foregoing discussion assumes that a risk of some significance exists. Counsel need not and should not always stop negotiating whenever the other party offers terms that are minimally agreeable to the client. Indeed, to do so would frequently display more interest in the offer than is warranted, signal the other party to raise its expectations and to take a harder line than it planned to take, and decrease the chances of attaining the best available agreement. In other words, to *always* accept, or to always stop to check with the client as soon as the first agreeable offer is obtained, is very poor negotiating indeed.

The necessity of a consultation with the client is, therefore, a matter of judgment. Counsel must weigh the probability and the consequences of the loss of the offer due to nonacceptance against the realistic probability and the consequences of negotiating a more favorable agreement.

For the other side, of course, the same requirements and principles are applicable. Thus, to successfully reach closure on one's proposal, it must at least meet the minimum requirement of the other party's bottom line.[129] In addition:

1.   The less that the other party believes that it can obtain further concessions; *and*

---

[126] Paplow, *Negotiating Settlement of a Personal Injury Action-Defendant*, in Attorney's Guide to Negotiation 10-10 (1979); Smiley v Manchester Ins, 71 Ill 2d 306, 375 NE2d 118 (1978).

[127] *See* §7.05.

[128] Paplow, *supra* note 126; Smiley v Manchester Inc, 71 Ill 2d 306, 375 NE2d 118 (1978).

[129] G. Kennedy, J. Benson & J. McMillan, Managing Negotiations 102 (1982) [hereinafter Kennedy]. The authors are British and write from a very competitive perspective of labor negotiations.

2. The more that the other party fears that failing to accept will result in no agreement being reached; creates

3. An increased likelihood that the move for closure will succeed

Therefore, counsel may need a persuasive presentation in moving for closure to convince the other side that factors (1) and (2) exist.

At times, a party's assent or acquiesence to a settlement proposal will be clear even though it is implicit, rather than expressed. In this situation, closure can be accomplished in a bona fide way by expressing an understanding that there is, in fact, an agreement.[130] Provided that this is a fair conclusion, this approach has the benefit of not asking whether there is really an agreement, since that question may cause the other negotiator to have second thoughts. If the other negotiator responds that there is no agreement, counsel should obtain feedback by requesting an explanation of the reasons preventing agreement at that point.[131]

A different type of move for closure consists of an inducement to act now through the offer of some additional concession.[132] It can be presented through many of the tactics outlined in the following chapters.[133] At times, the additional concession may involve either a unilaterally large concession by one party, or one or more reciprocal, large concessions by both parties.

Example 3-28

The plaintiff's attorney (P) contacts the defense attorney (D) because the court requires that they prepare an extensive, final pretrial order. The following conversation occurs:

D: You know, preparing this will involve a lot of time and effort on both sides. If we are going to settle, it makes sense to do so now that discovery is closed and before we spend days preparing the final pretrial order.

P: That certainly makes sense. I'm always willing to discuss settlement.

D: We've been very far apart, but I can move fairly substantially if you can.

P: Well, your last offer was $50,000.00 and my last demand was $350,000.00. It's true that we both know a lot more about the case and that perhaps we were both somewhat extreme. I could come down to $275,000.00.

D: That's still rather high, but I can offer $115,000.00

P: We're still $160,000.00 apart, although I still have room to talk.

D: Look, let's not fence around, will you take $170,000.00?

---

[130] C. Karrass, Give & Take: The Complete Guide to Negotiating Strategies and Tactics 38 (1974).

[131] *Id* 38.

[132] *Id;* Kennedy, *supra* note 129.

[133] *See* **chs 4-7.**

P: I could take $180,000.00.[134]

D: OK.

At other times, moving for closure may involve a purposefully concise negotiation because of a relative lack of value and significance, or because one or both sides are particularly anxious to settle. Under these circumstances, moving for closure may involve anything from small or relatively small concessions to large concessions, and the concessions may be reciprocal or more one-sided.

Example 3-29

In a case which eventually will involve a jury trial unless otherwise resolved, the initial written discovery has been completed, and the depositions of the plaintiff and of a key liability witness have been taken. The result is that the plaintiff's attorney has reevaluated his case, and now believes that, although his client is sympathetic and suffered serious damages, the chance of proving liability is extremely dubious. The defense attorney believes that she has a strong case, but is still concerned that the plaintiff could survive a motion for a directed verdict and prevail on jury sympathy. In addition, the costs of defense must be considered. Accordingly, the defense attorney contacts the plaintiff's lawyer, and to the latter's surprise, raises the possibility of settlement.

D: Although we believe that we will prevail at trial, we would be willing to settle now for a small amount to avoid further expenses.

P: (feeling cautiously elated, but speaking in a neutral tone): I admit that the deposition did not go as well as I expected. I'm interested in settling, but small is a relative term, and I still could win a sizable verdict.

D: I can offer $7,000.00.

P: (despite having a bottom line of less than $7,000.00; judging that this defense attorney in this type of case would not be employing Bulwareism): That's not unreasonable, but it's a bit lower than I had in mind. I know that I could settle for $13,000.00.

D: I can't go that high, although I am sure that the client would offer a little more than $7,000.00.[135]

P: Look, we both know where we're headed. Instead of my saying $11,500.00 and your saying $8,500.00 and my saying $10,500.00 and your saying $8,500.00, why don't we go on to other cases and agree on $10,000.00?

D: I really can't go to $10,000.00, but I can get $9,000.00.

---

[134] Note that the absence of articulated reasons for the positions is generally a poor negotiating practice. See §10.03.

[135] The negotiators are failing to state reasons for their positions. They should be doing so unless, in context, the reasons are apparent. See §10.03.

P: (deciding not to press for anymore): We can accept that.

Moving for closure means creating a firm agreement. It can include complet-ing all of the attendant documentation as well has having the parties execute those documents. Usually, where the agreement is to be reduced to writing, however, there is a gap between the close of the negotiation and the execution of the documents that memorialize the agreement. Sometimes, a substantial danger of repudiation exists during this time. If so, the closure strategy also includes formulating and completing any feasible steps that are reasonably use-ful to attempt to guard against such repudiation in that interim period, as well as all of the steps that are necessary for a final closing of the transaction or settlement. For example, a letter confirming the agreement can be transmitted.

Movement for closure is applicable not only to the entire negotiation, but also to settling a particular issue within the negotiation. Final agreement on the issue is reached so that the parties move forward and focus on the remaining issues. Such focusing on the various separate issues that are involved can be helpful. Usually, movement for closure on an issue is done with the more easily settled issues, while discussion of the more difficult issues is deferred. This can promote an overall agreement by creating a more favorable atmosphere for the negotiation. It also can encourage a final agreement by creating a com-mitment by the parties to reach agreement due to the investment of time and effort that already has produced partial success.[136]

One caveat concerning moving for closure on an issue is that counsel should be careful that this does not interfere with executing a problem solving or other strategy. As discussed above, because of the different values that the parties may attach to different issues, problem solving sometimes can involve exchang-ing concessions on one issue for concessions on another issue to the mutual satisfaction of both parties.[137] Thus, before moving for closure on an issue if a problem solving or other strategy is being used involving tradeoffs between issues, careful consideration should be given to whether a different use and resolution of that issue could be employed to more favorably resolve other issues and thereby effect a better overall agreement for the client.

§3.16 Combining Strategies

Various strategies have been outlined one by one for clarity. In negotiating, though, it often is not effective to choose, implement, and remain with a single strategy throughout the negotiation. Furthermore, the concede first strategy is always used and the moving for closure strategy only can be utilized during particular portions of the negotiation. Those two strategies, therefore, must be used in conjunction with other strategies.[138] A typical combination of strate-gies would be HRESSC and moving for closure. Another blend would be prob-

---

[136] See §5.18 on creating a psychological commitment to reach an agreement.
[137] *See* §§3.08 & 3.09.
[138] *See* §§3.07 & 3.15.

lem solving, concede first, and move for closure. Any permutation or combination is possible.

The necessity or desirability of changes in the choice of strategy can arise in a number of ways. A strategy may be tried and discarded because it did not achieve those gains that were thought to be possible. Since this is not unusual, potential changes in strategy can and should be part of the overall negotiating plan.[139] Even with careful planning, unforeseen events during the negotiation itself can lead to previously unplanned, but carefully chosen, changes in strategy.

Strategy changes may be sequential in nature, or they may be issue oriented. Sequential changes in strategy are those that occur over time during the negotiation based on counsel's constant and continual reevaluation of the process. Issue oriented changes in strategy occur in multiple issue negotiations in which there are different strategies for different issues. For this reason, negotiations should be planned on an issue-by-issue basis, as well as on an overall basis.[140]

Example 3-30: Issue Oriented Strategy Changes

The client has a medical malpractice case against a teaching hospital. Aside from the serious, permanent injury that she suffered due to the malpractice, the client also has serious medical conditions that will very likely require medical care at a substantial cost in the future. Additionally, the client is without funds and on public aid, which will be cut off in the event of a settlement or a successful verdict. This apparently will necessitate the client's having to pay her own future medical bills from the settlement or verdict, unless doing so exhausts those funds so that she returns to being destitute and on public aid again!

The client's goals are to obtain as much money as possible, but also to avoid the danger that any recovery will be consumed by future medical expenses. Accordingly, these dual goals are analyzed as two separate issues for which two separate strategies are chosen. To maximize the dollar amount of the settlement, the HRESSC strategy is selected. With regard to future medical expenses, a problem solving strategy is chosen. The latter strategy then is effectuated by making a monetary concession on the settlement amount in exchange for free future medical care from the hospital. While the strategies and their implementation were closely intertwined, the client's goals may not have been achieved without employing both strategies to deal with distinct, albeit related, issues.

Example 3-31: Sequential Strategy Changes

An antitrust defendant, after initial sparring, has a very low opening offer. Later, it makes some small concessions, and then engages in a strategy of no further concessions. The defendant's offer is below the plaintiff's

---

[139] See §§9.05 and **9.11** regarding planning strategy and modifying plans.
[140] *See* **chs 8 & 9.**

bottom line, and consequently is rejected. The plaintiff, who had been using the HRESSC strategy, switches to no further concessions, because the plaintiff's attorney finds the defense's strategy to be offensive. Negotiations break down, and two years pass while discovery is conducted and the case awaits trial on a crowded court docket. Finally, the case is set for trial. One week before the trial date, at a pretrial conference, the judge suggests that another effort be made to settle the case, since "there ought to be room for movement by both sides." At this point, the defendant accepts the judge's suggestion, using it as a graceful way of dropping its strategy of no further concessions.[141] Again using the judge's recommendation as its explanation, the defendant now switches to a concede first strategy, followed by the HRESSC strategy. Seeing that some progress towards a settlement is being made, the judge continues the case for two weeks during which time the negotiations continue. On the day of the rescheduled trial, a settlement is reached.

Strategy changes may not be successful if the prior strategy has undermined the current one. A prior strategy can undermine the current one if it leads the other negotiator to believe that counsel is disingenuous or just using ploys. For example, a negotiator may not be successful in moving from a no concessions strategy to a problem solving strategy. Difficulty could well arise because the other negotiator refuses to believe that the problem solving strategy is being used in good faith and, instead, believes that it is a ploy in light of the earlier use of the hard strategy of no concessions.

Furthermore, clear signals must be given for the change in strategy, unless the strategy is being deliberately disguised. Otherwise, if, because of mixed messages or unclear signals, the other party does not recognize that counsel is switching strategy, the strategy switch cannot be effective.[142] A failure to have the strategy change recognized differs from the type of credibility problem raised above regarding the prior strategy's lingering effects. This problem stems from a lack of clarity in presenting the new strategy, rather than from a disbelief in the bona fides of the strategy being employed. Thus, the former is more of a substantive dilemma, while the latter is purely a communications failure.

§3.17   Summary and Review

    I. Credibility
        A. Crucial
        B. Appearance of:
            1. Attitude
            2. Preparation
        C. Honest Behavior

---

[141] See §5.19 regarding saving face.
[142] See ch 10 regarding effective communications.

   D. Creating By:
      1. Allies
      2. Actions
      3. Status
II. No Concessions
   A. Unilaterally define the only possible agreement
   B. Most useful where (a) great disparity of power, or (b) equally attractive alternative available if offer rejected
   C. Also used if weak but can inflict devastating consequences
   D. Effect of Time:
      1. Power and needs can change
      2. May be too short for other strategies
   E. Can be used to avoid negotiation costs
   F. A method to extend equal offers to various parties
   G. Limited if need flexibility or it violates custom
   H. If its use is miscalculated, the attempt may block an otherwise acceptable agreement
   I. May temper with a nonaggressive tone
   J. Consider for aggressive, competitive, or self-centered goals
   K. Thirteen countermeasures
III. No Further Concessions
   A. To force the other party to make the last concession
   B. For the overall agreement or an issue
   C. Timing is critical
IV. Making Only Deadlock-Breaking Concessions
   A. Brinkmanship
   B. Dangerous
   C. Consider for aggressive, competitive, self-centered goals
   D. Countermeasures:
      1. Deadlock
      2. Creation of movement
V. HRESSC
   A. High Realistic Expectations With Small Systematic Concessions
   B. The most generally useful strategy
   C. Realistically high opening position
   D. Small, not too rapid concessions
   E. Systematic, planned concessions, including no or low cost ones
   F. For competitive, aggressive, self-centered, or defensive goals
   G. Also for any competitive elements within cooperative goals
   H. Countermeasures:
      1. HRESSC
      2. No concessions
      3. No further concessions
      4. Deadlock-breaking concessions only
      5. Problem solving
VI. Concede First
   A. At opening stages of entire negotiation or one issue

    B. To create goodwill and movement

    C. Allows for demand of a reciprocal concession

    D. Relinquishes only limited value

    E. Must be used with other strategies

    F. Can backfire by raising the other party's expectations

    G. Do not use if weak or will be perceived as being weak

    H. Consider for competitive, cooperative, self-centered or defensive client goals

    I. Consider for aggressive client goals if the other party is not the target to be injured

    J. Countermeasures: refusal to reciprocate

    K. Also may be used by the other party to lead to movement in the desired direction

VII. Problem Solving

    A. Second most generally useful strategy

    B. Four steps: (1) procedural agreement (2) identification of problems (3) determination of common interests and limiting separate needs (4) discovery of solution

    C. Necessary conditions: (1) mutual desire and agreement to use (2) real mutual interests so the parties operate in good faith (3) jointly defined problems (4) win/win solutions, not capitulation

    D. Separation of needs and interests from positions

    E. Cooperative, sensitive demeanor

    F. Creativity and brainstorming

    G. Ideas from critically examined principles, precedent, or community practice

    H. Best for cooperative goals

    I. Useful for aggressive, self-centered, defensive, or competitive goals *only* if a cooperative element exists

    J. Countermeasures: (1) refusal to participate and (2) suggest win/lose solutions articulated as win/win ones

VIII. Purposes Other Than Agreement

    A. Can be used for any goal

    B. But can poison the atmosphere if it is discovered

    C. Delay

    D. Discovery

    E. Influencing the client or others

IX. Moving For Closure

    A. In total or on an issue

    B. To gain certainty of benefits without risk of losing them

    C. For all goals

    D. Used with other strategies

X. Combining Strategies

    A. Any permutation or combination possible

    B. Sequential changes

    C. Issue oriented shifts

Informational Tactics

4

§4.01 Introduction

Sir Francis Bacon, the 17th century English philosopher, perceptively regarded negotiation as a process of discovery.[1] While negotiation is more than just that, discovery is an important aspect of the process. Each party seeks discoveries from the other and tries to influence the discoveries by the other party through control of the information that is being given. In many ways, negotiation is a process of giving, withholding, and analyzing information.

For all negotiations, information about the other party is critical.[2] The information may be explicit or implicit. For instance, refusals to disclose information can provide knowledge that is as significant as facts learned in other ways.[3]

Information about the other party will persuade counsel that an agreement either is, or is not, likely to be feasible. If counsel perceives that an agreement is feasible, the same information also will affect counsel's understanding of the

---

[1] Karrass, Give & Take: The Complete Guide to Negotiating Strategies and Tactics 7 (1974).

[2] H. Cohen, You Can Negotiate Anything 101-04 (1982). In Cohen's words, "[I]nformation is the heart of the matter." *Id* 101.

[3] R. Givens, Advocacy: The Art of Pleading a Cause 442 (Shepard's/McGraw-Hill, Inc 1985).

best manner in which to structure the optimal agreement that is possible in a particular negotiation. Thus, it is through the exchange of information that the negotiators create the framework for the settlement or the deal, or conclude that no agreement is possible and terminate the negotiation.

In this process, the negotiators seek mutual interests and common ground, since agreement requires that some need(s) of each party be met. In this way, also, the negotiators decide whether contemplated strategies and tactics should be followed or altered. The types of information include knowledge concerning the needs, interests, and positions of the other party, as well as any other facts which bear on an assessment of the minimum offer that is likely to be agreeable to the other party.[4]

In litigation, the strength of each party's case is normally an important factor in negotiating. There, information about witnesses, documents, legal arguments, precedent, and all of the other factors that affect liability and damages, necessarily also affect the analysis of the lawyer and that of the client regarding the appropriate level for settlement. Even with liberal rules of discovery, the information disclosed during negotiations can provide revelations.[5] This often occurs because the information was not previously disclosed, because it was not known that the other attorney knew the information, or because the real significance of the information was not understood before the negotiation.

In any negotiation, knowledge of the other party's strategy can influence both counsel and the client. For instance, if the other party's strategy is known to be one of no concessions, counsel's analysis of the negotiation will be quite different than if the other party's strategy is known to be that of problem solving.

Informational tactics fall into three major categories. These three categories are:

1.   The disclosure of information (*See* §§**4.02, 4.07 & 4.08**)

2.   Creating facts through actions that alter the existing facts (*See* §**4.03**)

3.   Obtaining information (*See* §§**4.04-4.08**)

Before proceeding with a detailed discussion of these specific tactics, it should be noted that their use is both essential and pervasive. Informational tactics are critical in every negotiation, regardless of the client's goals, regardless of the strategy being implemented, and regardless of the other tactics being used. As explained at the outset, negotiation is, in large part, the process of disclosing and withholding information to persuade the parties to assent to some type of agreement, or to decide that an agreement will not be feasible and that the negotiation should be terminated.[6] There can be no negotiation without engaging in informational tactics.[7]

---

[4] H. Cohen, *supra* note 2, at 104.

[5] See §**3.12** regarding the strategy of negotiating to obtain information and **ch 8** and **9** regarding planning.

[6] See §**1.02** on the process of negotiation. See also §**9.03** regarding setting the bottom line and §**3.04** on no further concessions.

[7] H. Cohen, *supra* note 2, at 19. According to Cohen, information is one of the "three

Five of the seven primary informational tactics are used in every negotiation. In addition, informational bargaining occurs fairly often. Only fact creation occurs less frequently.

Counsel always engage in some disclosures of information. Conversely, counsel also are always involved in obtaining some information. Indeed, even the initial offer is sometimes, at least in part, an information seeking tactic.[8] Frequently, disclosures of information and seeking information will begin as part of the preparation for the actual negotiating.[9] Often this is an integral part of the planning process, because obtaining information may be a prerequisite to counsel's effective planning and choice of strategy and noninformational tactics.[10] Less obviously, disclosing information before any actual bargaining occurs may be essential to favorably influencing the other party's planning and choice of strategy and tactics.[11]

Like the other more often used types of informational tactics, fact creation can be used for all client goals, employed with all strategies, and utilized in conjunction with any other tactic. However, as explained further below, in many negotiations, it will not be appropriate or viable to use the fact creation tactic. That is because, in many negotiations, the opportunity to legitimately alter the factual context will not exist.

The focus on the full range of information tactics emphasizes valuable but often overlooked aspects of negotiation, as well as the more popular ones. American negotiators generally are accustomed to relatively short negotiations and are skilled at argument, but lack skills in:[12]

1. Asking questions
2. Obtaining information
3. Listening
4. Using questions as a tool of persuasion

In addition, American negotiators tend to ignore or to hurry through phases accepted in some countries as the first two stages of a negotiation, establishing

---

crucial elements (that) are always present" in negotiations. *Id.* (Cohen's other two crucial elements are time and power. *Id.*)

[8] Stevens, *Strategy and Collective Bargaining Negotiations,* in G. Bellow & B. Moulton, The Lawyering Process 526-27 (1978). Where the initial offer or demand reflects a high, but realistic expectation, it can function as an information seeking device by eliciting a response that illuminates the other party's position. *Id.*

[9] H. Cohen, *supra* note 2, at 102.

[10] See **§8.03** regarding gathering information prior to the negotiation.

[11] H. Cohen, *supra* note 2, at 104.

[12] J. Graham & Y. Sano, Smart Bargaining 19 (1984).

rapport and an exchange of pertinent information.[13] Counsel must be careful to expend sufficient time and energy on those stages, since those efforts, or the lack thereof, can affect the subsequent stages of persuasion and concessions, and agreement or termination of the negotiation.

§4.02   The Disclosure of Information

Information disclosure can change the entire course of a negotiation. Disclosure may stimulate a fresh analysis through facts that one side knows which would otherwise be unavailable to the other side.[14] The information can alter the lawyer's analysis either because it was previously unknown, or because the other side was thought to be unaware of it.

Negotiators are expected to be truthful in their statements, but not to disclose all that they know.[15] A key negotiating skill is the ability to determine what information should be disclosed during the course of a negotiation. The selective disclosure of information is one of the most important tools available to persuade the other negotiator or the other party to alter its position. It requires judgment in balancing:

1.   The likely intended and unintended effects of the disclosure
2.   The likely intended and unintended effects of nondisclosure

The latter becomes an even more significant concern when the information is explicitly or implicitly sought by the side. A refusal to disclose in the face of an actual or tacit request for the information will create an inference in the mind of the other party. Counsel must anticipate that inference and decide whether the likely inference from withholding the information is more helpful or harmful than disclosure of the information.

Disclosure may be designed to motivate the other party or its negotiator to accept a particular position. It also can be structured to create previously unknown alternatives. In many negotiations, a lack of information can lead to a lower gain for each of the parties. This can occur where each is trying to maximize its own gains, but both fail to realize that an alternative exists which will lead to a better result for each of them through a previously uncontemplated compromise between their first choices.

This dilemma is illustrated below. (The parties are designated as "A" and "B"; "VA" is value to A and "VB" is value to B on a scale of 1, as the lowest value, to 10, as the highest value).

---

[13] *Id* 13.

[14] H. Raiffa, The Art and Science of Negotiation 219 (1982).

[15] W. Fallon, AMA Management Handbook 5-48 (1983).

Figure 4-1

A's First Choice	B's First Choice
VA 10 and VB 1	VA 1 and VB 10

Known Compromise
VA 3 and VB 3

Unknown Alternative
VA 6 and VB 5

As illustrated above, the two known compromises are further away from the first choices of the parties and have less value for both than the unknown alternative. A lack of information has prevented the parties from discovering this preferable alternative. At times, only through the disclosure of information by the parties themselves can the best alternative become known, with its benefits for both sides.

Counsel may need to reveal some or all of the client's goals and the client's specific needs or interests as long as it does not reveal a bargaining weakness that outweighs the benefit of the disclosure. By doing so, counsel may be able to clearly establish to the other party that any agreement must be structured within certain parameters.[16] That may be helpful regardless of what strategy is being followed. In addition, such a disclosure, by identifying the relevant issues, may particularly facilitate any problem solving strategy.[17] Without knowing the goals, needs, and interests of the parties which are relevant to the problem, the lawyers may not be able to identify or solve the problem impeding agreement.

Being selective means that counsel are conscious and in control of the information that they are communicating. Example 4-1 demonstrates the need for selectivity and control in making disclosures.

Example 4-1

Plaintiff (P) and defense (D) counsel are in the midst of discussing an imminent trial and the possibility of settlement.

P: Are you still planning to call Wittner as a witness?

D: I'm not sure. She moved, and we're having trouble locating her.

P: Your expert certainly does not come across well. You ought to take that into account.

D: I will.

Defense counsel has revealed that he cannot locate a major witness and lacks confidence in the defendant's expert. Unless these disclosures were

---

[16] *See* R. Fisher & W. Ury, Getting to Yes, Negotiating Agreement Without Giving In 109 (1981) [hereinafter Fisher].

[17] *Id* 11, 41-42 and 51. Fisher and Ury note that the "interests define the problem." *Id* 42. This is consistent with their "principled negotiation" general approach of focusing on interests, not positions. Thus, Fisher and Ury stress talking about interests and being sure that the parties are aware of each other's real interests.

justified by very specific and compelling reasons, it was a major error to reveal such unfavorable information. The defendant's bargaining position now is weaker because of disclosures that gained nothing.

Selectively disclosing information includes not only verbal but also nonverbal communications. For example, counsel's physical actions or tone may be inconsistent with the message that he or she is articulating. Selectivity extends both to information that is given directly and to information that is transmitted indirectly through the inferences that can be drawn from the communication. Accordingly, counsel should be acutely aware of how the other negotiator may perceive a nonverbal communication, including those inferences that the other negotiator may draw from the tone and physical presentation which accompany a particular statement or action.

Example 4-2

The purchaser's lawyer listens very carefully to a long proposal that is put forth by the vendor's attorney. As the vendor's attorney is explaining the entire proposal, the purchaser's lawyer appears to be taking almost verbatim notes. Then, the purchaser's attorney says smoothly: "My client does not have the slightest interest in that proposal or in anything like it."

If there was really no possibility of interest in the proposal or in a related proposal, then why did the lawyer listen so carefully for a long time and take virtually verbatim notes? While it is possible that the lawyer was initially confused about the direction that the proposal was headed, it is unlikely that the purchaser's attorney would have listened and taken notes in that manner unless there was at least some interest in some aspect of the proposal or in a somewhat similar plan. At best, the attorney has sent a confusing, mixed message.[18] At worst, the lawyer has unintentionally disclosed information that he wanted to conceal: that the proposal was of some interest. Thus, one should be attuned to any inconsistency between the verbal and the nonverbal signals from either oneself or from the other negotiator.[19]

The selective disclosure of information also means avoiding verbal slips which indicate one's true position when one is attempting to project a different stance.

Example 4-3

BUYER'S LAWYER: Would you take $18,000.00, I mean $15,000.00?

---

[18] See **§10.03** regarding the need for clarity in sending communications to the other side.

[19] Oatley, *Negotiating Techniques For Lawyers*, 6 Advoc Q 214, 231 (1985).

Although the "$18,000.00" could be a mistake, it also can be a verbal slip prematurely disclosing a willingness to make a $3,000 concession.

Example 4-4

> BUYER'S LAWYER: We would consider paying $15,000.00 to $18,000.00.
>
> SELLER'S LAWYER: Well, at $18,000.00 you are at least getting closer to a price that we could accept.

In Example 4-4, the buyer's lawyer has not selectively disclosed information unless he is trying to communicate that $18,000.00 is an acceptable price because the other lawyer is almost certainly going to focus on the favorable end of any range that is given.[20]

In addition, the selective disclosure of information involves decisions regarding the timing of those disclosures that ought to be made. The negotiator must determine:

1.   Which information should be disclosed at the outset of the negotiating process or of the negotiation itself

2.   What information ought to be held until the negotiation focuses on a particular fact, issue, or argument

3.   The information is to be saved until the parties become deadlocked

The timing of the disclosure should be calculated to maximize or minimize its impact, depending on which of those effects is sought.

The total amount of time that is available for the negotiation also is a subject on which a conscious decision about disclosure may well be needed. Counsel should withhold information about the amount of time available for the negotiation if that fact forms an apparent constraint which could force the negotiator to accept a less favorable outcome. On the other hand, it should be disclosed if it creates a useful deadline that pressures the other side to concede more.[21]

Example 4-5

Counsel has traveled to a different city or a foreign country to negotiate. He has a deadline by which he must depart for home. If that information may indicate that counsel is under time pressure to accept the best available deal before having to depart, counsel should avoid revealing the departure deadline.[22]

At times, disclosure of certain information is legally required. For instance:

---

[20] Nolan, *Settlement Negotiations,* 11 Litigation 17, 20 (1985).

[21] *See* §5.26.

[22] M. Zimmerman, How to Do Business with the Japanese 101 (1985); H. Cohen, You Can Negotiate Anything 93-95 (1982).

1. In many securities matters, state and federal laws mandate that certain disclosures be made[23]
2. Required franchise disclosures similarly are governed by law[24]
3. A seller of real property may be liable for undisclosed, known latent defects, depending on the circumstances of the transaction.[25]

Where disclosure is legally mandated, the degree of selectivity is limited, and the categories of information required to be disclosed must be recognized.

The most persuasive type of disclosure can be to reveal just enough to get the other negotiator to draw his or her own conclusions, without realizing that the conclusions were, in fact, subtly suggested. In contrast, direct conclusions should be stated where:

1. The other negotiator may not understand a more subtle approach; or
2. The other negotiator has, in fact, already drawn the conclusion

Some disclosures are intended to be directly persuasive in answering or countering apparently significant, negative factors. This should be done where such factors are known to and recognized by the other party.[26]

Example 4-6

"If I were in your place, I'd be concerned about that aspect. I think, however, you will find that, in practice, it actually functions to. . . ."

Example 4-7

"Although you probably think that creates a disadvantage, it really doesn't work out that way. Any disadvantage is more than balanced by the four positive factors. . . ."

By anticipating those factors which the other party will view as negative or problematic, the attorney may be able to restructure a planned proposal and the accompanying explanation to defuse the potential problem or issue. The restructuring can eliminate the undesirable factors, or conceptualize them in a less negative or even in a positive manner.

Not only can such understanding enable one to give a more persuasive presentation, it also can lower the defenses of the other party and create an atmosphere of trust. This occurs because such understanding demonstrates to the

---

[23] 69 Am Jur 2d *Securities Regulation-Federal* §§123-66 & 169-80 (1973); 69 Am Jur 2d *Securities Regulation-State* §§33-34 & 47-58 (1973).

[24] 62 Am Jur 2d *Private Franchise Contracts* (1987 Supp §§4.3-.7) (1972).

[25] 77 Am Jur 2d *Vendor and Purchaser* §§329-335 (1975).

[26] Of course, one normally refrains from raising "red flags" when the other party does not know of them or does not recognize their significance.

other party that its needs are being comprehended, acknowledged, and responded to realistically.[27]

Often, it may be normal and expected for one or both parties to disclose a substantial amount of factual data and projections to the other party. For instance, in negotiating a merger, a joint venture, or a partnership agreement, the types of information that may be expected to be provided by the seller can include:

1. Itemized records of past and present revenues

2. Itemized records of past and present expenses

3. Records of accounts receivable

4. Information concerning anticipated income in both the short term and the long term

5. Data regarding anticipated expenses for both the short term and the long term

6. Figures showing the past and present salaries, bonuses, and fringe benefits of partners and/or executives

7. Indications of which employees are the key ones

8. Information regarding the retirement or other pertinent personal plans of partners and/or executives

9. Data concerning assets, credit, and capital investments

10. Information about financial obligations and liabilities, including pension and profit sharing plans

Whether and how such information should be disclosed to protect or defuse potential claims of reliance by the recipient of the information should be a concern for all of the lawyers involved in the transaction. Concern means that a professional judgment must be made on the nature and extent of any risks, and on the appropriate measures to be taken. Determining which measures are appropriate depends on:

1. Those risks

2. The benefits of the deal if desired risk-reducing measures are rejected by the other party

In purely, or primarily, competitive negotiations, it also may be normal and expected for a party to disclose a substantial amount of information. This occurs, for instance, in attempting to settle a personal injury claim without having to file suit. In such cases, the plaintiff's attorney always will provide some, and will sometimes provide all, of the following to the defendant's insurance company:

---

[27] Fisher and Ury advise the negotiator to "acknowledge ... (the other party's) interests as part of the problem." Fisher, *supra* note 16, at 52.

1. Basic biographical information about the plaintiff
2. The names and addresses of the hospitals and doctors that treated the plaintiff
3. Information regarding the plaintiff's employment
4. A basic description of how the accident occurred
5. Medical bills
6. Medical records
7. Medical reports from treating physician(s)
8. Medical reports from consulting physician(s)
9. Reports from other experts, such as an economist, an occupational therapist, a vocational therapist, etc., concerning damages and disabilities
10. Reports from experts regarding liability
11. A verification from the plaintiff's employer of salary and time lost from work
12. The police report of the accident
13. Witness' statements
14. Photographs of the scene, the plaintiff after the accident, and any vehicles, machinery, etc. that were involved in the accident
15. Signed authorizations for the insurance company to obtain medical and employment records

This list illustrates some of the types of information which, if available, the lawyer may choose to reveal in order to generate a desired offer from the insurer without having to file suit.

The common types of information listed above, and similar types of information, are often disclosed for two reasons. First, the insurer will not settle without documenting its file so that the settlement is shown to be justified. Second, even if there is no settlement and a suit is filed, most, if not all, of this information will be obtained by the defense in discovery in any event. Again, the benefits of disclosure must be weighed against any detriments from revealing particular information, either at a specific point in the negotiation or at any time.

Most often, the first four types of information are given over the telephone, and the rest is sent to the defendant's insurer with an appropriate cover letter. At times, however, more information will be provided, and the means of communication will differ.

A more expansive form of disclosure that sometimes is used by plaintiffs' attorneys in basically competitive litigation negotiations is the settlement brochure.[28] In personal injury actions, where these brochures are used more often than other types of cases, settlement brochures can involve all of the information listed above, as well as such items as:

---

[28] Skolrood, *Negotiating Settlement Of A Personal Injury Action-Plaintiff,* in Attorney's Guide to Negotiation (1979); Tober, *The Settlement Conference,* 15 Trial Law Q 42, 45 (1983);

1. A statement of the facts
2. A memorandum on the legal issues
3. A memorandum concerning any medical issues
4. A memorandum on the likely damages award

All of the information is packaged together in a comprehensive, persuasive manner.[29] Of course, in a non-personal injury case, the format would be the same, although the specific types of data and issues would vary.

Another more extensive than normal form of disclosure is the "open file" approach. As the name implies, this involves opening up all or most of one's file to the other side except for privileged matter sought to be protected and within the limits of sound discretion. In addition to providing the type of documentary information mentioned above, the open file also can include allowing written or recorded statements or oral, nonrecorded interviews or questioning of the client, experts, or other key witnesses.[30]

Both the settlement brochure and the open file approach are deviations from the usual types of litigation disclosures and should be employed cautiously when one or the other seems to be appropriate in a particular case. They are premised on two concepts. The first is that the disclosure will be persuasive both through the quality and/or quantity of the material being presented. The second premise is that the material ultimately would be divulged anyway through discovery, briefs on motions, or other pretrial procedures. The criteria that should be considered before employing such methods in a case include the following:

1. Is the other party or its insurer likely to be receptive to this approach?
2. Is the other negotiator likely to be receptive to this type of approach?
3. Do the dual premises described above really apply to this particular case?
4. Is the case worth expending any extra time and expense involved in utilizing these methods?
5. Is the case perceived to be sufficiently significant by the other side so that it will devote the necessary time and any expense needed to fairly evaluate the information that is being transmitted to it?
6. If a settlement is achieved, how do the anticipated time, effort, and costs which will have been saved compare to those anticipated if the case were to be settled at a later point or if the case proceeded to trial?[31]

Annotation, Werchick, *Settling the Case-Plaintiff*, 4 Am Jur Trials 289 (1966); For a sample of a settlement brochure see *Annotation*, Belli, *Sample Settlement Brochure*, 4 Am Jur Trials 411 (1966).

[29] *See* Tober, *The Settlement Conference*, 15 Trial Law Q 42, 45 (1983); Belli, *Sample Settlement Brochure*, 4 Am Jur Trials 411 (1966).

[30] Anatomy of Personal Injury Case-1 (Continuing Legal Education Satellite Network, Advanced Legal Studies, NY, NY, G. Spence & R. Rose, 1986).

[31] As always, the time value of money and the potential for an award of prejudgment interest need to be considered in evaluating the advantages of an early settlement.

If applicable, the time, effort, and expense of an appeal should be figured into the last calculation. It is possible that these approaches will be successful only in a limited number of cases.[32] Nevertheless, if used in carefully selected cases, even that may yield an overall benefit.[33]

Verbal and written narratives are the most common forms of communicating disclosures of information. However, charts, graphs, drawings, photographs, videotapes, various types of documents such as financial statements, and any other type of non-narrative visual communication all can and should be utilized when appropriate.[34] This may be necessary for situations in which a narrative will not persuasively communicate the message so that it is received, understood, and motivates the desired response. Even where it is not a matter of absolute necessity, it can be more persuasive to supplement the narrative presentation with tangible displays.

Similarly, tours and demonstrations also can be an effective means of persuading the other party of the value of a business, service or product. The same is true with respect to convincing the other party of a factual issue where litigation or potential litigation is involved.[35] Although in a nonlitigation context, such techniques often are thought of as "sales" ploys, they are effective negotiation tools in a variety of contexts and should not be overlooked.

Avoiding disclosure without creating distrust and without any misrepresentations is a crucial part of the selective disclosure of information. Some inquiries can be responded to by answers carefully and clearly framed with only the most favorable information, as long as no misrepresentation results from the partial answer. Deflection is responding in a way that moves slightly or completely off of the direct subject of the inquiry, and also may be useful. Deflection techniques include:[36]

1. Answering a question that was not asked as if counsel understood that to be the question that was asked

2. Refusing to agree with a portion of or an assumption within a question

3. Being deliberately ignorant of the answer to an anticipated question, so that the response simply indicates a lack of knowledge

---

[32] Anatomy of a Personal Injury Case-1 (Continuing Legal Education Satellite Network, Advanced Legal Studies, NY, NY, G. Spence & R. Rose, 1986).

[33] *Id.*

[34] In other words, anything that could be used as either real or demonstrative evidence may be helpful, regardless of whether the negotiation involves a litigation, or a nonlitigation matter. For information regarding such visual displays, see D. Siemer, Tangible Evidence: How to Use Exhibits at Trial (1984). Although Siemer's discussion is in the context of presenting exhibits at trial, much of the information is applicable to negotiation as well.

[35] Although written in the context of trial presentations, see generally, *id.* As Siemer points out in discussing "views" of the scene: "The inaccuracies inherent in verbal communication are enormous. Words mean different things to different people." *Id* 15.

[36] C. Karrass, Give & Take: The Complete Guide to Negotiating Strategies and Tactics 8-9, 88 (1974).

Unless used carefully and selectively, deflection can create distrust. For that reason, it should be used sparingly during any negotiation.

At times, a simple and direct refusal to disclose the information being sought can be appropriate where the requested information is either:

1. Sensitive and, at least in the perception of the party being asked to make the disclosure, not of legitimate concern to the party requesting it

2. Information that is simply not a subject for disclosure at all

The latter category can include such things as the amount of one's authority. In litigation, at times it can also include facts and arguments when counsel is not willing to engage in a detailed discussion of the strengths and the weaknesses of his or her case.

In deciding which technique to use to avoid a real answer to an inquiry, counsel must balance the following factors:

1. The need to be perceived as honest and candid, rather than as disingenuous, in order to create or to preserve trust

2. Whether the information should be disclosed in part or avoided directly so that the negotiation proceeds in a desired direction

3. How the other negotiator and the other party will react to either a deflection or to a direct refusal to answer, including the inferences which may be drawn by them

Frequently, a direct refusal to answer should be accompanied by an explanation of the reasons that the inquiry is unfair or improper. In this way, a potential adverse reaction to the refusal to answer may be defused.

An entirely different type of information disclosure is the "snow job."[37] In this type of disclosure, the negotiator attempts to obscure important information within a mass of other information. The major countermeasures are:

1. To demand carefully drawn categories of information, with the information produced within the predetermined classifications

2. To painstakingly peruse all of the information with sufficient time allocated to allow an effective review

To preserve credibility, as well as to avoid potential charges of fraud at times, an attorney should not disclose information as a fact unless he or she is relatively certain of it after reasonable inquiry.[38] Unless openly acknowledged, guessing or speculating easily can lead to inaccuracies which are discovered later. If information requested by the other negotiator is not known, counsel should either:

---

[37] *Id* 197.
[38] Credibility is of great importance. *See* **§3.02.**

1.   Admit a lack of knowledge

2.   Deflect the inquiry

A last caveat is in order regarding inadvertent disclosure. Generally, attorneys should assume that their counterparts can read upside down and will read anything that is left out in view.[39] Although it is certainly the less usual situation, depending on the nature of the matter and its value to the parties, the possibility of surveillance, espionage, electronic eavesdropping, etc. may need to be considered, and measures may be required to guard against or to neutralize such intrusive information gathering attempts by the other party.

§4.03   The Creation of Facts

Communication by action can be effective and persuasive.[40] The tactic of creating facts consists of actions by the attorney or by the client that legitimately add to or alter an existing factual situation. It does not involve dishonesty or deceit, but instead is a bona fide enhancement of a party's factual posture or presentation.

Example 4-8

A house is for sale. To improve its appearance and to increase its value and the price that can be obtained for it, it is painted.[41] The increase in the price is much greater than the cost of painting, so that the incremental revenue is greater than the incremental variable cost. Thus, the result is a net profit.

Example 4-9

In actual or potential litigation, an investigation leading to the discovery of a previously unknown, important, credible witness produces at least the new fact of a solid witness with significant testimony. Where the new witness's information could not have been presented through anyone else, new facts also are created in the sense that previously unknown or unprovable facts now can be put into evidence. The witness may be a fact witness or an expert witness.

Example 4-10

A party, seeking to sell its business, is concerned that a potential buyer will be skeptical of the financial data which was compiled by the seller's internal bookkeeper, even though the data is accurate. Accordingly, the

---

[39] W. Coffin, The Negotiator: A Manual For Winners 149 (1973).

[40] R. Givens, Advocacy: The Art of Pleading a Cause 438 (Shepard's/McGraw-Hill, Inc 1985).

[41] Williams, *Leviathan's Program* (Book Review), The New York Review of Books, June 11, 1987, at 33.

seller creates a new fact by obtaining an audited financial statement from an independent, reputable accounting firm, which presents essentially the same financial information as the party's own bookkeeper had prepared. (The same situation could occur with respect to a party seeking financing.)

Example 4-11

A written or verbal description of a new service or product has been presented during the negotiations, but the potential purchaser either does not accept or does not accurately comprehend the description. Therefore, prior to any further bargaining, a demonstration of the service or the product is given. The demonstration thereby "creates" a new, persuasive fact of the realities of the service or the product since, in the negotiation, that fact did not previously "exist" in the potential purchaser's mind.

Painting, or even cleaning a house that is for sale, may display the same structure in an entirely different way. Having the new witness alters the truth that can be proven in a courtroom. An internal bookkeeper's financial information may be discounted or considered with great uncertainty, whereas the addition of an audited financial statement, verifying the previously uncertain economic data, can change the posture of the negotiation.[42] A written or verbal description of a product or of a service may contain its attributes, but still leave an unpersuaded audience. An effective demonstration can impress that same audience far more than the most clever and eloquent written or verbal description.[43] In this sense, each of the examples portrays a fact which, in effect, did not exist before. For the purpose of persuasion and influencing the other party, a fact does not exist until the other party either believes it or at least is sufficiently convinced to take it seriously.

Another type of fact creation relates to win/win offers that are based on "new facts."[44]

Example 4-12

Discounts for early payment are offered to secure a sales contract. The discounts are important to the buyer, but have relatively little cost to the seller.

Example 4-13

Guaranteed tonnage is very significant to a carrier because it reduces the possibility of a serious cash flow problem. It is offered by the shipper to secure more favorable terms for a shipping contract. The guarantee has

---

[42] Whether the audited financial statement will succeed in doing so will depend on the importance that the other party attaches to the data, and the validity, or invalidity, with which the other side perceives the audited statement.

[43] Of course, written or verbal descriptions can be highly effective in many instances.

[44] For a discussion of win/win outcomes, see §5.06.

no cost to the shipper, which needs to have that much of its product transported anyway.

Example 4-14

The future cost of insurance is uncertain. The parties agree to pass through any increase in insurance costs. Both sides benefit by having a formula that ensures fairness, and that avoids a protracted dispute about the correct dollar estimate of future cost increases.

These three examples consist of possible new facts which can be created by counsel and the client during a negotiation. The first two examples create win/win results, because the new facts have far more value to the other party than for counsel's own client, for whom the offer entails nonexistent or small costs.[45] The last example illustrates a resolution that equitably solves a problem for both parties.[46] All of them involve the creation of new facts which permit the making of a new, more attractive and valued offer.

Disclosing information to outside parties can create new operative facts. Public pronouncements demonstrate commitment to a position.[47] Unless it is considered a bluff, a publicly announced position forces the other party to consider whether agreement with the public position or further concessions are necessary. The persuasiveness of the public position can come from the knowledge that:

1. There is a natural reluctance to accept the loss of face entailing by compromising a public position without receiving a valuable concession
2. The position has greater value to the party stating it than was previously understood by the other side
3. Contrary to the other side's prior belief, the party's position is less flexible or is inflexible

Threats of potential adverse changes can be new facts that create uncertainty.

Example 4-15

"We cannot prevent some of our members from engaging in a wildcat strike, if they decide to go out."

Example 4-16

"We believe your client, although a key employee wanting to buy the company, has been misappropriating certain amounts. If this deal is not made on these terms, we will audit and investigate fully. On the other hand, if he buys the business on these terms, we'll consider the matter closed."

---

[45] See §§**5.06** and **5.08** regarding win/win outcomes and concessions with little or no cost to the party offering them.

[46] See §**3.08** regarding the problem solving strategy.

[47] W. Rusher, How to Win Arguments 95 (1981).

Example 4-17

"If it's not resolved today, we'll institute litigation. I have an emergency, temporary restraining order and the other papers ready, and we'll see you in court tomorrow. But let's see what we can do together to prevent that."

Threats can be based on matters totally controlled by one party. They also may involve matters outside of the control of the party making the threat, such as the wildcat strike. Either way, the fate of the party receiving the threat is in its own hands.[48] That party either can accept the offered terms and avoid the threatened consequences, or accept the risk posed by the threat or the threatened consequences themselves.

To be credible, the rumored, threatened, or other potential action must appear to present a real danger, and not merely be a bluff. Personal credibility and historical precedent often are the key factors which determine whether the danger is viewed as real or not.

Depending on what precipitates a threat, on the context of the negotiation, and on whether the other party has been given a reasonable opportunity to prevent the threatened action, threats need not be presented as a hostile posture. A party may wish, or may need to appear, not to be acting aggressively, either to:

1.   Maintain a relationship with the other party
2.   Impress interested third parties, including the media and the public

To avert the appearance of aggression, a threat can be presented coolly, as a matter of fact which the other party can avoid by being reasonable. The same purpose may be achieved by expressing some reluctance to make threats, but explaining that the other side's refusal to fairly compromise has forced this position to be taken.

When a threat is a hostile gesture, it may be presented with an explanation as to why it is justified.

Example 4-18

"Given the agreements and promises that have been violated by your client, we have no choice but to file suit unless we receive these provisions that ensure penalties for such conduct in the future."

Example 4-19

"The serious grievances which we have outlined were deliberately caused by your client and have placed my client in an intolerable position. Accordingly, unless the situation is altered immediately, we will have to seek an injunction."

---

[48] C. Karrass, Give & Take: The Complete Guide to Negotiating Strategies and Tactics 228 (1974).

Countermeasures to threats include:

1. Counterthreats
2. Being indifferent to the threats

Litigation, or the persuasive threat of it, creates new facts. These include potential fees and costs that may not be recovered, as well as an uncertain outcome if the matter is decided at trial or on appeal. The uncertainty of a judge's ruling or a jury's verdict in the future provides an incentive, often the major incentive, for settlement.[49]

In criminal cases, new facts can occur through such actions as:

1. A change in attitude on the part of the victim or another witness, including a reluctance to relive a traumatic experience[50]
2. A successful motion to suppress evidence
3. Granting of a motion to suppress a statement
4. Denial of a motion to suppress

Changes in bargaining rules also constitute new facts which can have a tremendous impact on negotiations.

Example 4-20

In 1975, an arbitration ruling altered the rules of free agency for baseball players. Four years later, players' salaries had more than doubled.[51]

Similarly, legal research can constitute a means of creating operative facts through the discovery of precedents which may affect the outcome of a case if the matter is resolved through adjudication rather than settlement.

A significant part of effective negotiating is the ability to present facts persuasively.[52] Thus, it is clear that the creation of facts that the other party finds convincing and significant can be a vital tool to improve one's position in the negotiation.

§4.04   Listening for Information

The corollary tactic to the selective disclosure of information is the effective acquisition and comprehension of information. This is a two-stage process. First, the information must be elicited or discovered. Second, it must be perceived and understood.

---

[49] H. Raiffa, The Art and Science of Negotiation 315 (1982).

[50] Roberts, *Negotiation in a Criminal Case-Prosecution,* in Attorney's Guide to Negotiation 12-11 (1979).

[51] H. Raiffa, *supra* note 49, at 104.

[52] See §5.10 regarding debating the issues.

Regarding the latter point, verbal information can be difficult to perceive and understand far more so than written information. Lawyers, like many other people, often are more interested in talking than in listening. Consequently, they frequently are thinking about what they are going to say when they start to speak again, rather than carefully listening to what is being said by someone else.[53] Counsel also may have preconceived ideas about what is expected to be said by the other negotiator. They then fail to perceive what is really being said and instead think that they heard what they wanted or expected to hear.

Careful listening is a skill that is crucial for an effective negotiator so that the negotiator can endeavor to discern the other side's real position.[54] The attorney not only must hear each word but also must perceive what is actually being said, rather than what is expected or desired to be said.[55] Further explanation on how to listen effectively is provided in the section on receiving information.[56]

§4.05   The Funnel Approach

Attorneys, like business executives, often cut off and block available information from being perceived.[57] Even when broad information is needed, they lapse into the gathering of information by asking narrow questions of someone who wants or is willing to disclose information. Rather than attempting to elicit a complete narrative, they launch into cross-examination style questions. That is, they ask narrow, sometimes leading, often yes or no type questions. This is a much more difficult and less effective means of obtaining complete information from a willing source.

Anyone doubting that conclusion should attempt a simple experiment. Follow these steps:

1.   Ask someone to think of an interesting or exciting experience
2.   Attempt to learn all about that experience by asking only questions that can be answered "yes" or "no," and instruct the person responding to answer only "yes" or "no"
3.   Lastly, attempt to learn about the same or a different experience by encouraging the person responding to explain what occurred so that you can see and feel it happen. Instruct the other person to be cooperative. Speak only to encourage the other person to continue, to give guidance if the account becomes confusing, or to stop an irrelevant disgression

---

[53] G. Nierenberg, The Art of Negotiation: Psychological Strategies for Gaining Advantageous Bargains 45 (1968).

[54] R. Fisher & W. Ury, Getting to Yes: Negotiating Agreement Without Giving In 33 (1981); H. Cohen, You Can Negotiate Anything 106 (1982).

[55] G. Kennedy, J. Benson & J. McMillan, Managing Negotiations 40 (1982); H. Cohen, *supra* note 54, at 217.

[56] *See* §10.04.

[57] M. Schoenfield, Presentations at continuing legal education programs and seminars for business professionals.

The old television show, "What's My Line," provides a further example of the problem with narrow questions. The premise of the show was that the panelists would attempt to determine a guest's occupation by asking only yes or no type questions. The yes or no question often failed to generate sufficient information, which made deducing the occupation difficult and interesting. If broader or narrative type questions could have been asked, it would have been easy to always determine the occupation, and there would have been no show. This lesson is underscored by a famous incident on the show, in which the panel failed to discover that the guest's occupation was the governor of Georgia. The guest, Jimmy Carter, later became known to everyone.

No one can anticipate all situations. Narrow questions can miss important details or unexpected portions of a story. Such questions should be saved for uncooperative sources, and to fill in any details that may be missing from the initial account.

The funnel approach is a structure for obtaining broad information from a totally or somewhat willing source, including those who are only reluctantly cooperative.[58] It begins with asking general questions which often seek a narrative response. After broad questions and encouragement exhaust the speaker's willingness or ability to disclose information, narrower and narrower questions are posed, seeking more specific or detailed information.

This method for obtaining information is applicable to negotiations.[59] In many situations, there is a "casual" general question like: "How's business?" However, that question may not be so casual at all. Rather than just being perfunctory and polite conversation, it can be a highly effective, information gathering device for the negotiation. The question can lead to disclosure of key information, such as:

1. Whether the party has excess capacity or is overextended

2. The party's sales growth or decline

3. Cash flow problems that the party is experiencing or that it fears will occur

4. Difficulties with accounts receivable that the party is experiencing or that it fears will occur

5. The ease or the difficulty that the party has in securing capital, financing, or lines of credit

6. The party's plans for expanding or reducing its operations

7. The strength or weakness of the party's management

8. Problems with the quality of a product or of a service that the party is marketing

---

[58] M. Schoenfield & B. Pearlman Schoenfield, Interviewing and Counseling 58 (1981).

[59] The same type of inquiries may be asked of one's own client to acquire information needed to interview and counsel the client regarding the client's goals and counsel's recommendations for the negotiation. *Id. See* **ch 2.**

9.   The loss of, or the need to acquire, a major customer or supplier

As these examples indicate, a routine question can perform an important intelligence gathering function. Responses to the simple, "how's business" question can reveal:

1.   Factors affecting the price or the value of a property, service, product, business, or other subject of the negotiation
2.   The needs, interests, strengths, and weaknesses of the other party

Eliciting these types of information can be extremely valuable for analyzing one's position. The information can help to avoid either undervaluing or overvaluing the client's position, as well as to establish the appropriate settlement range.

Example 4-21

Prior to an upcoming negotiation, the negotiators for the two sides happen to meet.

NEGOTIATOR A: How's business?
NEGOTIATOR B: We're basically doing very well. With our expansion, next year our profits should skyrocket. But right now, the expansion has caused real cash flow problems. If anything happens to interrupt our present production, we would be in serious trouble.
NEGOTIATOR A: Well, hopefully we can avoid that situation.

If Negotiator A represents the union and Negotiator B represents management in an upcoming labor negotiation, it is axiomatic that this conversation should never take place from B's perspective. Negotiator B has disclosed vital information that will allow Negotiator A to accurately set high realistic expectations for the union, to accurately assess management's settlement point, and to know how to pressure management. This example graphically illustrates just how informative the simple, "how's business" type of inquiry can be, as well as the need for selective disclosure of information.

The general, less direct form of probing is the first stage of the funnel approach. Often, the first stage is done as a low-key, offhand, vague, not too important part of the conversation. The inquiry is made to sound as if it is not part of the real negotiation, but rather just routine conversation. In this way, the other party or negotiator may be less alert to guarding against inadvertent disclosures of important information. This casual first stage should be followed by more narrow, direct questions, as may be appropriate.

The funnel approach also can start with more direct, but still general, probes as well.

Example 4-22

"Have you ever had a bad or an unsatisfactory experience with _____ or in this type of deal before? (If so) What happened?"

Example 4-23

"To help me to structure the best deal that I can for both clients, what are your client's objectives and needs?"

Example 4-24

"How do you judge the success of this kind of program?"

Example 4-25

"Do you basically like the present offer, although you may want some changes, or are we operating in totally different areas?"

An opening may be created by acknowledging a lack of understanding and then framing the inquiry in terms of the other's perceptions.

Example 4-26

"Maybe I don't understand. Explain how you see it."

These types of direct inquiries can be made when either:

1. The other negotiator or the other party will want to respond in an attempt to influence the structure of the proposed arrangement

2. Counsel wants to place the burden of not being able to consider restructuring the existing proposal, or of not being able to consider any further concessions, on the unwillingness of the other side to provide the requested information.

The latter usually is triggered by two types of situations. In the first, the attorney choosing direct inquiry believes that the information is such that the other party will not divulge it. The attorney wants to precipitate the situation of a refusal to disclose the information in order to create a rationale or a pretext to block further movement in the negotiation. This is effective only if the information request is reasonable, so that the attorney appears to be acting legitimately. Clearly, asking for the other negotiator's bottom line or ultimate authority, and then refusing to negotiate further without that disclosure, will not be viewed as legitimate. In the second type of situation, counsel is willing to proceed, but needs the requested information to do so, and wants to be able to blame the other party for creating an impasse if the information is not forthcoming. This can be especially important if the parties are attempting to influence the other negotiator's client or client's constituency, allies, or other third parties.[60]

The funnel approach can be a response to volunteered information, permitting counsel to explore the true content of the information.

Example 4-27

The proposed lease from the landlord contained a proportionate pass through of all building operating expenses and real estate taxes in excess of $750,000. Counsel for the tenant first inquired into the operating expenses using broad questions.

"What expenses are included in operating expenses?"
"How are operating expenses expected to rise during the four-year lease term?"
"Are any real estate tax reassessments scheduled during the lease term?"

Counsel next followed up with narrower questions, including:

"How have operating expenses risen recently?"
"What were the total operating expenses in each of the last three years, and what was the amount of each category of the operating expenses in that time?"
"Are there any items of deferred maintenance, or expected major maintenance, replacement, or repair that may occur during the lease term?"

Lastly, counsel sought to verify the figures that were reported.

"Can we have a copy of the building's profit and loss statement for the last three years, or at least that portion that shows the operating expenses?"

In this way, the funnel approach was used to explore a factual issue.

For many uses of the funnel approach, the lawyer must be aware of issues and problems from previous experience or from prenegotiation information gathering. Unless the attorney possesses the necessary substantive knowledge, important matters may be overlooked. For instance, in a lease negotiation, if the lawyer does not know the difference between usable and rentable space, an entire area of concern may be missed.

Information should be checked, rather than blindly accepted.[61] A degree of skepticism is healthy. Statistical analyses, computer models, and other asserted facts, if significant but not self-evident, should at least be probed using the funnel method. Even so, other, more concrete verification techniques should be employed if they are warranted and feasible. These include references, sam-

---

[60] See **§6.02** regarding transmitting information to the other negotiator's client, **§6.05** regarding dealing with allies, and **§6.06** concerning influencing third parties.

[61] C. Karrass, Give & Take: The Complete Guide to Negotiating Strategies and Tactics 196 (1974).

ples, demonstrations, affidavits, inspections, warranties, opinion letters, etc. Proof or confirmation of asserted "facts" may be demanded from the other party, or obtained independently of the other party.

The countermeasure is selective information disclosure. Guarded responses are necessary. At time, a full and open response is fine. At other times, the request for information must be resisted.

§4.06   Sources of Information

The client is the first source of information, as well as one which always continues to be available. When the client is an entity, potential sources of information should not be limited to the key decision makers and the top staff. For instance, at times in a labor negotiation, the best source of information can be the line supervisors, who may have insights into problems, issues, costs, facts, or analysis that are unknown to higher levels of management.[62] Similarly, in other contexts, supervisors, technical staff, or other workers may have information that the top levels of management do not have.

In negotiations, counsel naturally and properly focus on the other party and its negotiator as major sources of information. These certainly are important sources of information in every negotiation.

However, other sources can be important as well. Indeed, in many negotiations, the preparation for the negotiation will begin by gathering information from these other sources. As noted above, this investigative work may be critical to the eventual success of the negotiation.[63] Prior, similar negotiations can provide facts, standard or specialized terms, and market values. Factually similar negotiations with the same party may reveal its true needs, interests, and intentions. Even factually dissimilar negotiations can impart significant insights into the strategies normally employed by the same party or the same negotiator and the credibility of either one or of both.[64]

Attorneys, both inside and outside of one's own office, who have interacted with the same party or the same negotiator, can provide valuable information and insights from that experience. Similarly, clients or others with prior interactions also can be valuable sources.

In addition, reference sources may be utilized, depending on the nature of the situation and the type of information that is being sought. University or association studies and reports may be available. Professional societies, their publications, and other periodicals can reveal facts about a party, the market, etc. Continuing legal education books, forms, and other legal material can provide information on the structure, terms, values, or prices which should be considered. In personal injury, civil rights, and other types of litigation in which precedent can help to predict the likely outcome of the case, reports of jury

---

[62] W. Fallon, AMA Management Handbook 7-105, 7-106 (1983).

[63] *See* **§4.01.**

[64] G. Nierenberg, The Art of Negotiation: Psychological Strategies for Gaining Advantageous Bargains 48-50 (1968).

verdicts, administrative rulings, reports of settlements and cases reported on appeal may provide data on the size of damage awards, the facts needed to support an award of a certain amount, and the findings required to sustain a judgment on appeal.

Of course, these are only the starting points for the analysis of the negotiation. Each situation must be evaluated independently, in light of the needs and the positions of the parties. Prior agreements with different parties must be viewed with a special caution. These almost inevitably are the product of compromise, rather than the ultimate structure with all of the terms that either party wished that it could have obtained in the agreement. They must be scrutinized for ways to improve the terms for the client.

Consultants and experts also are sources of information. In the transportation field, a consultant may know the most cost efficient mode for shipping, the strengths and weaknesses of specific carriers, and the market rates. Appraisers, contractors, and engineers can be used in determining the value of a particular building. In antitrust litigation, an economist can help define the relevant market and the market shares of those within it, as well as issues such as the ease of entry into the market. In personal injury cases, experts and consultants include doctors, occupational or vocational therapists, economists, actuaries, accident reconstruction specialists, and specialists in any product that may be involved. Indeed, the possibilities are almost limitless.[65]

The government may be another fertile source of information. Governmental studies can contain important data or other facts. In negotiating with a governmental agency, its own rules or rulings can reveal limitations on its negotiating authority.[66] In any industry or profession in which there is government regulation, those regulations and the record of their promulgation may be helpful. Moreover, information about the other party may well be available from the government through a freedom of information request, subject to the relevant privacy and freedom of information restrictions.[67]

For some transactions, inspections are a source of information for the buyer. These include purchases of:

1. Real estate

2. Businesses[68]

3. Machinery, equipment, and other goods when their quality or quantity should be verified before an agreement is reached and/or prior to making full payment

---

[65] One national service that locates experts for attorneys advertises that it has over 8,000 experts in over 3,000 categories.

[66] Wise, *Negotiations with the Internal Revenue Service,* in Attorney's Guide to Negotiation 2-16 (1979).

[67] See the federal Freedom of Information Act (FOIA), 5 USC §552 *et seq.* Some states and municipalities have analogous statutes.

[68] Marcus, *Representing the Purchaser of a Small Business,* in Attorney's Guide to Negotiation 5-29 (1979).

In more unusual situations, investigators can assist as a source of information. These include "corporate intelligence" and "competitor intelligence" firms.[69] To decide whether to request authorization from the client to employ an investigator, the lawyer must consider:

1. The potential benefits from the information to be sought
2. The likelihood of obtaining that information
3. The risk of embarrassment or of offending the other party if the investigation is discovered
4. Any danger that illegal acts may occur during the investigation
5. Costs

These considerations must be balanced in deciding whether the use of a private investigator is sound or not.

§4.07   Bargaining for Information

A reluctant or recalcitrant source of information may be persuaded by astute reasoning. Sometimes, however, counsel must bargain for information. In such instances, the information itself becomes the subject of a negotiation, as something of value is traded for specific information.

With third parties, the trade can involve anything from goodwill to money. The means of obtaining the information are confined only by legal and ethical restrictions, such as the laws regarding bribery, insider trading, the theft of corporate and business secrets, the disclosure of various categories of information by government officials, and privileged information.

In the negotiation itself, there can be either explicit or implicit trades of information. In the latter situation, counsel may make a disclosure with the clear, albeit unstated, expectation that it will lead to a reciprocal release of information from the other negotiator. This is analogous to the concede first strategy.[70] If the other negotiator fails to respond, counsel can try to demand a reciprocal disclosure. If that fails, counsel should, at least for a period of time, refuse to make any further disclosures, unless there is a specific agreement on mutual disclosures.

In an explicit informational trade, a party may offer to disclose certain information if different information held by the other side also is revealed. At times, parties are reluctant to provide disclosures because of fear that one-sided disclosures of information will lead to an imbalance in the information known to the parties, thereby creating a corresponding disadvantage in the negotiation. When such a problem arises, the explicit trading of information can open up communications between the parties in a productive fashion. Assuming that

---

[69] *Far From Being Cloak-and-Dagger, Corporate Spying Becomes Workaday Stuff,* Chicago Trib, Dec 22, 1987, §5, at 3, col. 1.

[70] *See* **§3.07.**

the parties are acting in good faith, trading can alleviate that fear by eliminating the possibility that the flow of information will be in only one direction.

§4.08   Information through Discussion

One of the most common methods for exchanging information is discussion. This can be in the form of a conversation, a debate, or an argument. What form the discussion takes will depend on the situation, the parties, and the negotiators.

Except to the extent that an adversarial posture is required, a less adversarial discussion is likely to be more productive. A less adversarial form of the discussion allows the negotiators and the parties to be more easily focus on the content of the message, rather than on its style of delivery. The key is to find the style (conversation, debate, or argument), the phrasing, and the tone that persuasively conveys selective information to the other party and its negotiator, as well as which effectively elicits information from them.

The more adversarial debate or argument style is appropriate in a number of situations. First, it is appropriate where the other negotiator will be overwhelmed. This is the exception, rather than the usual case. Since unsuccessful attempts to overwhelm often lead to resentment and to increased resistance, or at least to the latter, the attempt is likely to be counterproductive unless it is successful.

Debating or arguing in an adversarial style also is fitting where the other negotiator is determined to interact on that level, and initial efforts to engage in a less adversarial dialogue have been or apparently would be futile. One may conclude that such efforts have been or would be futile in the absence of a demonstrated willingness and ability on the part of the other negotiator to respond in kind. In these circumstances, the more adversarial level is necessary to avoid creating the impression that counsel, or counsel's client, can be intimidated.

Furthermore, the need of the client, of the client's constituency, or of other third parties to hear a more adversarial posture can make the use of such a style appropriate. This may occur either initially or during some other point in the process. The attorney, however, must function as a counselor, and not adopt an unsuitable or counterproductive antagonistic manner just because the client has hostile feelings towards the other party or its negotiator. The client's desires may be skewed by highly charged, emotional misconceptions. One of the functions of attorneys is to act without the personal animus that can cloud the judgment of clients who are caught up in their personal feelings. Indeed, that is one of the reasons why it is difficult to represent oneself in a negotiation.[71] Zealous advocacy should be based on an objective assessment of the situation as to what will benefit the client. For an attorney to fail to properly counsel the client, and to enact a charade only because it reflects the client's desires without regard to consequences, is poor representation.

---

[71] H. Cohen, You Can Negotiate Anything 87-88 (1982).

Since discussion is an often used and useful general method for selectively disclosing information and also for eliciting information, it is an option that can be utilized for all client goals and for all strategies.

Asking the other negotiator questions during the discussion can be an effective technique for discovering information, even if the information generated is the manner in which the other negotiator attempts to avoid answering the question.[72] Simply remaining silent can cause the other negotiator to continue to talk, thereby revealing more information than perhaps was intended.[73] These two techniques can be used in conjunction with each other.

Releasing information in a discussion should not necessarily be resisted. One of the reasons that parties, with basically the same goal, can disagree regarding how to achieve the goal, is a difference in the information that they possess.[74] Thus, particularly where a problem solving strategy or cooperative goals are involved, it may be important to discuss and to share information about pertinent data, the clients' needs, opinions, etc.[75] Indeed, in such situations, brainstorming sessions seeking creative solutions can be an effective means of discussion.[76]

During the discussion portion of a negotiation, there may be facts or other information that should not be disclosed. Commonly, counsel do not want to disclose their authority. In litigation, the attorney can want to avoid revealing certain facts and arguments, or be unwilling to engage in a discussion of the strengths and the weaknesses of the case in detail. One purpose may be to avoid revealing key, secret information prior to the trial, when the risk of alerting the adverse party, who then will be better prepared at trial, outweighs the likelihood that disclosure will lead to settlement. Another purpose can be to avoid either a waste of time because disclosure would either be fruitless, or an admission of weakness. In these situations, generalities and deflection can be used to avoid unwanted disclosure to the other party.

Example 4-28

"We both know that we have evidence and arguments to present, and we both know what they are. I'm not going to waste both of our time by debating what we already know, since we are not going to agree that either of us is right. Do you want to discuss numbers or don't you?"

Good deflection requires shifting the discussion to another topic. In addition, questions about authority can be handled in several ways. The response might be astonishment that anyone would ask such a question and expect a serious answer. Alternatively, inquiries about authority can be met with an outright

---

[72] Note, *An Analysis of Settlement,* 22 Stan L Rev 67 (1969) in G. Bellow & B. Moulton, The Lawyering Process 513 (1978).

[73] Oatley, *Negotiating Techniques for Lawyers,* 6 Advoc Q 214, 225-26 (1985).

[74] H. Cohen, *supra* note 71, at 159.

[75] *Id* 159.

[76] G. Nierenberg, The Art of Negotiation: Psychological Strategies for Gaining Advantageous Bargains 54 (1968).

refusal, perhaps coupled with an indication of a willingness to make a recommendation to the client depending on counsel's opinion at the end of the negotiating session.

Principles and policies are especially useful tools for discussion in a negotiation with a governmental or other entity which:

1. Has a goal that is a policy objective or is premised on certain principles
2. Has a decision maker and/or a negotiator who is truly influenced by that policy goal or principles

Examples of policy goals and principles are justice in a criminal prosecution, protecting or enhancing the environment, and preventing or redressing age, race, sex, religious, or physical capability discrimination. When such policy considerations or principles constitute a key motivating factor for the other side, a good opportunity may exist for discussion to be used to shape or to explain offers and positions. The discussion should seek to influence the other party through the use of its own policy or principle.

Example 4-29

> "I realize that, as an EEOC[77] attorney, you are trying to protect the rights of blacks whom you believe should have been but were not hired. However, in protecting those rights, you have proposed a back pay award which would be devastating to the company. I'm sure this is inadvertent. Perhaps you are unaware of the company's precarious financial position, especially with regard to debt and its relationship with its lenders. In fact, even if the government were to prevail at trial and win a large back pay award, the result would bankrupt the company. So the real result would be to throw all of the current workers, including a number of minority workers, out of work. It would just create an illusory back pay award and hiring order, since the company would be forced out of existence. That result will not advance the government's policy objectives. But, I think there is a middle ground if you are willing to be flexible without abandoning any of your policy objectives."

Informal or "off-the-record" discussions can lead negotiators to a revealing degree of candor. Counsel's guard may drop because of the spontaneity, the informality, and the feeling that a higher degree of candor is expected in talking as one professional to another outside of the formal negotiation. An attorney should initiate such an informal discussion whenever it will be advantageous, but be extremely wary of being drawn into one. There are times, however, when the ability to candidly comment "off-the-record" or informally to the other negotiator provides a face-saving or less threatening means of disclosing information.

---

[77] Equal Employment Opportunity Commission.

§4.09 Summary and Review

    I. In large part, negotiation is an informational process

   II. Informational tactics are used in every negotiation

  III. Selective Disclosure of Information
- A. Consciously decide whether disclosure creates a more advantageous effect than withholding information
- B. To influence persuasively and thereby motivate the other party
- C. Can facilitate problem solving
- D. Timing of disclosures must be calculated to maximize or minimize impact
- E. Legally required disclosures
- F. Decisions whether to reveal client goals, needs, and interests
- G. Countering actual or perceived negatives
- H. Expected disclosures
- I. Settlement brochure and open file
- J. Visual aids
- K. Avoiding disclosure without creating distrust and without misrepresentation, through the use of favorable information, deflection, direct refusals to answer, and snow jobs
- L. Do not state anything as a fact unless reasonably certain of it

  IV. Creation of Facts
- A. Legitimately add to or alter the facts
- B. Physical
- C. Win/win offers
- D. Use of third parties
- E. Threats
- F. Litigation, including its cost, changed witness or victim attitudes, and judicial rulings
- G. Legal precedent

   V. Listening for Information

  VI. Funnel Approach
- A. For sources at least somewhat willing to disclose information
- B. Start with broad, general questions
- C. May be presented as casual and offhand
- D. Follow-up with narrower and narrower questions
- E. Check information as appropriate
- F. Countermeasure: selective information disclosure

 VII. Sources of Information
- A. Clients
- B. Other lawyers
- C. Others having experience with the other party, its negotiator, or similar situations
- D. Reference material
- E. Prior agreements as models
- F. Consultants and experts
- G. The government
- H. Inspections

      I. Private investigators
VIII. Bargaining for Information
      A. In the negotiation or with third parties
      B. Trade for information or something else of value
      C. Can open the flow of information if one party otherwise fears
         that disclosure will not generate reciprocity
  IX. Information through Discussion
      A. Conversation, debate, or argument
      B. Less adversarial versus more adversarial style and tone
      C. Use of questions
      D. Utilizing silence
      E. Selectivity
      F. Generalities and other deflections
      G. Use of the other party's own policies and principles
      H. Informal, off-the-record discussions

General Tactics

5

§5.01 Introduction

While strategy is concerned with broad approaches, tactics are maneuvers designed to implement strategy. They are the immediate steps which counsel takes to move the negotiation in the direction established by the client's goals, by the overall planning, and by the strategy that the negotiator has selected.

The tactics described in the following sections provide a wide variety of ways in which to advance a negotiation. A great diversity of tactics are discussed to maximize the negotiator's choice and selection so that optimal effectiveness can be achieved. The tactics will be explained and, when applicable, will be related to those strategies which they either are best suited to implement or for which they are particularly unsuitable.

A number of the tactics described below will involve making concessions. Many negotiators tend to fall into patterns in making concessions.[1] Successful negotiators tend to make smaller concessions and be less predictable by using a more varied pattern of concessions. Using concession patterns as a clue during the negotiation will be analyzed further in §9.11 on the implementation and adjustment of a negotiating plan.

§5.02 Requiring Preconditions

Preconditions are demands which must be agreed to before the remainder of the negotiation proceeds. Although often articulated as demands that must be met before a negotiation can commence, they are, in fact, the first stage of some negotiations. In addition, preconditions can be used as the first stage of a phase or for an issue in a negotiation.

Preconditions are unilaterally chosen by a party and then are presented as non-negotiable items. In many respects, preconditions are like the strategy of no concessions, except that they are limited to gaining an initial agreement on certain points.[2] In this way, they differ from simply deciding that an issue should be negotiated with compromises first as part of establishing an agenda.[3] Although at times, minor adjustments may be compromised, the basic premise of the precondition is not negotiable.

The nature of preconditions may be procedural, substantive, or a combination of the two. Procedural prerequisites are ground rules that will govern all

---

[1] C. Karrass, Give & Take: The Complete Guide to Negotiating Strategies and Tactics 75 (1974).

[2] See §3.03 regarding the no concessions strategy.

[3] *See* §9.07.

or a portion of the remainder of the negotiation. They could be such prerequisites as:

1. An understanding that audited financial statements will be provided to verify financial conditions
2. The presence or the absence of the clients at the site of the negotiation
3. Whether or not the negotiations will be conducted in secret
4. The place at which the physical meeting to conduct the negotiations will occur[4]

Substantive preconditions are items which one party or the other ultimately seeks to gain, or refuses to include in the negotiation. Possible substantive preconditions are such items as:

1. Whether price concessions are or are not negotiable
2. Whether the parties will or will not be equal partners or shareholders if an agreement is reached to form a new partnership or corporation
3. Whether the defendant is ready to pay realistic damages, not merely nominal damages or the cost of defense
4. Whether installment payments will be permitted

As noted above, sometimes procedural and substantive preconditions can be combined. Two examples of such combinations are:

1. A nation demanding, if it negotiates with a group, that its willingness to negotiate does not mean that it recognizes the legitimate status of the group
2. If an agreement is reached on all of the other issues, the payment of reasonable attorney's fees also will be negotiated[5]

If either of two conditions exists, then preconditions can be effectively demanded. One of these conditions is that the demanding party has sufficient power or leverage to unilaterally impose a prerequisite as a trade-off for the other party's right to negotiate the remaining issues. The second situation that is conducive for preconditions is that the preconditions are reasonable from the perspective of both of the parties because they clarify an essential issue, for which there can only be total agreement or total disagreement, and without which it is pointless to continue. Since the issue is critical and since no real middle ground exists, preconditions avoid the possibility that the parties will be completely wasting their time and expense by attempting to negotiate. The

---

[4] The location where the negotiators are to physically meet can have psychological or political value to the negotiators, to the parties, or to outsiders whom the parties wish to influence.

[5] Deferral of negotiating attorney's fees is ethically required in negotiating a settlement in a class action. See §6.08 regarding class actions.

waste would result if one party were absolutely unwilling to agree to a basic term that was considered unequivocally essential by the other party.

This tactic should be employed with caution, and refrained from in most negotiations. The other party or its negotiator may resent its use. They may view it as a direct form of coercion or an attempt to unfairly gain concessions without relinquishing anything in return. Whether such resentment will occur depends on the custom and practice for that type of negotiation, whether the requirement of a precondition is presented harshly or softly, the personality of the other negotiator and of the other party, and whether the precondition seems fair or appropriate. Preconditions based on reasonableness are less likely to generate resentment than those that rely on pure power.

To the extent that resentment may be caused by employing this tactic, that effect must be weighed against the potential benefit if the preconditions are successfully imposed. This analysis includes whether one party will refuse to negotiate at all, retaliate, or adopt a harder line on the remaining issues in order to compensate for acquiescing to the preconditions.

In light of these dangers, counsel must be especially careful in analyzing the potential, unintended effects before attempting to impose a precondition in the following situations:

1. The client's goal is cooperative
2. The plan for the negotiation includes the use of a problem solving strategy
3. A long-term relationship between the two parties is at stake

In those instances, an affable, congenial atmosphere is more likely to result in a successful negotiation. Demanding agreement on a precondition can prevent or destroy that type of atmosphere. Accordingly, counsel must analyze whether a risk exists that any attempt to impose preconditions will be counterproductive. If so, that risk must be weighed against the chances of and the potential benefits from successfully imposing the desired preconditions.

Countermeasures include direct refusal, which is a no concession strategy applied to the precondition. Unless the other party will be intimidated, that usually should be combined with the face-saving tactic,[6] in order to allow the party demanding the precondition to continue gracefully without receiving it. Another countermeasure is to demand a reciprocal precondition if that alternative is available.

§5.03 Making or Avoiding Making the First Offer

A lawyering myth, that used to be heard more often, is that a good negotiator

---

[6] *See* §5.19.

never makes the first offer, or always tries to avoid making the first offer.[7] In a program on negotiating during the mid-1970s, a participant asked Mark Schoenfield: "What will happen when we learn to negotiate better so that we always avoid making the first offer? I mean if everyone starts taking these programs and stops making the first offer, no one will ever make the first offer!" That obviously has not happened. It has not happened because, in fact, sometimes it is better to make the first offer, and sometimes it is better to refrain from making the first offer.[8]

A realistic first offer can establish the "ball park" or range in which the negotiation will be played out.[9] Such an offer can set the basic area of agreement, normally with a fair amount of room for maneuvering left for the remainder of the negotiation. It can do so by influencing the other side's perception of what is possible or reasonable to attain in the negotiation.[10]

The term "realistic first offer" simply refers to a position that is neither so high that it is absolutely disregarded, nor so low that it concedes too much. When a negotiator is in a position to make such a realistic first offer, it can be advantageous to do so in an attempt to establish the parameters of the negotiation.

Whether the negotiator is in a position to make a realistic first offer is a function of the amount and the quality of information that is in the negotiator's possession. Making the first offer can be counterproductive if it is so unrealistically high that either it suggests to the other side that no agreement is possible when that is not true, or it is simply not taken seriously.[11] Making the first offer also can be counterproductive if it is so low that it concedes too much and discloses more about the offeror's bottom line than is prudent.[12] Avoiding these pitfalls requires having sufficient information to assess properly the other party, the other negotiator, and the particular situation.

Of course, the negotiator may not have, or may be uncertain about, whether he or she has adequate information from which to derive a realistic first offer. Without sufficient information, it is advantageous to wait for the other party to make the first offer. This is because that offer will provide additional information to use in assessing the bargaining range and the potential outcomes.

One exception occurs when time constraints exist which force counsel to make the first offer. The time needs of the client must outweigh the risks of making a first offer with insufficient knowledge. In this situation, the lawyer should err on the side of aiming too high, rather than too low.

Generally, this tactic can be used with any client goal or strategy. The caveat to that statement is that in some types of negotiations, the accepted norm may

---

[7] Some commentators believe that making the first offer should generally be avoided. *See* Oatley, *Negotiating Techniques for Lawyers*, 6 Advoc Q 214, 228-29 (1985).

[8] Note, *An Analysis of Settlement*, 22 Stan L Rev 67 (1969), in G. Bellow & B. Moulton, The Lawyering Process 533-34 (1978).

[9] *Id* 533-34.

[10] S. Goldberg, E. Green & F. Sander, Dispute Resolution 47 (1985).

[11] *Id.*

[12] *Id;* Note, *supra* note 8.

be for one side to virtually always make the first offer. For instance, in a personal injury case in which a suit has not yet been filed, the negotiation normally occurs between plaintiff's lawyer and the defendant's insurance company. In these situations, it is normally the plaintiff's lawyer who has to make a "settlement demand" before the insurer is willing to make a settlement offer. This pattern has become so pervasive that the chance to tactically decide whether to make or to avoid making the first offer is severely limited. Fortunately for personal injury plaintiffs' attorneys, such attorneys usually should be in the position of having sufficient information to make a realistic first offer.

In some fields, custom permits the imposition of bidding and written proposal procedures. When appropriate, a party can thereby force the other party to make the first offer by requiring written bids or proposals. The bids may constitute the entire negotiation, or at least the major portion of it.

§5.04   Demanding Responses to Offers and Positions

In order to assist other attorneys, two very experienced attorneys once attempted to demonstrate an effective negotiation. One attorney had planned extremely carefully with a series of positions and reasons for each of those positions. He did most of the talking. The other attorney never responded in a definite way to the first attorney's positions. Instead, she would look incredulous, question whether he was really serious in some of his reasoning, and smile or laugh quietly as part of her response. Although she did not refuse his offers outright, he kept making more and more concessions in an attempt to achieve an agreement. In fact, he went so far in his concessions that he actually exceeded his settlement authority! It is ironic and interesting that all of this occurred in a demonstration designed to show how to negotiate.

In the demonstration, the first lawyer neglected to utilize a basic tactic. He failed to get clear and absolute responses to his offers. Rather, he assumed that the other negotiator's reactions to his reasoning and her manner were refusals of his offers. Instead of demanding that she accept or reject his proposals, he just kept making further concessions. In effect, he was bargaining against himself. His error was compounded to the point of malpractice by making concessions which exceeded his authority.

Counsel must demand that offers be accepted or rejected before making further concessions.[13] Otherwise, unnecessary concessions will be made when a more favorable agreement could have been reached by staying with the prior position.

In order to ensure that both parties avoid unnecessary concessions when counsel believes that an offer or certain terms have been accepted, recapitulation and summarization should be used.

---

[13] Tober, *The Settlement Conference,* 15 Trial Law Q 42, 43 (1985); Erisman, *Settlement Do's and Don'ts,* 24 Trial 112 (1988).

Example 5-1

"At this point, let me reveiw what we've agreed on and what is still open. . . ."

The attorney must pin down that terms are actually accepted, as opposed to just receiving an acknowledgment that the terms are understood and will be considered.[14] Those two types of responses sometimes can be confused in the vagaries of a discussion.

Example 5-2

"That's an interesting idea that we haven't considered before. I think that I like it."

The problem with this response is that it may be an acknowledgment to consider the idea, and not an acceptance of it. Therefore, the meaning of the response must be clarified.

Clarification of an ambiguous response generally should be accomplished by stating one's own understanding that there is agreement on the point, rather than by questioning the other negotiator about whether it has been agreed on in fact. This is because the question might be interpreted to mean that a serious issue remains about whether there should be an agreement at this point. Such a question may generate doubts and second thoughts unnecessarily.

Demanding definite responses to offers and to positions is very different from demanding agreement on the reasons that justify the offer or the position. For many reasons, the other attorney or party may be absolutely set against agreeing with counsel's reasons, or at least unwilling to articulate and admit agreeing with the reasons. Acknowledging the correctness of a reason may involve separate damage to the party even beyond the particular issue that is being discussed. It may be viewed as an important precedent to avoid, either for future transactions or in other litigation. In addition, it could be perceived as a factual admission that will be used for other issues in the negotiation. It also might involve the loss of prestige or of face.

Regardless of the motive underlying the refusal to agree with the reason for the offer, the most important concept is that disagreements about reasons rarely need to be resolved, provided that the parties agree on the terms of the offer itself. When an agreement can be reached within acceptable terms, it is almost always best to allow the disagreement about the reasons that justify the agreement to remain. Furthermore, a party should be allowed to tacitly agree for the reasons stated by the other party, even if it refuses to acknowledge that those are the reasons which led it to assent to the offer. It is substantive agreement that is crucial.

Agreement on the reasons themselves should only be sought in those relatively infrequent situations in which it is difficult to separate the reasoning behind the agreement from the manner in which the agreement will be imple-

---

[14] M. Zimmerman, How to Do Business with the Japanese 116 (House 1985).

mented. Thus, if the manner in which the accord is to be implemented cannot be absolutely specified and is subject to interpretation, then it may be important to agree on the rationale of the agreement. In this manner, it may be possible to avoid or to minimize future problems in interpreting the accord, or at least to have some objective guidance when such questions do arise. This is similar to what counsel sometimes do to interpret a legislative act by looking for the expressed rationale in statutes or by examining legislative history to attempt to determine legislative intent.

A negotiator must be aware of any natural tendency to expect or to demand directness, when implicit communication could better reveal the response to an offer or position.[15] Similarly, a tendency to avoid or to break silences may interrupt the other side, prevent it from considering how to respond, and block the opportunity to learn important information.[16]

The tactic of demanding responses to offers and to positions applies to all client goals and to every strategy, with one exception. If the purpose of the negotiation is for something other than agreement, then the response becomes irrelevant. Normally, however, without such feedback, the negotiator cannot properly evaluate the parties' positions.

In many negotiations, the negotiator lacks final authority, but does exert considerable influence or control over the ultimate decision maker. A definite response in that situation would be: "I will recommend acceptance." Similarly, a key inquiry to obtain a response for needed feedback could be: "Will you recommend acceptance of this proposal?"

Countermeasures to demands for the acceptance or rejection of offers include:

1. A lack of authority
2. The need for clarification, factual information, or to explore other issues before responding
3. Silence, if it is likely to force the other side to fill in an uncomfortable gap by talking, thereby making additional concessions, disclosing further information,[17] or explicitly or implicitly withdrawing its demand for feedback
4. Silence as a form of refusal to the demand for a response,[18] unless it will create or exacerbate a counterproductive antagonism between the negotiators

At times, an acceptance or rejection needs to be expressed. Where the other party has presented a totally unrealistic proposal, the four most useful responses generally are:

---

[15] J. Graham & Y. Sano, Smart Bargaining 14 (1984).

[16] *Id.*

[17] J. Nierenberg & I. Ross, Women and the Art of Negotiation 69 (1985).

[18] *Id.*

1. Probe to discover the other side's perception of the benefits in order to (a) uncover previously unknown or undervalued aspects, (b) gain insight into the other party's true needs, interests, goals, pressures, and situational constraints, and (c) obtain an understanding of the other side's perception of one's own client and oneself regarding each of those factors

2. Reject firmly with an explanation of the reasons that counsel believes that the offer is unrealistic

3. Make an equally unrealistic counteroffer as protection against an attempt to use the "split the difference" tactic[19]

4. Present a realistic counteroffer, and specify that any suggestion to split the difference will be rejected, because the other party's offer was completely unrealistic[20]

§5.05 Reciprocity

Related to the concept of demanding definite responses to offers and positions is the idea of reciprocity. The reciprocity tactic is to demand a concession in return for a concession. The demand is made on the basis that it is only fair to give a concession after one is received, and that the other negotiator now "owes one." At times, the demand also might be made in terms of a legitimate need for feedback regarding whether the other side is willing to modify its position further, or the other party's belief as to a reasonable range to be discussing. The point of reciprocity is to avoid repeated concessions by the first party without obtaining anything in return.

Reciprocity also occurs in the context of requiring a counteroffer by the other side in response to counsel's making the first settlement demand. Initial offers by the parties are not concessions, but the principle is the same. Counsel wants to avoid bidding against himself or herself by requiring some reciprocal movement by the other negotiator.[21]

This tactic may not work, however, if the demand, offer, or concession does not present a reasonable position that justifies reciprocity.[22] Even if a mistake has been made, and on reevaluation the position is determined to be unreasonable by its proponent, an effort still should be made to obtain reciprocity on the basis that the position was taken in good faith.[23] Additionally in this situation, reciprocity also might be sought on the basis that one needs to know what the other side considers to be reasonable. This is particularly applicable where

---

[19] See R. Givens, Advocacy: The Art of Pleading a Cause 50 Shepard's/McGraw-Hill, Inc 1985 Supp 1986). See also **§5.16.**

[20] R. Givens, *supra* note 19. See also **§5.16.**

[21] Nolan, *Settlement Negotiations,* 11 Litigation 17, 20 (1985); Davis, *Settlement Negotiations: Strategy and Tactics,* 21 Trial 82, 83 (1985); Erisman, *Settlement Do's and Don'ts,* 24 Trial 112 (1988).

[22] Nolan, *supra* note 21; Davis, *supra* note 21.

[23] Davis, *supra* note 21.

an initial counteroffer is sought in response to a first demand. With three exceptions, this tactic can be used for all client goals and with all strategies. The exceptions are those aggressive client goals inconsistent with concessions, and the strategies of no concessions and no further concessions.

Regardless of whether an attorney is using this tactic or it is being used by the other negotiator, an attorney must realize that negotiators often feel compelled to respond to an offer with a counteroffer, and to respond to receiving a concession with an increased willingness to give a concession. Although this frequently is reasonable, there also is a norm of reciprocity which sometimes operates blindly. Negotiators can feel that the customary and normal way of proceeding is to make automatic counteroffers and reciprocal concessions.

That inclination must be resisted. There is no rule or requirement that negotiators behave that way. Rather, counteroffers should be extended only if it is consistent with one's strategy and tactically appropriate to do so. Similarly, counsel need not and must not automatically make a concession just because one is received.

Although this point may appear obvious when it is focused on, lawyers continue to engage in such counterproductive behavior, apparently without even realizing in many instances that they are doing so. The countermeasure is awareness and the use of judgment in consciously deciding whether to reciprocate.

§5.06   Win/Win Proposals

The problem solving strategy consisted of working with the other party to discover mutually beneficial approaches and concessions that eliminated the other party's objections to an offer.[24] This was achieved either through mutual gain by expanding the pie or by concessions at little or no cost to one party but valued by the other. Similar types of mutually beneficial proposals also can result from the creative analysis of the parties by one negotiator, with or without input by the client. Offering win/win proposals is a tactic which consists of generating mutually beneficial resolutions without input from the other party or its negotiator.

Of course, win/win possibilities do not exist every time. The potential for discovering win/win situations depends on being able to capitalize on differences between the parties' beliefs, values, projections, trade-offs, discount rates (a special case of intertemporal trade-offs), and risk preferences.[25]

This tactic can be employed to further any client goals and to advance any strategy with two exceptions. The exceptions are negotiating for purposes other than agreement strategy, and certain aggressive client goals where a win/win proposal would be inconsistent with weakening or destroying the targeted person or entity.

Win/win proposals can take a vast array of forms. They are limited only by client goals, situational constraints, willingness, and creativity.

---

[24] See §3.08 on the problem solving strategy and §8.09 on planning win/win proposals.
[25] H. Raiffa, The Art and Science of Negotiation 286 (1982).

Example 5-3

An agreement is reached to handle billing so as to reduce costs and to split the cost savings.

Example 5-4

A transaction is structured in order to increase the tax benefits for one party while proportionately reducing the cash cost to the other party sufficiently so that both benefit.

Example 5-5

In the sale of a business, uncertainty about liabilities has created a dilemma for a potential purchaser which has resulted in a need to offer a lower price to obtain the buyer's agreement. As an approach for creating a win/win outcome, the seller's attorney considers altering the proposed deal so as to sell the assets, rather than the corporate stock or other forms of ownership, of the present business. An asset sale will avoid the uncertainty regarding the business's liabilities for the buyer, while leaving the seller with the liabilities which it would have had to face anyway. Fortunately, the asset sale did not involve nonassignable contracts as a key item for the purchaser. If it had, the purchaser would have had to purchase the entity itself to capture those contractual rights.

Example 5-6

Another method for structuring the sale of a business is to set a flexible price based on future operations.[26] This technique creates a win/win proposal by making payment to the seller fluctuate, depending on the revenue generated by the buyer after it assumes control. Usually, the price is a percentage of revenue for a set period of time. Although supposedly a win/win solution, the seller can lose dramatically if:

1. The buyer is inept
2. After the sale, outside forces in the market undercut the business's ability to generate revenue
3. The buyer is dishonest and engages in skimming, maintains false books and records, etc.
4. The percentage is of net revenue, and the buyer manipulates salaries and costs to lower the net revenue

Possible safeguards include some guaranteed payment, monitoring procedures, and the use of gross, rather than of net, revenue as the measuring standard. Even so, the attorney must counsel the seller thoroughly concerning the risks of being, in effect, a limited partner with the buyer, bal-

---

[26] Marcus, *Representing the Purchaser of a Small Business,* in Attorney's Guide to Negotiation 5-13 (1979).

anced against the possibility of receiving more money from the percentage than could be obtained with a fixed price.

In Example 5-6, a future contingency was utilized. This generally should be used as a basis for resolution only if:

1. It is clearly defined, so that the parties cannot disagree on whether the contingency occurred

2. Information will be readily available to determine whether the contingency has occurred

Example 5-7

The parties were interested in entering into an agreement for the licensing of technology. The potential licensee disliked the customary terms of a minimum royalty for the item, or of any royalty. Taking this into account, an appealing offer was prepared that omitted those terms. Instead, payment was based on a simple formula using a shared cost savings with an inflation index that in fact led to a higher total income than the normal royalty fee.[27] This was a win/win proposal, because it removed all risks from the licensee, since payment was required only if the licensee achieved a cost savings from the use of the technology.

Win/win proposals are especially useful with cooperative client goals, the problem solving strategy, and the HRESSC strategy. Even when the HRESSC strategy is employed in what appears to be a competitive negotiation, win/win proposals can be tactically employed to obtain an acceptable agreement.[28] A common example of this is structuring a settlement in a personal injury case. Although the case involves a basically competitive negotiation, structuring a settlement may create a win/win situation in the right circumstances.[29] Class actions also can be, at times, particularly appropriate for this tactic by providing the class members with free or discounted goods or services from the defendant instead of or in addition to a monetary settlement. In this way, the value of the settlement to the class can be greater than the cost of the settlement to the defendant.[30]

---

[27] M. Zimmerman, How to Do Business with the Japanese 115 (1985).

[28] *See* **Example 3-30.**

[29] See **§7.03** regarding structured settlements.

[30] Kempf, Jr. & Taylor, *Settling Class Actions,* 13 Litigation 26, 27 (1986). Examples of this type of settlement in class actions include: Phemister v Harcourt Brace Jovanovich, Inc, No 77-C-39 (ND Ill 1984) (BAR/BRI courses and books); *In re* Cuisinart Litig, 1983-2 Trade Cas (CCH) ¶65,860 (D Conn 1978) (kitchenware products); and Zipkin v Genesco, Inc, [1980] Fed Sec L Rep (CCH) ¶97,594 (SDNY 1980) (securities).

Example 5-8

A party is unwilling or unable to pay monetary damages as such. Instead, the same benefit to the plaintiff was obtained through a new long-term contract, certain credits, and a compromise of a prior debt.[31]

In criminal cases, alternative dispositions provide win/win opportunities. Within the criminal court system itself, the use of court supervision, either by that term or its local equivalent, can satisfy the prosecution by providing a finding of guilty plus possible costs and fines. The defendant avoids incarceration and any record of a conviction, has the case dismissed after a period of good behavior, and often can expunge the record of the arrest. Other potential win/win alternatives may include restitution, community service, entering into the armed forces (if a less serious crime was involved), and informally agreeing to rely on polygraph test results.[32] The latter two may not be available, either because of the criminal record or other aspects of the particular defendant, or the controversy about the degree of reliability for polygraph test results.

This topic is discussed further in **§8.09** concerning planning possible win/win outcomes.

§5.07   Concessions of Greater Value to One Party

Many concessions are of equal value for both of the parties to the negotiation. A dollar flowing from one party to the other normally has the same value to each of the parties. Other concessions with objectively defined monetary values usually also have the same value to both parties, unless they are of different value to a party for idiosyncratic reasons.

Other concessions can have vastly different values for each party. Even the same number of absolute dollars can have different subjective, psychologically real values for each party depending on each party's economic status and cash flow requirements, and the emotional impact of either having to pay or being the recipient of the funds.

Example 5-9

A plaintiff in a personal injury case is and always has been poor. In addition, he has serious medical problems that cause him to have a relatively short life expectancy. Moreover, his medical condition renders him unable to work. Thus, his only opportunity to ever have a substantial amount of money is through a settlement or a verdict in his case. Liability in the case is questionable, but the injuries are so severe that a fair and reasonable settlement would be $250,000.00. Nevertheless, defense counsel assesses the plaintiff's situation and offers $100,000.00. Although

---

[31] R. Givens, Advocacy: The Art of Pleading a Cause 48 (Shepard's/McGraw-Hill, Inc 1985 Supp 1986).

[32] Penn, Jr., *Negotiation in a Criminal Case-Defense,* in Attorney's Guide to Negotiation 13-12 (1979).

his attorney accurately advises the plaintiff that the case is worth $250,000.00, the plaintiff accepts the offer. He accepts it because the $100,000.00 is worth far more to him than it would be to most people, and he is averse to risk when it comes to possibly not recovering anything at trial.

Example 5-10

In a commercial litigation case between two businesses, the defendant knows that the plaintiff is having serious cash flow problems. Accordingly, the defendant makes an offer that is substantially less than the case is worth, but which also is sufficient to solve the plaintiff's cash flow crisis. The plaintiff makes a business decision that the short-term benefits of accepting the offer outweigh the long-term detriments of settling for less than the case is really worth.

Example 5-11

A plaintiff in a tort case is substantially motivated by principle and the desire not to let the defendant "get away with it." The defendant is uninsured. A fair and reasonable settlement would be $25,000.00. The plaintiff accepts an offer of $18,000.00, however, feeling that the amount is sufficiently high so that the defendant did not "get away with it."

It can be advantageous to disguise the value of an item to the client, which is or will be the subject of bargaining. If the other party believes that the item is of a lesser value to one's client than it is in fact, a concession of less value may be demanded as a trade-off for the item. In some instances, however, revealing the value of an item may be necessary in order to obtain it.

An ideal concession is one that involves something that is not essential for the client to retain and that is of far greater value to the other party.[33] It therefore can be used as a direct trade-off, or to extract a concession for something else that is of far greater value to the client for a net gain.

This differs from the win/win tactic and does not expand the pie for mutual gain.[34] Here, the concession does involve some real cost or sacrifice for the client. It leads, however, to a disproportionately favorable benefit and, thus, it is advisable to offer it.

Many entities emphasize short-run financial results and focus heavily on each quarter. If so, counsel who is negotiating with such an entity may be able to trade long-run concessions, of greater value to the client, for short-run concessions that are more valued by the entity.

In a multiple issue negotiation, a variation of this tactic is to purposefully

---

[33] See Oately, *Negotiating Techniques for Lawyers*, 6 Advoc Q 214, 224 (1985). Oately advises trying to have apparent concessions to give to the other party in order to obtain the points that counsel is really seeking.

[34] See §5.06 on win/win tactics.

include demands that one is willing to trade off for other concessions.[35] To be effective, these must be apparently reasonable, bona fide demands.[36] In reality, however, they are included merely, or at least primarily, as concessions that the other side will perceive as being valuable and which can be traded for a "reciprocal" concession.

Another variation is to use a number of small concessions to demand reciprocity for a concession which the client values more than all of the smaller concessions combined. As long as the aggregate value of the smaller concessions that are given to the other party arguably equals or exceeds the value of the single, large concession now being demanded, the demand should be presented in those terms.

Example 5-12

"I agreed to your demands on delivery, guarantees, and discounts. All I'm asking in return is for the terms for servicing. That's certainly less than what I've given you."

The tactic of using a concession or concessions of far greater value to the other party can be used with most client goals and strategies. There are, however, four exceptions to their use. These exceptions involve the no or no further concessions strategies, the strategy of negotiating for purposes other than agreement, and certain aggressive client goals. To review, this tactic is not applicable to the no or no further concessions strategies, because those strategies do not permit offering any concessions.[37] This tactic also is irrelevant to or inconsistent with the strategy of negotiating for purposes other than agreement, for a party then is merely using the negotiation as a pretext for a different objective.[38] Finally, in some aggressive client goals, the other party in the negotiation is the target of the aggression, rather than the target being some third party.[39] In those instances, an offer of a concession that is of greater value to the other party almost always is inconsistent with the objective of weakening or of destroying the other party. This tactic, however, is not always inconsistent with such aggressive goals. Whether the two are inconsistent depends on the particular situation.

Example 5-13

The aggressive goal is to acquire a competitor. Offering a concession of greater value to the competitor in order to acquire it is consistent with that aggressive goal.

---

[35] Note, *An Analysis of Settlement,* 22 Stan L Rev 67, in G. Bellow & B. Moulton, The Lawyering Process 527-28 (1978).

[36] Id.

[37] *See* §§3.03 & 3.04.

[38] *See* §§3.10, 3.11, 3.12, 3.13, & 3.14.

[39] See §2.02 regarding aggressive client goals.

§5.08   Trial Proposals

Trial proposals are offers that are made as a sudden shift to a new type of arrangement or to significantly different terms than were previously indicated, discussed, or proposed. This sudden shift is distinguished by the fact that it is not part of a logical sequence in a series of offers. Trial proposals are made with great uncertainty as to whether there will be acceptance or rejection by the other party. The purpose is to attempt something different, and then to gauge the reaction of the other negotiator and of the other party. Even if it is rejected, a trial proposal still may elicit a reaction that provides important information about the other party's vital interests and about its real positions.

Trial proposals are useful for suddenly shifting the focus of the negotiation, especially when the parties have been unable to progress from their respective fixed positions. They can be used with any client goal or strategy except those of the no or no further concessions strategies. They are, however, less likely to be applicable where the only issue is the amount of money to be paid. When combined with the win/win tactic, trial proposals are especially effective.[40]

To the extent that a trial proposal involves a large concession, it should be offered only after a cautious evaluation. When large concessions are made suddenly, there is a danger that the concession will be larger than necessary to achieve the agreement. In addition, a sudden large concession may create the impression that further large concessions will be forthcoming if the other party just rejects the offer or makes additional demands. Therefore, it is essential that trial proposals involving large concessions be phrased especially firmly, with persuasive reasons given for the position that is being taken. This minimizes the possibility that the trial proposal will be perceived as a sign of weakness, or as a willingness to make further large concessions.

Trial proposals are commonly referred to with certain slang expressions such as: "We should float a trial balloon;" or, "Let's run it up the flagpole and see who salutes." Despite these colloquialisms, the trial proposal or "trial balloon" tactic should be taken seriously. Its effectiveness should not be underestimated when used in the manner explained above.

§5.09   Bargaining

Bargaining consists of an offer to exchange one specific item for another. It may be a certain amount of money for merchandise, property, or a release. It could be increasing the price in order to obtain agreement by the seller for more liberal payment terms. Such a price increase can include the imposition of interest on later payments, thereby increasing the real price. In professional sports, the bargaining could consist of offering a tackle and a draft choice for a speedy and strong split end. The essence of bargaining is: "I will give you X for Y."

---

[40] See §5.06 regarding the win/win tactic as well as §3.08 on the problem solving strategy and §8.09 on planning possible win/win outcomes.

Usually, bargaining becomes a series of offers and counteroffers. To avoid the appearance of unbridled "horse trading" or just throwing numbers back and forth, it is especially important to state reasons for one's position.[41]

People often appreciate items more that are perceived as having been earned, or won, rather than merely given away. In the context of some negotiations, the value of a particular concession will be clear. At other times, the value of a concession will be unclear. Counsel must be careful not to give the impression that a concession has little value by not requiring the other party to bargain or otherwise work to obtain it. An exception exists in some cooperative negotiations when the concession carries a goodwill utility beyond its own intrinsic worth.

The importance of one's own and of the other party's bottom line or settlement point already has been discussed.[42] It also may be helpful in bargaining to set a point somewhat above the bottom line for use as a check point at which one should reevaluate the negotiation before agreeing to any further concessions.[43] This may help to avoid having to retreat to the previously planned bottom line, or it may provide an opportunity to decide that additional information acquired during the negotiation requires that a previous plan be adjusted.[44]

Bargaining is extremely useful for competitive goals, and is useful for other client goals, as well as any strategy that includes the use of concessions. If used for the strategy of purposes other than agreement, counsel must offer either:

1. Unacceptable, but perhaps interesting, proposals
2. Proposals leading to partial agreement to encourage continued negotiation, but without creating a complete and final agreement

Many of the written materials on negotiation underemphasize bargaining. They concentrate on the cooperative and the problem solving areas which are more in vogue, or creative approaches that are used less often. Yet, bargaining remains one of the most used and useful tactics. It also can be innovative when combined with the win/win tactic.[45]

§5.10 Debate

Debate is an exchange of views on one or more offers, positions, or reasons designed to persuade the other party or its negotiator to agree or acquiesce. The agreement or acquiescence is to either:

1. Accept a proposal, position, or reason

---

[41] See §5.10 on discussions.

[42] See §§8.08 & 9.03.

[43] R. Fisher & W. Ury, Getting to Yes: Negotiating Agreement Without Giving In 106 (1981). Fisher and Ury refer to this as formulating "a trip wire." Id.

[44] Id.

[45] See §5.06.

2.   Withdraw or desist from advocating an offer, position, or reason

Persuasion to withdraw or desist can be created by a debate which influences the other side's view of values, facts, law, principles, needs, or interests. It also can be generated by a debate which demonstrates the futility of continuing along a particular line or approach.

Because debate involves an exchange of the views that each side is advocating, it differs from informational tactics, in which one negotiator gives or seeks to obtain certain information. However, it often is combined with informational tactics, such as selective information disclosure[46] or the funnel approach.[47]

Debate can be used for all client goals and strategies. A reasonable debate can be an especially effective tactic for persuading parties that a proposed term or a complete agreement is fair or otherwise worthy of acceptance. Persuasion of fairness is most important with a cooperative client goal or with the problem solving strategy. In those situations, it often is combined with an exploration of the needs of the parties using informational tactics.

In addition, debate may be coupled with other tactics. For instance, it can be important as a part of bargaining in terms of explaining and defending reasons for the positions that are being taken.[48]

Example 5-14

> In a civil rights case, there are multiple counts and multiple plaintiffs, some of whom are plaintiffs in just one count, and some of whom are plaintiffs in several counts. The defense offers to pay $2,000.00 to each plaintiff in Counts I through V and $10,000.00 to each plaintiff in Counts VI and VII, but it wants Count VIII dropped, because the liability is far less clear, and the political sensitivity is much greater. The lawyers vigorously debate the merits of Count VIII, citing cases and arguing the witnesses' testimony. Plaintiffs' counsel states that:
>
> P: You know, I understand your feelings about Count VIII, but I have two problems with your just wanting that dropped as part of an overall settlement. First, even though we both know that I have problems with my witnesses, it's worth something in settlement value. Leaving that aside for the moment, though, there are two plaintiffs in that count, Smith and Johnson. Now Smith is involved in some of the other counts, so that he decides whether to trade off Count VIII in return for settling the other counts. Johnson, though, is involved only in Count VIII. Now you can't expect him to drop that for nothing. In fact, you're putting me in an impossible situation. I can't tell Johnson to take nothing so that everyone else, including me, can get paid. There's no way that I can or should suggest that to him. He has a legitimate claim. If I did,

---

[46] *See* §4.02.

[47] *See* §4.05.

[48] See §5.09 on bargaining.

he should fire me and file a complaint against me to the Commission on Attorney Registration and Discipline. You don't want to put me in that position, do you?

D: No, let me take this back to my supervisor.

P: OK, and when you do, just consider this from my perspective. See if there's a way to offer a reasonable amount to Johnson on some agreed amended version of the complaint that alleviates your problems. Or settle the rest and we'll try Count VIII.

Because the debate tactic functions to influence the other party to move in a specific way, it is not sufficient to merely engage in directionless argument. An essential element is to explicitly or implicitly place the desired answer or direction of movement clearly in the mind of the other side. Equally essential, the other side then must be persuaded to accept it.

Persuasion means convincing the other party or its negotiator to move in the desired direction. It is accomplished by altering the other's view or perceptions on:

1.   The merits of the subject
2.   The usefulness of a position for the purpose of the negotiation

Example 5-15

In the debate phase of a negotiation, a lawyer seeks to demonstrate that the market value of an item is different from what the other party actually believes, or claims to believe it to be. The attorney will attempt to convince the other party that his or her position on value is correct, without pressing for an explicit acknowledgment from the other side to allow for face-saving.[49] Because the other side may not be convinced of the "facts" being argued, the lawyer also will seek to convince it that its asserted market value will not be accepted by the lawyer's client. This would have a beneficial effect as well, by forcing the other party to accept that its concept of the market value will not be the basis for an agreement.

If possible, the persuasive argument should be aimed at showing how counsel's position will meet the underlying requirements, wants, and goals of the other party.[50] As one writer has observed: "If you want to persuade people, show the immediate relevance and value of what you're saying in terms of meeting *their needs and desires.*"[51] (Emphasis in original.)

If an offer is met by skepticism or an objection, the attorney should:[52]

---

[49] *See* **§5.19.**

[50] *See* H. Cohen, You Can Negotiate Anything 85-87 (1982).

[51] *Id* 87.

[52] *See* XEROX, Professional Selling Skills 2 (1976).

1. If needed for clarity and to avoid any misunderstanding, restate it in the form of a question

2. Respond directly to the perceived problem, with proof if possible

3. When appropriate, restate and stress the overall benefits of the proposal while minimizing any drawbacks

Indifference to an offer may require probing to discover or to clarify a party's needs.[53] The funnel approach can be very helpful in this process, allowing counsel to elicit areas of general need and then to focus in on the details of the need(s).[54]

Productive debate requires concentrating on specific substantive or procedural items to cause a modification or reversal of the other side's views. It is not productive to engage in personal attacks or personality conflicts with charges of bad faith or of attitude problems,[55] with three exceptions. These exceptions are:

1. To the extent that doing so is useful as part of focusing on the process[56]

2. In explaining the basis for a demand or for a rejection of an offer where the basis cannot or should not be presented less antagonistically

3. As part of a persuasive argument on the strength of one's own case in litigation, or potential litigation

Persuasive argument for the debate tactic includes:

1. Weaving legal and factual themes into "a coherent and credible whole"[57]

2. Presenting strengths, facing or diminishing weaknesses, and forcing the other side to argue its weaknesses[58]

One of the most powerful argumentative techniques is to take a point considered to be a weakness by the other side and to reasonably present it as a strength. A willingness to discuss the point, combined with a reasonable argument that it is not a weakness, can discourage the other negotiator who thought that a persuasive flaw had been discovered. This technique is a popular one with politicians and has been described as the "central principle of political jujitsu: the very openness with which one faces and discusses a weakness acts as powerful evidence that there is in fact no weakness at all."[59]

---

[53] *Id.*

[54] *See* §4.05.

[55] R. Givens, Advocacy: The Art of Pleading a Cause 474-75 (Shepard's/McGraw-Hill, Inc 1985).

[56] See §5.21 regarding focusing on the process.

[57] J. McElhaney, Trial Notebook: A Practical Primer on Trial Advocacy 4 (1981).

[58] T. Mauet, Fundamentals of Trial Techniques 300-01 (1980).

[59] J. Greenfield, Playing To Win: An Insider's Guide to Politics 257 (1980).

Regardless of whether the discussion will be in the style of an informal debate or an issue-oriented argument, planning to determine the issues will enhance the effectiveness of the attorney's presentation and responses. How issues are defined can be determinative.[60] The issues must be implicitly or explicitly agreed on for the process to progress.[61] Nevertheless, the issues should be defined as favorably as possible. The best definitions of issues tend to lead to positions with unassailable premises.[62]

In giving reasons for a bargaining or other position being taken, it may well be useful to rely on objective criteria as the basis of the reasons.[63] With governmental officials, the appeal often should be based on justice and specific principles that they are supposed to be seeking to attain as part of their official duties.

In criminal cases, the objective criteria for defense counsel's appeal to the prosecution includes any particular mitigating circumstances as well as equal treatment for similarly situated defendants. The latter factors mainly consist of the seriousness of the crime, age, criminal record, and restitution to the victim.[64] At the same time, defense counsel must avoid deprecating the seriousness of the crime or the criminal justice system's deterrent effect on potential offenders, since those also are criteria for the prosecution to follow.[65] The presentation, both explicitly and implicitly, should demonstrate that a balancing of the factors favors the defendant's negotiating position. This approach can be combined with arguments based on any weaknesses in the prosecution's case. It also can be combined with any self-interest that the prosecutor may have, such as saving time and easing an overcrowded docket. Naturally, the same basic approach with different factors can be used in civil cases as well.

Objective criteria may be drawn from any number of sources, including:

Precedent and common practice[66]

Morality, decency, and the public interest[67]

Verdicts or settlements that have been reported in similar cases[68]

Knowledge generally recognized by those in the field

---

[60] *Id* 25.

[61] *Id* 28.

[62] *Id* 17.

[63] As noted earlier in **ch 3,** the use of objective criteria is one of the cornerstones of Fisher and Ury's "principled negotiation" approach.

[64] Roberts, *Negotiation in a Criminal Case-Prosecution,* in Attorney's Guide to Negotiation 12-13 (1979).

[65] *Id* 12-14.

[66] R. Fisher & W. Ury, Getting to Yes: Negotiating Agreement Without Giving In 86 (1981) [hereinafter Fisher]; H. Cohen, *supra* note 50, at 80.

[67] H. Cohen, *supra* note 50, at 79.

[68] Oatley, *Negotiating Techniques for Lawyers,* 6 Advoc Q 214, 220 (1985).

Example 5-16

An insurance adjuster (A) and plaintiff's counsel (P) are discussing an automobile accident in which the insured rear-ended the client. Immediately afterwards, the client complained of neck and back pain, and sought medical care. She was diagnosed and treated as having neck and back strain, i.e., whiplash.

A: We seriously question whether your client was really hurt. The x-rays were negative, there are no objective findings by the doctor, and there was basically no damage to her car.

P: Let's be serious. You know, or you ought to know, that soft tissue injuries do not show up on x-rays, and that neither a lack of other findings by the doctor or a lack of property damage means that you can't have whiplash. In fact, she was driving a jeep wagon, so it wasn't damaged, but that didn't stop her from being whipped back and forth by the impact. As to the doctor, he diagnosed and treated her for neck and back strain, and that would be his testimony. And in fact, that is consistent with the medical literature, even without other findings. So, how are you going to be better off by forcing me to file suit and go to trial assuming we can reasonably resolve this now?

On the other hand, a negotiator must not overrely on or be unduly influenced by factors that might be considered to be objective criteria. If the other negotiator is citing an agreement negotiated by someone else, even in a similar matter, one may decide that the agreement was not negotiated satisfactorily and simply choose to reject its use as precedent. Also, with respect to reported verdicts and settlements, one must take great care that the cases are truly similar. This is particularly important where even the same type of injury may have drastically different consequences for different people. It is always essential to consider every case on an individualized basis. While reported verdicts and settlements can be a useful guide, they never can be as significant as the facts of the particular case that is being negotiated.

Debate through various forms of a persuasive argument aimed at the negotiator sometimes can cause a change in the other party's position when all else fails. At times, it is essential for the argument to appeal to the other negotiator's personal interests in order to create the necessary motivation for the other side to modify or reverse its position.[69] Appeals to reason or principle can be countered by challenges to their validity or applicability.[70]

There are times when difficulty in reaching an agreement, or the best agreement, may be due to differences in how the issues are perceived by the parties and/or the negotiators. This can result from the differing emotions of the parties and/or negotiators. In such instances, discussing the perceptions or the

---

[69] See §5.29 on appeals to the personal interests of the negotiator or the decision maker.

[70] W. Rusher, How to Win Arguments 66, 77 (1981).

emotions may help lead to a resolution of the differences.[71] One clue that emotional forces are the motivating factor can be a debate that degenerates into counterproductive argument with each side speaking mainly to hear itself and listening only to formulate its next clever or cutting response. A common reason to argue is to release aggressive tension.[72] Countermeasures to a genuinely angry, argumentative presentation include:

1.   Changing the tone[73]
2.   Focusing on the process while acknowledging the legitimacy of the feelings[74]
3.   Responding in kind, if that will shock or intimidate the other side into refraining from angry argument, rather than intensifying the anger

If a highly charged, argumentative form of debate is being attempted as a ploy to intimidate, then the third countermeasure, or calmly ignoring the tone, are appropriate. Regardless of the verbal or nonverbal communication selected in response to an angry argument, it is crucial that the lawyer remain poised and inwardly calm in order to think clearly.[75]

Key countermeasures in a negotiators' debate include:

1.   Contrary facts
2.   Citing precedents or laws, or attacking their interpretation or relevance
3.   Revealing purported facts to be mere assumptions[76]
4.   Acknowledging a mistake in an argument, but promptly replacing it with a new point[77]
5.   Using or distinguishing analogies[78]
6.   Permitting the other side to abandon positions tacitly, and thereby avoid or lessen a loss of face

§5.11   Conditional Proposals

Conditional proposals are offers which are contingent on either resolving all of the remaining issues in the negotiation, or on resolving certain specified remaining issues. This differs from bargaining in that the tactic involves an offer of X for Y, but the offer is conditioned on subsequently reaching agreement on one or more other issues.

---

[71] Fisher, *supra* note 66, at 26 & 31.

[72] *Id* 8.

[73] *See* §5.14.

[74] *See* §5.21.

[75] W. Rusher, *supra* note 70, at 15.

[76] *Id* 72.

[77] *Id* 132.

[78] *Id* 103.

Example 5-17

"I'm willing to meet your price on the initial shipments if we resolve the volume discount on the subsequent orders."

Example 5-18

"We will agree to consider your office's investigators to be exempt from restrictions on political hiring and firing if we settle the remaining three categories of employees without creating too large a number of total exempt employees. However, if we cannot decide those three categories within the aggregate numerical constraint that I have outlined, we will have to reexamine the investigator category."

The use of conditional proposals is appropriate for client goals and strategies that involve the following circumstances:

1. Multiple issues
2. A relationship between all or some of the issues so that trade-offs between issues are possible
3. A concern that the other party may make high demands on issues being negotiated later in the process, so that there may be a legitimate need to later reexamine earlier issues and the issue-by-issue subagreements in view of the emerging totality of the proposed overall agreement

Example 5-19

A hospital wants a doctor who is finishing her residency in cardiology to relocate to a different state and maintain her practice in the hospital's area. There are numerous issues involved in the potential agreement. With respect to the benefits to the doctor, these issues include:

1. The amount which the hospital will pay the doctor
2. The time over which that amount will be paid
3. The nature and extent of various fringe benefits that the hospital will provide, including such benefits as professional liability insurance, life insurance, disability insurance, and moving expenses
4. The length of time for which these benefits will be provided
5. Whether free office space will be provided, and if so, how much and for how long
6. Whether loans will be given to provide the doctor with working capital, and if so, how much and on what terms

As to the doctor's obligations under the potential contract, the issues include:

1. The length of time that the doctor is obligated to maintain her practice in the hospital's area

2. The definition of the boundaries of that area

3. The circumstances under which the doctor would not be obligated to maintain her practice

4. The extent, if any, to which secondary offices could be opened outside of the hospital's area

5. The amount of the hospital's damages and of the physician's obligations should she breach the contract

6. The definition of maintaining the physician's practice, including such considerations as vacations, time spent on continuing medical education, and maternity leave

The hospital presents a relatively comprehensive proposal which appears to be a reasonable first offer. The situation is conducive to the doctor's attorney employing conditional proposals because the three criteria described above are present. Part of the hospital's offer would obligate the physician for a period of four years. In structuring a counteroffer, the doctor's lawyer, among other things, seeks higher amounts of compensation and loans. In presenting the counteroffer, counsel for the physician informs the hospital's negotiator that the inclusion of the four-year time period in the counteroffer is conditional upon the acceptance of the rest of the counteroffer.

§5.12 Power

In international negotiations, the tactic of power can be exercised through such means as the granting or withholding of economic assistance, trade sanctions, and the threat or use of various levels of military force and violence.[79] To the extent that one party truly has power over the other to force an agreement on its terms, the use of power will be effective on the immediate issues. To the extent that long-term relationships or issues are important considerations, however, power must be exercised with a view towards its long-term effects, both those effects that are intended and those that are unintended.

The party with less power often resents the use of power to force it to acquiesce. That resentment can lead to overt or covert resistance and attempts to undermine or to sabotage the forced agreement, or to retaliate in other ways. Those potential adverse effects must be weighed against the benefits of exercising power to determine whether or not to employ the tactic. Both long-term and short-term effects must be anticipated.

In addition, the potential ramifications for constituent groups or third parties must be examined in two respects. First, one must decide whether the views of any or all of these entities, individuals, or groups have a sufficiently signifi-

---

[79] For example, in 1987, both India and China sought to bolster their respective negotiating positions by moving sophisticated military equipment and additional troops into a disputed border area. *China, India, Raising Ante In Border Feud*, Chicago Trib, June 28, 1987, §1, at 6, col. 1.

cant impact to be taken into account. Second, if their views are to be taken into account, there must be an evaluation of what views are likely to emerge from an exercise of power in light of historical positions, short-term and long-term vital interests, and any immediate situational pressures or constraints. The questions to be considered include whether the exercise of power will be:

1. Perceived as legitimate or illegitimate
2. Intimidating or cause an immediate counterreaction
3. Viewed as creating a precedent for the future, or as an aberration

To the extent that the exercise of power is tied to a legitimate rationale, and therefore is perceived by the other side as justified but unwelcome, the use of power is less likely to provoke a hostile reaction.[80] A related factor is that such a perception may alleviate the other side's problem of self-esteem, since the need to save face itself could lead to an antagonistic reaction.[81] For the same reasons, if power is being exercised by threatening the other party, it often is better to issue the threat with a nonthreatening style.[82] This assumes, however, that a threatening manner will cause the other party to react to save face, rather than become intimidated. If it will be intimidated by a threatening style, that style should be considered in light of any long-term effects.

The same principles that apply to negotiations in the international arena of nations also apply to negotiations in business, torts, criminal prosecutions, and other areas in which lawyers become involved. The potential benefits from exercising power must be weighed against the likelihood and seriousness of unintended, adverse effects that can arise from anger, jealousy, or resentment by the less powerful, or outsiders who feel slighted or threatened.

Power can take many forms. A party may have effective control in various ways, such as being able to:

1. Offer extremely attractive economic benefits to the other party
2. Cause the other party to incur extremely high costs if litigation is not avoided
3. Cause the other party to suffer high economic losses unless an agreement is reached
4. Create delay in the resolution of a claim for years if the matter has to be litigated
5. Threaten noneconomic sanctions which constitute an unacceptably high risk to the other party

---

[80] D. Druckman, Negotiations: Social-Psychological Perspectives 28 (1977).

[81] *See* Brown, *Face-Saving and Face-Restoration in Negotiation,* in D. Druckman, Negotiations: Social-Psychological Perspectives 284 (1977). See also **§5.19** regarding saving face.

[82] G. Bellow & B. Moulton, The Lawyering Process 560 (1978).

Example 5-20

> The client is arrested at home, without a warrant, at night, after a noncon-
> sensual entry by the police in the absence of probable cause or exigent
> circumstances. The arrest is for murder and armed robbery. Following
> the arrest, the client then is held for an undue length of time before being
> brought before a magistrate for a hearing on probable cause and a bond.
> Defense counsel's analysis is that the client's Fourth Amendment rights
> have been violated, and liability against the police for a §1983 civil rights
> claim is clear.[83] On the other hand, although the criminal case against
> the client appears weak, the prosecution now appears to have developed
> sufficient evidence to bring the case to trial, although it seems unlikely
> that conviction can be obtained. The client, while maintaining that he is
> innocent, is nevertheless understandably concerned that there might be
> any chance he could be convicted, particularly in light of the seriousness
> of the charges and his prior criminal record. After several rounds of nego-
> tiations, and with a date set for trial of the criminal case, the prosecution
> offers to dismiss all of the charges in return for a release from the client
> on his civil rights claim. Despite the likelihood that he will be found not
> guilty, and that he would then obtain a substantial verdict or settlement
> on his civil rights claim, the client agrees to the offer. He signs the release,
> and the prosecution dismisses the charges. The possibility of being con-
> victed of murder and armed robbery was too powerful for the client to
> withstand that threat.[84] The prosecution's power came from its threat and
> the potentially drastic, although unlikely, adverse consequences.

There are, however, legal and moral restrictions on the use of power. For
example, threatening to dump toxic waste on someone's property to force them
to sign an agreement would be illegal, immoral, and grounds to void any such
"agreement" on the basis of duress.

Usually though, issues of legality and morality are not the relevant factors,
because the types of power being contemplated are neither illegal nor immoral.
In most instances, the key factor in deciding whether to employ power is effectiveness. The decision to exercise, or to refrain from exercising, power is made
normally on the pragmatic grounds of long-run and short-run efficacy.

Due to the negative reactions that can result from the exercise of power,
it should be chosen as a tactic only after an especially cautious analysis of certain
client goals and strategies. Cooperative goals generally are inappropriate for
the power tactic. At a minimum, it will be perceived as being at least somewhat
inconsistent with being cooperative. Competitive and aggressive goals usually

---

[83] *See* Llaguno v Mingey, 763 F2d 1560 (7th Cir 1985) (en banc). *See also* Payton v New
York, 445 US 573 (1980).

[84] Whether the prosecution's offer was ethical and whether the release is enforceable
are open to question. Depending on the circumstances and the "voluntariness" of the
agreement, a release of a claim for civil rights violations in consideration for dismissing
a criminal prosecution can be constitutional and enforceable. Town of Newton v Rumery, 408 US __, 107 S Ct 1187 (1987).

are ideal for the use of the power tactic, assuming that sufficient power exists, and assuming the absence of conflicting goals. It also can be useful for self-centered and defensive goals, depending on the factors and the analysis outlined earlier in this section.

With regard to strategies, and assuming the requisite degree of power, the power tactic is an ideal tactic for the strategies of no concessions, deadlock-breaking concessions only, and HRESSC, since it eliminates or decreases the need to make concessions. It also may be helpful with the strategies of negotiating for purposes other than reaching an agreement and of moving for closure, again depending on the specific factors in the particular negotiation.

For the problem solving strategy, however, counsel may decide to refrain from or temper the use of power to the extent that its exercise will be perceived as inconsistent with problem solving. The danger is that the power tactic may so undermine the problem solving strategy that the strategy itself will become totally ineffective.

Countermeasures to the use of power include creating realistic, adverse potential effects on the party using or contemplating the use of power. These effects may be either short-term or long-term. The potential gain from the use of power must be outweighed by the potential loss in a cost-benefit risk analysis. This can be done directly by the targeted party itself or through allies.[85] In order to constitute an effective countermeasure, the threatened countereffect must be known or communicated to the party employing or considering the use of power.

§5.13   Bluff

Bluff simply refers to taking a position as if that position were absolutely fixed without the possibility of further modification, when that is not really true. Instead, counsel is prepared to back down if strongly challenged. Such a position may take two forms. The first is a purportedly non-negotiable offer or counteroffer. The second type of bluff is threatening to cause an adverse consequence for the other party if it refuses to agree to certain terms, when the lawyer knows that the client cannot or will not do so.

The obvious dilemma in bluffing is that, once caught bluffing, counsel's credibility becomes either very low or nonexistent. A common consequence is that the other negotiator is forced or encouraged to push hard on all of the remaining issues, in order to determine whether other bluffs are being attempted.

Being caught bluffing will affect not only that negotiation, but also all future negotiations with that party or with that negotiator. It also is likely to affect other negotiations with other negotiators and parties, since one's reputation tends to become known. This even occurs in large legal communities, because lawyers tend to operate within certain segments of the general legal community, based on their areas of practice and prominence.

Do attorneys ever try to bluff? They certainly do. What can go wrong? Consider the following example from an actual negotiation:

---

[85] *See* §6.05.

Example 5-21

The negotiation was to buy out the interest of one partner in a very successful business. On Monday, the parties' attorneys negotiated and reached agreement on the price and the other basic terms. By late Tuesday morning, the buyers' lawyer had prepared a draft agreement and transmitted it to the seller's attorney for a scheduled 2:00 p.m. closing. Each lawyer remained in his office. The negotiation of various terms continued through a series of telephone conferences and exchanges of draft agreements. By 6:30 that evening, counsel were still negotiating the drafting of the terms. Seller had agreed that the mutual releases would not bar the buyers' potential indemnification claim against the seller if customers sued because of certain specified actions of the seller. However, the seller's attorney suddenly inserted a paragraph which, in the event of such a third-party suit by a customer, would require the buyers to assert that the seller had acted properly in the buyers' defense of the action. The buyers previously had adamantly refused to agree to such a term, and it negated the indemnification exclusion negotiated earlier that day. The buyers' attorney (B) then called the seller's lawyer (S).

> B: Paragraph seven has to come out. You know that my clients cannot and will not take that position with their customers.
>
> S: Tell them that I assure them that it will not hurt them to do it.
>
> B: They're really not interested in assurances. They will not do this and cannot be expected to do something so detrimental to their long-run relationships with their customers.
>
> S: It can't come out.
>
> B: Are you saying that it's non-negotiable? You stuck it in after we've agreed to the contrary and now it's non-negotiable? Is that your position at this hour?
>
> S: Yes. You tell them that they are fools if they blow the deal over this.
>
> B: I'm not going to debate with you over who is behaving like a fool. But, if this was your plan, you've wasted everyone's time. If this is non-negotiable, that's it. I'm going home. I'm telling my clients to tear up the certified check which has been sitting here most of the day and I'm going home. Goodbye.
>
> S: Wait. The seller, Byron, is standing right here. Let me put him on. Byron, talk to Mark about that paragraph seven.
>
> BYRON: What about paragraph seven?
>
> B: Byron, your lawyer tells me it's non-negotiable. You know that they can't agree to this. If this was non-negotiable, you've wasted two days of your time and money and their time and money.
>
> BYRON: OK. Take it out. Now we have a deal.

In this process, the seller's attorney grossly miscalculated his position. He lost all of his credibility by his unsuccessful bluff. In addition, by placing his client into the position of having to personally admit the bluff and back down, he certainly did not enhance his standing with his own client.

One method for extricating oneself from an unsuccessful bluff is to seek "new information." The lawyer, in planning the bluff, should think about what to do if caught, and should consider whether anything can be referred to as "new information" which ostensibly became known after the position was taken. If so, the lawyer can attempt to escape from the dilemma of an unsuccessful bluff by acting as if the change of a previously unalterable position or threat was due to learning some new and totally unanticipated information. Whether this maneuver is feasible will depend on the plausibility of the "new information" cited, the lawyer's own demeanor, as well as the level of skepticism of the other party and its negotiator. Successful execution of the "new information" ploy will prevent a loss of face and credibility from a bluff that is called by the other party.

Countermeasures include calling the bluff by an outright refusal to acquiesce. This may or may not involve creating new facts which directly alter the threatened consequences of the bluff.[86] Additionally, counsel may use selective information disclosure[87] and debate,[88] as well as face-saving,[89] to persuade the other negotiator that the bluff rests on seriously erroneous premises.

§5.14   Tone

The tone of a negotiation is its general mood. It may be:

1. Relaxed or tense
2. Friendly or hostile
3. Trusting or suspicious
4. Cooperative or competitive
5. An atmosphere of an acknowledged, mutual desire to work out an agreement, or a reluctant exploration of the possibilities for an agreement

Tone is an unavoidable, ever-present element in every negotiation. "Every negotiation has a climate. And more than any other single factor, this climate will control the results of the negotiation. If you control the climate, you probably control the proceedings—for better or worse."[90] Although that may overstate the importance of tone, there can be no doubt that tone has a significant impact on many negotiations.

---

[86] See §4.03 regarding creating new facts.
[87] See §4.02.
[88] See §5.10.
[89] See §5.19.
[90] J. Nierenberg & I. Ross, Women and the Art of Negotiation 47 (1985).

The tone can be important in determining whether the negotiation actually will progress to an agreement. Even when the parties' bottom lines overlap, thereby creating a potential zone of agreement, often negotiators must be willing to expend the time necessary to explore each other's positions in order to find that zone of agreement. If the negotiation is unpleasant or unnecessarily difficult, a negotiator may decide that the tone indicates a process that is not likely to result in a satisfactory offer. This then can become a self-fulfilling prophecy.

Unless, in light of long-run and short-run interests, it will be productive to intimidate or overwhelm the other side, the negotiation should not be conducted in such a way so that one side feels that it is being astutely manipulated into an unfavorable deal. This can create a defensive or hostile reaction that makes it more difficult to achieve a good agreement. Lawyers need to be careful about this trap, since the value of clever argument has been ingrained into them from law school, if not before.

Counsel must anticipate and observe the other negotiator's reactions to the tone and feel of the negotiation. Persuasion means convincing the other negotiator to desire a specific course of action. It does not mean getting the other negotiator to concentrate on:

1.   Retaliation
2.   Face-saving ploys
3.   Scoring debating points

An exception exists if, by maneuvering the other negotiator into engaging in one or more of those three acts, counsel can obtain substantive concessions without countervailing long-term or short-term losses or problems.

Tone is especially significant to the extent that some relationship beyond the present negotiation is contemplated. The relationship either can be some type of working relationship under the terms of the contemplated agreement, or future negotiations for contemplated or possible additional transactions. All other factors being somewhat equal, people prefer to deal with those that they like, followed by those that they do not dislike. Those disliked are obviously the least preferred. Negotiators are no different. In deal making, to the extent that a negotiator is liked, that person has established an advantage in the negotiation.

Furthermore, when a working relationship or long-term series of transactions between the parties is an objective in the negotiation, difficulty or unpleasantness during the negotiation may be interpreted as indicating that the party will be difficult or unpleasant in the relationship itself. The tone then becomes a decidedly substantive, negative factor in deciding whether to enter into an agreement at all. Even when an agreement is still possible, a distasteful tone can increase the economic and noneconomic price that has to be paid in order to compensate for the expected irritation, bother, and aggravation.

In most deal-making and transactional matters, the tone of the negotiation generally should be professionally pleasant. Normally, the parties have come together without coercion, and have authorized the negotiation because of an interest in reaching an agreement within each party's self-determined limita-tions. They have not sent their negotiators to do battle, except to the extent that, at times, very tough negotiating stances need to be taken. Even if one party is or desires to appear less interested in making a deal, a disinterested or more distant tone need not be unpleasant.

In litigation, the tone tends to be more adversarial, because the negotiators' alternative to settlement is to continue to do battle through the remainder of the litigation process and trial. This in part reflects the often ambivalent feel-ings of the parties towards negotiating versus fighting. This does not mean, however, that the tone in litigation should be unpleasant, or that it should be so adversarial that it tends to lead to a power struggle between the negotiators in which they lose sight of the real interests, goals, and issues of the negotiation. A trial lawyer must be able to demonstrate the inner confidence and the willing-ness to proceed to trial that makes his or her negotiating position stronger. It is this display of confidence and willingness to proceed to trial, rather than mere tone alone, that is effective in litigation negotiations. Of course, the other side's perception of counsel's trial abilities may also influence its negotiating decisions.

Generally, the attorney should not generate an atmosphere that feels like pressure to his or her counterpart. That does not hold true, however, if pres-sure is likely to be successful because of the needs and constraints of the parties, as well as the negotiators' personalities. Frequently, though, a low-key, but assertive, posture may be best. Being low-key and assertive means: "[A]void the hard sell . . . coax the (other party) into appreciating one's point of view . . . adopt a self-effacing and humble role while at the same time being quietly forceful whenever necessary or appropriate."[91]

Tone also can be useful in encouraging the other party and its negotiator to be psychologically committed to making a deal. Counsel can adopt a profes-sional level of enthusiasm for making a deal or settlement because of the inevi-table benefits for both parties. This can be effective in motivating the other party and its negotiator to really want to reach an agreement if at all possible.

Regardless of whether the context is deal making or litigation, a more adver-sarial tone is appropriate for several purposes. First, it can counter the aggres-sive tone of the other negotiator or of the other party and demonstrate the ability to resist being intimidated or pressured. Second, when it is very likely to succeed in intimidating or pressuring the other party or its negotiator with-out offsetting negative effects, a more adversarial tone should be used. Third, this type of tone can provide a temporary display of emotion to appropriately underscore and reinforce a particular point, argument, or reaction. Its use may be necessary so that the negotiator's demeanor does not conflict with his or her words, thereby destroying or decreasing his or her persuasive power.

A temporary change of tone, through a controlled display of emotion, can be effective in conveying or in emphasizing the message being articulated by counsel. A constant or a very predictable display of emotion tends to be viewed

---

[91] M. Zimmerman, How to Do Business with the Japanese 97 (1985).

as part of the negotiator's personality or as a mere tactic, and therefore it loses its persuasive force. In contrast, a temporary, controlled, appropriate display of anger, skepticism, amusement, bewilderment, or other emotion can persuade the other party and its attorney of the depth and the sincerity of the statements that counsel is making. It even may be the persuasive factor necessary to convince the other side of the correctness of the statement.

Using an unexpected tone can be an effective means of delivering a message. If loudness is expected, soft intensity may be used to capture the listener's attention, avoid prepared psychological defenses, and, thereby, take the listener off guard. Similarly, loudness can make a point when only moderate tones were expected. The loudness should not be so much that it is offensive, but rather it should be sufficient to make the listener feel the speaker's deep belief.

Even a quite dramatic display can be effective in the right situation with the right negotiators, although generally less dramatic means should be utilized.

Example 5-22

The prosecutor was young, inexperienced, nice, and not a very strong person. He had agreed to a plea bargain under which the defendant would receive probation. The agreement was well within reason for offenses of a similar nature by an offender with neither previous convictions nor arrests for serious offenses. In other words, it was a fair deal for both the government and the defendant. However, the pair of defense attorneys anticipated that there would be a problem. The arresting officer and the victim had strong feelings of racial animosity against the youthful offender. They were likely to attempt to pressure the prosecutor into reneging on the agreement before the case was called in court that afternoon. The two defense attorneys prepared a contingency plan to be used in the event that the prosecutor attempted to renege on their agreement. Both defense attorneys were known to be assertive, but not particularly loud or hostile. The prosecutor entered the courtroom. The court call was not scheduled to begin for 30 minutes. Only the pair of defense attorneys were there. The prosecutor spoke first. "I'm really sorry fellows, but the victim and the cop are furious with me. I just can't go through with our deal. I'm going to have to ask for at least six months of jail time." One of the defense attorneys stood up immediately. Without saying a word, he picked up his file and hurled it across the room, scattering papers all over the floor. Then he turned and faced the prosecutor, with a look of fury and disgust on his face. There was a moment of silence. Then he spoke. The anger in his voice made it shake. "You S.O.B.," he said in a low voice. Then he screamed, "Who in the hell do you think that you are?!" Without looking again at the prosecutor, who appeared to be in shock, he paced furiously around the room in circles, waving his hands and arms and yelling, "How can you do this? You made me spend 45 minutes counseling my client to take this deal. Then you're going to renege on me because some bigoted bastards want you to ruin my client. You do this and I will never deal with you again. I'm going all over this building telling everyone about what you pulled and that they better not deal with you because you don't keep your word. Just go to hell." Then he strode rapidly out of the courtroom, slamming the door and leaving his partner and the prosecutor alone in the room with the scattered papers. The room was absolutely quiet. Coming out of a stunned silence, the prosecutor spoke. "He's really upset with me, isn't he?" The remaining defense attorney, who had not spoken at all, looked at the prosecutor and nodded affirmatively. A determined look came over the prosecutor's face. "He's right," the prosecutor said. "I'm going to keep our bargain. I'll be right back." He left the room to confront the victim and the officer. Almost as soon as the prosecutor returned, the case was called. The plea bargain was kept, and the young offender received probation instead of a term of incarceration.

One method to counter an emotional tone is to indicate understanding, but to focus on the facts.[92] The factual explanation should demonstrate that counsel's position is reasonable and fair.

Example 5-23

"I understand your frustration. But you must not realize the ramifications of what you're asking. First of all. . . ."

Some negotiators' effectiveness is affected by the other negotiator establishing a tone of personal like, respect, or approval. Their guard may drop, or their aggressive pursuit of certain demands may diminish. In dealing with such an individual, counsel should use that fact and behave in a personally friendly, respectful, and approving manner.

A negotiator must have the self-awareness to realize if he or she is vulnerable to such an approach because of a need to be "liked and approved of,"[93] and must avoid being influenced by it if the client will suffer. It does not matter whether the other negotiator's conduct is genuine or manipulative. In neither event should an attorney permit personal gratification to prejudice the client's interests.

In shifting from a competitive goal, win/lose strategy to a cooperative goal, win/win strategy, counsel often must also shift the tone of the negotiation. However, many lawyers confuse the tone of the negotiation with whether the negotiators are being competitive or cooperative. This error can create a significant flaw in their analysis of the negotiation. Just because a negotiator has a cooperative tone of voice does not mean that he or she is being cooperative.

Example 5-24

In a lease negotiation, the lessor's attorney started with an unreasonably low position, but articulated it as if she was engaged in problem solving

---

[92] C. Karrass, Give & Take: The Complete Guide to Negotiating Strategies and Tactics 56 (1974).

[93] *Id* 119.

and being cooperative. The other negotiator sounded mildly adversarial, but really tried to engage in problem solving. His opening position was quite reasonable. As the negotiation continued, the lessor's attorney continued to use a cooperative tone, but initially refused to make any concessions. The more adversarial sounding lessee's attorney made a large initial concession. During the balance of the negotiation, the two engaged in bargaining. The lessor's attorney, with the more cooperative tone, made fewer and smaller concessions, while the lessee's attorney with the adversarial tone made more and larger concessions.

That example occurred at a National Institute for Trial Advocacy Negotiation Program demonstration. The audience's reaction was that the lessor's attorney had been cooperative, while the lessee's lawyer had been competitive. Yet, on further examination and analysis of the behavior of each of them, the audience discovered that the tone of the negotiators had deceived them. A quite different picture emerged when the audience focused on the behavior of the negotiators and their concession patterns.

Mere tone and firm commitment to client goals of cooperation or competition should not be confused.[94] Positions, process, concessions, and all behavior, including tone, must be considered before a decision can be made about whether a negotiator is engaged in competitive or cooperative negotiating. It is essential to do this in order to properly analyze the other party and its negotiator during the negotiation itself. Only in that way can effective adjustments be made based on the true intentions and behavior of the other party and its negotiator, rather than on mere tone and style.

Tone is an integral part of all negotiations. Every negotiator has some tone in every negotiation. It cannot be avoided. The question is whether the negotiator's tone is congruent with the positions being articulated, and thus persuasive. Counsel must set the proper tone and control it with such variations as may be necessary during the course of the negotiation.

§5.15   The Use of Alternative Opportunities

In the background of some negotiations, there are known, specific opportunities with outside parties that are alternatives to the positions being presented by the other party. The opportunity may be a different building, being supplied by a different party, a different business or investment opportunity to become a partner, a shareholder, etc. The alternative opportunity is something that is mutually exclusive with the deal being presented, so that the client can do only one or the other. In these situations, the alternative to reaching an agreement is not to be without any agreement, but rather to be in an agreement with a different party through a separate negotiation.

A negotiator must beware of inadvertently foregoing a potential alternative opportunity while pursuing a negotiation. At times, multiple, simultaneous negotiations are essential to maintain the client's options.

---

[94] See §§2.03 & 2.04.

Example 5-25

A professional practice was for sale. Due to the limited market for the practice, there was a significant danger if any viable, potential purchaser was lost before a sale actually was made. Counsel negotiated simultaneously with several possible buyers until the best available deal was identified, and a written agreement was executed.

In addition, each such alternative opportunity constitutes leverage with the other party to the extent that the alternative opportunity is comparable to the one being presented in the current negotiation.[95] Counsel can use and present the alternative opportunity, since the client cannot be reasonably expected to accept a deal which is inferior to one which is clearly available from a different source.

Furthermore, alternative opportunities provide both a measure of the market value and the market terms for such transactions or settlements. They also create a floor below which no transactional agreement will be considered because a better deal awaits elsewhere. Any uncertainty about the existence of an alternative opportunity must be analyzed based on the potential benefits versus the risk that the opportunity is illusory.

In examining the market, the alternative opportunity need not presently exist, although it certainly is a more powerful bargaining chip if it is currently available. However, past history, which indicates that similar opportunities will be available in the near future, can be used to formulate an alternative opportunity position. Such a position can be persuasively based on a reasonably expected opportunity.

Alternative opportunities can result from legitimate fact creation.[96] Their existence or absence can be an active, rather than a passive, factor. By successfully searching for or having the client explore for genuine alternative opportunities, counsel has created a new operative fact in the negotiation that must be responded to by the other party and its negotiator. They cannot ignore it completely, even if they refuse to match or exceed it.

Employing this tactic necessitates planning and preparation, since counsel must be aware of specific alternative opportunities. It requires knowledge of the market and its prices, customs, values, and practices. The requisite knowledge may already be known to the negotiator, or may come from some other source, including the client.

The alternative opportunity tactic differs from the bluff tactic, since the assertion that an alternative opportunity exists is true. An attorney who strongly suspects that the claimed alternative opportunity is a mere bluff may weigh the risks of being mistaken and call the bluff or demand verification that the purported opportunity exists.

---

[95] *See* H. Cohen, You Can Negotiate Anything 52-58 (1982).
[96] *See* §4.03.

Example 5-26

> "If I am going to be able to get my client to take this seriously, I will need a copy of a written offer from this other source."

Such a direct challenge can be appropriate, although it does create the danger that the other party will be unwilling to relent because of a fear of losing face, even if it wants to retract the bluff.

More often, a less aggressive but firm approach will be more effective in leading to the retraction of a bluff, without requiring any overt or otherwise embarrassing admission that the other party was bluffing. This approach always includes some statement that provides an opportunity for the other side to escape from the bluff without a loss of face.

Example 5-27

> "If you can really get the same thing, especially when quality is taken into account, and get it at that price, then you should do business with them instead. We cannot and will not sell at that price, because there is no margin for a reasonable return. Before you make your final decision, however, you ought to closely evaluate the qualitative factors, because there is no way that they can come close to our quality at that price unless they are just selling below cost one time before they raise the price on you. From what I know, I don't think that you will find the quality is the same. In fact, you're going to find that all you've bought are new headaches. But, obviously, it's your decision."

This firm, face-saving approach ignores that portion of the bluff which asserts that the position was fixed and final. Instead, the approach affords a method for further reconsideration and modification of the position.

In Example 5-27, quality was used for that purpose. Each negotiation will be different. The constant principle is to refuse to act as though the position (i.e., bluff) of the other negotiator was stated as fixed and final, and to present a face-saving opportunity for the other negotiator to move away from that position and to proceed with the negotiation.

Due to the possibility of a bluff, the alternative opportunity tactic often leads into initiation of debate, funnel approach, or informational bargaining tactics.[97] Furthermore, apart from the question of a bluff, the negotiators may discuss or argue about whether the other opportunity is truly comparable in two respects. First, counsel may inquire to try to determine whether the alternative opportunity is certain, tentative, or illusory.

Example 5-28

> A medical practice was for sale. The attorney for one potential purchaser probed during the negotiation to ascertain whether any legitimate, seri-

---

[97] See §§5.10, 4.05, 4.07 & 4.08.

ous rivals existed with means to make a comparable, or superior offer to the offer that was being planned.

Second, differences in the opportunities are identified and explored to evaluate whether the opportunities are really comparable, or whether one is distinctly advantageous. Quantitative or objective differences can be disposed of relatively quickly once they are identified. However, qualitative and subjective differences often are difficult or impossible to measure. For this reason, qualitative or subjective differences usually are the focus of the most difficult portions of a discussion to determine whether the opportunities are equivalent, or whether one is better than the other.

The attorney must be sensitive to two reactive factors in deciding whether to employ the alternative opportunity tactic. In some situations, the relationship between the parties is such that the client's loyalty is a positive negotiating factor that has real value to the other party. Reliance on an alternative opportunity will undermine that loyalty factor. If it is appropriate or necessary to use the tactic despite its detrimental effect on the loyalty factor, the negative impact should be tempered by suitable explanation.

Example 5-29

"You and Fred have done business together for a long time. You know that he has remained loyal to you, even when there have been some disadvantageous differences in the deals for him. And he knows that you've been good and fair with him, at times going out of your way for him. He appreciates your loyalty, as I'm certain that you do his. But look at the choice that he's facing. It would be irrational and virtually suicidal to throw away such a great opportunity out of loyalty. And he's not even asking you to match it penny for penny. All that he's asking is for you to come close enough to offer a rational opportunity for a business decision in your favor."

The explanation should be framed in terms of a loyal but reasonable person or entity who is being driven away by the other party's unwillingness or inability to present a rational alternative in the negotiation.

The second reactive factor in deciding whether to employ the alternative opportunity tactic is the perception of the other party. Will it be viewed as either:

1.   An unfair threat
2.   The equivalent of asking competitors to bid back and forth against each other in a setting in which such bidding is considered inappropriate

The latter is sometimes derogatorily referred to as being "whipsawed." Some parties may resent and refuse to participate in such a process. That reaction can be based on the nature of the parties' relationship, the qualitative or personal nature of the product or service, or whether it is customary to operate in this manner in the particular type of negotiation. For many negotiations, however, matching, or at least responding to, a competitive offer or position is the custom rather than the exception.

These two potential, unintended, negative reactive effects must be weighed against the often powerful leverage created by a realistic and legitimate position that no agreement will be entered into that does not favorably compare with specific alternative opportunities.

The alternative opportunity tactic can be utilized with any client goal and strategy. It can demonstrate reasons for and justify a range of positions. The following examples illustrate some of these positions.[98]

Example 5-30

Counsel represents a manufacturer and decides to employ the no concessions strategy in making an offer to purchase raw materials from a potential supplier. The appropriateness and fairness of the offer is explained on the basis that a different supplier is willing to accept virtually the same offer.

Example 5-31

In a commercial transaction involving financing, one of the unresolved issues is the rate of interest that will be charged. Utilizing problem solving, an agreement is sought by resolving an issue based on the terms available from alternative opportunities. "Let's see what interest rates are commonly being used in these types of deals, and we'll match the best one commonly available."

Example 5-32

In a different commercial transaction, one of the issues is the base price of the unit. The alternative opportunities provide a basis for a necessary concession. "If that's the price they're quoting, I will meet it. And you'll know that you're still getting superior workmanship."

§5.16   Splitting the Difference

One of the most frequently invoked tactics is to split the difference. The difference may be dollars, the date for closing the transaction, or anything else that is capable of being split in half to resolve an issue.

This tactic can be used with all client goals and with almost all strategies. It cannot be utilized with the strategies of no concessions, no further concessions, or of negotiating for purposes other than an agreement except as a ploy, since those strategies are concerned with resolving differences through a compromise.

---

[98] Using the alternative opportunity tactic is a concrete method of negotiating based on objective criteria. As noted in **ch 3,** this is one of the four cornerstones of Fisher and Ury's "principled negotiation" approach.

Splitting the difference is especially useful for three strategies. It can be used to be a deadlock-breaking concession.[99] Second, in problem solving, splitting the difference can be a "reasonable" method of resolving the difference between the parties' positions.[100] Third, this tactic can be the method for closing the agreement by splitting the only remaining difference that has been preventing a complete agreement.[101]

Splitting the difference is effective when:

1.   The parties have reached a point at which the difference between their positions is relatively small

2.   Each party realizes that the other's position is at least somewhat reasonable, so that the split is fair

Under these two conditions, splitting the difference is a rational and appropriate method for resolving the issue.[102] Since each party has a reasonable position, and the difference between them is relatively small, it may be difficult or impossible to bridge the difference in any other way. Neither party may be willing to move more than halfway either out of a fear of losing face, a desire for a fair agreement with equal compromises of good faith disputes, or both. The split preserves fairness while avoiding a loss of face.[103]

The optimal time for a split of the difference is when in addition to the two conditions described above being present, the other party's position is already within the range of counsel's settlement authority. In this way, a split improves an already acceptable offer.

When the difference between the parties is truly relatively small or proportionately unimportant, even unreasonable differences can be appropriate to split. It just may not be worth either the cost in time and energy or the risk of losing a potential agreement to refuse to split what, in context, is a minor, but unreasonable difference. In doing so, however, one must guard against allowing a precedent to be established that leads the other party to become unreasonably stubborn on remaining issues because it expects to be able always to resort to splitting any difference.

Avoiding such a harmful precedent can be accomplished in two ways. One method is to explain at the time of the split that the split is being agreed to

---

[99] *See* §3.05.

[100] *See* §3.08.

[101] *See* §3.15.

[102] This helps to explain the frequency with which splitting the difference is suggested by judges in settlement conferences. In the "Lloyd's of London formula," the judge asks each side to assess the probabilities of liability and of a damages award if the jury finds liability. If and when the parties are within a reasonable range, the judge then suggests that they split the difference. Menkel-Meadow, *Judges & Settlement,* 21 Trial 24, 27 (1985). Thus, the "Lloyd's of London formula" appears to encompass the optimal conditions for using the split the difference tactic.

[103] Of course, if the split is suggested by a judge pursuant to the "Lloyd's of London formula" in a settlement conference, avoiding a loss of face is even easier. *See* Menkel-Meadow, *supra* note 102, at 27.

on this particular issue for certain stated reasons, but that such a split should not be expected on future issues. Another method is to refuse to agree to split the difference on future issues if the other party attempts to establish a pattern of extracting small, last concessions by haggling and then demanding a split of the difference. The consequences of failing to avoid such a pattern is what is commonly known as being "nickled and dimed to death."

There is also a narrow exception to the general rule against splitting a relatively large difference. Splitting a larger difference is appropriate when:

1. The result of the compromise is within the negotiator's authority

2. Other tactics have been tried without avail

3. The parties are deadlocked

4. Further negotiations using other tactics appear futile, or there is a time problem making closure on the issue important

The apparent fairness and ease of splitting the difference often creates considerable impetus for its use. However, the analysis must not be superficial or automatic.

The splitting the difference tactic should not be used as a method to bypass proper negotiation or because the negotiator is lazy. Relatively large differences should not be split, because other tactics can be used to explore resolutions in the more favorable area of the bargaining range. By splitting the difference, counsel ignores the potential for a more favorable agreement when considerable latitude still exists. Cost effectiveness is the key.

Counsel must guard against an opposing negotiator who manipulates the negotiation, so that splitting the difference results in a more favorable outcome to the other party. This tends to occur in one of two ways. The other negotiator may set his initial position artificially high, planning to resort to a split of any remaining difference. This then leads to a better outcome for the other party, because the artificially high initial position has skewed the bounds of the difference unduly towards one end of the bargaining range. The other method to similarly manipulate the negotiation is to make consistently smaller concessions than are extracted. Again, this leads to that party's being situated more advantageously at the time that a splitting of the difference occurs. While guarding against such manipulation, a negotiator should use these maneuvers if they are likely to be successful rather than counterproductive.

§5.17   Focus/Downplay

In analyzing a negotiation, counsel should consider the subjects on which the other party focuses, and those which the other party avoids. These subjects and patterns can provide clues to that party's real interests.

The tactic of focus/downplay consists of giving a false clue. The negotiator focuses on items of less interest and downplays items of real interest for a time.[104]

That pattern of behavior makes it appear that the item of real interest has less value to the client than it does in reality. If successful, it leads to obtaining the item at a lesser cost because the other party underestimates its value to the client.

A basic example of this tactic can be found in the following purchase of transportation by an entrepreneur in the Old West.

Example 5-33

"[Y]ou just don't like to be without something to ride. I liked the looks of the mule best of all. . . . Knowing my man I went to Jenks and told him that I wanted to buy one of his horses. A sly look came into his eyes and he told me he'd only deal for the mule."[105]

In this way, our Western entrepreneur purchased the mule, which was the transportation which he really wanted, while manipulating the seller into believing that the mule was his last choice. Similarly, by creating an appearance that the most desired object is less desirable, the purchaser tends to minimize its cost.

The converse can also be true for a seller. The seller similarly might focus on an item that is of less interest to him, which therefore he is more ready, in reality, to sell. By creating an appearance that the lesser desired item is more valuable to him to retain, the seller may be able to increase the price that he can obtain.

§5.18   Creating a Psychological Commitment for Agreement

In some negotiations, it is possible to encourage the other party and its negotiator to have a psychological commitment to reaching an agreement. For this tactic, the substantive "carrots" or "sticks" are not directly important. Rather, counsel uses the process of negotiation itself to create a strong motivation for the other negotiator to achieve an agreement if that is at all possible given the absolute and final limits of his or her authority. The term "absolute and final limits" refers to the fact that, if successful, this tactic even can lead the other negotiator to seek more flexible authority in order to reach an agreement. Likewise, using the negotiation process to create strong motivations to reach an agreement also can be directed against the other party. If successful, it leads to the other party's increasing its negotiator's authority and lowering its bottom line.

One method of creating such a powerful, psychological incentive and commitment is to focus on, and even be professionally enthusiastic about, the bene-

---

[104] *See* McLintock, *Social Motivation in Settings of Outcome Interdependence*, in D. Druckman, Negotiations: Social-Psychological Perspectives, 53-54 (1977).

[105] E.L. Doctorow, Welcome to Hard Times (1960).

fits that an agreement will mean for both parties.[106] The emphasis is on the benefits flowing from the general concept of the agreement, without regard to the details of the terms.

A second method is to focus on the benefits from the points already resolved. Even conditionally resolved points should be used in this effort.[107]

While in some negotiations, apparent coolness and disinterest by the client will be necessary to avoid being perceived as overly eager and therefore weak, in other negotiations, that perception is less of a concern. If the client is in a position of relative strength, or at least parity, with the other party, counsel may be able to afford to display enthusiasm without causing a perception of weakness. Especially in some deal-making or transactional matters, some degree of enthusiasm about the end result for the parties can encourage the other party and its negotiator to more vigorously and more flexibly seek to resolve any differences, and to find a way to reach an agreement.

At times, the negotiator personally will be the focus, since the stated benefit will be for the negotiator's personal interests.

Example 5-34

"You know, if we can pull this off, you will have made one of the largest deals that they're going to see. It certainly won't hurt you a bit in the company."[108]

Example 5-35

Counsel was representing a client claiming certain government benefits. The official with whom counsel was negotiating was an overworked, low-level bureaucrat, although able to render a favorable decision for the client. "You know, not only are these claims fair, but if we can work out an agreement now, it will close the files and save everyone a lot of unnecessary paperwork."

The work group phenomenon is another factor that can create a psychological commitment to reaching agreement among the negotiators. When negotiators repeatedly deal with each other, they can become dependent on one another to facilitate their work. The group may consist of prosecutors and public defenders, insurance company adjusters and attorneys, and others who regularly or periodically interact with each other.[109] Each of the negotiators in the group has a load of assignments, responsibilities, and personal goals. In order to manage their duties, they are dependent on each other to a degree, since no one member of the group can make agreements happen without some cooperation from the others. Often, they ask each other for small accommodations

---

[106] See §5.14 on tone.

[107] See §5.11 regarding conditional proposals.

[108] See §5.29 on appealing to the other negotiator's personal interests.

[109] Lewis, Goetz, Schoenfield, Gordon & Griffin, *The Negotiation of Involuntary Civil Commitment,* 18 Law & Soc Rev 629, 634 (1984).

and favors. To a degree, an unconscious divided loyalty emerges, since each of the negotiators becomes a part of the group of negotiators, with feelings for the group as well as for the client.

The work group phenomenon raises two points for negotiators who find themselves a part of such a group because of the nature of their duties. These points consist of awareness and opportunity.

First, they must be aware of the tendency to act against the client's best interests in order to assist another negotiator from the group who requests a personal favor. This does not exclude giving personal favors to other negotiators which will benefit the client in the long run because reciprocal favors will be granted.[110] It does exclude those favors, however, that will not be returned for the present client, although the negotiator personally or other clients may benefit from reciprocity. This restriction, though, is limited to favors that negatively impact on the present client, since only those favors create a prohibited conflict of interest.

The second point is that, when it is advantageous for the negotiator's own client, counsel should exploit any opportunity created by the work group phenomenon. The decision to use this tactic must be made only after consideration of the long-term and the short-term effects, since reciprocity is likely to be demanded.

Sometimes within, and other times apart from, an actual work group, an attorney will negotiate an agreement with someone with whom there are likely to be future negotiations. The future negotiations may involve either the individual negotiator, that person's law firm, or the negotiator's employer or client. To encourage a psychological commitment towards reaching agreement again in the future, counsel should act appreciative of the deal, with as much professional respect and camaraderie as appropriate in view of the negotiators' personalities and the way in which they interacted during the negotiation. The negotiator who leaves a negotiation feeling good about the outcome will be far easier to deal with in the future than one who feels disappointed or upset about the result. The latter will wait to use the next negotiation to make up or get even for the prior negotiation. That creates an additional burden which should be avoided whenever possible.

Another method for creating a psychological commitment to reaching agreement is by negotiating in a manner that causes the other party and its negotiator to expend a great deal of time, energy, and effort towards reaching an agreement.[111] Once that time, energy, and effort is expended, the other party and its negotiator normally become more reluctant to cease negotiating without achieving some form of agreement. To do so is to admit failure, in that all of the work on the negotiation was wasted. This is especially likely to occur if the time and effort also involves a substantial out-of-pocket cost, so that a monetary

---

[110] See §5.05 regarding reciprocity.

[111] H. Cohen, You Can Negotiate Anything 71 (1982); R. Fisher & W. Ury, Getting to Yes: Negotiating Agreement Without Giving In 27 (1981). Fisher & Ury phrase this as: "Give them a stake in the outcome by making sure they participate in the process." *Id.*

loss is created by the failure to achieve an agreement. In a multi-issue negotiation, the other party may be induced to invest more time, energy, effort, and expense by deferring the more difficult issues for last and reaching at least conditional agreement on the easier issues.[112]

The higher the investment of resources in the negotiation (regardless of whether they are economic or noneconomic), the more anxious a party is likely to be to attain an agreement. Consequently, the negotiator must guard against becoming too committed to reaching an agreement. Counsel must be wary of performing less assertively or making unnecessary concessions because of undue fear that no agreement will result from all that has been invested in the negotiation.

In deal making, especially acquisitions, the general mood can tend to be that the deal is wanted so "let us get it done." The negotiators and the clients may become unduly concerned with losing the deal rather than with:

1.   Achieving the optimal deal available

2.   Avoiding a bad deal

This overeagerness to gain a deal can lead to an unwarranted emphasis on a cooperative goal and on the problem solving strategy, when the party would achieve a more favorable agreement by at least some or additional use of a competitive goal and other strategies with a variety of tactics.

Another variation has been called "supercrunch."[113] A group of competitors are invited to a meeting by a party with which they wish to do business. They are presented with difficult demands or requirements by that party. The party using supercrunch then tries to get each of the competitors, in the presence of the group, to commit to attempting to meet its demands or requirements. If a substantial number of commitments are attained, pressure is placed on the competitors to return with favorable bids or proposals that do, in fact, meet the demands or requirements.

In disputes, including litigation, a different attitudinal issue arises. The client and its negotiator may be ambivalent about whether to settle or to fight. This leads to an issue about the timing of the negotiations.[114] It also can induce an undue psychological commitment against settlement, even when a favorable result could be reached that is not likely to be exceeded at trial. The negotiator must guard against an inappropriate psychological commitment not to settle a matter, as well as against an inappropriate psychological commitment to settle. A negotiator must beware of blindness and loss of perspective from being too enamored with either the battle or with peace.

In litigation, fear of trial can create a powerful psychological commitment towards settlement. This can arise from a lack of preparation for trial, insecurity

---

[112] H. Cohen, *supra* note 111, at 72; Davis, *Settlement Negotiations: Strategy and Tactics,* 21 Trial 82, 83 (1985).

[113] C. Karrass, Give & Take: The Complete Guide to Negotiating Strategies and Tactics 211-13 (1974).

[114] See **§7.10** regarding timing in litigation negotiations.

as a trial lawyer, the weakness of the case, undue reluctance to present a difficult case, or the cost of the trial to the client. The latter factor may arise because the client cannot afford the cost, or is unwilling to expend the cost, or is likely to be dissatisfied with the cost given the probable outcome of the trial. Cost effectiveness is a valid reason to settle, as are trial realities. Fear of a difficult trial, however, must be resisted.

Some negotiators attempt to cause the other party to become psychologically committed to a deal through a "lowball" offer.[115] The "lowball" offer consists of:

1. A great initial price
2. Hidden costs through extras once the basic price is accepted

The "lowball" is more likely to be successful if disguised by a presentation that makes the hidden costs appear customary or otherwise to be fairly expected. A countermeasure to guard against such a "lowball" maneuver is to demand full information about the items that are included or excluded before indicating acceptance of the deal.[116]

The "lowball" maneuver is an extreme, short-run measure. It can cause such resentment and distrust that the other party terminates the negotiation. If it works at all but is recognized, it normally will work only once with a party or a negotiator. Unless the other side is a complete fool, once is more than enough to teach the lesson and to create:

1. A very guarded approach to any future interactions
2. A refusal to negotiate with the party, its negotiator, or both

The long-run loss of credibility often outweighs any short-run gain from this ploy. Depending on the circumstances, it also may be considered unethical, deceptive, or, in extreme cases, fraudulent.

§5.19   Face-Saving

The face-saving tactic is the taking of an action or the making of a statement that permits the other party or its negotiator to back down from a position or to make additional concessions without being embarrassed.[117] The creation of an opening for further movement without losing face can motivate concessions or other shifts in position which would otherwise never occur. It is not at all unusual for a party or a negotiator to stubbornly refuse to act, even when that may be costly, rather than suffer personal embarrassment or a potential

---

[115] C. Karrass, *supra* note 113, at 105-07.

[116] *Id* 106.

[117] This is in contrast to situations in which the focus is on saving counsel's own face.

loss of respect from the other party, its negotiator, or others who might learn of the incident.[118]

The problem of not allowing a need to save face to impede movement is inherent in the nature of negotiating. It has been observed that negotiators face an innate contradiction, needing to "be firm without appearing rigid, and at the same time (being) willing to yield without appearing too conciliatory."[119] This makes the need for ways to save face part of the basic fabric of negotiation.[120]

One method of implementing this tactic is simply to ignore the other party's assertion that this is a final or non-negotiable position. The negotiator continues to proceed as if that position never was stated. If, of course, the other party again asserts that its position is final or non-negotiable, it will have to be treated as such. The other party, however, may be secretly relieved to have its threat of finality ignored so that it can change its position without embarrassment or humiliation.

Another method of allowing the other party to save face is to provide new information about the matter at issue. This can save face in either of two ways. First, the information may provide a new and real reason for the other party to alter its previously fixed position. Alternatively, the information may function as a pretext that permits the other party to act as though it has received new knowledge which justifies a change in its previously fixed position. Either way, the new information effectively allows the other party or its negotiator to save face.

A third method of saving face for the other party or negotiator is to offer what is, in reality, a token or meaningless additional "concession" in return for the other side's making a meaningful change in its position. This allows face to be saved by creating the fiction that the other side improved its bargain or engaged in a reciprocal trade, rather than the reality that it made a concession.[121]

The fourth method is to interpret the other side's position differently than it was really intended, so that the other side does not have to indicate that it is changing its position. Such an interpretation must be communicated in a way that is neither condescending nor unfair.

In each of the following examples, the other negotiator has just made a "final offer." The responses are designed to permit additional movement without forcing an implicit admission that the assertion that the offer was "final" was a lie or a bluff.

---

[118] Brown, *Face-Saving and Face-Restoration in Negotiation,* in D. Druckman, Negotiations: Social-Psychological Perspectives 275 (1977); Rubin, *Negotiation,* in S. Goldberg, E. Green & F. Sander, Dispute Resolution 60-64 (1985); H. Cohen, You Can Negotiate Anything 189-93 (1982).

[119] *See* D. Druckman, Negotiations: Social-Psychological Perspectives 31, 41 (1977).

[120] Brown, *supra* note 118, at 278.

[121] *See* D. Druckman, *supra* note 119.

Example 5-36

Counsel knows that the other side's "final offer" was not intended to include the inventory. Nevertheless, the response is: "That offer is acceptable as long as it includes the inventory." To allow face to be saved, the responding negotiator acts as if the other side's intent not to include the inventory is not known. Therefore, the response is actually a demand for an additional concession.

Example 5-37

"Your offer does not cover the allocation of price among the assets for tax purposes. As you know, that can have different effects on the buyer and seller. Depending on that allocation, we may have a deal. Let me suggest. . . ."

Example 5-38

"I think that you either misinterpreted or were not given some critical information. Let me try to explain it to you, because I think that then you will agree that it wouldn't make sense for us to accept the last offer given the way that you structured it. However, an adjustment to the structure will make it work for both of us."

Recognizing a subtle request by one too embarrassed or reluctant to directly ask can be important. If it is advisable to do so in order to create movement in a desired direction, the request can be granted, without explicitly referring to the implied request, thereby allowing the other party to save face.[122] This also can generate gratitude that pays dividends in various ways throughout the balance of the negotiation.

In general, the less threatening, intimidating, and aggressive that counsel appears, the easier it is for the other party and the other negotiator to save face.[123] This is particularly true when the other negotiator or party perceives counsel's approach to be unfair or unjustified.[124] Conversely, the easier it is for the other side to justify its decision to make a concession or to compromise as the correct, competent, effective choice under the circumstances, the less it feels threatened with a loss of face.[125] To the extent that a proposal, in form or in substance, can be made consistent with the other side's values and self-image, it will be easier for them to accept the proposal without a loss of face.[126]

---

[122] In Japanese, "haragei" refers to the use of an allusive suggestion for important requested favors without a direct request. M. Zimmerman, How to Do Business with the Japanese 107 (1985).

[123] Brown, *supra* note 118, at 283.

[124] *Id* 284.

[125] Rubin, *supra* note 118, at 61.

[126] R. Fisher & W. Ury, Getting to Yes: Negotiating Agreement Without Giving In 29 (1981).

Techniques to break an impasse while allowing the other side to save face include altering the terms, tone, or the participants, such as:[127]

1.   Modifying the payment terms

2.   Changing the negotiator or the negotiation team leader

3.   Altering the allocation of risk

4.   Modifying the time of performance

5.   Changing or adding guarantees of satisfaction

6.   Altering or adding a grievance mechanism

7.   Changing strategy with a concomitant change in tone

8.   Modifying or adding options

9.   Changing specifications

10. Adjusting terms

11. Using a mediator, an arbitrator, or some other means of alternative dispute resolution

12. Creating a joint study committee

13. Focusing on the lack of information, or the inaccurate information on which the other negotiator had been relying through no fault of his or her own

14. Telling a funny story, as long as it is appropriate

Face-saving is not used with an aggressive client goal if that goal includes embarrassing or humiliating the other party or its negotiator. That type of situation, though, is rare. For other types of aggressive client goals, other client goals, and for any strategy, face-saving should be used as necessary to avoid or break deadlocks where a party or its negotiator has backed itself into a psychological corner from which it does not know how to escape.

§5.20   Inserting New Issues

When negotiations begin, the negotiators normally already know or quickly define the issues. This often is done with generalities and assumptions about the common meaning of what is included in the issues.

Example 5-39

In a sale of a home, it is assumed, without discussion, that the issues will include such items as the amount of the purchase price, a sum to be held in escrow, the date by which the transaction will close, and the terms of the mortgage contingency clause. Whether other matters are issues, such

---

[127] C. Karrass, Give & Take: The Complete Guide to Negotiating Strategies and Tactics 24-25, 60 (1974).

as a liquidated damages clause, or the inclusion of certain fixtures, is quickly determined.

In planning for the negotiation, counsel may decide to save certain issues for possible use later in the negotiation. The purpose of this tactic is to be able to trade off on the new issues to gain concessions on other issues, if the need arises. Planning for the probable or contingent use of the new issues tactic differs from setting an agenda.[128] Establishing an agenda means having certain issues negotiated before others in order to deal with the easiest or the hardest first or to see how the negotiation of certain issues unfolds before reaching other issues. Under the inserting new issues tactic, one or more issues are purposefully withheld until another issue or a certain problem is reached, regardless of when in the negotiation process that point occurs. The withheld issue then is injected into the process, while the other issue or a problem still is being considered. At that point, the new issue can be bargained away for greater concessions on the issue or problem already being negotiated.

Example 5-40

Corporation A is negotiating with Corporation B for the acquisition of B's wholly owned subsidiary, Corporation C. The manner in which certain aspects of the transaction are structured will affect the potential tax benefits and liabilities of each company. Prior to beginning the actual negotiation, A's counsel already knows basically how B wants to structure those aspects of the transaction. In planning its approach to the negotiation, A's counsel purposely decides to create and save an issue concerning B's accounts receivable to see what develops in the negotiation of structuring the transaction and the resulting tax consequences. The accounts receivable issue can be injected and traded off to obtain concessions on the tax aspects.

A different version of injecting new issues is to disassemble a proposed package deal. The parties then bargain about the component parts of the deal, and the final agreement may be limited to one or some of the components, rather than the complete package. The new issue consists of a more limited scope to the negotiation than originally existed.

Example 5-41

The client is seeking to purchase machinery and equipment with installation and servicing. The original issue is the price and other terms for the package. It is possible for the client to purchase the various components of the deal separately. In order to explore for further concessions, counsel inquires into whether the purchase of each component separately is a potential alternative with the seller. If the components can be bargained for separately, the attorney then negotiates at least the price portion of

---

[128] See §9.07 regarding planning agendas.

each component. Next, these prices are compared to the original price for the entire package. Attempts can be made to obtain discounts for buying either the entire package or combinations of components. If advantageous, a portion of the items sought may be purchased from the seller with the remainder obtained from other sources.

Even if the use of the new issues tactic has not been planned, counsel must be aware of its potential use in the event that an opportunity to do so arises. Such an opportunity can occur spontaneously through creative thought. It may be that the attorney will suddenly think of an issue that can be effectively utilized with this tactic. Also, the actions or positions taken by the other party can create a new issue which the counsel had not included in planning for the negotiation. The issue may be one which the other party purposely injects into the negotiation as a separate issue, or it inadvertently may arise as a result of the actions or positions taken by the other party.

Example 5-42

The litigation concerned whether a substantial "gift" from a living, elderly person was obtained through fraud or duress. The plaintiff was the elderly person. Other family members who were supporting the litigation would benefit directly or indirectly under the plaintiff's will and trust. The defendant was the recipient of the gift. The new issue injected by the defendant was a proposed agreement not to challenge the will and trust if allowed to retain the gift.

Example 5-43

The client owes money, but has financial difficulties that prevent it from being able to simply pay the full amount that is due. In order to save litigation and collection costs, as well as to be more confident that it will actually receive payment, the other party is willing to compromise on the amount that is owed. It is not, however, willing to compromise the amount nearly as much as had been hoped or as much as is needed. Accordingly, counsel injects a new issue to ameliorate the cash flow problem, that of spreading the payment through installments rather than making one total payment.

Injecting new issues sometimes can be used to save face while settling a losing negotiation when outside parties are of concern. This occurs when a party believes that its real goals cannot be achieved, but that it needs to reach an agreement and win something so that it can save face. Usually, a party resorts to creating a new issue which it can win. The party then uses that to claim that the negotiation was successful. The claim of success is directed towards the public, business associates, or whoever else has an opinion or reaction that is of concern to the party.

The new issues tactic can be employed with any client goal and strategy. Especially when a cooperative client goal or a problem solving strategy is involved, care must be taken to inject the new issue in a manner that appears to be legitimate and fair. Otherwise, the tactic will be perceived as a bad faith attempt to use a functional irrelevancy as a bargaining chip.

Example 5-44

After extensive negotiations and an oral agreement, a draft agreement has been prepared by B and transmitted to A, the other party's negotiator. Certain terms intended by B were implicit throughout the negotiation and were expressly referred to by B in reaching an oral agreement. The negotiators now are meeting to discuss the draft.

A: In reviewing this and looking at how it will work again, we can't live with sections 2.03 and 3.06 unless we receive a 10 per cent volume discount. I know we agreed in general, but this just wasn't clear to us.

B: We have spent hours and hours in working out this deal and it always was understood that it would be structured in the manner that the draft reflects. No volume discounts were ever mentioned.

A: That may have been your understanding, but we certainly never intended to agree to do that. And we now realize that the deal is unfair without a volume discount.

B: There have been any number of references to the structure in these provisions and you never once questioned it.

A: Well, it wasn't really clear to us until we saw it on paper. Then the full import hit us.

B: It was discussed sufficiently to be clear. I just think that you are now just trying to get an extra concession because you think that we are locked into this deal. We are not locked in though, and I do not intend to be pressured in this way.

The example illustrates the problems and distrust that can arise when the new issue is injected in connection with issues already resolved. It is critical to inject the new issue for increased bargaining leverage on an existing issue before agreement is reached on that existing issue. Otherwise, inserting a new issue will and should be viewed as a dishonest and bad faith negotiation ploy. When considered to be in bad faith, it can lead to a breakdown in the entire negotiation because of a refusal to deal with a party operating in bad faith. In addition, it leads to a loss or serious diminution of the negotiator's personal credibility for operating in bad faith.

Difficulty can arise inadvertently if the parties or the negotiators honestly differ about whether there was an agreement on the initial issue before a party sought to use the new issue tactic. The disagreement can generate a controversy over whether the injection of the new issue is an attempt to renege on a prior agreement on earlier issues. This difficulty usually can be avoided through periodic summaries or recapitulations of:

1.   The issues completely agreed on at that point

2.   The issues agreed on only conditionally[129]

3.   The issues that still are totally open

For the latter two categories (issues for which there is conditional agreement or no agreement), the injection of a new issue into the existing issue is a legitimate, proper bargaining mechanism to gain increased leverage.

A countermeasure to last minute, additional demands, when agreement is virtually complete, is to treat the demand as though it forces all of the issues to be reopened.[130] Other countermeasures include a refusal to negotiate the new issue at all, inserting one's own additional issues, or termination of the negotiation.

§5.21   Focusing on the Process

Separate and apart from the substantive issues, negotiations can break down or become impaired by events in the process of the negotiating. The negotiators or the parties may clash or become embroiled in disputes struggling over how to conduct the negotiation. The process itself then becomes disrupted, sometimes to the extent that the negotiation does not proceed productively.

The tactic of focusing on the process consists of:

1.   Stopping the negotiating activities and reflecting on the situation

2.   Getting the negotiators to agree that the negotiation has been sidetracked by a problem in the process which does not involve the substantive interests of the parties, and that they want to get back on track

3.   Using informational tactics,[131] problem solving,[132] or debate[133] to obtain agreement of the negotiators on a way to proceed effectively with the substantive issues for the parties, which resolves or ameliorates the blockage or procedural problem that has stymied progress

4.   Return to negotiating substantive issues

To the extent that a more cooperative attitude is likely to result from articulating the cause of the problem, counsel should do so. This must be phrased without accusations, and in a nonjudgmental manner. Similarly, face-saving can be crucial in motivating the other negotiator to productively focus on the process.[134] It does so by allowing the other negotiator to escape from a dilemma of his or her own making.

---

[129] See §5.11 regarding conditional proposals.

[130] R. Lewicki & J. Litterer, Negotiation 155 (1985).

[131] See ch 4.

[132] See §3.08.

[133] See §5.10.

[134] See §5.19

Focusing on the process may address:[135]

1. The causes of past conflicts
2. Each negotiator's or each party's perception of the other side
3. Obtaining a climate for constructive discussion

The problem may be that the negotiators are locked in a power struggle after an emotional outburst because of a disagreement concerning the manner in which the negotiation will proceed. This might involve which issue to negotiate first, some other aspect of whose agenda will control, whether to engage in problem solving, or the extent to which the merits of each parties' case should be debated. Focusing on the process is used to resolve the procedural dispute, so that the negotiators can return to attempting to resolve the substantive concerns. The negotiators may bargain and trade concessions on the process to be followed, just as they would for the substantive agreement itself.

A procedural dilemma also may arise from a negotiator's becoming concerned due to distrust, confusion, or misunderstanding the manner in which the other is proceeding in the negotiation. This can lead to a breakdown in progress on the substantive issues, because the negotiator becomes concerned about inadvertently or unnecessarily weakening his or her position due to a tactic or strategy that the other side is thought to be using. The dilemma is exacerbated if the negotiators on both sides engage in this behavior simultaneously.

Example 5-45

Jolton believes that progress will occur for a cooperative client goal only if a problem solving strategy is conducted by both parties. However, she is concerned that the other party is disingenuously only pretending to engage in a cooperative, problem solving approach, while actually being quite competitive and using a deadlock-breaking concessions only or HRESSC strategy. Jolton knows that proceeding with a problem solving strategy will be ineffective, and could even be disadvantageous if the other party unfairly manipulates the problem solving strategy. Therefore, she feels stymied and unable to proceed in any direction. In order to stimulate progress, Jolton switches to the focus on the process tactic, seeking to determine whether problem solving is a viable choice.

JOLTON: I'm trying to think the problem through with you and solve it, but you seem to just want to talk about more concessions. I don't see how we'll get anywhere that way.

GREEN: First, I thought you were just arguing with me. From my standpoint, the problem is a little different. Perhaps we should discuss how we see this point, and try to see if we can agree on the problem.

---

[135] R. Lewicki & J. Litterer, Negotiation 306 (1985).

The focus on the process tactic can provide a solution by having the negotiators articulate their concerns, misunderstandings, confusion, or disagreements about the manner in which the other negotiator is proceeding. They then discuss or otherwise negotiate and agree on the process of the negotiation.

Example 5-46

A taxpayer sues a private corporation which supplied services to a local governmental entity. The taxpayer claims that the corporation overcharged the government under the terms of the service contract with counts alleging breach of contract and fraud. The taxpayer's attorney (P) and the corporation's attorney (D) have been involved in a lengthy negotiation session.

D: Going back to the numbers, are you willing to go well below $700,000 or not? From prior discussions with my client, I can tell you that the client does not expect to pay anything like that. There would be no way for me to convince the company to go above the $600,000 range.

P: I think that this can settle, but we can talk about how. I really don't want to make any further concessions at this point until you talk to your client and get authority.

D: Do you just want to waste more time while I do that? I don't want to play games.

P: I don't want to either. However, you're going to your client. I expect that, whatever I say now in terms of a number, you're going to come back and demand a lower number because your client will expect further concessions. And, if I give you a best number now, I will not be in a position to give you those expected concessions. We could become deadlocked because your client has false expectations of further concessions when there really aren't any left to give.

D: That's not going to happen.

P: You mean that you can guarantee that your client will not demand further concessions once I give you a number below $700,000?

D: I can sell $600,000.

P: $600,000 will not do it.

D: Then what will do it? Give me your best number. (Defense counsel is demanding that plaintiff's counsel reveal his authority.)

P: (deflecting the demand to reveal his ultimate authority): Let's see if we can compromise and agree on how to proceed. I want you to understand that a number significantly above $600,000 but on the lower end of the $600,000 range ultimately will be acceptable and to get authority so that this can be settled with one last concession on my part.

D: Alright. I'll do that.

By focusing on the process, the negotiators have found the means to reach a settlement.

Focusing on the process can consist of identifying certain conduct by the other negotiator and promising to make the conduct known if it persists. Counsel may halt or restrain outrageous demands or behavior by the other negotiator if he or she:

1. Correctly perceives that the other party does not want a breakdown of the negotiation over its lawyer's excessive demands or offensive conduct
2. Verbally identifies the conduct
3. Openly makes a record of it
4. Acknowledges an intention to explain to the client the reasons that negotiation is not feasible

The likelihood that these actions will be successful is greatly enhanced if the parties have a close relationship, so that they communicate with each other directly, as well as through their attorneys.

If confronted by the focus on the process tactic being invoked by the other negotiator, counsel must think rather than react precipitously. Instincts should be used, as well as an intellectual analysis. The lawyer should consider his or her objectives and determine how to react to most likely achieve those objectives. Counsel's reaction should not be based on satisfying some immediate, inner feelings.

If confronted by an accusation that one has unnecessarily created difficulties in a negotiation, the lawyer should first consider, as objectively as possible, the source of the accusation and its credibility. If and only if the source has some credibility, the possibility should be considered that:

1. A mistake about market values or other facts has been made
2. Something has been misinterpreted
3. Information is lacking
4. There has been a miscalculation of strategy, tactics, or tone

A negotiator must neither:

1. Become unsettled or uncertain just because of personal criticism or attack
2. Be blind to the possibility that, since no one is perfect, an error has been made

To retain a generally confident attitude, counsel should not accept such criticism or attack unless clearly convinced that it is justified.

Countermeasures to such criticism or attack include:

1. If the comments were justified, switch strategy, or tactics, perhaps with an explanation that the problem was not intentionally created
2. If the comments were justified, and after consulting with the client, change a substantive position

3. If the comments were sincere, but misguided, explain why they were mistaken

4. If the comments were sincere, but mistaken, reject their accuracy, acknowledge the other person's sincerity, and switch strategy or tactics as a good faith effort to proceed

§5.22 The Creation of Movement

At a certain point in some negotiations, the parties may become bogged down or may reach an impasse. The atmosphere can be marred by intransigence and polarization. In many instances, both sides are responsible for the dilemma, while at other times, only one negotiator or party is responsible.

Regardless of who is responsible for creating the situation, a negotiator needs to be cognizant of it when it occurs. Counsel then must decide whether the client's interests and directions necessitate that the negotiator assume the burden of trying to get the negotiation unblocked and moving again. This may be contrary to the negotiator's personal feelings that the other party or its negotiator created the situation and therefore should have the burden of correcting it. Those personal feelings must be set aside, though, and the issue should be analyzed on the basis of the client's best interests and instructions. Sometimes this will necessitate consultation with the client. The decision that must be made in these situations is whether to take the initiative and act to move the negotiation forward, sometimes with the use of dramatic steps.

If the decision is made to act to create movement so that the negotiation can proceed again, the analysis begins with an examination of the reasons for the lack of progress. Often, this examination will lead to the use of other tactics in conjunction with creating movement. The tactics which tend to be particularly useful in these situations are:

1. Information disclosure[136]
2. Fact creation[137]
3. Face-saving[138]
4. Injecting a new issue[139]
5. Focusing on the negotiation process[140]
6. The use of allies[141]
7. The use of media or community pressure[142]

---

[136] *See* **§4.02.**
[137] *See* **§4.03.**
[138] *See* **§5.19.**
[139] *See* **§5.20.**
[140] *See* **§5.21.**
[141] *See* **§6.05.**
[142] *See* **§6.06.**

8.   Alternative dispute resolution[143]

9.   New instructions for the negotiator[144]

10.   Changing negotiators[145]

Although other tactics such as those listed above often are used to help generate progress, the creation of movement merits separate consideration because it arises in response to a particular problem and is then of paramount importance. Many negotiations fail, despite the existence of a zone of agreement due to the fact that the parties' bottom lines overlap. This failure occurs even though, by definition, such negotiations should produce an agreement. The negotiation is doomed because an impasse arises and neither negotiator assumes responsibility for generating movement, or they are insufficiently creative or inadequately skilled to find a way to create movement. Through proper planning and knowledge of negotiation strategy and tactics, the negotiator should be able to often create movement when that is in the client's best interests, so that a zone of agreement is not wasted.

The analysis of the cause of the impasse and the creation of movement may involve recognizing and understanding one's own emotions, as well as those of the client, the other negotiator, and the other party.[146] In this regard, it may be that one participant's perception of another's intentions or of the facts is not accurate.[147] If so, that participant's perception may need to be altered through persuasion.[148] It also may be necessary to let the other party or its negotiator "let off steam" before further progress can be made.[149]

Whether negotiations have broken down due to a failure of communication, rather than substantive or procedural problems, should also be considered. The negotiator should be sure that both sides understand both what each one wants and what has been sought from the other.[150]

Where there are multiple issues involved, but one issue is causing the impasse, creating movement can involve a decision to temporarily agree to disagree on that portion while attempting to make progress on other issues.[151] If such progress is made, there may be more flexibility on the bypassed issue.[152]

---

[143] *See* **§6.07.**

[144] H. Raiffa, The Art and Science of Negotiation 129 (1982).

[145] *Id.*

[146] *See* R. Fisher & W. Ury, Getting to Yes: Negotiating Agreement Without Giving In 30 (1981).

[147] *Id* 25-27.

[148] *Id* 27.

[149] *Id* 31.

[150] *Id* 45-47. Fisher & Ury caution that: "If you have no idea what they think they are being called on to do, *they* may not either. That alone may explain why they are not deciding as you would like." (Emphasis in original.) *Id* 47.

[151] *Id* 72.

[152] See **§5.18** concerning creating a psychological commitment to reaching an agreement.

It may also be possible to circumvent the issue that has deadlocked the negotiation by agreeing on a procedure whereby it can be resolved in the future, rather than remaining blocked because a substantive agreement cannot be reached.[153]

§5.23 Deadlock

Deadlock is the creation of an impasse, sometimes as a prelude to termination giving the other party a final opportunity to compromise. Another function is as a temporary or interim tactic to test the other side's strength and resolve.[154] Therefore, deadlock should be used only when there is:

1. A good chance of success
2. A relatively low risk that the other party will react so strongly that it terminates the negotiation or otherwise causes a serious long-run problem in the negotiation
3. A face-saving way has been planned to break the deadlock if necessary through the creation of movement, unless the client is at its bottom line and the only alternatives are capitulation by the other party or termination of the negotiation[155]
4. Closure is inappropriate or not feasible[156]

One method of producing a temporary deadlock is to insist on unspecified concessions.

Example 5-47

"I've done all I can do at this point. You'll just have to do better if we're going to reach agreement."

Deadlock can be especially useful in implementing a strategy of negotiating for delay, rather than agreement.[157] This is a third function of the deadlock tactic, which is different from a test of strength or resolve. A party may welcome a deadlock when a delay produces its own benefit. For instance, management may welcome a deadlock and consequent strike if the strike:

1. Allows for reducing large inventories without having to pay fixed labor costs[158]
2. Saves wages which then are used to fund an important portion of the eventually agreed-to wage increase

---

[153] R. Fisher & W. Ury, *supra* note 146, at 72.

[154] C. Karrass, Give & Take: The Complete Guide to Negotiating Strategies and Tactics 49 (1974).

[155] See §§5.19 and 5.22 regarding face-saving and creation of movement, respectively.

[156] *See* §3.15.

[157] *See* §3.11.

[158] H. Raiffa, The Art and Science of Negotiation 81 (1982).

The dynamics of a prolonged deadlock are important. Research indicates "a highly polarized, unproductive conflict is characterized by the following dynamics:"[159]

1. Feelings of anger, resentment, tension, hostility, mistrust, frustration, and futility

2. Communicating to criticize and blame, and to block criticism and blame

3. A blurring of the issues

4. Personalization of the conflict

5. Focusing on areas of wide disagreement, instead of areas of agreement

6. Each side locking into its position

7. Each side tending to unite as a team against the other side

Some countermeasures to create movement and to break a deadlock respond to and alter the above listed conditions. Such countermeasures include:

1. Focusing on the process to acknowledge the legitimacy of feelings, enhance understanding, and, if possible, depersonalize the issues[160]

2. A return to, or an initial use of, productive information disclosure and information bargaining, instead of hurling accusations[161]

3. An adjournment to reduce tensions and to create an environment for a "fresh start"[162]

4. Redefining the issues

5. Switching to a problem solving approach[163]

6. Using a win/win proposal to alter the pattern of the dynamics[164]

7. Fact creation to demonstrate the strength or resolve to resist the other side's demands and pressures

Linkage is an additional countermeasure to deadlock, and a form of injecting a new issue.[165] Sometimes linking more than one negotiation together can obviate the basis of an impasse. Although complicated, this can be useful if the linkage is practical. One may creatively open an entire new series of possibilities by linking the present negotiation to:[166]

1. Other pending negotiations with the same party

---

[159] R. Lewicki & J. Litterer, Negotiation 281 (1985).

[160] *See* §5.21.

[161] See §§4.02 & 4.07, respectively.

[162] *See* §5.24.

[163] *See* §§3.08 & 3.09.

[164] *See* §5.06.

[165] *See* §5.20.

[166] H. Raiffa, supra note 158, at 13.

2.   Other pending negotiations with a different party

3.   Future negotiations with the same party

4.   Future negotiations with a different party

Another approach to breaking a deadlock is a variation of the concede first tactic.[167] One party makes a unilateral concession. The concession is accompanied by an explicit statement that it is a one-time attempt to reduce tension, and the other party is asked to reciprocate in a specific way. Lastly, a threat to terminate the negotiation is the ultimate test of a deadlock.

Due to the danger of termination and the hostility or frustration which can be produced, deadlock rarely should be used with a cooperative client goal. Moreover, it should be used cautiously whenever termination of the negotiation is a concern.

§5.24   Adjournment

The tactic of adjournment is to temporarily stop the negotiation and resume it later. The negotiation is to be resumed either at a specified time or at a time to be established by mutual agreement. This tactic is used for four purposes. These purposes are:

1.   To regroup

2.   To change the mood

3.   To obtain authority

4.   To deal with other matters

At times, the negotiator may need to adjourn the negotiation to regroup. This occurs when the negotiator is unable to gain momentum or is otherwise stymied. It can occur because a decision must be made whether to proceed with further concessions at or approaching one's bottom line. Also, the negotiator may need a break because of feeling frustrated, defensive, or angry due to the belligerence or uncooperative attitude of the other party.[168]

At these times it may be best to adjourn if counsel believes that having time to analyze the negotiation process will lead to being able to act more effectively when negotiations are resumed. For instance, pressure for an immediate decision usually should be resisted if doubt exists, since it generally is not necessary.[169] In dire situations, an immediate decision can be required despite uncertainty and doubts. This will lead to closure or termination of the negotiation.[170]

At other times, the mood of the other negotiator, the other party, or one's own client is such that it is seriously impeding or preventing the progress to

---

[167] See §3.07.

[168] R. Lewicki & J. Litterer, Negotiation 5, 19 (1985).

[169] W. Coffin, The Negotiator: A Manual For Winners 11 (1973).

[170] See §3.15.

be made in the negotiation. If that mood appears to be temporary, a period of adjournment is needed to allow time for the mood to improve.

Sometimes an adjournment is necessary because the client has to be consulted about modification of the authorized negotiating authority. The length of such an adjournment will depend on the client's availability, and the amount of time needed to counsel and to confer with the client, as well as to obtain the client's decision regarding the bottom line. This need can arise from a new and different approach in the negotiation which was unanticipated, so that the negotiator lacks authority to respond to it. It also can arise because different authority appears to be needed if an agreement is to be achieved due to the positions taken by the other party on the anticipated issues.

On occasion, an adjournment also becomes necessary due to the negotiator's having a scheduling conflict. Since adjournment causes a loss of momentum and prevents closure, adjournments due to scheduling conflicts should be avoided if the momentum is good or if closure is appropriate.

In seeking an adjournment, counsel may reveal the real reason for it or it may be necessary to use a pretext. The decision on what reason to give should be based on the criteria used for selective information disclosure.[171]

Regardless of the actual reason for adjournment, it allows for a clearer assessment of positions and of the process to be made, since there is more time for such analysis and fewer distractions to thought than occur during the dynamic process of the negotiation itself. This may be a positive or a negative factor for each side, depending on:

1.   Which negotiator and party will benefit more from the time for such an analysis

2.   Whether the negotiator is so confused or otherwise in trouble that the time is needed regardless of the potential benefits to the other side

The adjournment tactic can be employed with any client goal and with all strategies, except for closure. In fact, it is the exact opposite of closure. Therefore, it should not be utilized when closure is appropriate.[172]

Adjournment should be resisted if:

1.   It will benefit the other negotiator more, and counsel can continue without losing self-control and the ability to act effectively; *and*

2.   It is likely to leave a counterproductive residue of hostile feelings

At times, negotiations involve marathon bargaining sessions. Such bargaining sessions are structured to test endurance. Sometimes the side which is less tired, or which can function better while being tired, finally prevails in a negotiation. In these circumstances, physical toughness is helpful, and mental toughness is essential. A good negotiator knows when to:

---

[171] *See* §4.02.

[172] See §3.15 regarding closure.

1. Use an endurance advantage

2. Refrain from attempting to exploit an endurance advantage because the attempt will be counterproductive due to the hostility it generates in the other side

3. Refuse to become locked into an endurance test in which there is a significant danger that the other side will prevail

Adjournment often includes setting a specific time and place for the next meeting.[173] This may consist of an agreement to confer within a set or "reasonable" time and to schedule the next session. However, if an impression of disinterest, lack of optimism about the potential for an agreement, or an atmosphere of general uncertainty is desired, a different method should be employed. Under these conditions, an open-ended adjournment may be useful. That type of adjournment leaves open the scheduling of the next session or, perhaps, the question of whether the negotiation will even continue. The latter option should not be chosen unless the client is prepared to accept either:

1. A termination of the negotiation unless the other party initiates further contact

2. The initiation of further contact if the other side does not initiate, with the risk that it may fail

§5.25 Patience

While a negotiator may need to be relentless and tireless at times, patience can be a negotiating virtue as well. Unless the other party or its negotiator is susceptible to being pressured into the desired decision, pressing too quickly for an agreement can lead to resistance in and of itself. Undue pressure may produce a perception that a proposal's creator fears a calm analysis because it will reveal undesirable, hidden facets. After calm analysis, however, the other side may feel comfortable with the proposal.

In addition, "acceptance time" can be needed simply to adjust one's thinking to new ideas.[174] Only once the new ideas are comfortably absorbed can the negotiation proceed.

Patience also can demonstrate resolve and firmness when rhetoric fails to do so. This increases in importance if a "deadline" approaches and the pressure on both sides to take some action escalates.[175] It can convince the other side that a position is real and not subject to change, at least not without receiving a major concession. In this manner, patience can lower the other party's expectations and wear it down.[176]

---

[173] W. Coffin, The Negotiator: A Manual For Winners 54 (1973).

[174] See C. Karrass, Give & Take: The Complete Guide to Negotiating Strategies and Tactics 1 (1974).

[175] H. Cohen, You Can Negotiate Anything 98 (1982).

[176] C. Karrass, supra note 174, at 143; H. Cohen, supra note 175, at 83.

Deadlines are a major countermeasure to patience.

§5.26   Deadlines

Deadlines should be used to limit the time period for acceptance of an offer whenever:

1.   An open offer may cause the loss of alternative opportunities that cannot be fully pursued while the offer is outstanding

2.   A decision is needed because costs must be incurred or actions must be taken unless the offer is accepted

3.   The cost basis or other factors can change, and it is awkward or difficult to revoke the offer

4.   It will cause a procrastinating party to make a decision

Example 5-48

In a case in litigation, either a settlement must be reached or relatively substantial costs have to be incurred for depositions, experts, and further legal fees. The offer takes into account the fact that those costs have not yet been incurred, and, correspondingly, a deadline for acceptance is placed on the offer.

Example 5-49

The statute of limitations is approaching. Thus, either a settlement must be reached or suit has to be filed. Accordingly, the plaintiff offers to settle, but sets a deadline for the defendant to accept.

Example 5-50

A relatively significant offer in the form of a binding estimate is made. The estimate takes into account current costs, but those costs are liable to increase in the future. Therefore, a deadline for acceptance is utilized.

A reason for imposing a deadline should be given to the other party, so that the deadline appears to be both fair and firm.[177] If there is no apparently legitimate reason for the deadline, except to apply pressure, the deadline is unreasonable and arbitrary.

Artificial, unfair deadlines can be perceived as a high pressure power play, and thereby lead to resentment on the part of the other side. Assuming that the other party cannot be overwhelmed or intimidated by a deadline, that resentment will be counterproductive to reaching an agreement. At times, it will lead the other side to reject any agreement, or, at least, any agreement

---

[177] See C. Karrass, Give & Take: The Complete Guide to Negotiating Strategies and Tactics 46 (1974).

based on the deadline, in order to clearly demonstrate its ability to resist such pressure.

Sometimes deadlines are negotiable. If non-negotiable and credible, they create a time pressure to increase the speed and/or size of concessions in order to reach an agreement. Therefore, deadlines can be used to speed up the negotiation process, although care must be taken to avoid deadlines that:

1. Prematurely and unnecessarily cause a termination of the negotiation without an agreement
2. Have to be withdrawn with a consequent loss of face and credibility

If a failure to agree has greater adverse consequences for one party than the other, the deadline strengthens the latter's position while weakening that of the former. Lastly, in protracted or complex negotiations, interim deadlines on certain issues may be set to determine whether it is worthwhile to expend further time, energy, and costs on the negotiation.

If confronted by a deadline, the attorney should analyze whether it really is advantageous to the other party to force a decision. If not, one should generally be skeptical of whether the deadline is real, or is a bluff which one can attempt to change.[178] Deadlines are often more flexible than negotiators realize.[179] The other party may be willing to alter an artificial deadline, especially if offered a face-saving reason to do so. Modifying the deadline to reasonably accommodate the needs and the interests of both parties is an example of a face-saving reason.

In addition to utilizing a face-saving demand for modification, another countermeasure is to change the benefit or the appropriateness of the deadline.[180] This may involve:[181]

1. Increasing the cost to the other party of enforcing the deadline
2. Reducing the cost to the client if the deadline is enforced

Example 5-51

The party being confronted with a deadline believes that it has the power to force a withdrawal of the deadline by increasing the cost to the other party of invoking it. "We will not negotiate at all unless that ultimatum is withdrawn, and no further public threats are made while negotiations proceed."

Another countermeasure to deadlines is to create an incentive for reaching a prompt agreement.[182] The incentive obviates the other party's need for a deadline.

---

[178] *Id* 46-47.

[179] H. Cohen, You Can Negotiate Anything 98 (1982).

[180] C. Karrass, *supra* note 177, at 95.

[181] R. Lewicki & J. Litterer, Negotiation 85 (1985).

[182] *Id* 154.

When a client imposes a deadline on its own negotiator and no corresponding pressure is placed by the other party on its counsel, the first negotiator tends to be weakened. The negotiator facing an impending deadline from the client then is liable to lower his or her aspirations, soften positions, and increase the rate and the speed of concessions. It has the same effect as a deadline successfully imposed by the other party.

§5.27   Dealing with Those Who Lack Authority

Counsel may be confronted by a negotiator who lacks real control over whether his or her client will enter into an agreement. For these purposes, real control can be considered either having formal authority to make binding compromises, or having sufficient influence on the client to have, in effect, informal binding authority.

This situation is not one in which the negotiator could get traditional negotiating authority to bind the client, but has failed to do so. Rather, it is one in which the nature of the other party or its policies dictates that its negotiator proceed without binding authority, and then submit the resulting proposal for a decision. Thus, such a party will insist that the negotiation proceed although its negotiator lacks authority, and that the result be transmitted to the appropriate superior for a final decision.

The approval that is of concern here is not perfunctory, but rather is that of the real decision maker, who independently analyzes the proposed agreement, even though the negotiator's views may be considered. In such instances, the other negotiator functions more to screen and probe information, and to shuttle messages back and forth between counsel and the other side's real decision maker, than in other negotiations.

This situation must be distinguished from that in which the other side's ultimate decision maker is normally or always a perfunctory player in the process, because the other negotiator's recommendations are normally followed. If that is the case, the other negotiator should be treated as having final authority, since, in effect, his or her informal authority is ordinarily final. This principle is adhered to even if the other party must personally execute documents, if execution is simply a formality and not a time to reevaluate before deciding whether to agree.

At times, the other negotiator may not reveal whether he or she has real authority. The presence or absence of authority also may not be inherently apparent. If there is a question about whether one with real authority is present, the question should be pressed.[183] Such an inquiry does not request that any specific authority be disclosed, but is restricted to whether the negotiator has authority to enter into a yet unspecified agreement. In addition, other possible sources of information should be considered to learn the other lawyer's true role.

---

[183] C. Karrass, Give & Take: The Complete Guide to Negotiating Strategies and Tactics 12 (1974).

A typical setting, in which one is confronted by a negotiator without authority, is a government bureaucracy, in which the negotiator is expected to fully negotiate and to obtain concessions without being able to make binding concessions. Of course, not every governmental bureaucracy functions this way for every negotiation.[184]

Many times, government bureaucracies function in this way because the decision makers are elected boards, elected officials, or high ranking administrators in a large agency or department. For purposes of controlling the demands on their time, they refuse to invest time monitoring negotiations until a possible final result is presented. As a matter of law, however, the result cannot be final until a decision maker at this level approves it.

Example 5-52

In litigation in which the County is a party, a judge sets a pretrial settlement conference, and instructs the attorneys either to have settlement authority or to bring a representative of the client who has authority. The County's attorney explains that the County cannot comply with that instruction because, as a matter of law, any settlement has to be approved by the County Board at its regular monthly meeting. The attorney further explains that, accordingly, all that he can do is to negotiate a tentative agreement and make a recommendation which may or may not be followed.

When confronted by a lack of formal authority, counsel initially must analyze the situation in terms of the following factors:

1.   The potential for making the other negotiator's authority a precondition
2.   The other negotiator's influence
3.   The other party's approach towards concessions

First, can the other party be forced to provide a negotiator with real authority so that this dilemma can be avoided? Can this be demanded as a precondition to substantive negotiations?[185] Second, what is the other side's procedural attitude approach to further concessions? Does it operate merely by approving or disapproving the negotiated proposal, or does it always or often demand further concessions so that another stage of negotiation is foreseen?

The tactic for dealing with those who negotiate without authority depends on the answers to these questions. When a precondition demanding that the

---

[184] For instance, in dealing with claims against the government brought pursuant to the Federal Tort Claims Act, counsel for the Veteran's Administration has only $25,000 of authority. If the matter goes into litigation, the local United States Attorney's office's authority is limited to $200,000. Higher amounts have to be approved directly by high ranking Justice Department officials in Washington, D.C., who are then the real decision makers and who independently analyze any proposed settlement. *See* 28 USC §2671 *et seq.*

[185] See **§5.02** concerning preconditions.

other negotiator obtain authority before the negotiation proceeds appears to be viable, that maneuver should be attempted first. A variation of this, which has the same effect, is to demand that the other negotiator be replaced by a superior who does have authority.[186] If such a precondition is not feasible, or is unsuccessful, then the tactic must shift.

The next step depends on the answer to the question of the other negotiator's influence. If the other negotiator, either individually or in combination with other subordinates who are directly involved in the negotiation (even those who may not be present), has significant influence with the ultimate decision maker, then the negotiation should be aimed at a proposal which the other negotiator will support. A proposal that is supported by the other negotiator is desired under these circumstances, because that support will make the other party's ultimate approval far more probable and possibly certain.

To obtain such support from the other negotiator, some concessions, either real or apparent, may be essential. In this way, the other negotiator feels that his or her superior will approve of their recommending an agreement that was won from the other party through hard, skillful bargaining.

Appeals to the other negotiator's self-interest may also be employed. Counsel should indicate how the other negotiator will be viewed favorably by others because of a pending proposal, or will otherwise benefit from reaching an agreement and having it approved.

In part, one negotiates for a firm commitment from the other negotiator to support a proposed agreement. Unless the answer already was volunteered, counsel should directly inquire whether the other negotiator will recommend the tentative agreement. Counsel should demand that the other negotiator unequivocally state that the proposal will be recommended. Unless the other lawyer agrees immediately, one then should seek a firm commitment from the other negotiator to make a strong recommendation to the other party. The following types of statements may be used:

> "I expect you to make a strong recommendation."
>
> "I trust that you're going to push this to gain approval."
>
> "If I convince my client to go this far, will you do your best to convince your side to accept it?"

Whether to state this as a question or as an expectation depends on the other negotiator's personality and the relationship between the negotiators. These should be considered to anticipate whether the other negotiator will react more favorably to being asked, or to being told that the recommendation is expected. In either case, definite feedback must be obtained from the other negotiator so that a clear commitment or refusal is received.

Even if the other lawyer is influential with his or her client, counsel must analyze whether to demand that a proposal be transmitted to the other party without or against the other lawyer's recommendation. Unless clearly fruitless,

---

[186] Rodgers, *Negotiating and Settling Personal-Injury Cases,* 23 Trial 108 (1987).

the other negotiator's refusal to recommend or opposition should not deter counsel from pressing an appropriate position if necessary. The factors to be considered are whether:

1. The position has a reasonable chance of acceptance
2. Further concessions are unacceptable at all or unwise at that time
3. An overriding counterproductive reaction will occur from the other negotiator or the other party

If the other negotiator lacks such influence on the real decision maker, counsel's viewpoint shifts. In these situations, the negotiation now aims for an acceptable proposal that is anticipated to have a likelihood of approval by the other side before clear feedback is received. The degree of likelihood is affected by any need for closure at that point. If closure is not needed, informational tactics[187] or a trial proposal[188] can be used to generate feedback for further evaluation. Unfortunately, counsel sometimes must negotiate for the best proposal that seems appropriate at that time, even though it also seems unlikely to be approved by the other side.

Lastly, the answer to the third issue can also necessitate further changes in this tactic. If the other party normally operates, or may be operating, with the expectation that it can demand additional concessions after a tentative agreement is submitted to its real decision maker, then counsel must withhold some potential concessions so that they are available when additional demands are made. If, instead, the other party operates by accepting or rejecting tentative agreements without demanding further concessions, one should submit the best proposal that seems appropriate at that point. Again, this is dependent on whether a need for closure exists.

When faced with a setting in which no further concessions are likely to be sought, but in which rejection is a significant possibility, it is especially important that counsel begin the negotiation with a relatively high position and make a series of concessions before the proposal is transmitted. This allows the other negotiator to appear to have forced a better agreement for his or her side than one's client wanted to make. Receiving a proposed agreement that appears to contain concessions which were reluctantly made due to forceful bargaining by the other negotiator can influence the ultimate decision maker's opinion of the proposal. It can cause the real decision maker to perceive that the agreement is more favorable to its side than the agreement is in reality and thereby increase the chances that it will be approved.

Another situation involving a lack of authority on the part of the other negotiator that can arise is to be confronted by the position that compromise is impossible as a matter of policy on an issue. Counsel then must use information gathering to determine who established the policy, who has the power to change it or to make an exception to it, and the feasibility of altering or obtain-

---

[187] *See* **ch 4.**
[188] *See* **§5.08.**

ing an exception to the policy. Attempts to alter or obtain an exception to a policy can occur directly within the negotiation or through other avenues of approach to whoever has the authority to make the desired decision. If it is to be accomplished outside of the negotiation itself, the issue becomes whether this is to occur with the knowledge of the other negotiator, or secretly. Three criteria should be considered in deciding this question. These are:

1. The reaction of the other negotiator and of any other relevant persons
2. The other negotiator's goodwill
3. Any ethical prohibitions on direct communications between a lawyer and a party represented by counsel

Counsel must anticipate the reaction of the other negotiator, as well as of anyone else who needs to be considered. If there is a significant possibility that the other negotiator or someone else will act with influence to prevent the desired decision if disclosure is made, then a secret approach should be considered unless the second and third criteria dictate to the contrary.

In considering the second criteria, counsel must gauge whether the other negotiator's goodwill is of value. A secret approach to obtaining a policy change or exception without the other negotiator's knowledge may embarrass the other negotiator. It also can cause the other negotiator to resent what may be perceived as an improper attempt to circumvent his or her role. If the effort to alter or obtain an exception to the policy is successful, the other negotiator certainly will learn of it. Even if it is unsuccessful, the other negotiator may well discover the attempt. The risk of a negative reaction by the other negotiator must be evaluated in view of the likelihood of, and the benefits from, a successful attempt to affect the policy.

§5.28   Surprise

The tactic of surprise consists of unveiling startling new terms during a negotiation. The terms are structured to be, at least superficially, much more attractive to the other side. They are presented to catch the other party and its negotiator off guard. The negotiator introducing the surprise offer then presses for an immediate agreement. That negotiator points out, through a spontaneous and innocent sounding but well-planned presentation, the ways in which the new proposal meets the other side's prior objections or problems, and how it fulfills the other party's needs, interests, and goals. Demands, issues, and events also can be presented as surprises during the negotiation for a persuasive impact.

The tactic of surprise should be used only if:

1. It is likely to move the other party in the desired direction
2. The party introducing the surprise is desperate

The reason for exercising a degree of caution before engaging in a tactical surprise is that it can backfire. Instead of being persuaded, the surprise and

the attempt to induce a quick decision can cause the other p
tor to become distrustful or fearful, or to lose face. Any on
may lead that party or its negotiator to harden its position i.
moved towards the desired agreement.[189] When the other neg\
such a surprise, a countermeasure should be employed unless
clearly offers a net advantage for the client.

The counter to the tactic of surprise is to slow the process dow\ ⸗ounsel
can ask questions and insist on further explanations and elaborations. It is
appropriate to acknowledge a need for time to study the new proposal or the
new information. It also is fitting to firmly resist any pressure and to demand
an adjournment, if necessary, to allow adequate time to consider the matter.
This resistance to pressure and insistence on adequate time to respond applies
regardless of whether the negotiation is being conducted in person, by telephone, or through written communications.

Such countermeasures are equally necessary, even if they seem more difficult
to maintain, when surprise is skillfully used in conjunction with a deadline.[190]
On the other hand, this is by no means to suggest that it is always advantageous
to combine the tactics of surprise and deadlines. Indeed, there are undoubtedly
times when such a combination will:

1. Engender a reaction of resistance
2. Make the surprise seem more suspicious, and therefore make it more
    likely to produce adverse, rather than beneficial, effects

This should be carefully considered in planning the surprise.[191]

§5.29 Appealing to the Personal Interests of the Other Negotiator or a Non-Party Decision Maker

All negotiators have their own personal combinations of business, professional, social, psychological, and economic interests, even when they are not
negotiating for their own personal benefit. Likewise, when the real decision
maker is not personally the party, that decision maker also brings a similar set
of personal interests to the process. These personal interests are different
from, and may conflict with, those of the party being represented. During the
negotiation, an attorney must be aware of and exploit all legitimate opportunities to influence the other negotiator or the other party's real decision maker
through appeals to the personal interests of either one or both.

---

[189] C. Karrass, Give & Take: The Complete Guide to Negotiating Strategies and Tactics 215 (1974).

[190] See §5.26 regarding deadlines.

[191] See §9.08 concerning planning the timing of the negotiation.

Example 5-53

The strike of the professional football players in 1987 may have been caused by an appeal to a negotiator's personal interests in a negotiation 10 years earlier. The 1977 negotiation resulted in a collective bargaining agreement that arguably traded away the players' free agency rights for mandatory union dues and a closed shop. At that time, the union was financially weak. One commentator attributes the 1977 tradeoff to an appeal by management to the personal aspirations of the then head of the union to strengthen the union's treasury.[192]

Assuming that the real basis for resolving the 1977 professional football players strike was a negotiator's personal aspirations, it provides a sophisticated example of a successful appeal to such personal interests that shaped the structure of an agreement.

Appeals to personal interests may be particularly useful when the other negotiator is a government official or a member of another bureaucracy that may not wish to risk personal embarrassment. Any threat must be gauged based on the other negotiator's personality and likely reaction, as well as one's power to fulfill the threat. This analysis also applies to threats of negative personal consequences to other types of negotiators.

Example 5-54

"Look, we are negotiating with you because our general contractor has technical legal responsibility for the subcontractor's violation of Davis-Bacon requirements for these workers.[193] The violations were not our fault. In fact, as you have seen, we were defrauded by the subcontractor also. We are attempting to work this out with you in good faith. You are here under federal law as the United States government. The question has come up regarding whether we should withhold from the wages due and remit the withholding directly to the I.R.S. You take the position that we should just pay it to the workers and deal with the I.R.S. later if we are challenged, and that you will not help to clarify this with the I.R.S. Now, I recognize that there are different agencies, but this still is one country. There is only one federal government. You can't tell me one position as one agency, and then subject me to a possible contrary position by another agency when your only authority comes from the federal government. If you persist in saying that we must immediately agree to direct payments without I.R.S. clarification, we will be forced to make this into a political issue with our elected officials, and a media issue as well. It will be a good one. One federal agency, or I should say one particular

---

[192] *Former Agent Puts the Blame for NFL Strike*, Chicago Trib, Sept 24, 1987, §4, at 2, col. 4.

[193] Davis-Bacon concerns the wages paid by contractors under contracts with the federal government. *See* 40 USC §276a *et seq.*

middle level career service bureaucrat, threatening citizens to force them to possibly violate the law as interpreted by a different agency. Do you really want to force me to put you personally and your agency in that position? Doesn't it make sense to you to work together to clarify this with the I.R.S.? That won't cost you anything."

Example 5-55

"I have a client here on a minor charge. It is a misdemeanor that everywhere else would mean supervision, so that this young woman does not wind up with a criminal record. Supervision was a program for minor, first drug offenders sponsored by the State's Attorney, your office. Now you are telling me that, in this little branch court in the suburbs away from the main office, you don't like the program, so you will not use it?! You won't use your own office's program?! If you don't agree to use it now, I'm going to a telephone. And you are not going to want to think about all of the people that I'm going to call."

For attorneys, statutory fee award cases can create a potential divergence of the plaintiff's negotiator's interests and those of his or her client. In settlement negotiations, the fee for the plaintiff's attorney may be a point for personal appeal, unless before the negotiation begins, it has been explicitly provided for in the attorney-client contract. To avoid conflicting interests, fees can be based on a percentage of any settlement or otherwise be tied to the results. Court awarded fees still would be applied for in the event the case is decided on a verdict, rather than a settlement, with a provision to substitute or credit the awarded sum. In class actions, to avoid conflicting interests between class counsel's personal economic aspirations and relief for the class, there generally are two restrictions that should be followed:

1. Fees for class counsel cannot be negotiated until the relief for the class has been tentatively settled[194]
2. The court must approve any fees[195]

§5.30 Combinations of Tactics

Even more so than with strategies, tactics are used in combination with other tactics.[196] As described earlier, informational tactics are an integral part of every negotiation regardless of the client goal, the strategy, or the other tactics

---

[194] H. Newberg, Class Actions §§11.09 & 15.34 (Shepard's/McGraw-Hill, Inc 1985); McDonald v Chicago Milwaukee Corp, 565 F2d 416 (7th Cir 1977).

[195] Manual for Complex Litigation Second 171, in I (pt 2) J. Moore, Moore's Federal Practice (1986).

[196] See §3.16.

involved.[197] Tactics can be employed in any combination, as long as the tactics chosen do not undermine one's position by conflicting with each other in context, or creating an undesired impression of inconsistency. Whether the perception of inconsistency is desirable depends on whether it is:

1. Advantageous, in that it keeps the other side off balance
2. Disadvantageous, in that it creates an image of confusion, weakness, or unfairness that is counterproductive

§5.31 Summary and Review

  I. Preconditions
     A. Basically non-negotiable demands which must be agreed to before the remainder of the negotiation proceeds
     B. Required as a tradeoff for the right to commence or continue negotiating
     C. May be at the outset of the negotiation, or for a phase or issue
     D. Can be procedural or substantive
     E. Necessary conditions: (1) Power or (2) Clarify a term essential to deciding whether to invest time and energy in further negotiation
     F. Can be dangerous, so use with caution, especially for a cooperative client goal, problem solving strategy, or long-term relationship
  II. Making or Avoiding Making the First Offer
     A. Realistic first offer can establish the basic range for the negotiation
     B. Making the first offer effectively requires sufficient knowledge to be realistically high without conceding too much
     C. Client's time needs can dictate making the first offer
     D. Custom can affect who makes the first offer
     E. Useful for all client goals and strategies
  III. Demand Responses to Offers and Positions
     A. To avoid unnecessary uncertainties
     B. Clarify an ambiguous response by stating an understanding that the point has been agreed on by the parties, if it is reasonable to do so
     C. Allow agreement on substance without requiring agreement on reasons, except if that is important to interpret the agreement in the future
     D. For all client goals and strategies, except for purposes other than reaching agreement
     E. Includes the negotiator's agreement to recommend the proposal to the client

---

[197] *See* **ch 4.**

    F. Countermeasures include lack of authority, expressing a need for more information or to explore other issues first before responding, or silence

    G. Respond to unrealistic proposals with probes of the other side's perceptions, a firm rejection with an explanation, an equally unrealistic counteroffer, or a realistic counteroffer coupled with the caveat that splitting the difference is unacceptable

IV. Reciprocity

    A. Can be a demand for a reciprocal concession based on fairness

    B. Also can be a demand for a counteroffer after one's offer is rejected

    C. Requires that the offer is reasonable to justify reciprocity

    D. For all client goals, except aggressive ones inconsistent with concessions, and all strategies except no concessions or no further concessions

    E. Pitfalls of the norm of reciprocity: inappropriate concessions

    F. Countermeasures: awareness and judgment

V. Win/Win Proposals

    A. Unilaterally generate a mutually beneficial proposal that either expands the pie or involves little or no cost to one party but is valued by the other

    B. Not always possible

    C. Generate by concentrating on differences between the parties' beliefs, values, projections, tradeoffs, and risk preferences

    D. Use for client goals except those aggressive goals aimed at weakening or destroying the other party, and for strategies of no concessions, no further concessions, and negotiating for purposes other than reaching agreement

    E. Especially useful for cooperative client goals, and the problem solving and HRESSC strategies

VI. Concessions of Greater Value to One Party

    A. Either objective or subjective value

    B. May downplay the value of an item in order to obtain it

    C. Ideal concession has much greater value to the other party than to the client, resulting in a substantial net gain

    D. Can consist of demands inserted solely to be traded off later, or a series of small concessions to be traded for a larger one

    E. Use for client goals except certain aggressive ones not permitting concessions, and for all strategies except no concessions, no further concessions, or negotiating for purposes other than agreement

VII. Trial Proposals

    A. A sudden shift to significantly different arrangements or terms with great uncertainty about whether it will be accepted or rejected

    B. If rejected, it still may provide valuable information from the other side's reaction

C. Good for shifting the focus

D. Useful for all client goals and strategies except no concessions or no further concessions

E. Avoid large concessions, unless they are absolutely necessary or a firm reason can be provided to prevent being perceived as weak

VIII. Bargaining

    A. Offer to exchange one item for a specified other item

    B. Use reasoned positions

    C. Extremely useful for competitive goals, and useful for other goals and all strategies which permit the use of concessions

IX. Debate

    A. An exchange of views to persuade the other side to agree or acquiesce

    B. Requires creating an answer or direction of movement, and not stopping with a directionless argument or an unclear point for movement

    C. Useful with all client goals and strategies

    D. Often coupled with other tactics

    E. Concentrate on specific substantive or procedural items

    F. Carefully define issues

    G. Avoid personal attacks or personality conflicts unless necessary

    H. Persuade with strengths, facing or diminishing weaknesses, forcing the other side to argue its weaknesses, and citing objective criteria as the basis for reasons whenever feasible

    I. Motivate change by showing how the other side's needs can be met, and probe those needs as necessary in order to do so

    J. Appeal to negotiator's personal interests if appropriate

    K. Countermeasures

        1. Do not be awed by supposedly objective criteria

        2. Challenge the validity or applicability of reasons or principles

X. Conditional Proposals

    A. Offer conditioned on resolving some or all remaining issues

    B. Appropriate for all client goals and strategies involving multiple issues with possible trade-offs between issues

XI. Power

    A. Ability to force agreement on immediate issues

    B. Exercise only after careful consideration of any intended and unintended short-term and, especially, long-term effects

    C. Evaluate ramifications with constituent groups and third parties

    D. Various forms of power

    E. Legal and moral restrictions

    F. Appropriate for all client goals and strategies except, generally, for cooperative goals and the problem solving strategy

    G. Countermeasures include creating a sufficiently adverse potential effect to outweigh the gain from exercising power on a cost-benefit risk analysis

XII. Bluff
  A. Falsely taking a position as nonmodifiable or as able to create a consequence
  B. If bluff is called, destroys or seriously undermines credibility
  C. Maneuver out of having bluff called through "new information"
  D. Countermeasures include an outright refusal to acquiesce, selective information disclosure, debate and face-saving

XIII. Tone
  A. The atmosphere or climate of every negotiation
  B. Can affect whether agreement will result
  C. Unless pressure will work, avoid making the other side feel they are being manipulated into an unfavorable deal
  D. Anticipate and observe the other side's reaction to tone
  E. Consider long-run effects
  F. Generally, pleasant and nonadversarial or less adversarial tone for deal making, while more adversarial, but generally not unpleasant for litigation
  G. Use of assertive, but low-key, tone unless pressure, adversarial, or enthusiastic tones are indicated
  H. Enthusiasm for mutual benefits of agreement can create an atmosphere that increases the probability of agreement
  I. Temporary changes in tone can be persuasive
  J. One counter to an emotional tone is indicating understanding while focusing on the facts
  K. Use and guard against self need to receive a tone of respect, approval, or being liked, if it may cause inadvertent weakness
  L. Tone may need to change to be consistent with a shift in strategy
  M. Do not focus on tone and be misled about substantive concession patterns

XIV. Use of Alternative Opportunities
  A. With an outside party
  B. Mutually exclusive with reaching agreement in present negotiation
  C. May necessitate simultaneous negotiations with different parties
  D. Constitutes leverage in the negotiation
  E. Provides a measure of market terms and values, and a floor for any agreement depending on the degree of certainty that it is truly available
  F. Can result from legitimate fact creation
  G. May demand verification or other proof if suspect a bluff or face-saving tactics
  H. As an alternative, use informational tactics to probe whether the opportunity is certain or uncertain, and comparable or more or less advantageous
  I. Requires consideration of two reactive factors:
    1. Loyalty issue

2. Whether the other side will perceive it as a threat or an inappropriate demand for bids or being whipsawed

J. Can be used with any client goal or strategy

XV. Splitting The Difference

A. Use with all client goals

B. For all strategies except no concessions or no further concessions, or negotiating for purposes other than agreement unless used as a ploy

C. Especially useful for deadlock-breaking concessions only, problem solving, and closure

D. Effective when (1) a relatively small difference exists, and (2) a split is fair

E. Unreasonable but proportionately unimportant difference can be appropriate to split if a cost-benefit risk analysis concludes that a resolution is preferable to investing time and energy or risking loss of an available agreement

F. Beware of creating an always split the difference precedent, and communicate an unwillingness to do so to the other party

G. Split large difference if (1) within authority and (2) total deadlock after exhausting other approaches or (3) time problem dictates moving for closure

H. Do not use as an easy way to avoid more difficult negotiation unless cost effective

I. Manipulate with high initial offer and giving smaller concessions than those received if possible, while guarding against such manipulation

XVI. Focus/Downplay

A. Give false clue of interest and value

B. To minimize cost of obtaining an item as a purchaser, or maximizing its price as a seller

XVII. Creating a Psychological Commitment for Agreement

A. Using the process of negotiation itself

B. May display professional enthusiasm for benefits to both parties from general concept of reaching agreement or points already resolved

C. Avoid enthusiasm for agreement if client needs to appear disinterested to prevent being perceived as overly eager or weak

D. May focus on benefits for the negotiator personally

E. Use work group if possible to undermine the negotiator's loyalty to the other party, while resisting it for oneself to prevent conflicts of interest

F. Avoid becoming overly psychologically committed to reaching agreement or unduly fearful of losing a deal, while seeking to get the other side to become too psychologically committed because of its expenditures of time, effort, and costs, or through "supercrunch"

G. In litigation, beware of becoming so enamored of battle that one is blinded to an advantageous settlement, or unduly fearful so that one's position is undervalued

H. Lowball: Hidden costs are sprung after the offer is accepted in a dangerous maneuver that, unless successfully disguised, can create deep distrust; counter by demanding full information before responding to an offer

XVIII. Face-Saving

A. Encourage a change of position by creating a justification for the other party which avoids embarrassment

B. Reasonably ignoring assertions of non-negotiable positions

C. Cite new information

D. Make a meaningless concession that can be treated as real

E. Interpret the other side's position without becoming condescending or unfair

F. Recognize subtle requests by those too embarrassed or reluctant to ask directly

G. Behave in a nonthreatening, nonintimidating manner

H. Make proposals that appear consistent with the other party's values and self-image

I. Break a deadlock while allowing the saving of face by altering the terms, tone, or participants

J. Tell an appropriate and funny story

K. Use with all client goals and all strategies except an aggressive one if it is aimed at humiliating or embarrassing the other side

XIX. Inserting New Issues

A. To create an opportunity to gain or make concessions

B. Often requires planning so that issues are saved until needed, although it may arise spontaneously through creative thought

C. Includes disassembling package deals

D. Use to make a losing negotiation appear to be a victory to outside parties

E. Avoid appearing to be unfair or in bad faith by using before agreement is reached on the issue against which the tradeoff will be made

F. For any client goal and strategy

G. Countermeasures include refusing to negotiate the new issue, demanding the reopening of all issues, injecting one's own additional issues, or termination of the negotiation

XX. Focusing on the Process

A. Use when the parties or negotiators clash or struggle over how to conduct the negotiation, rather than the substantive terms for the parties, to the extent that the negotiation cannot proceed productively

B. Four steps: (1) Stop and reflect; (2) Negotiators agree to resolve blockage; (3) Resolve the blockage; (4) Return to negotiating substantive issues

      C. Be nonaccusatory if that will lead to cooperation

      D. Can arise due to a power struggle, emotional outbursts, distrust, confusion, or misunderstanding

      E. Allows discussion of concerns, misunderstandings, confusion, or disagreements about how to proceed in the negotiation

      F. Includes threats to reveal conduct to others

      G. Countermeasures: (1) Reflect carefully and accept or reject without becoming unsettled; (2) Switch strategy or tactics if appropriate; (3) Explain reasons for agreeing or disagreeing with the other negotiator's analysis of the process

XXI. Creation of Movement

      A. Take the initiative when the negotiation is bogged down, if appropriate for the client's goals

      B. Failure to take the initiative can doom the negotiation even when a zone of agreement exists

      C. May use information disclosure, fact creation, face saving, injecting a new issue, focus on the process, allies, media or community pressure, alternative dispute resolution, new instructions, or a change of negotiators

      D. Can necessitate overcoming emotional or communications difficulties

      E. If one issue is creating an impasse, it may be better to defer that issue while resolving others

XXII. Deadlock

      A. Create temporary impasse to test the other side's strength and resolve

      B. Use as a temporary measure when there is a low risk that the other side will terminate, one has a face-saving way to break the impasse if necessary, and closure is inappropriate

      C. Also useful for delay under a strategy of negotiating for purposes other than reaching agreement

      D. Can lead to hostility, frustration, and locking in of positions

      E. Countermeasures include linkage with other negotiations as a form of injecting a new issue, focus on the process, informational tactics, adjournment, redefining the issues, problem solving, win/win, fact creation to demonstrate strength or will to resist, concede first as an explicitly one-time maneuver, and a threat to terminate the negotiation

XXIII. Adjournment

      A. A temporary halt of the negotiation which is understood to be resumed later

      B. To regroup, change mood, obtain authority, deal with other matters

      C. Allows each side time to think, which may be a positive or negative factor depending on the status of the negotiation

      D. For all client goals and strategies, except for closure

    E. Use marathon bargaining only if physically and mentally at least as tough as the other negotiator, and it will not create counter-productive hostility in the other side

    F. Open-ended adjournment can be used to create an impression of disinterest or general uncertainty, if the risk of termination does not mandate against it

XXIV. Patience

    A. Use when pressure will not work, by allowing the other side to have time to absorb new ideas and become comfortable after calm analysis

    B. Can demonstrate fairness or resolve, causing the other party to lower its expectations

    C. Deadlines are a countermeasure

XXV. Deadlines

    A. Use to avoid loss of alternative opportunities, because actions must be taken unless an offer is accepted, if the cost basis of the offer is subject to change, or to force a procrastinating party to make a decision

    B. Give a reason for the deadline so that it does not appear to be an artificial power play which can cause resentment

    C. Can create time pressure increasing the size and speed of concessions if a failure to reach agreement has greater adverse consequences for one party than the other

    D. May lead to premature termination of negotiation

    E. Countermeasures include a face-saving attempt to force modification if the deadline is a bluff, fact creation changing the benefit or appropriateness of enforcing the deadline, and creating an incentive for prompt agreement obviating the need for a deadline

    F. If one negotiator faces an internal deadline imposed by the client while the other does not, that negotiator may be forced into weakening positions planned or undertaken

XXVI. Dealing with Those Who Lack Authority

    A. The other negotiator lacks formal authority

    B. The other negotiator may screen, probe, and messenger information, or also may have real influence over the decision maker

    C. If unsure about whether the other negotiator has any real authority or substantial influence, it is legitimate to ask without seeking the substance or details of the authority

    D. Use other forms of information gathering as well, to learn the other negotiator's influence or lack of it

    E. Consider requiring a negotiator with authority as a precondition

    F. Evaluate whether the other party is likely to demand further concessions once any proposal is transmitted to its decision maker, and withhold some concessions if appropriate

    G. If the other negotiator has influence over a decision maker, press for an agreement to recommend a proposal

    H. Demand proposals be transmitted to the other party without or against the other negotiator's recommendation if further concessions are unwise, and the attempt will not be clearly fruitless or counterproductive

    I. Negotiate to appear to have been forced to make concessions, if that will cause the other negotiator to be more enthusiastic about advocating the proposal as having been won and thereby make it more appealing to the other party

    J. Circumvent an obstinate or unreasonable negotiator unless the attempt is likely to be counterproductive or is ethically prohibited

    K. If confronted by a policy prohibiting needed or desired concessions, probe to determine whether modification or exceptions are possible and, if so, the identity of the person with the power to act

XXVII. Surprise

    A. Unveil startling new terms that are at least superficially more attractive than the prior terms

    B. Press for immediate agreement

    C. Persuade with explanation of how the offer meets the other party's objections, problems, needs, interests, or goals

    D. Use if it is likely to succeed, or due to desperation

    E. Be cautious, since it can backfire if the other party resents, distrusts, or becomes fearful

    F. Counter by slowing the process

    G. May combine with a deadline, unless that will engender too much suspicion or resistance

XXVIII. Appeals to Personal Interests of Other Negotiator or a Non-Party Decision Maker

    A. Exploit legitimate opportunities to influence the outcome by appeals to the personal, business, professional, social, psychological, and economic interests of the other negotiator

    B. The same principle applies to the personal interests of the other party's decision maker, if that person or group is distinct from the other party itself

    C. The appeal may consist of threatening negative personal consequences, depending on the power to fulfill the threat and the other negotiator's personality, which determines the probable reaction

XXIX. Combinations of Tactics

    A. Generally should be utilized

    B. Use inconsistency if it will keep the other side off balance

    C. Avoid inconsistency if it creates an impression of confusion, weakness, or unfairness that is counterproductive

Tactics Involving Other Parties

6

§6.01   Introduction
§6.02   Active Client Participation
§6.03   Negotiating Teams
§6.04   Judicial Settlement Conferences
§6.05   Allies
§6.06   Media or Community Pressure
§6.07   Alternative Dispute Resolution
§6.08   Class Actions
§6.09   Multiple Parties
§6.10   Gifts and Entertainment
§6.11   Summary and Review

§6.01   Introduction

Some tactics involve the participation or involvement of persons other than the two primary negotiators. This happens when the negotiator chooses to use active client participation, negotiating teams, media or community pressure, allies, or alternative dispute resolution.[1] At other times, the participation of others is required by law or ordered by a court.[2] Whatever the precise situation, counsel must understand and take into account the roles played by these additional participants and their effect on the process, in order to effectively negotiate in these circumstances.

---

[1] *See* §§6.02, 6.03, 6.05, 6.06, & 6.07.
[2] *See* §§6.04 & 6.08.

§6.02   Active Client Participation

During the course of a negotiation, the client is always involved as the ultimate decision maker on substantive settlement decisions. In some negotiations, the client plays an additional, more active role by directly participating in negotiation sessions.

The decision on the degree of client involvement does not depend on the client goal or the strategy that is chosen. The tactic of active client participation can be implemented with any client goal or strategy. Instead, the decision to use or to refrain from using this tactic is based on pragmatic criteria. The factors that determine its efficacy, and thus whether it should be chosen for a specific negotiation, are described below.[3]

The first factor concerns any negotiations conducted directly by the client before counsel became involved. Some clients, regardless of their level of skill and the advisability of doing so, negotiate the price and other basic terms before engaging counsel. This can be effective for the client who has excellent negotiating skills and a knowledge of the market values and practices. It can be quite disadvantageous, though, for clients who lack that degree of skill and knowledge. However, the lawyer may not have an opportunity to influence the prospective client's decision to do so. Once the basic terms have already been agreed to, counsel must attempt to create as many protections and gain as many advantages as possible within the framework instituted by the client.

Certain clients are skilled negotiators who are active and experienced in the very type of negotiation that is being conducted. Usually, these are sophisticated business clients who are perfectly capable of negotiating the basic terms of the matter themselves. In addition, to be effective, the client is not overly emotional regarding the issues or parties in the specific negotiation. Counsel's role in such situations is:

1.   To provide advice on the tax, financial, or other substantive or legal matters within the lawyer's expertise

2.   At times, to assist in or to negotiate certain terms or portions of the agreement that are deemed to be technical matters for counsel

3.   Normally, to document the agreement

In such instances, the client may initiate the negotiation of the basic framework and the key terms without counsel, and may participate actively throughout the negotiation. Other times, counsel will handle the negotiation. In addition, the client and the attorney may decide to use some hybrid system of joint or alternating participation.

Assuming that direct, active client participation is not the normal course, the analysis for deciding whether to choose active client participation begins

---

[3] On occasion in litigation, a judge will require that the client be present at a pretrial conference to discuss settlement. Of course, to the extent that this is required, there is no choice about having some degree of client participation. *See* **§6.04.** Also, at times in litigation, the parties' depositions are used to try to further the negotiation. *See* **§7.04.**

by examining the advantages of having the client absent from the negotiating sessions. The reason to commence the analysis from this perspective is because the client's absence from the negotiating sessions is generally more effective than the client's presence.

In most instances, the client has sought legal representation due at least in part to the lawyer's supposed negotiating skills, as well as particular, needed substantive knowledge. To the extent that the attorney is the one with the negotiating skills, the client should be directly involved in the actual negotiating sessions only if there is a distinct, definite advantage in doing so.

The client's absence can prevent negotiating errors. If the client is present, various mistakes can occur due to the client's lack of negotiating skill or because of the client's personal involvement. In part, the attorney serves as a "buffer" to prevent heated exchanges between the party and the other side that can poison the atmosphere and destroy an opportunity for a good settlement.[4]

The client, verbally or nonverbally, may disclose information which should not be disclosed at all, or at least not at that time.[5] This disclosure may be made by actual statements or admissions, questions that the client asks, or visible reactions to the other negotiator's offers or positions, among other methods of direct or indirect communication. It often is difficult or impossible for many clients to play the proper role on a negotiation team.[6] This role includes, if necessary, being silent and impassive except for certain controlled reactions that are desired as part of the negotiation plan. A client can reveal an eagerness or anxiety that indicates a weakness or a willingness to accept the other party's position without obtaining further concessions. The lawyer is supposed to be a professional sufficiently skilled to control such verbal or nonverbal disclosure of information.

If the client is present, the client also may mistakenly and prematurely accept the other party's offer, while counsel is properly still seeking to improve the offer through further negotiations.

The client's presence also may cause the negotiator to err. A negotiator, who perceives that the client expects to hear certain things said, may make the mistake of posturing just to satisfy the client's perceived expectations. That posturing, though, may be wasteful and even counterproductive to the extent of blocking progress in the negotiation.

Similarly, the client's presence usually prevents the type of candid exchange that two skilled, professional negotiators engage in when they are alone. The degree of candor is not in violation of the client's interests, but instead, it furthers those interests by searching to determine whether a middle ground exists for agreement. The ability to candidly exchange selective information is a crucial one for a professional negotiator.

In addition, when the client is present, counsel may need to refrain from appearing to be overly friendly or candid with the other negotiator, because

---

[4] Sandels, *Negotiation in Business Litigation,* in Attorney's Guide to Negotiation 11-6 (1979).

[5] See **§4.02** regarding disclosing information.

[6] See **§6.03** concerning the use of negotiating teams.

the client can mistake professional friendliness or candor for disloyalty. This tendency by clients is more prevalent in litigation, with its often hostile undertones, than in deal making, although it can be present in both situations. The danger is especially strong in criminal cases. If a criminal defense attorney is overly friendly with the prosecutor, the client may even view such conduct as a conspiracy by the attorneys against him or her.[7]

If the client is going to be present, and if friendliness or special candor is fitting, unless the client already understands that fact, it should be explained to the client in advance. It may be known that the client already has that understanding if either:

1. The client is well known to the lawyer
2. It is a business matter with a sophisticated client in which the degree of friendliness or candor is not unusual

On the other hand, the client's presence at some negotiations may be beneficial in a variety of ways. These include:

1. Expediency
2. Unity
3. Relationship
4. Communication

The client's presence can expedite matters because the client is there to answer questions and to make decisions. However, this function also can usually be accomplished without the client's physical presence at the negotiation through telephone conduct with the client.

However, the client who is able to avoid unwarranted disclosures and premature acceptances can demonstrate a unity of position with what is being articulated by counsel. This strengthens the client's position. Nevertheless, any potential benefit from demonstrated unity must be weighed against the possible inhibition of a candid exchange between the negotiators.

The client's presence may benefit the relationship between the parties when a goal of the negotiation is for the parties to embark on a working relationship with each other. In these situations, the parties' presence at the negotiation can begin their relationship of working together, as well as provide a common, clear understanding of the terms and spirit of the agreement. The parties may be able to experiment with developing a methodology for working together by using problem solving to resolve disputes and disagreements. Their experience with each other in the negotiation gives the parties an opportunity to decide whether they are sufficiently compatible for the contemplated working relationship.

Not every negotiation for a working relationship, though, requires the active participation of the clients. In many instances, they will have previously inter-

---

[7] Penn, Jr., *Negotiation In A Criminal Case-Defense*, in Attorney's Guide to Negotiation 13-7 (1979).

acted or be interacting outside of the negotiation sessions anyway. That inter-action may be sufficient for them to determine whether they can have a good working relationship.

In other instances, the clients' participation should be limited to certain por-tions of the negotiations. This can largely avoid the potential difficulties arising from the client's attendance described earlier, while still providing an opportu-nity for the clients to work together in the negotiation as an experiment to determine their compatibility.

Lastly, there may be a time for the clients to be encouraged to negotiate directly. At least in part, this may be without counsel, or with only a minimal presence of counsel. Although unusual, this is sometimes helpful in continuing or reestablishing a working relationship between the parties. This is not in any way an attempt to unethically communicate directly with a party who is repre-sented by counsel. Its purpose is to allow limited, direct interaction between the clients on issues that are best left to them. Several examples will illustrate this point. One of the ways in which this can occur is where there has been prior client-to-client negotiating in the same transaction.

Example 6-1

The seller and the purchaser of an industrial building had negotiated the price before either engaged an attorney. An inspection of the premises revealed a latent defect in the roof, although the cost of repair was rela-tively small in comparison to the purchase price. Nevertheless, the cost of repair was still a significant sum. Both clients desired to meet at the site, view the roof, and determine an appropriate adjustment of the price that they had previously set without legal advise. Their desire to do so without lawyers was based on avoiding further legal fees, resolving the matter on the spot, and their own comfort with their ability to negotiate a fair price. They, in fact, quickly succeeded in negotiating a fair compro-mise of the issue.

Lawyers' schedules can create an expediency issue. On rare occasions and under extreme circumstances, the undue unavailability of the party's attorney may necessitate direct negotiation between the parties. This should be strictly limited to rare and extreme occasions, as otherwise, it would be an unethical attempt to circumvent the party's lawyer. Extremely careful planning with the client almost invariably is essential for such a direct client negotiation.

Example 6-2

The seller of a medical practice needed a quick decision by a potential purchaser. The seller's attorney's repeated efforts to contact the buyer's lawyer were unsuccessful, because the purchaser's lawyer was never avail-able and did not return any of the phone calls. The seller, therefore, was forced to contact the potential buyer directly in order to communicate the requirement of a quick response to the seller's offer.

As noted above, one of the circumstances which can make direct client-to-client negotiating desirable is when the reestablishment of a working relationship is sought.

Example 6-3

Two law firms previously had a working relationship with each other before one instituted litigation against the other concerning a contingent sublease of space. With authorization from the law firm clients, counsel for the parties had worked out an agreement which basically resolved the matter. The agreement included one firm's subleasing certain space to the other firm. The nature of the sublease required some future interaction between the parties. However, because of the litigation, the parties had not been speaking to each other for the most part. A few minor details remained to be resolved. Both negotiators agreed to have client representatives present to discuss and to settle those details. The client representatives were both partners from the law firms. As the two negotiators observed the client representatives begin to interact in a fruitful manner, they proceeded into an adjacent room ostensibly to discuss the form of the documentation that was needed. The negotiators deliberately left the client representatives together, however, so that they would have an opportunity to reestablish a working relationship. When the two negotiators returned, the minor details had been settled, and the client representatives were talking in a relaxed manner.

If the other negotiator appears to be blocking a settlement or misinterpreting the situation, a session with the clients present can be useful. Counsel then can communicate directly to, or at least in front of, the other party. This may either deter the behavior that is blocking progress, or eliminate the misunderstanding. To avoid potential errors by one's own client, counsel may seek to have only the other party present if that:

1.   Is feasible
2.   Will not inhibit the other party from really participating

Another form of direct client participation is through statements to the public or to other third parties that are designed to influence the outcome of the negotiation. This aspect will be examined in §§6.05 and 6.06 regarding the use of allies and media or community pressure.

In litigation, the clients' presence in the negotiating process can occur at a pretrial settlement conference, or even at a deposition. These situations will be discussed in §§6.04 and 7.04, respectively.

§6.03   Negotiating Teams

Lone negotiators are, in general, more common than negotiating teams with multiple members. The reasons for this general practice are the cost-benefit ratio, style, and potential conflict among the negotiators.

The relative costs and benefits from using a negotiating team may not justify its use. It often is not cost effective to have more than one negotiator. Frequently, a second or additional negotiators will not add anything of sufficient significance to justify their involvement.

Even aside from the cost factor, working as part of a negotiating team may conflict with the style of the person in charge of handling the negotiation. That negotiator may prefer to work alone, and may not feel the need for any assistance in the actual negotiating sessions.

Negotiating teams also have the potential for internal conflict. Multiple negotiators may act inconsistently with each other. Such inconsistency weakens their party's position, unless it is done as a deliberate role-playing maneuver (as discussed later in this section). Although one negotiator will be designated as the leader, the other(s) may make disclosures or otherwise react in ways that are counterproductive to the approaches being taken by the leader. Even when the other team members are not supposed to make statements, their nonverbal reactions can disclose information that was not intended to be disclosed. In addition, it often is extremely difficult for team members to be present without becoming more actively involved than was planned. This is because, either correctly or due to ego, at some point the other team members may strongly believe that they have something to add which the team leader has missed.

There are, however, five potential benefits in using a negotiating team instead of a lone negotiator. These potential benefits must be compared to the factors discussed above that favor a single negotiator in order to determine the efficiency of using the team approach. The potential benefits are:

1. Active client participation
2. Specialized knowledge
3. Collective judgment
4. Notes and observation
5. Role playing

The first potential benefit is that of active client participation when such participation is desirable. The factors for deciding whether this is desirable in a specific negotiation were examined above.[8]

Second, there may be a need for specialized knowledge of law, engineering, personnel, the facts, or some other area involved in the substantive issues under consideration. If no one negotiator possesses all of the necessary knowledge, and there is a need to have someone with the knowledge physically present in the negotiating sessions, a team approach should be used.

The third potential advantage can be found in the old adage, "two heads are better than one." The nature of the negotiation may be such that the collective wisdom and judgment of more than one negotiator is desired in the negotiating session itself. Most often, this occurs when a creative, new approach appears to be necessary.

---

[8] *See* **§6.02.**

It also may be that the negotiation is sufficiently complex that an additional person is useful to keep notes on the interaction during the negotiating session. This can be for purposes of having a periodic recapitulation during the course of the negotiation. Moreover, the otherwise uninvolved team member may be in a better position to observe the process than the leader, who must constantly interact with the other side as well as observe. Thus, the notes and observations of the less involved team member can be utilized for analysis during the negotiation process, during breaks, or between sessions.

The other potential benefit is that the team approach creates the possibility of role playing. In one type of scenario, a team member is designated as the information gathering player, while another observes during this stage.

The best known team role playing is that which is commonly known as "Mutt and Jeff" or "good cop and bad cop." In these roles, one negotiator is hard, tough, and difficult, while the other is nice, reasonable, and more accommodating. Together, they seek to manipulate the other party's negotiator with this psychological ploy. Perhaps unfortunately, this approach is so well known that it is generally no longer effective. In fact, when multiple negotiators on the same team spontaneously and genuinely disagree so that a "Mutt and Jeff" situation exists in reality, the other party's negotiator may refuse to believe that their actions are honest.

Since the "Mutt and Jeff" game is so well known, if it is to be effective, the team must utilize a creative, dynamic version of it to disguise it sufficiently. The roles may be used only at certain points. Team members also can switch roles at various points. Any other version that disguises the true nature of the tactic can be used as well.

Countermeasures against the "tough guy" half of a "Mutt and Jeff" team include:

1. Exhaust the "tough guy" by not responding and then ignore him or her[9]
2. Bypass the "tough guy"[10]
3. Use an unreasonable "tough guy" yourself[11]
4. Publicly blame the "tough guy" for sidetracking the negotiation[12]
5. Terminate the negotiation, either temporarily or indefinitely with the express explanation that it is due to the "tough guy's" conduct[13]
6. Predict what the "tough guy" is about to do, or identify the tactic that is being used and the tough's guy's role in it so that the other side becomes reluctant to engage in a known charade[14]

---

[9] C. Karrass, Give & Take: The Complete Guide to Negotiating Strategies and Tactics 80 (1974).

[10] *Id.*

[11] *Id.*

[12] *Id.*

[13] *Id.*

[14] *Id.*

7.   Identify the tactic and terminate the negotiation, either temporarily or indefinitely, with the express explanation that it is due to the use of the tactic

8.   Threaten to use countermeasures two, four, five, and six unless the "Mutt and Jeff" routine ceases

Some of these countermeasures involve predicting, describing, or identifying what the other negotiators are doing. These countermeasures can cause them to feel embarrassed or angry at having been unmasked or having lost face. If this causes the other negotiators to lose their emotional equilibrium, the time may be ripe to push for a concession or movement.

Example 6-4

".... So now if you are ready to stop playing good guy-bad guy in particular, and games in general, perhaps we can make some progress. Now there is really no valid reason why we should not agree to. . . ."

Whenever team negotiations are used, especially careful planning is essential. Responsibilities must be established for gathering data and needed information beforehand, as well as for handling logistics. The functions and the roles of each of the members of the team must be defined for the planning stage and in the negotiating sessions themselves. The team members all must clearly understand their duties and responsibilities. All must be aware of the limits on information disclosure, concession patterns, and positions.

A leader is essential. The designated leader must have firm control over the other members. Quiet directives and adjournments should be employed freely by the leader to maintain that control.

During the negotiation, the leader must be in a position to maintain both physical control and continuity of the team. At the same time, the leaders of each team normally should be across from, or next to, each other.[15] The purpose of this is to:[16]

1.   Facilitate communications

2.   Allow a clear view of nonverbal communication

3.   Demonstrate the leader's power within the team

The leader may not always be an attorney, even though there is an attorney on the team. A negotiating team for a labor union may be structured as:

1.   A leader and main spokesperson

2.   A note taker

3.   A financial expert

---

[15] C. Karrass, *supra* note 9, at 187.

[16] *Id.*

4. A production expert

5. An attorney who, unlike the union members themselves, does not have an ongoing working relationship with management

By not having an ongoing working relationship with management, unlike the union members, the lawyer is freer to:

1. Criticize management

2. Raise difficult points

3. Be a target for management's criticisms

This point regarding the attorney's role on a negotiating team is not just limited to labor-management negotiations. It may be applicable whenever the other party's negotiating team has members with whom the client needs to maintain a good, close, working relationship. Similarly, if the other side also is employing such a negotiating team, it may be preferable to focus on the other party's lawyer when making criticisms or in focusing on difficult points. Whether these general criteria are advantageous to follow in a particular negotiation also depends on the specific individuals that comprise the rest of the team, and how they will behave if the lawyer is the focus of the attention.

When faced with a negotiating team, in both planning and the ongoing assessment during the negotiation, it must be decided which members of the team are going to be the focus of communications. In addition to the considerations concerning attorneys noted above, this assessment may vary during the negotiation depending on the issues and on spontaneous developments. The person or persons to be focused on should be either:

1. Those who are more receptive and are capable of convincing other members of their team

2. The difficult member(s) who must be neutralized either by showing that they are not intimidating, or by overwhelming them

The number of negotiators can be important. Some people tend to become intimidated and overwhelmed when they are outnumbered. Others do not care. Still others react defensively and become hardened. If the latter reaction is a significant possibility, the negotiator should take steps to indicate the size of the negotiating team to his or her counterpart.

The corollary is that if a negotiator fears being outnumbered, then the following precautions should be utilized:

1. An agreement should be sought in advance regarding the size of the negotiating team

2. A team should be assembled which avoids the possibility of being seriously outnumbered

The latter option should not be chosen, however, where there is concern that this will inadvertently result in outnumbering the other side, thereby causing it to have a defensive reaction.

At the same time, unwieldy numbers of team members must be avoided. Beyond a certain size, the danger of internal conflicts and a loss of coordination of efforts outweighs the benefits of adding members to the negotiating team. The appropriate, maximum number for a given negotiation will depend on the nature and scope of the negotiation, as well as on the potential team members' specialized talents and personalities.

§6.04 Judicial Settlement Conferences

Judges may act as mediators to:[17]

1. Facilitate negotiations

2. Impose deadlines to prevent protracted negotiations

3. Deflate unrealistically high aspirations

4. Suggest potential positions or principles for a compromise

5. Oversee the process

Unlike some but not all independent arbitrators, judges can have conflicting goals. Case management concerns can dictate pressure on one or more parties regardless of fairness. Unhappiness with a litigant's position can consciously or unconsciously affect subsequent judicial rulings if no settlement is reached. For these reasons, some court systems designate a separate judge to conduct the settlement conference. If the trial judge also is the settlement judge, counsel may want to either have or refrain from having a judicial settlement conference, due to its potential impact on subsequent stages of the case. Of course, counsel may not be given a choice in the matter.

A settlement conference may be spontaneous, short, and informal. It may consist of a colloquy in open court. Longer discussions in the form of a full, scheduled conference are prevalent as well, with the agreed agenda being settlement. Depending on the court system, the judge, and whether the case is criminal or civil, a judge first may require the parties to waive any right of disqualification based on statements that are made in the settlement conference. This is so that the judge avoids being trapped into a recusal for cause.

For some pretrial settlement conferences, the judge or local court rules may require that the client be present. Where a party is a corporation or a governmental body or agency, the requirement will be for a representative of the party to be present, often a representative with settlement authority or decision-

---

[17] H. Raiffa, The Art and Science of Negotiation 225-26 (1982).

making power.[18] The purposes of this requirement usually involve authority and persuasion. The court wants the matter to be settled and seeks to facilitate a settlement by having the decision maker with the ultimate authority present. This avoids the necessity of adjournment while the lawyers leave to confer with their clients.[19] As to persuasion, the court may believe that it can best influence the parties with the court's opinions if the parties hear those views directly from the judge.

The latter point requires serious consideration of potential positive and negative effects. To the extent that counsel believes that the other attorney is unwilling or unable to convince the opposing party of the realities of the case so that a realistic negotiation can be held, counsel may welcome and encourage the requirement that the parties be present. This also can be true if counsel wants his or her own client to hear certain views expressed by the court in order to reinforce counsel's advice and to persuade an unrealistic client to be realistic about a potential settlement.

Those potential benefits from having the judge express his or her views directly to the clients must be weighed against three potential detriments. These detriments consist of a possible lack of skill on the part of the judge, the potential for undue pressure by the judge on the client, and the reaction of a weak client.

Many judges are not particularly skilled at fairly mediating or otherwise facilitating a settlement. They can lack the mediation or "people skills" necessary to properly play their role at such a settlement conference.

Some judges desire simply to force a settlement, if at all possible, by unduly pressuring both parties or the weaker party.[20] This often takes the form of pressure to split all differences, or to otherwise agree without due regard for the realities of the case. Such undue pressure is especially difficult to resist when the judge is the trier of fact.[21] Even when there will be a jury trial, though, the judge can influence the jury in both subtle and overt ways,[22] as well as by pre-

---

[18] At times, with some government entities, it will not be possible to have a representative with authority or the ultimate decision maker present due to the legal structure of the government. See §5.27 regarding dealing with those who lack authority.

[19] If this is the court's only concern, being able to reach the client by phone during the pretrial conference may be a viable alternative to having the client present if the latter would be difficult.

[20] At the opposite end of the scale are those judges who are totally ineffectual at moving the parties towards a settlement because they do no more than inquire as to the parties' positions or inclination towards settlement.

[21] Indeed, to avoid any appearance of undue pressure, many judges refuse to be involved in settlement conferences if they will be the trier of fact unless the case is settled. Others, however, take the position that their taking an active settlement role will not bias their role as the trier of fact in a bench trial. Manual For Complex Litigation Second 154, in I (pt 2) J. Moore, Moore's Federal Practice (1986).

[22] A judge may subtly influence a jury through physical expressions, tones, and attitudes which are impossible to capture on the record for appeal. The Supreme Court has long recognized the enormous influence which the trial judge can exert over the jury. Starr v United States, 153 US 614 (1894); Quercia v United States, 289 US 466 (1933). In reversing a murder conviction due to the trial judge's comments, the *Starr* court noted

trial rulings. Accordingly, counsel and the client do not want to anger or upset the judge during the settlement conference if it can be avoided. Therefore, the lawyer and the client will need to plan and be prepared to be as accommodating as possible to the court, with the caveat that they will not compromise their objectives unless they are genuinely persuaded by the merits of the judge's comments. This includes consideration of the likely outcome of a trial if the judge will be the trier of fact and has indicated views on the liability or damages issues.[23]

The attorney must learn to persuade the court that a settlement is not feasible and, if necessary, to withstand pressure from the court to settle without offending the judge. If the judge's rulings will, or may be, affected, the lawyer must counsel the client about that danger before the client decides on a final position.

A weak client can also create a severe problem. The client may be weak in the sense that he or she is likely to be overwhelmed by the judge's comments and pressure, when in fact the judge is just probing and would pressure the other party if the client displayed some resistance. A client should be prepared by proper counseling to play an effective active role, or a passive one with counsel taking a strong lead.

The most effective means of judicial settlement pressure, however, may be simply setting a date for trial.[24] A judicial settlement conference is most likely to be effective if a relatively near trial date has already been set, or if the parties know that such a trial date will be set if the case does not settle.[25]

§6.05 Allies

Allies are those who can favorably influence the other party and its position in the negotiation. The tactic of using allies is appropriate with any strategy and with any client goal. Its only limitations are:

1. Whether allies exist
2. The cost of using allies
3. Whether using allies will backfire

The initial question is whether any persons or entities who are potentially effective allies exist in the particular situation. Often, there is no one with the

---

that when a jury hears the trial judge speak, the judge's "lightest word or intimation is received with deference, and may prove controlling." *Starr*, 153 US at 626, *quoted with approval in Quercia*, 289 US at 470. Especially if the issues are close on the merits or if it is a matter of the trial court's discretion, a judge can overtly affect the jury through rulings on motions in limine, on evidentiary objections, and on jury instructions.

[23] To prevent the expression of such views, some court systems use a judge other than the trial judge to conduct settlement conferences.

[24] G. Spence, Trial By Fire 168 (1986).

[25] See also §7.10 regarding the timing of settling litigation.

requisite degree of influence who can be brought into the negotiation, either due to their unwillingness or their lack of power.

The next issue is cost. The assistance of the potential ally may not be free. It can involve either an economic cost, a noneconomic cost, or both. The ally's assistance itself may be the subject of an entire, separate negotiation. The potential cost of the ally's assistance must be weighed against the potential benefits of the proposed intervention.

The last issue needing to be evaluated is whether there is any possibility that the attempt to involve the potential ally will backfire, and that the potential ally instead will lend its support to the other side. This can occur from belief, principle, self-interest, or from a refusal to pay the economic or noneconomic costs demanded by the potential ally.

The ally can have its own agenda or priorities. For example, an international or sister union's participation in the negotiation process can shift the focus to items which are not of real interest or of significant value to the local union.[26]

In considering whether the ally tactic is viable in any given negotiation, three sources of allies should be considered. These are:

1. Internal allies
2. Parties already involved
3. External, but influential parties

Internal allies are sympathetic persons who are either inside the other party (where it is an entity), or inside the other negotiator's law firm. Any effective appeal to such potential allies cannot compromise their relationship with their own side. Of course, the ethical restrictions against communicating directly with the other party where it is being represented by counsel also must be observed. Additionally, the difficulty of a lawyer's interfering with a matter being handled by another lawyer within the same firm must be considered. Whether such allies are willing to act will depend on their own self-interest, their relationship with each party and negotiator, their position within their entity's hierarchy, and the difficulty of accomplishing the request.

In both transactional matters and litigation, potential allies may be found among the involved parties. For transactional matters, such other parties may be directly concerned, or they may be indirectly affected by the results of the negotiation. In litigation, there may be more than two parties in the case, as well as potential additional parties. Also, as discussed earlier, the judge is a potential ally in negotiating a matter that is in litigation, depending on the judge's degree of activism in settlement negotiations and the judge's view of the case.

The third category of external, but influential allies encompasses such people as family, friends, business associates, and governmental officials. It includes anyone who is not presently involved or directly affected, but who has influence over the other party, and may be willing to become an ally.

---

[26] Mandle, *Collective Bargaining Negotiation*, in Attorney's Guide to Negotiation 14-9 (1979).

Example 6-5

In the negotiations between the United State and Panama regarding the Panama Canal, American officials were sometimes in conflict among themselves. Pentagon officials leaked the conflict to the press, which stimulated increased congressional opposition to a new treaty.[27] For the Pentagon officials who opposed the proposed treaty, various members of Congress were allies or potential allies.

Example 6-6

When the professional football players struck in 1987 and the owners decided to continue to play games with substitute players, a critical economic factor was how the television networks and their advertisers would react to the substitute games. For both sides, the networks and their advertisers were crucial potential allies. One of the key reasons that the strike failed was that the networks and most of the advertisers supported the substitute games.

To the extent that a choice exists, one decision that needs to be made is who should contact the potential ally. Factors to be taken into account in making this decision include:

1. Personal influence, friendship, or the potential ally's feeling of indebtedness to the contact for past help
2. A status of at least equal seniority between the contact and the potential ally based on their positions of leadership, seniority, or other professional or social standing

For ongoing relationships, the repeated use of an ally can lead to an overdependence on that ally. The ally then is positioned as the pivotal force in the negotiation. This gives the ally the ability to wield power and influence. It also allows it to commence or increase demands for benefits in return for its continuing support. Moreover, the parties may become so dependent on the ally's intervention that they lose their capacity to negotiate alone with each other. If the ally then disappears or refuses to intervene, the parties must learn how to interact and negotiate productively without the ally.

Example 6-7

In 1987, the Chicago school teachers union engaged in a strike. During past strikes, the union and the school board had depended on the mayor of Chicago, the governor of Illinois, and the state legislature to intervene with additional funds for wage increases. The historical role of these mutual allies created a dependence on outside intervention for a financial

---

[27] H. Raiffa, The Art and Science of Negotiation 181 (1982).

bailout on the monetary issues. This time, however, the outside political officials refused to become involved. The parties appeared rather lost as they attempted to negotiate without their former allies.[28]

The dangers of becoming overly dependent must be considered against the short-run benefits provided by the ally, as well as the party's ability to maintain the alliance.

Allies, of course, can be extremely beneficial. A continuing alliance should be viewed as a separate, but interrelated, long-run negotiation in itself. Planning a negotiation must include the negotiation with the ally, or that subject should be the focus of specific, separate planning.[29]

In some negotiations, deadlocks or difficulties can arise which counsel attributes to the unreasonable, aggressive, or uncompromising personal attitude of the other negotiator, rather than the other party's instructions, interests, needs, or goals. A tactical assessment then must be made about whether it is feasible to remove the other negotiator from the negotiation. If possible, the removal usually is accomplished through internal or external allies.[30] This may be done by the allies discrediting the other negotiator, thereby causing the other party to replace the other negotiator. Another way in which the allies can act is by providing a channel to bypass the other negotiator. If the latter means are under consideration, counsel must not violate the ethical restrictions on communicating with a party who is represented by counsel.

Before seeking to have allies provide a means to negate an unreasonable negotiator, counsel must consider the likelihood that the effort will be successful. Counsel must further consider the risk, that if the attempt fails, it will strengthen the relationship between the other party and its negotiator, because the other party may believe that the attempted bypass just demonstrates that its negotiator is doing a good, tough job.

In criminal cases, police officers may be potential allies in the negotiation. In that situation, care should be exercised not to alienate the officers. Instead, if possible, defense counsel should seek to build rapport with the officers, since they can influence the prosecution's negotiating position.[31] Similarly, defense counsel may need to talk to the victim, who can also influence the prosecutor's view of a proper plea bargain. Care must be exercised in talking to the victim to avoid charges of misconduct or becoming a witness for the purpose of impeachment.[32]

---

[28] *A lesson learned at last?*, Chicago Trib, Sept 13, 1987, §4, at 1, col. 1.

[29] See ch 8 & 9 regarding planning.

[30] C. Karrass, Give & Take: The Complete Guide to Negotiating Strategies and Tactics 29, 57 (1974).

[31] Penn, Jr., *Negotiation in a Criminal Case-Defense*, in Attorney's Guide to Negotiation 13-8 (1979).

[32] In any contact with the victim defense counsel should, if feasible, avoid direct contact through the use of investigators or at least avoid being alone with the victim. Whatever the contact, defense counsel should beware of the potential for charges of obstruction of justice or bribery. *Id.*

§6.06   Media or Community Pressure

Some negotiations directly involve or affect public issues or the public interest. Often in such negotiations, the parties and their negotiators are sensitive to media accounts and to the community's response to its perception of the positions of the parties in the negotiation. These types of negotiations can include interactions involving only private parties. This occurs when the public is judging the parties and is in a position to affect at least one of the parties, as it would be as a consumer of one of the parties' products or services.

In these types of situations, the negotiator must consider effectively communicating the client's message to the media and to the public either to create pressure on the other party or to avoid pressure on one's own side. Positions must be tailored for their persuasive impact on the media and the public. The thrust may well include appeals to decency and to the public interest. Public statements, press conferences, news releases, copies of pleadings or orders in litigation, and other aspects of a public relations effort must be evaluated and used as appropriate, within the limits of any applicable disciplinary rules.

Example 6-8

In the 1987 professional football players strike, both the union and the owners made concerted efforts to win the support of both the media and the fans in order to bring pressure on each other.

Example 6-9

In strikes of government employees that disrupt or curtail services that have a strong impact on the community, both sides usually make an effort to pressure the other through the media and community support. In the 1987 Chicago teachers strike, each side not only attempted to direct media and community pressure against the other, but also sought to employ it, albeit unsuccessfully, on the mayor, the governor, and the state legislature as potential allies.

§6.07   Alternative Dispute Resolution

Due to the rising costs and delays in traditional litigation through our judicial systems, alternative dispute resolution has been an increasingly popular topic of discussion and has become more frequently used. In addition, it can encourage and allow the parties to structure the settlement process to fit their own needs. Even when the process can theoretically be tailored to meet these needs within the judicial system, such efforts usually fail. These failures tend to be due to a combination of custom and a mental attitude of the parties, as well as their negotiator-litigators, which often is more attuned to doing battle than to creatively tailoring a settlement process.

The structure of the alternative dispute resolution is necessarily the first item for discussion in determining whether to use it. The only exception to such tailoring occurs when the litigation or dispute arises from the breach of an agreement that specifies a particular form of alternative dispute resolution.

Alternative dispute resolution also can alter the process created by conventional litigation if, in a particular case, it provides:[33]

1. A more efficient and economical discovery mechanism
2. Incentives for each party to investigate and realistically evaluate its own situation
3. A means for a dialogue between the parties
4. Feedback from a respected, neutral source regarding the realities of the parties' positions which may motivate them to make difficult decisions instead of procrastinating

Additionally, the neutral mediator can propose solutions which the parties either are unaware of or are afraid to suggest. All of the above discussion assumes that the alternative dispute resolution process is functioning at its best.

Tailoring the process may be substantive or procedural.

Example 6-10

When the partnership was formed, no provisions were drafted into the agreement regarding dissolution if the partners later disagreed on basic business decisions. The statutory remedy provided only for a sale of the assets and payment of the liabilities. Due to the nature of the business, the sale of the assets, including goodwill, would not be very profitable compared to the ongoing operations. The operations were capable of being divided. This more profitable solution for both parties was agreed on as part of the initial negotiation regarding the form, procedures, and issues for alternative dispute resolution. The specific division of the business operations then was resolved through arbitration.

The tactic of alternative dispute resolution can be used regardless of the client goal or of the strategy being employed. Its usefulness depends on its form, the quality of the personnel involved, the costs, its length, and the expected results. All of these factors must be compared with the same factors applied to a resolution through the judicial system.

Much of alternative dispute resolution, such as mediation, nonbinding arbitration, summary jury trials, and mini-trials is not binding on the parties. Nonbinding alternative dispute resolution can be disadvantageous to a party who is less able or less willing to bear the expenses of proceeding through both nonbinding and binding phases, such as a mini-trial and a real trial.[34] This can cause significant, unfair pressure on that party to capitulate or to acquiesce, rather than face the additional expense of litigation or trial. If the ability or determination to pay future costs rather than agree to an otherwise undesirable settlement might be a factor, the attorney should consult with the client about

---

[33] Henry, *ADR and Personal Injury Litigation,* 23 Trial 73 (1987).

[34] R. Givens, Advocacy: The Art of Pleading a Cause 53 (Shepard's/McGraw-Hill, Inc 1985 Supp 1986).

that consideration before agreeing to engage in a nonbinding alternative dispute resolution procedure.

Alternative dispute resolution can be applied to either future use or present use. As to the former, in drafting agreements that require an ongoing relationship and future interaction between the parties, other than just a mechanical periodic payment of a specific sum, the parties may wish to provide a mechanism to resolve any future breaches and disputes. As explained above, these provisions can provide a tailor-made structure for resolving any future differences that may arise. In contrast, the present use of alternative dispute resolution arises when the parties either contemplate or are already engaged in litigation. Regardless of its usage, the same cost-benefit analysis outlined above applies.

There are various types of alternative dispute resolution mechanisms. Mediation and arbitration are the two most popular forms. Mediation is nonbinding. It tends to be preferable when the following conditions exist:[35]

1. A neutral has a reasonable likelihood of facilitating voluntary agreement by the parties

2. The parties need to be able to work together in a continuing relationship after the matter in issue is resolved

Arbitration tends to be more useful than mediation if:[36]

1. A settlement is too unlikely without a neutral decision

2. The parties' relationship will end once the dispute is resolved

However, the likelihood of success of mediation or arbitration balanced against costs and time factors ultimately is the crucial analysis. Arbitration also can be used after a failed mediation, regardless of whether the parties' relationship will continue after the current conflict is concluded.

Mediation

A mediator explores the views and the positions of the parties to discover whether the parties have a zone of agreement. If so, the mediator encourages the parties to make concessions, or clarifies a misunderstanding if that is the stumbling block preventing an agreement, rather than a need for concessions. The mediator does not express his or her own views on the merits of each side's positions, but rather is a facilitator of understanding and movement.

With mediation, the neutral tends to be passive at first while seeking to learn the parties' true positions and priorities. Then, the mediator becomes more active. In the active stage, the mediator will facilitate or press for concessions

---

[35] Cooley, *Arbitration vs Mediation*, 66 Chicago B Rec 204, 205 (1985).
[36] *Id* 205.

without a loss of face, or create alternative proposals for the parties to consider.[37]

Timing is essential, since mediation cannot succeed unless the parties are ready to compromise.[38] Mediation is most effective under the following circumstances:[39]

1.   The bargainers are inexperienced

2.   The parties have become overly committed to their positions

It is less effective if:[40]

1.   A party is stymied by internal disagreement

2.   There are major differences in the parties' expectations or in economic positions

3.   The conflict between the parties is intense, with many issues, or strong disagreements on priorities

The mediation process usually consists of eight distinct stages. These are:[41]

1.   Initial contact with the mediator

2.   Preparation by the parties

3.   An introductory phase in which the parties and the mediator set the procedures to be followed, and the mediator seeks to establish credibility and control of the process

4.   The parties state the problems and the issues

5.   There is clarification of the problems and the issues

6.   An effort is made to create and to analyze new solutions

7.   A solution is selected

8.   Before drafting a written agreement for the parties to sign, the basic terms of the agreement are summarized and, if necessary, clarified

Some of the benefits which mediation can achieve are to:

1.   Propose realistic expectations[42]

2.   Bring the parties together to communicate[43]

---

[37] R. Lewicki & J. Litterer, Negotiation 303 (1985).

[38] *Id* 304.

[39] *Id* 304-05.

[40] *Id* 305.

[41] Cooley, *supra* note 35, at 209.

[42] C. Karrass, Give & Take: The Complete Guide to Negotiating Strategies and Tactics 111 (1974).

[43] *Id;* H. Raiffa, The Art and Science of Negotiations 108-09 (1982).

3.   Listen and moderate the parties' discussion dispassionately, while establishing a productive atmosphere and easing any interpersonal conflicts[44]

4.   Obtain confidential information from the parties to determine if a zone of agreement exists, and provide appropriate feedback regarding a potential zone of agreement[45]

5.   Search for joint gains and stimulate mutually helpful inventive thinking[46]

6.   Suggest compromises that the parties would be unwilling to propose themselves[47]

7.   Deflate unreasonable claims and loosen the parties' commitments to certain positions[48]

8.   Persuade the parties to accept new ideas that they would be more hesitant to accept if the ideas had been put forth by the other side[49]

9.   Help the parties to clarify their values and their bottom lines by considering the implications of not reaching an agreement[50]

10. Get the parties to ask themselves: "What decisions do I want my opponent to make and what must I do to help him or her make that decision?"[51]

11. Provide a way for a party to save face while changing positions.[52]

12. Articulate rationales for an agreement in order to promote acceptance of the proposal[53]

The mediation role, however, can vary depending on the mediator's degree of leadership regarding procedures as well as within the bargaining sessions.[54]

One of the forms which mediation can take is the one-text mediation approach.[55] In a one-text mediation, the mediator obtains information about the issues and then circulates draft proposals or ideas to get feedback from the parties.[56] The mediator then submits a final proposal with a recommenda-

---

[44] C. Karrass, *supra* note 42; H. Raiffa, *supra* note 43.

[45] H. Raiffa, *supra* note 43.

[46] C. Karrass, *supra* note 42; H. Raiffa, *supra* note 43.

[47] C. Karrass, *supra* note 42.

[48] H. Raiffa, *supra* note 43.

[49] C. Karrass, *supra* note 42.

[50] H. Raiffa, *supra* note 43.

[51] C. Karrass, *supra* note 42.

[52] *Id;* H. Raiffa, *supra* note 43.

[53] H. Raiffa, *supra* note 43.

[54] *Id* 218.

[55] R. Fisher & W. Ury, Getting to Yes, Negotiating Agreement Without Giving In 113 (1981).

[56] *Id* 118.

tion that both sides accept it, and each party must either accept or reject the suggested agreement.[57]

Mediation has become increasingly popular in matrimonial litigation. In some jurisdictions, an attempt to mediate is required by the court. This, however, has both positive and negative aspects.[58] Among the positive features are:[59]

1.   A reduction of court caseloads

2.   A lowering of legal costs

3.   Sometimes being a superior means of resolving highly emotional battles, such as custody battles

4.   A tendency to produce agreements which the parties abide by longer than they would decrees imposed by a judge

On the other hand, though, negative facets of such a system can be:[60]

1.   Unfairness and useless delay if the mediators are of poor quality

2.   A weaker party may be pressured into an unfair agreement

In major corporations, internal conflicts are frequently dealt with by CEOs exercising their power through effective informal mediation, rather than by using pure power to just announce a decision.[61] In the same way, a mediator can effectively wield power without being the final adjudicator.

Arbitration

Arbitration is a format in which private individuals, rather than judges or the parties themselves, decide the merits of each side's position. There are two types of arbitration, nonbinding and binding. The names express the difference between the two. The only difference is that nonbinding arbitration is advisory, while binding arbitration yields a decision that the parties must accept. The results of binding arbitration are enforceable in court.[62]

Nonbinding arbitration still involves having a neutral render a decision, although it is only advisory. In this respect, however, it differs from mediation in which the mediator seeks to facilitate a fair agreement without issuing a decision on who should prevail.

Binding arbitration involves relinquishing control over the outcome to a decision maker who may be an unknown quantity. However, the parties can structure the process so that they have a right to choose the arbitrator(s). This

---

[57] *Id.* This mediation approach was used to achieve the Camp David accord between Israel and Egypt. *Id.*

[58] *Peace Talks,* Chicago Trib, April 8, 1987, §5, at 1, col. 2 & 7, col. 1.

[59] *Id.*

[60] *Id.*

[61] H. Raiffa, *supra* note 43, at 183.

[62] *See* 6 CJS *Arbitration* §149 *et seq.* (1975).

helps to create a greater likelihood that the parties will perceive that there is fairness throughout the procedure.

The decision makers may be specialists in the particular field in which the issue arises, such as real estate, securities practices, etc. Normally, there is either one arbitrator or three arbitrators. If there is one arbitrator, either the parties agree on a particular arbitrator, or the parties agree to use an arbitrator from an agreed-on organization. If there are three arbitrators, each party normally appoints an arbitrator, and those two arbitrators then jointly choose a third arbitrator to prevent the possibility of a deadlock.

Example 6-11

Where a settlement cannot be reached on a claim under an uninsured motorist provision in an automobile insurance policy, the policy normally provides for binding arbitration. Typically, the policy also provides that there will be three arbitrators, one chosen by the insurer, one chosen by the insured, and the third chosen by the first two arbitrators

Arbitration may prove to be advantageous or detrimental, depending on the particular case. Potentially, some of the key advantages of arbitration are:[63]

1. A fresh view with creative and/or face-saving solutions from the arbitrator.
2. Less costs than a prolonged dispute that could result in litigation, deadlock, or strike.
3. A faster resolution than litigation

On the other hand, the potential negative consequences include:

1. Decreasing the negotiator's efforts due to a reliance on the arbitration
2. Chilling the parties' willingness to compromise, because the arbitrator may split the difference
3. Less of a commitment on the part of the parties to carry out the decision imposed by the arbitrator than if the parties had reached a voluntary agreement, which is important if good faith efforts by a party are needed to implement the decision.
4. Expenses which may equal litigation, depending on the procedure[64]
5. Often the grounds for appealing a bad arbitration decision are narrow, such as the decision's exceeding the arbitrator's authority or being "manifestly unjust"[65]

To the extent that all of the needs of both parties are not sufficiently known, the outcome may not be optimal, but still it may be preferable to a continued

---

[63] C. Karrass, *supra* note 42, at 190.

[64] Bayer & Abrahams, *The Trouble with Arbitration,* 11 Litigation 30 (1985).

[65] *Id* 32.

impasse.[66] In addition, a lack of knowledge of the facts or of the applicable legal principles will impair the arbitrator's determination. Therefore, as in a trial, counsel must strive to present persuasively all of the important information, and thereby to influence the arbitrator's decision.

The process follows its own rules for identification of the issues, discovery, presentation of the evidence, and the applicable rules, standards, and guidelines for the decision maker to use as criteria for making a ruling. At times, the rules borrow from those used by the judicial system. The arbitration process usually is similar to that of a lawsuit. It generally consists of the following stages:[67]

1. The initiation of arbitration
2. Preparation by the parties
3. One or more prehearing conferences
4. The hearing itself
5. The arbitrator's decision

The differences between arbitration and litigation procedures, as well as the quality of the decision maker, can be critical. Any potential arbitration matter must be analyzed to determine whether disadvantageous procedural and decision maker differences exist under either system.[68]

One particular form of binding arbitration is final offer arbitration. This has been utilized to resolve major league baseball players' salary disputes since 1974. In a final offer arbitration, each party simultaneously submits a final offer. The arbitrator then must select the more appropriate of the two positions. The arbitrator cannot choose any other outcome. This mechanism is therefore strictly a win/lose form of arbitration. As such, it often carries with it significant risk and uncertainty. Accordingly, it can provide an effective incentive to settle before the arbitrator's decision in order to eliminate the risk and uncertainty.[69]

In nonbinding arbitration, the arbitrator's decision is only as effective as the decision maker's ability to influence the parties' settlement positions. This depends on the parties' personalities, predisposition to respect the advisory opinion, respect for the arbitrator, analysis of why the arbitrator reached his or her decision, and the alternatives to accepting the nonbinding decision. Nonbinding arbitration is more effective than one might suspect. If unsuccessful, though, it adds an additional layer of expenses to the total cost of obtaining a resolution of the dispute.

Prior to arbitration, one party may attempt to generate a favorable position by bargaining the other party down. This creates a bargaining range with fig-

---

[66] H. Raiffa, *supra* note 43, at 35.

[67] Cooley, *supra* note 35, at 206.

[68] Bayer & Abrahams, *The Trouble with Arbitration,* 11 Litigation 30, 31-32 (1985).

[69] H. Raiffa, *supra* note 43, at 110.

ures on the table that are relatively advantageous for the first party.[70] The theory is that the arbitrator will learn of the parties' prearbitration range and be influenced by it. Some arbitrators' analyses are affected by the parties' last offers, if those offers are known to the arbitrator. In those instances, the last offers establish the outer parameters for the arbitrator's decision.

This is a prearbitration tactic to be used when possible, and to be guarded against if the other negotiator attempts to use it. The countermeasure is to maintain a relatively high (or low, as the case may be) position. The countermeasure should be employed if both of the following conditions apply:

1. There is a likelihood of arbitration because the negotiation will become deadlocked

2. Smaller concessions are being offered by the other party than those which it demands, thereby creating a danger that an unfavorable prearbitration bargaining range will be revealed to the arbitrator

Summary Jury Trials

A recent development in alternative dispute resolution is the summary jury trial.[71] These are really specialized forms of nonbinding arbitration. Summary jury trials are conducted by a real judge using real jurors.[72] This procedure allows the parties to present their evidence and arguments in an abbreviated form and to receive an advisory decision from the "trier of fact." Typically, the procedure is completed within one day with the attorneys telling the "trier of fact" what their witnesses would testify to, rather than actually having the witnesses speak.[73] What the attorneys represent regarding the testimony must be done in good faith based on depositions, interviews, records, etc.[74] Any exhibits that could be used at trial can also be used in this process. If a party is an individual, the party should be present for the summary jury trial, or if the party is an entity, a representative with settlement authority should be present.[75] At times, though, if a government entity is a party, it may be impossible to have a representative who has settlement authority present due to the legal requirements for settlement authorization.[76] The presence of the client

---

[70] C. Karrass, *supra* note 42, at 190.

[71] The term mini-trial has also been used to refer to this procedure, although that term is not technically correct. Rieders, *Summary Jury Trials,* 23 Trial 93 (1987).

[72] *Id.*

[73] In some summary jury trials, however, live witnesses are used. Manual For Complex Litigation Second 157, in I (pt 2) J. Moore, Moore's Federal Practice (1986). Some summary jury trials also take two days. *Id.*

[74] Rieders, *supra* note 71.

[75] *Id* 94.

[76] *See* §5.27 regarding negotiating with someone who lacks authority. Some would say that a summary jury trial is not appropriate in cases where the government representative lacks settlement authority. Rieders, *supra* note 71.

or the client's representative means that the summary jury trial entails active client participation with the tactical considerations involved in active client participation in the negotiating process.[77]

An issue exists concerning whether courts can force parties to engage in summary jury trials as a means of facilitating settlements.[78]

Mini-Trials

A mini-trial is similar to a summary jury trial, but instead of a real judge and real jurors, a mini-trial uses designated persons to play those roles. More typically, a mini-trial is conducted as if it were a bench trial.[79] After the cases have been presented, the "judge" acts as a mediator.[80] If a settlement is not reached through mediation, the parties are informed of the "judge's" decision.[81]

Alternative Resolution Summary

Alternative dispute resolution does not replace negotiation. The parties and their negotiators should employ the same types of negotiation goal analysis, planning, strategy, tactics, communication techniques, and drafting methods that are used in any other form of negotiation. These must be channeled and adapted, however, to fit the particular format of the alternative dispute resolution method that is being utilized. For arbitration and summary or mini-trials, trial tactics are necessary as well.

Alternative dispute resolution may, at times, be used as a ploy. If it is not binding, it can be part of strategies that do not seek agreement, such as those of delay or discovery.[82] The countermeasure is to require expeditious and binding procedures.

The strategy of negotiating not to seek an agreement, but instead to influence third parties, can be the reason for a publicized call for alternative dispute resolution.[83] Even if seeking an agreement is desired, such a publicized call for alternative dispute resolution may well be a tactical ploy involving allies, media pressure, or community pressure.[84]

Example 6-12

In the 1987 professional football players strike, the union appeared to be in an ever-weakening position. Late in the strike, the union publicly

---

[77] See §6.02 on active client participation in the negotiating process.

[78] See In re Strandell v Jackson County, 838 F2d 884 (7th Cir 1988). The Seventh Circuit held that parties cannot be compelled to participate in summary jury trials. Id.

[79] See Manual For Complex Litigation Second 157, in J. Moore, Moore's Federal Practice (1986).

[80] Id.

[81] Id 157-58.

[82] See §§3.11 & 3.12 regarding negotiating for purposes of delay and discovery, respectively, rather than to reach an agreement.

[83] See §3.14.

[84] See §§6.05 concerning allies and 6.06 regarding media and community pressure.

called for a return to work coupled with the use of alternative dispute resolution procedures. The union's public proposal was for a resumption of games combined with immediate mediation, followed, if necessary, by binding arbitration. To some experts, the union's public offer to submit all of the issues to alternative dispute resolution was a ploy to appear to be reasonable and thereby win fan and media support, since the owners were all but certain to reject the proposal.[85]

The countermeasure to such a ploy is to publicly unmask it, thereby making the other side appear to be Machiavellian and disingenuous.

§6.08 Class Actions

Settling class actions involves certain specialized considerations and requirements.[86] It must be kept in mind from the beginning that the settlement will have to satisfy not only the particular known clients who are the class representatives, but also the unnamed members of the class, at least to the extent that they choose to take an interest in the matter, as well as the judge who will have to approve the settlement.[87] Although, theoretically, the client goals of the individual clients who are the class representatives will be the same as the goals of the class as a whole, care should be taken to make certain that this consistency is maintained.

The proposed agreement and the course of the negotiation are subject both to judicial review and to the review of interested parties, such as the members of the class.[88] Counsel will need to disclose the entire agreement, its effect on the members of the class, whether its effect will vary among the class members, and why the agreement is fair.[89] Counsel also may well have to disclose how the settlement was reached, although the extent to which this is examined in detail will vary from case to case, depending on the circumstances and on whether objections to the settlement are raised.[90] On occasion, there may be a protracted, contested hearing as to the fairness of the settlement.[91] The interested parties even have a right to discovery regarding the settlement process.[92]

---

[85] *Labor-Management Experts Ponder Players' Tactics,* Chicago Trib, Oct 13, 1987, §4, at 3, col. 1.

[86] *See* Manual For Complex Litigation Second 223-36, in I (pt 2) J. Moore, Moore's Federal Practice (1986).

[87] *Id.* 224-30; Kempf, Jr., & Taylor, *Settling Class Actions,* 13 Litigation 26 (1986); Rules 23(e) and 23.1 of the Fed R Civ P mandate that class actions "shall not be dismissed or compromised without the approval of the court."

[88] Kempf, Jr., *supra* note 87; J. Moore, *supra* note 86, at 224-30.

[89] J. Moore, *supra* note 87, at 225-26.

[90] *Id* 225-30.

[91] *Id* 229-30.

[92] Kempf, Jr., *supra* note 87. The denial of such discovery was held to be an abuse of discretion by the district court in *In re* General Motors Engine Interchange Litig, 594 F2d 1106, 1124 (7th Cir 1979).

Thus, the settlement negotiations should be conducted as if they were "public events,"[93] to the extent that the conduct of the negotiators may be scrutinized later.

To avoid conflict of interest charges, class counsel should not negotiate regarding attorney's fees until the substantive terms for the class have been resolved.[94] Agreements regarding fees for class counsel also are subject to judicial review.

§6.09   Multiple Parties

Having more than two parties involved in a negotiation tends to geometrically increase the number and the complexity of both the issues and the possible alternatives. However, the same strategies, tactics, planning procedures, communications techniques, and drafting skills are used as with a two-party negotiation.

§6.10   Gifts and Entertainment

In business deals, clients sometimes legitimately utilize giving gifts to the other party or entertaining the other party. This should be strictly distinguished from bribes or other improprieties. Lawyers obviously should not be presenting gifts to the attorney for the other party to influence that attorney's representation. Sometimes, though, business gifts and entertainment can be useful, proper, and even expected. Accordingly, they should be considered when appropriate in a business context.

§6.11   Summary and Review

    I. Active Client Participation
        A. In the negotiation sessions
        B. Possible for any client goal or strategy
        C. Some clients conduct a portion of the negotiation before involving counsel, leaving certain items already resolved
        D. Certain clients who are experienced and skilled in particular types of negotiations, and are not unduly emotional about the specific issues or parties, can be effective participants
        E. As a general rule, negotiate without the clients present to avoid errors unless there is a distinct advantage to having one or more clients present
        F. A client's presence can impede communication and cause undue posturing

---

[93] Kempf, Jr., *supra* note 87.

[94] H. Newberg, Class Actions 255 (Shepard's/McGraw-Hill, Inc 1985); Prandini v National Tea Co, 557 F2d 1015 (3d Cir 1977); McDonald v Chicago Milwaukee Corp, 565 F2d 416 (7th Cir 1977).

    G. Avoid appearing overly friendly or candid with the other lawyer if the client may misinterpret that as disloyalty

    H. Used for expediency, demonstrating unity of negotiator and client, to establish or repair relationships between clients, and to directly communicate with the parties

    I. May be limited to certain phases of the negotiation, if at all

    J. Can include client-to-client negotiations of certain issues without counsel, after counsel completes some phases of the negotiation

II. Negotiating Teams

    A. Lone negotiator more common because of cost-benefit ratio, style, and potential conflict or inconsistency among negotiators

    B. The potential benefits from the team approach are:
   1. Active client participation
   2. Specialized knowledge
   3. Collective judgment
   4. Notes and observation
   5. Role playing

    C. Role playing includes information gatherer and observer, as well as "Mutt and Jeff"

    D. Countermeasures to "Mutt and Jeff" tough guy include exhaust without responding and ignore, bypass, be tough back, publicly blame the other side for sidetracking the negotiation, terminate the negotiation pointing out that this conduct is the basis, openly predict the behavior, or threaten to take these measures

    E. Team negotiation requires especially careful planning of the roles for gathering information beforehand, logistics, planning, information disclosure, concessions, positions, and observation

    F. Critical to have a leader with firm control using directions and adjournment as necessary, and being physically positioned to exercise leadership

    G. If the rest of the team has an ongoing relationship with the other party while the lawyer does not, the lawyer can criticize and raise difficult points more freely than the others, as well as serve as a target for criticism

    H. Focus communications on the other team's member who is: (1) more receptive; or (2) more difficult, thus requiring neutralization

    I. Consider the number for the team in terms of whether being outnumbered may be a disadvantage, outnumbering the other team will intimidate or cause a harder defensive reaction, coordination problems, the nature and scope of the negotiation, personalities, and the need for specialized talents

III. Judicial Settlement Conferences

    A. Judge as mediator to facilitate negotiations, impose deadlines, deflate unrealistic expectations, suggest positions or principles for compromise, and oversee the process

B. If the trial judge is involved, it can affect later rulings depending on the judge
C. May require clients to be present for authority and to influence them directly
D. The presence of parties may have a positive or negative effect depending on their respective personal strengths, possible lack of judicial skill at mediating, and potential undue pressure
E. If the client will be present, plan with and counsel the client to be prepared to play an effective role, either active or passive

IV. Allies
A. Those who can favorably influence the other party
B. Limited by whether they exist, costs, and potential backfire
C. Gaining an ally's assistance can be the subject of an entirely separate negotiation
D. For all goals and strategies
E. May be internal, other involved parties, or external
F. May require appeal to ally's self-interest
G. One with a relationship, status, and skill should be the contact person
H. Avoid becoming overly dependent
I. Allies can assist in having an unreasonable negotiator for the other party removed or bypassed. However, a failed attempt may strengthen that negotiator's position with his or her client

V. Media or Community Pressure
A. For negotiations involving public issues or public interest
B. Seek to take persuasive positions that pressure the other party or avoid pressure on one's own client

VI. Alternative Dispute Resolution
A. To avoid cost and delay in the judicial system
B. Allows a tailoring of the process better than the judicial system
C. At its best, it may be advantageous to litigation by being more efficient for communicating information, creating incentives for realistic self-examination by each party, providing a means for dialogue, generating feedback from a respected neutral, and having the neutral propose solutions which the parties are not aware of or are afraid to suggest
D. Nonbinding will be a disadvantage to a weaker party without sufficient energy or resources for both that phase and litigation if there is no settlement, since it will be under tremendous pressure to settle
E. May be drafted into agreements to resolve future disputes
F. The mediator helps the parties discover whether a zone of agreement exists and clarifies any misunderstandings, but does not express a definite view on the merits
G. Mediation is nonbinding and useful when a neutral is reasonably likely to influence the parties who are ready to compromise

H. Arbitration is preferable to mediation when a voluntary agreement is unlikely without a neutral's decision

I. Arbitration can be binding or nonbinding. The latter differs from mediation in that a decision is rendered by the neutral instead of only seeking to facilitate voluntary agreement of the parties

J. Beware of a party who attempts to bargain one side down more than it concedes before the arbitration in order to skew the range for a resolution in its favor
   1. Counter by refusing to engage in that type of concession pattern
   2. Use this maneuver if it is available

K. Potential negative consequences include undue reliance on arbitration without sufficient efforts to resolve the matter first, chilling compromises because the arbitrator may split the difference, less commitment to an arbitrated decision than a voluntary one if good faith efforts by a party are necessary, expenses that can equal litigation depending on the procedures, often narrow grounds for appeal, and sometimes disadvantageous procedural differences from litigation for a particular matter

L. Summary jury trials also can produce an advisory opinion, and are a form of nonbinding arbitration

M. Mini-trials are bench trial versions of the summary jury trial approach, with the addition of an attempt by the judge to mediate the dispute after the trial, but before issuing a ruling

N. Negotiation goal analysis, planning, strategy, and tactics still are used in alternative dispute resolution, with the addition of trial tactics for arbitration and summary or mini-trials

O. A public demand can be part of a tactic to create allies or community and media pressure. Counter by unmasking the ploy

P. May be used as a ploy for discovery or delay under the strategy of negotiating other than for agreement. Countermeasure to require expeditious and binding procedures

VII. Class Actions
   A. Settlement must satisfy the interests of the class and be approved by the court
   B. Class counsel's fees should not be negotiated until the substantive relief for the class has been at least contingently resolved subject to agreement on fees for class counsel

VIII. Multiple Parties
   A. Increases complexity of issues and analysis
   B. Use same planning methods, strategies, and tactics as a two-party negotiation

IX. Gifts and Entertainment
   A. Sometimes customary in business matters
   B. Avoid bribery and ethical violations

Litigation Related Tactics

7

§7.01   Introduction

All of the tactics discussed in the preceding chapters are applicable in matters involving litigation or potential litigation. Some tactics, however, are exclusively or primarily applicable to litigation or to claims which will result in litigation unless they are settled. These litigation tactics are the subject of this chapter.

In analyzing litigation tactics, one must consider the conditions under which the negotiation commences. For transactional or other deal-making negotiations, the parties normally are voluntarily interacting because they are motivated by a potential, mutual gain.[1] The litigation context is quite different. The parties may be involuntarily locked in a negotiation by events beyond some or all of the parties' control, rather than a free, mutual decision. In this context, seeking to avoid a loss is as common a motivation as the possibility of a unilat-

---

[1] At times, however, one or both of the parties seek to avoid a potential loss.

eral gain. Unlike deal making, both avoiding a loss and unilateral gain are far more prevalent motivations than mutual gains.

Several other conditions also tend to characterize litigation negotiations as opposed to transactional matters.

1. *Uncertainty.* The parties feel an uncertainty or ambivalence about negotiating, rather than fighting. This is in contrast to the more positive atmosphere of a transaction, in which the entire purpose of interacting is to try to reach an agreement.

2. *Rigidity.* Often due to ambivalence, frustration, fear, or anger, the parties are more rigid and less prone to compromise, at least initially. Usually, they have previously attempted to resolve the matter with each other, but have failed miserably. This failure commonly leaves a degree of skepticism about whether the matter can be settled at all.

3. *Suspicion.* The parties feel that they cannot trust each other.

The negotiating alternative may include a loss for both parties instead of an economic gain for either.[2] Nevertheless, avoiding further loss may not be the motivating force for a party. For instance, fees and costs can exceed the incremental value of the concession demanded by each party, and yet the parties may remain unwilling to agree to the compromises that are necessary to reach an agreement. This unwillingness may be because one or both of the parties perceive the potential compromise as exceeding the market value of the case, otherwise being unfair, or violating some emotional or psychological need. Thus, a protracted conflict may continue despite a lack of a direct motive for pure gain, in an economic sense.

§7.02 Litigation

Instituting litigation is itself a tactic which so profoundly impacts on negotiation that it should be considered as a separate tactic. It operates separately from the negotiation itself. In some respects, litigation is a form of fact creation[3] and power. Sometimes, it is part of creating movement.[4] This tactic increases the cost of failing to agree, and may expand the stakes with claims of compensatory, punitive, and treble damages, as well as claims for costs and attorney's fees. In addition, litigation can only be evaluated for settlement purposes after sufficient information is known to plan for a trial, so that the strengths and weaknesses of the case can be assessed.[5] Negotiation may need to be delayed awhile to acquire the necessary information.

For the purposes of this section, litigation includes the threat of litigation, as well as actually being in litigation. If taken seriously, the threat of litigation

---

[2] Although this possibility exists in some non-litigation situations, it is more common in litigation.

[3] *See* §4.03.

[4] *See* §5.22.

[5] Lubet & Schoenfield, *Trial Preparation-A Systematic Approach*, 12 Trial Law Q 16 (1978).

can have the same negotiating impact as the filing of a suit. Used as a threat which can be avoided "reasonably," it may force the other party into a decision to agree in order to save the cost of retaining litigation counsel for an initial evaluation and response. This factor is not applicable for parties which have their regular counsel handle the matter or already have engaged litigation counsel to evaluate the case or demonstrate their willingness and ability to litigate.

If new to the scene, the appearance of litigation counsel in response to the threat of litigation usually has one of two effects on the negotiation process. There may be lowered client expectations, due to a less favorable than expected assessment of the potential litigation. This can result in an increase in the flexibility of the positions being taken in the negotiation. In contrast, the other effect can be increased intransigence. This is due to the client's readiness to use its fresh "hired gun" to fight, or to a favorable assessment of the possible litigation.

The litigation evaluation by counsel may or may not be accurate or realistic, but the client usually relies on it and does not have any other assessment as a crosscheck. The litigator should make the evaluation based on the law and the known facts, without regard to the lawyer's personal interests due to any effect on attorney's fees. Regrettably, some lawyers unethically allow their assessment of the case to be influenced by the fact that a prompt settlement can eliminate potentially substantial fees.[6]

In litigation, settlements can occur on the eve of trial, during trial, or after trial, even while the case is on appeal. Counsel therefore must be mentally prepared to negotiate at any stage of the litigation. However, it is critical that potential or actual negotiations never reduce one's efforts in a way that would endanger the chance for success at trial or on appeal.

Openness to realistic negotiation, combined with a readiness to effectively engage in a trial or appeal, is essential. It also is in the client's best interest, although it is not always an easy course for the litigator. Indeed, one commentator has observed that: "In fact, sitting down and talking settlement in the early stages of litigation may take more guts and efficiency than proceeding mindlessly with litigation."[7]

A party can benefit by continuing to litigate vigorously to maintain momentum in the litigation while negotiating.[8] The effects of a continuing show of strength must be balanced against any direct costs and, if applicable and valued, against a loss of goodwill or further deterioration of a relationship.

Creative lawyering to expedite cases may be essential to force the other party to engage in realistic settlement negotiations. If the motion has a reasonable basis, motions for temporary restraining orders and preliminary injunctions can be used for this purpose. To succeed in generating meaningful negotia-

---

[6] C. Karrass, Give & Take: The Complete Guide to Negotiating Strategies and Tactics 196 (1974).

[7] Nolan, *Settlement Negotiations,* 11 Litigation 17 (1985).

[8] R. Givens, Advocacy: The Art of Pleading a Cause 463 (Shepard's/McGraw-Hill, Inc 1985). This is also applicable to strikes, boycotts, and other types of hostile action.

tions, the motion must create sufficient pressure to overcome the other party's emotional, economic, or other types of reluctance to settle realistically at that time.

Where the parties have an ongoing working relationship, the impact of actual or threatened litigation on that relationship must be evaluated before deciding that litigation should be instituted. Injecting litigation into a relationship can cause it to deteriorate or remain intransigent. Similarly, charges and counter-charges should be anticipated and evaluated in terms of any potential positive or negative effect on customers, business associates, and others whose attitudes are of concern.

To the extent that the suit will receive publicity, the effect of that publicity on future negotiations should also be considered.[9] Will the publicity cause the other party to weaken or harden its position?

Even if the suit will not receive publicity, a complaint that is perceived as inflammatory by a defendant may be taken so personally that the dispute becomes a matter of principle, and settlement becomes more difficult. How-ever, some defendants can be intimidated by a fear of having strong allegations adjudicated against them. This should be considered in terms of drafting the complaint. Even the cause of action itself can be perceived as a personal attack. For instance, by definition, a malpractice claim must allege professional negli-gence. Of course, a good cause of action must be alleged regardless of the defendant's feelings. On the other hand, a weak claim must be considered in terms of whether it adds bargaining leverage or whether it may create a more hostile defendant bent on not settling in order to seek vindication.[10] This is particularly important if the allegations are personally made against the indi-vidual(s) who will make the settlement decisions for the other party.[11]

Litigation often is the only feasible method for resolving a dispute. It can establish a precedent for protecting the client's rights now and in the future. Even when potential costs and delays are taken into account, it can be the only viable means of attaining the client's goal.

Litigation is especially useful for a no concessions or for a no further conces-sions strategy. It also can be useful in eventually effectuating all other strategies except for that of concede first. Depending on the circumstances, litigation can be appropriate for any type of client goal. Of course, at times, it will be inappropriate for certain cooperative and defensive goals.

The existence of litigation can serve as a shield to provide protection against continuing or renewed injurious acts. Even without the issuance of a temporary restraining order or a preliminary injunction, a defendant may be reluctant to expose itself to further liability, and may desist from the same or variations of the conduct that already is being challenged in the lawsuit.

---

[9] See **§6.06** regarding media and community pressure.

[10] Potter, *Settlement of Claims and Litigation: Legal Rules, Negotiation Strategies, and In-House Guidelines*, 41 Bus Law 515, 528 (1986).

[11] *Id* 528.

Example 7-1

An antitrust suit is filed against a company alleging predatory pricing practices. After the suit is filed, the company alters its discount policies.

Example 7-2

In 1985, the city of Chicago and a company that it hired sent out notices to hundreds of thousands of alleged "scofflaws" demanding that they pay over $100 million in alleged "fines" and "costs." A class action suit was filed in federal court pursuant to 42 USC §1983, claiming that the notices violated due process.[12] The plaintiffs filed a motion for a preliminary injunction, and the defendants filed a motion to dismiss. The district court ordered that an amended complaint be filed. In response to one of the plaintiffs' claims, the defendants modified their demand notices, but continued to issue them. An amended complaint was filed attacking both the original and the new demand notices. A motion for a preliminary injunction incorporating the amended complaint was filed, and the defendants again moved to dismiss. The motions were extensively briefed, and eventually the district court ruled that the demand notices did violate due process. Long before that ruling, however, in response to the amended complaint and the briefs, the city and the company had completely halted their demand notice program. The plaintiffs had achieved the effect of a preliminary injunction without one being issued.

Thus, litigation can provide important protection while it is pending.

The same pressure that yields that protection may affect the defendant's bargaining position and willingness to negotiate, and may even affect its bottom line. Furthermore, to the extent that the willingness to litigate is perceived as a sign that such willingness will occur in the future, it may deter the other party in the future. The other party may decide, in retrospect, that the expense and the aggravation of the suit outweighed the benefits that it gained from the behavior challenged in the complaint, regardless of the outcome of the suit.

§7.03   Structured Settlements

A particular type of win/win tactic, the structured settlement, merits a separate discussion.[13] A structured settlement is a settlement device that is used primarily in the personal injury field. Instead of the typical, single, lump sum payment, a structured settlement involves a series of payments over time. Commonly, a structured settlement involves an initial, relatively large payment, followed by a long-term series of smaller payments. The latter, for instance, can provide a monthly income to the plaintiff.

---

[12] Horn v City of Chicago, No 85-C-6838 (ND Ill 1987), No 87-1174, 87-1175, 87-1936 (7th Cir).

[13] J. Eck & J. Ungerer, Structuring Settlements (Shepard's/McGraw-Hill, Inc 1987).

Structuring is flexible to meet the anticipated needs of the plaintiff.[14] The long-term series of payments can incorporate such features as increases to offset inflation and periodic larger payments.[15] The length of the plan can be for a specified number of years, or the plaintiff's lifetime, or whichever of the two is longer or shorter.[16]

Typically, the defendant or its insurer funds the payments through the purchase of an annuity.[17] The annuity is owned by the defendant or its insurer with the plaintiff as the beneficiary.[18]

In the right case, a structured settlement can be advantageous to both sides. For the defense, the advantage is that the cost of the settlement is normally less than that which the defense would have to pay to provide a regular lump sum settlement.[19] The cost of the structured settlement is the cost of the annuity, plus any initial payment to the plaintiff that the defendant or its insurer is itself providing. That cost is the present value of the settlement. For the plaintiff, the advantages are a long-term or lifetime stream of tax-free income.[20] This may be important to the plaintiff, if the plaintiff needs such an income because:[21]

The plaintiff has a permanent complete, or partial, disability

The plaintiff is faced with long-term or permanent large expenses for medical or personal care

There are spendthrift considerations for the plaintiff

---

[14] Halpern, *A Plaintiff's Alternative to Structured Settlements*, 23 Trial 83 (1987).

[15] Dannings, Johnson & Lesti, *Structuring Settlements: A Negotiating Guide*, 15(3) Trial Law Q 30, 31-32 (1983) [hereinafter Dannings].

[16] *Id* 32-33.

[17] Given the long-term nature of the payments, and the fact that once the defendant or its insurer purchases the annuity it may have no further liability for the payments, the reliability and the stability of the company providing the annuity is extremely important. Therefore, plaintiff's counsel always must insist that the annuity come from at least an A+ rated annuity company which belongs to a state guarantee fund. McNay, *The Other Side of Structured Settlements*, 23 Trial 79, 81 (1987). If possible, a AAA rated life insurance company is preferable for the source of the annuity. *But see id.* Of course, if the defendant is itself a sufficiently large and stable enough entity, and it retains the ultimate responsibility for the payments to the plaintiff, then the concern about the company providing the annuity is alleviated.

[18] This is an essential element of a structured settlement so that all of the payments to the plaintiff, like the normal personal injury settlement, are deemed by the IRS not to be income. Rev Rul 79-220, 1979 2CB 74; IRC §§104 & 130. If the plaintiff owns the annuity, or is considered to have constructive receipt of it, the payments will be considered to be income like any other investment owned by the plaintiff. Rev Rul 79-220; IRC §130; McNay, *The Other Side of Structured Settlements*, 23 Trial 79, 81 (1987). Counsel must also be careful to meet all other requirements necessary to avoid having the payments considered to be income by the IRS. *Id* 81.

[19] It has been suggested by one plaintiff's lawyer that a structured settlement savings of 10 per cent for a defendant is reasonable. Halpern, *supra* note 14.

[20] The Internal Revenue Service has ruled that, just as a normal lump sum personal injury settlement is not taxable income, the payments generated by a properly structured settlement also are not income. Rev Rul 79-220, 1979 2CB 74; IRC §§104 & 130.

[21] Halpern, *supra* note 14.

The extent to which a structured settlement will meet these needs for the plaintiff must be weighed against the present value of the settlement.[22] It also must be weighed against the long-term investment possibilities and their tax consequences for the plaintiff had a nonstructured settlement been obtained.[23]

The latter consideration may vary with the economic condition of the country.[24] Generally, the economic factors that make structured settlements more attractive are:

Higher present interest rates

Lower future, anticipated interest rates[25]

Higher present and anticipated, future tax rates[26]

Lower future, expected inflation

Part of the information that is needed by plaintiff's counsel in negotiating or evaluating a structured settlement proposal is the present value of the settlement. Most often, defense counsel have become unwilling to disclose their actual cost.[27] At times, defense lawyers have argued that such a disclosure would cause the Internal Revenue Service to view the plaintiff as being in constructive receipt of the annuity, thereby making the income from it taxable.[28] The IRS, however, has taken the opposite position, and has stated that disclosure to the plaintiff of the cost or the present value of the settlement does not convert the proceeds of the settlement into taxable income.[29] In any event, if the defense will not disclose their actual cost, plaintiff's counsel must determine

---

[22] In making this determination, the fact that structured settlements are inflexible once the annuity has been purchased should also be considered. McNay, *supra* note 17; Halpern, *supra* note 14.

[23] Halpern, *supra* note 14; Winslow, *Tax Reform Preserves Structured Settlements*, 65 Taxes 22, 23 (1987). It has been suggested that, at times, a favorable plaintiff's alternative to a structured settlement may be to invest a normal, lump sum settlement in a single premium whole life insurance policy, possibly through a trust. Halpern, *supra* note 14, at 84-89.

[24] Halpern, *supra* note 14, at 84-89.

[25] *Id* 83.

[26] McNay, *supra* note 17, at 79-81.

[27] Dannings, *supra* note 15, at 33-34; Halpern, *supra* note 14.

[28] Counsel must take extreme care to evaluate this and any other tax question to insure that the settlement is structured so that the payments to the plaintiff are not taxable.

[29] IRS Priv Ltr Rul 8333035 (May 16, 1983) states that:

> On March 21, 1983, the Internal Revenue Service issued a ruling that you will have neither actual nor constructive receipt, nor the economic benefit of the present value of the amount invested in the annuity, and the periodic payments will be excludable from your gross income under section 104(a)(2) of the Internal Revenue Code. In that ruling, we cited Rev. Rule. 79-313, 1979-2 C.B. 75; and Rev. Rule. 79-220, 1979-2 C.B. 74; for the proposition that a corporation will be considered the owner of an annuity if the annuity is subject to the general creditors of the corporation. The corporation can change the beneficiary of the policy, and the beneficiary does not have the right to accelerate any payment or to

the actual or approximate cost (i.e., the present value) through an appropriate consultant.[30]

Knowing the present value of the structured settlement also is necessary so that plaintiff's counsel's fees can be calculated under a contingent fee contract. Although fees sometimes can also be structured, more commonly the fees are paid from the larger first payment of the structured settlement.[31] If plaintiff's counsel receives its fees immediately, its percentage should be based on the present value of the settlement.[32] It would be clearly unfair to the client for counsel to presently receive a percentage of the total payments, rather than of the present value. Accordingly, in order to ethically calculate the fee, plaintiff's counsel also needs to know the present value of the structured settlement.

Example 7-3

A structured settlement is negotiated in a case in which the plaintiff is eight years old and has suffered a certain degree of permanent disability. The present value of the settlement is $900,000. It is agreed that the settlement will be structured as follows:

1. An initial payment of $400,000

2. Monthly payments of $3,000 initially and increasing every year by 3 per cent

3. Additional payments of $50,000 at ages 18, 21, 25, and 30

---

decrease the amount of the annual payments specified. *You have asked for a clarification of the above ruling because of your concern that your knowledge of the existence or cost of the annuity might cause you to be in constructive receipt of that annuity.*
Based on the language in section 1.451-2(a) of the regulations, the Service has consistently taken the position that knowledge is not determinative in deciding a question of constructive receipt, but that unqualified availability is decisive. Rev. Rule. 68-126, 1968-1 C.B. 194; Rev. Rule. 73-99, 1973-1 C.B. 412; Rev. Rule. 74-37, 1974-1 C.B. 112; and Rev. Rule. 76-3, 1976-1 C.B. 114; all set forth conclusions consistent with this position.
Based on the information submitted in the original ruling request, *we conclude that disclosure by defendant of the existence, cost, or present value of the annuity will not cause you to be in constructive receipt of the present value of the amount invested in the annuity.* (Emphasis added.)

It should be noted that, although this seems to leave no doubt as to the position of the IRS, a letter ruling is not precedent.

[30] Dannings, *supra* note 15, at 33-34.

[31] Structuring fees involves the deferral of income for counsel, as opposed to the exclusion of income for the client. Accordingly, the tax requirements and ramifications of such structuring for counsel's tax liability need to be determined on an individual basis with appropriate consultations from tax experts as counsel deems necessary. Counsel's contract with the client, the client's feelings and needs, and any applicable state law can affect whether counsel has a choice in structuring the fee or in being paid in full at the time of the settlement. *See* Sayble v Feinman, 76 Cal App 3d 509, 142 Cal Rptr 895 (1978); Cardenas v Ramsey County, 322 NW2d 191 (Minn 1982); and *In re* Chow, 3 Haw App 577, 656 P2d 105 (1982).

[32] *See* Donaghy v Napoleon, 543 F Supp 112 (DNJ 1982); Landgraf v Glasser, 186 NJS 381, 452 A2d 713 (1982); Merendion v FMC Corp, 181 NJS 503, 438 A2d 365 (1981); and Johnson v Sears, Roebuck & Co, 291 PaS 625, 436 A2d 675 (1981).

It is further agreed that the payments are guaranteed for 20 years, or life, whichever is longer, and that an annuity to fund the payments will be purchased by the defendant for the benefit of the minor plaintiff from a AAA-rated life insurance company. The initial payment of $400,000 is to be used to pay the plaintiff's attorney's fees and expenses with the balance being put into a trust.

§7.04   Depositions

In litigation, when both clients are present at a deposition, their interaction or noninteraction should be treated as a part of the negotiation. As part of the negotiation strategy and tactics, counsel must carefully plan with the client, so that the client knows how to behave in the presence of the adverse party.

In addition, the questions that are posed and the answers that are given in the presence of the parties, including volunteered information if necessary, may present opportunities to directly communicate with the opposing party. This may be particularly significant when counsel suspects that the other attorney has not adequately informed the other party of certain facts or issues.

Although it is more common for clients to be present only at their own depositions, the client's presence at other depositions also presents a potential opportunity to affect the negotiating process. Again, the client's statements or nonverbal behavior provides a means to communicate to the other side, which may aid subsequent settlement efforts.

In addition, the questions posed to the other party and any admissions that are elicited can be viewed as both a means of communication and of fact creation.[33] On occasion, the impact of the inquiries and admissions may be sharpened by questioning the other party as if conducting a tough cross examination, as opposed to the usual discovery deposition type questions. Such an approach is the exception rather than the rule, and should be used only where:

1.   There is a reasonable possibility that it will result in a settlement

2.   Discovery is either not needed or also can be obtained during the deposition

3.   The "cross examination" during the deposition will not adversely affect the real cross examination if a trial is necessary by previewing a line of questioning and allowing the other party to be better prepared for it

§7.05   The Policy Limits Letter

If an insurance carrier refuses to settle a liability claim in bad faith, the carrier can become liable for whatever verdict is eventually awarded, even if that

---

[33] *See* §§4.02 & 6.03.

amount is in excess of the policy limits.[34] To help build a case that such additional liability against the insurer exists in these circumstances, plaintiff's counsel should put the insurer on notice of a potential claim in excess of the policy through a policy limits letter. This written demand for the policy limits can place the insurer in the position of having to pay a judgment above the limits of its policy if it rejects the claimant's demand.[35] The policy limits letter should:

1. Describe how all necessary information has been provided to the insurer

2. Note that the company's liability is clear and summarize why it is clear

3. Summarize the extent of the damages and describe why they clearly exceed the policy limits

4. Note that the company has had more than enough time to investigate and to evaluate the claim

5. Demand the policy limits

6. State that, if the demand is not met, the claimant will hold the insurer responsible for the total damages in excess of the policy limit

7. Set a time limit for the company to settle for the policy limits

8. Where the insurer owes its duty of good faith and fair dealing to its insured, who is not the claimant, ask that a copy of the letter be sent by the insurer to its insured[36]

As state law varies, the law of the applicable jurisdiction should be checked to determine whether a policy limits letter can be effective, and, if so, whether any special conditions precedent exist to pursue a bad faith claim in excess of the policy limits.

§7.06 Loan Agreements

Loan agreements can sometimes be utilized where there are multiple defen-

---

[34] This stems from the requirement in most states that insurance companies owe a duty to their insurers of good faith and fair dealing. J. Appleman, Insurance Law and Practice §§8878 & 8878.85 (1981).

[35] Skolrood, *Negotiating Settlement Of A Personal Injury Action-Plaintiff*, in Attorney's Guide to Negotiating 9-27 (1979).

[36] Generally, the insurer owes its duty of acting in good faith and of fair dealing only to its insured. J. Appleman, *supra* note 34, at 8878.85. At times, the claimant will be the insured. At other times where liability insurance is involved, the claim will be against the insured. In the latter situation, the plaintiff transmits the policy limits letter, not the insured. Assuming that there is no settlement and that a bad faith claim is being pursued to collect more than the policy limits, the plaintiff will first have to obtain a judgment against the insured. If a judgment in excess of the policy limits is rendered, the plaintiff can then negotiate an agreement with the insured to obtain an assignment of the insured's rights against the insurer. *Id.*

dants.[37] This type of device developed in a commercial insurance setting in the 1800s and, more recently, it has been used in tort cases.[38] In this kind of agreement, the plaintiff settles with a defendant for a noninterest-bearing loan, which is repayable only under specified, limited circumstances. Depending on the agreement, repayment will be required only to the extent that either:[39]

1. Plaintiff recovers from a second defendant
2. Plaintiff's subsequent recovery from a second defendant exceeds the amount of the loan

Example 7-4

Plaintiff settles with defendant X pursuant to a loan agreement for $25,000. Plaintiff goes to trial against defendant Y and loses. The plaintiff is not required to pay defendant X.

Example 7-5

In a personal injury case, plaintiff's counsel expects a verdict for $25,000 to $40,000. Plaintiff settles with defendant X pursuant to a loan agreement for $25,000 which is repayable to the extent that the plaintiff recovers from the second defendant. Plaintiff goes to trial against defendant Y, but obtains a verdict of only $15,000. When Y pays that judgment, plaintiff has to pay the $15,000 to defendant X while retaining the original $25,000.

Example 7-6

Plaintiff settles with defendant X, pursuant to a loan agreement for $25,000 which is repayable only to the extent that the plaintiff's recovery from the second defendant exceeds the amount of the loan. Plaintiff goes

---

[37] The law of the pertinent jurisdiction must be checked, both to be sure that such agreements will be upheld and enforced, as well as to ascertain any particular requirements that must be met.

[38] Reese v Chicago, Burlington & Quincy RR, 55 Ill 2d 356, 303 NE2d 382, 385 (1973); see 13 ALR3d Insurance: Validity and Effect of Loan Receipt or Agreement between Insured and Insurer for a Loan Repayable to Extent of Insured's Recovery from Another, 42 (1967). The practice began with marine insurers, and became common in the nineteenth century as a result of battles between shippers' insurance companies and the common carriers used by the shippers concerning who ultimately paid for negligently caused damage to the shipments. Reese. The insurers began to give loans to their insureds while they litigated against the allegedly negligent carriers. Id Such loan agreements were approved by the Supreme Court in Luckenbach v WJ McCahan Sugar Refining Co, 248 US 139 (1918). Notwithstanding this long-standing background, in 1973 the Illinois Supreme Court noted that: "Despite the fairly well-developed case law concerning insurer's loan receipts, we have found few cases dealing with this device when used by potential joint tortfeasors . . . . " Reese, 55 Ill2d at 362, 303 NE2d at 386.

[39] See 62 ALR3d Validity and Effect of "Loan Receipt" Agreement between Injured Party and One Tortfeasor, for Loan Repayable to Extent of Injured Party's Recovery from a Cotortfeasor, 1111, 1113-15 (1975).

to trial against defendant Y and obtains a verdict of $15,000. Plaintiff owes defendant X nothing and nets $40,000. Had the verdict been for $35,000, plaintiff would have retained $50,000 and defendant X would have been repaid $10,000. Had the verdict been for $100,000, plaintiff would have retained $100,000 and defendant X would have received all of its money back.

Some jurisdictions approve of loan agreements and treat them as such.[40] Other jurisdictions refuse to treat these agreements as creating a loan, and instead construe them as some other type of settlement agreement, such as a covenant not to sue.[41]

An example of a relatively simple loan agreement is as follows.

Example 7-7

Loan Agreement

Docket N.: 76 L 11705

Harris Trust and Savings Bank, as guardian of the Estate of John B. Hopp, Jr., plaintiff, hereby acknowledges receipt from United State Fire Insurance Company, paid on behalf of Dr. Mel Feinberg, one of the defendants, of the sum of SEVEN HUNDRED FIFTY THOUSAND and No/100 DOLLARS ($750,000.00) as a loan, which said sum it promises to repay to the United States Fire Insurance Company, at the time of and in the event of recovery by it by means of judgment, compromise, settlement or in any other manner whatsoever, from any person, persons, corporation, corporations, or any other legal entities, causing or liable for loss or damages sustained by John B. Hopp, Jr., as a result of medical treatment administered to John B. Hopp, Jr., in 1972. This Agreement is in no way to be construed as evidence of wrongdoing or fault on the part of Dr. Mel Feinberg, and Dr. Feinberg makes no admission of fault.[42]

The loan agreement allows the parties additional flexibility in negotiating a settlement. It permits a potential new incentive for a defendant to settle by holding out the prospect that the defendant will receive some or all of its money back.

State law is likely to require that the terms of the loan agreement have to be disclosed to the nonsettling defendant(s).[43] If the plaintiff needs to rely on witnesses who are affiliated with the settling defendant to prove its case against the nonsettling defendant(s), a loan agreement may affect how the trier of fact

---

[40] *Id* 1115-17.

[41] *Id.*

[42] *See* Harris Trust & Savs Bank v Ali, 100 Ill App 3d 1, 425 NE2d 1359, 1364 (1981).

[43] See, for example, *id* 1365. *See generally* 62 ALR3d *Validity and Effect of "Loan Receipt" Agreement between Injured Party and One Tortfeasor, for Loan Repayable to Extent of Injured Party's Recovery from a Cotortfeasor,* 1111 (1975).

perceives the credibility of those witnesses. That potential credibility problem needs to be evaluated as part of the decision on whether to consider or to accept a loan agreement.

§7.07 "Mary Carter" Agreements

Loan agreements are sometimes classified as a related but distinct form that has become known as a "Mary Carter"[44] agreement.[45] Like loan agreements, "Mary Carter" agreements involve cases in which there are multiple joint tort-feasors, and a settlement is reached with less than all of the joint tortfeasors.[46] In a "Mary Carter" agreement, there is an agreement as to the maximum liability for the settling tortfeasor, with a provision that either that amount will be reduced in relation to how much is obtained from the nonsettling tortfeasor, or that a recovery from the nonsettling tortfeasor will eliminate the settling tortfeasor's obligations.[47]

"Mary Carter" agreements may not provide for dismissing the settling defendant from the suit, and sometimes are defined as being secret agreements between the parties to the settlement.[48] Yet, in an apparent contradiction, they

---

[44] The term, "Mary Carter" agreement, comes from the use of this type of agreement in the case of Booth v Mary Carter Paint Co, 202 So 2d 8 (Fla Dist Ct App 1967); 65 ALR3d *Validity and Effect of Agreement with One Cotortfeasor Setting His Maximum Liability and Providing for Reduction or Extinguishment Thereof Relative to Recovery against Nonagreeing Cotortfeasor,* 602, 604-605, n 1 & 3 (1975). Mary Carter was overruled on other grounds in Ward v Ochoa, 284 So 2d 385 (Fla 1973).

[45] *Compare* Manual For Complex Litigation Second 164-65 in J. Moore, Moore's Federal Practice (1986) and Annotation, *supra* note 44, at 607.

[46] J. Moore, *supra* note 45; Annotation, *supra* note 44, at 604.

[47] Annotation, *supra* note 44, at 604, n 1. *See also* 62 ALR *Validity and Effect of "Loan Receipt" Agreement between Injured Party and One Tortfeasor, for Loan Repayable to Extent of Injured Party's Recovery from a Cotortfeasor,* 1111, 1113-15 (1975).

[48] J. Moore, *supra* note 45; Annotation, *supra* note 44, at 605 and 614-17, nn 3, 32, and 34. In Booth v Mary Carter Paint Co, 202 So 2d 8, 10 (Fla Dist Ct App 1967), the court described the agreement at issue as follows:

An agreement between . . . the defendants, B.C. Willoughby and Harry Lee Sutton, and . . . the plaintiff, J.D. Booth, provides: "1. That the maximum liability, exposure or financial contribution of the defendants, B.C. Willoughby and Harry Lee Sutton, shall be $12,500.00."

The agreement further provides:

Second, that in the event of a joint verdict against Willoughby and the Mary Carter Paint Company exceeding $37,500.00, that the plaintiff will satisfy said judgment against Mary Carter Paint Company entirely, with no contribution from Willoughby and Sutton. Provided, however, that if the Mary Carter Paint Company is not financially responsible to the extent of $37,500.00, the defendant Willoughby will contribute an amount of money between Mary Carter Paint Company's actual responsibility and the figure of $37,500.00, but not to exceed $12,500.00.

Third. Willoughby and Sutton agreed that in the event of a verdict for all the defendants, they would pay the plaintiff $12,500.00; and in the event of a verdict against Mary Carter Paint Company less than $37,500.00, that Willoughby and Sutton would contribute the sum $12,500.00.

Fourth, Willoughby and Sutton shall continue as active defendants in the active

probably will have to be disclosed.[49] As with loan agreements, care must be taken to check the validity, requirements, and effects concerning the proposed agreement in the applicable jurisdiction.

§7.08 Contribution Statutes

Contribution statutes can create an incentive to settle where there are multiple defendants with joint and several liability. For example, the Illinois contribution statute states, in part, as follows:

    (c) When a release or a covenant not to sue or not to enforce judgement is given in good faith to one or more persons liable in tort arising out of the same injury or the same wrongful death, it does not discharge any of the other tortfeasors from liability for the injury or wrongful death unless its terms so provide but it reduces the recovery on any claim against the others to the extent of any amount stated in the release or the covenant, or in the amount of the consideration actually paid for it, whichever is greater.

    (d) *The tortfeasor who settles with a claimant pursuant to paragraph (c) is discharged from all liability for any contribution to any other tortfeasor.*

---

defense of said litigation until all questions of liability and damages are resolved between the plaintiff and the other defendants.

Fifth, that should the conditions laid down in the agreement result in any financial responsibility on the part of Willoughby and Sutton, they will pay the plaintiff within five days after the questions of liability and damages between the plaintiff and the other defendants are settled or concluded. In paragraph 6 we again find the provision that the financial responsibility, exposure, or liability of Willoughby and Sutton shall not exceed the sum of $12,500.00.

Seventh, is is stated:

"It is the intention of the parties hereto that this agreement shall be construed as a conditional agreement between them as to financial responsibility only, and that it shall in no wise constitute, or be construed to constitute, a release, settlement, admission of liability, or otherwise, and shall have no effect upon the trial of this case as to liability or extent of damages, nor shall said agreement be revealed to the jury trying said case."

Eighth, it was agreed that the contents of this agreement would be furnished to no one, unless so ordered by the court, and

Ninth, that the terms and conditions specified in the agreement, which are dependent upon a jury verdict, should be equally applicable and binding on the parties in the event plaintiff Booth amicably settles the issues of liability and damages with Mary Carter Paint Company.

Although the Mary Carter court upheld this agreement, subsequently, the Florida Supreme Court, in Ward v Ochoa, 284 So 2d 385, 387-88 (Fla 1973), rejected the secrecy provisions of the agreement, at least where such an agreement is "sought to be discovered under appropriate rules of procedure," and held that the agreement could be admissible at trial. *Id* 387.

[49] J. Moore, *supra* note 45; 65 ALR3d *Validity and Effect of Agreement with One Cotortfeasor Setting His Maximum Liability and Providing for Reduction or Extinguishment Thereof Relative to Recovery against Nonagreeing Cotortfeasor,* 602, 605, and 614-17, nn 3, 32, and 34.

(e)   A tortfeasor who settles with a claimant pursuant to paragraph (c) is not entitled to recover contribution from another tortfeasor whose liability is not extinguished by the settlement."[50] (Emphasis added.)

The protection from liability to a codefendant for contribution, that the statute provides to a defendant who settles with the plaintiff, can create a strong incentive to be the first defendant to reach a settlement with the plaintiff. The stronger incentive is most likely to be with the defendant who is apt to be the target of a successful contribution claim between codefendants.[51] If this situation exists, and the defendants appear to be unaware of it, the plaintiff may make them aware of it if that will create a tactical advantage.

Example 7-8

In a personal injury case, the two defendants are jointly and severally liable. The facts of the case are such that if either one is found liable, both will be liable. Plaintiff's injuries are severe, and, if the plaintiff prevails on the issue of liability, the likely verdict is $150,000. The plaintiff, however, has difficulties in proving liability, and his chances of doing so are perhaps 50-50. Defendant X has a contribution claim against defendant Y. If the plaintiff does prove liability, defendant Y believes that it will be held liable for 80 per cent of the plaintiff's damages under X's contribution claim. The applicable contribution statute has the same provisions as the Illinois statute. Defendant Y views its potential exposure and mathematical break-even point as follows:

$150,000 verdict with 80% contribution = $120,000 of potential exposure

50% chance of having to pay $120,000 = $60,000

Defendant Y also accurately assesses the fact that the plaintiff has to be concerned with losing at trial and recovering nothing. Accordingly,

---

[50] Ill Rev Stat ch 70 para 302. The other paragraphs of 302 are as follows:

(a) Except as otherwise provided in this Act, where 2 or more persons are subject to liability in tort arising out of the same injury to person or property, or the same wrongful death, there is a right of contribution among them, even though judgment has not been entered against any or all of them.

(b) The right of contribution exists only in favor of a tortfeasor who has paid more than his pro rata share of the common liability, and his total recovery is limited to the amount paid by him in excess of his pro rata share. No tortfeasor is liable to make contribution beyond his own pro rata share of the common liability.

(f) Anyone who, by payment, has discharged in full or in part the liability of a tortfeasor and has thereby discharged in full his obligation to the tortfeasor, is subrogated to the tortfeasor's right of contribution. This provision does not affect any right of contribution nor any right of subrogation arising out of any other relationship.

[51] Compare the effects of Ill Rev Stat ch 70 para 302 (d) and (e)(1987).

defendant Y opens settlement talks with the plaintiff. The two parties settle for $50,000. Defendant Y is satisfied that it settled for $10,000 less
than its most likely value of $60,000. The plaintiff would have settled with
both defendants for a total of $75,000 ($150,000 times 0.5). Instead, he
now has $50,000, with his chances of recovering $150,000 just as good
as they were before he settled with Y. Thus, he feels that he can afford
to take the risk of proceeding to trial. Moreover, a realistic settlement
with defendant X could result in an additional $50,000. That figure is
derived as follows:

$150,000 verdict minus $50,000 setoff for the settlement with
Y = $100,000

50% chance of a verdict = $50,000

Thus, while Y may have saved $10,000 from its mathematical break-even
point, the plaintiff has increased a total realistic settlement with both
defendants from $75,000 to $100,000. Due to the provisions of the contribution statute, the early settlement between the plaintiff and Y has helped
both of them at the expense of X, whose likely exposure has significantly
increased.[52]

§7.09 Offers of Judgment

Rule 68 of the Federal Rules of Civil Procedure states as follows:

At any time more than 10 days before the trial begins, a party defending
against a claim may serve upon the adverse party an offer to allow judgment to be taken against him for the money or property or to the effect
specified in his offer, with costs then accrued. If within 10 days after the
service of the offer the adverse party serves written notice that the offer
is accepted, either party may then file the offer and the notice of acceptance together with proof of service thereof and thereupon the clerk shall
enter judgment. An offer not accepted shall be deemed withdrawn and
evidence thereof is not admissible except in a proceeding to determine
costs. If the judgment finally obtained by the offeree is not more favorable
than the offer, the offeree must pay the costs incurred after the making
of the offer. The fact that an offer is made but not accepted does not preclude a subsequent offer. When the liability of one party to another has
been determined by verdict or order or judgment, but the amount or
extent of the liability remains to be determined by further proceedings,
the party adjudged liable may make an offer of judgment, which shall have
the same effect as an offer made before trial if it is served within a reason-

---

[52] For convenience, this example did not include the parties' litigation costs in calculat-
ing their settlement positions or exposure. Of course, in reality, this factor would also
be taken into account.

able time not less than 10 days prior to the commencement of hearings to determine the amount or extent of liability.

A number of states have similar rules.[53] Some states also have analogous rules that allow a plaintiff to make an offer of judgment and provide for prejudgment interest if the plaintiff ultimately achieves a verdict in excess of the offer.[54]

For federal court actions, the costs that can be shifted to the plaintiff are set forth in the statute that defines general federal court costs.[55] Typical expenses included within § 1720 are fees paid to the Clerk of the Court, witness fees, and court reporter's costs.

Rule 68 is probably underutilized as a negotiating tactic.[56] A Rule 68 offer can be made only by a defendant.[57] There is no cost to the defendant if the plaintiff rejects the offer.

Under the proper circumstances, a Rule 68 offer of judgment can place significant pressure on the plaintiff to accept the offer. Of course, to do so, the offer must be realistically high to create concern by the plaintiff that a verdict will not exceed the offer. Also, the offer should be made early enough to maximize the potential cost to the plaintiff to the extent possible.[58]

A Rule 68 offer of judgment is most useful when it is quite probable that the defendant will be found liable at trial. In fact, the rule was particularly intended for cases in which it is highly likely that the plaintiff will prevail, although the extent of the damages is unclear.[59] The cost-shifting provisions of Rule 68 do not apply if the defendant prevails at trial.[60]

The usefulness of Rule 68 to a defendant in a given case depends on the following criteria:

1. Can the defendant realistically evaluate the potential liability and the potential damages so as to be able to make an advantageously low but still realistic offer of judgment?

2. Is the defendant willing to settle the case for that relatively low but realistic amount?

3. Are the future costs sufficiently high to constitute a meaningful threat to the plaintiff, if the offer of judgment is rejected and the plaintiff recovers less than the offer?

4. Is it likely that the plaintiff will win at trial?

---

[53] *See* Delta Air Lines v August, 450 US 346, 356-58, nn 18-22 (1981).

[54] Varon, *Promoting Settlements & Limiting Litigation Costs By Means of the Offer of Judgment: Some Suggestions for Using & Revising Rule 68,* 33 Am U L Rev 813 (1984).

[55] 28 USC § 1720.

[56] Varon, *supra* note 54, at 815 & 848.

[57] Delta Air Lines v August, 450 US 346, 352 (1981).

[58] *See* Varon, *supra* note 54, at 843.

[59] Delta Air Lines v August, 450 US 346, 355-56 (1981).

[60] *Id.*

5. Is the plaintiff entitled to recover statutory attorney's fees as costs if the plaintiff prevails?

Regarding the last of the five criteria listed, a Rule 68 offer of judgment must not exclude, either explicitly or implicitly, statutory attorney's fees where those fees have been statutorily defined as costs.[61] For example, in civil rights and employment discrimination cases, the federal statutes provide that a prevailing plaintiff obtains attorney's fees as part of the costs.[62] This must be distinguished from statutes that award attorney's fees to prevailing plaintiffs, but do so as a separate and distinct item from the costs.

If the offer of judgment explicitly includes attorney's fees and other costs, then that is the total offer.[63] Where attorney's fees are defined as costs, if the offer of judgment does not explicitly include attorney's fees, then the court will add on the attorney's fees and the other costs to the amount of the Rule 68 offer.[64] If a prevailing plaintiff, who is entitled to attorney's fees as part of the costs, has rejected a Rule 68 offer of judgment, whether the plaintiff has surpassed the offer of judgment is determined by comparing the judgment obtained plus costs, including attorney's fees up to the date of the offer, to the amount of the offer.[65] The attorney's fees incurred after the date of the offer are disregarded in making that determination.[66]

If the plaintiff does not exceed the rejected offer, then the defendant will not be liable for any attorney's fees accrued after the offer was made.[67] An early, realistic offer of judgment therefore can put particular pressure on a plaintiff and on plaintiff's attorney where statutory attorney's fees are involved.

In civil rights and employment discrimination cases, even if the defense succeeds in shifting its costs to the plaintiff by using Rule 68, defense attorney's fees apparently cannot be shifted to the plaintiff under Rule 68.[68] This result occurs because, under 42 USC §1988, the defendant can receive attorney's fees only if civil rights or employment discrimination suits are vexatious, frivolous, or brought to harass or embarrass.[69]

If the defendant is in a better position than the plaintiff to evaluate the case early, and the defendant makes an offer of judgment, the plaintiff will be at

---

[61] Marek v Chesney, 473 US 1 (1985); Simon, *The New Meaning Of Rule 68: Marek v. Chesney and Beyond,* 14 NYU Rev L & Soc Change 475, 513-14, n 189 (1986).

[62] *See* 42 USC §§1983, 1988, & 2000(e) *et seq.*

[63] Marek v Chesney, 473 US 1 (1985).

[64] *Id.*

[65] *Id;* Grosvenor v Brienen, 801 F2d 944 (7th Cir 1986).

[66] Marek v Chesney, 473 US 1 (1985).

[67] *Id;* J. Moore, *supra* note 45, at 173, n 11.

[68] Crossman v Marcoccio, 806 F2d 329 (1st Cir 1986) (holding that Rule 68 cannot make the plaintiff responsible for the defendant's attorney's fees); Marek v Chesney, 473 US 1 (1985), Brennan, Marshall, and Blackmun, JJ, *dissenting,* 473 US at 13, n 15; Grosvenor v Brienen, 801 F2d 944, 946, n 4 (7th Cir 1986) (strongly suggesting in dicta that such a fee shift is impermissible). The Supreme Court has not ruled on this issue.

[69] Christianburg Garment Co v EEOC, 434 US 412 (1978).

a significant disadvantage in trying to evaluate whether to accept the offer. The plaintiff should seek to avoid this dilemma through research and investigation prior to filing suit, as well as by early discovery.[70]

§7.10   Timing

The vast majority of cases do settle.[71] They are more likely to settle, however, when the timing of the settlement provides an extra incentive to settle. These also are the times when a judicial settlement conference is most likely to be effective.[72]

It is important for counsel to recognize the timing issue, both to know when it is advantageous for the client to settle, and also to know when the time is ripe to approach the other side to attempt to reach a settlement. The latter point may be more important to plaintiffs' lawyers, since it is generally the defense which needs the extra incentive to become interested in settling.[73]

Once a suit has been filed, a settlement can, of course, be reached at any time. However, settlements tend to occur when:

1. The defendant will save a relatively significant amount of litigation expenses

2. Defense counsel will avoid a significant amount of pretrial preparation

3. Both parties will save a relatively significant amount of litigation expenses

4. Both parties' counsel will avoid a significant amount of pretrial preparation

5. There is relatively little, or no, time left to settle before the trial will commence[74]

The amount constituting a relatively significant amount of litigation expenses generally depends on the sums at stake in the case and the resources of the parties.

These incentives are mostly likely to be present at the following points:

---

[70] Simon, *supra* note 61, at 491-94. It has been suggested that, if the plaintiff does find itself in this dilemma, it should seek an extension of time to respond to the offer as well as accelerated discovery, so that it can adequately evaluate the offer. *Id* 494-97. It is questionable, however, whether such an extension is permissible under the language of the rule. Staffend v Lake Central Airlines, 47 FRD 218 (D Ohio 1969), held that no such extensions are permissible.

[71] Perschbacher, *Regulating Lawyers' Negotiations,* 27 Ariz L Rev 75, n 2 (1985).

[72] See **§6.04** concerning judicial settlement conferences.

[73] Naturally, this generality does not hold true in every case.

[74] As the trial approaches, many lawyers become more realistic about the weaknesses and the problems of their case, as well as about the risks of going to trial. G. Spence, Trial By Fire 168 (1986). In the context of large personal injury cases, it has been suggested that such cases tend not to settle until the time of trial nears. Davis, *Settlement Negotiation: Strategy and Tactics,* 21 Trial 82, 84 (1985).

1. After the initial written discovery has been completed, but prior to the time to start taking all or most of the depositions

2. If expert testimony is essential, after the written discovery, nonexpert's depositions, and perhaps the deposition of plaintiff's expert, but either before the defense has to disclose its expert, or before its expert's deposition is taken

3. If final pretrial order is required, after all, or virtually all, discovery has been completed, but before the expenditure of time and effort to prepare an extensive final pretrial order

4. When a firm trial date is relatively imminent, but a settlement will still avoid the cost and the effort of substantial final trial preparations

5. When the trial is about to commence[75]

A number of incentives cause these points. The first two time points are basically influenced by the economics of saving litigation costs. In addition, settlements at the first point listed may occur in those cases in which either there was no opportunity to settle the case before filing suit, or the case clearly should have been settled without the need for a suit.

Example 7-9

A city lacks procedures for settling civil rights claims unless a lawsuit is filed. Where the plaintiff's liability case appears to be strong and the damages are relatively small, the city is inclined to reach early settlement to avoid unnecessary expenses.

Example 7-10

Plaintiff's insurance company for a major medical policy refuses to pay the medical bills that the plaintiff has submitted because it claims that the plaintiff made misrepresentations when he completed the company's application for coverage. Specifically, the insurance company asserts that the plaintiff falsely denied receiving psychiatric treatment, counseling, or therapy. In fact, the plaintiff had received therapy from a psychologist. Plaintiff's counsel points out to a representative of the insurer that, under the applicable law, the application for the policy will be construed narrowly and strictly against the company. Plaintiff's counsel then argues that psychiatry and psychology are two distinct professions. None of this sways the company's representative, and a lawsuit is filed. After reviewing the matter, defense counsel for the insurance company concludes that the plaintiff will prevail and quickly settles the case. In this instance, no discovery at all was needed before a settlement could be reached.

The time point involving substantial final pretrial orders arises from a combination of economics and the personal interests of the attorneys who have to

---

[75] This is sometimes referred to as "settling on the courthouse steps."

expend the time to prepare it. As a practical matter, the importance of the attorney's personal interests may be affected by whether the attorney is paid by the hour, salaried by his or her client, or is working on a contingency basis. This should be considered in evaluating the likely attitude of opposing counsel.

Settlements at the last time point listed are motivated by economics and the personal interests of counsel. They also can result from the following factors:

1. One or more parties' realization that a trial is not worth whatever may be gained
2. One or more parties' fear of losing at a trial
3. The parties' realization that a trial is not worth the cost in time and inconvenience
4. Because of the pressure and the stress that trials tend to cause for both the parties and their attorneys
5. There is no time left to either delay or to ignore the matter
6. A combination of these factors

These six factors also operate to cause settlements in cases in which a trial is about to begin, or sometimes after the trial has begun. There is probably nothing more that a judge can do to effectively encourage a settlement then to set a meaningful trial date in the relatively near future.[76]

Just as it is easier to settle cases when the timing of the settlement negotiations creates an economic incentive to settle, the opposite is also true. If realistic settlement negotiations do not take place soon enough, it is possible that the litigation costs that have been incurred will make it more difficult to settle the case. This is because those expenditures lower the amount that the defendant is willing to pay in settlement.

A plaintiff's expenditure of costs can cause the plaintiff to demand a higher settlement, possibly a higher settlement than the defendant is willing to pay. The passage of a long period of time also may cause the plaintiff to raise its bottom line unless some special need for money arises.

Example 7-11

Had a medical malpractice claim been settled early, the plaintiff would have been willing to settle for as little as $25,000. Five years have now passed, and the defendant's insurance company has steadfastly refused to discuss a settlement until the case is set to go to trial in three days. In preparing for the trial, the plaintiff has incurred $7,000 in expenses, and the trial expenses will be an additional $3,000. The plaintiff's attorney estimates that the odds on liability are 50-50, and that a verdict for the plaintiff probably will be in the area of $70,000. The plaintiff considers the attorney's estimate that the results of a trial are likely to be either minus $10,000 (if the defendant prevails), or plus approximately $70,000

---

[76] G. Spence, *supra* note 74. See also §6.04 regarding judicial settlement conferences.

(if plaintiff prevails). With this counseling in mind, but also being aggravated by the five-year wait and the defendant's delay in being willing to negotiate, the plaintiff insists on a bottom line of $35,000. The defendant has had $15,000 of expenses and anticipates that a trial will cost an additional $8,000. Defense counsel evaluates the probable outcome of a trial somewhat differently than does the plaintiff's attorney. The defendant's insurer decides that it will offer a maximum of $25,000 to settle the case. No settlement is reached, and the case goes to trial. The delay in settlement has meant that the opportunity for an economically favorable settlement for both sides has been lost.

In certain cases, emotions affect negotiation timing. This can occur in any type of case, but more often it occurs in more emotional contexts such as matrimonial litigation. For example, parties in divorce cases can have strong emotional feelings and needs that affect their settlement positions, especially in the early stages of the case. They may feel guilt and fear public knowledge of their problems and secrets, as well as the possible or actual involvement of family, friends, and associates.[77] These fears tend to lower their settlement aspirations. The parties may feel anger and self-righteousness, and may have been influenced by stories of supposedly "great" settlements that have been received by others.[78] If so, settlement aspirations tend to be higher. They also can feel uncertainty and anxiety about finances and future relationships.[79] This leads to feelings of a need for security, which again tends to raise settlement ambitions. Emotional influences from cash flow problems or from child custody or support issues may affect settlement goals in either direction depending on the particular circumstances and the persons involved. As a result of the usual presence of strong emotions, at least initially, it often is especially important in matrimonial cases to wait to negotiate until the client is ready to be realistic.[80] On the other hand, if the other party's emotions have rendered his or her settlement objectives unreasonably low, the opportunity exists to present a favorable offer that may be accepted only if it is tendered early.

Like emotions, an entity's internal policies also can produce an optimal time to settle.

Example 7-12

For accounting and planning purposes, an insurance company has an internal policy of preferring to close files by the end of its fiscal year. As the end of its fiscal year approaches, its adjusters and their supervisors are therefore more prone to settle claims in order to reach the administrative goal of reducing the number of open files.

---

[77] Zavett & Friedman, *The Negotiation of Matrimonial Cases,* in Attorney's Guide to Negotiation 6-5, 6-6 (1979).

[78] *Id* 6-6 & 6-9.

[79] *Id* 6-5.

[80] *Id* 6-35.

§7.11   Criminal Cases

The nature of criminal cases creates its own set of considerations regarding negotiation timing. Criminal cases almost invariably involve litigation or threatened litigation. In a small percentage, the negotiation will occur to prevent the filing of charges. Almost all criminal negotiations, however, occur in the context of a pending prosecution. In addition to other tactics, discussion, win/win, and the creation of facts are especially useful.[81]

One important distinction between criminal and most civil negotiations is that, in criminal cases, the judge has an independent responsibility to evaluate the appropriateness of a suggested disposition.[82] The vast majority of criminal cases result in a negotiated plea.[83] To make the system function in a bureaucratic sense, some judges are less inclined to independently review a proposed disposition than they are to quickly close a case. Others review each case more carefully. Defense counsel especially should not engage in negotiations without ascertaining whether the resulting agreement is likely or certain to be approved by the court. This includes considering the judge's sentencing tendencies.

Most often a negotiated plea will involve an agreement regarding a recommended sentence between the prosecution and the defense. At times, however, the agreement will be for the prosecution not to make any recommendation, although the judge may receive one from a probation department.

§7.12   Summary and Review

I. Litigation
   A. Unlike transactions or deals, parties may be pushed together by outside events rather than mutual decision and may seek unilateral gain or to avoid a loss rather than mutual gain. There often is uncertainty about whether to negotiate, greater rigidity against compromise initially, and suspicion
   B. Emotional and psychological needs can cause a party to take positions that are economically unwise
   C. Fact creation can profoundly change the stakes, and may necessitate delay to obtain information needed to evaluate the case
   D. A threat of litigation perceived as serious can motivate the other party to settle rather than expend fees and costs

---

[81] See §5.10 on discussion, §8.09 regarding win/win outcomes, and §4.03 about the creation of facts. These sections all contain portions focused on the criminal case.

[82] Roberts, *Negotiation in a Criminal Case-Prosecution*, in Attorney's Guide to Negotiation 12-24 (1979). In some civil cases, the judge also has a special duty to independently evaluate the fairness of any settlement. For example, in class actions, the court must adjudicate whether a settlement is fair and reasonable before the settlement is final. Fed R Civ P 23(e); Armstrong v Board of School Directors, 616 F2d 305 (7th Cir 1980). See §6.08 regarding class actions. Other types of civil cases in which a negotiated settlement normally must be scrutinized by the court include juvenile neglect and abuse cases and personal injury settlements for minors.

[83] Penn, Jr., *Negotiation in a Criminal Case-Defense*, in Attorney's Guide to Negotiation 13-3 (1979).

    E. The appearance of new counsel for litigation can raise or lower client expectations, depending on the attorney's evaluation of the case, or create a client mind-set to use its new weapon

    F. Counsel's evaluation must ignore the impact of prompt settlement on fees from the standpoint of the lawyer's personal interests

    G. Litigation often adversely impacts any remaining relationship between the parties; and that must be analyzed before choosing the tactic if such relationship is important to the client. This includes considering customers or associates who may hear of the charges and counterchanges

    H. Be mentally prepared to negotiate at any stage without reducing efforts in a way that endangers the chance of success at trial or appeal

    I. Negotiations may be expedited through motions for injunctive relief

    J. In deciding whether to litigate, consider whether there will be publicity and, if so, the effect on the parties and any relevant others

    K. Similarly, any intimidating or inflammatory effects from decisions on how to draft the complaint must be considered

    L. Especially useful for no concessions or no further concessions strategies, and can be used for all other strategies except concede first

    M. Can be utilized for all client goals, but may be inappropriate in a particular situation for cooperative and defensive goals

    N. Can serve as a deterrent to further acts by the defendant

II. Structured Settlements

    A. A specialized win/win tactic

    B. A stream of payments over time generally not subject to taxation

    C. Must be evaluated against present value and investment potential of a lump sum payment

III. Depositions

    A. If contact between the parties is possible, the client participation analysis applies from **§6.02.**

    B. Provides an opportunity to disclose information to the other party through questions, responses to questions, and nonverbal communication

IV. Policy Limits Letter

    A. To challenge a bad faith refusal to settle by an insurer

    B. Can make the insurer responsible for damages above the policy limits

    C. Depends on state laws

V. Loan Agreements

    A. Can be used where there are multiple defendants

    B. One defendant settles for a noninterest-bearing loan repayable only to the extent that either:

1. Plaintiff recovers from a second defendant
2. Plaintiff's subsequent recovery from a second defendant exceeds the amount of the loan

C. Can affect the perceived credibility of a witness
D. Disclosure may be required

VI. "Mary Carter" Agreements
    A. For multiple defendant cases where less than all defendants settle
    B. The settling defendant's monetary obligation is reduced by any recovery from one or more other defendants
    C. Disclosure may be required

VII. Contribution Statutes
    A. Protects a settling defendant against claims by other defendants
    B. Can provide an incentive to settle before other defendants

VIII. Offers of Judgment
    A. Federal Rule 68 and some state's rules
    B. Pressures a plaintiff by shifting costs if the plaintiff does not receive a judgment in excess of the offer
    C. Most useful where the plaintiff is quite likely to prevail
    D. Structure depends on whether an award of attorney's fees is possible
    E. A defendant with more knowledge of the case can pressure a plaintiff by an early offer of judgment. The countermeasure for plaintiff is anticipation, prelitigation investigation, and early discovery

IX. Timing
    A. Litigation tends to settle when one or more parties can save significant expense, time, or effort
    B. Also, litigation tends to settle when trial is imminent
    C. Expenditure of costs can make it more difficult to settle
    D. Delay can lead a plaintiff to raise its demands
    E. Emotions can affect optimal timing
    F. A party's internal policies may affect the timing of a negotiation

X. Criminal Cases
    A. Judges must evaluate a plea bargain
    B. Defense counsel must determine or estimate whether the judge will accept a plea bargain, and the judge's sentencing tendencies

Systematic Planning: The First Stages

8

§8.01   Introduction

Effective planning generally is the most important element in successful negotiation. Many commentators acknowledge the critical importance of planning.[1]

Consider the following example: Your job is to negotiate the sale of 100,000 pounds of Jeftod, a raw material used in manufacturing. The cost to produce Jeftod is $2 per pound. A potential purchaser is BARP. You enter the office of their vice-president, Laurjen, whom you have never met before. Initially, you exchange greetings and sit down in large chairs separated by a marble table. After mentioning the weather, Laurjen says: "Let's get right to the point. We need 25,000 pounds and will pay $75,000. Can we make a deal?" How should you respond? Obviously, you do not have sufficient information to respond at this point. Should you accept the offer, since the profit margin

---

[1] See for example, R. Lewicki & J. Litterer, Negotiation 45 (1985); *Negotiations, or The Art of Negotiating*, in W. Zartman, The 50% Solution 48 (1976).

would be 50 per cent? Or should you make a counteroffer? If you do make a counteroffer, how much should it be?

Some people do not plan at all. Others plan for a negotiation by simply attempting to think about it in a general, unstructured way. Acting as though the negotiation was some amorphous cloud, they just think about whatever points come to mind. By doing so, they cover certain important points, but at the same time, they are unlikely to think of all of the important points.

Systematic planning is an important means of creating a thorough, well-prepared negotiating plan. Just as simple checklists can be useful to insure that nothing is overlooked in other contexts,[2] systematic planning can perform that same function. Of course, systematic planning involves far more than a mechanical checklist, since each step requires careful analysis of a range of possibilities.

Moreover, the uncertain and fluid nature of negotiation can make it a stressful experience.[3] Systematic planning reduces the stress by increasing the negotiator's personal effectiveness and control over the situation.

Systematic planning for a negotiation consists of a series of 14 steps. These steps provide a methodology to determine goals, decide what information should be analyzed, analyze that information, plan strategy and tactics, and formulate a series of potential offers and tradeoffs, as well as a sound bottom line position.

By preparing systematically, the negotiator can avoid many pitfalls and negotiation nightmares. A common one is underestimating or overestimating the other party or its negotiator.[4] To avoid unwittingly falling into this trap, planning steps 3 through 13 provide a guide for the analysis. The other side then should be given the benefit of the doubt as to questions about its strengths and abilities. This will avoid underestimating them until these areas can be probed during the negotiation.

Ineffective planning can lead to a failure to make a favorable agreement, or to the making of an agreement that is less favorable than one which is potentially available. These problems are illustrated below in the following examples.

---

[2] Kim, O'Connor & Hianik, *Drafting the Contract for the Purchase and Sale of a Business,* in Buying And Selling Businesses 6-16 (1987). Checklists, adjusted as necessary to fit the particular matter, may be particularly useful in certain types of business transactions such as a sale of assets or a sale of stock. *Id.* Such a negotiating checklist, with any revisions that occur due to the course of the negotiation, then may be used as an framework for drafting a written agreement. *Id.*

[3] Watson, *Meditation and Negotiation: Learning to Deal with Psychological Responses,* 18 U Mich JL Ref 293, 304 (1985). The negotiation process necessarily involves ambiguity and uncertainty. *Id.* This is psychologically difficult to tolerate and the tolerance for ambiguity and uncertainty varies from individual to individual. *Id.* Watson notes that: "A skilled negotiator must be able to tolerate such ambiguity for prolonged periods of time." *Id.* The negotiators', as well as the clients', capacity for such tolerance will strengthen or weaken their negotiating positions. *Id.* See §8.07 concerning evaluating strengths and weaknesses.

[4] W. Coffin, The Negotiator: A Manual for Winners 14 (1973).

Example 8-1

Prior to negotiating, the seller and the buyer have each established a "bottom line" which is the "worst" deal that each would be willing to make. Seller is willing to sell for $120 per unit or better. This is the Seller's Bottom Line (SBL). Buyer is willing to buy at $140 per unit or less. That is the Buyer's Bottom Line (BBL). Prior to any negotiation, the parties are positioned as shown below:

Figure 8-1

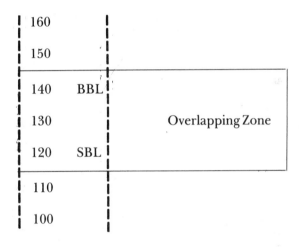

Unless the parties offend each other, miscommunicate, or fail to take positions within their own range of acceptable prices, they will reach agreement on price, since the price that the seller is willing to accept (SBL) is below that which the buyer is willing to pay (BBL). There is a zone of overlapping prices acceptable to both Seller and Buyer from $120-$140 per unit. Thus, Buyer and Seller should be able to achieve a deal, since a zone of mutually acceptable prices exists.

In an effective negotiation, each will strive to make the deal as close to the other party's bottom line as possible, without knowing exactly what that bottom line is and without "blowing" an acceptable deal.

Example 8-2 Failure to Obtain or Consider Information

Assume the same situation as in Example 8-1, except that Seller, through inaccurate gathering or assessment of information, makes a critical planning error. He overlooks one of the buyer's needs, or fails to consider it as an important constraint on the buyer. This error leads Seller to decide that he may be able to obtain a price of $180/unit. He opens the negotiation with a $180/unit demand (Seller's Opening Position, or SOP).

Figure 8-2

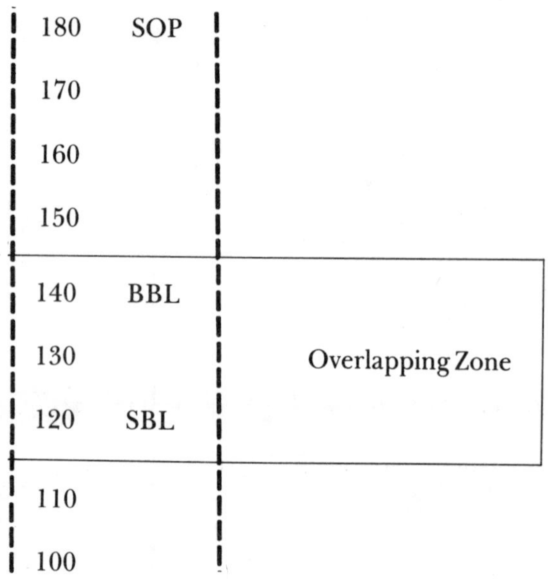

```
  180    SOP

  170

  160

  150
 ┌──────────────────────────────────────┐
  140    BBL

  130            Overlapping Zone

  120    SBL
 └──────────────────────────────────────┘
  110

  100
```

Buyer decides that Seller's demand is so far outside of the range of acceptable alternatives that no counteroffer should even be made, and the negotiation breaks down without a deal being made, despite the fact that the parties have a zone within which they could agree.

Example 8-3 Failure to Close an Acceptable Deal

A second potentially disastrous planning error is for Seller to decide that he will not close the deal today unless he gets a least $150/unit, mistakenly believing hard bargaining always is best. Seller now opens at $160/unit (SOP). The buyer, who actually needs to make the deal today, counters at $140/unit, the highest price that he is willing to pay (Buyer's Opening Position, or BOP).

Figure 8-3

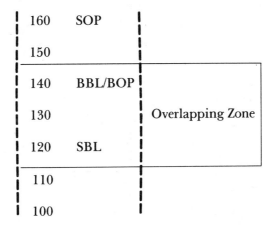

Seller decides to wait in order to see if Buyer offers a higher price, but intends to accept the $140/unit offer in a few days if Buyer stays firm. However, Buyer, needing the deal today, locates another seller who is willing to sell at $140/unit, and makes the purchase there instead. Thus, due to a miscalculation, Seller fails to make a deal that was in fact $20/unit above his bottom-line price.

Example 8-4 Making a Less Favorable Deal than Possible

Another type of planning error is underestimating the potential deal. Seller fails to carefully analyze market forces and situational pressures. Thinking that he is unlikely to get more than $125/unit, he devises an opening position of $130/unit. The buyer's bottom line is actually $140/unit. Now, at the start of the negotiation, the parties are positioned:

Because Seller's Opening Position (SOP) is below Buyer's Bottom Line (BBL), Seller cannot achieve the optimally available deal for Seller of $140/unit. Seller has started the negotiation too low at $120/unit. Poor planning has led to a less favorable deal than was possible.

Example 8-5 Uncontrolled Horse Trading

Seller has not planned the type of concessions to make. Buyer offers $100/unit. Seller counters with $150/unit. Buyer offers to "split" the difference at $125, although he is really willing to pay $135/unit. Seller agrees to $125, a relatively large concession, and never explores whether a smaller concession would suffice.

Figure 8-4

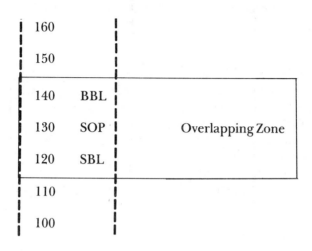

Example 8-6 Deadlock on Nonessential Points

Some points are essential, while others are merely desirable. If the negotiator has not analyzed which points are desirable but not essential, he or she may deadlock a negotiation by engaging in unnecessarily dangerous arguments and positions on a point which is not essential.

Example 8-7 Lack of Objectivity Due to Relationships

Negotiators may stop taking a hard, objective look at the potential deal because of the relationship with the other party or the other party's negotiator. While the value of the relationship cannot be ignored, it normally should not overwhelm all other factors. Long-standing relationships must be examined periodically, especially concerning negotiation goals and expectations to determine whether a better deal is available through harder bargaining or from another source.

In addition, the "work group" effect should be guarded against, so that the negotiation is approached objectively. The work group effect refers to the unwillingness to be confrontive that can occur when negotiators with supposedly different interests are involved in repeated negotiations in which they need cooperation from each other to complete their assignments. A classic example is the public defender and the local prosecutor. If they have to process a large number of cases through the courtroom each day, they may unconsciously develop a mutual goal of processing cases, instead of focusing on each negotiation with the interests of their respective clients in mind. An insurance adjuster may develop a similar work group arrangement with a public adjuster, in which each unconsciously compromises the client's interests. Systematic planning reduces the chances of being influenced by the work group effect, since the negotiator focuses on the particular negotiation, planning how to carefully and creatively achieve the best possible result.

§8.02   The System

Due to the fact that the information realistically available to a negotiator is never complete and is never without a degree of uncertainty, planning the perfect negotiation is impossible. Nevertheless, effective, systemic planning will greatly reduce negotiating errors and will greatly increase counsel's control of the negotiation. This, in turn, will significantly increase the number of optimal or nearly optimal deals that are achieved.

The 14 steps for systematic planning are outlined below. The amount of time spent on each step will vary greatly with each negotiation. That variance is dependent on such factors as experience or whether the negotiation is one of a large number of somewhat relatively simple, repetitive negotiations, or whether it is a single, relatively complex, more unique negotiation. The basic fourteen steps for systematic planning, however, remain the same. These steps are listed below.

1. Gathering information prior to the negotiation
2. Determining the client's goal(s)
3. Identifying issues
4. Analyzing the market and customary terms
5. Assessing strengths and weaknesses
6. Estimating the other party's bottom line and opening position
7. Considering win/win outcomes
8. Setting the opening position
9. Setting the bottom line
10. Choosing strategies and tactics
11. Considering concessions and tradeoffs
12. Determining an agenda
13. Analyzing timing
14. Choosing the mode(s) of communication

The first seven steps are discussed in the following sections. The remaining seven steps are described in Chapter 9.

Although detailed, the planning process is not inordinately time consuming or unwieldy. Proper planning certainly takes longer than no planning at all. It may or may not take longer than sloppy and ineffective planning, but it tends to avoid errors of oversight or miscalculation.

Through practice and familiarity with the steps, the time expended decreases. Using experience, but being careful not to become sloppy or fall into unthinking patterns, the time can be adjusted for the nature and context of the negotiation. Repetitious negotiations, especially of small tort cases, certain small transactions, and some criminal matters, can be done more quickly. Thus, with experience in utilizing the planning system and adjustments for the type of negotiation, the steps outlined provide an effective and efficient method to improve a negotiator's performance for any type of negotiation.

Providing cost-efficient services is a vital consideration. Judgment must be exercised so that an appropriate amount of time is devoted, providing the quality of service to which the client is entitled without creating undue cost. This potential dilemma is no different for planning than for other aspects of lawyering. Proper and systematic planning is a necessity for competent representation. Used correctly, systematic planning is an essential, cost-effective element in providing high quality services to clients.

§8.03   —Step 1: Prenegotiation Information Gathering

The first step in planning is to obtain any information needed and available regarding:

Your client's goals

The issues

The relevant market

The vital interests of each party and of each negotiator

The strengths and weaknesses of each party and of each negotiator

The indications of the other party's bottom line

Any effects or influences from the current economic, social, and political climates[5]

This step in the process occurs as early as is feasible and precedes any actual negotiating.[6]

Example 8-8

A licensor of technology is gathering facts prior to the beginning of the negotiation. The information obtained includes:[7]

1.   The efforts that the potential purchaser has made to develop or to acquire the same or the equivalent technology

---

[5] Mandle, *Collective Bargaining Negotiation,* in Attorney's Guide to Negotiation 14-3 (1979).

[6] H. Cohen, You Can Negotiate Anything 102 (1982).

[7] M. Zimmerman, How to Do Business with the Japanese 110-11 (1985).

2.   The benefits, both economic and otherwise, that the potential purchaser is likely to obtain from acquiring the technology

3.   The cost and the delay that the potential purchaser will incur in order to implement the technology if it is procured

This information will help to indicate the value of the technology in question. The methods and sources for obtaining this information were previously discussed.[8] Naturally, the available information is invariably limited and its reliability is often questionable. Therefore, tentative inferences should be made with caution and subjected to reevaluation as additional information becomes known.

Example 8-9

A collective bargaining agreement is to be negotiated. The employer's negotiator is planning for the negotiation, and is engaged in prenegotiation information gathering. This preparation includes:[9]

Updating himself on the law with respect to the applicable statutes, judicial decisions, and administrative rulings

Reviewing the current contract and related company documents, such as employee handbooks, pension or profit sharing plans, incentive programs, job evaluation procedures, work rules, posted company policy statements, etc.

Obtaining data about employees, including seniority information, the history of prior negotiations, information on all grievances and their resolutions since the last collective bargaining negotiation, the mood of the bargaining unit

Facts about the members of the bargaining unit's negotiation team, including information concerning their personalities

The nature of the information needed for planning varies, depending on the factors involved in the specific negotiation. However, the major categories of information that pertain to planning are discussed in the following sections which outline the steps in the planning process.[10]

After completing the prenegotiation information gathering of the available data, the planner may be struck by the gaps or the uncertainties in the accessible information. Next a determination should be made regarding the information which counsel will seek to learn or to confirm during the course of the negotiation.[11] The results of this determination then are utilized in subsequent planning steps regarding choices about tactics in general and informational tactics

---

[8] See **ch 4** on Informational Tactics.

[9] Mandle, *supra* note 5, at 14-5.

[10] See the following sections in **chs 8 & 9**.

[11] J. Graham & Y. Sano, Smart Bargaining 51 (1984).

in particular, as well as for analyzing the agenda.[12] Later, the identification of missing or uncertain information also will be used during the negotiation itself as the negotiator probes and evaluates.

§8.04 —Step 2: Determining the Client's Goals

At the outset, the general goals for the negotiation must be determined with the client who makes the ultimate decision.[13] Establishing the client's goals allows the negotiator to plan more precisely, since planning is required for each goal. The nature of the negotiation and the factors involved in the particular negotiation will determine the type of goals that are involved, as well as the specifics of each particular goal.

Example 8-10

A business transaction is being negotiated. The goals include the price, quality of the goods, due dates for delivery, cost and the means of financing, dependability of the other party, length of the contract, and obtaining options to renew.

Example 8-11

A dispute between neighbors has resulted in a lawsuit. One of the goals is to get the parties talking again, so that they can deal with each other in the future, thereby avoiding further legal expenses.

Example 8-12

An elected public official is faced with potential hiring restrictions due to budgetary constraints. The official desires to maintain a certain number of those job positions outside of the local civil service system, so that those jobs can be given to political allies.

If, as usually occurs, the client has multiple goals in mind, a priority needs to be placed on each goal. This is done so that the relative importance of each goal is ascertained for purposes of subsequent planning.[14]

Next, decisions must be made concerning whether it is essential to achieve all of the goals, and whether some goals are more important than other goals. Essential goals relate to vital interests, while desirable goals concern nonvital interests.

It may be that even though more than one goal is deemed to be essential, nevertheless, even those essential goals can be given different levels of priority. Similarly, desirable, but nonvital goals should also be prioritized. Both long-run and short-run goals must be included in this process of setting priorities.

---

[12] *See* **ch 4** & **§9.07.**

[13] G. Kennedy, J. Benson & J. McMillan, Managing Negotiations 24 (1982) [hereinafter Kennedy]; see **ch 2** regarding client goals.

[14] Kennedy, *supra* note 13. (1982).

Example 8-13

A store selling meat decides that the price and the quality of the meat are its crucial goals. The store also considers free advertising to be desirable, but nonessential. Depending on its profits, the market, or a variety of other factors, the store either may be willing to sacrifice some degree of quality to obtain meat at a lower price, or it might elect to pay more to receive a higher quality of meat in the anticipation that this will increase its sales. On the other hand, even if the store is willing to sacrifice some degree of quality to cut its costs, the store will not buy rotten meat at any price. Similarly, there will be a cost which the store is unwilling to bear no matter what quality meat can be obtained. Thus, planning is needed to establish a relationship between the vital goals of price and quality. This price/quality relationship will not only assign a priority to one or the other of the two goals, but it also will create limits on the tradeoffs between them. Furthermore, there may be some tradeoff from either or both goals for free advertising. The client must decide on these goals and their priorities.

The identification and prioritization of goals leads to the issues to be negotiated. In Example 8-13, concerning the meat store, the potential issues to be discussed with the client are:

Issue One: Price alone—Essential goal

Issue Two: Quality alone—Essential goal

Issue Three: Price and Quality if negotiated jointly—Two essential goals

Issue Four: Free advertising—Desirable goal

Issue Five: Free advertising with some tradeoff of price or quality— One desirable goal and two essential goals

There are five potential issues, since the meat supplier has to choose whether to negotiate: (1) price, but not quality; (2) quality, but not price; (3) both price and quality; (4) to obtain free advertising; and/or (5) to trade price, quality, or both for free advertising.

Even when only money is involved, and no nonmonetary issues such as quality, the identification and prioritization of the issues is critical.

Example 8-14

A person intends to purchase a new car. The prospective buyer plans for three different issues:

1. Negotiating a reduction from the sticker price
2. Bargaining over the amount the car dealer will pay for the prospective buyer's car in a trade-in

3. Deciding whether to keep the present car unless a trade-in of a certain value can be achieved

Example 8-15

A contract for a professional baseball player is scheduled to be negotiated. The issues that the player's agent plans for include:

1. The base salary
2. Various incentive clauses, such as for hitting more than 25 home runs, having a batting average of more than 300, etc.
3. Deciding whether some payments should be deferred into the future to minimize the tax consequences for the player, but with guarantees to ensure payment if the team files for bankruptcy before all of the payments have been made
4. Deciding whether a low interest loan is desirable and negotiating the terms of such a loan

Example 8-16

A union and management are engaged in one of a periodic series of negotiations. For management, the potential short-run, favorable benefit of a one-sided agreement may be shortsighted. The potential for creating a "difficult climate for the next negotiation" due to a union attitude of "militancy, unreasonable demands or personal grudges" needs to be analyzed.[15] If there is a reasonable likelihood of causing long-run difficulties, but short-run gains, then the long-term and the short-term goals must be prioritized.

After the client initially states the goals, and during the process of setting priorities and separating essential from nonessential goals, the lawyer may need to counsel the client about the legal aspects of those goals. Antitrust, securities, estate, tax, contractual, and other legal ramifications may need to be explained, so that the goals can be established and prioritized with a proper understanding of the real implications of each goal.

Many people have a natural tendency to focus more on the immediate future than on the long run. The attorney must ascertain whether the client has considered any long-term implications, and should also counsel the client if it appears that the client has not carefully compared the long-run benefits and detriments with those in the short-term. Certainly, short-term goals can be more important than long-term goals.[16] In some instances, however, the client may be thinking of pressing too hard and focusing only on the immediate potential deal, rather than establishing a more beneficial long-term relation-

---

[15] Mandle, *Collective Bargaining Negotiation,* in Attorney's Guide to Negotiation 14-3 (1979).

[16] Kapov, *International Business-Government Negotiations,* in W. Zartman, The 50% Solution 435 (1976).

ship.[17] Immediacy sometimes masks true worth and leads to overvaluing the short-term effects at the expense of far more important long-term consequences. Accordingly, care should be taken that less valuable short-run objectives do not cause the loss of more valuable long-run ones.[18]

Some clients need to be cautioned about engaging in business with those who may not operate in good faith. The greatest business relationship on paper can sour quickly and lead to grave problems if one party acts in bad faith to the detriment of the other. The more important long-term consideration may be to avoid dealing with such parties.

Balancing distant and immediate risks, benefits, and detriments is extremely important for negotiations that involve long-term relationships, since, as a general rule: "An agreement which is not fair to the other side will be honored mostly in the breach and in the long-run is not beneficial to either party."[19] The most durable agreements fairly address the needs of both of the parties.[20]

Fairness, though, is a relative term, and clients normally want the most advantageous deal possible, without creating an untenable situation. Therefore, the analysis is whether an obtainable agreement is so unfair that the other party will not fulfill its obligations. If there is a significant risk, the advantages must be weighed against the consequences of a breach.

Lastly, client goals must be sufficiently specific, so that the attorney can use the goals as a structure for discussing bottom line authority in the negotiation with the client.[21] The client may state goals which are inadequate for this purpose without further clarification. Examples of such statements are:

> "Make the best deal that you can."
>
> "Get as much as possible."

Clarification could include:

1. The criteria or factors which will to be used to determine whether a possible deal is the "best deal"
2. Whether there is a minimum number that is acceptable

When such clarification is necessary, the funnel approach and client counseling should be employed to assist the client in considering the real meaning of each contemplated goal in the context of the negotiation.[22]

Thus, each goal generates its own issue, and has its own priority in relationship to any other goal. To the extent that tradeoffs between goals are feasible, additional issues will emerge. These latter issues consist of each combination

---

[17] J. Graham & Y. Sano, Smart Bargaining 15 (1984).

[18] W. Coffin, The Negotiator: A Manual for Winners 12 (1973).

[19] Rifkin, *Negotiating Patents, Trade Secrets and Know-How Licenses,* in Attorney's Guide to Negotiation 15-13 (1979).

[20] R. Lewicki & J. Litterer, Negotiation 15 (1985).

[21] *See* §9.03.

[22] *See* §§2.01 & 4.05.

of goals that are subject to tradeoffs as a separate new issue. In turn, each issue then becomes the focal point for the subsequent planning steps.

§8.05   —Step 3: Identifying the Issues

Once the goals are known, the issues that are to be negotiated must be identified. Issues arise in those areas in which the parties' goals are or may conflict. The areas of conflict then are analyzed for the specific points to be negotiated. This can be done on an issue-by-issue basis, as issues with subissues, or both. In addition to this, the analysis must include whether the issues may be intrinsically linked or not. If there is linkage, the potential packages of issues and subissues should be identified as well.

An issue can also arise in an area in which there is no conflict between the parties' goals, but a negotiator creates the issue as a tradeoff in an effort to gain reciprocity through a variation of the concession that is of greater value to one party tactic.[23] Identifying the real issues can help counsel to recognize when the other negotiator is using this tactic and artificially creating an issue.

Some refer to each party's agenda of issues as its "bargaining mix."[24] The combined bargaining mixes provide a picture of the issues to be negotiated.

Issues can be initially categorized as economic or noneconomic. Each economic and noneconomic issue is then classified involving the long run, the short run, or both the long run and short run.

The definition of the issues may turn into a key part of the negotiation. Defining issues one way or another, in and of itself, can alter the outcome of the negotiation. If an issue is defined as accounting for sales proceeds held by a marketing agent, the potential outcome is far more limited than if it is defined as the fraudulent diversion of sales proceeds with treble or punitive damage.

The process of identifying issues next seeks to anticipate how the other side will define the issues. Modification of issues can be made if appropriate in light of the expected views of the other side. The attorney must choose whether to initially define issues to:

1.   Create room to negotiate the definitions of the issues
2.   Gain immediate acceptance of a favorable or a fair definition

If a favorable definition is likely to be accepted by the other party, or rejected without serious negative consequences, it should be attempted.

Before proceeding further, the client goals must be reexamined in the context of the issues that have been identified and the information that has been gathered at this point. Clarification may be required. Adjustments should be considered, if client goals appear to be unrealistic in view of the issues that have emerged. If clarification or possible adjustment of goals is needed, further client counseling is essential.

---

[23] See §5.08 regarding this tactic and the variation being discussed.
[24] R. Lewicki & J. Litterer, Negotiation 60 (1985).

After the issues have been identified and the client goals have been reexamined, counsel can then focus on each issue and each combination of issues in terms of:

1.   The information that has been gathered and that still is needed[25]
2.   The specific benefits and detriments flowing from the issue as they affect each client goal[26]
3.   The relevant market[27]
4.   Strengths, weaknesses, and interests of each party[28]
5.   The other party's probable opening position and bottom line[29]
6.   Possible win/win outcomes[30]
7.   The opening position[31]
8.   The bottom line[32]
9.   The strategies and tactics to be chosen[33]
10.   Potential concessions and tradeoffs[34]

These steps are considered in the following sections. While focusing on those steps, issues may be redefined or modified. New issues can emerge. Counsel must then review the prior steps to determine whether modifications should be made based on the newly recognized or redefined issues.

§8.06   —Step 4: Analyzing the Market and Customary Terms

Everything that is negotiated has a market. Houses, cars, raw materials, singers, and even accountants have prices based on their value within their market. Even when it is somewhat unique, such as a beautiful old painting, the market value of the item must be taken into consideration in planning for a negotiation, although any subjective value to the client will influence or control the opening position and the client's bottom line.[35]

---

[25] *See* §8.03.
[26] *See* §8.04.
[27] *See* §8.06.
[28] *See* §8.07.
[29] *See* §8.08.
[30] *See* §8.09.
[31] *See* §9.02.
[32] *See* §9.03.
[33] *See* §9.05.
[34] *See* §9.06
[35] Market value assumes the existence of available comparisons to what is being negotiated.

Each market has its own aspects. For instance, in labor negotiations, data must be obtained and analyzed regarding compensation rates, both in terms of wages and fringe benefits.

Another aspect of a market is supply and demand. This can include the size of the market, when that will affect the value of the item being negotiated.[36]

Example 8-17

The negotiation is for production of a custom made item. Fixed costs to begin production are $750,000. The size of the potential sales market will affect the profit margin to be negotiated. Assume that the gross profit margin based *only* on variable costs is $5 per unit. Using this cost structure, 150,000 units must be sold before the break-even point is reached. Thus, the extent of the potential market is critical. Uncertainty as to the size of the market may lead to a demand by the manufacturer for a sharing of the initial fixed costs to commence production, or to other approaches to spread the risk.

Types of market practices may also be a consideration. Whether credit is extended and, if so, the nature of the credit terms, may be a virtual "given" in the negotiation. Audited financial statements will be expected in certain transactions. The international licensing of technology will necessitate giving the right to manufacture the product in a particular country.[37] Various disclosures of information can be required by law in certain types of transactions.

Information about the market must be evaluated. Market value is a consideration, but it is not a guide in and of itself. Long-run and short-run factors can affect the price and the economic terms of a given transaction or settlement, either elevating it above, or depressing it below, the true market value. The same principle applies to market practices. Some may be too fixed to be modified, but others can be transformed as part of a negotiation depending on the parties and the context.

Negotiation Methods

In addition to the market value and practices, the market's customs and norms also need to be analyzed regarding negotiation methodology. Union officials in traditional labor negotiations expect to be able to demonstrate their zeal to their constituents by initially venting various complaints, regardless of whether they involve directly negotiable issues. A rug merchant in a Middle Eastern bazaar will be disappointed if the customer walks away after hearing the "price" without haggling for the real price. Negotiators from certain foreign cultures expect a period of formalities and pleasantries before getting down to business. They can reject attempts to negotiate without engaging in these preliminary stages. Thus, unless the market customs and norms are

---

[36] Rifkin, *Negotiating Patents, Trade Secrets and Know-How Licenses,* in Attorney's Guide To Negotiation 15-19 (1979).

[37] M. Zimmerman, How to Do Business with the Japanese 114-15 (1985).

understood, the negotiator may fail, either by not understanding the other negotiator, or by not being understood by the other negotiator. At the same time, realistic consideration should be given to whether unorthodox approaches will yield better results.

Summary

The negotiator must know or learn as much as possible about market values, practices, norms, and customs, in order to assess their potential effect on each aspect of the negotiation. A failure to properly analyze the market can lead to disastrous consequences. At this point, counsel should estimate the other party's view of the market. In part, this is based on the information known to be possessed by the other party. Although completed for the moment, the market analysis always is subject to change as new information emerges.

After the market is analyzed, the information gathered, the client goals, and the issues should be checked for gaps, inconsistencies, or other errors. Adjustments should be made as needed, with the client's participation and decision making to the extent that any change in client goals is considered.

It is possible, of course, that the reexamination of the earlier planning steps during this or any other stage will lead to a recognition of a flaw in the analysis of the current step. This possibility can never be ignored.

§8.07 —Step 5: Assessing Strengths and Weaknesses

After establishing the client's goals and analyzing the market, further information and analysis is required before determining the positions that will be taken. The fifth step in planning the negotiation is to determine one's own strengths and weaknesses and to estimate the strengths and weaknesses of the other side. This includes the strengths and the weaknesses of each party and each negotiator.

The other side's strengths and weaknesses can be only estimated, since the available information will be incomplete and contain uncertainties.[38]

The extent to which this estimate should affect one's decisions naturally will vary with the degree to which the estimate is considered to be reliable.

Effective planning can change or diminish potential weaknesses, or points which the other party may perceive as "negatives." First, the potential weaknesses and/or the potential perceived negatives must be recognized. Once they are recognized, responses to these points need to be prepared. Such points must be responded to, if possible, or they will remain a source of concern to the other party throughout the negotiation. The response may be based on fact creation, which can:

1.   Create a strength for one's side

---

[38] G. Kennedy, J. Benson & J. McMillan, Managing Negotiations 33 (1982).

2. Diminish or eliminate a weakness for one's side

3. Create a weakness for the other side[39]

Naturally, as a general rule, weaknesses and points that the other party is likely to perceive negatively should not be mentioned if the other party is unaware of them. Two exceptions exist to this general rule. First, respond anticipatorily to the weakness or to the negative point if the other negotiator or the other party is certain to think of it during the course of the negotiation. This will enhance an appearance of strength and confidence. Second, one should respond if disclosure of the weakness or the negative point is required by law.

The nature of the parties' relationship is a critical factor in the assessment of strengths and weaknesses. At least in the setting of a commercial transaction, the parties' relationship can be categorized in one of the following four ways:[40]

1. *Total Independence:* Each party has at least one viable other option

2. *Mutual dependence:* Each is equally without another viable option

3. *Uneven dependence:* Both lack a viable alternative, but one needs an agreement more than the other

4. *One-sided dependence:* Only one of the parties lacks a viable alternative

To determine or to estimate strengths and weaknesses, at least three factors should be considered. These factors are:

1. The party's vital interests
2. The situational pressures and constraints
3. The other negotiator

Vital Interests

During the negotiation, the parties will take positions and articulate various reasons which may be real or which may be mere pretexts. Strengths and weaknesses, however, are best assessed by examining one's own vital interests and those of the other party. A party which realizes that it can fulfill or affect another party's vital interest has identified a strength for itself.

Example 8-18

A prospective applicant for a loan realizes that the bank's vital interests are receiving the repayment of the loan, plus having suitable security if the bank perceives that a realistic danger of nonpayment exists.

---

[39] *See* §4.03.

[40] Kane & Esposito, *Representing Clients in Negotiation of a Commercial Real Estate Transaction,* in Attorney's Guide to Negotiation 7-3 (1979).

Example 8-19

> A prospective supplier of a bakery analyzes the bakery's vital interests
> to be the quality of the goods being supplied, the price of those goods,
> and the certainty that the goods will be promptly delivered.

Goodwill can be a vital interest. Goodwill can operate either from the client
towards the other party, or as something which the client desires to have from
the other party. In some large scale negotiations, goodwill between the parties
is a necessary, albeit implicit, requirement to negotiate.[41] In such cases, though,
goodwill alone may not be a sufficient incentive to negotiate in the absence
of more concrete reasons.[42]

Price is not always the most vital interest, although it usually is at least one
of the vital interests. Price may be subordinate to such factors as "warranties,
time, performance, technical service, warehousing, quality, insurance, time
payments, innovative ideas, and assurance of supply. . . ."[43]

To ascertain the other party's vital interests, counsel determines or estimates:

1. Why does the other party want this deal?
2. What does the other party really want?

The parties' vital interests reveal the needs of each party. Satisfying those
needs is what the negotiation is really all about. These needs also are factors
to be evaluated in assessing the relative strengths and weaknesses of each party
as it approaches the negotiation.

Needs and interests can be affected by the relative power of each party. For
example, bargaining may be motivated by such a distribution of power between
the parties that each party perceives the need to compromise.[44]

Planning should include methods for fulfilling the other party's need[45] to
the extent necessary or appropriate. In addition, an understanding of, and sensitivity to, the needs of the other side can contribute to a good rapport by demonstrating empathy and building trust.[46]

Example 8-20

> "Your client needs cash flow. Our proposal meets that need by. . . ."

---

[41] Rothchild, *Racial Stratification and Bargaining: The Kenya Experience,* in W. Zartman, The
50% Solution 235 (1976).

[42] *Id.*

[43] W. Fallon, AMA Management Handbook 5-48 (1983).

[44] Rothchild, *supra* note 41.

[45] This encompasses the concept in Fisher and Ury's "principled negotiation" approach
that the parties should focus on options that are mutually satisfying to their basic interests. R. Fisher & W. Ury, Getting to Yes: Negotiating Agreement Without Giving In
14 (1981) [hereinafter Fisher].

[46] Kane & Esposito, *supra* note 40, at 7-7.

Meeting the other party's needs creates strength for one's own position by making it attractive to the other side while still achieving one's own goals. This type of persuasive offer tends to be more effective than relying on threats.[47]

Interests are a key. There cannot be an agreement unless all of the parties believe that it is in each of their interests to agree to the same terms. The interests may be positive or negative, and different for each party. They can include:

1.   Attaining an outcome that is perceived as fair
2.   Getting as much as possible
3.   Avoiding a loss

It is absolutely critical, for both the planning and the negotiation stages, that the negotiator act with the understanding that an agreement is never reached unless the agreement is perceived by each party to be in its best own interests because the terms are more advantageous than continuing without an agreement.

Example 8-21

The plaintiff in a personal injury suit has suffered certain disabilities and "needs" a guaranteed income of $50,000 per year for ten years. Plaintiff's counsel is expected to insist on at least $500,000 to settle the suit. The defendant is unable to pay that much in a lump sum settlement. After making this assessment of the plaintiff's needs, however, defense counsel investigates the cost of an annuity that would provide the plaintiff with the desired guaranteed income of $50,000 for ten years. Upon learning that the cost of the annuity is far less than $500,000, defense counsel proceeds to plan to offer the plaintiff a structured settlement.[48]

Each party's valuation of the items at issue and of the possible outcomes should be assessed based on the parties' respective interests. For an agreement to be reached in a transactional setting, the parties either must value the subject matter somewhat differently, or the agreement must create more for them to divide than if there were no agreement.[49] (That is, the "pie" must be enlarged.)[50] A buyer and seller will not contract to purchase an item if they value it exactly the same, because there would be no gain or profit for either. For instance, an item will not be sold for a dollar unless the seller values a dollar more than the item and the buyer values the item more than the dollar. Agreement occurs when:

1.   Each party relinquishes something in return for something else from the other party which it values more

---

[47] *See* Fisher, *supra* note 45, at 82.

[48] See **§7.03** regarding structured settlements.

[49] W. Zartman, The 50% Solution 10 (1976).

[50] *See* **§2.04.**

2.   Each party gains something of greater value from a third party than that which it relinquishes, as in a joint venture

3.   A combination of the above

In these situations, agreement becomes more likely the more that the parties' values differ or the more additional items will become available if an agreement is reached.[51]

In order to estimate which of the other party's interests are vital to it, five overlapping issues should be analyzed. These issues are:

1.   The other party's real needs

2.   The other party's background

3.   The other party's need for an agreement

4.   The personal feelings of the other party and of the other negotiator

5.   Other influences on the other party

Evaluating these overlapping issues entails raising and attempting to answer a variety of questions. The answers to these questions will lead to the estimation of the other party's vital interests, as opposed to its nonvital interests.

Just as vital interests can reveal needs, real needs can reveal vital interests. The other party's real needs often must be distinguished from the positions that the other party takes and from what it claims its needs to be.[52] Various questions should be considered in trying to ascertain the other party's real needs. These include:

Why is the other party interested in the possibility of negotiating the matter?

Are there significant resources that the other party has been willing to commit to the negotiation?

What does the other party expect to receive?

Why would what the other party expects to receive be important to the other party?

What problems does the other party have that a negotiated agreement could eliminate or alleviate?

What plans or desires does the other party have that a negotiated agreement could facilitate or fulfill?

How many and what different interests does the other party have?[53]

---

[51] W. Zartman, *supra* note 49, at 11.

[52] H. Cohen, You Can Negotiate Anything 68 (1982). Cohen suggests that: "In all negotiations, there are two things being bargained for: 1. The specific issues and demands, which are stated openly 2. The *real needs* of the other side, which are rarely verbalized." (Emphasis in original.) *Id.*

[53] *See* Fisher, *supra* note 45, at 48-49.

Are there deeper, more basic needs underlying the apparent or supposed needs of the other party?[54]

Is the party seeking justice or fairness, and if so, is its quest aimed at procedural or substantive matters, or a combination of the two?[55]

What are the experiences of the other party in similar situations?

Regarding the last question listed, these prior experiences can indicate two important factors:

1. Whether the other party is strong or weak, taking into account any changes in the other party's structure or condition since the past incident(s)

2. Whether the other party should be expected to repeat or to modify its behavior based on the results of the prior negotiation(s)[56]

The second factor in ascertaining vital interests is the other party's background. It must be considered in a search for any events that have occurred which provide clues regarding the issues or the items which are deemed to be most or more important by the other party. In some cases, it may be necessary to take this analysis one step further, and to consider whether the other party's perception of which issues or items are important to it really accurately reflects the other party's needs. If not, planning should take into account how to alter the other party's perception; assuming, of course, that such a change in the other party's perception would be beneficial to one's own positions. In addition, the negotiator must analyze whether the other party's perception of its own needs and interests can be altered in a way that creates a more favorable context for the negotiation.

Part of the analysis of background includes the training, occupations, career mobility, and tradition of the person or people involved. Differences in those matters can yield differences in philosophy and values.[57] These differences can provide opportunities for, or create impediments to, reaching agreement. For instance, such differences may lead to misunderstandings and ineffective communication unless care is exercised to prevent that from occurring. On the other hand, differences in values may make reaching an agreement easier by

---

[54] H. Cohen, *supra* note 52, at 68-70; Fisher, *supra* note 45, at 49-50. Fisher and Ury note that basic human emotional needs, such as the need for security, a sense of belonging, recognition, and control over one's life, may be the real needs behind the other party's negotiating demands. *Id.*

[55] Bartos, *How Predictable Are Negotiations,* in W. Zartman, The 50% Solution 39 (1976).

[56] For example, in the context of labor negotiations, has the other party "won or lost" from prior strikes? *See* Mandle, *Collective Bargaining Negotiation,* in Attorney's Guide to Negotiation 14-6 (1979).

[57] Strauss, Schatzman, Ehrlich, Bucher & Sabshin, *The Hospital and Its Negotiated Order,* in W. Zartman, The 50% Solution 115 (1976).

allowing more opportunities for the use of win/win solutions and reciprocal concessions that are of a greater value to one side than to the other.[58]

If the parties' share some mutual background, that may be significant. An initial inquiry, therefore, is whether the parties have some mutual history. If so, analyzing the significance, if any, of that mutual background raises such questions as:

> Has the parties' previous relationship been friendly or hostile?
>
> During the parties' prior relationship, did anything happen from which insights can be gained regarding the other party's needs, concerns, and priorities?
>
> Similarly, if there have been any prior negotiations between the parties, did anything happen which can provide clues regarding the other party's needs, concerns, and priorities?

The mutual background includes prior agreements. If a prior agreement exists on the same or analogous matters, it usually is a reference point for the negotiation. In addition, past history between the parties can influence the tone and the goals of the present negotiation.[59] This is especially true if a party perceives that the prior agreement was unfair or unsatisfactory, and this has generated a desire to make up for the prior terms, retaliate, or at least to insist on better terms that are perceived as completely fair and satisfactory.

The nature and the extent of the other party's need for an agreement is the third crucial factor in trying to determine the other party's vital interests. Overlapping questions that arise with respect to the other party's need for an agreement include:

> How much does the other party need to reach an agreement in the negotiation?
>
> What are the consequences to the other party if the matter is resolved through an agreement?
>
> What are the consequences to the other party if the matter is not resolved through an agreement?
>
> What are the alternatives for the other party if the matter is not resolved through an agreement?[60]
>
> Assuming that the settlement zones of the parties overlap, what are the range of outcomes if an agreement is reached?
>
> What are the range of outcomes if no agreement is reached?
>
> Of the possible outcomes if no agreement is reached, what is the most likely outcome?

---

[58] Menkel-Meadow, Legal Negotiation: A Study Of Strategies in Search of a Theory, 4 Am B Found Res J 905, 916 (1983). *See* §§5.06 & 5.08.

[59] M. Zimmerman, How to Do Business with the Japanese 114 (1985).

[60] Raiffa, *The Art & Science of Negotiation,* in S. Goldberg, E. Green & F. Sander, Dispute Resolution 46 (1985). See §5.15 concerning the use of alternatives.

Of the possible outcomes if an agreement is reached, what is the most likely outcome?

If no agreement is reached, what are the odds that the most likely outcome will occur?

If no agreement is reached, is there a significant possibility that some extreme outcome will occur?

Is the other party willing to take risks, or is the other party adverse to taking risks?

Taking into account the likely and the extreme possible outcomes of an agreement and of no agreement, and further taking into account the willingness of the other party to take the types of risks involved if there is no agreement, what will the other party's goal(s) probably be during the negotiation?

Personal feelings are the fourth factor in ascertaining vital interests, and they can also affect a negotiation. These may be either the personal feelings of the party or of the negotiator. In this regard, during the planning stage, counsel should consider:

Whether any personal favoritisms or likes of the other party or of the other negotiator are likely to influence that party's goal(s) or priorities

Whether any personal dislikes of the other party or of the other negotiator are likely to influence that party's goal(s) or priorities

Often, hidden factors exist, such as power, prestige, ego acceptance, job security, and personal prejudice.[61]

Lastly, assessing the other party's vital interests requires considering other influential ramifications. Here, one ought to ask whether there are any other factors which may influence the other party's willingness or ability to negotiate, to agree on various issues, to avoid reaching an agreement, or to choose certain strategies or tactics. The types of factors that may be involved include:

Psychological effects and conditions

Family pressures

Social norms, mores, customs, and pressures

Business norms, mores, customs, and pressures

The economic situation and economic pressures, both in the long run and in the short run

The political situation and political pressures, both long-term and short-term.

---

[61] T. Warschaw, Winning By Negotiation 193 (McGraw-Hill, Inc 1980).

Example 8-22

The other party is a businessman who is in serious financial difficulties. Nevertheless, the other party's business continues to operate and continues to be extended credit by its present suppliers. The client is owed money by this businessman. The debt that is owed to the client arises out of past dealings between the two parties. There are no longer any dealings between the parties. However, the present suppliers may be another influence on the other party. Some of the questions that are considered in the planning stage include:

Will the other party threaten to go bankrupt?

If so, how serious is that threat?

Will the other party veto the use of a threat of bankruptcy for fear that his present suppliers will refuse to continue to extend credit?

Example 8-23

A lawsuit against the city generates publicity. There is some public sentiment both for and against the city's actions that led to the suit. Plaintiff's counsel's planning needs to take into account:

Whether the city officials fear that negotiating, or compromising enough to reach an agreement, will have adverse political consequences for them.

If so, will the City be unwilling to negotiate, or unwilling to compromise enough to reach an agreement, due its officials' fear of an unfavorable political reaction?

Situational Pressures or Constraints

In addition to their vital interests, the parties may be limited, or at least affected, by situational pressures or constraints. That phrase refers to particular forces or concerns that are outside of the direct scope of the negotiation, which cause a party either to rule in or out potential types or aspects of agreements, or at least to seek to include or avoid them. Although these forces or concerns can overlap with the type of vital interests discussed above, they arise from specific temporary forces or personal idiosyncracies, rather than intrinsic, general needs. Examples of such situational pressures and constraints are:

A strong personality on the part of either party, determined to take risks and able to withstand uncertainty[62]

Whether an argument, term, or agreement, unless rejected, will become a costly precedent in the future

---

[62] Watson, *Mediation and Negotiation: Learning to Deal with Psychological Responses,* 18 U Mich JL Ref 293, 304 (1985). Clients who are weak in this sense may create problems by being overanxious to accept a settlement.

Whether an argument, term, or agreement, if it is accepted, will become a useful precedent in the future

Excess capacity of a seller, so that additional sales will help to defray the seller's fixed costs

High total costs, fixed costs, or variable costs of a seller of goods and services

Any unique or special qualities of an item that is being offered for sale, or that is sought to be obtained

The business, social, political, or personal power possessed by a party[63]

Any business, social, political, or personal power that will affect the other party[64]

Fear of or concern about litigation

In pending litigation, the immediacy of a trial

The existence of an actual or of a potential competitor who may make a deal with one party which would preclude the other party from making a desired deal

Projected shortages or excesses, which make short-term or long-term contracts more or less desirable

Expected fluctuations in price or in costs, which make short-term or long-term contracts more or less desirable

A potential negative comment to third parties by one party about the other party that could create a stigma which the targeted party would prefer to avoid

Example 8-24

A consultant is in a fee dispute with a former client, an influential business. The consultant decides to compromise the fee, rather than have the former client criticize the consultant's work to others in the industry because of dissatisfaction with the fee.

Example 8-25

With the trial scheduled for the near future, a party or a key witness feels emotionally incapable of testifying about an experience which has left the person psychologically traumatized. The negotiating positions shift accordingly.

---

[63] *See* Redelaway, *Gorbachev The Bold* (Book Review), 34 NY Rev Books 21 (May 28, 1987); Ash, *World War to Cold War* (Books Review), 34 NY Rev Books 44 (June 11, 1987).

[64] *See* Watson, *supra*, note 62.

Example 8-26[65]

In 1987, the leader of the Soviet Union sought to modify the "party line" on a variety of issues, in an attempt to reform, to a degree, the economic and political systems. His proposed reforms were subject to review by the Soviet Politburo, whose members also possess various levels of formal and informal organizational power. Gorbachev's ability to implement his package of reforms was constrained by this situation as other members of the Politburo did not owe their careers to him and had a common interest in preventing him from gaining too much personal power, to the extent it threatened their own power.

Example 8-27[66]

The "Big Three" leaders in World War II, Roosevelt, Churchill, and Stalin, faced a variety of situational constraints in negotiating with each other. These particularly included their domestic political concerns, as well as the "lesser" actors and social and political conditions "on the ground" in the disputed lands. Local conditions were important determinants of the available options.

A sufficiently strong situational pressure or constraint can become or create a new vital interest.

The Other Negotiator or Representational Decision Maker

Assuming that the other party is represented by a negotiator, rather than being directly involved in the negotiation, the personal interests and the personality of the other negotiator must be taken into account.[67]

Example 8-28

A lawyer is negotiating a very large business loan with an account representative of a major financial institution. The account representative has a quota of such loans which she is expected to generate. Accordingly, finding and structuring loans which will be approved by the credit department of the financial institution directly involves her personal interests. Due to that, the lawyer is able to obtain information willingly from the account representative on the lender's needs and perceptions, so that they can try to structure a mutually acceptable loan. Part of the information obtained is that an initial rejection of the loan by the credit arm at a foreign headquarters was due to their unwillingness or inability to recognize the local market, in which a below investment grade company still could

---

[65] Redelaway, *supra* note 63.

[66] Ash, *supra* note 63.

[67] *See* Hermann & Kogan, *Effects of Negotiators' Personalities on Negotiating Behavior,* in D. Druckman, Negotiations: Social-Psychological Perspectives (1977).

go to the equity market. With this information, the lawyer and the account representative successfully restructure and split the loan among three financial institutions on a participating basis.

An assessment also must be made of who is, for practical purposes, making the decisions for the other side.[68] If the other negotiator lacks authority, then the personality and interests of the ultimate decision maker should also be considered whenever that decision maker is a representative of the other party, rather than the other party itself.[69] If the other party is an organization, the decision maker will always be a representative.

Aspects of personality to consider include:

1. Truthfulness

2. The need to be controlling

3. A tendency to seek conflict or be adverse to conflict, or to be competitive rather than cooperative[70]

4. A desire to avoid a reputation for softness[71]

5. Any desire to project or to maintain any other certain personal image

6. A weakness against certain manipulations, because his or her client's interests will be subordinated to the negotiator's personal interests[72]

7. A willingness to take risks, and an ability to tolerate uncertainty[73]

As to the last factor listed, unless an individual is willing to take some risks and is able to withstand substantial uncertainty, that person will not be able to consistently obtain the results that should be obtained. To do so requires the courage to trust one's judgment, and to take the responsibility for making decisions on which much may depend.[74] The willingness to take some risks

---

[68] Fisher, *supra* note 45, at 47. See §5.27 regarding negotiating with those who lack authority.

[69] See §5.27 on negotiating against those without authority.

[70] Williams, *Legal Negotiation and Settlement,* in S. Goldberg, E. Green & F. Sander, Dispute Resolution 50 (1985); H. Cohen, *supra* note 52, at 117-18. *See also* Menkel-Meadow, *supra* note 58, at 915.

[71] Bartos, *supra* note 55, at 486.

[72] Negotiators seek and will fight to maintain an "image of competence" as much or more than for the "bottom line." Fuich, *Observations on the Negotiating Process,* in Attorney's Guide to Negotiation 1-4, 1-5 (1979).

[73] Karrass, *The Negotiating Game,* in G. Bellow & B. Moulton, The Lawyering Process 453 (1978); H. Cohen, *supra* note 52, at 60-61.

[74] Both Karrass and Cohen speak of risk taking in terms of the courage that it requires and of the power that it gives. Karrass, *supra* note 73; H. Cohen, *supra* note 52, at 60-61. Karrass states, in part, that: "People assess risk differently even when they have the same information. . . . Courage plays a part in the decision to make a concession, to hold one's ground, or to force a deadlock." Karrass, *supra,* at 453. Cohen describes risk taking in negotiating as blending courage and common sense. Cohen, *supra,* at 60.

and withstand uncertainty also gives the negotiator or decision maker a certain degree of power.[75]

Another perspective for assessing personal factors in a negotiation is to classify those negotiators, representative decision makers, or parties who tend to always negotiate the same way. Such a chosen style reflects a choice, either conscious or unconscious, based on personal feelings or needs. One commentator separates the types into "jungle fighters," "dictators," "dream merchants," "soothers," and "win/win."[76]

In this categorization, "jungle fighters" can be charming or intimidating. They see the negotiation as a win/lose war. Jungle fighters can be countered by refusing to react emotionally, not displaying fear, placing issues in perspective, demonstrating that the negotiator is not aiming to destroy them, showing that they lack power and will be embarrassed unless they relent, or overpowering them if that is appropriate.

"Dictators" are viewed as seeking to win by maintaining power and control. The best countermeasures are logical appeals to their self-interest, refusing to react emotionally, allowing them apparent power and control while obtaining crucial substantive gains, demonstrating the existence of power to destroy them without embarrassing them, or using that power if necessary.

Manipulators are labeled "dream merchants" in this series of categories. The countermeasures are to refuse to be manipulated, to twist the manipulation to the negotiator's own advantage, or to exploit a personal weakness of the other side.

The category of "soothers" is seen as denying the existence of problems or unfavorable facts. The counter is to probe carefully, be secretly distrustful, use their fear of direct stress and confrontation, and exploit their need to be liked and respected.

The last category of "win/win" consists of those who are pragmatists, committed to achieving agreement through mutuality. The countermeasures are favorable win/win tactics, careful bargaining to take advantage of their willingness to make concessions for mutuality, and exploiting their willingness to try new approaches and to take calculated risks.

Furthermore, situational pressures on the other negotiator, the other party, or the other side's representative decision maker may create incentives or disincentives for reaching an agreement apart from the real vital interests of the other party. A negotiator may be influenced by the personal need for a commission, to replace a former customer who the negotiator is blamed for losing, avoiding criticism, etc.[77]

---

[75] Karrass, *supra* note 73; H. Cohen, *supra* note 52, at 60-61. Karrass considers one of the sources of negotiating power to be the "balance of uncertainty and courage." Karrass, *supra*, at 453. Similarly, Cohen refers to the "power of risk taking." Cohen, *supra*, at 60.

[76] T. Warschaw, *supra* note 61, at 18-59, 183-89.

[77] Allowing such personal needs to affect the negotiation to the actual or possible detriment of the client would, of course, raise serious ethical issues.

Example 8-29

In a lawsuit against a government entity with the trial date three days away, the judge holds a settlement conference. The plaintiff's attorney agrees to reduce her demand to $15,000. The judge strongly recommends that the government agree to pay the $15,000. The plaintiff's attorney assures the judge that the client will follow her recommendation, and that the plaintiff's approval is a formality. The government attorney lacks authority, but agrees that the demand is reasonable and to recommend its acceptance, while further stating that his recommendations usually are followed. Both because it appears that the case is settled and to create pressure for both parties to approve the settlement, the judge changes the trial date to a status date, and states that the court "will expect to be able to dismiss the case as settled on that date." When the attorneys report back on the status of the tentative settlement, the plaintiff's attorney reports that her client will accept $15,000. The defense attorney, however, informs the judge that the government has refused to raise their prior offer of $5,000. The judge tells the attorneys to wait until the end of the court call, at which time they will hold another pretrial conference in chambers. In that conference, in response to the judge's questioning, the government's attorney expresses his own dissatisfaction with his recommendation's being rejected, and explains that the rejection was based largely on departmental budgetary problems. The judge then expresses strong dissatisfaction both with the rejection of the court's settlement recommendation and with the scheduling problems for the court's trial calendar that have been caused by "my reliance on the assurance that the attorney's settlement recommendations would be followed." After some further discussion, the government's attorney agrees to take the matter up with a higher level to try to overturn the government's current position and to fight as hard as he can to come back with settlement authority for $15,000. In fact, the government's attorney does intend to do just that. He will do so partially because he believes that $15,000 is a fair settlement. His primary motivation, however, is that he considers his own credibility, prestige, and reputation to be at stake because he must prove that he can deliver when he indicates that he can obtain approval of a settlement.

Negotiators representing well-known parties may enter the negotiation with "the reputations and legacy of their predecessors."[78] When a negotiator receives an inherited reputation, that attorney must decide whether the reputation is advantageous or disadvantageous for the specific negotiation. If not, the negotiator must prepare specific actions to dispel the unwanted reputation. If it is the other negotiator who arrives with an inherited reputation, probes should be made to ascertain whether the inheritance is genuine or an illusion.

---

[78] R. Lewicki & J. Litterer, Negotiation 54 (1985) [hereinafter Lewicki].

Analysis

Considering all of these factors, the relative strengths and weaknesses of each party should be estimated. At this point, the need for obtaining additional information before and during the negotiation may become apparent.

The importance of this section cannot be overstated. The vital interests and the situational pressures or constraints on the other party, its negotiator, and any relevant decision maker, including personality and personal interests, reveal their requirements and their desires. It is those requirements and desires which govern their conduct during the negotiation and motivate their willingness or unwillingness to agree on particular points.[79] Understanding the other party's perspective is a crucial part of the planning process.

All negotiations occur in the context that each party can influence the outcome for the other.[80] Thus, understanding the other party's perspective requires taking into account any ways that the other party may have been influenced already by the client or counsel.

At this point, anticipation of the other party's view is required. Counsel must analyze how the other party is likely to view the strengths, weaknesses, and interests of:

1.   Itself and its negotiator

2.   The client and counsel personally

After the anticipation phase of the analysis, the prior steps are reexamined. Counsel should focus on whether the actual and perceived strengths, weaknesses, and interests of each party and its negotiator requires modification of the first four steps. In addition, the review of the prior steps may reveal corrections to be made in the current step.

§8.08   —Step 6: Estimating the Other Party's Bottom Line and Opening Position

Prenegotiation planning also involves estimating the other party's bottom line.[81] Based on the information derived from steps one, three, four, and five, the sixth step in systematic planning is to estimate the other party's bottom line. The psychological and other needs and interests of the other party must be considered, as well as those of its negotiator or representative decision maker.[82] The crucial question is what is the worst deal which might realistically be expected to be acceptable to the other party? To do so "realistically," consider that the negotiation will occur on your lucky day, but will not equal your

---

[79] H. Cohen, *supra* note 52, at 69.

[80] Lewicki, *supra* note 78, at 25.

[81] Raiffa, *The Art and Science of Negotiation,* in S. Goldberg, E. Green & F. Sander, Dispute Resolution 46 (1985); Karrass, *The Negotiating Game,* in G. Bellow & B. Moulton, The Lawyering Process 458 (1978).

[82] *See* §8.07.

wildest fantasy. This avoids underestimating, while keeping the estimate within the boundaries of reality.

Each party's bottom line will be affected by:

1.   The value which it places on an outcome
2.   The economic and noneconomic costs which it attaches to delay, negotiating difficulties, or termination of the negotiation

Each party's bottom line also is affected by its anticipation of the other party's bottom line. Therefore, to estimate the other party's bottom line, the negotiator must envision the other side's assessment of the negotiator's own client's bottom line.

These appraisals can be very difficult if the other party apparently desires fairness. The reason for this is that fairness can be very enigmatic.[83] The planner must seek objective substantive and procedural bases for fairness.[84] Such objective criteria may include the market or legal requirements. In conjunction with estimating the other party's bottom line, also project the other party's likely highest expectation. If the other party is unrealistic, this factor should be taken into account.

After examining the other party's likely highest expectation, the other party's opening position should be estimated based on the appraisal of its highest likely expectation. As part of estimating the other side's opening position based on its anticipated highest likely expectation, the following questions should be asked.

1.   Whether the other side is likely to open at or above its highest expectation in order to build in tradeoffs and concessions, or to compensate against possibly underestimating.
2.   If the other party is expected to open above its highest expectation, how far above is it likely to be?

Perceptions and expectations of the value of items or of the likelihood of gaining them affect each party's positions. The chances of reaching agreement vary directly with the reality of expectations.[85] If a negotiator makes unrealistic demands without properly counseling the client about the situational realities, the demands themselves may reinforce the client's unrealistic expectations, or create unrealistic expectations by a client constituency group, such as a union.[86] Therefore, proper counseling of the client is essential to avoid sabotaging an otherwise acceptable potential agreement.

Similarly, since perceptions affect expectations, counsel may need to plan to alter the other party's perceptions. Otherwise, the anticipated expectations

---

[83] H. Raiffa, The Art and Science of Negotiation 268 (1982).

[84] *See* R. Fisher & W. Ury, Getting to Yes: Negotiating Agreement Without Giving In (1981).

[85] W. Zartman, The 50% Solution 402 (1976).

[86] *See* Raskin, *The Newspaper Strike*, in W. Zartman, The 50% Solution 476 (1976).

of the other party may render reaching the optimal, or perhaps any, agreement unlikely. Strategy, tactics, reasoned positions, and communications all can be planned to impact and to change the other party's perceptions and expectations.

For planning purposes, the other party's estimated bottom line and its estimated highest expectation form tentative parameters for the negotiation. In keeping with the system of issue-by-issue analysis, these estimates are made for each issue. Assuming that one's own bottom line overlaps with the estimated bottom line of the other party, this creates tentative zones of agreement.[87]

This phase of planning included anticipating multiple goals and issues, and alternative packages of linked items which may be sought by the other party. Single or separate issue planning, and linear thinking without combinations and permutations is inadequate if the negotiation is likely to be at all sophisticated or complex.

Once the expected opening substantive position of the other party is ascertained, the negotiator next must consider the manner in which the other party will open the negotiation in terms of timing, agenda, strategy, and tactics. Counsel must decide whether to block, counter, or manipulate the likely opening(s) of the other side. Potential openings of one's own should be analyzed, including possible "scripts" of actions and responses.

"Scripting" refers to one's thoughts about the expected words of the other negotiator, either responding to counsel's opening, or initiating his or her own action. The negotiator plays out, in his or her own mind, the next statements which will be made, those then expected by the other negotiator, etc. This mental process is continued until the projected event is complete.[88] The planner practices for the negotiation with a pictorial "setting, characters, and dialogue."[89] Usually, alternative actions and reactions should be mentally played out to avoid being blindsided in the actual negotiation by tunnel vision in the planning stage.

The negotiator, however, must remain ready for the fluid dynamics of the actual negotiation. Prepared responses can be quite helpful in keeping control, so long as the negotiator uses them only if they are still truly appropriate given whatever actually occurs during the negotiation itself.

The earlier steps should now be crosschecked with the estimates of the other party's bottom line and opening position. Any necessary adjustments should be made.

---

[87] See §8.01 regarding zones of agreement.

[88] Most people have done such scripting in one setting or another, whether for an important personal conversation, a job interview, or for attorneys, for an oral argument or a cross-examination.

[89] T. Warschaw, Winning By Negotiation 172-73 (McGraw-Hill, Inc 1980).

§8.09 —Step 7: Considering Win/Win Outcomes

Often, negotiations involve win/loss issues. What one party gains is necessarily lost by the other party. For example, if the only issue is price, the seller who demands $30,000, but who agrees to accept $25,000, has "lost" the $5,000 difference, while the buyer has "won" a corresponding $5,000. Many issues are win/lose, either entirely or in part.

In contrast, other issues involve win/win outcomes.[90] Those are the outcomes in which the gain to one party comes without cost to the other party.

These win/win outcomes fall into two categories:

1. Gain to one party without a corresponding loss to the other party
2. Mutual gain[91]

Gain to One Party without a Corresponding Loss to the Other Party

The first type of win/win results occur when one party gains, but the other party does not suffer a corresponding loss and wins because an agreement is reached. In other words, the concession costs the party making it either absolutely nothing or so very little as to be insignificant, but is of significant value to the party receiving it. Some examples of this type of win/win outcome are as follows.

Example 8-30

The parties enter into a risk-free consulting contract. The consultant agrees that a fee will not be paid unless the annual savings in costs exceeds the fee. The company hiring the consultant gains the services without the risk that the expense of hiring the consultant will exceed the benefit that the consultant will provide. Assuming that the consultant is able to ascertain, in advance, that the savings in costs to the client are virtually certain to be greater than the fee, the consultant makes the concession of a risk-free contract without incurring any real cost to itself. Thus, a win/win result is achieved.

Example 8-31

Herb is selling his car to Sam. Cars of this make and model are rare. Herb agrees to include a bicycle rack in the deal for the same price. Sam wants the bicycle rack, and racks which fit this particular type of car are difficult to find. Herb already has the rack and he has no use for it once he sells

---

[90] For a discussion concerning the distinction between planning win/win outcomes, as compared to using a problem solving strategy or employing win/win tactics, see Menkel-Meadow, *Toward Another View Of Legal Negotiation: The Structure of Problem Solving,* 31 UCLA L Rev 754, 818-19 (1984).

[91] G. Bellow & B. Moulton, The Lawyering Process 579-80 (1978); Menkel-Meadow, *supra* note 90, at 809. *See also* R. Fisher & W. Ury, Getting to Yes: Negotiating Agreement Without Giving In 11-12 (1981).

the car. Selling the bicycle rack separately to someone else is not practical for Herb, because since it only fits this rare type of car, the rack has no value to most third parties.

Example 8-32

The seller is asked to deliver raw materials on one-day notice so that the buyer can minimize its inventory levels. However, weekend deliveries are especially costly for the seller. The buyer's factory accepts deliveries on Saturday, although it does not do any actual manufacturing on the weekends. It really does not matter to the buyer whether raw materials that are ordered on a Friday are delivered on Saturday or on Monday. For these reasons, the buyer agrees to a "concession" that orders which are placed on Fridays can be delivered on Mondays, instead of on Saturdays. The seller secures a savings in its variable costs without any real cost being incurred by the buyer.

Example 8-33

A clothing store owner has cash flow problems, and therefore wants 30-day payment terms from the store's suppliers (i.e., payment is not due for 30 days after delivery.) This will allow the clothing store to sell most of the clothes that it receives before it has to pay for them. The wholesaler agrees, but adds a small interest charge to cover the lost use of the money for 30 days. The store owner solves the store's cash flow problems without having to take out commercial loans, which would be at least as costly as the wholesaler's interest charge. The small interest charge prevents the wholesaler from losing anything by granting the concession of 30-day payment terms. The wholesaler, though, does not really gain anything except the overall agreement, since the small interest charge is simply equal to the lost use of the funds (i.e., the discounted cash flow).

As the examples illustrate, gain to one party without a corresponding loss to the other party typically occurs where the parties have different needs.[92] It occurs where the parties are not in a linear, zero-sum type of negotiation. Under these circumstances, one party's needs can be satisfied without taking something away from the other party. The party giving the noncost concession wins rapport and, at times, the ability to later demand reciprocity.

Mutual Gain

Negotiation often is conceptualized as involving a "pie" with only a set number of pieces available to be divided.[93] However, negotiation for mutual gain alters the size of the pie. It consists of expanding the pie by creatively thinking of new terms which, in effect, add more pieces to, and thereby expand, the

---

[92] Menkel-Meadow, *supra* note 90, at 809.
[93] *See* H. Cohen, You Can Negotiate Anything 149-50 (1982).

pie.[94] When this can be done and the parties share the benefits, they have effected a win/win outcome with mutual gain. The following are illustrations of how parties can mutually gain by expanding the pie.

Example 8-34

Two companies are negotiating a comprehensive sales contract. As part of this contract, the corporations agree to set up a new terminal-to-terminal computerized billing system which will reduce the administrative costs for each of the companies.

Example 8-35

A trucking company is operating with 20 per cent unused capacity on one particular route. The company agrees to give an extra discount to a shipper for additional volume above that which is presently shipped on the run. The carrier is thus able to fill its previously unused capacity, while the shipper saves money through the additional discount. Both parties win without any significant cost to either of them.

Example 8-36

A company intends to pay one of its employees a bonus in November. The employee's personal tax situation is such, however, that the employee prefers to wait two months, so that taxes on the bonus will not have to be paid for an additional year. The company's tax situation is basically unaffected by when it pays the bonus. The employer agrees to defer payment of the bonus for two months, until January. The company benefits by gaining an additional two months of interest on the bonus money, while the employee's loss of the interest is more than offset by the lessening of his tax liability.

Example 8-37

In planning for a negotiation to attempt to settle a law suit between two parties, defense counsel anticipates that it will be difficult to agree on a purely monetary settlement amount. The circumstances are such, though, that the defendant is willing to provide shares of stock in one of its subsidiaries to the plaintiff, and it is likely that the plaintiff will be interested in such an arrangement. If the settlement can be safely characterized as a long-term capital gain for the plaintiff because it is acquiring an equity interest in the defendant's subsidiary, the plaintiff will obtain a substantial tax savings, as compared with what the plaintiff would have to pay in taxes from a simple monetary settlement. After checking with a tax specialist, the defendant's attorney concludes that a settlement could be so characterized for tax purposes. Defense counsel further concludes

---

[94] *See* id 149-51.

that the tax savings to the plaintiff will lead it to accept a lower settlement, thereby achieving a gain for both parties and making a settlement feasible.[95]

Plan so as to Attain Win/Win Results Whenever Possible

Being able to foresee or to imagine a win/win outcome often is not obvious, and these opportunities probably are missed more often than is realized.[96] When the negotiation concerns a matter that is in litigation, or that may result in litigation unless a settlement is reached, the planning process should consider win/win outcomes, even if they are outcomes that a court would not be able to order.[97] Many times the addition of a win/win outcome to the negotiation as a whole, or to a particular issue within a multi-issue negotiation, makes the difference between reaching an agreement and not having any agreement at all.

These facts underscore the importance of planning to achieve win/win results whenever it may be possible to do so. In considering whether such results can potentially be created in a specific negotiation, counsel must consider the needs and the objectives of the parties, negotiators, and any relevant decision makers. The focus is on whether those needs and objectives are totally compatible, wholly in conflict, or somewhere in between.[98] The critical question is whether the needs and objectives of both parties can be wholly or partially achieved through a win/win outcome.[99]

Win/win results often involve the substance of the ultimate agreement that is negotiated. Frequently, substantive win/win outcomes can pertain to the rate, manner, and/or timing of payment.[100] Some of the more common means of effecting such win/win outcomes are the use of structured settlements and payment plans, although indicia or guarantees of the deferred payments may be appropriate.[101] They also can involve procedural matters.[102] Procedural matters can involve a method to be followed which achieves a fairness goal or saves face. It also may concern such things as continuances, the timing of discovery, other scheduling matters, or publicity.[103]

---

[95] *See* W. Fallon, AMA Management Handbook 5-48 (1983).

[96] G. Bellow & B. Moulton, The Lawyering Process 580 (1978).

[97] Menkel-Meadow, *supra* note 90, at 789.

[98] *Id* 794 & 818-19.

[99] H. Cohen, *supra* note 93, at 161.

[100] G. Bellow & B. Moulton, The Lawyering Process 580 (1978).

[101] With regard to structured settlements, see **§7.03.** As to payment plans, it should be noted that receiving full payment over time may be less certain than if one lump sum payment is required. This is likely to depend on the economic strength of the payor and on whether any guarantees of payment or any penalties for nonpayment are included in the agreement.

[102] G. Bellow & B. Moulton, The Lawyering Process 580 (1978).

[103] *Id.*

Furthermore, contract negotiations generally are more likely to contain opportunities for win/win planning.[104] This logically follows, since business agreements are typically entered into because it is believed that they will economically benefit both parties.[105]

Another aspect of many negotiations that is ripe for win/win planning is the tax consequences of the agreement.[106] This can arise in contract negotiations, settlement in certain types of litigation, as well as in various other negotiating contexts.[107] To the extent that it is possible to do so, the other side's view of win/win outcomes must be anticipated. If this leads to an awareness of any additional actual or potential win/win outcomes, they are added into the analysis.

Next, as before, counsel reevaluates the prior steps based on the analysis formed in this step, and checks the analysis formed in the present step against the information gathered and the judgments made in the earlier planning stages. As before, any needed adjustments then are made to the result of the prior planning stages, as well as for the current step.

§8.10 Summary and Review

    I. Systematic Planning

        A. Is critical

        B. Ineffective planning can prevent any agreement even when one could be reached, or lead to a less favorable agreement

        C. Common errors include a failure to obtain or consider information, failing to close an acceptable deal, making a less favorable deal than possible, uncontrolled horse trading, deadlock on non-essential points, and a lack of objectivity due to relationships

        D. Do it in a cost-effective way

    II. Step 1: Prenegotiation Information Gathering

        A. Obtain any information that is needed and available

        B. Including your client's goals, the issues, the market, vital interests of each party and its negotiator, strengths and weaknesses of each party and negotiator, indications of the other party's bottom line, and effects or influences from current economic, social, and political climates

        C. Identify informational gaps and uncertainties for probes and evaluation during the negotiation, especially regarding informational tactics and setting the agenda

    III. Step 2: Determine the Client's Goals

---

[104] *Id.*

[105] Menkel-Meadow, *supra* note 90, at 809-10.

[106] Potter, *Settlement of Claims and Litigation: Legal Rules, Negotiation Strategies, and In-House Guidelines,* 41 Bus Law 515, 525 (1986).

[107] *See* **Example 8-36** for an illustration of the kind of miscellaneous situation in which tax consequences can give rise to a win/win outcome through proper planning.

A. Ultimately the client's decision

B. Plan for each goal

C. Identify and prioritize the goals with the client

D. Separate essential and desirable goals

E. Includes long-run and short-run goals

F. Counsel the client on legal ramifications so the real implications of each goal are understood, as well as for careful consideration of long-term versus short-term benefits if necessary

G. Goals must be sufficiently concrete to be later translated into authority with the client

H. Each goal becomes an issue, and each combination of goals with tradeoffs between them also becomes an issue

IV. Step 3: Identifying the Issues

A. Issues arise where parties' goals are or may conflict

B. Analyze on an issue-by-issue basis, subissues, or packages of linked issues and subissues

C. Beware of artificially created issues being used as tradeoffs

D. Categorize as economic or noneconomic, and as long-run, short-run or both

E. Defining the issue can affect the outcome, and the definition should be formulated, in light of the other party's views, as favorably as feasible

F. Next, reexamine client goals in view of the information gathered and the issues, and counsel the client if goals need clarification or adjustment

G. Each of the remaining planning steps must be done for each issue or combination of issues

V. Step 4: Analyzing the Market

A. Everything has a market

B. Includes supply and demand

C. Consider market practices regarding expected and non-negotiable terms, some of which may be set by law

D. Market value and terms can vary over time, and some terms may be negotiable in one context and non-negotiable in another

E. Practices and norms can affect or limit negotiation methods, although unorthodox approaches should be considered

F. Estimate the other party's view of the market

G. After the market is analyzed, check the information gathered, client goals, and issues for gaps, inconsistencies, or other errors. Adjust as necessary with the client

VI. Step 5: Assess Strengths and Weaknesses

A. Identify strengths and weaknesses of the client, each other party, and every negotiator

B. Planning can change or diminish actual or perceived weaknesses, create strengths, or create a weakness for the other party

    C. Mention weakness which the other party is unaware of only if (1) the other side is certain to think of it anyway or (2) disclosure is required by law

    D. Consider the parties' relationship regarding any dependence or independence

    E. Based on (1) vital interests, (2) situational pressures and constraints, and (3) the other negotiator's personal interests, pressures, and constraints

    F. Vital interests reveal needs, strengths, and weaknesses. Plan to utilize strengths and the other side's weaknesses, avoid or alter own weaknesses, and fulfill interests and needs of the other party to the extent necessary or appropriate

    G. Build rapport by understanding and being sensitive to the other side's needs

    H. Generally more persuasive to articulate a position in terms of meeting the other side's needs than as a threat

    I. Needs and interests can be for positive gain, fairness, or avoiding a loss

    J. No agreement will be reached unless each party agrees its interests are better met by this agreement than continuing nonagreement

    K. A transactional agreement requires that the parties value the items being exchanged differently, or that the agreement will enlarge the pie

    L. Estimate which of the other party's interests are the vital ones based on its real needs, background, need for agreement, personal feelings, and other influences

    M. Consider altering the other party's perception of its interests and needs if that creates a more favorable negotiation context

    N. A prior relationship between the parties can provide clues

    O. Requires analysis of benefits and risks from agreement and nonagreement

    P. Take into account situational pressures or constraints

    Q. Evaluate the other negotiator's personal interests and personality, and those of any representational decision maker

    R. Decide whether to accept or disavow any inherited rather than earned reputation, and probe reputations inherited by others to determine whether it is deserved or an illusion

VII. Step 6: Estimate the Other Party's Bottom Line and Opening Position

    A. Use information from steps 1, 3, 4, and 5

    B. The other side's bottom line is affected by its value of an outcome, the economic or noneconomic costs of delay or negotiating difficulties or termination, and its anticipation of your side's bottom line

    C. Estimate the other side's bottom line as your lucky day, but not your wildest fantasy, to avoid underestimating or being unrealistic

    D. Estimate the other party's likely expectations, regardless of whether they are realistic

    E. Estimate the other side's opening position based on whether it is likely to be higher than its highest expectation to create room for tradeoffs or compensate against underestimating, and, if so, how much higher

    F. Unrealistic demands may create or reinforce unrealistic client expectations, thereby reducing the chance for an otherwise acceptable agreement

    G. The other party's bottom line and opening position must be estimated for each issue and combination of issues

    H. Next, anticipate the way that the other party will seek to open the negotiation, and devise moves to block, counter, or manipulate

    I. Review prior steps for errors or modifications in prior or current step

VIII. Step 7: Consider Win/Win Outcomes

    A. Gain to one party without a corresponding loss to the other party, in which the giver wins rapport and, at times, the ability to later demand reciprocity

    B. Mutual gain by expanding the pie

    C. Use whenever possible, and explore needs and objectives in a search for opportunities

    D. May be substantive or procedural

    E. Anticipate the other party's view of win/win outcomes

    F. Recheck prior steps for errors or modifications in those or the current step

Systematic Planning: The Second Stages   9

§9.01   Introduction

Having completed the first seven planning steps, the first stage of planning is concluded. That stage was principally concerned with gathering information, analyzing information, and making judgments and estimates about the parties and the negotiators, as well as actions and positions to be expected from the other side. Steps 8 through 14 form the second stage of planning. Using the first stage as a basis, in the second phase, decisions are made by the negotiator regarding specific positions to take, and which strategies and tactics to employ during the course of the negotiation.

§9.02   —Step 8: Setting the Opening Position

During planning step 7, the negotiator estimated the other party's bottom line, expectations, and opening position, as well as planned opening moves to commence the negotiation. Step 8 consists of establishing the initial substantive position.

The opening position must be established in a reasonable, but not overly modest, manner. High, realistic expectations are a key to successful negotiation.[1] If expectations are too low, the negotiator may fail to demand as much as could be gained through a higher demand. Studies indicate that high opening positions generally lead to more favorable settlements than more modest or low ones.[2] Although high aspirations lead to better results if an agreement is reached, they also lead to more deadlocks.[3] Indeed, unrealistically high aspirations can frighten off, create feelings of futility, or offend, thereby driving the other party away from the negotiation.[4] The reasonable opening position therefore is established using realistically high expectations.

The information generated in steps 1 through 7 is utilized to determine the content of a realistically high expectation in the particular situation. The information consists of:

1. The client's own goals

2. The issues

3. Market values and practices

4. Each party's vital interests, relative strengths and weaknesses, situational pressures and constraints, as well as the personal interests and the personality of the other negotiator and any relevant decision maker

5. Estimates of the other party's highest position, expectations and bottom line, and one's own planned opening moves

6. Any potential win/win outcomes

As part of this analysis, the negotiator must analyze anticipated reactions by the other party and its negotiator to potential opening positions that are under consideration.

Note that one's own high expectation and opening position should be somewhat higher than the estimate of the other party's bottom line. This provides a margin of error against underestimating the potential gain.[5] It also builds in room for a concession if one is necessary for psychological reasons, such as that the other party will feel like a failure unless at least one concession is extracted.[6]

---

[1] *See* J. Graham & Y. Sano, Smart Bargaining 41 (1984).

[2] R. Lewicki & J. Litterer, Negotiation 90 (1985).

[3] C. Karrass, Give & Take: The Complete Guide to Negotiating Strategies and Tactics 4 (1974).

[4] Thus, it has been advised that the opening position should be "within the ballpark." Erisman, *Settlement Do's and Don'ts,* 24 Trial 112 (1988).

[5] G. Bellow & B. Moulton, The Lawyering Process 531 (1978) (citing I Belli, Modern Trials 754 (1954)).

[6] *Id.*

Utilizing and analyzing all of this information, a high, realistic opening position is established, not only for the entire negotiation, but also for each issue, and for any combination of issues. Such combinations consist of groups of issues which involve potential tradeoffs between the issues.

Example 9-1

A company that provides a variety of computer and data processing services is preparing for contract negotiations with a potential major customer. After going through steps one through six, the company prepares opening positions for an entire package of services, for each separate service that will be offered, and for several combinations of services involving possible tradeoffs with the customer taking more services in return for a lower price per service.

Since the opening position establishes a limit on that which can be gained for the client, the lawyer may consult with the client before a final determination is made. The client should be counseled regarding the factors and potential difficulties which should be considered. A client may have information which alters the analysis. Counsel may recommend or determine the opening position, depending on the client's level of negotiating sophistication and involvement with formulating substantive positions.

The result of this analysis and consultation is the planned opening position. It may or may not actually be used. Whether the planned opening position is actually used depends on whether it still seems appropriate when the first offer or counteroffer is to be made. That determination is based on the actions taken, and the information generated, up to that point in the negotiation.

The opening position must also be structured as a reasoned posture.[7] This means that a persuasive argument is planned for the opening position, just as persuasive reasons will be planned for alternative positions.

One caveat is that driving too hard of a bargain may be dangerously counterproductive if it leads to the other party's later repudiating the bargain, or if it results in a lack of necessary good faith efforts by the other party in carrying out the agreement. A contract which is, or which becomes, unprofitable for the other party can cause disastrous consequences, unless compelling reasons exist for compliance with the contractual terms. This danger most often occurs in negotiations for long-term relationships in which it is important that the other party's performance meet a certain level of quality.

Since the other side's expected opening position and reaction to one's own planned opening position already have been anticipated, the negotiator can turn to a review of the previous steps. One's planned opening position may alter the decisions and analysis made in the first phase of planning regarding information gathering, client goals, issues, the market, strengths, weaknesses,

---

[7] Raiffa, *The Art and Science of Negotiation,* in S. Goldberg, E. Green & F. Sander, Dispute Resolution 46 (1985). Raiffa suggests that part of preparing one's persuasive reasoning should include arguments regarding fairness, and concerning the likely result if the matter were arbitrated.

interests, the other party's anticipated bottom line and win/win outcomes. This review can possibly alter the lawyer's view of the planned opening position, leading to modifications of it.

§9.03   —Step 9: Setting the Bottom Line

A crucial part of planning is to set the bottom line.[8] At some point, not making any agreement at all is preferable to the best deal that the other party is willing to offer. At that point, no further concessions are to be made, and the negotiation is terminated. The bottom line is the absolute point beyond which it would be better to reject any offer or demand.[9] This, of course, is the crucial point for the client, who must decide it with the assistance of counseling, as needed.

Just as in establishing the opening position, all of the information generated by the previous steps is used in setting the bottom line. Also as with determining opening positions, bottom lines are established for the negotiation as a whole, as well as for each issue in a multi-issue negotiation. Similarly, if there are potential tradeoffs between issues, a bottom line should be established for each relevant combination of issues.

Example 9-2

A couple is interested in purchasing a house. Given their goals and interests, the issues for them are the price of the home, its quality, the number of bedrooms, and the number of bathrooms. They decide that their bottom line for each of these issues is as follows:

Price: $200,000

Quality: High

Bedrooms: Four

Bathrooms: Two

They further decide, however, that they are willing to trade off between the price and the number of bedrooms, so that their bottom line for the combination of these two issues is $170,000 and three bedrooms.

The client must authorize the bottom line position, since it is the client who has to make the ultimate decision about whether to agree to specific terms. Before that authorization, the attorney must counsel the client about the legal

---

[8] C. Karrass, *The Negotiating Game,* in G. Bellow & B. Moulton, The Lawyering Process 458 (1978); Raiffa, *The Art and Science of Negotiation,* in S. Golberg, E. Green & F. Sander, Dispute Resolution 20, 46 (1985). Raiffa uses the phrase "reservation point" for the bottom line.

[9] R. Fisher & W. Ury, Getting to Yes: Negotiating Agreement Without Giving In 104 (1981) [hereinafter Fisher]. Fisher and Ury refer to this as the "Best Alternative To A Negotiated Agreement," or "BATNA." *Id. See also* S. Goldberg, E. Green & F. Sander, Dispute Resolution 20 (1985).

aspects and ramifications of the potential agreement. Any relevant tax considerations must be explored, either through counsel's own expertise or that of a tax attorney or accountant.

Settlement bottom lines for litigation may require more counseling and advice than usual, if the client lacks experience in such matters. For instance, this frequently can occur for matrimonial clients,[10] criminal defendants,[11] and personal injury plaintiffs.

In addition to strictly legal aspects, to the extent that the attorney has knowledge and expertise in other relevant areas, the attorney should also counsel the client about any pertinent business, social, political, and personal factors which the client either may not be aware of or may not have fully considered. In this respect, the attorney should consider a potential agreement as a whole, examining both the legal and the nonlegal issues. The American Bar Association's Model Code of Professional Responsibility[12] and the ethical guidelines for each state provide guidance regarding the scope of the lawyer's responsibilities in advising the client.

The client may be enthusiastic to rush into "a great deal" without first fully analyzing it. The attorney then will have to explain the need for caution and the role of the lawyer in watching out for certain pitfalls. Examples of unanticipated problems based on the lawyer's experience can help explain the advisability of a thorough analysis.

The client's input should be sought with respect to all potential terms, especially the advantages and disadvantages of noncash substantive terms.[13] The counseling process must be an interactive one. At the same time, counsel should explain those areas of the proposed agreement that are beyond his or her expertise and require the assistance of other professionals, such as engineers, appraisers, etc.

In rendering advice, the attorney must try to ensure that the client understands, as well as hears, the advice that is being given.[14] Often, it is helpful to begin with an overview listing all of the alternatives to be considered, so that the client knows the framework for the decisions before considering each alternative. In addition to those alternatives known to the lawyer, the client should add any other alternatives which ought to be considered.

After the lawyer and the client jointly establish the list of alternatives, each alternative must be examined. The order for examining the alternatives may

---

[10] Zavett & Friedman, *The Negotiations of Matrimonial Cases*, in Attorney's Guide to Negotiation 6-5 (1979).

[11] *See* Penn, Jr., *Negotiation in a Criminal Case-Defense*, in Attorney's Guide to Negotiation 13-13, 13-14 (1979).

[12] American Bar Association's Model Rules of Professional Conduct, Rule 2.1, states that: "In representing a client, a lawyer shall exercise independent professional judgment and render candid advice. In rendering advice a lawyer may refer not only to law but to other considerations such as moral, economic, social and political factors, that may be relevant to the client's situation."

[13] Sandels, *Negotiation in Business Litigation*, in Attorney's Guide to Negotiation 11-6 (1979).

[14] M. Schoenfield & B. Pearlman Schoenfield, Interviewing and Counselling (1981).

depend on whether some decisions cannot be made until after other matters are decided. Except as to those decisions which are necessarily deferred, the alternatives should be considered beginning with the most aggressive and working down to the least aggressive. Since clients usually are most intrigued by more aggressive ideas, this allows attention to be given first to the ideas that are more likely to be the initial focus of the client's thoughts.

In this sense, more aggressive does *not* mean attacking or quarrelsome. Rather, it refers to the alternatives which appears to be seeking the highest and the most favorable outcome, regardless of the chances for success. In litigation, for example, the most aggressive alternative always is to go to trial. It is extremely rare that a settlement will contain all of the benefits that are at least theoretically obtainable through a totally favorable judgment. The dollars paid by the defendant through a settlement will be less than the dollars potentially awardable as damages. Likewise, in criminal cases, the most aggressive alternative is to go to trial, since a defendant will be better off with an outright acquittal than with any plea bargain. In transactional negotiations, the most aggressive alternative will, of course, vary, depending on the particulars of the specific negotiation.

Example 9-3

In negotiating a particular business lease for raw space, the cost for the improvements or "build-out" desired by the lessee was substantial. The most aggressive alternative for this issue in the negotiation was to have the other party bear those costs.

To focus effectively on each alternative, counsel should explain the particular risks and benefits associated with that choice, as opposed to the other alternatives. To the extent possible, the chances that each benefit and risk will actually occur must be assessed.

Example 9-4

An attorney is counseling the client regarding a major case arising out of a business transaction.

Before deciding on our bottom line, let's review our choices. We can go to trial and let the jury decide. Our case is strong, with our chances of prevailing clearly better than even, but probably less than 75 per cent. If the jury finds liability, our damages should be around $650,000. However, if the jury decides against liability, you will not receive the business vindication you're talking about, as well as not recovering the funds. All of this must be balanced against the settlement possibilities. Recovery of 50 per cent will solve your cash flow problem and, as we've discussed, be viewed as a vindication by your business associates. Of course, a 50 per cent settlement gives up your claim to the other roughly $325,000. We could set our bottom line at higher than 50 per cent, since your chances of recovery are higher than that. Based on the strength of our case and what we know about the defendant, I suggest aiming for 70 per cent, but settling for half or above, depending on how you feel about the risks involved. Since this is your money, it is your judgment about how to weigh the risks that is important.

Normally, the lawyer should make a recommendation about whether to settle at a given level or within a given range. The only exception to this is the highly sophisticated client who may need an evaluation of the risks and benefits, but who does not require advice beyond that. *Sophisticated* means quite knowledge-able in the area under consideration. In fact, with some sophisticated clients who are very familiar with a particular type of transaction or circumstance, the client will have determined the bottom line without advice. The attorney then needs to provide advice only if there is reason to believe that the client is unaware of some factor or has miscalculated the situation.

In the end, the client must decide on and must authorize the bottom-line position, that position which has to be achieved or there cannot be an agree-ment. In doing so, the client really is determining that, at a given point, non-agreement is the preferred alternative. This may involve proceeding to trial, waiting for another potential purchaser, etc., depending on the situation. The bottom line divides the least acceptable alternative for agreement from the point at which not agreeing is better. It is essential that this concept be under-stood by the client.

Counsel should caution against unrealistic bottom lines, unless alternative opportunities or proceeding to trial are preferred to a realistic bottom line. These two situations tend to arise when:

1. The other party has misvalued its position and refuses to be realistic
2. The same benefits can be attained more advantageously elsewhere
3. In litigation, a defendant's economic problems influence it to be much lower in its position than it otherwise would be, even though the defen-dant is not judgment proof and has assets to offer

In cautioning against an unrealistic bottom line, counsel's goal is: "Don't let GREED prevent a settlement."[15] In other words, a good settlement should not be lost because of unrealistic expectations.

The attorney must also consider the timing of the counseling, in terms of whether the client is ready to hear and heed the advice that is being given.[16] The timing of the advice may be critical. Up to a certain point in the process, the client may not be ready to be realistic. It may be pointless to counsel a client with strong, but unrealistic, expectations until the lawyer knows that the other party will agree to realistic terms. Premature advise may produce the erroneous impression that the lawyer simply is too soft. In other instances, only the passage of time will alleviate anger or other emotions sufficiently for reason to be heard by the client.

---

[15] Lee, *Some Comments on Negotiation and Settlement,* 10 Am J Trial Advoc 181 (1987).
[16] *See* §7.10.

Since the other side's bottom line was anticipated in step 8, the negotiator now should use the planned bottom line to reexamine the earlier steps regarding prenegotiation information gathering, the client goals, identifying the issues, the market, strengths, weaknesses and interests, the other party's expected bottom line and opening position, possible win/win outcomes, and the client's opening position. This review may also lead to adjustment of the planned bottom line if a flaw is revealed.

To the extent that a need for adjustment of an earlier step becomes apparent, the most likely adjustment is to one's own opening position. If the planned opening position and bottom line do not allow sufficient room for an expected need to have concessions available, one or the other must be adjusted. Unless it is clear that the bottom line should be adjusted based on further counseling of the client, the adjustment should be made to one's own opening position to hedge against setting both it, and the bottom line, too low.

Just as something may occur that makes counsel decide not to use the planned opening position, the planned bottom line can be subject to change. Generally, any such change will be based upon new information that is obtained during the course of the negotiation.[17] Sometimes, the change can result from outside events affecting the client. Any change in the bottom line must be the client's decision, again with counseling by the lawyer, as necessary.

For this reason, as well as for general rapport with the client, the client should be kept informed of the status of the negotiation. This also allows the attorney to check on whether the client's goals have changed. The lawyer may not need to question the client, but instead can reiterate the positions so that the client has an opportunity to interject changes or raise questions that cause a reevaluation.

It should be noted that, unlike most other steps, the bottom line is *not* reexamined based on how the other side is expected to react to it. The bottom line is based on alternatives to not reaching agreement, *regardless* of the likelihood of agreement. Interim bottom lines are the exception to ignoring the likelihood of achieving the position. An interim bottom line is a limit established for a phase of a negotiation, to determine whether it can be achieved. If that phase is completed without achieving it, a final or different interim bottom line is determined or, if predetermined, simply implemented. Since use of interim bottom lines can cause a loss of credibility or face if perceived as a bluff, the same measures should be taken to avoid such consequences as outlined in the section on bluffs.[18]

The true bottom line of each party determines whether any agreement is possible, and if so, the range within which it will occur. Assuming that the bottom lines do not change during the negotiation, any agreement must occur at or between the bottom lines of each party. This is sometimes described as the settlement range set by the resistance points of the parties.[19]

---

[17] Fisher, *supra* note 9. *See also* S. Goldberg, E. Green & F. Sander, Dispute Resolution 20 (1985).

[18] *See* §5.13.

[19] M. Saks & R. Hastie, Social Psychology In Court 122 (1978).

If information obtained during the negotiation or outside events cause the client to modify a bottom line already announced to the other side, the shift may cause a loss of credibility or face if the initial position appears to have been an unsuccessful bluff. Therefore, it is critical that the new bottom line be explained with reasons which persuasively demonstrate that the old bottom line was not a bluff.

§9.04 —An Exception: Limited Authority

Employing the concept of limited authority is an exception to the step for planning the bottom line. Since using the theory of limited authority presupposes that the negotiator is unaware of the client's bottom line, the negotiator does not plan a bottom line. Reasons for giving the negotiator only limited authority include:

1. When the negotiator or the party believes that doing so will be an excellent method for resisting pressure from the other side for concessions

2. To maintain harmony at the bargaining table by having the responsibility for resistance to movement by a decision maker who is not present[20]

3. As a reason for direct information gathering in order to be able to inform the decision maker[21]

Limited authority sometimes is employed whether there is a reason for it or not, because it is part of the party's general negotiating policy and procedure. At other times, it is chosen for a specific negotiation.

Planning for the use of limited authority is conducted in conjunction with its possible use as a tactic.[22] If confronted by this tactic, counsel should probe to determine whether the limited authority is a tactical ploy, or whether it is part of the other party's basic policy and procedure. The countermeasures are the same as those for dealing with negotiators without authority.[23]

§9.05 —Step 10: Choosing Strategies and Tactics

Continuing to use the analyses from the prior steps, including which approach(es) characterize the client's goal(s), choices are made from among the potential strategies and tactics.[24] The potential strategies, singularly, or in combination, are:

Personal credibility[25]

---

[20] J. Graham & Y. Sano, Smart Bargaining 12 (1984).

[21] *Id.*

[22] *See* **§5.27.**

[23] *See* **§5.27.**

[24] *See* **chs 3-7.**

[25] *See* **§3.02.**

No concessions[26]

No further concessions[27]

Deadlock-breaking concessions only[28]

HRESSC[29]

Concede first[30]

Problem solving[31]

Purposes other than reaching an agreement, including delay, discovery, influencing the client, and influencing third parties[32]

Moving for closure[33]

Likewise, for each strategy chosen, one or more tactics are planned regarding:

Disclosing information[34]

Creating facts[35]

Listening for information[36]

Using the funnel approach[37]

Using sources of information[38]

Bargaining for information[39]

Informational discussions[40]

Requiring preconditions[41]

Making or avoiding making the first offer[42]

Demanding responses to offers and to positions[43]

---

[26] *See* **§3.03.**
[27] *See* **§3.04.**
[28] *See* **§3.05.**
[29] *See* **§3.06.**
[30] *See* **§3.07.**
[31] *See* **§3.08.**
[32] *See* **§§3.10-3.14.**
[33] *See* **§3.15.**
[34] *See* **§4.02.**
[35] *See* **§4.03.**
[36] *See* **§4.04.**
[37] *See* **§4.05.**
[38] *See* **§4.06.**
[39] *See* **§4.07.**
[40] *See* **§4.08.**
[41] *See* **§5.02.**
[42] *See* **§3.03.**
[43] *See* **§5.04.**

Reciprocity[44]

Win/win proposals[45]

Trial proposals[46]

Concessions that are of greater value to one party[47]

Bargaining[48]

Discussion[49]

Conditional proposals[50]

Power[51]

Bluff[52]

Tone[53]

The use of alternative opportunities[54]

Splitting the difference[55]

Focus/downplay[56]

Creating a psychological commitment for agreement[57]

Saving face[58]

Inserting new issues[59]

Focusing on the process[60]

Creating movement[61]

Adjournment[62]

Patience[63]

---

[44] *See* §3.05.
[45] *See* §5.06.
[46] *See* §3.07.
[47] *See* §5.08.
[48] *See* §5.09.
[49] *See* §5.10.
[50] *See* §5.11.
[51] *See* §5.12.
[52] *See* §5.13.
[53] *See* §5.14.
[54] *See* §5.15.
[55] *See* §5.16.
[56] *See* §5.17.
[57] *See* §5.18.
[58] *See* §5.19.
[59] *See* §5.20.
[60] *See* §5.21.
[61] *See* §5.22.
[62] *See* §5.24.
[63] *See* §5.25.

Limited authority[64]

Surprise[65]

Appealing to personal interests[66]

Deadlock[67]

Deadlines[68]

Active client participation[69]

Negotiating teams[70]

Judicial settlement conferences[71]

Allies[72]

Media or community pressure[73]

Alternative dispute resolution[74]

Class actions[75]

Litigation[76]

Structured settlements[77]

Depositions[78]

Policy limits letter[79]

Loan agreements[80]

"Mary Carter" agreements[81]

Contribution[82]

Offers of judgments[83]

---

[64] *See* §5.27.
[65] *See* §5.28.
[66] *See* §5.29.
[67] *See* §5.23.
[68] *See* §5.26.
[69] *See* §6.02.
[70] *See* §6.03.
[71] *See* §6.04.
[72] *See* §6.05.
[73] *See* §6.06.
[74] *See* §6.07.
[75] *See* §6.08.
[76] *See* §7.02.
[77] *See* §7.03.
[78] *See* §7.04.
[79] *See* §7.05.
[80] *See* §7.06.
[81] *See* §7.07.
[82] *See* §7.08.
[83] *See* §7.09.

Timing[84]

Alternative strategies and tactics usually should be chosen for flexibility. The order of their intended use then must be tentatively determined in advance, subject to adjustment as the negotiation unfolds. Basic considerations affecting these choices are the expected dynamics of the negotiation, the nature of the client goals, and whether there is more than one issue involved, only money is at stake, or a win/win outcome is possible.

The strategy or strategies and the tactic or tactics that are chosen generally should include those needed to deal with four common negotiating dilemmas. These four quandaries are as follows:

1. How can the subject of negotiating be introduced where raising that possibility will be awkward?[85]

2. What actions can be taken as initiatives to break a deadlock, or to get the negotiating process moving again if it becomes bogged down?[86]

3. What methods will induce the other party or the other negotiator to become psychologically committed to reaching an agreement?[87]

4. To the extent that prior planning steps indicate a need for further information, which usually occurs, what is the most effective way to engage in the information gathering tactics?[88]

To the extent that these dilemmas are anticipated, the means to handle them should be considered in the planning stage.

The strategic and tactical choices must be analyzed in view of those anticipated to be made by the other side. The analysis includes possible reactions of the other side to planned choices in strategy and tactics. Likely countermeasures must be evaluated.

Through this anticipation, the choice of strategy and tactics is refined. Changes are made if problems are revealed due to the expected choices or moves of the other side. As with other steps, best and worst case scenarios may be useful.

One major caveat applies to anticipating the other side's conduct in planning strategy and tactics. The planner must focus on initiating actions, as well as reacting to the other side's anticipated conduct. A negotiation planner cannot become controlled or paralyzed by the expected moves of the other side. Although anticipation is critical, it can be overemphasized. The criticism has been made that many negotiators spend too much time and effort trying to

---

[84] *See* **§7.10.**

[85] This dilemma can be difficult in terms of avoiding the appearance of weakness or the appearance of being overly eager. But see **§5.03** concerning making the first offer.

[86] *See* **§5.20.**

[87] Potential methods include inducing the other side to expend such efforts that it will not want its efforts to have been "wasted," or the lure of future business. *See* **§5.18.**

[88] Virtually every negotiation involves the use of information gathering as a vital tool because of the number of unknowns which normally exist. *See* **§4.01.**

anticipate the other side.[89] Such overly reactive thinking is: "[L]ikely to make negotiators feel threatened and defensive, and make them less flexible and less creative in their negotiating behavior."[90]

During the planning stage itself, the negotiator may be able to affect the negotiation that is going to be conducted. Counsel can engage in the information gathering strategy before the negotiation starts, thereby learning more about the market, the other party, the other negotiator, or the situation that is to be negotiated.[91] Potential sources of information can be utilized, including public documents, media reports, experts, persons who have had contact with the other party, those who have been in similar situations, or others with relevant knowledge. Furthermore, it may be possible to create new facts or new issues before the negotiation.[92] The new facts may influence the other party's positions. The new issues may affect the bargaining process by creating potential tradeoffs or concessions.

After refirming the choice of strategy and tactics, those choices and the earlier nine steps are then reviewed. Errors in the present or any earlier step are corrected.

§9.06 —Step 11: Considering Concessions and Tradeoffs

Along with strategies and tactics, concessions and tradeoffs should also be planned, unless the only chosen strategy does not permit concessions under any circumstances. Normally, however, some concessions are expected. In part, parties tend to expect concessions because they want and believe that they will be able to shape the other party's actions during the negotiation.[93]

Concessions can be structured directly or creatively. For example, "nonspecific compensation" is a concession which is totally unrelated to what is demanded in return, except in terms of its value.[94]

Such tradeoffs need not be even logically related, as long as their values correlate.[95] This is possible, since an item often has a different value to each party.

The differing values on items, which create the opportunity for tradeoffs, flow from the parties' economic and noneconomic views of benefits and detriments. Parties may place different values on future versus present benefits or costs. One may place great value on security or peace of mind, which can be satisfied at little or no cost to the other. It has been suggested that a tradeoff

---

[89] R. Lewicki & J. Litterer, Negotiation 65 (1985).

[90] *Id.*

[91] See **ch 4** regarding information tactics.

[92] *See* **§4.03.**

[93] R. Lewicki & J. Litterer, Negotiation 91-92 (1985).

[94] *Id* 120.

[95] Mandle, *Collective Bargaining Negotiation,* in Attorney's Guide to Negotiation 14-18 (1979).

should be viewed as "a process of weighing and sorting and judging and deciding, finally, which option will work most effectively for you and the other person."[96]

The estimated value of the item to the other party indicates the necessary value of the item(s) to be chosen as a tradeoff. At times, trial proposals are used to test those estimates.[97]

A high, realistic opening position and the bottom line already have been established. In between, there is an area with room to maneuver. This area is called the anticipated zone of agreement. This is illustrated below for a case in which there is one issue and three potential concessions that are anticipated.

Figure 9-1

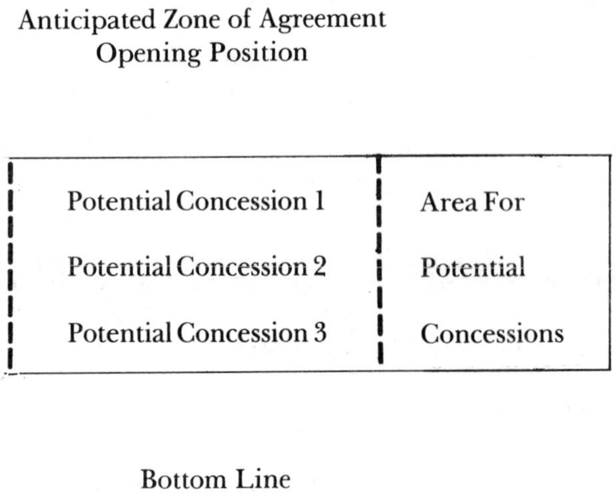

Anticipated Zone of Agreement
Opening Position

Potential Concession 1	Area For
Potential Concession 2	Potential
Potential Concession 3	Concessions

Bottom Line

For each potential concession, a rationale is developed, so that the new position appears to be reasonable and firm in the absence of new information or a concession by the other party. This is essential for the negotiator to present persuasively the present position being taken.

The nature and the order of the planned concessions must be determined for each issue or combination of issues if linkage exists which allows for tradeoffs between issues. A multiple issue negotiation with potential tradeoffs between issues could have the following anticipated zone of agreement and planned concessions:

---

[96] T. Warschaw, Winning By Negotiation 110 (McGraw-Hill, Inc 1980).

[97] See §5.08 regarding trial proposals.

Figure 9-2   Anticipated Zone of Agreement

Issue One	Issue Two	Combination of Issues 1 & 2
Opening Position	Opening Position	Opening Position
Potential Concession A	Potential Concession C	Trade-off F
Potential Concession B	Potential Concession D	Trade-off G
	Potential Concession E	
Bottom Line	Bottom Line	Bottom Line

In Figure 9-2, there is a separate opening position, potential plan for concessions with rationales for each, and a bottom-line position for each of the two issues, as well as for the combination of the issues.

Planning for concessions and for tradeoffs accomplishes several important functions. First, it allows for the creation of apparent concessions which are not real concessions. A negotiator may bargain about an issue that is not particularly important to the client, just so that it can later be conceded for a reciprocal concession that is of real value to the client.

Example 9-5

In a negotiation for a lease, the lessee's attorney bargains for an early time of possession, just so that the issue of early possession may be conceded to arrange for a smaller security deposit.

Example 9-6

A developer is negotiating with a community group concerned with the size and configuration of the planned unit development. The developer's bottom line will depend, in part, on the following factors:

1. The developer's relative political clout compared with that of the community group
2. The developer's ability to pass on costs
3. Any general zoning or permit issues
4. The availability of alternative sites

The developer's building plans and specifications include certain extra stories on the building, which it would find acceptable to actually construct, but which also function as a potential tradeoff for concessions from the community group.

Another important function of this planning step is that a number of relatively small concessions can be generated for potential use, thus avoiding large changes in one's position which might pass up more favorable opportunities for settlement. A third function is that persuasive reasons for each potential position can be conceived. This may not be as easy to do in the middle of the actual bargaining. Lastly, careful tradeoffs can be calculated, such as the present dollar value of changes in pricing in comparison to changes in credit terms. Again, it may be far easier and more practical to make such calculations in advance, rather than during the actual negotiating session.

Next, the other party's likely tradeoffs and concessions are envisioned. This includes anticipating reactions to one's own planned tradeoffs and strategy. Adjustments are made in planned tradeoffs and concessions based on the expected behavior of the other party. As before, after any adjustments, the present step is reviewed and crosschecked with the prior steps.

§9.07 —Step 12: The Agenda

The term *agenda,* in the context of negotiation, refers to the order in which actions will be taken, issues will be considered, or concessions will be made during the negotiating process. A decision first must be made as to whether to set an agenda. At least twelve factors should be considered in reaching this decision. These factors are whether:

1. The initial phase of the actual negotiation should be utilized to reduce tension or to build rapport

2. Information gathering is needed before resolving certain issues, so that your position is not undervalued or so that win/win opportunities are not missed

3. There should be selective information disclosure at an early stage, because the other party will be more inclined to concede more if it knows the information

4. There will be a need to disclose, obtain, or exchange information about interests, needs, goals, or perhaps, about opening positions at the first session(s), and then to adjourn to evaluate, revise, or formulate proposals before a subsequent negotiating session

5. Is it better to make the first offer or to wait to receive an offer, and is that affected by any customs regarding who makes the first offer?[98]

6. It is important to get at least tacit agreement on how the issues are defined before proceeding with other portions of the negotiation[99]

7. A certain issue or issues must be resolved before other issues can be discussed

---

[98] For example, in personal injury litigation, the plaintiff's lawyer customarily makes the initial demand. *See* Paplow, *Negotiating Settlement of a Personal Injury Action-Defendant,* in Attorney's Guide to Negotiation 10-8 (1979).

[99] *See* **§8.05.**

8.   Relatively easy issues should be negotiated first to create goodwill, rapport, and momentum

9.   It is better to negotiate the hardest issue first, before expending time and energy on other issues, which will be a wasted effort unless the hardest issue can be resolved

10.   An order or a package of issues should be defined and agreed on to influence the outcome of the negotiation by establishing the starting point and the sequence of what will be discussed

11.   The other party is unprepared for an extended negotiation

12.   Valuable insights are likely to be gained by allowing the other party to set an agenda, thereby discovering which areas the other party wishes to cover first or avoid

Example 9-7

One commentator suggests negotiating general provisions first, because these are the easier issues. He cites the advantages of avoiding controversy at the start, since these tend to be standard terms, setting a positive initial tone, and preventing quibbling over these details at the end of a difficult negotiation.[100]

Example 9-8

Panama was negotiating the Panama Canal pact with the United States. The easier issues were negotiated first, and the harder ones were deferred until later. The compensation issue was deferred until last. That may have been because the Panamanian government did not want to be perceived by its domestic constituency as "having sold out" in the early stages.[101]

Agendas in negotiations themselves often have two phases.[102] First, potential alternatives are sought through informational tactics. Later, other tactics are used to endeavor to isolate and shape an acceptable solution.

A party's view of the image to be projected by its agenda can be affected by whether a party should be characterized as the one pursuing an agreement, or the one who is being pursued for an agreement. The pursuer generally wants to generate interest and to avoid complications.[103] On the other hand, the pursued usually wishes to avoid appearing very interested, and to allow the pursuer to make the first moves in order to gain information.[104]

Additionally, a decision must be made about whether the negotiation should or is likely to consist of a single session or of a number of sessions over a period

---

[100] Rifkin, *Negotiating Patents, Trade Secrets and Know-How Licenses,* in Attorney's Guide to Negotiation 15-35 (1979).

[101] H. Raiffa, The Art and Science of Negotiation 178 (1982).

[102] Bartos, *How Predictable Are Negotiations,* in W. Zartman, The 50% Solution 486 (1976).

[103] X. Frascogna, Jr. & H. Hetherington, Negotiation Strategy for Lawyers 195 (1984).

[104] *Id.*

of time. Multiple sessions can result from such causes as a party's need to consult with an expert, a negotiator's need to check with higher authority, or the necessity of a complicated calculation of unanticipated possible benefits or costs. Delay can also be used if a group decision is required.[105]

Similarly, serial agreements may be anticipated with separate, but binding, agreements at each stage of the process.

Example 9-9

The negotiation concerns obtaining access over the client's neighbor's property in order to repair part of the client's adjoining property. Counsel's plan for the negotiation involves the following sequence of events:

1. An initial agreement for access on a single day in order to make minor repairs

2. All goes well with the initial agreement, thereby creating confidence on the neighbor's part that the client's contractor will be careful in utilizing the access and will avoid damaging property or inconveniencing the neighbor

3. A second major agreement for longer access to perform major repairs, which will be achieved through the trust and confidence generated by the contractor's conduct during the initial, minor repairs

The confidentiality of disclosures can be a preliminary, but a crucial, issue on an agenda. Agreement on confidentiality may be necessary before other issues can be reached.

Example 9-10

An inventor is negotiating with a company regarding the manufacturing of one of her inventions. Both parties are concerned with the effects of a confidentiality provision in the event that they are unable to agree on a manufacturing contract with royalties. From the company's perspective, it may not want to be bound, except to the extent that the inventor has, or can obtain, a patent. Otherwise, the company may be unable to avoid being precluded from proceeding with its own efforts in that area without paying the inventor.[106] For the inventor, a broad provision is desirable to protect against potential later claims by the company that disclosures were not utilized.

Even if counsel does not have a strong commitment to an agenda, opening moves should be planned and loosely scripted. This prepares counsel for the important opening portions of the negotiation and avoids hesitancy or becom-

---

[105] Kapov, *International Business-Government Negotiations,* in W. Zartman, The 50% Solution 435 (1976).

[106] *See* Rifkin, *Negotiating Patents, Trade Secrets and Know-How Licenses,* in Attorney's Guide to Negotiation 15-6 (1979).

ing lost at the start. Even so, quick modifications may be appropriate based on the initial dynamics and substantive positions.

Assuming an agenda is planned, the other side's planned agenda and its reaction to the intended agenda must be envisioned. Potential conflicts or counterproductive aspects may require adjustment of the planned agenda.

The planned agenda then is reviewed against the prior steps. If the analysis reveals any inconsistencies, gaps, or errors, the plans are adjusted appropriately.

Even when planning to set the agenda, the negotiator should avoid fighting over control of the agenda unless one of the following conditions applies:

1. Counsel really cannot negotiate unless certain portions of the desired agenda are followed

2. The power struggle over the agenda is essential to establish the necessary psychological climate for the rest of the negotiation, including demonstrating to the other party that one will not be pushed around

Otherwise, however, struggles over the agenda are counterproductive. Such struggles frequently are a waste of time and effort. Worse, they can even lead to a total breakdown of the entire negotiating process because of the antagonisms that may develop. Thus, battles over an agenda should be avoided unless the exceptions outlined above apply.

Example 9-11

In 1964, negotiations between India and a fertilizer consortium degenerated into a struggle over whether the agenda should consist of negotiating the substantive details or the procedure for an agreement in principle.[107] This struggle probably was avoidable, and arose partially due to a lack of sound planning.[108]

If necessary, however, the agenda itself may be the subject of negotiation. This can include procedures to be followed by the parties during the negotiation, time periods for the sessions, the right to caucus, and the confidentiality of discussions during and after the negotiation.[109] If the agenda is to be negotiated, the planning must include the point during the negotiation at which to negotiate the agenda. In other words, an agenda can include the negotiation of the agenda by the parties. The same strategies and tactics apply to negotiating the agenda as apply to any other item to be negotiated.

---

[107] Kapov, *supra* note 105, at 443.

[108] *See id* 445.

[109] Mandle, *Collective Bargaining Negotiation,* in Attorney's Guide to Negotiation 14-14 (1979).

§9.08 —Step 13: Timing

A decision must be made regarding the most advantageous time to commence negotiations. Each party's goals, vital interests, situational pressures and constraints, as well as the personal interests and the personality of the negotiator, should be taken into account. Both parties must be ready to negotiate to seriously seek an agreement. If early negotiations fail to reach an agreement, the same considerations apply to when to reopen negotiations.

The optimal time to negotiate is:

1. When one's side is under less pressure to make an agreement than the other side

2. Before the needs of one's side become more pressing, creating added pressures

3. When enough is known about the situation to negotiate intelligently

As to the latter point, in transactional matters, the value of the subject matter must be ascertained. This includes inspection of buildings or tests of new types of machinery for flaws, as well as information about market price. In litigation, cases should not be settled until the case is properly evaluated[110] with sufficient facts and legal principles or precedents known for a competent analysis. A need for additional information must be balanced against the worth of an early settlement or deal before:

1. An existing weakness or problem for the client is uncovered by the other side; *or*

2. A likely future weakness or problem develops

These factors should be evaluated and balanced in view of the time-consuming and costly efforts that may be expended uselessly if the other party learns of such weaknesses or problems.

In dispute situations, the parties often initially need to release some of their anger and frustration, or to prove their willingness to be tough. They then must engage in conflict for a period of time before they are ready for a realistic resolution reached by mutual agreement.

If litigation has been instituted, either before any negotiations or after initial negotiations did not result in a settlement, the litigation process itself affects planning the timing of negotiations. This is because of the deadlines, pressures, and costs involved in the litigation process. For a detailed discussion of these influences, see **§7.12.**

Since the client's needs can dictate the timing of the negotiation, timing sometimes is a decision for the client. In any event, any priorities regarding timing must be established through consultation with the client.[111]

---

[110] Lee, *Some Comments on Negotiation and Settlement,* 10 Am J Trial Advoc 181 (1987).

[111] Kane & Esposito, *Representing Clients in Negotiation of a Commercial Real Estate Transaction,* in Attorney's Guide to Negotiation 7-8 (1979).

The time when both parties are ready to negotiate seriously to seek an agreement will be affected by each side's deadline for reaching an agreement.[112] Indeed, frequently, an agreement will not be reached until at least one party's deadline for concluding the negotiation is reached, or even exceeded.[113]

Deadline in this context is used to mean the time by which a party, or its negotiator, feels that it needs to obtain an agreement.[114] A deadline may be absolute, such as the time by which a particular business deal must be achieved or the opportunity to make the deal will have passed. A deadline may be apparently absolute, such as a firm trial date that the judge will not alter; although some cases settle even during the trial. It also may be created by the other party. Frequently, however, a deadline is a date simply chosen by a party, and it may be subject to negotiation, such as a strike deadline.[115] In the latter situation, counsel must consider the likelihood of negotiating a change in the deadline, and the risks and benefits of attempting to proceed past the deadline.[116]

Since a party tends to feel more pressure to compromise as its own internal deadline approaches, it is preferable to be in the following positions,[117] unless using the deadline tactic:

1. To know the other side's deadline

2. To not have one's own deadline known by the other side, at least in an adversarial negotiation (it may be necessary to have both sides know each other's deadlines in a transactional, cooperative negotiation)

3. To have a more flexible or a later deadline than the other side

Being in the above situations is advantageous, because counsel is helped by knowing when the other side is under some type of deadline pressure, while avoiding a similar perception by the other side.

The timing of a negotiation also may depend on whether long-run contracts are reviewed periodically. A periodic review can reveal whether the agreement still represents a sufficient mutuality of interest.[118] In this manner, the need or the opportunity to renegotiate more favorable terms may be discovered.

Timing may depend on the urgency with which a transitional negotiation is needed to restructure a current agreement. The urgency of the need to restructure can dictate the timing of such a renegotiation.

---

[112] H. Cohen, You Can Negotiate Anything 91-99 (1982).

[113] *Id* 91-92. Cohen also suggests that most concessions will occur relatively shortly before the party's deadline. *Id* 92.

[114] See **§5.26** regarding the tactical use of deadlines.

[115] H. Cohen, You Can Negotiate Anything 96-97 (1982).

[116] *Id* 96-98.

[117] *Id* 92; *see* **§5.26.**

[118] M. Zimmerman, How to Do Business with the Japanese 111 (1985).

Example 9-12

A trucking firm leased its trucks under a long-term leasing agreement. Unfortunately for the firm, the market price for such leases had dropped dramatically since it entered into its current lease. This created an overwhelming competitive advantage for the firm's competitors. In turn, the competitive disadvantage for the business caused a loss of revenue, placing the firm in a precarious financial position. It became imperative to seek an immediate restructuring of the economic terms of the lease in order to avoid financial ruin for the trucking firm.

The other party's timing needs and reaction to the intended timing must be anticipated. The timing can be modified if problems foreseen by the expected needs or reaction of the other party outweigh any benefits from the intended timing.

The timing of some negotiations is more structured than that of others. Serious labor negotiations are scheduled, but litigation negotiations may evolve out of a chance meeting at the courthouse.[119] Counsel should not negotiate terms merely because of a chance encounter if he or she is unprepared to do so, or if the timing is not advantageous. However, even when counsel is not ready to proceed, the occasion can be used to gather information. This requires active listening, with little or no disclosure of information.[120]

Timing raises the issue of having a single, versus a sequential, negotiation. If the negotiation will, or is likely to, consist of multiple sessions, then the timing of each session must be considered. This also applies to structuring successive negotiations which are self-contained, but periodic. For example, labor or contractual negotiations can occur yearly or on some other regular basis.

Lastly, reexamine the prior steps and the present step in light of each other. Any needed adjustments in the plans then should be made.

§9.09   —Step 14: The Mode(s) of Communication

After deciding that the time is right to negotiate, the final step is to determine which mode of communication should be utilized. Choices must be made among face-to-face meetings, telephone communications, letters, other written communications, and combinations of methods. The advantages and disadvantages of these choices are analyzed in §10.05.

The analysis must include anticipating the other party's reaction to the mode of communication. The negotiator must consider whether a particular mode will be perceived as awkward, inappropriate, offensive, a pretext for delay, or for any other reason trigger an adverse response. If an adverse response is a significant possibility, the benefits and detriments of using another mode must be considered.

---

[119] Skolrood, *Negotiating Settlement of a Personal Injury Action-Plaintiff,* in Attorney's Guide to Negotiation 9-1 (1979).

[120] *See* §4.04.

Lastly, the means of communication may impact the timing of the negotiation. Any potential delays must be taken into account. Effects on timing must be considered against the benefit or problems with the planned method, or with alternative modes of communication. If timing will be affected, then, again, the anticipated reaction of the other side regarding altered timing must be considered, and any necessary adjustments in the prior or present planning steps should be made.

§9.10   Multiple Party Interactions

Multiple party interactions may involve parties who are "on the same side," as well as those with positions on opposite sides of the negotiation. Multiple party negotiations should be analyzed on the basis of which sides have multiple parties, and also on the basis of the type of negotiation involved, such as transactional or adversarial.

Multiple party negotiations tend to involve an increased interdependence between the parties. There is a corresponding tendency towards a loss of autonomy and the ability to manipulate other parties' affairs.[121]

In litigation, for instance, where there is a single plaintiff and multiple defendants, the basic question is whether the negotiation will be conducted as if there is only one combined defendant, or as if each defendant has a separate interest. Thus, the defendants should consider whether to agree on terms for negotiating with the plaintiff among themselves, and then to present a united front to the plaintiff. This may depend on the agreement that can be reached among the defendants. It should be noted, however, that it is possible for the defendants to present a united negotiating position to the plaintiff, even though they are by no means in agreement among themselves as to their relative responsibilities.[122]

Assuming that a group of defendants agrees on a united front, the plaintiff must then either accept that position and negotiate with the defendants as a group, or attempt to negotiate with the defendants individually. That decision will depend on the needs and interests of each of those parties and whether the negotiation with the group is likely to proceed advantageously. Even if the

---

[121] Morse, *The Bargaining Structure of Nato: Multi-Issue Negotiation in an Independent World*, in W. Zartman, The 50% Solution 86 (1976).

[122] An extreme example of this occurred during the multi-district federal litigation that arose as a result of the DC-10 crash in Chicago in 1979. *In re* Aircrash Disaster Near Chicago, Illinois, On May 25, 1979 (MDL 391). Over one hundred cases were consolidated in the Northern District of Illinois for pretrial purposes. There were two defendants, the airline and the manufacturer of the plane, each with its own attorneys. At one point during the overall litigation, the defendants began to actively litigate between themselves. The dispute between the defendants concerned their percentage of the total liability to the plaintiffs, as well as the responsibility for the loss of the aircraft. In fact, while the plaintiffs had scheduled and had taken some nine depositions on the question of liability, the defendants scheduled and began to take some three hundred depositions. Nevertheless, at all times, the defendants presented an absolutely united front with respect to negotiating settlements with the plaintiffs.

plaintiff negotiates with the defendants as a group, the plaintiff may still want to try to split the defendants, through the arguments that it presents or through the settlement proposals that it makes.[123]

On the other hand, assuming that the defendants do not agree to negotiate as a group, the plaintiff then has the opposite situation to consider. Here, the plaintiff must decide whether it will be more advantageous to negotiate individually with the defendants, or whether it would be preferable to try to maneuver the defendants into a group negotiation.

In a transactional matter, those who appear to be allied may, in fact, have different interests and goals. If so, this can lead to the opportunity for a series of separate negotiations similar to those discussed above in the context of litigation. For instance, joint venturers who are seeking a contract with another party may not be in agreement as to their priorities and bottom lines. The same may be true of a group of lessees who are negotiating with their landlord concerning improving the services provided at their building. The issue for the other party is whether to attempt to separately influence or otherwise split the group.

An extremely important caveat, however, applies to transactional negotiations, particularly those that need to be conducted with at least an apparently cooperative approach. In this situation, if one party is perceived as trying to split allies, the resulting ill-will may destroy the chance of reaching an agreement. Accordingly, great caution must be exercised with regard to being perceived as attempting to split allies in a transactional or cooperative situation.

Multiple parties can make reaching agreement more difficult.

Example 9-13

In a labor strike against newspapers, it was far easier for the publisher's group to disagree with the group of unions than to agree.[124] The publishers required unanimity for an agreement.[125] The unions could agree based on a majority vote, but any union could cause a shutdown by commencing or remaining on strike.[126]

Regardless of whether a negotiation involves litigation, labor relations, or a transaction, or whether it is adversarial or cooperative, multiple party negotiations require that each party be separately considered at each step of the planning process. One's own ally's vital interests must be analyzed, since counsel will be negotiating with the ally and attempting to avoid being split apart from the ally unless, of course, that is to the client's advantage. Thus, each step of the planning process will entail additional considerations and analysis for each of the parties that is involved in the negotiation.

---

[123] See §§7.06, 7.07, & 7.08 regarding various tactics that the plaintiff may employ to split multiple defendants.

[124] Raskin, *The Newspaper Strike*, in W. Zartman, The 50% Solution 475 (1976).

[125] *Id.*

[126] *Id.*

§9.11 Implementation and Adjustment

During the negotiation, counsel initially must implement the negotiation plan. Implementation requires a commitment to doing, rather than merely trying to do. A commitment to merely try can create a mind-set for a half-hearted attempt. An attitude to just "try" is insufficient. Unless something significant and unforeseen occurs justifying alterations, the opening moves should be performed as planned. This should be done even if the plan is followed imperfectly, rather than merely trying to do so.[127]

The necessary mental commitment requires gathering energy, completely focusing on the interaction, and refusing to allow fatigue or distractions to undermine performance. A lawyer must never allow becoming worn down or being distracted to adversely impact the outcome of a negotiation. Yet, this does occur, due to improper mental and physical conditioning and attitude. Mental toughness, the ability to concentrate, and a willingness to accept the challenge are crucial, even in a cooperative or problem-solving negotiation. If necessary, adjournments can be used to deal with fatigue.[128] Scheduling can avoid "jet lag," if that is a problem.

The opening moves are important, and restraint should generally be used if possible in the beginning of the negotiation.[129] The opening and the initial stages are used partially to determine or at least to get an indication of the other side's predispositions. These predispositions may concern strategy, tactics, positions, or motives of either the other party or its negotiator. If such predispositions can be identified, then the best means to influence them can be considered. The ways in which those predispositions are likely to affect the other side's reactions can also be appraised.

Sometimes, in complex negotiations, notes are made to keep track of positions and points of agreement. These also can be utilized to uncover patterns of behavior and goals.[130]

In analyzing the other side's conduct, it must be recognized that, not infrequently, negotiators or parties make shortsighted choices,[131] are not ruled strictly by a desire to maximize economic gain, or are unpredictable. Such conduct may seem irrational, but analysis during the negotiation must not ignore the possibility that the other party or its negotiator may be shortsighted, economically irrational, or unpredictable. Information gathering and trial balloons[132] may be used to discern the reasons for such conduct. Similarly, they may be employed to detect patterns that make seemingly unpredictable activity predictable. At the same time, negotiators must be mentally ready for the unexpected, since no one can always anticipate or analyze perfectly.

---

[127] J. Small, Comments at the National Institute of Trial Advocacy Southeast Regional (Oct 19, 1987) (Chapel Hill, North Carolina).

[128] *See* **§5.24.**

[129] X. Frascogna, Jr. & H. Hetherington, Negotiation Strategy for Lawyers 63 (1984).

[130] Sandels, *Negotiation in Business Litigation,* in Attorney's Guide to Negotiation 11-19 (1979).

[131] R. Lewicki & J. Litterer, Negotiation 133 (1985) [herinafter Lewicki].

[132] *See* **§5.07.**

Economic or utility models must be balanced against "human imponderables."[133] Game theory cannot be relied on alone, since it tends to assume rationality in decision making.[134] If used, game theory must be adjusted to include subjective values, which may not be objectively rational. Feelings and emotions can be the motivating forces.[135]

Deciphering the other side's thinking and motivations is complicated by what has been called: "[T]he dilemma of trust—that is, (negotiators) must infer the other's true intentions or preferences while knowing that the other is attempting to inflate, magnify or justify these preferences."[136]

For example, smaller concessions tend to be made as a party is forced to approach its bottom line.[137] If the concession pattern leads to the conclusion that the other party's bottom line is different than expected, further planning is required. Since each negotiator is seeking to decode the messages that are being received, an astute negotiator will inject messages that falsely suggest or imply nearness to the client's resistance point.[138]

Unpredictability can be advantageous in forcing the other party to adopt a worst case scenario analysis, and to increase its uncertainty and the resulting level of stress. For instance, in the early 1970s, the unpredictable and rash personality of Malta's leader strengthened his bargaining position against Great Britain, because the British feared that he would move politically away from them and towards Libya and the Soviet Union.[139]

On the other hand, irrationality or unpredictability may make negotiation impractical. A lack of consistent values during the course of the negotiation[140] and other types of irrational behavior can make it impossible to negotiate normally. The resulting frustration or disgust can lead to a termination of the negotiation, especially if the value of a future working relationship with the unpredictable party is believed to be diminished or destroyed.

After the opening moves and analysis, use the properly prepared, flexible plan, considering the various alternatives from the actions of the other negotiator. In addition, the planning process should be repeated during the negotiation as often as necessary, in order to take into account new information acquired during the negotiation itself.

In repeating the planning process, check the accuracy of one's theories about the other party and its negotiator, including focusing on personalities. There

---

[133] W. Zartman, The 50% Solution 18-19 (1976).

[134] *Id* 26.

[135] de Felice, *Negotiations, or The Art of Negotiating,* in W. Zartman, The 50% Solution 49 (1976).

[136] Lewicki, *supra* note 131, at 323.

[137] *Id* 92.

[138] M. Saks & R. Hastie, Social Psychology in Court 124-25 (1978).

[139] Wriggins, *Up for Auction: Malta Bargains with Great Britain 1971,* in W. Zartman, The 50% Solution 220 (1976).

[140] For instance, one of the problems that has been faced in trying to negotiate with some airline hijackers has been their lack of consistent values during the bargaining. Baldwin, *Bargaining with Airline Hijackers,* in W. Zartman, The 50% Solution 421-22 (1976).

are some pure, one-dimensional personality types in terms of their actions while negotiating. Of course, many others are multi-dimensional. Counsel must probe to ascertain the other negotiator's style.

Unless the real decision maker or those exerting influence is clear at the outset, part of the assessment is to identify that person or persons. The negotiator can then focus on those who must be reached.

Counsel may need to adapt with further planning if the other party or its negotiator tends to have difficulty with attitude changes, short-term learning, cognition, or perception. Such adaptation may take the form of:

1. Increasing the clarity or the simplicity of the messages that are being communicated

2. Altering or modifying strategy and/or tactics

3. Changing the expressed reasons for positions

4. Changing positions

5. Adjusting timing to make proposals earlier or to lengthen deadlines[141]

In addition, an adjustment can be necessary if the other side has difficulty making decisions.

Replanning may be a split-second mental process during a negotiation session, or a more time-consuming effort during an adjournment or between sessions. Either way, it should be a conscious process using the same, specific systematic planning framework. This will help to avoid blind reactions which are not well thought through, and that may well prove to be ill conceived.

While some degree of action based on one's feel for the negotiation is appropriate and inevitable, careful analysis is necessary. Thoughts should not be rationalized to artificially place them within definitional categories.

Rather, in an important sense, the analysis always returns to the most basic and yet profound question: "What's really going on here?"[142]

One crucial aspect of that question involves sub-questions about the process:

1. Is the process moving in a direction?

2. If so, what is the direction?

3. Is that direction the most advantageous or even advantageous at all?

By focusing on these questions, the negotiator can be alert to maintain or to change the current course of action.

Choices must be made between firmness and flexibility. One factor is whether the behavior of the other side tends to be predictably symmetrical or asymmetrical.[143] If it is symmetrical, then:

---

[141] See §§5.26 & 7.10.

[142] J. McKnight, Seminars at Center for Urban Affairs and Policy Research, Northwestern University (Chicago, Ill 1979-1980).

[143] W. Zartman, *supra* note 133, at 30.

1. Firmness will be met with firmness
2. Flexibility will lead to reciprocal flexibility

If it is asymmetrical, then:

1. Firmness will lead to flexibility by the other side
2. Flexibility will cause the other side to stand firm

Another type of adjustment may concern long-term and short-term goals. If priority long-run goals cannot be met at the present time, then the analysis must shift to evaluate whether short-run measures can be used to build towards long-term goals.

§9.12   Conclusion

The planning steps apply to all types of negotiations, as illustrated by the following examples.

Example 9-14

The new case involves an accidental shooting which has left the 20-year-old, single client permanently disabled.

Step 1: *Information Gathering.* Medical records, including evaluations by physiatrist, occupational therapists, and physical therapists are obtained. Other information reveals that there is a strong case of negligence against the owner of the gun, but no products liability case against the manufacturer. The owner's homeowner's policy covers the accident and has a policy limit of $1,000,000. Nothing is known about the individual claims representative, but the insurance company is considered to be normally relatively reasonable.

Step 2: *Goals.* The client's goals are to maximize the recovery against the insurance policy, at least recover enough to provide for herself, since she can no longer work, but not to seek money personally from the owner of the gun, who is a relative.

Steps 3, 4, and 5: *Issues; Market; Strengths and Weaknesses.* The major issues are negligence and damages. The market is considered in terms of the likely jury award to this particular client, as well as reported verdicts and settlements for similar injuries. The strength of the case is that there are strong facts demonstrating negligence, and a very badly injured and sympathetic victim. The weakness of the case is that the client is very uneasy about having to testify and thereby relive everything that has happened to her, and also that both the client and her family are worried about how she will be able to take care of herself if the defendant somehow prevails at a trial. An additional concern is that, if a suit is necessary, the court docket is so backlogged that it will be at least four years before the case will be reached for trial.

Step 6: *Other's Bottom Line and Opening Position.* Based on preliminary conversations, it is believed that the insurance company would prefer to settle the case without a suit. Furthermore, the company apparently knows that, if the case does go to trial, it will probably lose, but that there also is a realistic possibility of a no liability verdict. It is also believed that the company will want to save some money if it agrees to an early settlement. The insurance company's bottom line is estimated to be $900,000, and its expected opening position about $400,000.

Step 7: *Win/Win Outcomes.* The possibility of a win/win outcome is considered, and it appears that such an outcome may be feasible through a structured settlement.[144]

Step 8: *Opening Position.* In light of the foregoing, a decision is made to make an opening demand of $960,000. This will be presented as a reasonable demand, given the strong liability case, the reasonable possibility that a verdict would be in excess of the $1,000,000 policy limit, and the savings in litigation expenses to both sides.

Step 9: *Bottom Line.* After discussions with the client, a bottom line of $850,000 is established, with the possibility that the present value of such a settlement could be somewhat lower if a structured settlement seemed to warrant it.

Figure 9-3

Issues	Cash Settlement	Structured Settlement
Bottom Line	$850,000	Present Value of $775,000 with an initial cash payment of at least $330,000 and a structure that provides a satisfactory lifetime income

Step 10: *Strategy and Tactics.* A HRESSC strategy seems to be clearly appropriate.[145] Facts will be "created" by retaining experts on firearms and on econom-

---

[144] See **§7.03** regarding structured settlements.
[145] *See* **§3.06.**

ics, and by obtaining reports from them.[146] These reports will then be transmitted to the insurance company. All other pertinent information, such as the police reports and the medical records, also will be provided to the insurance company. The information will be sent in the form of a settlement brochure.[147] It is further decided to make the first offer, since that is the normal procedure in this type of case; counsel intends to rely primarily on bargaining and discussion,[148] after using selective information disclosure in transmitting the settlement brochure.

Step 11: *Concessions and Tradeoffs.* Three potential concessions are planned, if it seems necessary to move from the opening position towards the bottom line. These will be explained using rationales of trying to be reasonable and avoiding the time and costs of litigation.

Figure 9-4

Opening Position: $960,000

Anticipated	Area for	Potential	Concession 1
Zone of	Potential	Potential	Concession 2
Agreement	Concessions	Potential	Concession 3

Bottom Line: $850,000 (cash settlement)

Step 12: *Agenda.* It is not clear whether the negotiation will require more than one session, although this appears likely. In any event, there does not seem to be a need for setting a formal agenda beyond initially transmitting the settlement brochure, pursuant to the selective information disclosure tactic.

Step 13: *Timing.* The negotiation is planned to begin within 30 days of when all of the information has been submitted to the insurance company. The insurer is to be advised that there is a strong interest on the plaintiff's part either to reach a prompt settlement or to file suit. There is no definite deadline, but there also is no intention to let the negotiation drag on for months, given the amount of money involved and the interest that could be earned on that

---

[146] *See* §4.03.
[147] See §4.02 regarding settlement brochures.
[148] *See* §§5.03, 5.09, & 5.10.

money. It is hoped that the insurer will feel a general deadline pressure to avoid having a lawsuit filed.

Step 14: *Communication Mode.* Despite the large amount of money that is involved, it is anticipated that the negotiating will take place on the telephone, because that is the customary mode of communication in this area for this type of negotiation. Having systematically planned the negotiation, counsel is now ready to proceed.

Example 9-15

Counsel is retained to negotiate an employment agreement for a doctor who has completed her residency and has an additional one year's experience. The potential employer is a group of doctors in the same specialty, who are in a partnership.

Step 1: *Information Gathering.* Information is gathered through the client, as well as other doctors, regarding the market for a doctor in this specialty with this level of experience, in terms of salary, fringe benefits, and the potential for a future partnership. The client has already been given a proposed contract by the partnership. That proposal indicates the partnership's positions on various issues.

Steps 2 and 3: *Goals and Issues.* The client's goals are to:

1. Obtain a salary and fringe benefits that are reasonable for the employment market that she is in (a short-term goal)
2. Obtain reasonable provisions for pregnancy/maternity leave, should she have children in the future (a long term-goal)
3. Maintain a good relationship with the other doctors, with a view to becoming a partner after being an employee for a year or two (a long-term goal)

The various potential fringe benefits are each considered individually as separate issues. These potential fringe benefits include:

1. Malpractice insurance
2. Major medical insurance with pregnancy coverage
3. Disability insurance
4. Paid vacation time
5. Paid sick leave time
6. Paid pregnancy/maternity leave time
7. Paid time for continuing medical education
8. Expenses for continuing medical education
9. Expenses for membership in professional societies and associations
10. Provisions regarding a car phone
11. Provisions regarding a home computer

The client considers an overall financial package of salary and fringe benefits to be an essential goal. Among the different types of fringe benefits, however, some are deemed to be essential, such as having the partnership pay her malpractice insurance premium. Others are considered to be only desirable, such as having the partnership provide a good disability insurance policy. Reasonable provisions for pregnancy/maternity leave also are regarded as essential, as is the maintenance of a good relationship, so that the prospects for a future partnership are not compromised.

Additional issues include:

1. The length of the contract
2. Whether any references to, or specific provisions for, a future partnership will be included in the contract, and, if so, the terms
3. Provisions for terminating the contract by either party

It is determined that the client's goal is for a two-year contract, with a provision that, if both parties wish to enter into a partnership agreement, discussions regarding such an agreement will begin at least six months prior to the expiration of the current contract.

Step 4: *Market.* As noted above, the market for various of the contractual substantive terms is considered. The partnership's attorney prepared its contract proposal and will negotiate for it, so that it is anticipated that the usual negotiation methods in the market will be employed, including some direct contract between the clients, depending on the future developments. (If the partnership were negotiating through one of its members, rather than through an attorney, this might affect the negotiating methods).

Step 5: *Strengths and Weaknesses.* It is known that the partnership has a vital interest in securing the services of a young doctor in the client's specialty who the partners believe is both well-qualified and personally compatible with them. It is also known, given the partnership's employment offer, that the partners believe that the client meets those criteria. Apparently, no one else is currently under consideration for the position. On the other hand, it is not vital to the partnership that the client be hired, and there are undoubtedly other doctors who could also meet the partnership's needs. If there is no agreement, the partnership will be inconvenienced by a delay in filling its need for another doctor in the client's specialty, but it can certainly cope with that, if necessary. Similarly, the client has a vital interest in obtaining this type of position, and would like it to be with this particular medical group. If there is no agreement, however, the client certainly will be able to find other employment opportunities that also meet her needs. Thus, the strengths and the weaknesses seem roughly equal, with both parties personally anxious for an agreement, but with both parties also able to withstand the possibility of not reaching an agreement.

Step 6: *Other's Opening Position and Bottom Line.* The other party's opening position has already been presented in its draft contract. The partnership's bottom line and its expectations are now estimated, using its contract proposal as the starting point. The contract proposal is fairly reasonable, although it omits certain desired fringe benefits and any reference to pregnancy/maternity leave. It is believed that the partnership is willing to make some concessions to improve the contract for the client, since it would not be reasonable for the partnership to be using a no concessions strategy on all of the various contractual issues.

Step 7: *Win/Win Outcomes.* The partnership's proposal has no reference to a car phone or a home computer, although both of these items would be beneficial to the client's medical practice, and therefore also beneficial to the partnership. Either a tradeoff on salary or a requirement by the employer that the client obtain these items will have favorable tax consequences for the client. Thus, there will be a gain to the client without a corresponding loss to the partnership. The partnership's proposal also does not have provisions for time off for purposes of continuing medical education. A provision for this will be included in the counterproposal on behalf of the client, and may be viewed as a win/win outcome, since both parties will gain from the client's obtaining a certain amount of continuing medical education.

Steps 8, 9, and 10: *Opening Position; Bottom Line; Strategy and Tactics.* Next, a high realistic opening position is established for each issue, except for some of the fringe benefits for which the original offer is already satisfactory. A bottom line is also considered for each issue, and for those issues that can be traded off against each other. Counsel and the client consider the idea of demanding increases in all of the offered fringe benefits, even those that are already quite acceptable, in order to create potential concessions that are of greater value to the partnership than to the client. It is rejected because, in this particular negotiation, there is a danger that seeking to increase every aspect of the initial offer would be perceived as an unrealistically high position, and that could adversely affect the chances of reaching an agreement. As referred to above, both a HRESSC and a win/win strategy are planned.

Step 11: *Concessions and Tradeoffs.* These are planned for the salary and fringe benefit issues. It is noted that there are many potential cross-issue tradeoffs among the salary, each potential fringe benefit, the length of the contract, possible future partnership references or provisions, and termination provisions. In light of the multi-dimensional nature of this negotiation, it is recognized that this step may very well need to be replanned as the negotiation progresses and the initial plan is implemented and adjusted.[149]

Steps 12, 13, and 14: *Agenda; Timing; Communications Mode.* The planned agenda is to prepare and submit a written counterproposal on behalf of the client, followed by a discussion between the attorneys. Timing is not an issue, because both sides are eager to reach an agreement and are ready to negotiate. Written communications and proposals will be used, as well as face-to-face meetings and telephone calls.

A sound plan for a negotiation almost always has alternatives and is multi-dimensional. As each step is completed, earlier steps are reexamined to consider whether any modification is needed. Issue-by-issue planning is required, as is cross-issue planning to the extent that tradeoffs between issues are required or desirable.

The importance of effective planning cannot be overstated. By following this system for planning, the negotiator will be as well-prepared as possible. At the same time, the negotiator must be ready and able to act and to react appropriately once the negotiation commences. The plan that is formulated is not designed to be blindly followed as a preconceived, unchangeable scenario. Rather, it is intended to provide definite guidelines and adaptable tools. The secret is to be: GOALS RIGID AND MEANS FLEXIBLE.[150] While not abandoning goals, an effective negotiator must be willing to recognize and to use unanticipated means to achieve those goals. Similarly, it may be necessary to recognize and to discard means that are not working effectively. The negotiator's goals are to obtain or to exceed the client's bottom line.

Although the negotiator's goals should be rigidly maintained unless the client changes them or their priorities, that does not mean that even the client's bottom line is always absolutely unchangeable. Information received during the course of the negotiation may justify altering the bottom line, with, of course, the client's authorization.

Tough, but flexible implementation of the plan allows the negotiator to exploit opportunities that would otherwise be lost. This approach enhances the chances of achieving a successful result.

A final note of caution is warranted. Never underestimate the other party or its negotiator, and, in litigation, the strength of its case or the ability of its trial counsel. Bold acts can be appropriate, if tempered by realism and a touch of humanity. History constantly reminds us that many a brave but grave error can be traced back to foolishly underestimating or ignoring the other side's true capabilities. General Custer and the Light Brigade gave rise to moving poems, books, and movies as tributes to folly. While a lawyer in most negotiations is unlikely to inspire such artistic endeavors, the possibility of a less dramatic form of folly cannot be ignored.

---

[149] *See* §9.11.

[150] *See* R. Fisher & W. Ury, Getting to Yes: Negotiating Agreement Without Giving In 54-55 (1981).

§9.13 Summary and Review

I. Step 8: Setting the Opening Position
   A. The initial substantive position
   B. Use high but realistic expectations to avoid underestimating or overestimating to the point of causing deadlock or termination
   C. Use information from steps 3 through 7
   D. Set opening position above estimate of other party's bottom line to guard against underestimating and to allow for one or more concessions, if needed
   E. Establish for the entire negotiation each issue and any combinations of issues which may involve potential tradeoffs between issues
   F. May be the client's decision with counseling as needed, depending on client's level of sophistication and substantive involvement
   G. Also plan reasons to justify it
   H. May or may not be used, depending on the actual way that the negotiation unfolds
   I. Driving too hard of a bargain can lead to repudiation or lack of good faith efforts

II. Step 9: Set the Bottom Line
   A. The point at which no agreement is better than any available agreement
   B. Use information from steps 2 through 8
   C. Establish for the entire negotiation each issue and each combination of issues where there can be tradeoffs between issues
   D. This is the client's decision ultimately, after listening to the client's own views and counseling the client on legal, business, social, political, and personal factors as appropriate
   E. Use outside experts for input, if needed
   F. Generate a list of alternatives with client, and analyze each generally, taking the most aggressive first and the least aggressive last. The analysis includes risks, benefits, and the chances that each will occur
   G. Counsel generally makes a recommendation, except for highly sophisticated clients
   H. Caution against unrealistic bottom lines, unless the alternatives to agreement are preferable to a realistic bottom line
   I. Time the advice for when the client is psychologically ready to hear it
   J. Reexamine the earlier steps and this one for possible errors or adjustments
   K. The bottom line is set based on the alternative to reaching agreement, rather than the likelihood of achieving it, except for interim bottom lines during phases of the negotiation, which create the same dangers as bluffs

    L. Subject to change during the negotiation, so communicate with the client during the negotiation about the status of it

    M. If changed, avoid looking like the initial opening position was a failed bluff

    N. Exception for limited authority, in which the negotiator deliberately does not know the client's bottom line to resist pressure for concessions, maintain harmony in the negotiation by blaming someone not present, and demand information for the decision maker

III. Step 10: Choosing Strategies and Tactics

    A. Strategic choices are:

      1. Personal credibility

      2. No concessions

      3. No further concessions

      4. Deadlock-breaking concessions only

      5. HRESSC

      6. Concede first

      7. Problem solving

      8. Purposes other than reaching an agreement, including delay, discovery, influencing the client, and influencing third parties

      9. Moving for closure

    B. Tactical choices are:

      1. Disclosing information

      2. Creating facts

      3. Listening for information

      4. Using the funnel approach

      5. Using sources of information

      6. Bargaining for information

      7. Informational discussions

      8. Requiring preconditions

      9. Making or avoiding making the first offer

     10. Demanding responses to offers and to positions

     11. Reciprocity

     12. Win/win proposals

     13. Trial proposals

     14. Concessions that are of greater value to one party

     15. Bargaining

     16. Discussion

     17. Conditional proposals

     18. Power

     19. Bluff

     20. Tone

     21. The use of alternative opportunities

     22. Splitting the difference

     23. Focus/downplay

     24. Creating a psychological commitment for agreement

25. Saving face
26. Inserting new issues
27. Focusing on the process
28. Creating movement
29. Adjournment
30. Patience
31. Limited authority
32. Surprise
33. Appealing to personal interests
34. Deadlock
35. Deadlines
36. Active client participation
37. Negotiating teams
38. Judicial settlement conferences
39. Allies
40. Media or community pressure
41. Alternative dispute resolution
42. Class actions
43. Litigation
44. Structured settlements
45. Depositions
46. Policy limits letter
47. Loan agreements
48. "Mary Carter" agreements
49. Contribution
50. Offers of judgments
51. Timing

C. Choose alternative strategies and tactics for flexibility, but tentatively decide on planned order of use subject to adjustment as the negotiation unfolds

D. Generally include strategies and tactics available to initiate negotiations if that is awkward, break deadlocks, get the process moving if it becomes bogged down, induce the other party or its negotiator to become psychologically committed to reaching agreement, and gather any information indicated to be needed by the prior planning steps

E. Refine choice of strategies and tactics by considering anticipated reactions and countermeasures by the other side

F. Focus on initiating action, not merely responding to anticipated actions by the other side

G. Take planned measures that are available before the negotiation starts and which can influence its outcome, such as fact creation

H. Review prior steps, and make any appropriate modifications to this or the prior steps

IV. Step 11: Consider Concessions and Tradeoffs

A. Plan for concessions and tradeoffs unless the only strategy chosen precludes them

   B. Some concessions and tradeoffs are generally expected
   C. Can be logically unrelated, as long as related in value to that being demanded in return
   D. Tradeoffs flow from different values placed on the same item by each party
   E. Plan potential concessions for the area between the opening position and the bottom line
   F. Create a rationale for each concession, so that the new position appears fixed and firm in the absence of new information or a concession by the other party
   G. Plan for each issue or combination of issues if tradeoffs are possible between issues
   H. Includes creation of apparent concessions that are really unimportant to the client
   I. This planning allows a number of relatively small concessions and tradeoffs, with rationales for each, and well-calculated tradeoffs, all of which helps avoid lost opportunities for a more favorable agreement
   J. Anticipate the other party's likely tradeoffs and concessions, as well as its reactions to your own, and make adjustments if necessary
   K. Review prior steps, and modify prior or present steps if appropriate
V. The Agenda
   A. The order of actions, issues, and concessions
   B. The 12-factor approach to directing whether to set an agenda based on the need to: build rapport, gather information, disclose information, adjourn after initially obtaining or releasing information, make or refrain from making the first offer, agree on the issues, resolve some issues before other issues, resolve easy issues just to create momentum, negotiate the hardest issues first to avoid wasting time on easy ones, agree on the definitions and sequences or packages of issues to be discussed, catch the other party unprepared for extended negotiation, or gain insights by allowing the other party to set the agenda
   C. Often use informational tactics first, seeking alternatives and then other tactics
   D. Influenced by whether a party wants to appear to be the pursuer or the pursued
   E. Affected by any need for multiple sessions
   F. Consider serial agreements
   G. May need to agree on confidentiality of information to be disclosed
   H. Plan opening moves, even if you do not intend to set an agenda
   I. Consider other side's likely agenda or reactions and modify as necessary

    J. Check against prior steps, and adjust this or prior steps if appropriate

    K. Avoid power struggles over the agenda unless (1) the sequence of the negotiation is critical or (2) the power struggle is necessary to create respect from the other side

    L. The agenda itself may be negotiated

VI. Step 13: Timing

    A. Decide when it is most advantageous to negotiate

    B. It is advantageous if one is under less pressure than the other side, before coming under additional pressure, if one knows sufficient information to negotiate intelligently, before the other side uncovers a weakness or problem, and prior to a weakness or problem developing for the client

    C. May need to let a party's anger dissipate

    D. Litigation affects timing

    E. Decided by or in consultation with the client

    F. Avoid being under pressure from an internal deadline or having that known to the other side, while seeking to determine whether the other side is under an internal deadline

    G. Need for restructuring of existing agreement, including based on a periodic review process

    H. Anticipate the other party's timing needs or reactions to intended timing

    I. Include single, sequential, and periodic negotiations

VII. Step 14: The Mode(s) of Communication

    A. Choose between face-to-face, telephone, written, or combinations

    B. Consider the other party's reaction

    C. Can cause delay, thereby affecting timing

VIII. Multiple Party Interactions

    A. Parties on the same or different sides

    B. Evaluate seeking to split the other side if it consists of multiple parties by considering the needs and interests of each, as well as whether a group negotiation is likely to proceed advantageously, but be cautious in transactional and cooperative negotiations

    C. If in a group of plaintiffs or defendants, consider whether to negotiate as a group or separately

    D. Must consider each ally and opposing party separately at each step of the negotiation process

IX. Implementation and Adjustment

    A. A strong mental attitude is critical

    B. Perform opening moves as planned, unless a significant unforeseen event occurs

    C. Use opening stages to learn about the other side

D. For complex negotiations, notes may aid in keeping track of positions and points of agreement, as well as identifying patterns of behavior and goals

E. Consider the possibility that other side is shortsighted, controlled by noneconomic factors, or unpredictable

F. Be ready for the unexpected

G. Inject false clues, suggesting you are at or near your bottom line, if that is advantageous

H. Unpredictability can (1) advantageously force the other party to adapt a worse case scenario or (2) create frustration or disgust, causing a termination of the negotiation, especially if it diminishes or destroys the unpredictable party's value for a future working relationship

I. After the opening moves, use alternatives in the plan if appropriate, considering the actions of the other negotiator

J. Repeat the planning process during the negotiation as needed, based on new information acquired

K. Adjust if the other party or negotiator has problems with attitude changes, short-term learning, cognition, perception, or making decisions

L. Planning during the negotiation may be quick or lengthy, but it must be conscious, using the same steps and methods of analysis as prenegotiation planning

M. Evaluate whether the process is moving in a direction, and, if so, whether it is an advantageous or the most advantageous direction

N. Watch for whether the other side's actions are symmetrical or asymmetrical with one's own

O. If priority long-run goals cannot be achieved, consider whether short-term measures can build towards long-terms goals

X. Conclusion

A. Have alternatives and be multi-dimensional

B. Reexamine each step in light of earlier steps

C. Plan issue-by-issue, and for cross-issues if tradeoffs are possible

D. Be Goals Rigid and Means Flexible

E. Reexamine bottom lines, if appropriate

F. Client must authorize bottom-line positions

G. Never underestimate the other party or its negotiator, or, in litigation, the other side's case or its trial attorney

Effective Communication

10

§10.01   Introduction

Negotiation is a process which consists of exchanging information. This exchange may be by design or through inadvertence. Outcomes are affected by imperfect information, so each negotiator seeks to cause the other to behave as desired by attempting to control and manipulate information through communications.[1]

Some studies suggest that communications, in a negotiation resulting in agreement, often proceed through three distinct stages.[2] These stages are:[3]

1.   Early statements and defenses of positions, building strong arguments, and demonstrating some form of power, including persuasion

2.   Searching for solutions, using the factors and limitations established during the first stage

3.   Striving together to find settlement terms which satisfy the negotiators and the clients

---

[1] W. Zartman, The 50% Solution 14-15 (1976).

[2] R. Lewicki & J. Litterer, Negotiation 176 (1985).

[3] *Id.*

329

As noted throughout the preceding chapters, effective communication skills are essential for a negotiator.[4] The communication process is an integral part of negotiations and forms the medium through which the negotiators decide whether to agree and, if so, at what point agreement will be reached. The skills used encompass both the sending of information and the receipt of information. The information that is sent must persuade the other negotiator to accept the sender's message. Methods to transmit information persuasively will be covered in **§10.03.** Conversely, in order to receive information properly, the recipient should recognize all clues, both verbal and nonverbal, and effectively analyze them. Techniques for correctly receiving information will be discussed in **§10.04.** Different modes of communication are discussed in **§10.06.**

These communication principles and techniques apply to all negotiations, regardless of the particular client goals, strategies, or tactics that are involved.

§10.02   Polite Communications versus Power Struggles

Most of the time, the communication process will and should be a polite one. The negotiators will avoid attempting to intimidate each other. They will listen carefully to what is being said, being alert for both clues and positions. Each will give the other an opportunity to speak. At times, they will encourage the other to speak in order to gain additional information. The degree of friendliness and assertiveness may vary, and the words may be spoken forcefully and even a bit roughly. It need not be at all docile. However, the process of communicating should generally be a polite one, with each negotiator having an opportunity to give and to receive information.

A polite communications process has at least there major benefits for the negotiators. These benefits are that it:

1.   Facilitates the disclosure of information
2.   Also facilitates careful listening
3.   Avoids unnecessary power struggles

A polite communications process provides the negotiators with an opportunity to disclose information. By facilitating disclosures, the maximum desired flow and exchange of information tends to occur. This then is limited only by the negotiators' respective judgments about whether to disclose information. The polite mode, however, avoids the cutting off of valuable information which a negotiator is willing to disclose. The more useful information that is disclosed to a negotiator, the more that negotiator enjoys an increased basis for knowing which strategy, tactics, and positions to choose, and for determining whether to continue negotiating.

Polite communications also aids the negotiator's ability to listen carefully. By taking turns, even in a rough fashion, each negotiator can concentrate on

---

[4] See in particular, **chs 1 & 4.**

carefully listening to the other, rather than on interrupting or fighting to speak. Careful listening is extraordinarily important so that the negotiator really, consciously hears and recognizes all of the information that is being disclosed.

Finally, polite communication avoids unnecessary power struggles. Power struggles can waste time, create counterproductive hostility, and even lead to a breakdown in the negotiation process itself. Polite communication avoids such undesired effects.

Three major exceptions exist to the general rule that polite communications are to be preferred to power struggles. Interruptions, a refusal to listen, and a struggle to control the communications process are appropriate when:

1. It is feasible to control the outcome of the negotiation by dominating the communications process

2. The other negotiator insists on attempting to dominate the communications process, and it is essential to avoid domination, and substantive points cannot be won by diverting the other negotiator into focusing on winning control of the communications process while unintentionally losing substantive ground

3. The other negotiator insists on engaging in undue repetition, to the point that any benefits from appeasing the other's ego are outweighed by the waste of time

With respect to undue repetition, no one should have to listen passively to the same points being made over and over again. This is especially true if the points are lengthy ones. Except if ego appeasement will yield substantive results, undue repetition need not be tolerated. In this situation, breaking out of the polite communications mode is normally not one's first choice. Instead, one can first attempt to summarize what has been said. Alternatively, counsel can try to deal with the process.[5]

Example 10-1

In a contract negotiation between two businesses, the other negotiator has been engaging in undue repetition. Counsel employs summarization in order to maintain a polite communications mode. "Now, because you're repeating the cost points that you told me earlier, let me say that I understand your position on costs. You've told me that your costs without any profit margin are $2.48 per unit. I understand that."

Example 10-2

In seeking to settle a matter that is in litigation, counsel is faced with unduly repetitious arguments from the other negotiator. Trying to maintain a polite communications mode, counsel chooses to focus on dealing with the process of the negotiation itself: "You keep repeating the same points about your perceptions of the strength of your case and the weakness

---

[5] *See* §5.21.

of mine. In fact, you've used the same phrase several times. I recognize the points that you're telling me, although I absolutely disagree with the weight that you give to each point. We disagree on the possibility of liability and the likely damages, even if liability were to be found. I want you to understand that you are not, you clearly are not, going to change my view of the case just by repeating yours. If you wanted to make certain that I understood your view, I assume that you now know that I do understand it. If you want to make progress, we need to move on, rather than just repeat the same points to one another."

If one can dominate the communication process and thereby dominate the outcome of the negotiation, then one should do so. If, however, domination of the communication process will lead to a breakdown in the negotiation as the other negotiator refuses to participate, it will be counterproductive. Similarly, it can also be counterproductive if it causes the other negotiator to harden positions because of frustration at being unable to otherwise communicate, the desire to avoid being dominated, or anger.

As with the use of power as a tactic, long-run as well as short-run effects must be taken into account.[6] In analyzing (a) whether it is likely to be possible to dominate the communications process, as well as (b) whether such dominance will have a positive or negative effect on the ultimate outcome of the negotiation, the other negotiator's personality must be given special consideration, along with the vital interests and personality of the other party. Personalities may lead the other party or its negotiator to balk at attempts at communications dominance, just as with power tactics.[7] This can happen not only when the other party is an individual, but also with corporations or other organizations that have personalities as entities, resulting from either one or more strong leaders within the entity or the entity's need to maintain an image of strength.

With certain exceptions discussed below, counsel should avoid being dominated. If the other negotiator seeks to dominate the communications process, it will normally be necessary to assert oneself. Initially, as in preventing undue repetition, the summarization and dealing with the process tactics can be used. However, if those tactics fail, the negotiator may have to use interruptions, loudness, tone, and blunt phrasing to achieve at least parity and avoid being dominated.

Example 10-3

After being harrangued for ten minutes with no end in sight, and after being unable either to summarize what the other negotiator has said, or to deal with the process because the other negotiator has just refused to stop talking, counsel suddenly shouts, "Wait!" The negotiator, uncertain of whether this is a sign of capitulation, pauses. Speaking both force-

---

[6] *See* §5.12.

[7] *See* §5.12.

fully and more loudly than normal, counsel states: "Negotiation is impossible without give and take, and without both sides listening to each other. Apparently you intend only to speak and not to listen, or even to give me the courtesy of being able to speak. That being the case, I am going to leave now. If I am mistaken, and you are willing to stop talking and to listen to my position, say so."

If the other negotiator is seeking to dominate the communications process, one should consider whether that can be allowed for a period of time without adversely affecting the outcome. At times, in fact, the desire of the other negotiator to dominate the communications process can be manipulated in order to achieve a more positive outcome. This type of mental judo can occur either when the other negotiator is (1) disclosing information unwisely, (2) bargaining against himself or herself, or (3) so intent on ego gratification through this domination that substantive points are relinquished.

One should always be alert for the possibility that the other negotiator is foolishly disclosing information. In seeking to dominate the communication process, the other negotiator may talk and talk to the point at which information is being disclosed regardless of whether it is wise to do so. This includes lawyers who want to teach other lawyers how much they know. Sometimes, this desire to teach during a negotiation is due to differences in age or experience, attraction between the sexes, or a feeling of inferiority which the other negotiator seeks to overcome by playing the role of teacher.[8] The other negotiator may also talk too much in response to counsel's remaining silent, as if expecting to hear more.[9] To the extent that valuable information can be obtained by allowing the other negotiator to "dominate" the communication process without losing control of the outcome, permitting such temporary dominance can be an effective means of manipulating the other negotiator into unwisely disclosing more information than could otherwise be obtained.

Trying to dominate the process can, on occasion, unwittingly lead to bargaining against oneself. This is an even less skillful attempt to dominate the communication process than becoming carried away with trying to teach the other negotiator. Bargaining against oneself means that the other negotiator, seeking to control the communication, fails to demand feedback due to simply talking too much. Instead, the other negotiator takes a position, talks, does not receive a clean rejection or counteroffer, while continuing to talk and "dominate" the communication process. In reality, the negotiator who falls into this trap is not only not truly dominating the communication process, but is also failing to control the outcome of the negotiation. Getting caught up in winning the communication process in this manner, while losing sight of the fact that the real victory comes only with the outcome of the negotiation, occurs more frequently than many negotiators realize. A skillful negotiator recognizes when to allow the negotiator to "dominate" the communication process and thereby manipu-

---

[8] Of course, each negotiator must guard against falling into this trap.

[9] *See* Oatley, *Negotiating Techniques for Lawyers*, 6 Advoc Q 214, 225-26 (1985).

late the "domination" into having that other negotiator bid against himself or herself.

Lastly, the other negotiator may be so intent on the ego gratification of apparent dominance that substantive points are more easily relinquished. This does not occur through a lack of feedback, but rather because the negotiator loses sight of the pattern being created by concessions and tradeoffs.

§10.03   Sending Information—Only Deliberate Disclosures

Certain information should or must be disclosed to successfully negotiate. At the very least, positions must be disclosed. Often, facts, needs, and vital interests should be disclosed so that the other party knows the points to be met if an agreement is to be reached. Sometimes a fine line must be drawn between trusting the other side sufficiently to disclose enough information to reach an agreement and distrusting the other side enough so as to withhold information that could enable it to dominate the bargaining.[10]

The key in disclosing information is to consider the effect of the disclosure. How will disclosure advance the negotiation from the perspective of the party and its negotiator? If it will not advance the negotiation, then disclosure should not be made. The likelihood and benefit of persuasion must be weighed against any countervailing risk of creating problems or exposing a weakness. These principles include verbal and nonverbal disclosures.

Example 10-4

A settlement offer of $100,000 is made by the defendant's attorney. The plaintiff's bottom line was $75,000. The plaintiff's attorney responds that the offer is more reasonable, but that it is still not acceptable. Despite that statement, the plaintiff's attorney's eyes unconsciously widened, and he seemed to become more relaxed. Reading these signs, the defense attorney responded that $100,000 was a very good offer, and that he hoped that the plaintiff would consider it. The plaintiff's attorney agreed to do so, and the case settled for that amount. The defendant's bottom line actually was $140,000, but the plaintiff's attorney nonverbally signaled too much interest in the $100,000 offer.

Example 10-5

In negotiating a business transaction, in an effort to create enthusiasm for the proposed project, one of the negotiators talks far too much about how interested her client is in working with the other party. In doing so, she reveals that her client is likely to have some serious problems, at least in the short run, if the deal falls through. As a result, the other negotiator is able to insist on more concessions than anticipated.

---

[10] M. Saks & R. Hastie, Social Psychology in Court 121 (1978).

Being selective and deliberate in the disclosure of information is very difficult. It is even more difficult, since nonverbal disclosures must be controlled as well. However, this needs to be done, because lawyers often react unconsciously or behave in certain ways out of habit without considering the cues being given to the other negotiator. Yet, deliberate disclosure requires attaining a high degree of consciousness about, and control over, one's verbal and nonverbal information disclosures.

Using Rationales

Communicating persuasively is essential, since the communication is wasted unless it is believed. To give communications of positions a persuasive force, rationales should be included. These rationales may or not be the most important reason for the client or the negotiator, but they are real and plausible. While a rationale may disguise a party's real reason when it is advantageous to do so, material misrepresentations must be avoided.[11] The goal is to establish a position which will require the other party to accept it, or, depending on the strategy or tactic chosen, make a concession to have the position altered.

Example 10-6

In a wrongful death case, the defendant's attorney indicates that the settlement offer can be raised, but argues that the plaintiff should be willing to settle for less than what has been demanded, because a jury is unlikely to award that much. The plaintiff's attorney responds by lowering the demand, and expresses the rationale that, while not agreeing with everything that the defense attorney has said, a jury might not award as much as had been demanded. In reality, the true reason for the plaintiff's concession is because a key damages witness for the plaintiff may be unable to cope emotionally with the stress of testifying.

Three exceptions exist to the general principle that positions should be communicated with rationales to make the positions believable. These exceptions are when (1) the rationale is inherently clear, (2) no plausible rationale exists, and (3) the only plausible rationale involves a material misrepresentation or other breach of a legal or ethical duty.

For some positions in the context of a given negotiation, the rationale will be inherently clear. Thus, there will not need to be any explicit statement of the rationale.

Example 10-7

The case obviously involves a strong breach of contract claim with the damages indisputably amounting to $10,000. The claimant's attorney offers to settle for $9,000, in a context which clearly indicates that the small discount is being offered just to get the matter resolved.

---

[11] *See* **ch 12.**

The second exception to communicating positions accompanied by a ratio-nale is when none exists. In rare instances, no rationale exists. This ought to be an extremely unusual occurrence, since often, when no other rationale exists, the negotiator can find a rationale through one of the following three methods:

1. The split the difference tactic[12]
2. The tactic of reciprocity[13]
3. The use of precedent

As to the last method, the precedent may be with this client, drawn from other clients, with the other side, or it may involve other parties who are altogether unrelated to the present negotiation. What is important is that the precedent indicates that the position taken is reasonable and fair.

Persuasion is achieved by appealing to the other side's needs and interests, whether those be economic or noneconomic. The appeal may be to positive psychological or tangible benefits, or to avoiding negative detriments. There-fore, arguments and other forms of information disclosure are most persuasive if presented from the other side's point of view. The presentation may be in terms of the alternative to agreement for the other party being:[14]

1. A lost opportunity
2. Litigation
3. Other less attractive consequences

Indeed, it has been suggested that the presentation should always be in terms of alternatives even when, in effect, giving an ultimatum.[15]

A sound basis or some source may be needed to be stated to make the infor-mation credible. Otherwise, it may be disregarded, or at least discounted, as unreliable.

Focusing at first on establishing rapport between the negotiators can enhance one's persuasive powers. One method is to concentrate initially on those points which the negotiators basically concur on, thereby building momentum towards reaching an agreement, or at least towards substantially narrowing any disagreement. One especially effective technique is a response that first refers to the portion of a statement which can be agreed with, before rejecting the remainder of the assertions.[16] It is more persuasive to explain than

---

[12] *See* §**5.16.**

[13] *See* §**5.05.**

[14] X. Frascogna, Jr. & H. Hetherington, Negotiation Strategy For Lawyers 13 (1984).

[15] H. Cohen, You Can Negotiate Anything 44 (1982). Cohen refers to this as providing a "selection from a limited menu." *Id.*

[16] R. Lewicki & J. Litterer, Negotiation 265-66 (1985) [hereinafter Lewicki].

to just make statements,[17] so that the listener understands and is not forced to choose between blindly trusting the speaker or rejecting the idea. Sometimes, insinuations with indirect references, rather than direct proposals, are better at leading the listener to arrive at the desired thoughts.[18] Conclusions should be left unstated when the listener will form the desired conclusion and hold it more strongly because it is his or her own idea. Themes, analogies, and story-telling can be effectively used for this purpose.[19]

The issue of whether to offer conclusions to maximize the persuasive impact of the presentation depends on the listener's predisposition and ability to deduce the desired answer. For listeners with open minds, using implicit, but clear, conclusions is more effective, so that listeners draw their own conclusions and convince themselves.[20] If, however, listeners are firmly entrenched in their own ideas, then conclusions should be explicitly stated.[21]

The same principles for maximizing an audience's perception of communications in general also apply to maximizing the persuasive force of rationales.[22] These principles are that stimuli attract more attention, and are perceived and retained more effectively, when they are:[23]

1. Larger
2. More intense
3. Include a visual component with visible contrast to the surrounding material
4. Unique or novel
5. Presented first, so as to achieve a "primacy" effect
6. Presented last, so as to achieve a "recency" effect
7. Repeated, which may also tend to yield acceptance

Counsel should, however, refrain from repetitious presentations which either bore or offend the listener, who has already either accepted or rejected the information. The only exception is if the other negotiator will become worn down, instead of fighting back or remaining firmly entrenched in the prior position.

Other Techniques for Persuasion Force

In addition to expressing positions with rationales, counsel must state the position with a sense of conviction. A confident manner and, at times, a profes-

---

[17] S. Hamilton, What Makes Juries Listen 339 (1985).

[18] De Felice, Negotiations, Or The Art of Negotiating, in W. Zartman, The 50% Solution 54 (1976).

[19] S. Hamilton *supra* note 17, at 119-20.

[20] R. Lewicki *supra* note 16, at 189.

[21] *Id* 190.

[22] *Id* 163-64.

[23] *Id.*

sional level of enthusiasm add a convincing tone. The terms may be presented loudly or softly. The tone of voice can be forceful or matter-of-fact. The only important point is that, in the context of the situation and the negotiator's personality, the speaker appears to be sincere and to truly believe the words being spoken. If the speaker does not seem persuaded, despite the words spoken, the listener surely will not be persuaded.

As noted earlier, statements of rationales, facts, and positions cannot be effective unless considered credible by the listener. Even if the listener does not always agree with the speaker's rationales or facts, the listener will only be inclined to acknowledge them internally as the true thought of the speaker if the speaker treats them as real and not mere ploys. In this respect, it is the same as when counsel is talking to a jury in an opening statement or in a closing argument.

Another technique for persuasion in negotiations is to build in concessions. Some negotiators find it difficult or impossible to believe that the initial position or early positions do not have some built-in concessions.[24] They are more easily persuaded to believe in a position if they "earned" it by first extracting one or more concessions before the position is reached.[25]

The most useful other techniques for persuasion are:

1. Asking questions of the other negotiator

2. Not sounding judgmental about the other negotiator

3. Defining the problem that needs to be solved

In addition to obtaining information, questions can be utilized to give information or to stimulate thought.[26] Asking questions of the other negotiator may force the other negotiator to face the weaknesses of his or her case.[27] Antagonistic questions should be avoided unless, in less common circumstances, it is desirable and feasible to:

1. Antagonize to provoke an emotional, less controlled, or uncontrolled reaction

2. Intimidate

3. Counter hostile attacks by the other negotiator

4. Persuade by a confident or an embarrassing tone[28]

---

[24] For this reason, the no concessions strategy almost always requires either a strong rationale or standing firm in order to establish credibility. See **§3.03** regarding the no concessions strategy.

[25] See **§9.06** regarding planning concessions and tradeoffs.

[26] Of course, this is the basis of the Socratic method.

[27] Oatley, *Negotiating Techniques for Lawyers*, 6 Advoc Q 214, 225 (1985); R. Fisher & W. Ury, Getting to Yes: Negotiating Agreement Without Giving In 116 (1981) [hereinafter Fisher].

[28] See **§5.14** regarding tone as a tactic.

The latter may be quite difficult to do, and may run a substantial risk of offending the other negotiator.

If one can induce the other negotiator to recognize weaknesses through questions that raise the other's consciousness, it may be more persuasive than simply telling the other negotiator that such weaknesses exist. At the same time, pressing for an open acknowledgement of the weakness can be seen as an attack that requires a face-saving counterattack. Thus, seeking such an acknowledgment may be counterproductive unless the atmosphere is one of real openness and candor, or one of effective intimidation.

Speaking in terms of one's own reaction, rather than judgmentally about what the other negotiator has said, can minimize or avoid defensive responses.[29] The exception is that expressing a negative judgment about the other negotiator's behavior is appropriate if the other negotiator will be convinced that his or her actions have been unfair or misguided. The negative judgment must be limited to the other negotiator's specific behavior, and not aimed at the negotiator as a person, which is generally perceived as a highly antagonistic attack.

In addition, stating the problem that needs to be solved by the parties before proposing a position may induce the other negotiator to listen more closely to what is being said.[30] This is effective only if the definition is agreeable to the other side.

Persuasion can also involve timing. Some types of proposals, particularly if they are unusual or innovative, are not likely to be accepted immediately.[31] They may be acceptable, at least in a modified form, if there is sufficient time for the other side to consider and become more familiar with them.[32] Accordingly, these types of proposals should be introduced into the negotiation well in advance of either party's deadline for reaching an agreement.[33]

The way in which the negotiator is perceived by the other side can be bolstered by references who are known to the other side, or by appropriate prior activities that are credible or verifiable. They can demonstrate power, capability, and veracity. Mentioning prior situations in a gentle, matter-of-fact tone, sometimes cryptically and other times anecdotally, can convey a threat without being so hostile as to provoke a counterproductive reaction.

Clear Signals

Up to this point, the focus for the sender of the communication has been on deliberate disclosures and on persuasion. Both points are aimed at having the listener believe the message as intended.

However, the most deliberately chosen and persuasively stated message will be lost or confused if it is unclear. There is a need for clear, precise signals.

---

[29] R Fisher, *supra* note 27 at 37.

[30] *Id* 53.

[31] H. Cohen, *supra* note 14, at 104-05.

[32] *Id.*

[33] *Id.*

Mixed messages, therefore, must be avoided. Those are messages which, in context, seem internally inconsistent. Similarly, messages with potential multiple meanings are to be avoided also, since the speaker then cannot control which meaning will be chosen by the listener.

In seeking to transmit messages clearly, a negotiator must try to recognize the psychological needs of the other negotiator and the other party. It may be that these needs are neither articulated nor even understood by the other person.[34] These psychological needs, however, can filter the way in which the other person perceives the message.[35] Such psychological conditions can be too sensitive and too deeply rooted to be confronted directly. Instead, a negotiator may be forced to work around or within the confines set by the other's filtering process. Recognizing such perceptual limitations allows messages to be structured so that they are more likely to be received and understood as intended.

Mental filtering of information in negotiation which is usually unconscious commonly leads to misperceptions in terms of:[36]

1. Stereotyping based on demographic and social data
2. Generalizing from one attribute to other attributes
3. Not accepting information that contradicts a preexisting belief
4. Projecting one's own feelings or characteristics on to another
5. Screening out information which contradicts one's self image or image of another

These types of distortions impede and sometimes block communication. The resulting misperception can cause a negotiator to act contrary to the client's best interests. A negotiator must be alert to avoid mental filtering based on personal needs or defenses, since it creates misperception.

Reaching The Decision Maker

The client, as the real decision maker, will be apprised of the progress of the negotiation or of the lack of it, either during or at the end of the negotiating process. The client, however, is usually absent from all or most of the negotiating sessions. In the majority of such negotiations, counsel will be able to operate on the basis that positions and other information are being fairly communicated to the real decision maker for the other party. It is the lawyer's professional responsibility as a negotiator to communicate accurate and sufficient information to the client, so that the client can make a properly informed judgment about its own positions and can issue authority and direction to the negotiator.

In some negotiations, however, counsel may sense that the other negotiator is withholding or distorting the information being communicated to the other

---

[34] Lewicki, *supra* note 16, at 52.

[35] *Id.*

[36] *Id* 166-68.

party. This may be intentional or inadvertent. This problem usually stems from one of the following reasons:

1. Personal interest
2. Fear
3. Incompetence
4. Reporting to an intermediary

The other negotiator's personal interests may interfere with fair and accurate reporting to the other party, where those personal interests are to keep the negotiation going rather than to resolve or to terminate it. In addition, certain information may reflect unfavorably on the other negotiator. Similarly, if the other negotiator fears, correctly or incorrectly, the other party's reaction to learning certain information, inaccurate information may be communicated to the other party. Simple incompetence may be another explanation. The other negotiator's lack of competence in the communications phase of negotiation, or with communications generally, may result in the necessary information's not reaching the other party. Finally, the cause of the problem may be in the requirement that the other negotiator report through some chain of command to an intermediary rather than to the real decision maker. That intermediary may then be distorting or failing to accurately convey information about the negotiation to the real decision maker for the same types of reasons that a negotiator might do so (personal interests, fear, incompetence).

Whenever counsel believes that the other negotiator or some intermediary is blocking or failing to accurately convey information to the real decision maker for the other party, action should usually be taken in an attempt to correct that situation. Two exceptions to that rule exist. These exceptions are:

1. When the information is aimed at the other negotiator rather than the other party in any event, so that it has already reached its target
2. When progress in the negotiation is sufficiently good, so that there is no reason to disturb whatever is occurring by seeking to ensure that additional information reaches the real decision maker.

The decision about the sufficiency of the negotiation's progress, and whether it is likely to improve through communicating certain information to the real decision maker, requires a judgment based on the following factors:

1. The history of this or prior negotiations, including any applicable precedents
2. The other party's vital interests and any situational pressure or constraints
3. The personality of the real decision maker

If the exceptions do not apply, and an attempt should be made to ensure that the information reaches the real decision maker, a number of methods exist for doing so. These methods include:

1. An appropriate inquiry
2. An appropriate request
3. The client's or decision maker's presence
4. Written communications
5. Depositions

An appropriate inquiry in this situation entails counsel's asking questions of the other negotiator designed to determine first whether the information reached the real decision maker. If not, the next questions should lead into a discussion of *when* (not whether) that decision maker will be informed, so that the negotiations can continue.

Example 10-8

"How did he react to those facts?"

Example 10-9

"Does she understand that there is a substantial risk unless she authorizes a compromise on these issues?"

In deciding whether this method will be useful, counsel must gauge the honesty of the other negotiator and the corresponding reliability of any answer to the inquiry.

An appropriate request consists of counsel's requesting that the information be transmitted to the decision maker, and that the decision maker's reaction be reported back. Here again, counsel must assess the honesty of the other negotiator. In addition, counsel should consider whether the other negotiator will refuse to comply with the request because it is perceived as an infringement on the attorney-client relationship or as a breach of negotiation protocol. An explanation may alleviate the other negotiator's concerns, or correct any misperception of the reason for, and nature of, the request.

Example 10-10

"As this is a basic issue which affects the entire negotiation, we feel that we cannot proceed further until we have a response from your client, so that we are sure that we understand his views on this point."

Example 10-11

"My client does not feel that your client appreciates how critical this is from our point of view. Therefore, we are asking that you inform your client of exactly what I have explained regarding my client's needs and let us know of your client's response."

If neither an inquiry nor a request to the other negotiator seems to be sufficient, counsel can instead request or, if necessary, insist, that the decision makers be present at the next negotiating session. Before doing so, counsel should consider the potential impact, both beneficial and negative, that the presence of one or both clients may produce.[37]

Another option is the use of written communications. A letter or proposed settlement agreement can be designed to include all of the information desired to reach the real decision maker. The only issue is whether the other negotiator will actually show it to the decision maker. That issue can be dealt with in two ways. First, in certain contexts, counsel can seek the other negotiator's permission to send a copy of the written communication to the other decision maker.

Example 10-12

> Plaintiff's counsel is concerned that the other negotiator's real client in interest, an insurance company, is not receiving the necessary information regarding the plaintiff's position. Plaintiff's counsel has prepared, and is about to send, a settlement brochure to the defense attorney.[38] The plaintiff's attorney calls and tells the defendant's attorney that the settlement brochure is about to be sent, and asks if a copy of it can also be mailed directly to the insurance company. The expressed, though not the real, rationale is that this will simply save defense counsel's office the bother of copying and mailing the settlement brochure to the insurance company itself.[39]

The second means to ensure that the written communication reaches the real decision maker for the other party is to expressly request in the written communication that this be done. Particularly if a settlement offer or draft agreement is being transmitted, given the fact that, since the request and material are all in writing, communicating the offer normally is ethically required, and failing to transmit the offer can be malpractice, this approach places enormous pressure on the other attorney to transmit the communication properly.

If the matter involves litigation, a deposition of the other side's decision maker is another means of ensuring that information is being communicated properly. Some questions in the deposition may have a multiple function, including determining whether the opposing party is aware of certain information or issues, and, if not, informing the other party directly through questions. The deposition question must be properly framed under the applicable discovery rules.

Example 10-13

> In a personal injury case: "Are you aware that the plaintiff's medical bills are $10,000?"

---

[37] *See* §6.02.

[38] For a discussion of settlement brochures, see §4.02.

[39] Anatomy of A Personal Injury Case-1 (Continuing Legal Education Satellite Network, Advanced Legal Studies, NY, NY, G. Spence & R. Rose, 1986).

Example 10-14

In contract litigation: "Are you aware that the plaintiff had to spend an additional $50,000 replacing the goods that could not be used?"

Example 10-15

In a malpractice case in which the defendant's insurance policy gives the insured the right to veto a settlement: "Now, as you may know, according to the expert that we retained, there were three steps that should have been taken, and what I want to do is to ask if you have considered each of these. First, regarding step one, was . . . ?"

Example 10-16

In an employment discrimination case: "Now, would it be feasible to rehire the plaintiff if she were willing to be placed into a different department? . . . What about if she were willing to accept a position, even if it paid as much as 15 per cent less than what she had been making?"

§10.04   Receiving Information

During a negotiation, the lawyer may need to obtain information from the other party which was not available from other sources or which should be confirmed.

Example 10-17

In negotiating an agreement for a joint venture, it is crucial that the parties understand each other's intentions, and that they agree on future plans.[40]

This section will focus on receiving information efficiently, so that its meaning can be accurately recognized and properly used in the negotiator's analysis.

Before it can be received, the information first may have to be elicited. Freely flowing disclosure can be encouraged by appearing to listen attentively, without interrupting, arguing, or attacking. Not indicating that the information being disclosed is important can help to encourage further disclosures if an indication of the information's significance will cause the other negotiator to become guarded.[41] On the other hand, a lack of interest may cause the speaker to desist. In addition, reticence can be countered by questions, discussion (including challenging the other negotiator to defend a point), and informational

---

[40] W. Fallon, AMA Management Handbook 9-31 (1983). According to Fallon, misunderstandings about these matters are the most common source of problems in joint ventures.

[41] R. Givens, Advocacy: The Art of Pleading a Cause 442 (Shepard's/McGraw-Hill, Inc 1985).

bargaining.[42]

The receiving of information during a negotiation is a process consisting of three parts:

1. Listening
2. Assessing Cues
3. Analysis

Each part of the process will be discussed in the following three subsections.

Careful Listening

Listening is a key skill.[43] The first step for careful listening is to be open to receiving new information. This means avoiding the pitfalls that distort accurate perceptions discussed earlier, along with good focus on the disclosures and possible use of the funnel approach.[44] The other negotiator must be given the opportunity, and subtly or overtly encouraged, to speak, through pauses in one's own speech and broad inquiries.

Example 10-18

"So I can understand your concerns, have you or your client ever had a bad experience with this type of arrangement?"

Example 10-19

"How will you judge the success of this deal?"

Example 10-20

"What are your client's needs, concerns, and goals?"

Example 10-21

"What is it that makes you reluctant to agree to this proposal?"

Many lawyers consider listening to be an easy task which they do well. It is not easy, and often attorneys do not do it well. Listening carefully requires energy, concentration, and, for a good number of lawyers, work and practice to develop their skills.

Accurate listening requires concentration on both the verbal and nonverbal messages and not on what the listener will say next. It also requires giving verbal and nonverbal feedback to show understanding and consideration of the

---

[42] See §§4.07 and 4.08 regarding informational tactics with respect to bargaining and discussion.

[43] J. Graham & Y. Sano, Smart Bargaining (1984).

[44] *See* §§10.03, 4.04 & 4.05, respectively.

situation from the other person's perspective.[45] The negotiator must focus on the present and not on thinking back into the past on what occurred before, or forward into the future on what should or will happen next or later. The time for prospective or retrospective thought is after the information has been received, and during or after the evaluation of it. This concentration cannot be broken by fatigue, negative feelings from other events or from the present interaction itself, other tasks or obligations, or time pressures. The discussion should be adjourned if a loss of focus begins to occur and cannot be controlled.[46]

Strange or dramatic nonverbal communication may be a ploy to surprise, intimidate, or disorient the listener. If faced with such behavior, counsel either should not react at all, or should initially respond with firmness, at least until it can be determined whether the conduct is genuine or merely a tactic. Calmness is essential.

A negotiator must be alert for otherwise unconscious distortion of perception due to an emotional reaction to the other party, its negotiator, or their strategy or tactics. Without such awareness, the negotiator may act unwisely without due regard for costs and realistic effects. The two most common emotional problems for negotiators are undue anxiety and anger.[47] Since anyone can be subject to these emotions, a negotiator must be mentally prepared for them. At times, with mental preparation, the energy created by these emotions can be usefully channeled for productive concentration. At other times, deep breathing with tensing and relaxing muscles may dissipate their effects. Still, at other times, it may be necessary to take a break in the negotiating session.

Attorneys must be alert for information that contradicts their assumptions, preconceptions, or understandings. Otherwise, the information may be missed. Hearing what we expect to hear is a very human trait, not at all restricted to lawyers. However, lawyers are not immune from this trait.

As a learning experience, read the following example and write down the scene and activity that you visualize from the first sentence:

Example 10-22

"Jack drove from Boston to New York on the turnpike with Mary."[48]

Look at the written description of what you visualized. You may have shared certain common assumptions from this passage:[49] (a) Jack drove a car; (b) The car had four wheels; (c) Mary was in the same car as Jack. Yet, none of those assumptions need be true. Jack could have driven a bus, truck, motorcycle, or even a covered wagon during a special event. If a car was used, it could have been

---

[45] T. Warschaw, Winning By Negotiation 103-04 (McGraw-Hill, Inc 1980).

[46] See §5.24 regarding adjournment.

[47] T. Warschaw, *supra* note 45, at 147-54.

[48] Williams, *Leviathan's Progress* (Book Review), 34 NY Rev Books 33 (June 11, 1987).

[49] *Id* 34.

an experimental one with three wheels. Mary could have been following or leading Jack in a separate vehicle.

At times, it is safe and appropriate to rely on listening assumptions. It is neither necessary nor practical to always check every detail. Yet, careful listening distinguishes between:

1. The words said and any inferences drawn, so that the inference is consciously separated into an assumption to be evaluated
2. Those listening assumptions that are safe to rely on, and those that may be dangerous to rely on without verification

In negotiations, the lawyer must be especially careful not to mistake his or her own assumptions in listening for material facts and aspects of proposals or positions. Restatements and recapitulations can be used to verify that counsel's understanding is correct.

Example 10-23

"As I understand your client's account, it is . . . Is that right?"

Example 10-24

"Let me make sure that I have the structure of your proposal correctly in mind. Your client proposed that . . . Now, have I misstated or omitted anything?"

Careful listening consists of consciously and accurately learning all that is really being said, without gaps, mistakes, or unconscious substitution of those thoughts which either are expected or preferred. No one does this perfectly all of the time. Many do not do it well at all.

Although taken from an actual deposition, rather than from a negotiation, the following example illustrates the difficulty of listening and perceiving.

Example 10-25 Who's on First—What's on Second

The deponent was an executive employed by the plaintiff. He had asked the CEO for another company to join a lawsuit as a co-plaintiff. That CEO had replied, "You'll have to ask my lawyer." At the deposition, the following occurred:

DEFENSE ATTORNEY:	How did the CEO respond?
WITNESS:	You'll have to ask my lawyer.
DEFENSE ATTORNEY:	Answer the question.
PLAINTIFF ATTORNEY:	He just did.
DEFENSE ATTORNEY:	I'll try again. What did he say?
WITNESS:	You'll have to ask my lawyer.
DEFENSE ATTORNEY:	I'm asking you, and you have to respond.

PLAINTIFF ATTORNEY:	(stifling a laugh): That's responsive.
DEFENSE ATTORNEY:	I'm calling the judge. This is your last chance. Tell me what he told you.
WITNESS:	You'll have to ask my lawyer.
DEFENSE ATTORNEY:	That's it! I'm going to court.
PLAINTIFF ATTORNEY:	(laughing hysterically): Wait a minute. Let me explain . . .

All three had a good laugh after the explanation.

With technical information, negotiators may need to slow the pace of the discussion and recheck their understanding of the data. Follow-up questions can be used as clarification or as exploratory probes.

Example 10-26

"What is the additional cost if we also want _____?"

Example 10-27

"Are discounts available for other items or certain levels of volume?"

Example 10-28

"Can the manufacturing process meet these specifications, and if so, within what budgetary constraints?"

Example 10-29

"What if . . . or would you consider. . . ."

For the listener to restate or summarize what has been said tests whether the listener has understood the speaker's meaning. At times, this can even clarify the speaker's own understanding of the true meaning of what has been said.

Example 10-30

"Let me say this in my own words to make certain that we understand each other."

The technique of restatement and summarization also builds rapport. Responding to the other's expressions in this way tends to be perceived as demonstrating sensitivity to, and understanding of, the other side's positions, needs, and interests.

Accurately perceiving the other's sides messages and being responsive to them can be absolutely critical. For instance, the Cuban Missile Crisis of 1962 and the events in 1914 that led to the outbreak of World War I have been contrasted as examples of success and failure in perceiving the other side's efforts to de-escalate a crisis, act flexibly, and allow face to be saved.[50]

Special care should be taken with numbers. Calculations should be rechecked to avoid inadvertent, or occasionally deliberate, errors by the other side. Formulas for monetary issues should be translated into their real total dollar impact.

Example 10-31

"Let's see. The $5 concession per unit means $300,000."

Example 10-32

An offer to pay for certain property rights has been made in an amount of $10,000,000 spread unevenly over the course of ten years, according to a proposed payment schedule. On closer examination, given the extent of the deferrals and using a reasonable discount rate, it becomes apparent that the present value of the offer is only $3,200,000.

Percentages can also have a more subtle but dramatic effect than is apparent at first glance. Whether this analysis is done silently or is articulated depends on whether it is advantageous to share the result of the analysis. Therefore, counsel should generally make the necessary computations before discussing them. Only when the analysis is complete can a proper decision be made regarding whether to disclose the results.

Besides his or her own assumptions, a lawyer must separate out the facts that are really known by the speaker from the speaker's interpretations, assumptions, and hearsay.

Example 10-33

"We have a witness who says that your client ran a red light." If the assertion is not a bluff, did the witness actually see this, or is this an assumption by the witness based on pre- or post-occurrence observations, hearsay, or a combination of the two?

The possibility of assumptions by the witness, who now states the assumption as a fact, is in addition to credibility issues, because the witness is telling the truth as it is understood by the witness.

Example 10-34

"We have the financing." Is there a firm commitment from some source, or is the client, the other party, or its negotiator stating a perception based on a qualified commitment, an assumption, or some general comment?

Thus, the listener must distinguish between assumptions, opinions, hearsay, or first-hand observations and hard data. To do so may require questions and

---

[50] Holsti, Brady & North, *Measuring Affect and Action: The 1962 Cuban Crisis,* in W. Zartman, The 50% Solution 256-57, 276 (1976).

probing. Otherwise, an unwitting attorney may rely on information which is inadvertently inaccurate.

When negotiations are spread out over time, care must be taken that restatements of positions, offers, and demands are being made accurately. Careful listening can be ruined by a lapse of memory. While deliberate misrepresentation may or may not be likely, depending on the ethics of the other negotiator, honest misstatements by counsel or by the other negotiator can have an equally devastating effect unless promptly corrected. Particularly with numbers, notes should be routinely checked unless one's memory is absolutely fresh and clear on the point. The same precaution is true when reviewing settlement documents drafted by the other side, or when doing the drafting oneself.

The Assessment of Cues

In most negotiations, there is at least some uncertainty about the interests and the values of the other party and of its negotiator, as well as informational uncertainty and unequality.[51] Cues must be utilized to provide missing information.

Cues are indicators of the other party's true motives, interests, values, strategies, and tactics, as well as those of the other negotiator. The negotiator must distinguish between the intended, and the real, meaning of the other side's communications.[52] The latter may be cautious or face-saving, but still intentionally give cues as to its true needs or concerns. From these cues, inferences are drawn, and evaluations made, regarding the goals of one's own client, strategy, and tactics.

Part of this assessment is to differentiate between the other party's articulated positions and its bottom line. For instance, the other side's first offers or initial positions may be interpreted as reflecting high aspirations. The evaluation of the other party's bottom line considers that party's known and suspected needs, interests, and goals.

Any evident concession patterns can also be revealing to uncover how the other party really values items or links issues. Concession patterns may emerge for an additional reason as well. Commonly, negotiators tend to decrease the size of concessions as they approach the limits of their authority.[53] Thus, a pattern of smaller and smaller concessions can indicate the proximity of the other party's bottom line. On the other hand, it may be a false cue, deliberately placed by a sophisticated negotiator to subtly create a false impression.

The phrase "strategic misrepresentation" refers to feigning reluctance to agree to a demand in order to extract a reciprocal concession.[54] Although the demand is one which the negotiator is willing to agree to, or does not oppose, counsel deliberately appears to be reluctant, solely to justify linking the

---

[51] H. Raiffa, The Art and Science of Negotiation 274 (1982).

[52] Mandle, *Collective Bargaining Negotiation,* in Attorney's Guide to Negotiation 14-7 (1979).

[53] H. Raiffa *supra* note 51, at 128. *See also* H. Cohen, You Can Negotiate Anything 110-13 (1982).

[54] H. Raiffa, *supra* note 51, at 142.

demand to a counterdemand on another point.[55] Strategic misrepresentation can be distinguished from a genuine reluctance only through an analysis of the other side's needs, interests, and goals. It is a countermeasure to the search for cues.

Some cues indicate the personal style of the negotiator, such as:[56]

1. Being dominating

2. Responding logically or emotionally

3. Speaking directly or obscurely

4. Making others feel comfortable, as opposed to harried or threatened

5. Showing understanding, sensitivity, and encouragement, as opposed to appearing cold and unfeeling

6. Appearing confident, as compared to seeming hesitant, uncertain, or confused

7. Maintaining or avoiding eye contact

8. The presence or absence of facial expressions, and whether the expressions are tense or relaxed, or habitual, and involuntary rather than conscious

9. Mannerisms such as hand movements, head movements, stance, and posture

These can change, depending on the setting, the other persons involved, and the general state of the negotiator's health and emotions.[57]

As a part of the assessment of style, counsel should observe whether the other negotiator is confident and firm, unless reasonably persuaded to change. Strength in negotiation comes, in part, from appearing "appropriate" and "adaptable," while avoiding nervous mannerisms.[58]

A good negotiator uses nonverbal cues to strengthen verbal messages. The fundamental requirement for this is to convey the same central idea both verbally and nonverbally.[59]

Each negotiator must recognize whether he or she is using only one style for all types of negotiation. If so, the negotiator is being unduly limited. In addition, counsel should assess other negotiators who are encountered in different situations to determine whether they have but a single style or a wider repertoire. The more limited a negotiator's style, the more likely that negotiator can be frustrated by an inability to create movement and be manipulated by pressures or self-imposed limitations on available strategies and tactics.

---

[55] See also §§5.05 & 5.08 concerning reciprocity and concessions that are of greater value to one party.

[56] T. Warschaw, *supra* note 45, at 13, 89-92. *See also* R. Lewicki & J. Litterer, Negotiation 202-03 (1985) and M. Zimmerman, How to Do Business with the Japanese 117 (1985).

[57] T. Warschaw, *supra* note 45, at 13.

[58] *Id* 96.

[59] *Id* 93.

Such self-imposed limitations on strategy and tactics due to personal fears should be exploited.

The negotiator's behavior is affected not only by the negotiator's needs and interests, but also by those of the negotiator's client. Thus, when a party is absent, the negotiator's behavior provides indirect cues regarding the negotiator's client. When the real decision maker for a party is present, direct cues are given. This occurs when the party is an individual or someone with the ultimate decision-making authority. Representatives who are present, but who are not the real decision makers, provide only indirect cues and, just like the cues from the negotiator, those indirect cues are skewed by the representative's own needs and interests. In assessing cues, counsel therefore must distinguish between direct and indirect cues.

§10.05   Nonverbal Communication

Nonverbal information is critical to persuasion in face-to-face settings, because people rely significantly on visual cues in making decisions about credibility.[60] This is quite important, because oral communications tend to be more persuasive, although less remembered, than written communications.[61]

Cues can be verbal or nonverbal. Even when negotiations are conducted on a face-to-face basis, many negotiators ignore or miss most nonverbal cues. The reason that nonverbal cues are frequently missed is that the negotiators are looking away or are too concerned about what is going to happen next to notice the obvious.

The primary types of nonverbal cues are:

1.   Appearance
2.   Patterns
3.   Changes
4.   Verbal slips
5.   Fears/Avoidance
6.   Feedback

Appearance consists of nonverbal cues from the other negotiator or the other party, as well as the tone of their spoken words. Verbal pace and tone of voice are examples of nonverbal cues. People have ways and patterns of presentation. Personality, habit, and subcultural norms affect these patterns. Once these patterns are observed and recognized, one can watch for deviations from that person's normal pattern.

Of course, not every physical movement should be interpreted as an important nonverbal cue. The blinking of an eye may be due to a speck of dust or a new contact lens, rather than in response to statements that are being made.

---

[60] M. Saks & R. Hastie, Social Psychology In Court 109 (1978).
[61] Id 119.

In contrast, the negotiator who lights up like a Fourth of July fireworks display upon hearing an offer probably just conveyed a very important cue about his or her reaction to the offer. One who observes closely is likely to see clear nonverbal manifestations which convey messages that are neither subtle nor unclear. Attorneys often look away from the other negotiator or the other party to make notes during portions of the negotiations. Much of this note taking is unnecessary and leaves them looking down rather than looking at the other negotiator or at the other party during those times. While some notes may be helpful or essential, habitual and extensive note taking is not necessary for one with even an average memory and a willingness to concentrate. It is more harmful than beneficial, because it causes the negotiator to miss important nonverbal cues.

Looking away while listening or speaking can also stem from habit or from discomfort at watching others closely. Whatever the reason, it will lead to the same unfortunate results: many nonverbal cues will not be observed.

Looking away not only loses the opportunity for observing the other negotiator, but in itself can convey an unwanted message. A lack of eye contact might be perceived as indicative of weakness, uncertainty, guilt, or deception.[62] In contrast, good eye contact can be perceived as intimidating, honest, open, and challenging, or may help to maintain the other's attention.[63]

Anxiety regarding what to do next in the negotiation also causes many nonverbal cues to be missed. Too many negotiators jump ahead mentally and focus on their future moves, or on what they are going to say next, while failing to concentrate sufficiently on the interaction occurring presently within the negotiation.[64] This focus on the future, rather than the present, leads to a failure to see or to recognize some nonverbal cues. For the same reasons, it can also cause one to miss even verbal cues.

§10.06 Modes of Communication

Negotiations, including the communicating of information, offers, and rationales, can be conducted through various modes of communication. At times, the choice among meetings, telephone calls, letters, and other writings will be merely a matter of expediency or chance. Two lawyers may happen to meet at the courthouse, leading to a negotiation of a pending matter between them. More often, the choice among the modes of communication will be a conscious one, based on the advantages and disadvantages of each type of communication.

---

[62] W. Rusher, How to Win Arguments 120 (1981).

[63] *Id.*

[64] G. Nierenberg, The Art of Negotiation: Psychological Strategies for Gaining Advantageous Bargains 45 (1968).

Meetings

Formally scheduled meetings to negotiate generally indicate that the negotiators have implicitly or explicitly agreed that a serious effort will be made to reach an agreement. Otherwise, the negotiators have wasted time and energy preparing for and attending the negotiating session. Thus, it may be useful to have a preliminary discussion, prior to a formal meeting, to determine whether a meeting has a sufficient probability of being productive to warrant scheduling it. Accordingly, a negotiator can lose credibility by failing to make reasonable proposals and engage in reasonable discussions after scheduling a meeting to negotiate.

In a face-to-face setting, there is an opportunity for give and take, extensive discussion, and visual observation of the participants. The contact is more personal, and this may be either advantageous or disadvantageous in creating an atmosphere that is conducive to agreement.

Some types of negotiations involve formal meetings which are likely to be reported. This can be a detriment to the negotiation process. For example, negotiations in the 1962 New York City newspaper strike were criticized for a "lack of dependable channels for the confidential exchange of bargaining positions."[65]

Informal, private meetings and communications can be productive by allowing the negotiators to dispense with rhetoric, be open and candid with their views, and seek accommodation without a loss of face.[66] Informality can also aid the process by decreasing tension.[67] In order for this to work, the atmosphere must be one of trust that informal or off-the-record statements will not be publicized or used in some other way for a tactical advantage. Such understandings may be the subject of explicit negotiation and arrangement or of tacit understanding. Despite any accord on the use of statements and the informal nature of the setting, the negotiator must still be prepared through planning and on guard, since the negotiation process can be significantly influenced by occurrences in such meetings.

Many commentators believe that the site of the meeting has an important impact on negotiations.[68] Some think that one's own office provides a distinct advantage.[69] One thought is that making one's own office the site demonstrates power. Getting the other negotiator to travel a significant distance also may generate a psychological commitment to reaching an agreement due to the investment of time, energy, and expense.[70]

---

[65] Raskin, *The Newspaper Strike,* in W. Zartman, The 50% Solution 475 (1976).

[66] Mandle, *Collective Bargaining Negotiation,* in Attorney's Guide to Negotiation 14-20 (1979); Kapov, *International Business-Government Negotiations,* in W. Zartman, The 50% Solution 443 (1976).

[67] Kapov, *supra* note 66.

[68] *See* R. Lewicki & J. Litterer, Negotiation 143 (1985).

[69] X. Frascogna, Jr. & H. L Hetherington, Negotiation Strategy for Lawyers 85-86 (1984) [hereinafter Frascogna].

[70] See §5.18 regarding creating a psychological commitment for agreement.

Another consideration for the choice of site is how it will affect the available resources,[71] including the availability of information. It can be advantageous to meet at the other negotiator's office, provided that:

1. The other negotiator will not develop an undue sense of power by succeeding in imposing a choice of site
2. Any essential information is present or can be brought along or retrieved by telephone or telex, unless the opposite approach is desired, so that the unavailability of information is a convenient excuse to deflect inquiries or to require an adjournment
3. If a negotiating team is necessary for either side, its presence can be assured

If the choice of site is critical because it will affect perceptions of power, it may be preferable to:

1. Choose a neutral site
2. Plan more than one session, with the location of the meeting to alternate

The physical layout of the site can also affect the negotiating atmosphere. The setting of the room can create a tone of formality or informality. For example, a cooperative attitude may be fostered by having a living room style arrangement without the barriers of large tables or desks.[72] To the extent that creating a particular atmosphere is considered significant and can be affected by the meeting place, it is another consideration in choosing the site.

Travel to the other side's office may be necessary. However, with the proper attitude and care, there still should not be a "home field advantage" for the other negotiator. In this situation, counsel must be careful not to allow their performance to be adversely affected by:

1. Fatigue
2. The physical setting, including any impressive aspects of the site
3. Being outnumbered in the other side's office

Telephone Calls

A telephone call can be a good tool for specific information gathering before a meeting, either from the other negotiator or in order to plan and to obtain authority from the client. It also may be substituted for a meeting for a number of reasons. A telephone call may be preferred due to scheduling difficulties, as a more cost-effective device, or because the negotiation is expected to be relatively brief and simple.

Telephone calls permit discussion with some give and take, although usually less than at a meeting, because telephone negotiations tend to be shorter than

---

[71] J. Graham & Y. Sano, Smart Bargaining 58 (1984).
[72] Id 60.

those conducted at meetings. There is less of a commitment to negotiate required, since it is much easier to converse by telephone than to schedule a meeting. Telephone calls can be useful to define issues initially, establish rapport, and obtain background information without becoming as deeply immersed in substantive issues as in a meeting.[73]

Of course, personal contact is decreased, and nonverbal visual communication is nonexistent, when a telephone call is utilized rather than a meeting. This lack of visual cues can cause misunderstandings.[74] Tone of voice and verbal pace still remain, however, as potentially important cues to the other negotiator's thinking. In general, though, these factors and, in particular, the lack of face-to-face contact, may lessen the chances of reaching an agreement without a meeting.[75]

Since usually one does not know in advance that the other negotiator is going to call to initiate or to continue the negotiations, care must be taken that counsel who receives the call is sufficiently prepared at that time to proceed.[76] If not, it is important to defer the negotiation until there has been time to review the matter, and then to return the call to the other negotiator at that point. This is a form of adjournment.

Letters and Other Written Communications

Written communications are useful to transmit detailed, exact information.[77] The information can be presented without interruption. Letters, memoranda, telexes, settlement brochures, etc., can eliminate the confusion that sometimes occurs at meetings regarding what was said by providing a permanent record, as long as the writings themselves are clear, rather than ambiguous. Since written documentation of an agreement is normally required, some written communication usually occurs during the course of a negotiation.

Written communications slow the pace of the negotiation. This can be advantageous, disadvantageous, or neither, depending on the timing needs and interests of the parties.

One major disadvantage of a written communication is that it is not flexible. The negotiator, for instance, cannot engage in information gathering and then take a position. Instead, positions must be taken, unless a letter is limited to inviting the other party to make an offer, requesting the disclosure of information, or is only transmitting factual information to the other negotiator.

An exception to the usual lack of flexibility of a written communication is a draft of an agreement that already has been reached either orally or in a summary written form. Such a draft is circulated for discussion and revision. Using a writing is necessary to allow the negotiators and the parties to focus on the precise details and terms of the tentative agreement. This process may involve meetings or telephone calls to discuss the draft and alternative versions.

---

[73] Frascogna, *supra* note 69.

[74] H. Cohen, You Can Negotiate Anything 210 (1982).

[75] *Id.*

[76] *Id* 213-15.

[77] See §4.02 regarding settlement brochures.

Similarly, written materials may be necessary or useful at meetings to clarify, illustrate, or provide a more concrete form for information which will be a part of the basis for a negotiation. Construction drawings, charts, graphs, overlays, computer runs, other written forms of data, and other written references can all help to facilitate a meeting without destroying its flexibility. These can be supplemented or replaced by other visual forms of presentation, including videos, movies, slides, photographs, and models.

The second major disadvantage of a writing is that it can be a permanent record of a statement or a position. A party may not object to having a permanent record of an offer if it is accepted. However, the party may not want to have such a record if the other party rejects the offer, but shows it to third parties. In addition, the party or the negotiator may want or need to make certain statements without fear that a writing will be disclosed. For this reason, an agreement that such communications will be treated confidentially sometimes is essential. Even so, it may be best to refrain from making written comments about certain subjects or persons, and limit oneself to oral communications. On the other hand, there should be no hesitancy about having any significant representations or warranties in writing.

At times, counsel should reduce an offer to writing. This can be true even though a proposal is not fully developed, and only the approval of a basic concept or of a broad outline is sought. In certain instances, a precondition may be that the proposal is to be kept secret, at least unless it is accepted. However, the absence of any written document can help avoid inadvertent disclosures, as well as facilitate a denial in the event that a disclosure is made contrary to an agreement for secrecy. If these are serious concerns, an effort should be made to refrain from using a written proposal, at least until a substantive agreement is reached.

On the other hand, counsel may find it advantageous to have a record which is, or can be, made public. The written communication can then be used to influence allies, the media, the public, or others.[78]

This is not to discount the importance of written material. Seeing a proposal or a plan in a carefully written form can be far more persuasive than a brief verbal description. Matters that are reduced to writing can appear to be more significant, and can appear to reflect a greater commitment on the part of the writer. A high degree of organization, planning, and knowledge can also be demonstrated through writings. A written offer may be more easily scrutinized, discussed, and studied, than the same material presented verbally, since the latter is dependent on the memory or notes of the listener. All of this may increase the likelihood of reaching an agreement.

§10.07   Summary and Review

I. Outcomes are Affected by Perfect or Imperfect Information
   A. Seek to cause the other side to behave as desired through communications which control and manipulate information

---

[78] See §§6.06 and 6.07 regarding influencing allies, the media, and the community.

    B. Communication stages often are (1) build and defend positions to demonstrate some form of power, including persuasion, (2) search for solutions using the information from the first stage, and (3) strive together for satisfactory terms

II. Polite versus Power Struggle

    A. Generally be polite, so each negotiator can give and receive information, without necessarily being quiet or low key

    B. Polite mode facilitates selective disclosure and listening, while avoiding unnecessary and counterproductive power struggles

    C. Power struggles are appropriate when they (1) lead to control of the outcome, (2) avoid domination when a substantive victory cannot be achieved by permitting apparent procedural domination, and (3) stop wasteful repetition when appeasing the other's ego will not be productive

    D. Unsuccessful power struggles can create counterproductive frustration or hostility, and even cause a breakdown in negotiations

    E. Consider individual and entity personalities

III. Sending Verbal and Nonverbal Information

    A. Make only deliberate, selective disclosures

    B. Disclosure is appropriate if it will tend to persuade the other side to act as desired, considering any countervailing risks of creating a problem or revealing a weakness

    C. Use persuasive rationales with positions unless (1) the rationale is inherently clear, (2) no plausible rationale exists (rare) or (3) the rationale would involve a breach of a legal or ethical duty, such as a material misrepresentation. Splitting the difference, reciprocity, and precedent are often useful rationales.

    D. Persuade through appeals to the other side's economic and non-economic interests

    E. Disclose basis or source, if necessary to persuade

    F. Build rapport to enhance persuasion, including responding with points of agreement before stating points being rejected

    G. Explain, rather than demand blind trust, with implicit conclusions if the listener will be more convinced by figuring it out himself, and explicit conclusions otherwise

    H. Enhance persuasion by the size, intensity, visual impact, uniqueness, primary, recency, and reasonable repetition

    I. Persuasive force also results from acting convinced, building in concessions, pointed questions, avoiding judgmental behavior (unless the other will be convinced that the judgment is correct), defining the problem to be solved in a mutually agreeable way, timing that permits proper consideration to be given to the message, and references that demonstrate credibility or power

    J. Use clear signals, and avoid confusing, mixed messages

    K. Communicate with an awareness of the psychological needs of the other party and its negotiator, to avoid unwanted mental filtering, and be on guard against mental filtering by oneself, causing misperceptions

L. If the other negotiator is withholding or distorting information to the other party's decision maker and thereby creating a problem, use inquiry, request, presence of the person, written communications, and depositions

M. Encourage the disclosure of information by listening attentively without interruptions and not indicating its importance if doing so would cause the other negotiator to become guarded

N. Counter a reluctance to disclose by questions, discussions, challenging a point, and informational bargaining

O. Careful listening requires giving the other an opportunity to speak, concentrating on the verbal and nonverbal messages, and giving feedback to indicate understanding

P. React to strange or dramatic nonverbal information with a calm firmness, or refrain from reacting at all

Q. Be alert for otherwise unconscious emotional distortions or perceptions, and counter difficult emotional reactions by channeling the energy into concentration, deep breathing with tensing or relaxing muscles, or a break

R. Also be alert to avoid missing information that contradicts one's ideas because of a tendency to hear that which is expected or desired

S. Distinguish between the words heard and one's own inferences, so that the inference is evaluated as an assumption

T. Separate out verifiable facts from your own assumptions, opinions or hearsay knowledge, or those of the speaker, in order to decide whether verification is needed

U. Use restatements or recapitulation to avoid errors by corroborating one's own understanding, to build rapport, and to clarify the matter for the original speaker

V. Watch for verbal and nonverbal cues, including concession patterns, indicating the true motives, interests, values, strategies, and tactics of the other party and its negotiator. Distinguish between articulated positions and bottom-line ones.

W. Counter the search for cues with strategic misrepresentations, consisting of feigned reluctance

X. Exploit the other negotiators' self-imposed limitations on style, including a refusal or inability to use proper strategies and tactics due to personal fears

Y. Behave so that one's nonverbal actions are consistent with one's verbal actions. Watch for discrepancies with oneself, the other party, and its negotiator.

Z. Use good eye contact

AA. Changes in a person's normal pattern of nonverbal behavior can be significant

BB. Choose among meetings, telephone calls, and writings as modes of communication based on timing, impact, psychological commitment to negotiate seriously, and any need for privacy or confidentiality

CC. Use informal or off-the-record exchanges to encourage candor and avoid rhetoric, but be on guard

DD. The choice of site can indicate power, commitment, or a need to have or avoid having information available

EE. Physical layout can affect the atmosphere, but can be countered by mental attitude

Drafting

11

---

§11.01 Introduction

Drafting skills for three types of documents are essential in the negotiation process. These documents are:

1. Informational documents, i.e., letters and other written communications that convey information about needs, interests, general positions, conditions, scheduling, agenda, or other matters not described below

2. Proposals, i.e., sufficiently detailed offers that can be binding if accepted, although not in the form of a formal agreement

3. Formal agreements, such as contracts, releases, etc

Most of this section will focus on proposals and formal agreements.

With regard to informational documents, the drafter should apply the guidelines described for informational tactics and communications in Chapters 4 and 10, as well as in §§11.02 and 11.03. If the informational document is a settlement brochure or a policy limits letter, §§4.02 and 7.05, respectively, should be consulted. In drafting informational documents, organization, selectivity, clarity, and persuasiveness are the critical concepts. For example, a threatening letter must clearly reflect power, and not be so polite that it loses its effectiveness.[1] At the same time, unless the recipient can be intimidated by tone, the phrasing should not be so offensive as to provoke an angry, defensive reaction prompting the recipient to fight back rather than acquiesce.

Example 11-1 Too Polite

It is our wish that you accept this proposal. Please notify me promptly of your response. If you do not, and we cannot otherwise agree, we will be forced into litigation.

Example 11-2 Usually Too Aggressive

Since there is no question that we will prevail in court, sign within 24 hours or we will file suit.

Example 11-3

If this matter is not resolved within five days, we will proceed with litigation and such other steps as we deem appropriate.

The effects of other negotiating skills will vanish unless the negotiator can properly draft the documents that constitute or reflect the actual agreement. A relatively narrow exception to the need for skillful drafting exists for:

1. Oral agreements[2]
2. Litigation in which the settlement documentation consists of a simple agreed judgment
3. Litigation in which the settlement consists of a simple agreement that the defendant shall pay a specified sum to the plaintiff, at times with costs or fees, and in which the settlement documentation is a basic general release of the plaintiff's claim against the defendant

For other negotiated agreements, good drafting skills are critical to ensure that the client receives all of the benefits, and incurs only those costs that have been agreed to, by having an enforceable document that properly memorializes the agreement.

In drafting in substantive legal areas or in terminology with which counsel is not familiar from previous endeavors, counsel should usually begin by consulting either textbook or continuing legal education models, standard forms, or past agreements prepared by another lawyer. Two caveats must be remembered in starting this way:

---

[1] X. Frascogna, Jr. & H. Hetherington, Negotiation Strategy for Lawyers 5-6 (1984) [hereinafter Frascogna].

[2] Complex agreements should always be in writing, as should even simple agreements of real significance, unless custom or prior dealings strongly indicate to the contrary.

1. Counsel should begin with the working assumption that the model, form, precedent, or example being used is less than ideal to avoid blind acceptance

2. Counsel must also begin with the working assumption that the particular agreement being drafted is unique and cannot be entirely the same as the model, form, or example that is being used

With regard to the first caveat, characterizing an agreement as "ideal" means that it contains all conceivable terms structured in the most favorable possible way to one party, as if that party could control all of the terms, with the possible exception of the price. Prior agreements almost always are the result of a negotiated compromise. Therefore, their terms will normally be less than those ideal for either party. Similarly, models and forms typically reflect a moderate, less than "ideal" approach.

Nevertheless, it is with such an ideal in mind that one should commence drafting, limited only by the specific provisions that have been agreed on and the same type of realistically high expectations used for establishing one's initial position. Otherwise, counsel is mentally bargaining against the client by omitting or reducing terms that might be accepted by the other party through a more assertive approach. Such a less assertive method can result in a far weaker agreement than the one which is optimally available.

Regarding uniqueness, many agreements should reflect a degree of uniqueness based on the individualized needs, interests, and concerns of the parties, as well as on the idiosyncracies of the deal itself. Whenever models, forms, or examples are being utilized, they must be scrutinized in order to determine whether modifications should be designed based on any distinctive aspects of either the parties or the agreement. Furthermore, forms can become quickly outdated due to changes in substantive law or the economic environment.[3]

An additional, general consideration is whether a party needs, or may need, coercive power to force the other party to perform.[4]

Example 11-4

A $300,000 debt is settled for $100,000. Part of the settlement agreement, however, is that a failure to maintain the payment schedule will trigger a provision that the amount owed reverts to the $300,000 originally claimed and becomes due immediately. Personal guarantees of the debtor and his spouse are also required to reduce the risk of property transfers to avoid payment. Similarly, alternative dispute resolution provisions are considered, because all of the agreed acts will not occur simultaneously with the execution of the agreement.

---

[3] Hyman, *Drafting Contracts*, 68 CBA Rec 33 (1987).

[4] R. Givens, Advocacy: The Art of Pleading a Cause 452 (Shepard's/McGraw-Hill, Inc 1985).

Drafting agreements often involves a secondary negotiation process.[5] Although the agreement supposedly exists, it may change in sometimes subtle and often significant ways as it is drafted, and then drafts are exchanged and subsequently modified. It is in the drafting, discussion of drafts, and exchange of drafts that the secondary negotiation occurs. It is the secondary negotiation that results in the final form of the agreement. Counsel should consider whether the drafting process in a particular case is likely to involve a sufficiently substantive, secondary negotiation to necessitate the use of systematic planning steps.[6] If so, such drafting planning will include whether concessions are likely to be sought.[7]

§11.02   The Initial Draft

In drafting written agreements, whether they are agreed court orders, releases, contracts, or other types of documents evidencing agreement, the issue of which negotiator will do the initial draft arises. Although subject to review by the other negotiator and perhaps the other party, the drafter tends to exercise some discretionary control. The initial drafter places phrases and terms in to the proposed agreement, limited only by notions of fairness and the expectation of scrutiny by the other side. No terms should be included that are so unfair, in the context of the preceeding negotiation and the specific points of agreement, that they will seriously offend the other side or which may cause the entire deal to unravel, unless those risks are acceptable. This is especially true in cooperative arrangements, where maintaining a spirit of cooperation through reasonable drafting can be essential to prevent the deal from beginning to fall apart before it even commences. Apart from being generally fair, the proposed terms should also have a reasonable probability of passing the scrutiny of the other side, at least in the sense of obtaining its reluctant acquiescence to the drafted terms.

Determining which counsel initially drafts the provisions of the written agreement may be decided in a number of ways, such as:

1.   Through serious negotiation
2.   By an offer to do so with either the full agreement or the reluctant acquiescence of the other negotiator
3.   Through a request that the other attorney do so
4.   From unilateral action in which the attorney for one party just decides to draft a detailed proposed written agreement and transmits it
5.   By custom

If the decision is made according to custom, one party often starts with its standard agreement. This is common in real estate transactions where sellers and

---

[5] Frascogna, *supra* note 1, at 179.

[6] *See* **chs 8 & 9.**

[7] See **§9.05** regarding planning concessions and tradeoffs.

lessors usually have standard forms of agreement from which modifications are made, sometimes in the form of riders.

In order to determine whether counsel should care about being the initial drafter or should prefer to avoid that task, three primary criteria should be analyzed. These three criteria concern:

1. Control
2. Revisions
3. Costs

As discussed above, the initial drafter controls the original organization and phrasing of terms. This is important to the extent that discretion is to be used on items of significance, and in cases in which it will be difficult to obtain agreement on revisions. Thus, the first two criteria are very much interrelated. Counsel must assess the potential difficulty of negotiating revisions in view of the context and the timing of the negotiation. Assessing the possible difficulty of negotiating changes must take into account the other negotiator's personality and possible pride of authorship. Since some revisions normally are expected, a degree of modification should not be expected to generate hostility. However, with some attorneys, a complete rewrite of the draft will offend his or her pride of authorship, even though it may be necessary. Furthermore, a rewrite highlights the use of language and terms much more so than the initial draft does.

As to cost, in some instances when a need for extensive revisions is not anticipated, it may be more cost effective to allow the other attorney to prepare the initial draft. In these cases, counsel may prefer to avoid being the initial drafter.

The stage of the negotiation process can be an important factor in evaluating the cost effectiveness of preparing the initial draft.

Example 11-5[8]

> Counsel represents the seller of a small business. The sales contract will be relatively simple and have limited provisions. The seller's advantage in drafting the agreement must be weighed against the cost of preparing it before the buyer is finally committed to making the purchase.

Some commentators advocate always drafting first if possible.[9] That approach is too inflexible. It does, however, reflect the significance, at times, of who does the first draft. Since the initial drafter may have some advantage in controlling the final product,[10] counsel should prepare the first draft if there is any doubt about whether to do so.

---

[8] Frisch, Jr. & Rosenzweig, *Representing the Seller of a Small Business*, in Attorney's Guide to Negotiation 4-31 (1979).

[9] See, for example, Marcus, *Representing the Purchaser of a Small Business*, In Attorney's Guide to Negotiation 5-30 (1979).

[10] Sandels, *Negotiation in Business Litigation*, in Attorney's Guide to Negotiation 11-22 (1979).

§11.03 General Requirements

There are four general requirements in drafting written agreements to conclude a negotiation. These general requirements are to:

1. Use a high degree of precision in the terms and the language of the document

2. Be creative in order to generate the optimal written agreement

3. Anticipate that disputes will arise which require the written agreement to be enforced, and envision the nature of the disputes

4. Avoid losing the agreement that has been reached after closure except for the drafting

Written documents that evidence settlements or other agreements must be precise. The language should be clean and unambiguous. Not only the drafters and the parties, but any other reasonable person reading it, must reach the same conclusions about the rights and obligations of the parties. This preciseness should eliminate any need for parol evidence if a dispute arises. This high degree of precision should also eliminate a subsequent differing interpretation by one party due to a genuine initial misunderstanding, a failure of memory, or a malicious or greedy motivation.

Shorter, less complicated sentences should be used whenever longer sentences may be confusing or ambiguous. Plain English is clearer than long, complicated sentences. If long sentences are needed, they are easier to follow if they make their point early and then explain it, rather than starting with a long clarifying clause.[11]

Example 11-6 Poor Drafting

After acceptance of possession and payment of the balance of the down payment, and pursuant to the conditions of paragraphs six and seven, upon the lapse of more than thirty days from the date of any subsequent payment under the payment schedule shown on Exhibit A, and without the need to give notice or opportunity to cure, seller has the unqualified right to take back possession of the property for such default, with all amounts heretofore paid forfeited and the buyer thereby has all of its rights terminated.

Example 11-7 Better Drafting

Seller has the right to take back possession of the property if buyer fails to make any payment within thirty days of the date that a payment is due. Seller need not give notice or any opportunity to cure. This default provision is pursuant to paragraphs six and seven, and follows the payment

---

[11] Raymond, *Legal Writing: An Obstruction to Justice,* in Law Letters, Inc, Second Manual of In-House Training 190-93 (1983).

schedule shown on Exhibit A. All amounts previously paid are forfeited upon such default, and buyer's rights are terminated.

The drafter must aim to write so that the reader can understand on the first reading. Simplicity and lucidity are the goals.[12] It is more effective to use active, rather than passive verbs.[13]

Example 11-8 Passive

A security interest can be found in the buyer.

Example 11-9 Active

The buyer has a security interest.

Headings and subheadings can improve organization and clarity. Statements of purpose can aid courts in construing agreements.[14]

Precision requires the use of objective standards. Even then, the standards must be sufficient to be enforceable.

Example 11-10

In a contract for new real estate construction, the contract is precise in its use of architectural plans and specifications as objective criteria. Counsel is aware, though, that this is still inadequate unless the plans and specifications are sufficiently detailed to specify the items necessary so that compliance with the contract will result in the quality and value that the buyer expects to receive. Both counsel and the client, however, lack the expertise to analyze plans and specifications from these perspectives. Realizing this, the lawyer counsels the client, and advises that an expert, architect, contractor, or structural engineer should be consulted before the agreement is executed.

Exceptions to the requirement of exactness in drafting arise when:

1. A narrow ambiguity is no worse than the position that the other party will force into the agreement if the matter is explicitly set forth

2. It is in the client's best interest to have an ambiguity

3. Exactness is impossible

4. It is too difficult or unimportant to anticipate a future contingency and

---

[12] Younger, *In Praise of Simplicity,* in Law Letters, Inc, Second Manual of In-House Training 202-03 (1983).

[13] Hennings, *Everybody Agrees Legal Writing Is Bad But Not on What Needs to be Done,* in Law Letters, Inc, Second Manual Of In-House Training 213 (1983).

[14] R. Givens, Advocacy: The Art of Pleading a Cause 453 (Shepard's/McGraw Hill, Inc 1985).

draft responsive provisions, especially if there are strong mutual incentives for cooperation[15]

5.   The agreement can be terminated by either party if certain general conditions occur

Example 11-11

In a contract negotiation between a manufacturer and a retailer, the manufacturer is unwilling to guarantee delivery by a certain date and is unwilling to guarantee that it will commit a specific amount of its resources to the effort to provide delivery by a certain date. While recognizing that the contract has to have some indication of a delivery date to satisfy the retailer, the manufacturer wants the flexibility of not being locked into a precise date. Although receiving delivery by the particular date is important to the retailer, it still wants to enter in to the agreement, even though it cannot obtain the precise promises that it would like to have from the manufacturer. The parties agree that the written contract will provide that the manufacturer will use reasonable efforts to try to provide delivery to the retailer by the specific date.

From the retailer's point of view, Example 11-11 illustrates the first exception to the requirement that agreements should be precise. Although ambiguous, this is the best agreement that the retailer can obtain from the manufacturer. From the manufacturer's point of view, the example demonstrates the second of the exceptions. It is in the manufacturer's best interest to have some ambiguity regarding the date of delivery.

The third exception occurs when exactness is impossible to achieve. It may be impossible to be exact because:

1.   The parties cannot forecast or detail the precise conduct which will be needed

2.   In many cases, the task would be too time consuming

3.   The effort would result in undue rigidity and insufficient flexibility[16]

This is particularly true for matters which establish relationships over the course of time. In such cases, simple provisions should be used that can apply, without modification, despite unforeseen contingencies, technological changes, or shifts in the market.[17] One might say that the Constitution is the classic example of this type of drafting. Carefully detailed descriptions of aims, rather than means, can also be useful in such situations.[18] Care must be exercised so that in the absence of precision, the provisions do not create unin-

---

[15] *Id* 51 (Supp 1986).

[16] R. Givens, *supra* note 14.

[17] Rifkin, *Negotiating Patents, Trade Secrets and Know-How Licenses,* in Attorney's Guide to Negotiation 5-10 (1979).

[18] R. Givens, *supra* note 14.

tended inferences. At times, good faith may have to take the place of exactness. Good faith provisions, however, can be difficult to enforce.[19] Such difficulties generally stem from the potential for differring, reasonable interpretations of the exact conduct required by the provisions. Therefore, such provisions can lead to disputes, be an insufficient enforcement mechanism, or create a vague basis for a claim of breach.

In addition to being precise, the second general requirement in drafting is to be creative. Just as there can be a need for creativity in the negotiation itself, the drafter may need to create terms which precisely define the rights and obligations of the parties. This is done as favorably to one's own client as possible without overstepping the limitations discussed above regarding fairness and the expectation of scrutiny by the other side.[20]

The third general requirement in drafting is the ability to anticipate what can go wrong. If the parties have the same understanding of the terms of the agreement and abide by it, no problems will arise. Astute counsel must anticipate that something may happen, however, that will create difficulties or disputes leading to a need to rely on and enforce the written agreement. Such future problems typically originate due to:

1. Disagreement over the proper interpretation of the terms of the document

2. Unforeseen events for which provisions were not made

3. Economic or other difficulties affecting a party's ability to perform

4. Other changes of circumstances which create a motivation on the part of one party to repudiate the agreement or, at least, to fail to perform its obligations under the agreement properly.

Counsel needs to anticipate such potential problems and disputes. By doing so, provisions can be structured to guard against, or to provide for, significant contingencies that are realistic possibilities. Examples of provisions that are used to guard against, or to provide for, such contingencies include:

1. Enforceable liquidated damages clauses[21]

2. Other legally enforceable sanctions[22]

3. Covenants not to compete if terminated[23]

4. For closely held corporations or partnerships with a few

---

[19] R. Givens, *supra* note 14, at 52 (Supp 1986).

[20] *See* §11.02.

[21] *See* 22 Am Jur 2d *Damages* §§683-730 (1988) regarding limitations on liquidated damages provisions.

[22] R. Givens, *supra* note 14.

[23] *See* 54 Am Jur 2d *Monopolies, Restraints of Trade, and Unfair Trade Practices* §§542-564 (1971) concerning the limitations on covenants not to compete.

owner/operators, buy-sell provisions[24]

5. For the buyer in real estate transactions, a warranty that the premises will be in the same condition at closing as at the inspection conducted when the contract was signed, with all equipment and systems in proper working order

6. For the purchaser in real estate contracts for new construction, a warranty that the finished construction will pass the inspection of the local municipality and of an architect or structural engineer chosen by the purchaser, subject to arbitration if a dispute arises

7. Pass-throughs of increases in taxes, insurance, or other operating expenses

8. Default provisions to protect the seller of a business

The other general requirement is to draft an agreement which, while being precise, as creative as necessary, and anticipating any significant contingencies, avoids being a "deal killer." Unless the need for a particular provision outweighs the benefits of the deal, the lawyer should not risk becoming a "deal killer" by insisting on provisions that are not essential. Counsel certainly ought to engage in hard bargaining to attain the best possible agreement for one's client, but, at the same time, careful judgement must be exercised about the point at which to cease pressing for terms that are adamantly opposed by the other party.

Drafting can occur after a tentative agreement subject to execution of a final draft. A second way in which the drafting process may kill a deal is through delay. This potential pitfall stems from the same types of factors discussed earlier regarding the need for closure.[25] To the extent that documents must be executed before a firm, legally enforceable agreement exists, there can be no closure until the drafting process is complete.

Example 11-12

After three years, two business partners decided that their managerial views and styles were too divergent and conflicting, so they decided to split up. Lacking a buy-sell provision in their partnership agreement, the partners decided to divide the business' operations between themselves.[26] However, they were unable to resolve the issues of monetary compensation between themselves, and of responsibility for potential tax and other liabilities. Despite their failure to reach full agreement, each took his oper-

---

[24] A buy-sell provision sets up a mechanism by which one or more of the shareholders or partners can buy out the interests of the other(s). A formula for determining the sales price is included so that the question of price does not block the provision from operating effectively. The buy-sell provision may be triggered by a disagreement that results in the shareholders' or the partners' wanting to cease operating together, or by the retirement or the death of one of the shareholders or partners.

[25] See §3.15 regarding closure.

[26] *See* Frascogna, *supra* note 1, at 179.

ation as agreed on in the division, and began operating it as a separate new corporation. Several months later, they tentatively agreed on a payment of $150,000 from partner X to partner Y, subject to drafting an agreement resolving the remaining issues and establishing written terms. During the drawn-out drafting process while other issues remained open, X decided that the amount was too high, causing the negotiation to cease. Approximately one year later, X was willing to pay $51,000, while Y demanded $56,000. However, those positions were still subject to drafting an agreement resolving the other issues. Again, a lengthy drafting process ensued, during which the parties' views of the economics of the potential deal shifted, while other issues were still open. And, once again, the negotiation process terminated. Six months later, with additional counsel for X and new counsel for Y, the parties reopened the negotiation. After X threatened to institute litigation, Y agreed to the use of alternative dispute resolution.[27] A seven-hour, virtually nonstop mediation session resulted in an oral agreement. This time, X's attorney insisted that the parties draft and sign a written agreement before anyone left. Everyone agreed, in light of the history of these negotiations, that it would be wise to do so. Within one hour, the lawyers had drafted a two-page agreement which fully reflected all of the necessary terms, and the parties executed it.

Of course, it is not always feasible to draft an agreement on the spot within a relatively short time frame. The practicality of immediately drafting the agreement, however, should be considered unless:

1.   The drafting process is necessarily too complex to even think about engaging in it immediately

2.   The drafting process is not a concern for the reasons discussed in §11.01

Example 11-13

Two rival groups were engaged in competing with one another to purchase a local bank. On a Wednesday morning, both groups met separately with an attorney representing the bank's shareholders. Each indicated a willingness to pay a similar price for the stock. The shareholders' attorney responded that his clients would be interested in a firm written offer. The next day, one group transmitted a one-page, very simple, proposed written contract. The other group indicated that it would have its written offer ready by the following day, so the bank's shareholders waited. When the second group's offer arrived, it consisted of a forty-page, single-spaced draft contract containing numerous representations and warranties. Although it was somewhat financially advantageous, assuming that terms would ever be agreed on, the shareholders decided to accept and execute the one-page contract instead. They preferred a firm, straightforward

---

[27] *See* §6.07.

deal with only a single representation (that the last financial statement was materially correct), to a contract that created a potential for litigation because of many proposed representations and warranties. In addition, those proposals prevented the same assurance of finality implicit in the first offer, since many of them were unaccepted and would have to be negotiated.

§11.04   Formal Agreements

Formal agreements consist of contracts drawn with detail and specificity. They explain all of the terms of the settlement or the transaction, and reflect the full and complete agreement of the parties. The document may be labeled as an agreement, or it may be in the form of a letter. The essential quality of the document is that, properly drawn, it expresses the parties' intentions in their meeting of the minds, the parties' respective rights and obligations, and the consideration provided.[28] If correctly drafted, both the parties to the agreement and third parties will be able to read the document and understand those points.[29] A formal agreement can include exhibits or other documents incorporated by reference.

Three major exceptions exist to the general principle that the formal agreement contain all of the terms of the agreement. These exceptions involve the law, parol evidence, and unwritten modifications.

The relevant law at the time and place of the making of a contract is a part of the contract as a matter of law.[30] For instance, as a matter of law, implied warranties, an obligation to act in good faith, or various definitions may be part of the contract, even though they are not set forth within the contract.[31] This can be varied by the parties to the extent that the relevant law permits the parties to choose which state's law will govern the contract,[32] or expressly waive or disclaim particular aspects of the otherwise applicable law.

To the extent that the essential terms are present, but an ambiguity exists about their meaning, parol evidence of the parties' intentions can be intro-

---

[28] Sometimes only nominal consideration, such as ten dollars, is stated, accompanied by a general phrase such as "and the parties acknowledge other good and adequate consideration has been received."

[29] In drafting the document, it is important to keep in mind that third parties who have to interpret the document potentially include judges, mediators, and arbitrators. None of them will know the truth except as the evidence indicates.

[30] *See* 17 Am Jur 2d *Contracts* §257 (1964).

[31] See the UCC §§2-314 (implied warranty), 2-315 (implied warranty), 1-203 (obligation of good faith), 2-319 (definitions unless otherwise agreed) 2-320 (definitions unless otherwise agreed), 2-321 (definitions unless otherwise agreed), 2-322 (definitions unless otherwise agreed), and 2-324 (definitions unless otherwise agreed).

[32] *See* Restatement (Second) of Conflict of Laws §§186-188 (1969).

duced in the event of a dispute that results in litigation.[33] Parol evidence is evidence of the parties' intentions that is outside the "four corners" of the written agreement.[34] If the written agreement was intended to be the exclusive expression of the parties' agreement, however, extrinsic evidence may be limited to such areas as the course of dealing, the usage of trade, or the course of performance.[35] Similarly, where the essential terms are present, but a nonessential term is omitted, a court may imply the term based on a standard of reasonableness.[36]

---

[33] For instance, §2-202 of the UCC states as follows:

Final Written Expression: Parol or Extrinsic Evidence Terms with respect to which the confirmatory memoranda of the parties agree or which are otherwise set forth in a writing intended by the parties as a final expression of their agreement with respect to such terms as are included therein may not be contradicted by evidence of any prior agreement or of a contemporaneous oral agreement *but may be explained or supplemented*
(a) by course of dealing or usage of trade (Section 1-205) or by course of performance (Section 2-208); and
(b) by evidence of consistent additional terms unless the court finds the writing to have been intended also as a complete and exclusive statement of the terms of the agreement. (Emphasis added.)

The Official Comment to this Section states, in part, that:

1. This section definitely rejects:
(a) Any assumption that because a writing has been worked out which is final on some matters, it is to be taken as including all of the matters agreed upon;
(b) The premise that the language used has the meaning attributable to such language by rules of construction existing in the law rather than the meaning which arises out of the commercial context in which it was used; and
(c) The requirement that a condition precedent to the admissibility of the type of evidence specified in paragraph
(a) is an original determination by the court that the language used is ambiguous.

[34] *See* 30 Am Jur 2d *Evidence* §§1016-1022 (1967).

[35] The Official Comments to the UCC §2-202 state in part that:

2. Paragraph (a) makes admissible evidence of course of dealing, usage of trade and course of performance to explain or supplement the terms of any writing stating the agreement of the parties in order that the true understanding of the parties as to the agreement may be reached. Such writings are to be read on the assumption that the course of prior dealings between the parties and the usages of trade were taken for granted when the document was phrased. Unless carefully negated, they have become an element of the meaning of the words used. Similarly, the course of actual performance by the parties is considered the best indication of what they intended the writing to mean.
3. Under paragraph (b) consistent additional terms, not reduced to writing, may be proved unless the court finds that the writing was intended by both parties as a complete and exclusive statement of all the terms. If the additional terms are such that, if agreed upon, they would certainly have been included in the document in the view of the court, then evidence of their alleged making must be kept from the trier of fact.

See also UCC §2-202 set forth in note 33.

[36] See UCC §2-202 set forth in note 33.

Third, the formal agreement will not contain all of the terms if it has been modified by the parties without the execution of a subsequent formal writing documenting the modification. Such modifications, without the execution of a written document, can occur through a number of means. These include:

1. Oral agreements, unless precluded by an applicable statute of frauds[37]
2. Waivers[38]
3. The parties' course of performance with each other under the agreement which evidences a different intention by all of the parties than that reflected in the formal agreement[39]

To avoid, or to at least minimize, the possibility of disputes over whether an agreement has been modified, the drafter may include terms in the formal agreement to prevent disputed claims of modification.[40]

Example 11-14

It is further agreed that the provisions of this contract cannot be modified except in a writing signed by all of the parties.

Example 11-15

It is further agreed that a party's waiver of any right on one occasion shall not be deemed a continuing waiver for subsequent occasions.

For the most part, agreements of any real significance should be in writing, and should be signed by the parties, even if that is not required by law. This helps to prevent misunderstandings about rights and obligations. Moreover, this aids immeasurably whenever a party must enforce the terms of the agreement. Once there is testimony in dipsute about the terms, or even the existence, of an oral agreement, meeting the burden of proof can be difficult or impossible. In any event, doing so will certainly be far more difficult than if there is a properly written agreement. Furthermore, credibility issues can lead a trier of fact to a determination which, unknown to it, is actually contrary to the truth.

Nevertheless, oral agreements can be useful when the parties' relationship and level of trust, often combined with a lack of complexity, the stakes involved, and the local customs or practices, dictate that an oral agreement should be used. In more unusual situations, a party may be so offended by the suggestion that a "hand-shake" deal is insufficient, that the party refuses to proceed. However, in matters requiring counsel, written agreements should be the norm and should be utilized the overwhelming majority of the time, because the matters will usually involve complexity and significance.

---

[37] *See* UCC §2-209(3).
[38] *See* UCC §2-209.
[39] *See* UCC §§2-208 & 2-209.
[40] *See* UCC §2-209.

In addition, some matters are required to be in writing as a matter of law. These can include such matters as:

Contracts for the sale of real estate[41]

Securities offerings[42]

Consumer financing agreements[43]

Contingency fee agreements between lawyers and clients[44]

In multiple party litigation, a settlement may be between fewer than all of the parties. Moreover, regardless of whether litigation is actually pending, a settlement may involve:

1. Potential claims by the client against third parties who are not a part of the settlement agreement

2. Potential claims against the client by third parties who are not a part of the settlement agreement

Releases or covenants not to sue must be carefully drafted, pursuant to the law of the applicable jurisdiction, to:

1. Preserve any additional claims of the client to the extent possible[45]

2. Protect the client from any other claims, if possible, including any additional claims by the settling claimant and potential contribution claims by nonsettling claimants[46]

3. Avoid creating any admissions which might be used against the client in the future

In guarding against admissions, any potential for statements to be used by the government in criminal, civil, or administrative proceedings must be considered.

§11.05 —Standard versus Nonstandard Language

Standard language and terms have certain advantages. The meanings may be well understood, and may even have been adjudicated in prior litigation

---

[41] Exceptions exist to the Statute of Frauds general rule that a real estate contract must be written. 72 Am Jur 2d *Statute of Frauds*, §44 *et seq* (1974).

[42] 69 Am Jur 2d *Securities Regulation-Federal* §115 (1973).

[43] 15 USC §1632.

[44] For instance, the Illinois Code of Professional Responsibility requires that any contingency fee agreement between an attorney and a client must be in writing. Ill Rev Stat ch 110A Rule 2-106(c)(2) (1987).

[45] This includes minimizing any setoffs due to non-settling joint tortfeasors if possible. Dewey, *Traps In Multitortfeasor Settlements*, 13 Litigation 42 (1987).

[46] *Id; see also* §§**7.06, 7.07, & 7.08.**

with reported decisions. In addition, at least one group of competent lawyers believed that the language was sufficiently precise and meaningful to fulfill its purpose. These advantages must be considered against both the need for specialization and the potential for improvement. The parties' agreement may require somewhat specialized and particularized terms, or even completely different terms than the standard ones. Standard terms may need to be modified or expanded to reflect the idiosyncratic aspects of the agreement. Furthermore, counsel may be able to improve on the language that is customarily used. One area of improvement that should be frequently considered is the clarity of the language. Standard terminology often differs from plain English. To the extent necessary to avoid contractual ambiguities, plain English should be used.

The nonstandard portions of an agreement should be written clearly and understandably. The meaning must be both unambiguous and sufficiently broad to encompass any contingencies. When the nonstandard language is in the form of a rider to a form agreement, the rider should provide that the terms of the rider control over any inconsistent terms in the standard form. Such a provision will avoid patent ambiguities.

In complex agreements, headings and subheadings can be used to aid the reader. These provide both general guidance and a form of an index which eases the task of locating specific points.

§11.06 —Statutory Requirements and Case Law

Certain terms or specific language may be required as a matter of law. Statutory rules can impact on the drafting process, and some terminology may be required by specific statutes.[47] This includes disclaimers of points otherwise implied by law. In addition, case law can also create requirements for the provisions that need to be drafted.[48]

§11.07   Other Documents Evidencing Agreement

The best way to document an agreement is usually by a formal agreement executed by the parties. However, if custom or cost considerations militate against the use of a formal agreement, counsel need not rely on oral agreements alone. Several alternative methods exist to document the agreement.

Written Offers

A written offer, with other evidence, can establish the terms of the agreement.[49] Acceptance of the written offer may be shown in several ways. These

---

[47] See 15 USC §1632 and 69 Am Jur 2d *Securities Regulation-Federal* §§123-146(1973).

[48] For example, regarding notice provisions for settlement of a nationwide class action filed in a state court, see Phillips Petroleum v Shutts, 472 US 797 (1985).

[49] *See* 15A Am Jur 2d *Compromise and Settlement* §§7, 9, 11, & 49 (1976).

include oral statements, the other parties' conduct, and written acceptances.[50] Oral acceptance statements are naturally the most difficult to prove if they are disputed later. Conduct, as acceptance of a particular agreement, may also be difficult to prove later if it is disputed. The problem of proof is demonstrating not only that the conduct shows acceptance of an agreement, but also that it shows acceptance of that particular form of the agreement, rather than some other version of an agreement. Written acceptances are best from the standpoint of later enforcement. These may come close to, or may, in fact, constitute, a formal written agreement.[51]

The written offer may be in the form of a conditional letter. This type of letter indicates the basic terms, which are then conditioned on some act by the other party. At times, these conditions may include that the offeree tender a written acceptance to the offeror.

Written offers should normally contain an expiration date. Otherwise, they may be "accepted" much later, after a party no longer desires the transaction or settlement. A court then may be faced with adjudicating the validity of the alleged acceptance based on a standard of reasonableness, i.e., that the offer was extended for a reasonable time.[52]

Letters of Intent

Letters of intent state that a party seeks, or is willing, to enter into an agreement by outlining certain major terms, with the remaining provisions to be worked out later. Major terms could include, for example, the identity of the specific item to be purchased (such as particular land, services, goods, etc.) and the total price.

Often, letters of intent specify that they are subject to the resolution of all remaining terms in a formal, written agreement executed by the parties. This caveat is inserted to avoid having courts rule that an agreement has been reached on the major terms, that the minor terms can be implied by reasonableness and custom, and that therefore a complete and binding agreement exists. For the same reason that applies to offers, letters of intent should usually contain expiration dates.

Confirming Letters

A confirming letter is directed to the other party or its counsel. The confirming letter details the terms of the agreement. Since it is signed by only one

---

[50] 17 Am Jur 2d *Contracts* §§43-51 (1964).

[51] *See id* §§41, 43 & 44.

[52] The UCC §2-205 provides that:

Firm Offers

An offer by a merchant to buy or sell goods in a signed writing which by its terms gives assurance that it will be held open is not revocable, for lack of consideration, during the time stated *or if no time is stated for a reasonable time, but in no event may such period of irrevocability exceed three months;* but any such term of assurance on a form supplied by the offeree must be separately signed by the offeror.

(Emphasis added.)

party, it is less effective as proof of an agreement than a formal agreement. Furthermore, it is essential that delivery be through a means which can be proved in court later, if the need arises to rely on the confirming letter.

In the absence of a letter in response which denies the existence of an agreement or which contradicts the purported terms of the confirming letter, however, such a confirming letter provides powerful evidence in the event of a subsequent dispute. Therefore, it is imperative to respond to confirming letters that, in fact, do not reflect an actual agreement between the parties.

A purported confirming letter may be quite lengthy, so that a detailed response would be time consuming. When this situation arises, a short response may be preferable.

Example 11-16

Your July 17, 1987, letter is completely in error. There is not now, and there never has been, an agreement on the terms of the sale of the medical practice.

Example 11-17

Contrary to your August 5, 1987, letter, we have never agreed to deviate from the terms of our August 1, 1987, letter. If you wish to accept those terms, notify us in a writing delivered within 5 days from the date of this letter.

Notes and Memoranda

The terms of an agreement may be recorded in the internal notes or memoranda of a party. Since the other party has had no contemporaneous opportunity to respond, their probative value in the event of a dispute is less than that of confirming letters that are transmitted contemporaneously. Even to the extent that the notes or internal memoranda are perceived to reflect one party's understanding, the documents may not reflect the contemporaneous understanding of the other party(ies), unless they provide a specific account of the narrative interaction between the parties. If the documents record the words of each party, or at least the substance of their remarks, the documents can be used to derive the parties' understanding and intentions from their own spoken words, in the context of the overall conversation and surrounding events. Therefore, to the extent possible, notes or memoranda regarding an oral agreement should contain the comments of each person at the meeting, speakers in a telephone conversation, etc.

Four other factors can diminish or eliminate the probative value of notes or internal memorandums. These factors concern:

Memory

Authenticity

The contemplation of litigation

Hearsay

If the document was not made contemporaneously with the event, the writer's memory can be questioned. Unless provable by evidence, the authenticity of the alleged note or memorandum may be questioned. Self-serving internal documents written in the apparent contemplation of litigation can be viewed with a degree of skepticism by a judge or jury.

Depending on the circumstances, the admissibility of the document or its use as an exception to the rule against hearsay can be an additional problem. If the document was written by one present when the oral agreement was made, hearsay problems may be avoided through the exceptions for business records,[53] present recollection refreshed,[54] or past recollection recorded.[55] However, when the author was not even present at the conversation, but instead, wrote down an account of the conversation related by another, the hearsay on hearsay problems may render the documents inadmissible in the event of litigation. Therefore, the author should be one who was present at the time that the oral agreement was reached.

Court Orders

Agreements and settlements can also be documented by court orders in litigation. Two categories exist for such orders. First, an order can be expansive, in the sense that the order contains a complete account of the agreement. This is like a formal agreement, except that it is in the form of a court order.

Second, an order can be narrow, in that the order does not reflect the specifics of the settlement agreement. This lack of specificity may be because one or more of the parties wish to keep the particular terms secret. They could be concerned about the amount of money to be paid, or which party will be viewed as having prevailed. The objective may be to keep certain information from the public, creditors, employees, business relations, friends, etc. In such cases, the order will be relatively short and simple, reflecting only that the case is settled and dismissed. An order may also be drafted that way simply because the parties saw no need to set forth the settlement terms, or because it is the customary way that orders are drawn in a particular court.

With either the expansive or the narrow type of settlement order, the order can provide that the court will retain jurisdiction to enforce the agreement, or that the case will be reinstated in the event that a party violates the terms of the agreement. Even so, depending on the nature and the terms of the settlement, a narrow court order may not be sufficient to utilize in enforcing the terms of the agreement which are not stated in the order itself. This is particularly true with settlements involving nonmonetary provisions. For this reason, narrow orders normally are not employed with many types of nonmonetary settlements.[56]

---

[53] *See* Fed R Evid 803(6).

[54] *See* 81 Am Jur 2d *Witnesses* §§445-449 (1976).

[55] *See* Fed R Evid 803(5).

[56] For example, in trademark litigation, even if the defendant is willing to agree to change to an entirely unrelated trademark, the plaintiff may still insist on the entry of a detailed consent decree so that its rights can be readily enforced.

As long as the terms of the settlement can be shown in ways other than through the court order itself, such provisions for enforcement or reinstatement can still be effective, even though the details of the agreement are not contained in the order. Without provisions for enforcement or reinstatement in the court order reflecting the settlement, new litigation may need to be instituted in order to enforce the settlement agreement.

§11.08   Summary and Review

I. Draft with realistically high expectations, and avoid blindly following models, examples, or precedents

II. Build in coercive enforcement mechanisms, or alternative dispute resolution, if needed

III. Plan as appropriate for any secondary negotiation in drafting the terms

IV. Balance enhanced control from preparing the initial draft with cost effectiveness, including the practical feasibility of negotiating substantial revisions of the other lawyer's draft

V. Avoid terms that are so unfair in context of the deal that they create a risk of ruining the deal when they are seen by the other side, unless that risk is acceptable

VI. Be precise, creative, anticipate disputes, and avoid losing closure

VII. Use shorter, less complicated, plain English sentences for clarity

VIII. Avoid precision *only* if ambiguity is preferable for the client, exactness is impossible, it is too difficult or unimportant to spell out a future contingency, or a contingency permits a desired termination of the agreement

IX. Good faith provisions are subject to potential differing interpretations

X. Avoid a drafting process which leads to delays that risk repudiation of a tentative agreement

XI. Overly complicated proposals may be rejected in favor of simpler ones, especially if they are economically close in value

XII. Draw formal agreements with specificity to reflect all of the parties' understandings without ambiguity

XIII. Consider that the agreement may be interpreted in light of the law, parol evidence, and unwritten modifications, if permitted

XIV. Avoid oral agreements unless a high degree of trust and low stakes are present, or local custom or the relationship of the parties requires it. Be aware of whether a written agreement is required by law.

XV. Draft settlements, releases, and covenants not to sue with care, to preserve or avoid further claims

XVI. Use standard terms if they are well understood, and nonstandard terms if they are more easily understood or better reflect idiosyncratic aspects of the agreement

XVII. Include any terms required by law

XVIII. An agreement may be documented by a formal agreement, a written offer, letters of intent, confirming letters, contemporaneous notes and memoranda, and court orders

Ethics and Caveats

12

§12.01 The Negotiator's Self-Interest

The earlier discussion of credibility focused on the negotiator's need to be believed if he or she is to function effectively.[1] Ethics can be viewed as the legal, moral, and social constraints on negotiating behavior. To some degree, custom also is a factor, and this varies with the geographic area and the times.

For example, the specific outcome in *Brown v Board of Education*[2] resulted in part from internal and external negotiations involving the United States Supreme Court.[3] These included *ex parte* communications between Justice Frankfurter and a key attorney at the United States Department of Justice, who was one of his former law clerks. As that attorney recalled his *ex parte* relationship with Justice Frankfurter regarding the government's position in the case and the method by which the Court could frame a decision that would be politically acceptable to the nation:

> As I look now, I can see myself in *Brown v. Board of Education* as having
> been his junior partner, or law clerk emeritus, in helping him work out

---

[1] See **§3.02** regarding credibility.

[2] 347 US 483 (1954) and 349 US 294 (1955).

[3] Elman, *The Solicitor General's Office, Justice Frankfurter, and Civil Rights Litigation*, 100 Harv L Rev 817 (1987).

the best solution for the toughest problem to come before the court in this century.[4]

That recollection reflects a problem solving strategy, including using the tactics of allies and selective information disclosure. Of course, such *ex parte* communications would be highly unethical under present-day standards, even assuming that custom at that time permitted such behavior.

Apart from custom, and before examining the civil and criminal areas of practice, the negotiator's self-interest in ethical behavior should be noted. At a basic level, there are the issues of self respect, potential criminal or civil liability, and professional discipline. Obvious, but at times overlooked, constraints exist against coercion, duress, fraud, conspiracy to defraud or induce a breach of contract, or other conduct violating civil or criminal law. Beyond those concerns is credibility. An attorney can function more effectively if trusted and believed. Therefore, it is in the lawyer's self interest to behave ethically, because one's reputation becomes known. In large cities, lawyers most often practice within certain specialized areas and segments of the legal, business, and social communities. Even in a large metropolitan area with a large number of attorneys, one's reputation for truth and veracity often becomes known to those with whom a negotiation is being conducted.

Furthermore, if one negotiator suddenly feels that he or she has been misled during the negotiation by the other negotiator, the entire negotiation process can break down. The same is true if one negotiator believes that the other negotiator is reneging on an issue for which an agreement has already been reached. In such instances, both the attorney and the client can very well decide that any further negotiation will not be worthwhile. Their motivation may be either because of the highly distasteful treatment itself, or because they would no longer be comfortable attempting to rely on any agreement that might result. Even if the negotiation continues, such great caution may be exercised that the entire process becomes extremely difficult, if not wholly impractical.

§12.02   Civil Matters

In general, material misstatements of fact are banned.[5] Such misrepresenta-

---

[4] *Id* 844.

[5] The American Bar Association's Model Code of Professional Responsibility, DR 7-102 (1985), Representing A Client Within The Bounds Of The Law, states as follows:

(A) In his representation of a client, a lawyer shall not:

(1) File a suit, assert a position, conduct a defense, delay a trial or take other action on behalf of his client when he knows or when it is obvious that such action would serve merely to harass or maliciously injure another.

(2) Knowingly advance a claim or defense that is unwarranted under existing law, except that he may advance such claim or defense if it can be supported by good faith argument for an extension, modification, or reversal of existing law.

(3) *Conceal or knowingly fail to disclose that which he is required by law to reveal.*

(4) Knowingly use perjured testimony or false evidence.

(5) *Knowingly make a false statement of law or fact.*

tions can be considered to constitute fraud, as well as an ethical breach. They provide a basis to void an agreement.[6] Material misrepresentations can also create liability for compensatory and punitive damages.[7]

An issue arises when counsel makes a factually accurate statement which is not misleading, but the other negotiator draws an unwarranted inference. As long as counsel does not act in a manner which in any way confirms the unwarranted inference, counsel has not engaged in misrepresentation. In determining whether counsel has confirmed the unwarranted inference and therefore engaged in misrepresentation, silence as well as affirmative acts can be considered.

Even if the attorney is not responsible for the other negotiator's misperception, problems can arise. The other attorney may actually believe that counsel said something which was a misrepresentation. Although that belief is erroneous, it can lead to a genuinely believed assertion that there was a misrepresentation, and one-against-one contradictory testimony to determine who is believed by a judge or a jury. Even without claims of misrepresentation, an attorney who feels misled will be far more difficult to deal with in the remainder of the negotiation. Counsel therefore must decide whether to correct erroneous inferences, even if he or she is not responsible for the error. This requires balancing the potential gain from nonaction against the risks described above.

Virtually all negotiations involve seeking to persuade the other side that one's bottom line is higher than it really is, and that one's position is stronger than it really is, and may well involve such tactics as raising a false issue to create a basis for a later tradeoff.[8] These actions, and therefore the negotiating process itself, involve less than total openness and candor, and entail misleading the other side to a degree.[9] Such conduct, intrinsic as it is to the negotiation

---

(6) Participate in the creation or preservation of evidence when he knows or it is obvious that the evidence is false.

(7) Counsel or assist his client in conduct that the lawyer knows to be illegal or fraudulent.

(8) Knowingly engage in other illegal conduct contrary to a Disciplinary Rule. (Emphasis added.)

[6] *See* Perschbacher, *Regulating Lawyers' Negotiations,* 27 Ariz L Rev 75, 80, n 20 (1985); Virzi v Grand Trunk Warehouse & Cold Storage Co, 571 F Supp 507 (ED Mich 1983) (held that the failure of plaintiff's attorney to disclose plaintiff's death was unethical and voided the settlement that had been reached); Spaulding v Zimmerman, 263 Minn 346, 116 NW2d 704 (1962) (where court approval of a proposed settlement was sought, there was a duty on the part of the defendant to disclose that its medical examination of the plaintiff found an aneurysm of the aorta that was a result of the accident).

[7] Slotkin v Citizens Cas Co, 614 F2d 301 (2d Cir 1979) (holding a defense attorney liable for misrepresenting the amount of the defendant's insurance to plaintiff's attorney and to the court); Kath v Western Media, Inc, 684 P2d 98 (Wyo 1984) (suit for attorney's fees and court costs based on an attorney's failure to make required disclosures).

[8] *See* §5.08.

[9] White, Negotiation: *Machiavelli and the Bar: Ethical Limitations on Lying in Negotiation,* in S. Goldberg, E. Green & F. Sander, Dispute Resolution 69 (1985); Note, *Private Settlement as Alternative Adjudication: A Rationale for Negotiation Ethics,* 18 U Mich JL Ref 503, 525 (1985).

process, has long been established as ethically acceptable behavior.[10] On the other hand, as discussed above, material misrepresentations are improper. The ethical dilemma therefore becomes where to draw the line between ethically and necessarily seeking to create certain false impressions, and making unethical, specific, material misrepresentations.[11]

The American Bar Association's prior Code of Professional Responsibility did not include a general obligation on the part of a negotiator to be equitable or frank with the other side.[12] The ABA has, however, attempted to draw that ethical line through its Model Rules Of Professional Conduct. Those rules include the following:

Rule 4.1: Truthfulness In Statements To Others[13]
In the course of representing a client a lawyer shall not knowingly:

(a)   make a false statement of material fact or law to a third person; or

(b)   fail to disclose a material fact to a third person when disclosure is necessary to avoid assisting a criminal or fraudulent act by a client, unless disclosure is prohibited by Rule 1.6.[14]

Rule 4.2: Fairness To Other Participants[15]

---

[10] *See* White, *supra* note 9; Note, *supra* note 9.

[11] Perschbacher, *supra* note 6, at 127-28.

[12] Note, *supra* note 9, at 506. *See* Model Code of Professional Responsibility DR 7-102 in note 5.

[13] The ABA's Comment to this rule is as follows:
Misrepresentation: A lawyer is required to be truthful when dealing with others on a client's behalf, but generally has no affirmative duty to inform an opposing party of relevant facts. A misrepresentation can occur if the lawyer incorporates or affirms a statement of another person that the lawyer knows is false. Misrepresentations can also occur by failure to act.
Statements of Fact: This Rule refers to statements of fact. Whether a particular statement should be regarded as one of fact can depend on the circumstances. Under generally accepted conventions in negotiation, certain types of statements ordinarily are not taken as statements of material fact. Estimates of price or value placed on the subject of a transaction and a party's opinions as to an acceptable settlement of a claim are in this category, and so is the existence of an undisclosed principal except where nondisclosure of the principal would constitute fraud.
Fraud by Client: Paragraph (b) recognizes that substantive law may require a lawyer to disclose certain information to avoid being deemed to have assisted the client's crime or fraud. The requirement of disclosure created by this paragraph is, however, subject to the obligations created by Rule 1.6.

[14] Rule 1.6 deals with confidentiality between lawyers and clients.

[15] The ABA's comment to this rule is as follows:
Fairness: Fairness in negotiation implies that representation by or on behalf of one party to the other party be truthful. This requirement is reflected in contract law, particularly the rules relating to fraud and mistake. A lawyer involved in negotiations has an obligation to assure as far as practicable that the negotiations conform to the law's requirements in this regard.
Disclosure: Under the usually accepted conventions of negotiation, the parties have

(a) In conducting negotiations a lawyer shall be fair in dealing with other participants.

(b) A lawyer shall not make a knowing misrepresentation of fact or law, or fail to disclose a material fact known to the lawyer, even if adverse, when disclosure is:

(1) required by law or the rules of professional conduct; or

(2) necessary to correct a manifest misapprehension of fact or law resulting from a previous representation made by the lawyer or known by the lawyer to have been made by the client, except that counsel for an accused in a criminal case

---

only limited duties of disclosure to each other. Generally, a party is not required to apprise another party of background facts or collateral opportunities for gain that may accrue as a result of a transaction between them. Facts that must be disclosed do not include estimates of price or value that a party places on the subject of a transaction, or a party's intentions as to an acceptable settlement of a claim, or the existence of an undisclosed principal except where nondisclosure would constitute a fraud. A party is permitted to suggest advantages to an opposing party that may be insubstantial from an objective point of view. The precise contours of the legal duties concerning disclosure, representation, puffery, overreaching, and other aspects of honesty in negotiations cannot be concisely stated. They have changed over time and vary according to circumstances. They also can vary according to the parties' familiarity with transactions of the kind involved. Thus, the modern law of commercial transactions places duties of disclosure on sellers that go well beyond the classic rule of caveat emptor, and modern securities often must conform to elaborate disclosure rules. It is a lawyer's responsibility to see that negotiations conducted by the lawyer conform to applicable legal standards, whatever they may be.

In negotiation, as in litigation, a lawyer generally has no duty to inform an opposing party of relevant facts and circumstances. However, it is the lawyer's duty to be forthcoming when the lawyer or the client has misled another party with respect to a matter of fact or law, for in such circumstances the failure to act is the equivalent of actively misleading the other party. A lawyer should not induce a belief that the lawyer is disinterested in a matter when in fact he or she represents a client.

Whether there should be a further burden of disclosure on a lawyer has long been a matter of some controversy. Canon 41 of the Canons of Ethics required, in general terms, that "when a lawyer discovers that some fraud or deception has been practiced he should endeavor to rectify it," if necessary by undertaking to "inform the injured person or his counsel." A more limited requirement was imposed by DR 7-102(B) of the ABA Model Code of Professional Responsibility. The competing considerations are clear but difficult to resolve. A lawyer could properly be regarded as having a professional responsibility to see that negotiations under his or her auspices are informed on all sides. However, to make a lawyer responsible for an opposing party's information about the matter in negotiation exposes the lawyer to charges of misfeasance that can be easily contrived, and exposes the transaction to additional risk of being easily avoided on the ground of mistake. The likelihood of these consequences is especially severe when the facts concerning the matter in negotiations are inherently uncertain or complex, or where there is substantial discrepancy between parties' access to information about the matter. Counsel for the accused in a criminal case is subject to constraint against disclosing during negotiations facts that might incriminate the client. *See also* Rule 1.7. . . .

is not required to make such a correction when it would require disclosing a misrepresentation made by the accused.

   (c) A lawyer shall not:

      (1) engage in the pretense of negotiating with no substantial purpose other than to delay or burden another party;[16]

      (2) illegally obstruct another party's rightful access to information relevant to the matter in negotiation;

      (3) communicate directly with another party who the lawyer knows is represented by other counsel, except with the consent of the party's counsel or as authorized by law.

Rule 4.3: Illegal, Fraudulent Or Unconscionable Transactions[17]

A lawyer shall not conclude an agreement, or assist a client in concluding an agreement, that the lawyer knows or reasonably should know is illegal, contains legally prohibited terms, would work a fraud, or would be held to be unconscionable as a matter of law.

Another general guideline that has been suggested is that the duty to disclose information honestly in a negotiation is equivalent to the attorney's duty to disclose information honestly to the court in litigation.[18] The rationale of this proposal is that, since negotiation is an alternative to trial, the results of negotiations and trials should be essentially equivalent on an overall basis.[19] Of course, this suggestion is, at best, only indirectly applicable to transactional negotiations, since those are not a substitute for litigation.

States, by statute, by rule of their respective supreme courts, or by other regulation, may follow the American Bar Association's Model Rules, impose their own rules, or choose to remain silent on the subject. There is relatively little in terms of case law, statutes, rules, or regulations directly regarding the

---

[16] This should be considered in relationship to §§3.10-3.14.

[17] The ABA's Comment to this rule is as follows:

Although a lawyer is generally not responsible for the substantive fairness of the result of a negotiation, the lawyer has a duty to see that the product is not offensive to the law. There are many legal proscriptions concerning contractual agreements. Being a party to some types of agreement is a penal offense. Some types of contractual provisions are prohibited by law, such as provisions purporting to waive certain legally conferred rights. Modern commercial law provides that grossly unfair contracts are unconscionable and may therefore be invalid. Such proscriptions are intended to secure definite legal rights. As an officer of the legal system, a lawyer is required to observe them. On the other hand, there are legal rules that simply make certain contractual provisions unenforceable, allowing one or both parties to avoid the obligation. Inclusion of such provisions in a contract may be unwise but it is not ethically improper to include a provision whose legality is subject to reasonable argument.

[18] Note, *supra* note 9, at 504.

[19] *Id.*

conduct of negotiations.[20] In addition to the express law and rules, some guidance can be obtained by looking to the general law of contract, agency, tort, and malpractice.[21] Depending on the particular context of litigation, though, care must be exercised in applying some of those principles.[22] For instance, discovery rules may mandate some disclosures.

Statements or actions constituting ethical pressure on the other party, as compared to those that constitute an unethical threat, can vary, depending on the situation and on the parties' respective power.[23] Acts considered to be duress or deceit when directed against a powerless party may not be when used against a powerful party.[24] Threats of criminal prosecution are normally considered to be improper even where valid grounds exist for such a prosecution.[25] On the other hand, the Supreme Court in *Town of Newton v Rumery*, [26] that, in at least some circumstances, a release of a civil rights claim in return for the dismissal of a criminal prosecution does not violate due process, and is valid and enforceable. Nevertheless, if prohibited by state law, agreements based on a threat of criminal prosecution may be voidable by a state court, and the attorney who uses them to protect a client from civil liability could be deemed to have acted unethically and face personal liability or disciplinary sanctions.[27]

§12.03 Criminal Matters

The same general ethical constraints that govern civil cases also apply to criminal cases. In addition, the constitutional right to due process requires certain disclosures by the prosecution. Thus, in *Brady v Maryland*, [28] the Supreme Court held that the prosecution must disclose any exculpatory evidence to the defendant. Depending on the circumstances of the particular case, a failure to do so may be grounds to vacate a plea agreement.

A material misrepresentation by the government may also be grounds to vacate a plea agreement. In *United States v Schubert*, [29] the defendant's decision to plead guilty, rather than attempt to argue a defense of entrapment, was affected by the government's representation that its affiant was not a govern-

---

[20] Perschabacher, *supra* note 6, at 76-77.

[21] *Id* 79-80.

[22] *Id.*

[23] *Id* 80-88.

[24] *Id.*

[25] *Id* 88; Restatement (Second) of Contracts, §176(b) and Comment c (1979); *In re* Charles, 90 Or 127, 618 P2d 1281 (1980) (reprimanding an attorney for threatening a criminal prosecution during a negotiation).

[26] 107 S Ct 1187 (1987).

[27] For example, the Illinois Supreme Court's Code of Professional Responsibility, Rule 7-105, Threatening Criminal Prosecution, states that: "A lawyer shall not present, participate in presenting, or threaten to present criminal charges to obtain an advantage in a civil matter."

[28] 373 US 83 (1963).

[29] 728 F2d 1364 (11th Cir 1984).

ment informant. That representation was false. When the truth became known, the Court held that the defendant had a right to withdraw his plea of guilty.

Overcharging is the practice of charging a defendant with a more serious crime in order to create negotiating leverage. It allows a prosecutor to make a concession in plea bargaining by reducing the charge to the charge which should have been filed initially. Such overcharging by the prosecution to gain a negotiating advantage in plea bargaining is unethical.[30]

§12.04   Caveats

The first caveat is not to inform the other side of problems unless a disclosure is necessary. In seeking to operate fairly with the other lawyer, counsel may focus on an area as a problem for the other party that really was not of concern to that party beforehand, or even to which the other party had acquiesced and agreed.

Example 12-1

ATTORNEY A:	Now I know that you agreed to binding arbitration just before the break, but you sounded unsure about it.
ATTORNEY B:	Well, I'm not really certain if that's the right course of action for us.
ATTORNEY A:	Alright, why don't you think about it?
ATTORNEY B:	Actually, I don't think that I want arbitration at all.
ATTORNEY A:	Oh. Well, we're back to square one.

Generally, there is no need or requirement to alert the other party to concerns which it perhaps should have, but either does not have or does not recognize. Thus, in Example 12-1, Attorney A's concern for what Attorney B had done was both unnecessary and detrimental to A's client. Here, not only did negotiator A unnecessarily highlight the issue after having gained an agreement on arbitration, but A then also failed to move the discussion forward once the issue was again the subject of discussion at A's own initiative.

Three exceptions exist to the general rule that counsel should not create possible problems for the client by highlighting concerns for the other party which the other side has not raised. These three exceptions involve:

1.   Legal requirements

---

[30] Roberts, *Negotiation In a Criminal Case-Prosecution,* in Attorney's Guide to Negotiation (1979).

2. Short-term best interests
3. Long-term best interests

First, as noted above, case law, statute, or a rule may require disclosure.[31] If so, counsel must be aware of, and must comply with, these requirements. These include ethical standards and prohibitions.

The second exception for raising the other party's concern occurs when:

1. Counsel is quite confident that the other negotiator will raise the concern or problem anyway
2. Counsel has a good answer or solution to the concern or problem

In these situations, the anticipatory raising of the concern or problem demonstrates sensitivity to the other party's needs, and can create or enhance an atmosphere of trust.

The third exception occurs within the more general category of special actions for the sake of long-term relationship negotiations. Many negotiations concern a transaction or settlement in which the parties do not, and will not, have a continuing relationship. Other negotiations, however, are aimed at long-term relationships, such a partnerships, joint ventures, shareholder agreements, some manufacturing or supply agreements, certain employment contracts, labor-management collective bargaining agreements, etc. In negotiating an agreement that relates to a long-term relationship, one must consider the danger of repudiation or lack of good faith efforts that can arise if a party becomes disenchanted with the arrangement. Whenever these dangers exist and are significant in the potential long-term relationship, one's thinking should not be restricted to possible contingent, punitive measures to discourage breaches of the agreement. It is equally important to consider acting affirmatively to structure an arrangement which is not only advantageous to one's own client, but is also sufficiently beneficial to the other party to minimize or eliminate the dangers of repudiation or lack of good faith efforts in implementing the agreement.

Three types of negotiations raise these concerns. The first are those that seek to establish a present long-term relationship. The second are those aimed at continuing such a long-term relationship. The third are agreements which are designed to create an immediate, initial single transaction or short-term agreement that is planned as the first step towards establishing a long-term relationship.

If it is appropriate to take affirmative measures to structure an agreement with sufficient mutual benefit because of the specific long-term context involved, counsel has several options. A negotiator can raise matters that may be, or that may become, serious concerns for the other party if counsel:

1. Has an answer or solution in mind which he or she is confident will be acceptable

---

[31] *See also* §4.02.

2. Believes that demonstrating sensitivity to the issue has overall benefits for the negotiation that outweigh the risks of opening up a problem area

3. Determines that discovering the other party's reaction to and understanding of the issue is necessary

4. Finds that the concern is so likely to emerge later with potential serious consequences that it must be faced during the negotiation

Consultation with one's own client is usually critical in anticipating the other party's concerns and problems. It can also assist in deciding whether good solutions are presently known. Lastly, client consultations are often essential to determine whether a sufficient danger of repudiation or lack of good faith efforts exists to make affirmative measures to prevent such contingencies appropriate.

Two other types of affirmative actions should also be considered in such situations. First, one should ascertain whether it is feasible to generate publicity or credit for the other party, thereby creating or enhancing the psychological, social, business, or political value of the agreement. Second, to the extent that profit is an issue, counsel should determine whether the other party will, or can be, allowed sufficient profit to avoid a later desire to repudiate or sabotage the agreement by failing to employ reasonable, good faith efforts. An agreement that turns out to be unprofitable, or so much less profitable than alternatives as to be viewed as unprofitable, creates strong economic and psychological disincentives against full performance. Accordingly, counsel's own client may suffer a detriment, rather than gain a benefit, from a highly one-sided long-turn agreement.

Evaluating whether to create additional benefits for the other party is difficult. The potential dangers of pressing for a more one-sided agreement must be weighed against the potential benefits if the more advantageous agreement is made, and the other party does not repudiate or use less than proper efforts. Furthermore, the possibility of adjustments if difficulties arise must be considered against:

1. The problems of ascertaining the difficulties before any damage occurs

2. The potential adverse, precedential value of displaying a willingness to modify a favorable agreement

3. Any difficulties that will arise in salvaging the relationship and the basic structure of the deal

Example 12-2

Counsel represents a manufacturer of raw materials in connection with a contract between the client and a supplier, who is essential to the client in being able to maintain its operations without serious disruptions in production. Due to problems that the supplier is experiencing, an agreement is, or can be, reached that is very one-sided in favor of the client. Unless the agreement is made less one-sided and less favorable to the client, however, counsel and the client foresee the probability that the supplier will find itself forced in to bankruptcy. Since eliminating the essential supplier is against the client's own best interests, and since that is what is very likely to occur without additional voluntary concessions, the issue is clear, and the concessions need to be made.

Although Example 12-2 presents a clear picture, the issue is usually less than clear and requires careful evaluation.

The second general caveat is to consider alternatives to deadlock and statutory sales for dissolution when structuring entities. Some long-run agreements consist of establishing a new legal entity. It may be a corporation, partnership, or joint venture. Special issues arise when the entity is to be owned by a very small group so that deadlock issues can arise. The question then is whether traditional dissolution remedies would be effective and efficient, or whether an alternative arrangement should be structured into the agreement. The latter is often preferable to the sale of assets, which is the normal procedure under traditional legal measures. The creative mechanisms can include an outside director to avoid deadlock, alternative dispute resolution procedures in the event of deadlock, and methods for dividing the business assets, liabilities, and operations. Employment agreements, consulting contracts for owners, shareholder agreements, and ownership buy-out agreements can also be used to establish the parties' relationships so that the entity functions as the parties originally intended. This decreases the chances of a deadlock as well.

The third caveat is to obtain proper authorization and avoid conflicts of interest in representing multiple clients. In representing multiple clients in the same matter, counsel ordinarily cannot enter into any agreements unless:

1. Each and every client authorizes it
2. Some clients authorize it, and the remainder knowingly and intelligently do not object to the attorney's agreeing to it on behalf of the other clients after sufficient counseling so that they can make an informed choice
3. Some authorize it and the remainder do not waive their right to object to the agreement, but there is no conflict of interest between those clients seeking to enter into the agreement and those who oppose it
4. Some authorize it, and the agreement does not encompass the rights, claims, or defenses of the remaining clients, and their rights, claims, or defenses are entirely preserved

In some instances, clients may have initially agreed to be bound by a majority vote or by the decision of a particular member or members of the group of clients. However, a serious question exists regarding whether the client later remains bound by such an agreement when he or she is opposed to the decision that is made for the group.[32] If not, as with any serious conflict of interest among multiple clients in the same matter, the lawyer may need to withdraw.

---

[32] A. Kaufman, Problems In Professional Responsibility 45 (1975).

§12.05   Summary and Review

   I. Self interest in credibility and self respect
  II. Avoid criminal and civil liability, as well as disciplinary action, including for coercion, duress, fraud, or conspiracy to induce a breach of contract
 III. Beware of inadvertent material misrepresentations, or statements later perceived as such
  IV. Virtually all negotiations inherently involve a degree of information withholding or misdirection
   V. Brady disclosures for prosecution
  VI. Overcharging of a crime is unethical
 VII. Do not inform the other side of problems unless it is necessary to do so because of legal requirements, the other side will discover it later and counsel has a good solution, or to build or enhance a long-term relationship
VIII. Build in sufficient mutual benefit if concerned about potential repudiation or lack of good faith efforts
  IX. In creating new entities, owned by a small group, consider alternative to deadlock and statutory sale if dissolution occurs
   X. In representing multiple clients, beware of conflicts of interest or lack of authorization from all clients

Appendix A
A Working Guide for Negotiation

The Working Guide is a readily used structure to examine and plan for actual negotiations. It integrates and organizes the material into a succinct form for a comprehensive, step-by-step analysis. Using key words and phrases, it allows the reader to review the choices and information without having to search back through the text.

Systematic Planning

    I. Common errors include a failure to obtain or consider information, failing to close an acceptable deal, making a less favorable deal than possible, uncontrolled horse trading, deadlock on nonessential points, and a lack of objectivity due to relationships

   II. Do it in a cost-effective way

Step 1: Prenegotiation Information Gathering

    I. Obtain any information that is needed and available

   II. Including your client's goals, the issues, the market, vital interests of each party and its negotiator, strengths and weaknesses of each party and negotiator, indications of the other party's bottom line, and effects or influences from current economic, social, and political climates

  III. Identify informational gaps and uncertainties for probes and evaluation during the negotiation, especially regarding informational tactics and setting the agenda

Step 2: Determine the Client's Goals

    I. Client Goals
       A. Tangible or intangible
       B. Objective and subjective value
       C. Can shift or modify over time

      D. Affect choice of strategy and tactics, as well as tone

      E. Important in determining the client's bottom line

  II. Aggressive Client Goals

      A. Seek to undermine, deprive, damage, or otherwise injure a rival or opponent

      B. May be emotional choice and objectively illogical, but also can be objectively logical under an economic cost-benefit analysis

  III. Competitive Client Goals

      A. Seek to gain more than the other party

      B. Win/Lose

  IV. Cooperative Client Goals

      A. Agreement leads to mutual gain *rather* than a loss for one party corresponding to a gain for the other party

      B. Growing "pie," not a limited pie

  V. Self-Centered Client Goals—Client has an objective to achieve, regardless of what the other party receives

  VI. Defensive Client Goals—Seek to avoid a particular outcome

  VII. Combinations of Client Goals

      A. Multiple client goals are usually present

      B. May lead to conflicting client goals

      C. Can require establishing priorities for goals

      D. Sometimes conflicts between goals can be eliminated

      E. Ultimately the client's decision and counsel should form a team with the client

      F. Plan for each goal

      G. Identify and prioritize the goals with the client

      H. Separate essential and desirable goals

      I. Includes long-run and short-run goals

      J. Counsel the client on legal ramifications so the real implications of each goal are understood, as well as for careful consideration of long-term versus short-term benefits, if necessary

      K. Goals must be sufficiently concrete to be later translated into authority with the client

      L. Each goal becomes an issue, and each combination of goals with tradeoffs between them also becomes an issue

Step 3:   Identifying the Issues

  I. Issues arise where parties' goals are or may conflict

  II. Analyze on an issue-by-issue basis, subissues, or packages of linked issues and subissues.

  III. Beware of artificially created issues being used as tradeoffs

  IV. Categorize as economic or noneconomic, and as long-run, short-run, or both

  V. Defining the issue can affect the outcome, and the definition should be formulated, in light of the other party's views, as favorably as feasible

    VI. Next, reexamine client goals in view of the information gathered and the issues, and counsel the client if goals need clarification or adjustment

   VII. Each of the remaining planning steps must be done for each issue or combination of issues

Step 4:   Analyze the Market

      I. Everything has a market

     II. Includes supply and demand

   III. Consider market practices regarding expected and non-negotiable terms, some of which may be set by law

   IV. Market value and terms can vary over time, and some terms may be negotiable in one context and non-negotiable in another

    V. Practices and norms can affect or limit negotiation methods, although unorthodox approaches should be considered

   VI. Estimate the other party's view of the market

   VII. After the market is analyzed, check the information gathered, client goals, and issues for gaps, inconsistencies, or other errors. Adjust as necessary with the client.

Step 5:   Assess Strengths and Weaknesses

      I. Identify strengths and weaknesses of the client, each other party, and every negotiator

     II. Planning can change or diminish actual or perceived weaknesses, create strengths, or create a weakness for the other party

   III. Mention weakness which the other party is unaware of only if
        A. The other side is certain to think of it anyway, or
        B. Disclosure is required by law

   IV. Consider the parties' relationship regarding any dependence or independence

    V. Based on
        A. Vital interests
        B. Situational pressures and constraints, and
        C. The other negotiator's personal interests, pressures, and constraints

   VI. Vital interests reveal needs, strengths, and weaknesses. Plan to utilize strengths and the other side's weaknesses, avoid or alter own weaknesses, and fulfill interests and needs of the other party to the extent necessary or appropriate

   VII. Build rapport by understanding and being sensitive to the other side's needs

  VIII. Generally more persuasive to articulate a position in terms of meeting the other side's needs than as a threat

   IX. Needs and interests can be for positive gain, fairness, or avoiding a loss

X. No agreement will be reached unless each party agrees its interests are better met by this agreement than continuing nonagreement

XI. A transactional agreement requires that the parties value the items being exchanged differently, or that the agreement will enlarge the pie

XII. Estimate which of the other party's interests are the vital ones based on its real needs, background, need for agreement, personal feelings, and other influences

XIII. Consider altering the other party's perception of its interests and needs, if that creates a more favorable negotiation context

XIV. A prior relationship between the parties can provide clues

XV. Requires analysis of benefits and risks from agreement and nonagreement

XVI. Take into account situational pressures or constraints

XVII. Evaluate the other negotiator's personal interests and personality, and those of any representational decision maker

XVIII. Decide whether to accept or disavow any inherited, rather than earned, reputation, and probe reputations inherited by others to determine whether they are deserved or an illusion

Step 6: Estimate the Other Party's Bottom Line and Opening Position

I. Use information from steps 1, 3, 4, and 5

II. The other side's bottom line is affected by its value of an outcome, the economic or noneconomic costs of delay or negotiating difficulties or termination, and its anticipation of your side's bottom line

III. Estimate the other side's bottom line as your lucky day, but not your wildest fantasy, to avoid underestimating or being unrealistic

IV. Estimate the other party's likely expectations, regardless of whether they are realistic

V. Estimate the other side's opening position based on whether it is likely to be higher than its highest expectation to create room for tradeoffs or compensate against underestimating, and, if so, how much higher

VI. Unrealistic demands may create or reinforce unrealistic client expectations, thereby reducing the chance for an otherwise acceptable agreement

VII. The other party's bottom line and opening position must be estimated for each issue and combination of issues

VIII. Next, anticipate the way that the other party will seek to open the negotiation, and devise moves to block, counter, or manipulate

IX. Review prior steps for errors or modifications in prior or current step

Step 7: Consider Win/Win Outcomes

I. Gain to one party without a corresponding loss to the other party, in which the giver wins rapport and, at times, the ability to demand reciprocity later

II. Mutual gain by expanding the pie

   III. Use whenever possible, and explore needs and objectives in a search for opportunities

   IV. May be substantive or procedural

    V. Anticipate the other party's view of win/win outcomes

   VI. Recheck prior steps for errors or modifications in those or the current step

Step 8:   Setting the Opening Position

     I. The initial substantive position

    II. Use high but realistic expectations to avoid underestimating or overestimating to the point of causing deadlock or termination

   III. Use information from steps 3 through 7

   IV. Set opening position above estimate of other party's bottom line to guard against underestimating, and allow for one or more concessions, if needed

    V. Establish for the entire negotiation, each issue, and any combinations of issues which may involve potential tradeoffs between issues

   VI. May be the client's decision, with counseling as needed, depending on client's level of sophistication and substantive involvement

  VII. Also plan reasons to justify it

 VIII. May or may not be used, depending on the actual way that the negotiation unfolds

   IX. Driving too hard of a bargain can lead to repudiation or lack of good faith efforts

Step 9:   Set the Bottom Line

     I. The point at which no agreement is better than any available agreement

    II. Use information from steps 2 through 8

   III. Establish for the entire negotiation, each issue, and each combination of issues where there can be tradeoffs between issues

   IV. This is the client's decision ultimately, after listening to the client's own views and counseling the client on legal, business, social, political, and personal factors, as appropriate

    V. Use outside experts for input, if needed

   VI. Generate a list of alternatives with client, and analyze each generally, taking the most aggressive first and the least aggressive last. The analysis includes risks, benefits, and the chances that each will occur

  VII. Counsel generally makes a recommendation, except for highly sophisticated clients

 VIII. Caution against unrealistic bottom lines, unless the alternatives to agreement are preferable to a realistic bottom line

   IX. Time the advice for when the client is psychologically ready to hear it

    X. Re-examine the earlier steps and this one for possible errors or adjustments

XI. The bottom line is set based on the alternative to reaching agreement, rather than the likelihood of achieving it, except for interim bottom lines during phases of the negotiation, which create the same dangers as bluffs

XII. Subject to change during the negotiation, so communicate with the client during the negotiation about the status of it

XIII. If changed, avoid looking like the initial opening position was a failed bluff

XIV. Exception for limited authority, in which the negotiator deliberately does not know the client's bottom line to resist pressure for concessions, maintain harmony in the negotiation by blaming someone not present, and demand information for the decision maker

Step 10:   Choosing Strategies

I. Strategy Choices are
   A. Personal credibility
   B. No concessions
   C. No further concessions
   D. Deadlock-breaking concessions only
   E. HRESSC
   F. Concede first
   G. Problem solving
   H. Purposes other than reaching an agreement, including delay, discovery, influencing the client, and influencing third parties
   I. Moving for closure

II. The lawyer counsels the client and chooses the strategies and tactics, except when a strategy or tactic itself will directly impact the client's life

III. Credibility
   A. Crucial
   B. Appearance of
      1. Attitude
      2. Preparation
   C. Honest behavior
   D. Created by
      1. Allies
      2. Actions
      3. Status

IV. No Concessions
   A. Unilaterally define the only possible agreement
   B. Most useful where
      1. Great disparity of power, or
      2. Equally attractive alternative available if offer rejected
   C. Also used if weak but can inflict devastating consequences
   D. Effect of time

          1. Power and needs can change
          2. May be too short for other strategies
     E. Can be used to avoid negotiation costs
     F. A method to extend equal offers to various parties
     G. Limited if need flexibility or it violates custom
     H. If its use is miscalculated, the attempt may block an otherwise acceptable agreement
     I. May temper with a nonaggressive tone
     J. Consider for aggressive, competitive, or self-centered goals
     K. Countermeasures
          1. Appeal to higher authority within the other party
          2. Ignore and proceed by seeking concessions and tradeoffs
          3. Justify a concession with a cost-saving or win/win aspect
          4. As a seller, offer less, thereby increasing the price, in effect
          5. As a buyer, demand more be included, thereby lowering the price, in effect
          6. Terminate the negotiation session
          7. Information disclosure
          8. Fact creation
          9. Win/win proposals
          10. Insert a new issue
          11. Deadlock
          12. Surprise
          13. Litigation
  V. No Further Concessions
     A. To force the other party to make the last concession
     B. For the overall agreement or an issue
     C. Timing is critical
 VI. Making Only Deadlock-Breaking Concessions
     A. Brinkmanship
     B. Dangerous
     C. Consider for aggressive, competitive, self-centered goals
     D. Countermeasures
          1. Deadlock
          2. Creation of movement
VII. HRESSC
     A. High Realistic Expectations with Small Systematic Concessions
     B. The most generally useful strategy
     C. Realistically high opening position
     D. Small, not too rapid concessions
     E. Systematic, planned concessions, including no or low cost ones
     F. For competitive, aggressive, self-centered goals
     G. Also for any competitive elements within cooperative goals
     H. Countermeasures
          1. HRESSC
          2. No concessions
          3. No further concessions

          4. Deadlock-breaking concessions only

          5. Problem solving

VIII. Concede First

    A. At opening stages of entire negotiation or one issue

    B. To create goodwill and movement

    C. Allows for demand of a reciprocal concession

    D. Relinquishes only limited value

    E. Must be used with other strategies

    F. Can backfire by raising the other party's expectations

    G. Do not use if weak or will be perceived as being weak

    H. Consider for competitive, cooperative, self-centered, or defensive client goals

    I. Consider for aggressive client goals if the other party is not the target to be injured

    J. Countermeasures: refusal to reciprocate

    K. Also may be used by the other party to lead to movement in the desired direction

IX. Problem Solving

    A. Second most generally useful strategy

    B. Four steps

        1. Procedural agreement

        2. Identification of problems

        3. Determination of common interests and limiting separate needs

        4. Discovery of solution

    C. Necessary conditions

        1. Mutual desire and agreement to use

        2. Real mutual interests, so the parties operate in good faith

        3. Jointly defined problems

        4. Win/win solutions, not capitulation

    D. Separation of needs and interests from positions

    E. Cooperative, sensitive demeanor

    F. Creativity and brainstorming

    G. Ideas from critically examined principles, precedent, or community practice

    H. Best for cooperative goals

    I. Useful for aggressive, self-centered, or competitive goals *only* if a cooperative element exists

    J. Countermeasures

        1. Refusal to participate, and

        2. Suggest win/lose solutions articulated as win/win ones

X. Purposes other than Agreement

    A. Can be used for any goal

    B. But can poison the atmosphere if it is discovered

    C. Delay

    D. Discovery

    E. Influencing the client or others

XI. Moving for Closure
    A. In total or on an issue
    B. To gain certainty of benefits without risk of losing them
    C. For all goals
    D. Used with other strategies
XII. Combining Strategies
    A. Any permutation or combination possible
    B. Sequential changes
    C. Issue-oriented shifts

Step 11: Tactical Choices

I. Informational Tactics
    A. Selective disclosure of information
        1. Consciously decide whether disclosure creates a more advantageous effect than withholding information
        2. To influence persuasively and thereby motivate the other party
        3. Can facilitate problem solving
        4. Timing of disclosures must be calculated to maximize or minimize impact
        5. Legally required disclosures
        6. Decisions whether to reveal client goals, needs, and interests
        7. Countering actual or perceived negatives
        8. Expected disclosures
        9. Settlement brochure and open file
        10. Visual aids
        11. Avoiding disclosure without creating distrust and without misrepresentation, through the use of favorable information, deflection, direct refusals to answer, and snow jobs
        12. Do not state anything as a fact unless reasonably certain of it
    B. Creation of Facts
        1. Legitimately add to or alter the facts
        2. Physical
        3. Win/win offers
        4. Use of third parties
        5. Threats
        6. Litigation, including its cost, changed witness or victim attitudes, and judicial rulings
        7. Legal precedent
    C. Funnel Approach
        1. For sources at least somewhat willing to disclose information
        2. Start with broad, general questions
        3. May be presented as casual and offhand
        4. Follow up with narrower and narrower questions

      5. Check information as appropriate

      6. Countermeasure: selective information disclosure

    D. Bargaining for Information

      1. In the negotiation or with third parties

      2. Trade for information or something else of value

      3. Can open the flow of information if one party otherwise fears that disclosure will not generate reciprocity

    E. Information through Discussion

      1. Conversation, debate, or argument

      2. Less adversarial versus more adversarial style and tone

      3. Use of questions

      4. Utilizing silence

      5. Selectivity

      6. Generalities and other deflections

      7. Use of the other party's own policies and principles

      8. Informal, off-the-record discussion

    F. Sources of Information

      1. Clients

      2. Other lawyers

      3. Others having experience with the other party, its negotiator, or similar situations

      4. Reference material

      5. Prior agreements as models

      6. Consultants and experts

      7. The government

      8. Inspections

      9. Private investigators

II. General Tactics

    A. Preconditions

      1. Basically non-negotiable demands which must be agreed to before the remainder of the negotiation proceeds

      2. Required as a tradeoff for the right to commence or continue negotiating

      3. May be at the outset of the negotiation, or for a phase or issue

      4. Can be procedural or substantive

      5. Necessary conditions

        a. Power, or

        b. Clarify a term essential to deciding whether to invest time and energy in further negotiation

      6. Can be dangerous, so use with caution, especially for a cooperative client goal, problem-solving strategy, or long-term relationship

    B. Making or Avoiding Making the First Offer

      1. Realistic first offer can establish the basic range for the negotiation

      2. Making the first offer effectively requires sufficient knowledge to be realistically high without conceding too much

      3. Client's time needs can dictate making the first offer

      4. Custom can affect who makes the first offer

      5. Useful for all client goals and strategies

C. Demand Responses to Offers and Positions

      1. To avoid unnecessary uncertainties

      2. Clarify an ambiguous response by stating an understanding that the point has been agreed on by the parties, if it is reasonable to do so

      3. Allow agreement on substance without requiring agreement on reasons, except if that is important to interpret the agreement in the future

      4. For all client goals and strategies, except for purposes other than reaching agreement

      5. Includes the negotiator's agreement to recommend the proposal to the client

      6. Countermeasures include lack of authority, expressing a need for more information or to explore other issues first before responding, or silence

      7. Respond to unrealistic proposals with probes of the other side's perceptions, a firm rejection with an explanation, an equally unrealistic counteroffer, or a realistic counteroffer coupled with the caveat that splitting the difference is unacceptable

D. Reciprocity

      1. Can be a demand for a reciprocal concession based on fairness

      2. Also can be a demand for a counteroffer after one's offer is rejected

      3. Requires that the offer is reasonable to justify reciprocity

      4. For all client goals, except aggressive ones inconsistent with concessions, and all strategies except no concessions or no further concessions

      5. Pitfalls of the norm of reciprocity: inappropriate concessions

      6. Countermeasures: awareness and judgment

E. Win/Win Proposals

      1. Unilaterally generate a mutually beneficial proposal that either expands the pie or involves little or no cost to one party, but is valued by the other

      2. Not always possible

      3. Generate by concentrating on differences between the parties' beliefs, values, projections, tradeoffs, and risk preferences

      4. Use for client goals except those aggressive goals aimed at weakening or destroying the other party, and for strategies

of no concessions, no further concessions, and negotiating for purposes other than reaching agreement

5. Especially useful for cooperative client goals and the problem-solving and HRESSC strategies

F. Concessions of Greater Value to One Party

1. Either objective or subjective value

2. May downplay the value of an item in order to obtain it

3. Ideal concession has much greater value to the other party than to the client, resulting in a substantial net gain

4. Can consist of demands inserted solely to be traded off later, or a series of small concessions to be traded for a larger one

5. Use for client goals except certain aggressive ones not permitting concessions, and for all strategies except no concessions, no further concessions, or negotiating for purposes other than agreement

G. Trial Proposals

1. A sudden shift to significantly different arrangements or terms with great uncertainty about whether it will be accepted or rejected

2. If rejected, it may still provide valuable information from the other side's reaction

3. Good for shifting the focus

4. Useful for all client goals and strategies except no concessions or no further concessions

5. Avoid large concessions, unless they are absolutely necessary or a firm reason can be provided to prevent being perceived as weak

H. Bargaining

1. Offer to exchange one item for a specified other item

2. Use reasoned positions

3. Extremely useful for competitive goals, and useful for other goals and all strategies which permit the use of concessions

I. Debate

1. An exchange of views to persuade the other side to agree or acquiesce

2. Requires creating an answer or direction of movement, and not stopping with a directionless argument or an unclear point for movement

3. Useful with all client goals and strategies

4. Often coupled with other tactics

5. Concentrate on specific substantive or procedural items

6. Carefully define issues

7. Avoid personal attacks or personality conflicts, unless necessary

8. Persuade with strengths, facing or diminishing weaknesses, forcing the other side to argue its weaknesses, and citing objective criteria as the basis for reasons whenever feasible

9. Motivate change by showing how the other side's needs can be met, and probe those needs as necessary in order to do so
10. Appeal to negotiator's personal interests, if appropriate
11. Countermeasures
   a. Do not be awed by supposedly objective criteria
   b. Challenge the validity or applicability of reasons or principles

J. Conditional Proposals
   1. Offer conditioned on resolving some or all remaining issues
   2. Appropriate for all client goals and strategies involving multiple issues with possible tradeoffs between issues

K. Power
   1. Ability to force agreement on immediate issues
   2. Exercise only after careful consideration of any intended and unintended short-term and, especially, long-term effects
   3. Evaluate ramifications with constituent groups and third parties
   4. Various forms of power
   5. Legal and moral restrictions
   6. Appropriate for all client goals and strategies except, generally, for cooperative goals and the problem-solving strategy
   7. Countermeasures include creating a sufficiently adverse potential effect to outweigh the gain from exercising power on a cost-benefit risk analysis

L. Bluff
   1. Falsely taking a position as nonmodifiable or as able to create a consequence
   2. If bluff is called, destroys or seriously undermines credibility
   3. Manuever out of having bluff called through "new information"
   4. Countermeasures include an outright refusal to acquiesce, selective information disclosure, debate, and face saving

M. Tone
   1. The atmosphere or climate of every negotiation
   2. Can affect whether agreement will result
   3. Unless pressure will work, avoid making the other side feel it is being manipulated into an unfavorable deal
   4. Anticipate and observe the other side's reaction to tone
   5. Consider long-run effects
   6. Generally, pleasant and nonadversarial or less adversarial tone for deal making, while more adversarial, but generally not unpleasant for litigation
   7. Use of assertive, but low-key, tone, unless pressure, adversarial, or enthusiastic tones are indicated

8. Enthusiasm for mutual benefits of agreement can create an atmosphere that increases the probability of agreement
9. Temporary changes in tone can be persuasive
10. One counter to an emotional tone is indicating understanding while focusing on the facts
11. Use and guard against own need to receive a tone of respect, approval, or being liked if it may cause inadvertent weakness
12. Tone may need to change to be consistent with a shift in strategy
13. Do not focus on tone and be misled about substantive concession patterns

N. Use of Alternative Opportunities
1. With an outside party
2. Mutually exclusive with reaching agreement in present negotiation
3. May necessitate simultaneous negotiations with different parties
4. Constitutes leverage in the negotiation
5. Provides a measure of market terms and values, and a floor for any agreement, depending on the degree of certainty that it is truly available
6. Can result from legitimate fact creation
7. May demand verification or other proof if suspect a bluff or face-saving tactics
8. As an alternative, use informational tactics to probe whether the opportunity is certain or uncertain, and comparable or more or less advantageous
9. Requires consideration of two reactive factors:
   a. Loyalty issue
   b. Whether the other side will perceive it as a threat or an inappropriate demand for bids or being whipsawed
10. Can be used with any client goal or strategy

O. Splitting the Difference
1. Use with all client goals
2. For all strategies except no concessions or no further concessions, or negotiating for purposes other than agreement, unless used as a ploy
3. Especially useful for deadlock-breaking concessions only, problem solving, and closure
4. Effective when
   a. A relatively small difference exists, and
   b. A split is fair
5. Unreasonable, but proportionately unimportant, difference can be appropriate to split if a cost-benefit risk analysis concludes that a resolution is preferable to investing time and energy or risking loss of an available agreement

6. Beware of creating an always split the difference precedent, and communicate an unwillingness to do so to the other party
7. Split large difference if
    a. Within authority, and
    b. Total deadlock after exhausting other approaches, or
    c. Time problem dictates moving for closure
8. Do not use as an easy way to avoid more difficult negotiation unless cost effective
9. Manipulate with high initial offer and giving smaller concessions than those received, if possible, while guarding against such manipulation

P. Focus/Downplay
1. Give false clue of interest and value
2. To minimize cost of obtaining an item as a purchaser, or maximize its price as a seller

Q. Creating a Psychological Commitment for Agreement
1. Using the process of negotiation itself
2. May display professional enthusiasm for benefits to both parties from general concept of reaching agreement or points already resolved
3. Avoid enthusiasm for agreement if client needs to appear disinterested to prevent being perceived as overly eager or weak
4. May focus on benefits for the negotiator personally
5. Use work group if possible to undermine the negotiator's loyalty to the other party, while resisting it for oneself to prevent conflicts of interest
6. Avoid becoming overly psychologically committed to reaching agreement or unduly fearful of losing a deal, while seeking to get the other side to become too psychologically committed because of its expenditures of time, effort, and costs, or through "supercrunch"
7. In litigation, beware of becoming so enamored of battle that one is blinded to an advantageous settlement, or unduly fearful, so that one's position is undervalued
8. Lowball: Hidden costs are sprung after the offer is accepted in a dangerous manuever that, unless successfully disguised, can create deep distrust; counter by demanding full information before responding to an offer

R. Face Saving
1. Encourage a change of position by creating a justification for the other party which avoids embarrassment
2. Reasonably ignore assertions of non-negotiable positions
3. Cite new information
4. Make a meaningless concession that can be treated as real

5. Interpret the other side's position without becoming condescending or unfair
6. Recognize subtle requests by those too embarrassed or reluctant to ask directly
7. Behave in a nonthreatening, nonintimidating manner
8. Make proposals that appear consistent with the other party's values and self image
9. Break a deadlock while allowing the saving of face by altering the terms, tone, or participants
10. Tell an appropriate and funny story
11. Use with all client goals and all strategies except an aggressive one if it is aimed at humiliating or embarrassing the other side

S. Inserting New Issues
1. To create an opportunity to gain or make concessions
2. Often requires planning so that issues are saved until needed, although it may arise spontaneously through creative thought
3. Includes disassembling package deals
4. Use to make a losing negotiation appear to be a victory to outside parties
5. Avoid appearing to be unfair or in bad faith by using before agreement is reached on the issue against which the tradeoff will be made
6. For any client goal and strategy
7. Countermeasures include refusing to negotiate the new issue, demanding the reopening of all issues, injecting one's own additional issues, or termination of the negotiation

T. Focusing on the Process
1. Use when the parties or negotiators clash or struggle over how to conduct the negotiation, rather than the substantive terms for the parties, to the extent that the negotiation cannot proceed productively
2. Four steps
   a. Stop and reflect
   b. Negotiators agree to resolve blockage
   c. Resolve the blockage
   d. Return to negotiating substantive issues
3. Be nonaccusatory, if that will lead to cooperation
4. Can arise due to a power struggle, emotional outbursts, distrust, confusion, or misunderstanding
5. Allows discussion of concerns, misunderstandings, confusion, or disagreements about how to proceed in the negotiation
6. Includes threats to reveal conduct to others
7. Countermeasures

       a. Reflect carefully and accept or reject without becoming unsettled

       b. Switch strategy or tactics, if appropriate

       c. Explain reasons for agreeing or disagreeing with the other negotiator's analysis of the process

U. Creation of Movement

   1. Take the initiative when the negotiation is bogged down, if appropriate for the client's goals

   2. Failure to take the initiative can doom the negotiation, even when a zone of agreement exists

   3. May use information disclosure, fact creation, face saving, injecting a new issue, focus on the process, allies, media or community pressure, alternative dispute resolution, new instructions, or a change of negotiators

   4. Can necessitate overcoming emotional or communications difficulties

   5. If one issue is creating an impasse, it may be better to defer that issue while resolving others

V. Deadlock

   1. Create temporary impasse to test the other side's strength and resolve

   2. Use as a temporary measure when there is a low risk that the other side will terminate, one has a face-saving way to break the impasse if necessary, and closure is inappropriate

   3. Also useful for delay under a strategy of negotiating for purposes other than reaching agreement

   4. Can lead to hostility, frustration, and locking in of positions

   5. Countermeasures include linkage with other negotiations as a form of injecting a new issue, focus on the process, informational tactics, adjournment, redefining the issues, problem solving, win/win, fact creation to demonstrate strength or will to resist, concede first as an explicitly one-time manuever, and a threat to terminate the negotiation

W. Adjournment

   1. A temporary halt of the negotiation, which is understood to be resumed later

   2. To regroup, change mood, obtain authority, deal with other matters

   3. Allows each side time to think, which may be a positive or negative factor, depending on the status of the negotiation

   4. For all client goals and strategies, except for closure

   5. Use marathon bargaining only if physically and mentally at least as tough as the other negotiator, and it will not create counterproductive hostility in the other side

   6. Open-ended adjournment can be used to create an impression of disinterest or general uncertainty, if the risk of termination does not mandate against it

X. Patience
   1. Use when pressure will not work, by allowing the other side to have time to absorb new ideas and become comfortable after calm analysis
   2. Can demonstrate fairness and resolve, causing the other party to lower its expectations
   3. Deadlines are a countermeasure
Y. Deadlines
   1. Use to avoid loss of alternative opportunities, because actions must be taken unless an offer is accepted, if the cost basis of the offer is subject to change, or to force a procrastinating party to make a decision
   2. Give a reason for the deadline, so that it does not appear to be an artificial power play, which can cause resentment
   3. Can create time pressure, increasing the size and speed of concessions if a failure to reach agreement has greater adverse consequences for one party than the other
   4. May lead to premature termination of negotiation
   5. Countermeasures include a face-saving attempt to force modification if the deadline is a bluff, fact creation changing the benefit or appropriateness of enforcing the deadline, and creating an incentive for prompt agreement obviating the need for a deadline
   6. If one negotiator faces an internal deadline imposed by the client while the other does not, that negotiator may be forced into weakening positions planned or undertaken
Z. Dealing with Those Who Lack Authority
   1. The other negotiator lacks formal authority
   2. The other negotiator may screen, probe, and messenger information, or may also have real influence over the decision maker
   3. If unsure about whether the other negotiator has any real authority or substantial influence, it is legitimate to ask, without seeking the substance or details of the authority
   4. Use other forms of information gathering as well, to learn the other negotiator's influence or lack of it
   5. Consider requiring a negotiator with authority as a precondition
   6. Evaluate whether the other party is likely to demand further concessions once any proposal is transmitted to its decision maker, and withhold some concessions, if appropriate
   7. If the other negotiator has influence over a decision maker, press for an agreement to recommend a proposal
   8. Demand proposals be transmitted to the other party without or against the other negotiator's recommendation if further concessions are unwise, and the attempt will not be clearly fruitless or counterproductive

9. Negotiate to appear to have been forced to make concessions, if that will cause the other negotiator to be more enthusiastic about advocating the proposal as having been won, and thereby make it more appealing to the other party

10. Circumvent an obstinate or unreasonable negotiator, unless the attempt is likely to be counterproductive or is ethically prohibited

11. If confronted by a policy prohibiting needed or desired concessions, probe to determine whether modification or exceptions are possible and, if so, the identity of the person with the power to act

AA. Surprise
1. Unveil startling new terms that are at least superficially more attractive than the prior terms
2. Press for immediate agreement
3. Persuade with explanation of how the offer meets the other party's objections, problems, needs, interests, or goals
4. Use if it is likely to succeed, or due to desperation
5. Be cautious, since it can backfire if the other party resents, distrusts, or becomes fearful
6. Counter by slowing the process
7. May combine with a deadline, unless that will engender too much suspicion or resistance

BB. Appeals to Personal Interests of Other Negotiator or a Nonparty Decision Maker
1. Exploit legitimate opportunities to influence the outcome by appeals to the personal, business, professional, social, psychological, and economic interests of the other negotiator
2. The same principle applies to the personal interests of the other party's decision maker, if that person or group is distinct from the other party itself
3. The appeal may consist of threatening negative personal consequences, depending on the power to fulfill the threat and the other negotiator's personality, which determines the probable reaction

III. Tactics Involving Other Parties
A. Active Client Participation
1. In the negotiation sessions
2. Possible for any client goal or strategy
3. Some clients conduct a portion of the negotiation before involving counsel, leaving certain items already resolved
4. Certain clients who are experienced and skilled in particular types of negotiations, and are not unduly emotional about the specific issues or parties, can be effective participants

5. As a general rule, negotiate without the clients present to avoid errors, unless there is a distinct advantage to having one or more clients present

6. A client's presence can impede communication and cause undue posturing

7. Avoid appearing overly friendly or candid with the other lawyer if the client may misinterpret that as disloyalty

8. Used for expediency, demonstrating unity of negotiator and client, to establish or repair relationships between clients, and to directly communicate with the parties

9. May be limited to certain phases of the negotiation, if at all

10. Can include client-to-client negotiations of certain issues without counsel, after counsel completes some phases of the negotiation

B. Negotiating Teams

1. Lone negotiator more common because of cost-benefit ratio, style, and potential conflict or inconsistency among negotiators

2. The potential benefits from the team approach are
   a. Active client participation
   b. Specialized knowledge
   c. Collective judgment
   d. Notes and observation
   e. Role playing

3. Role playing includes information gatherer and observer, as well as "Mutt and Jeff"

4. Countermeasures to "Mutt and Jeff" tough guy include exhaust without responding and ignore, bypass, be tough back, publicly blame the other side for sidetracking the negotiation, terminate the negotiation while pointing out that this conduct is the basis, openly predict the behavior, or threaten to take these measures

5. Team negotiation requires especially careful planning of the roles for gathering information beforehand, logistics, planning, information disclosure, concessions positions, and observation

6. Critical to have a leader with firm control using directions and adjournment as necessary, and being physically positioned to exercise leadership

7. If the rest of the team has an ongoing relationship with the other party while the lawyer does not, the lawyer can criticize and raise difficult points more freely than the others, as well as serve as a target for criticism

8. Focus communications on the other team's member who is
   a. More receptive, or
   b. More difficult, thus requiring neutralization

      9. Consider the number for the team in terms of whether being outnumbered may be a disadvantage, outnumbering the other team will intimidate or cause a harder defensive reaction, coordination problems, the nature and scope of the negotiation, personalities, and the need for specialized talents

C. Judicial Settlement Conferences

      1. Judge as mediator to facilitate negotiations, impose deadlines, deflate unrealistic expectations, suggest positions or principles for compromise, and oversee the process

      2. If the trial judge is involved, it can affect later rulings, depending on the judge

      3. May require clients to be present for authority and to influence them directly

      4. The presence of parties may have a positive or negative effect, depending on their respective personal strengths, possible lack of judicial skill at mediating, and potential undue pressure

      5. If the client will be present, plan with and counsel the client to be prepared to play an effective role, either active or passive

D. Allies

      1. Those who can favorably influence the other party

      2. Limited by whether they exist, costs, and potential backfire

      3. Gaining an ally's assistance can be the subject of an entirely separate negotiation

      4. For all goals and strategies

      5. May be internal, other involved parties, or external

      6. May require appeal to ally's self interest

      7. One with a relationship, status, and skill should be the contact person

      8. Avoid becoming overly dependent

      9. Allies can assist in having an unreasonable negotiator for the other party removed or bypassed. However, a failed attempt may strengthen that negotiator's position with his or her client.

E. Community or Media Pressure

      1. For negotiations involving public issues or public interest

      2. Seek to take persuasive positions that pressure the other party or avoid pressure on one's own client

F. Alternative Dispute Resolution

      1. To avoid cost and delay in the judicial system

      2. Allows a tailoring of the process better than the judicial system

      3. At its best, it may be preferable to litigation by being more efficient for communicating information, creating incentives for realistic self-examination by each party, providing

a means for dialogue, generating feedback from a respected neutral, and having the neutral propose solutions which the parties are not aware of or are afraid to suggest

4. Nonbinding will be a disadvantage to a weaker party without sufficient energy or resources for both that phase and litigation if there is no settlement, since it will be under tremendous pressure to settle

5. May be drafted into agreements to resolve future disputes

6. The mediator helps the parties discover whether a zone of agreement exists and clarifies any misunderstandings, but does not express a definite view on the merits

7. Mediation is nonbinding and useful when a neutral is reasonably likely to influence the parties who are ready to compromise

8. Arbitration is preferable to mediation when a voluntary agreement is unlikely without a neutral's decision

9. Arbitration can be binding or nonbinding. The latter differs from mediation in that a decision is rendered by the neutral instead of seeking only to facilitate voluntary agreement of the parties

10. Beware of a party who attempts to bargain one side down more than it concedes before the arbitration in order to skew the range for a resolution in its favor
    a. Counter by refusing to engage in that type of concession pattern
    b. Use this manuever if it is available

11. Potential negative consequences include undue reliance on arbitration without sufficient efforts to resolve the matter first, chilling compromises because the arbitrator may split the difference, less commitment to an arbitrated decision than a voluntary one if good faith efforts by a party are necessary, expenses that can equal litigation depending on the procedures, often narrow grounds for appeal, and sometimes disadvantageous procedural differences from litigation for a particular matter

12. Summary jury trials can also produce an advisory opinion, and are a form of nonbinding arbitration

13. Mini-trials are bench trial versions of the summary jury trial approach, with the addition of an attempt by the judge to mediate the dispute after the trial, but before issuing a ruling

14. Negotiation goal analysis, planning, strategy, and tactics are still used in alternative dispute resolution, with the addition of trial tactics for arbitration and summary or mini-trials

15. A public demand can be part of a tactic to create allies or community and media pressure. Counter by unmasking the ploy

          16. May be used as a ploy for discovery or delay under the strategy of negotiating other than for agreement. Countermeasure is to require expeditious and binding procedures

    G. Class Actions

        1. Settlement must satisfy the interests of the class and be approved by the court

        2. Class counsel's fees should not be negotiated until the substantive relief for the class has been at least contingently resolved, subject to agreement on fees for class counsel

    H. Multiple Parties

        1. Increases complexity of issues and analysis

        2. Use same planning methods, strategies, and tactics as a two-party negotiation

    I. Gifts and Entertainment

        1. Sometimes customary in business matters

        2. Avoid bribery and ethical violations

IV. Litigation Related Tactics

    A. Litigation

        1. Unlike transactions or deals, parties may be pushed together by outside events rather than mutual decision, and may seek to avoid a loss or to experience unilateral gain rather than mutual gain. There is often uncertainty about whether to negotiate, greater rigidity against compromise initially, and suspicion

        2. Emotional and psychological needs can cause a party to take positions that are economically unwise

        3. Fact creation can profoundly change the stakes, and may necessitate delay to obtain information needed to evaluate the case

        4. A threat of litigation perceived as serious can motivate the other party to settle rather than expend fees and costs

        5. The appearance of new counsel for litigation can raise or lower client expectations depending on the attorney's evaluation of the case, or create a client mind-set to use its new weapon

        6. Counsel's evaluation must ignore the impact of prompt settlement on fees from the standpoint of the lawyer's personal interests

        7. Litigation often adversely impacts any remaining relationship between the parties, and that must be analyzed before choosing the tactic if such relationship is important to the client. This includes considering customers or associates who may hear of the charges and countercharges

        8. Be mentally prepared to negotiate at any stage without reducing efforts in a way that endangers the chance of success at trial or appeal

9. Negotiations may be expedited through motions for injunctive relief
10. In deciding whether to litigate, consider whether there will be publicity and, if so, the effect on the parties and any relevant others
11. Similarly, any intimidating or inflammatory effects from decisions on how to draft the complaint must be considered
12. Especially useful for no concessions or no further concessions strategies, and can be used for all other strategies except concede first
13. Can be utilized for all client goals, but may be inappropriate in a particular situation for cooperative and defensive goals
14. Can serve as a deterrent to further acts by the defendant
B. Structured Settlements
    1. A specialized win/win tactic
    2. A stream of payments over time generally not subject to taxation
    3. Must be evaluated against present value and investment potential of a lump sum payment
C. Depositions
    1. If contact between the parties is possible, the client participation analysis applies from §6.02
    2. Provides an opportunity to disclose information to the other party through questions, responses to questions, and nonverbal communication
D. Policy Limits Letter
    1. To challenge a bad faith refusal to settle by an insurer
    2. Can make the insurer responsible for damages above the policy limits
    3. Depends on state laws
E. Loan Agreements
    1. Can be used where there are multiple defendants
    2. One defendant settles for a noninterest-bearing loan repayable only to the extent that either
        a. Plaintiff recovers from a second defendant, or
        b. Plaintiff's subsequent recovery from a second defendant exceeds the amount of the loan
    3. Can affect the perceived credibility of a witness
    4. Disclosure may be required
F. Mary Carter Agreements
    1. For multiple defendant cases where less than all defendants settle
    2. The settling defendant's monetary obligation is reduced by any recovery from one or more other defendants
    3. Disclosure may be required
G. Contribution Statute

      1. Protects a settling defendant against claims by other defendants
      2. Can provide an incentive to settle before other defendants

H. Offers of Judgment
      1. Federal Rule 68 and some states' rules
      2. Pressures a plaintiff by shifting costs if the plaintiff does not receive a judgment in excess of the offer
      3. Most useful where the plaintiff is quite likely to prevail
      4. Structure depends on whether an award of attorney's fees is possible
      5. A defendant with more knowledge of the case can pressure a plaintiff by an early offer of judgment. The countermeasure for plaintiff is anticipation, prelitigation investigation, and early discovery

I. Timing
      1. Litigation tends to settle when one or more parties can save significant expense, time, or effort
      2. Also, litigation tends to settle when trial is imminent
      3. Expenditure of costs can make it more difficult to settle
      4. Delay can lead a plaintiff to raise its demands
      5. Emotions can affect optimal timing
      6. A party's internal policies may affect the timing of a negotiation

J. Criminal Cases
      1. Judges must evaluate a plea bargain
      2. Defense counsel must determine or estimate whether the judge will accept a plea bargain, and the judge's sentencing tendencies
      3. Flexibility, but tentatively decide on planned order of use, subject to adjustment as the negotiation unfolds

K. Combinations of Tactics
      1. Generally should be utilized
      2. Use inconsistency if it will keep the other side off balance
      3. Avoid inconsistency if it creates an impression of confusion, weakness, or unfairness that is counterproductive
      4. Flexibility, but tentatively decide on planned order of use, subject to adjustment as the negotiation unfolds
      5. Generally include tactics to initiate negotiations if starting the negotiation is awkward, break deadlocks, get the process moving if it becomes bogged down, induce the other party or its negotiator to become psychologically committed to reaching agreement, selectively disclose information, and gather any information indicated to be needed by the prior planning steps
      6. Refine choice of strategies and tactics by considering anticipated reactions and countermeasures by the other side

       7. Focus on initiating action, not merely responding to antici-
          pated actions by the other side

       8. Take planned measures that are available before the negoti-
          ation starts and which can influence its outcome, such as
          fact creation

   V. After tactical choices, review prior steps, and make any needed modifi-
      cations of the tactical or other steps

Step 12: Consider Concessions and Tradeoffs

    I. Plan for concessions and tradeoffs unless the only strategy chosen pre-
       cludes them

   II. Some concessions and tradeoffs are generally expected

  III. Can be logically unrelated, as long as related in value to that being
      demanded in return

  IV. Tradeoffs flow from different values placed on the same item by each
      party

   V. Plan potential concessions for the area between the opening position
      and the bottom line

  VI. Create a rationale for each concession, so that the new position
      appears fixed and firm in the absence of new information or a conces-
      sion by the other party

 VII. Plan for each issue or combination of issues if tradeoffs are possible
      between issues

VIII. Includes creation of apparent concessions that are really unimportant
      to the client

  IX. This planning allows a number of relatively small concessions and
      tradeoffs, with rationales for each, and well calculated tradeoffs, all
      of which helps avoid lost opportunities for a more favorable agreement

   X. Anticipate the other party's likely tradeoffs and concessions, as well
      as its reactions to your own, and make adjustments, if necessary

  XI. Review prior steps, and modify prior or present steps, if appropriate

Step 13: The Agenda

    I. The order of actions, issues, and concessions

   II. The twelve factor approach to directing whether to set an agenda
      based on the need to: build rapport, gather information, disclose infor-
      mation, adjourn after initially obtaining or releasing information,
      make or refrain from making the first offer, agree on the issues, resolve
      some issues before other issues, resolve easy issues just to create
      momentum, negotiate the hardest issues first to avoid wasting time
      on easy ones, agree on the definitions and sequences or packages of
      issues to be discussed, catch the other party unprepared for extended
      negotiation, or gain insights by allowing the other party to set the
      agenda

  III. Often use informational tactics, first seeking alternatives and then
      other tactics

   IV. Influenced by whether a party wants to appear to be the pursuer or the pursued

   V. Affected by any need for multiple sessions

   VI. Consider seeking initial agreement leading to further agreement(s)

  VII. May need to agree on confidentiality of information to be disclosed

VIII. Plan opening moves, even if you do not intend to set an agenda

   IX. Consider other side's likely agenda or reactions, and modify as necessary

   X. Check against prior steps, and adjust this or prior steps, if appropriate

   XI. Avoid power struggles over the agenda unless

     A. The sequence of the negotiation is critical, or

     B. The power struggle is necessary to create respect from the other side

  XII. The agenda itself may be negotiated

Step 14: Timing

   I. Decide when it is most advantageous to negotiate

   II. It is advantageous if one is under less pressure than the other side, before coming under additional pressure, if one knows sufficient information to negotiate intelligently, before the other side uncovers a weakness or problem, and prior to a weakness or problem developing for the client

  III. May need to let a party's anger dissipate

  IV. Litigation affects timing

   V. Decided by, or in consultation with, the client

  VI. Avoid being under pressure from an internal deadline or having that known to the other side, while seeking to determine whether the other side is under an internal deadline

  VII. Need for restructuring of existing agreement, including based on a periodic review process

VIII. Anticipate the other party's timing needs or reactions to intended timing

  IX. Include single, sequential, and periodic negotiations

Step 15: The Mode(s) of Communication

   I. Negotiation is a dynamic process of exchanging information to decide whether to agree and, if so, the optimal terms for agreement

  II. Effective Communications

     A. Outcomes are affected by perfect or imperfect information

       1. Seek to cause the other side to behave as desired through communications which control and manipulate information

       2. Communication stages are often

         a. Build and defend positions to demonstrate some form of power, including persuasion

         b. Searches for solutions using the information from the first stage, and

       c. Striving together for satisfactory terms

B. Polite versus Power Struggle

    1. Generally be polite, so each negotiator can give and receive information, without necessarily being quiet or low key

    2. Polite mode facilitates selective disclosure and listening, while avoiding unnecessary and counterproductive power struggles

    3. Power struggles are appropriate when they

       a. Lead to control of the outcome

       b. Avoid domination when a substantive victory cannot be achieved by permitting apparent procedural domination, and

       c. Stop wasteful repetition, when appeasing the other's ego will not be productive

    4. Unsuccessful power struggles can create counterproductive frustration or hostility, and even cause a breakdown in negotiations

    5. Consider individual and entity personalities

C. Sending Verbal and Nonverbal Information

    1. Make only deliberate, selective disclosures

    2. Disclosure is appropriate if it will tend to persuade the other side to act as desired, considering any countervailing risks of creating a problem or revealing a weakness

    3. Use persuasive rationales with positions unless

       a. The rationale is inherently clear

       b. No plausible rationale exists (rare), or

       c. The rationale would involve a breach of a legal or ethical duty, such as a material misrepresentation. Splitting the difference, reciprocity, and precedent are often useful rationales

    4. Persuade through appeals to the other side's economic and noneconomic interests

    5. Disclose basis or source, if necessary to persuade

    6. Build rapport to enhance persuasion, including responding with points of agreement before stating points being rejected

    7. Explain, rather than demand blind trust, with implicit conclusions if the listener will be more convinced by figuring it out himself, and explicit conclusions otherwise

    8. Enhance persuasion by the size, intensity, visual impact, uniqueness, primacy, recency, and reasonable repetition

    9. Persuasive force also results from acting convinced, building in concessions, pointed questions, avoiding judgmental behavior (unless the other will be convinced that the judgment is correct), defining the problem to be solved in a

mutually agreeable way, timing that permits proper consideration to be given to the message, and references that demonstrate credibility or power

10. Use clear signals, and avoid confusing, mixed messages

11. Communicate with an awareness of the psychological needs of the other party and its negotiator, to avoid unwanted mental filtering, and be on guard against mental filtering by oneself causing misperceptions

12. If the other negotiator is withholding or distorting information to the other party's decision maker and thereby creating a problem, use inquiry, request presence of the person, written communications, demands, and depositions

13. Encourage the disclosure of information by listening attentively without interruptions and not indicating its importance if doing so would will cause the other negotiator to become guarded

14. Counter a reluctance to disclose by questions, discussions, challenging a point, and informational bargaining

15. Careful listening requires giving the other an opportunity to speak, concentrating on the verbal and nonverbal messages, and giving feedback to indicate understanding

16. React to strange or dramatic nonverbal information with a calm firmness, or refrain from reacting at all

17. Be alert for otherwise unconscious emotional distortions of perceptions, and counter difficult emotional reactions by channeling the energy into concentration, deep breathing with tensing or relaxing muscles, or a break

18. Also be alert to avoid missing information that contradicts one's ideas, because of a tendency to hear that which is expected or desired

19. Distinguish between the words heard and one's own inferences, so that the inference is evaluated as an assumption

20. Separate out verifiable facts from your own assumptions, opinions, or hearsay knowledge, or those of the speaker, in order to decide whether verification is needed

21. Use restatements or recapitulation to avoid errors by corroborating one's own understanding to build rapport and to clarify the matter for the original speaker

22. Watch for verbal and nonverbal cues, including concession patterns indicating the true motives, interests, values, strategies, and tactics of the other party and its negotiator. Distinguish between articulated positions and bottom-line ones.

23. Counter the search for cues with strategic misrepresentations, consisting of feigned reluctance

24. Exploit the other negotiator's self-imposed limitations on style, including a refusal or inability to use proper strategies and tactics due to personal fears
25. Behave so that one's nonverbal actions are consistent with one's verbal actions. Watch for discrepancies with oneself, the other party, and its negotiator.
26. Use good eye contact
27. Changes in a person's normal pattern of nonverbal behavior can be significant
28. Choose among meetings, telephone calls, and writings as modes of communication based on timing, impact, psychological commitment to negotiate seriously, and any need for privacy or confidentiality
29. Use informal or off-the-record exchanges to encourage candor and avoid rhetoric, but be on guard
30. The choice of site can indicate power, commitment, or a need to have, or avoid having, information available
31. Physical layout can affect the atmosphere, but can be countered by mental attitude

Step 16: Multiple Party Interactions

I. Parties on the same or different sides
II. Evaluate seeking to split the other side if it consists of multiple parties by considering the needs and interests of each, as well as whether the group negotiation is likely to proceed advantageously, but be cautious in transactional and cooperative negotiations
III. If in a group of plaintiffs or defendants, consider whether to negotiate as a group or separately
IV. Must consider each ally and opposing party separately at each step of the negotiation process

Step 17: Implementation and Adjustment

I. A strong mental attitude is critical
II. Perform opening moves as planned, unless a significant unforeseen event occurs
III. Use opening stages to learn about the other side
IV. For complex negotiations, notes may aid in keeping track of positions and points of agreement, as well as identifying patterns of behavior and goals
V. Consider the possibility that other side is shortsighted, controlled by noneconomic factors, or unpredictable
VI. Be ready for the unexpected
VII. Inject false cues suggesting you are at or near your bottom line, if that is advantageous
VIII. Unpredictability can

A. Advantageously force the other party to adapt a worst case scenario, or

B. Create frustration or disgust, causing a termination of the negotiation, especially if it diminishes or destroys the unpredictable party's value for a future working relationship

IX. After the opening moves, use alternatives in the plan, if appropriate, considering the actions of the other negotiator

X. Repeat the planning process during the negotiation as needed based, on new information acquired

XI. Adjust if the other party or negotiator has problems with attitude changes, short-term learning, cognition, perception, or making decisions

XII. Planning during the negotiation may be quick or lengthy, but it must be conscious, using the same steps and methods of analysis as prenegotiation planning

XIII. Evaluate whether the process is moving in a direction, and, if so, that it is an advantageous, or the most advantageous, direction

XIV. Watch for whether the other side's actions are symmetrical or asymmetrical with one's own

XV. If priority long-run goals cannot be achieved, consider whether short-term measures can build towards long-terms goals

XVI. Effective negotiators are neither averse to conflict nor seek it

XVII. Effective negotiators avoid, create, minimize, or maximize conflict as appropriate in the long-run and the short-run to achieve the client's goals

XVIII. Have alternatives and be multi-dimensional

XIX. Re-examine in light of earlier steps, portions of the negotiation

XX. Plan issue-by-issue, and for cross-issues, if tradeoffs are possible

XXI. Be Goals Rigid and Means Flexible, unless client authorizes abandonment or modification of a goal

XXII. Re-examine bottom lines, if appropriate

XXIII. Client must authorize bottom-line positions, and any choices of strategies or tactics that may impact the client on a business, social, political, or personal level

XXIV. Never underestimate the other party or its negotiator, or, in litigation, the other side's case or its trial attorney

Step 18: Drafting

I. Draft with realistically high expectations, and avoid blindly following models, examples, or precedents

II. Build in coercive enforcement mechanisms, or alternative dispute resolution, if needed

III. Plan as appropriate for any secondary negotiation in drafting the terms

IV. Balance enhanced control from preparing the initial draft with cost-effectiveness, including the practical feasibility of negotiating substantial revisions of the other lawyer's draft

    V. Avoid terms that are so unfair in the context of the deal that they create a risk of ruining the deal when they are seen by the other side, unless that risk is acceptable

    VI. Be precise, creative, anticipate disputes, and avoid losing closure

    VII. Use shorter, less complicated, plain English sentences for clarity

    VIII. Avoid precision *only* if ambiguity is preferable for the client, exactness is impossible, it is too difficult or unimportant to spell out a future contingency, or a contingency permits a desired termination of the agreement

    IX. Good faith provisions are subject to potential differing interpretations

    X. Avoid a drafting process which leads to delays that risk repudiation of a tentative agreement

    XI. Overly complicated proposals may be rejected in favor of simpler ones, especially if they are economically close in value

    XII. Draw formal agreements with specificity to reflect all of the parties' understandings without ambiguity

    XIII. Consider that the agreement may be interpreted in light of the law, parol evidence, and unwritten modifications (if permitted)

    XIV. Avoid oral agreements unless a high degree of trust and low stakes are present, or local custom or the relationship of the parties requires it. Be aware of whether a written agreement is required by law

    XV. Draft settlements, releases, and covenants not to sue with care, to preserve or avoid further claims

    XVI. Use standard terms if they are well understood, and nonstandard terms if they are more easily understood or better reflect idiosyncratic aspects of the agreement

    XVII. Include any terms required by law

    XVIII. An agreement may be documented by a formal agreement, a written offer, letters of intent, confirming letters, contemporaneous notes and memoranda, and court orders

Step 19: Ethics and Caveats

    I. Self interest in credibility and self respect

    II. Avoid criminal and civil liability, as well as disciplinary action, including for coercion, duress, fraud, or conspiracy to induce a breach of contract

    III. Beware of inadvertent material misrepresentations, or statements later perceived as such

    IV. Virtually all negotiations inherently involve a degree of information withholding or misdirection

    V. Brady disclosures for prosecution

    VI. Overcharging of a crime is unethical

    VII. Do not inform the other side of problems unless it is necessary to do so because of legal requirements, the other side will discover it later and counsel has a good solution, or to build or enhance a long-term relationship

VIII. Build in sufficient mutual benefit if concerned about potential repudiation or lack of good faith efforts

IX. In creating new entities, owned by a small group, consider alternative to deadlock and statutory sale if dissolution occurs

X. In representing multiple clients, beware of conflicts of interest or lack of authorization from all clients

Bibliography

CASES

Aircrash Disaster at Chicago, Illinois, In re, May 1979 (MDL 391)

Armstrong v Board of School Directors, 616 F2d 305 (7th Cir 1980)

Booth v Mary Carter Paint Co, 202 So 2d 8 (Fla Dist Ct App 1967), *overruled on other grounds,* Ward v Ochoa, 284 So 2d 385 (Fla 1973)

Brady v Maryland, 373 US 83 (1963)

Brown v Board of Education, 349 US 294 (1955)

Brown v Board of Education, 347 US 483 (1954)

Cardenas v Ramsey County, 322 NW2d 191 (Minn 1982)

Charles, In re, 90 Or 127, 618 P2d 1281 (1980)

Chow, In re, 3 Haw Ct App 577, 656 P2d 105 (1982)

Christianburg Garment Co v EEOC, 434 US 412 (1978)

Crossman v Marcoccio, 806 F2d 329 (1st Cir 1986)

Cuisinart Litigation, In re, 1983-2 Trade Cas (CCH) ¶165,860 (D Conn 1978)

Delta Air Lines v August, 450 US 346 (1981)

Donaghy v Napoleon, 543 F Supp 112 (DNJ 1982)

General Motors Engine interchange Litigation, In re, 594 F2d 1106 (7th Cir 1979)

Grosvenor v Brienen, 801 F2d 944 (7th Cir 1986)

Harris Trust & Savings Bank v Ali, 100 Ill App 3d 1, 425 NE2d 1364 (1981)

Horn v City of Chicago, No 85-C-6838 (ND Ill 1987), No 87-1174, 87-1175, 87-1936 (7th Cir 1988)

Johnson v Sears, Roebuck & Co, 291 Pa Super 625, 436 A2d 675 (1981)

Kath v Western Media, Inc, 684 P2d 98 (Wyo 1984)

Landgraf v Glasser, 186 NJ Super 381, 452 A2d 713 (NJ Super Law Div 1982)

Llaguno v Mingey, 763 F2d 1560 (7th Cir 1985) (en banc)

Luckenbach v WJ McCahan Sugar Refining Co, 248 US 139 (1918)

Marek v Chesney, 473 US 1 (1985)

McDonald v Chicago Milwaukee Corp, 565 F2d 416 (7th Cir 1977)

Merendion v FMC Corp, 181 NJ Super 503, 438 A2d 365 (NJ Super Law Div 1981)

Newton, Town of v Rumery, 107 S Ct 1187, 94 L Ed2d 405 (1987)

Payton v New York, 445 US 573 (1980)

Phemister v Harcourt Brace Jovanovich, Inc, No 77-C-39 (ND Ill 1984)

Prandini v National Tea Co, 557 F2d 1015 (3d Cir 1977)

Quercia v United States, 289 US 466 (1933)

Reese v Chicago, Burlington & Quincy Railroad, 55 Ill 2d 356, 303 NE2d 382 (1973)

Sayble v Feinman, 76 Cal App 3d 509, 142 Cal Rptr 895 (1978)

Slotkin v Citizens Casualty Co, 614 F2d 301 (2d Cir 1979)

Smiley v Manchester Insurance, 71 Ill 2d 306, 375 NE2d 118 (1978)

Spaulding v Zimmerman, 263 Minn 346, 116 NW2d 704 (1962)

Staffend v Lake Central Airlines, 47 FRD 218 (D Ohio 1969)

Starr v United States, 153 US 614 (1894)

Strandell v Jackson County, 838 F2d 884 (7th Cir 1988)

United States v Schubert, 728 F2d 1364 (11th Cir 1984)

Virzi v Grand Trunk Warehouse & Cold Storage Co, 571 F Supp 507 (ED Mich 1983)

Ward v Ochoa, 284 So 2d 385 (Fla 1973)

Zipkin v Genesco, Inc, [1980] Fed Sec L Rep (CCH) ¶97,594 (SDNY 1980)

STATUTES

United States Code

5 USC §552 *et seq*

15 USC §1632

26 USC §104

26 USC §130

28 USC §1720

28 USC §2671 *et seq*

28 USC Fed R Civ P 23

28 USC Fed R Civ P 23.1

28 USC Fed R Civ P Rule 26-37

28 USC Fed R Civ P 68

28 USC Fed R Crim P 16

28 USC Fed R Evid 803(5)

28 USC Fed R Evid 803(6)

40 USC §276a *et seq*

42 USC §1983

42 USC §1988

42 USC §2000e *et seq*

State Statutes and Court Rules

Ill Rev Stat ch 70, para 302 (1987)

Ill Rev Stat ch 110A, Rule 2-106 (1987)

Ill Rev Stat ch 110A, Code of Professional Responsibility Rule 7-105 (1987)

Ill Rev Stat ch 121 1/2, para 701 *et seq*

Uniform Commercial Code

§1-203

§2-202

§2-205

§2-208

§2-209

§2-314

§2-315

§2-319

§2-320

§2-321

§2-322

§2-324

Regulations and Rulings

Treas Reg §1.451-2(a)

Rev Rul 68-126, 1968 1 CB 194

Rev Rul 73-99, 1973 1 CB 412

Rev Rul 74-37, 1974 1 CB 112

Rev Rul 76-3, 1976 1 CB 114

Rev Rul 79-220, 1979 2 CB 74

Rev Rul 79-313, 1979 2 CB 75

Priv Ltr Rul 8333035 (May 16, 1983)

Authorities

ABA Model Code of Professional Responsibility DR 7-102 (1985)

ABA Model Rules of Professional Conduct Rule 2.1

ABA Model Rules of Professional Conduct Rule 4.1

ABA Model Rules of Professional Conduct Rule 4.2

ABA Model Rules of Professional Conduct Rule 4.3

A Lesson Learned At Last?, Chicago Trib, Sept 13, 1987, §4, at 1, col 1

Anatomy of a Personal Injury Case-1 (Continuing Legal Education Satellite Network 1986)

J. Appleman, *Insurance Law and Practice* (1981)

Ash, *World War To Cold War*, 34 NY Rev Books, June 11, 1987, at 44

Baldwin, *Bargaining With Airline Hijackers*, in W. Zartman, *The 50% Solution* (1976)

Bartos, *How Predictable Are Negotiations*, in W. Zartman, *The 50% Solution* (1976)

Bayer & Abrahams, *The Trouble With Arbitration*, 11 Litigation 30 (1985)

I. Belli, *Modern Trials* 749 (1954), in G. Bellow & B. Moulton, *The Lawyering Process* (1978)

G. Bellow & B. Moulton, *The Lawyering Process* (1978)

D. Binder & S. Price, *Legal Interviewing and Counseling: A Client-Centered Approach* (1977)

Brown, *Face-Saving and Face-Restoration in Negotiation*, in D. Druckman, *Negotiations: Social-Psychological Perspectives* (1977)

China, India, Raising Ante In Border Feud, Chicago Trib, June 28, 1987, §1, at 6

W. Coffin, *The Negotiator: A Manual for Winners* (1973)

H. Cohen, *You Can Negotiate Anything* (1982)

Cooley, *Arbitration vs Mediation*, 66 Chicago B Rec 204 (1985)

Dannings, Johnson & Lesti, *Structuring Settlements: A Negotiating Guide*, 15 (3) Trial Law Q 30 (1983)

Davis, *Settlement Negotiations: Strategy and Tactics*, 19 Trial 82 (1985)

de Felice, *Negotiations, Or The Art of Negotiating* in W. Zartman, *The 50% Solution* (1976)

Dewey, *Traps in Multitortfeasor Settlements*, 13 Litigation 42 (1987)

E. Doctorow, *Welcome to Hard Times* (1960)

Draper, *American Hubris: From Truman to the Persian Gulf*, NY Rev Books, July 16, 1987, at 47

D. Druckman, *Negotiations: Social-Psychological Perspectives* (1977)

Elman, *The Solicitor General's Office, Justice Frankfurter, and Civil Rights Litigation*, 100 Harv L Rev 817 (1987)

Erisman, *Settlement Do's and Don'ts*, 24 Trial 112 (1988)

W. Fallon, *AMA Management Handbook* (1983)

Far From Being Cloak-and-Dagger, Corporate Spying Becomes Workaday Stuff, Chicago Trib, Dec 22, 1987, §5, at 3, col 1

R. Fisher & W. Ury, *Getting to Yes, Negotiating Agreement Without Giving In* (1981)

Former Agent Puts the Blame For NFL Strike, Chicago Trib, Sept 24, 1987, §4, at 2, col 4

X. Frascogna, Jr. & H. Hetherington, *Negotiation Strategy for Lawyers* (1984)

Frisch, Jr. & Rosenzweig, *Representing the Seller of a Small Business,* in *Attorney's Guide to Negotiation* (1979)

Fuich, *Observations on the Negotiating Process,* in *Attorney's Guide to Negotiation* (1979)

R. Givens, *Advocacy: The Art of Pleading a Cause* (Shepard's/McGraw Hill, Inc 1985)

S. Goldberg, E. Green & F. Sander, *Dispute Resolution* (1985)

J. Graham & Y. Sano, *Smart Bargaining* (1984)

J. Greenfield, *Playing To Win: An Insider's Guide to Politics* (1980)

Halpern, *A Plaintiff's Alternative to Structured Settlements,* 23 Trial 83 (1987)

S. Hamilton, *What Makes Juries Listen* (1985)

Hammer & Yukel, *The Effectiveness of Different Offer Strategies in Bargaining,* in D. Druckman, *Negotiations: Social-Psychological Perspectives* (1977)

Hennings, *Everybody Agrees Legal Writing Is Bad But Not On What Needs to Be Done,* in *Law Letters, Inc, Second Manual of In-House Training* (1983)

Henry, *ADR and Personal Injury Litigation,* 23 Trial 73 (1987)

Hermann & Kogan, *Effects of Negotiators' Personalities on Negotiating Behavior,* in D. Druckman, *Negotiations: Social-Psychological Perspectives* (1977)

Holsti, Brady & North, *Measuring Affect and Action: The 1962 Cuban Crisis,* in W. Zartman, *The 50% Solution* (1976)

Hyman, *Drafting Contracts,* 68 CBA Rec 33 (1987)

Kane & Esposito, *Representing Clients In Negotiation of a Commercial Real Estate Transaction,* in *Attorney's Guide to Negotiation* (1979)

Karrass, *The Negotiating Game,* in Bellow & Moulton, *The Lawyering Process* (1978)

C. Karrass, *Give & Take: The Complete Guide to Negotiating Strategies and Tactics* (1974)

Kapov, *International Business-Government Negotiations,* in W. Zartman, *The 50% Solution* (1976)

A. Kaufman, *Problems In Professional Responsibility* (1975)

Kempf, Jr. & Taylor, *Settling Class Actions,* 13 Litigation 26 (1986)

G. Kennedy, J. Benson & J. McMillan, *Managing Negotiations* (1982)

Kim, O'Connor & Hianik, *Drafting the Contract for the Purchase and Sale of a Business,* in *Buying and Selling Businesses* (1987)

Labor-Management Experts Ponder Players' Tactics, Chicago Trib, Oct 13, 1987, §4, at 3, col 1

Lee, *Some Comments on Negotiation and Settlement,* 10 Am J Trial Advoc 181 (1987)

R. Lewicki & J. Litterer, *Negotiation* (1985)

Lewis, Goetz, Schoenfield, Gordon & Griffin, *The Negotiation of Involuntary Civil Commitment,* 18 L & Soc Rev 629 (1984)

Lubet & Schoenfield, *Trial Preparation—A Systematic Approach,* 12 Trial Law Q 16 (1978)

Mandle, *Collective Bargaining Negotiation,* in *Attorney's Guide to Negotiation* (1979)

Manual For Complex Litigation Second in J. Moore, *Moore's Federal Practice* (1986)

Marcus, *Representing the Purchaser of a Small Business,* in *Attorney's Guide to Negotiation* (1979)

T. Mauet, *Fundamentals of Trial Techniques* (1980)

McClintock, *Social Motivation in Settings of Outcome Interdependence,* in D. Druckman, *Negotiations: Social-Psychological Perspectives* (1977)

J. McElhaney, *Trial Notebook: A Practical Primer on Trial Advocacy* (1981)

McNay, *The Other Side Of Structured Settlements,* 23 Trial 79 (1987)

Menkel-Meadow, *Judges & Settlement,* 21 Trial 24 (1985)

Menkel-Meadow, *Legal Negotiation: A Study of Strategies in Search of a Theory,* 4 Am B Found 905 (1983)

Menkel-Meadow, *Toward Another View of Legal Negotiation: The Structure of Problem Solving,* 31 UCLA L Rev 754 (1984)

Morse, *The Bargaining Structure of NATO: Multi-Issue Negotiation In An Independent World,* in W. Zartman, *The 50% Solution* (1976)

H. Newberg, *Class Actions* (Shepard's/McGraw-Hill, Inc 1985)

G. Nierenberg, *The Art of Negotiation: Psychological Strategies for Gaining Advantageous Bargains* (1968)

J. Nierenberg & I. Ross, *Women and the Art of Negotiation* (1985)

Nolan, *Settlement Negotiations,* 11 Litigation 17 (1985)

Oatley, *Negotiating Techniques for Lawyers,* 6 Advoc Q 214 (1985)

Paplow, *Negotiating Settlement of a Personal Injury Action-Defendant,* in *Attorney's Guide to Negotiation* (1979)

Peace Talks, Chicago Trib, April 8, 1987, §5, at 1, col 2 & 7, col 1

Penn, Jr., *Negotiation in a Criminal Case-Defense,* in *Attorney's Guide to Negotiation* (1979)

Perschbacher, *Regulating Lawyers' Negotiations,* 27 Ariz L Rev 75 (1985)

Potter, *Settlement of Claims and Litigation: Legal Rules, Negotiation Strategies, and In-House Guidelines,* 41 Bus Law 515 (1986)

Pruitt & Lewis, *The Psychology of Integrative Bargaining,* in D. Druckman, *Negotiations: Social-Psychological Perspectives* (1977)

H. Raiffa, *The Art and Science of Negotiation* (1982)

Raiffa, *The Art and Science of Negotiation,* in S. Goldberg, E. Green & F. Sander, *Dispute Resolution* (1985)

Raskin, *The Newspaper Strike,* in W. Zartman, *The 50% Solution* (1976)

Raymond, *Legal Writing: An Obstruction To Justice,* in *Law Letters, Inc, Second Manual of In-House Training* (1983)

Redelaway, *Gorbachev The Bold,* 34 NY Rev Books, May 28, 1987, at 21

Rieders, *Summary Jury Trials,* 23 Trial 93 (1987)

Rifkin, *Negotiating Patents, Trade Secrets and Know-How Licenses,* in *Attorney's Guide to Negotiation* (1979)

Roberts, *Negotiation In a Criminal Case-Prosecution,* in *Attorney's Guide to Negotiation* (1979)

Rodgers, *Negotiating and Settling Personal-Injury Cases,* 23 Trial 108 (1987)

Rothchild, *Racial Stratification and Bargaining: The Kenya Experience,* in W. Zartman, *The 50% Solution* (1976)

Rubin, *Negotiation,* in S. Goldberg, E. Green & F. Sander, *Dispute Resolution* (1985)

W. Rusher, *How To Win Arguments* (1981)

M. Saks & R. Hastie, *Social Psychology In Court* (1978)

Sandels, *Negotiation In Business Litigation,* in *Attorney's Guide to Negotiation* (1979)

M. Schoenfield & B. Pearlman Schoenfield, *Interviewing and Counseling* (1981)

T. Shaffer, *Legal Interviewing and Counseling* (1976)

D. Siemer, *Tangible Evidence: How to Use Exhibits at Trial* (1984)

Simon, *The New Meaning Of Rule 68: Marek v Chesney And Beyond,* 14 NYU Rev L & Soc Change 475 (1986)

Skolrood, *Negotiating Settlement Of A Personal Injury Action-Plaintiff,* in *Attorney's Guide to Negotiation* (1979)

G. Spence, *Trial By Fire* (1986)

Note, *An Analysis of Settlement,* 22 Stan L Rev 67 (1969), in G. Bellow & B. Moulton, *The Lawyering Process* (1978)

Stevens, *Strategy and Collective Bargaining Negotiations,* in G. Bellow & B. Moulton, *The Lawyering Process* (1978)

Strauss, Schatzman, Ehrlich, Bucher & Sabshin, *The Hospital and Its Negotiated Order,* in W. Zartman, *The 50% Solution* (1976)

Tedeschi & Bonoma, *Measures or Last Resort: Coercion and Aggression in Bargaining,* in D. Druckman, *Negotiations: Social-Psychological Perspectives* (1977)

Tober, *The Settlement Conference,* 15 Trial Law Q 42 (1983)

Note, *Private Settlement As Alternative Adjudication: A Rationale for Negotiation Ethics,* 18 U Mich JL Ref 503 (1985)

Varon, *Promoting Settlements and Limiting Litigation Costs By Means of the Offer of Judgment: Some Suggestions for Using and Revising Rule 68,* 33 Am UL Rev 813 (1984)

T. Warschaw, *Winning By Negotiation* (McGraw-Hill, Inc 1980)

Watson, *Mediation and Negotiation: Learning to Deal with Psychological Responses,* 18 U Mich JL Ref 293 (1985)

White, *Negotiation: Machiavelli And The Bar: Ethical Limitations On Lying In Negotiation,* in S. Goldberg, E. Green & F. Sander, *Dispute Resolution* (1985)

G. Willliams, *Legal Negotiation and Settlement* (1983)

Williams, *Negotiation: Legal Negotiation and Settlement,* in S. Goldberg, E. Green & F. Sander, *Dispute Resolution* (1985)

Williams, *Leviathan's Progress* (Book Review), 34 NY Rev Books, June 11, 1987, at 33

Winslow, *Tax Reform Preserves Structured Settlements,* 65 Taxes 22 (1987)

Wise, *Negotiations With The Internal Revenue Service,* in *Attorney's Guide to Negotiation* (1979)

Wriggins, *Up For Auction: Malta Bargains With Great Britain 1971,* in W. Zartman, *The 50% Solution* (1976)

XEROX, Professional Selling Skills (1976)

Younger, *In Praise of Simplicity,* in *Law Letters, Inc, Second Manual of In-House Training* (1983)

W. Zartman, *The 50% Solution* (1976)

W. Zartman & M. Berman, *The Practical Negotiator* (1982)

Zavett & Friedman, *The Negotiation of Matrimonial Cases,* in *Attorney's Guide to Negotiation* (1979)

M. Zimmerman, *How to Do Business with the Japanese* (1985)

Index

Z

LEGAL NEGOTIATIONS

Getting Maximum Results

**1995 Cumulative Supplement
Current to February 1, 1995**

Mark K. Schoenfield
Partner Schoenberg, Newman & Fisher,
Chicago
Member of the Illinois Bar

Rick M. Schoenfield
Partner Schoenfield & Swartzman,
Chicago
Member of the Illinois Bar

*Insert in the pocket at the back
of the bound volume.
Discard supplement dated 1994.*

Shepard's/McGraw-Hill, Inc.
P.O. Box 35300
Colorado Springs, Colorado 80935-3530

Supplement ISBN 0-07-172228-9

2300

New sections appearing in this supplement:

The Optimal Approach to Negotiating

1

§1.02 Negotiation as a Process

Page 4, text, add at end of section:

Negotiation training should be an important part of changing American business practices in order to better compete in a world economy. In looking at the fourteen steps advocated by Dr. Deming, the American visionary business teacher whose methods were adopted by the Japanese with incredible success, six of the steps should include negotiation training. These steps include:

1. Improve constantly the system of production and service
2. Adequate training on the job
3. Institute leadership
4. Break down barriers between departments
5. Institute a vigorous program of education and self-improvement
6. Put everyone in the company to work to accomplish the transformation

Recrafting America, Chicago Trib, Nov 6, 1991, §1, at 1.

§1.03 The Effective Negotiator

Page 6, text, add at end of section:

The opposite sides of the brain function with different types of thought processes. Therefore, it can be useful to recognize whether one is overly dependent on right-brain or left-brain thinking. Cooley & Stone, *Using*

Your Brain in Negotiation: Both Sides of It, CBA Rec 24 (Feb 1988). The literal functions of the brain are:

> Left: *Analytical*, linear, explicit, sequential, *verbal*, concrete, *rational*, active, goal-oriented
>
> Right: *Intuitive*, spontaneous, emotional, nonverbal, visual, artistic, holistic, playful, diffuse, symbolic, physical. (Emphasis added.)

Id. A truly effective negotiator is both analytical/rational (left-brained) and intuitive/creative (right-brained).

In negotiating or communicating with someone, it may be useful to know whether that person is right-brain or left-brain dominant, or fairly balanced. A dominance can suggest the most effective way to structure the information being communicated.

A basic clue is whether the person is right-handed, left-handed, or ambidextrous, since right-handed people are left-brained and left-handed people are right-brained. However, there are gradations of this as people may be extremely dominated by one side, moderately dominated, or not dominated by either side. Accordingly, a thorough analysis of whether someone is right- or left-brain dominant cannot be done based on very limited contact, since everyone will engage in certain actions characteristic of one side or the other. Over time, however, and for one's own self, a pattern can emerge.

For negotiations, left-brain dominant people prefer to acquire information and better learn it through reading, narrative explanation and facts, with details, specifications, and figures in an organized and logical manner. *Id* 29. The right-brain dominant person prefers and better understands visual imagery and creative exchanges of problem-solving ideas and concepts. *Id*.

§1.04   The Role of the Client

Page 6, text, add after first paragraph:

Much of the literature on negotiations and client counseling has been criticized for either ignoring or underemphasizing the role of client counseling in the negotiation process. Gifford, *The Synthesis of Legal Counseling and Negotiation Models: Preserving Client Centered Advocacy in the Negotiation Context*, 34 UCLA L Rev 811, 813-15 (1987). In contrast, see §§1.02, 1.03, 1.04, 2.02, 2.07, 2.08, 4.05, 4.08, 5.24, 8.04, 8.08, 9.02, 9.03, 9.11 (Supp), and 12.04 regarding client counseling.

The most difficult and frustrating aspect of negotiations for an attorney may well be counseling a client who insists on taking an unreasonable, unrealistic position and who insists on rejecting a good settlement offer. One must be careful not to unintentionally inflate a client's expectations. For instance, the client who wants to be kept informed as to "what we're asking for," must be carefully counseled that "what we're asking for is not what we realistically expect to get." In such a situation, it is essential that the attorney is confident that he, or she, has not only cautioned the client, but that the client has really heard and understood the cautionary language. Otherwise, months or years later, the client may be unable to accept a reasonable settlement.

A particularly difficult situation can arise where the attorney represents a minor whose parents insist on maintaining an unreasonable, unrealistic position and reject what is clearly a good settlement offer. Since the attorney cannot simply accept the settlement without the parents' consent, what can be done where the attorney is convinced that the parents' position is contrary to the best interests of the real client, the minor? Assuming that the case is in litigation, one option is for the attorney to arrange for a pretrial settlement conference so that the judge can succeed in mediating the situation. A more extreme option is to make a motion to have the court accept the settlement on behalf of the minor or to appoint a guardian for the limited purpose of accepting the settlement.

An attorney is obligated to inform the client of settlement offers and the failure to do so is a negligent breach of the attorney's duty to the client. *Moores v Greenberg*, 834 F2d 1105 (1st Cir 1987); *Patrick v Ronald Williams, PA*, 102 NC App 355, 402 SE2d 452 (1991). The *Moores* court stated that "as part and parcel of this duty a lawyer must keep his client seasonably apprised of relevant developments, including opportunities for settlement." 834 F2d at 1108. The First Circuit left open the question of whether this duty encompassed a duty to communicate a "patently unreasonable offer." *Id.* Since opinions about what constitutes a patently unreasonable offer may sometimes differ, it is prudent to inform the client of all settlement opportunities in a timely manner.

Merely being authorized to represent a client in a suit does not give the attorney any settlement authority. *United States v Beebe*, 180 US 343 (1901); *Michaud v Michaud*, 932 F2d 77 (1st Cir 1991); *Ford v Citizens & Southern National Bank*, 928 F2d 1118 (11th Cir 1991); *Humphreys v Chrysler Motors Corp*, 399 SE2d 60 (W Va 1990); *Patrick v Ronald Williams, PA*, 102 NC App 355, 402 SE2d 452 (1991); *King v King*, 199 Ga App 496, 405 SE2d 319 (1991); *Daniziger v Pittsfield Shoe Co*, 204 Ill 145, 68 NE 534 (1903); *Kazale v Flowers*, 185 Ill App 3d 224, 541 NE2d 219 (1989).

Settlement authority must come from the client who is the ultimate decisionmaker. ABA Model Rules of Professional Conduct Rule 1.2(a); *United States v Beebe*, 180 US 343 (1901); *Michaud v Michaud*, 932 F2d 77 (1st Cir 1991); *Ford v Citizens & Southern National Bank*, 928 F2d 1118 (11th Cir 1991); *Humphreys v Chrysler Motors Corp*, 399 SE2d 60 (W Va 1990); *Patrick v Ronald Williams, PA*, 102 NC App 355, 402 SE2d 452 (1991); *King v King*, 199 Ga App 496, 405 SE2d 319 (1991); *Daniziger v Pittsfield Shoe Co*, 204 Ill 145, 68 NE 534 (1903); *Kazale v Flowers*, 185 Ill App 3d 224, 541 NE2d 219 (1989).

Applying federal law, the First Circuit in *Michaud* explained that an attorney needs special settlement authority "because the decision to settle is the client's to make, not the attorney's." (932 F2d at 80.) Both *Beebe* and *Michaud* also held that there is a rebuttable presumption that an attorney's agreement to settle was authorized. In some jurisdictions, if an attorney enters into a settlement without special authority to do so, and the client refuses to consent to the settlement, the client is not bound by the lawyer's agreement. *United States v Beebe*, 180 US 343 (1901); *Michaud v Michaud*, 932 F2d 77 (1st Cir 1991); *Humphreys v Chrysler Motors Corp*, 399 SE2d 60 (W Va 1990); *Daniziger v Pittsfield Shoe Co*, 204 Ill 145, 68 NE 534 (1903); *Kazale v Flowers*, 185 Ill App 3d 224, 541 NE2d 219 (1989). Where a judgment is entered based on an unauthorized settlement, there is an issue of the time frame in which the judgment may be vacated under the law of various jurisdictions. *Compare United States v Beebe*, 180 US 343 (1901) *and Patrick v Ronald Williams, PA*, 102 NC App 355, 402 SE2d 452 (1991) (malpractice, in part, for agreeing to unauthorized settlement and, in part, for failing to timely vacate judgment based on the unauthorized settlement).

However, there is not unanimity among the jurisdictions regarding whether a client is bound by his or her attorney's unauthorized settlement. One approach is that attorneys have apparent authority to agree to settlements and that, therefore, under agency principles, a lawyer's consent to settle will bind the client, unless the other party is aware that the lawyer's authority was limited and did not include settlement authority. *Ford v Citizens & Southern National Bank*, 928 F2d 1118 (11th Cir 1991) (applying Georgia law).

Where the client can be bound by his or her attorney to an unauthorized, unwanted settlement, the client has a claim against the lawyer for malpractice. *King v King*, 199 Ga App 496, 405 SE2d 319 (1991). *See also Patrick v Ronald Williams, PA*, 102 NC App 355, 402 SE2d 452 (1991).

The Pennsylvania Supreme Court has held that even bad settlement advice cannot be the basis of a legal malpractice claim, unless an attorney fraudulently induces his or her client to settle. *Muhammad v Strassburger, McKenna, Messer, Shilobod & Gutnick*, 526 Pa 541, 587 A2d 1346 (1991), appeal pending before the United States Supreme Court (1991). In reaching that holding, the Pennsylvania Supreme Court explained that:

> This case must be resolved in light of our longstanding public policy which encourages settlements. Simply stated, we will not permit a suit to be filed by a dissatisfied plaintiff against his attorney following a settlement to which that plaintiff agreed, unless that plaintiff can show he was fraudulently induced to settle the original action. An action should not lie against an attorney for malpractice based on negligence and/or contract principles when that client has

agreed to a settlement. Rather, only cases of fraud should be actionable.

587 A2d at 1348.

The *Muhammad* court went on to note the following example of whether a settlement has been fraudulently induced:

> If the lawyer *knowingly* commits malpractice, but does not disclose the error and convinces the client to settle so as to avoid the discovery of such error, then the client's agreement was fraudulently obtained. (Emphasis in original.)

Id 1351.

In such a situation, the *Muhammad* court indicated that the settlement would still be valid because the fraud was on the part of the party's own attorney, but that the client would have a claim against the attorney for fraudulently inducing the settlement.

Client Goals

2

§2.05　Self-Centered Client Goals

Page 19, text, add at end of section:

Burton suggests that "a central concern . . . facing any public official using bargaining in discretionary decision making is how to imbue agency actions reached through informal negotiations with some of the same attributes of legitimacy which can usually be acquired only at the cost of lengthy and formalized administrative due process." Burton, *Negotiating the Cleanup of Toxic Groundwater Contamination: Strategy and Legitimacy*, 28 Nat Resources J 105, 135-36 (1988) (citing J. Freedman, *Crisis and Legitimacy* (1978)). Burton asserts that the attributes of the legitimacy of administrative actions are constitutionality, effectiveness, responsiveness and fairness. *Id* 110, 135-36. This could be viewed as a self-centered, intangible, and possibly vital goal.

An administrative agency may take a very hard-line, self-centered position if it takes its legislatively defined mission seriously. For example, the Chicago school finance authority, created by the state legislature, refused to ease rules on spending of future state reimbursements during a last-minute marathon bargaining session to avoid a teachers' strike. The finance authority stuck to its position, although a strike almost resulted, explaining that: "We're just doing what the legislature told us, trying to maintain fiscal responsibility in the school system." *Behind Closed Doors: How Chicago Averted a Teachers Strike*, Chicago Trib, Nov 24, 1991, §2, at 1. Other parties finally made significant compromises which still left a deep projected fiscal deficit. The whole process occurred in the context of shuttle diplomacy, with the mayor of Chicago playing the role of mediator. *Id.*

§2.06   Defensive Client Goals

Page 19, text, add at end of section:

Defensive negotiation goals can be based on avoiding potential liability from transactions. In negotiating loans on behalf of banks, savings and loans, and other financial institutions or lenders, one must be aware of potential securities fraud liability under §10(b) of the 1934 Securities Exchange Act. 15 USC §78j(b). The issue arises when the lender loans funds to projects which constitute securities transactions with investors through limited partnerships or private placement memorandum for deals such as: (1) long-term office building financing; (2) apartment building rehabilitation; (3) oil or gas exploration; (4) equipment leasing; (5) movie financing; or (6) the startup of a high-tech enterprise. Feldman, *Bank Liability for Securities Fraud,* Banking LJ 100, 102 (Mar/Apr 1990).

The lender's potential securities fraud liability is for aiding and abetting a fraud through recklessness, such as ignoring serious business or legal irregularities at the closing without notification to investors. *Id* 103, 107. The negotiator must be prepared to refuse to close a loan rather than create huge exposure for securities fraud damages to all of the investors. This position, of course, requires careful consultation with and authority from the client.

§2.07   Combinations of Client Goals

Page 22, text, add after Example 2-4:

Historically, the growth of unions before and shortly after World War II was often tied to negotiations with employers in which the union's organizational interests clashed with the short-run interests of its members. For example, when A. Phillip Randolph led the Brotherhood of Sleeping Car Porters against the Pullman Company in the early stages of that long and bitter struggle, he often made "recognition of the union" (an organizational goal and in the organizers' personal interests) a higher priority than wage increases for the porters (the constituents' short-run goal). Pinckney, *Keeping the Faith,* 37 NY Rev Books, Nov 22, 1990, at 29, 31. In the long run, Randolph's balancing of goals led to a recognized union and higher wages, as well as other important benefits for the employees.

Strategy

3

§3.02   Personal Credibility

Page 31, note 7, add:

It has been suggested that an attorney gains credibility in litigation by being one who: (1) is friendly, but professional; (2) can be relied on to fully investigate the case; (3) carefully prepares; (4) realistically evaluates the value of the case; and (5) is ready and willing to go to trial. Erisman, *The Art of Negotiating a Settlement*, 25 Trial 26, 28, 35 (Sept 1989).

Some of the same comments are made by Zmolek, who also notes the benefits of being diplomatic and courteous, rather than antagonistic, aggressive, or hostile. Zmolek, *Art of Negotiation: Strategies and Tactics*, 27 Trial 22 (Aug 1991). The appropriate use of humor may also be used to "break the ice," thereby, in effect, enhancing credibility. *Id* 23.

Page 31, note 10, add:

Where there is potential litigation, credibility may affect whether the other side will try to negotiate an agreement without instituting formal action. For example, interviews with public officials responsible for cleaning up and stopping pollution indicated that in deciding whether to negotiate a solution without filing a formal adjudicatory action, the officials considered:

1. Any past history of the polluter's dealing with government agencies
2. The magnitude of the contamination
3. How promptly the polluter reported the contamination
4. The polluter's responsiveness to cleanup suggestions
5. Their perception of the polluter's intent

Burton, *Negotiating the Cleanup of Toxic Groundwater Contamination: Strategy and Legitimacy*, 28 Nat Resources J 105, 136 (1988). In other words, the officials evaluated the polluter's credibility for negotiating in good faith with reasonable expectations and intentions.

Page 35, text, add after third full paragraph:

The impact of credibility on the negotiation process ranges from important to critical. In 1990, for example, the United Auto Workers negotiated new labor agreements with the Big Three domestic car manufacturers. The UAW targeted General Motors as the key negotiation, due to what Stephen Yokich, head of the UAW negotiating team, characterized as a lack of credibility: "The problem we had with the last contract was where GM didn't live up to the agreement; Ford has. The whole thing revolves around trust." *Shake Hands, Come Out Bargaining*, Chicago Trib, July 15, 1990, §7, at 1, cols 4-6.

The lack of trust had its roots in the prior 1987 agreement, which contained job-security provisions. GM, faced with overcapacity, closed some plants as "temporarily idled." *Id.* The union contested those closings as violating the job-security provisions, but lost the ensuing arbitration. However, that loss was not accepted by the union and led to bitter union pre-negotiation rhetoric.

The importance of direct, personal communications with key employees, to avoid personnel problems, is exemplified by Michael Jordan and the Chicago Bulls. After Jordan repeatedly, publicly criticized the Bulls' general manager, the Bulls' owner privately conferred with Jordan to present his views on why the general manager's actions were reasonable. The meeting was successful because of their ongoing relationship, which included mutual respect for each other's golf scores! *Conference with Reinsdorf Quieted Jordan*, Chicago Trib, Nov 17, 1991, §1, at 1. In many negotiations, personal relationships with credibility are a key factor.

§3.03   No Concessions

Page 39, note 35, add:

Similar observations about the market expectation of some give-and-take in personal injury negotiations have also been noted by other commentators. Zmolek, *Art of Negotiation: Strategies and Tactics*, 27 Trial 22, 23 (Aug 1991); Fuchsberg, *Ten Commandments for Successful Evaluation and Settlement*, 27 Trial 16, 16-18 (Aug 1991). Fuchsberg observed that this caters to the other negotiator's need for "ego satisfaction." *Id* 18. Of course, these observations have widespread application and are certainly not restricted to the area of personal injury negotiations.

§3.07   Concede First

Page 49, text, add after Example 3-10:

Example 3-10A

In an international negotiation, the United States maneuvered to have its position regarding short-range nuclear weapons prevail among the North Atlantic Treaty Organization (NATO) allies. *Bonn Walked into US Negotiating Trap*, Chicago Trib, June 1, 1989, §1, at 2. West Germany had demanded that the United States negotiate with the Soviet Union to reduce the number of short-range nuclear weapons based in Europe. *Id.* After an initial refusal, the United States conceded to such negotiation in principle and then demanded that the negotiating position have certain conditions. *Id.* Once the United States conceded first to the position of the West German position, the other NATO allies pressured West Germany into accepting the United States' stance on specific conditions to be demanded when negotiating that principle with the Soviet Union. *Id.* West Germany felt constrained to accept the United States' conditions in order to avoid being viewed as responsible for blocking short-range nuclear arms reduction talks with the Soviets. *Id.*

Example 3-10B

In the days leading up to the Persian Gulf War, Iraq failed in an effort to use a *concede first* strategy. After seizing Westerners and other foreigners in Kuwait and Iraq as hostages, Iraq altered its strategy and agreed to unilaterally release those hostages. Iraq then sought, but failed to obtain some reciprocal concession, even though it had conceded first by releasing its hostages.

These contrasting international examples suggest that the concede first strategy only works when the concession is viewed by the other side as legitimate. Since Iraq's hostage taking was viewed as an illegitimate attempt to obtain a bargaining chip, the release of the hostages was not seen as a true concession by the United States and its allies, but merely as giving up something to which Iraq had no right in the first place.

§3.09   Examples of Problem Solving

Page 59, note 109, add:

For an example of a problem solving approach to an actual negotiation concerning water usage in Denver, see Carpenter & Kennedy, *The Denver Metropolitan Water Roundtable: A Case Study in Researching Agreements*, 28 Nat Resources J 21 (1988).

Page 61, text, add at end of section:

As a reminder and example of the benefits of creative problem solving, consider this example: a developer bought a golf course and then encountered serious financial difficulties while seeking to have the property rezoned for multi-family housing. A bank had a $13 million first mortgage. The seller, who had received a significant downpayment, held a $7 million second mortgage. Without the rezoning, the property's value was problematic at $7-13 million. With rezoning, the value might increase to as much as $25 million. Rezoning was thought to require approximately six more months to complete.

The developer was without funds or cash flow, so the mortgage payments were two months in arrears. The bank then demanded a meeting of the parties. At that meeting, the developer asked for time to gain rezoning. He indicated, in factual detail, that rezoning had a good chance of causing interested parties to pay $17-25 million to take over the project. The bank responded that it could file a foreclosure within five days unless the developer raised funds, which he could not do. The negotiator for the second mortgagor pointed out that the filing of the foreclosure would trigger political fall-out which would kill any chance of rezoning for years. No one disagreed. The second mortgagor's negotiator then argued that, without rezoning, the bank was likely to incur a multi-million dollar deficiency through a foreclosure sale without rezoning. The bank unconvincingly attempted to act sanguine about its position. Then, using selective information disclosure, the bank revealed its needs:

1. A way to show federal regulators that it was acting diligently on a large, nonperforming loan;

2. Gaining sufficient control so that a later foreclosure filing would not take longer than if it were filed within five days.

That information disclosure was essential for the other parties to understand the bank's true needs and seek to meet them. The second mortgagor's negotiator then urged the parties to jointly engage in the problem solving strategy, in order to ascertain a method which would maximize the value of the property by continuing the rezoning process, and meet the bank's articulated needs. As a start to problem solving, he suggested:

1. Either a waiver of defenses to foreclosure or an assignment of the beneficial interest which the developer would have an option to reacquire for a set period of time;

2. The developer continue with the rezoning process;

3. Any agreement being confidential to avoid any adverse political impact that would jeopardize or preclude rezoning.

The parties then engaged in problem solving to refine those concepts into a final agreement.

§3.15   Moving for Closure

Page 73, text, add after first paragraph:

In sports, it has become common to have players seek to renegotiate their contracts based on compensation packages given to other players. *Contract? Oh That Old Thing*, Chicago Trib, Dec 11, 1988, §3, at 2. Thus far, the concept has extended only to players seeking more money. Management, however, still is not allowed to seek a downward renegotiation when a player's performance slips during the contract term. Both sides can use incentive clauses to tie compensation to performance without any renegotiation.

The danger of creating a norm that a contract can be renegotiated is nowhere more apparent than in professional football. More often than ever before, professional football players feel that they have a right to renegotiate multi-year contracts if they feel underpaid. Management, however, is not allowed to renegotiate multi-year contracts.

The prime 1990 example is Steve McMichael, star defensive tackle of the Chicago Bears. He demonstrated how a norm of contract renegotiation develops and affects the negotiation process. In 1989, McMichael demanded to renegotiate his multi-year contract, which had a base salary of $500,000 per year. *McMichael May Sit Out Season over Contract*, Chicago Trib, Feb 21, 1990, §4, at 3, cols 4-7. The Bears agreed to renegotiate, resulting in an agreement to add monetary incentive clauses for 1989 and 1990, plus a one-year contract extension through 1991 at $650,000. *Id.* Later in 1989, the Bears renegotiated the contract of their star defensive end, Richard Dent, to a salary of $1.2 million per year. *Id.* Before the 1990 season, McMichael then claimed that the Bears had misstated their true position during his 1989 renegotiation by saying that they did not renegotiate salary as a matter of policy and by saying that they were in poor financial shape. *Id.* McMichael then used those claims to demand another renegotiation of his contract and threatened to refuse to play at all unless his contract was renegotiated. *Id.*

This time, however, the Bears initially refused to renegotiate, leading McMichael to refuse to play in part of the pre-season. Later, the Bears agreed to another contract extension, which they treated as a new contract, rather than a contract renegotiation. The overall effect on future contracts and negotiations/renegotiations with McMichael, as well as other players, remains to be seen.

Balancing timing and closure risks are a critical part of negotiation choices. White House and congressional budget negotiators faced a political timing issue in July, 1990. *Politics Waylays Negotiations on Budget Deficit*, Chicago Trib, July 31, 1990, §1, at 3. If they reached a tentative agreement by the scheduled start of the congressional summer recess, there would be no time to pass legislation to implement it before Congress adjourned. During the summer recess, opposition to a specific budget agreement could be organized. For these reasons, the negotiators planned to avoid tentatively agreeing until Congress was ready to resume. *Id.* By doing so, the negotiators risked one of the dangers of delaying closure, that circumstances would change due to intervening events.

Informational Tactics

4

§4.01 Introduction

Page 81, text, add at end of section:

Successful negotiations by political lobbyists tend to be part of a long-term process to obtain information and create relationships as well as leverage. For example, the lobbyist in Chicago for the major utility, Commonwealth Edison, has constant contact with city aldermen and other political figures. "It's all part of the game of influence, of keeping in touch with politicians who always need something, because meeting that need may mean an advantage in later negotiations for higher rates, better [more favorable] regulations. . . ." *Playing Power Game at City Hall*, Chicago Trib, July 3, 1991, §1, at 1.

§4.02 The Disclosure of Information

Page 87, text, add after second full paragraph:

The timely disclosure of information may be an essential step in setting the stage for a successful settlement through its effect on the other party's expectations and planning. Insurance companies set a reserve when a claim is made which represents what the company expects it may eventually have to pay on the claim. Erisman, *The Art of Negotiating a Settlement*, 25 Trial 26, 28 (Sept 1989). That value is based on the information which the adjuster obtains. *Id.* Thus, if possible, the claimant's attorney will want to disclose information which will cause the reserve to be set at a higher, rather than a lower level. *Id.* Selective information disclosure provides the insurance adjuster with information about the nature and extent of the injury or loss which the adjuster needs for his or her file in order to justify payment of the claim. Cooperation in providing such information, in a timely manner, as well as timely updating of the information tends to generate goodwill. Twiggs, *Negotiating Claims with Insurance Adjusters*, 25 Trial 10 (May 1989).

Providing objective criteria for measuring the value of the claim will make it more reasonable for the adjuster to agree to pay in the range desired by the claimant's attorney. *Id.* Tax records, jury verdict reporters, medical and other expert reports, or the like, can all be used to create the desired objective criteria. *Id.*

Furnishing such objective criteria, as well as the usual documentation of medical bills, verification of lost wages, and so on may succeed in satisfying the insurance adjusters' and claims representatives' interests in closing files on a basis that they can justify as reasonable to their supervisors. *See* Rundlett III, *Negotiating a Small Personal Injury Claim*, 27 Trial 55 (Oct 1991).

Page 87, note 28, add:

Some settlement brochures are now being done on videotape. Erisman, *The Art of Negotiating a Settlement*, 25 Trial 26, 32 (Sept 1989). This should only be done, however, if the attorney feels comfortable using this method, if he or she believes that it will have a favorable impact on the other side, and if the damages justify the expense.

Page 89, note 34, add:

See Zmolek, *Art of Negotiation: Strategies and Tactics*, 27 Trial 22, 24 (Aug 1991), who suggests the use of photographs, X-rays, videotapes, medical illustrations, charts, and diagrams in order to graphically and persuasively present information in order to obtain a settlement.

§4.04 Listening for Information

Page 96, text, add at end of section:

Being a good listener when the other negotiator speaks is an excellent method of learning about both the weaknesses and the strengths of one's case. Erisman, *The Art of Negotiating a Settlement*, 25 Trial 26, 28 (Sept 1989).

Moreover, the other negotiator's failure to mention what you consider to be a key weakness in your case may indicate that the other negotiator has not realized the weak point in your case. Fuchsberg, *Ten Commandments for Successful Evaluation and Settlement*, 27 Trial 16, 18 (Aug 1991).

§4.05 The Funnel Approach

Page 100, text, add before last paragraph:

Direct requests for economic information can be used where the request appears legitimate. In professional hockey, the NHL Players

Association was to negotiate a new collective bargaining agreement in three months. In preparation for the negotiations, the union requested that the president of the league allow the union to inspect the owners' financial books. The union's position was that the economic data would permit them to negotiate for a "fair" share of the sport's revenue. *Where's the Info?*, Chicago Trib, Mar 31, 1991, §3, at 5.

§4.07   Bargaining for Information

Page 104, text, add at end of section:

For long-run, periodically continuing negotiations, negotiating for continuing disclosure of information should be considered a potential issue. Negotiating continuing access to information can have a dramatic effect on future negotiations. For example, National Hockey League players now receive disclosures about other players' salaries. *Money Talk*, Chicago Trib, Oct 17, 1990, §4, at 7, cols 5-6. For players underpaid in comparison to players of equal or lesser skills, other players' salaries can be used for leverage in their own salary negotiations. Yet, without systematic disclosure of the data, the opportunity for such leverage would be far less frequent. From management's perspective, of course, the data can be used at times to demonstrate that a particular player is not underpaid in comparison to his peers.

Whether or not the baseball salary push-pull syndrome will occur in hockey remains to be seen. Unlike baseball, hockey does not have an arbitration system. Yet, disclosed salaries of stars may be used by good players to push up their own salaries somewhat. That increase may then push up the mediocre players' salaries, which could bring the syndrome back full circle to stars' salaries.

General Tactics

5

§5.12　Power

Page 133, text, add after first paragraph:

The seven months of German reunification negotiations involved two parallel types of negotiations: internal and external. Ash, *Germany Unbound*, 37 NY Rev Books, Nov 22, 1990, at 11. During internal negotiations, West Germany's economic strength and inner political stability, in contrast to East Germany's economic weakness and lack of political stability, gave it great negotiating power. *Id.* This imbalance of power allowed West Germany to virtually set the structure of the unified country and the unification treaty in the internal negotiation. *Id.*

There also were external negotiations between West Germany and its World War II conquerors. In the political context of 1990, West Germany could basically ignore England and France, which lacked the political power to influence the outcome of the reunification negotiations. *Id.* Since the United States was a crucial party, but one whose support for reunification was quickly ascertained by West Germany, the crucial external reunification negotiation concerned West Germany and the Soviet Union.

That negotiation led to an agreement that the Soviet Union would support a reunified state as a member of NATO and end Soviet occupation of Germany. In turn, the newly united Germany would: (1) have a numerically limited army without atomic, biological, or chemical weapons; (2) pay significant reparation costs for the Soviet troop withdrawal; and (3) expand its economic ties with the Soviet Union to help in Gorbachev's modernization efforts. *Id.* Certainly, the Soviet Union's diminished power as a result of its worsening economic condition played a role in these decisions.

These negotiations are examples of the shifting nature of power and allies, as well as the effect of power and the costs of creating alliances.

Page 134, text, add after item' 5:

Often, the basis for power is different in negotiations involving litigation than in those for deal-making. In litigation, power tends to arise from the strength of one's case, counsel's abilities, and the capacity to bear the cost and delay. In litigation, parties who do not want to be together are forced to do so.

In deal-making, though, the parties generally want to be together. Power comes from being able to satisfy the needs of the other in a voluntary relationship. That may, however, vary with the availability of alternative sources or deals which meet the same needs.

Power can be apparent or inherent, or the product of the fact creation tactic. *See* §4.03. A coalition of groups may generate more political power as a united front than the aggregate power of each group as separate entities. In other words, the whole can be greater than the sum of its parts.

Power can be exercised to create positive or negative effects on the other party. Both positive and negative power can be economic or psychological, and may be based on business, political, social, or personal relationships. It can be manifested through the giving and withholding of technical or other information. Once power is invoked, there is an inherent danger that its use will lead to escalations in ever greater positive or negative ways. Each such usage may carry its own potential costs.

Power must be viewed separately with regard to each entity and every important individual involved. Otherwise, opportunities and dangers will be overlooked.

Page 135, text, add after Example 5-20:

The conduct of the Environmental Protection Agency (EPA) in the early 1980s provides an example of how a loss of power weakens negotiating effectiveness. Burton, *Negotiating the Cleanup of Toxic Groundwater Contamination: Strategy and Legitimacy*, 28 Nat Resources J 105, 116-17 (1988). During that time, the EPA's efforts to negotiate cleanups of pollution sites were undercut because the agency cut back on its ability to obtain enforcement through adjudication if negotiations failed. *Id.*

Page 135, text, add after second full paragraph:

The use of illegal power in negotiations is demonstrated by the *yakuza* and *sokaiya* in Japan. The *yakuza* is Japan's organized crime. *Sokaiya* are professional stockholders whose version of the protection racket is to sell protection from disruption at stockholder meetings and create violent disruption if their protection is rejected. While Japanese corporations are perceived as tough and tenacious negotiators, they often pay huge sums at home for what, in fact, is extortion for "donations," non-existent publications, and the like. *Japan Firms Behind 8 Ball*, Chicago Trib, Nov 26, 1990, §4, at 1, cols 7-8.

While such illegal uses of power are not advocated, awareness and anticipation of their use is important in various business settings. It is interesting to note how cultural differences play a role in these negotiations. Although various illegal protection rackets are not foreign to the United States, it is difficult to imagine large public corporations routinely paying huge sums to organized crime to avoid staged, violent shareholder disruptions. Of course, American public corporations have been known to compromise with organized political groups to avoid shareholder and other problems.

§5.14   Tone

Page 140, text, add after carryover paragraph:

Brinkmanship can be an extremely dangerous game, especially if the other party may react based on anger or a need to demonstrate forcefulness. The danger is that one may miscalculate the chances of an extremely adverse and potent reaction. For instance, the buyer of a country club had failed to make some required payments. He then abruptly revoked his proposal to restructure the payments without giving a reason. The sellers then almost filed suit against the buyer's principals, as guarantors, without attempting to negotiate further. Had such a suit been filed, the local papers would have printed the story, thereby undermining the buyer's credibility at a time when the buyer was attempting to sell equity memberships to generate cash flow. Fortunately for the buyer, it decided to reinstate the offer before suit was filed.

Page 140, text, add after first full paragraph:

A growing issue of concern and commentary is incivility among lawyers. Berkman, *Disagreeing Without Being Disagreeable*, Chicago Law 1 (Jan 1993). A reflection of the magnitude of that concern was the appointment of the Seventh Federal Judicial Circuit's Committee on Civility to study the problem. *Id.* Incivility tends to arise in the competitive atmosphere of litigation, rather than in the more cooperative atmosphere of transactions. Yet, incivility is clearly unnecessary in litigation.

One aspect of incivility is the failure to negotiate reasonable, cooperative resolutions of non-dispositive, procedural conflicts. According to a federal magistrate: "The problem I see is lawyers' inability to come up with reasonable compromises of their own positions on disputes which are not part of the merits. Most are not taking outrageous positions; they're taking extreme positions on the issues that exist. But with two lawyers taking extreme positions, nothing gets resolved." *Id* 61. In other words, there is a failure to negotiate these non-dispositive, procedural conflicts, even though there ought to be a zone of agreement in which they could be reasonably resolved. This creates unnecessary work and stress without advancing either side's interests in the case.

Another negative consequence may be that it poisons the feelings between the the two sides to the extent that potentially, mutually beneficial settlement negotiations are undercut. An experienced trial lawyer observed that: "A lot of times what you end up doing is making the other side so angry that they dig in their heels, and a case that could have been settled becomes a battle between lawyers who forget their clients." *Id* 64. Even if the attorneys do not become that narrowminded, senseless procedural fights can embroil the clients in costs and delays, resulting in a lose/lose situation in which cases, which should be settled, are not.

Examples of boorish behavior prone to poison the settlement process include:

1. Making unjustified attacks on the other party's honesty or integrity
2. Trying to raise questions about or take discovery about irrelevant, embarrassing aspects of the other party's life
3. Refusing to supply appropriate supporting documents
4. Demanding irrelevant documents
5. Taking outrageously extreme positions.

Magladry & Macpherson, *Now Cut That Out! Extremes of Boorish Behavior*, 30 Trial 43, 45-46 (July 1994).

To the extent that incivility is used as a conscious tactic, it is questionable at best, and often counterproductive. This may include failing to obtain as favorable a settlement as once was possible, because incivility in litigation sets the tone for the negotiation. Thus, litigation should be viewed as a long-term, involuntary relationship in which one must consider whether gaining a short-term, relatively insignificant advantage will result in long-term costs.

Some incivility is more of a reaction to stress and anger with the other side's arguments or postures rather than a conscious tactic. To react in such a manner, though, is to forget the negotiating maxim that one needs to separate people from positions. *See* R. Fisher & W. Ury, *Getting to Yes, Negotiating Without Giving In* (1981).

§5.16   Splitting the Difference

Page 149, text, add at end of section:

There is a different approach to the split-the-difference tactic. For those who prefer a sporting approach, the parties can use a coin flip to resolve the matter. Again, the difference should be relatively small and each party's position must be reasonable. The party initiating the idea should seek to narrow the range, if that ensures that either outcome would be acceptable. Even if the other party rejects the coin flip itself, it may make a concession which allows settlement. For example, A has offered to settle for $900,000, but will accept $850,000. B's offer has stood at $825,000.

> A: I realize that neither of us wants to budge. I'm confident that you would come up to $850,000, but that's really lower than I think is fair. Here's what I'll do. I'll flip a coin, and you'll call it in the air, or you can flip it and I'll call it. We let the coin hit, and however it lands without being turned over decides who wins. If I win, you pay $900,000. If you win, you pay $850,000. That's fair and more interesting, isn't it?

Of course, this should indicate to the other party that $850,000 would be acceptable, but that still means an additional $25,000 as a concession.

To be more hard-line without bluffing, the person proposing the coin flip can make it clear that $850,000 will not be acceptable except as part of a coin flip chance to get $900,000.

Instead of a coin flip, acceptable alternatives include darts or one hole of golf. However, dueling pistols are a thing of the past.

§5.18   Creating a Psychological Commitment for Agreement

Page 154, text, add at end of section:

See the end of Chapter 6 of the Supplement for this tactic's application to intra-organizational negotiations.

§5.25   Patience

Page 171, note 176, add:

The Japanese have become particularly known for their effective use of the patience tactic. Commerce Secretary Robert Mosbacher has stated that "part of the genius of the Japanese is subtlety and procrastination." *Japan Reneging on Trade Pledges 2 in Cabinet Say*, Chicago Trib, Mar 3, 1989, at §1, at 1.

§5.27   Dealing with Those Who Lack Authority

Page 175, text, add after Example 5-52:

Some negotiations are more effective at the other party's home office, in order to reach their real decisionmakers. Trying to break into the market for automobile parts in Japan, one small American manufacturer spent three years unsuccessfully seeking sales to the United States operations of Japanese auto makers. It then decided to visit top purchasing officials in Japan itself, after repeatedly hearing that decisions were made at the home office. The results were not immediately known, but the tactic appeared more promising. *Still Far Apart on Auto Parts*, Chicago Trib, Oct 6, 1991, §7, at 1.

§5.29 Appealing to the Personal Interests of the Other Negotiator or a Non-Party Decision Maker

Page 181, text, add at end of section:

There has been a surge of lobbying by Japanese corporations aimed at the federal government. Looking at the personal interests of federal government negotiators and decisionmakers who interact with Japanese business, some analysts believe that federal government officials are soft on Japanese business in order to create rapport so that they can be employed as lobbyists after leaving government service. Fallons, *The Great Japanese Misunderstanding*, 37 NY Rev Books, Nov 8, 1990, at 33, 34-35.

Unlike the military, which has built some barriers against the military service to military lobbyist career path, the Commerce Department, trade negotiators, and economic policymakers face no such restrictions. *Id.* This example demonstrates the importance of separating the negotiator's personal interests from those of the organization in assessing strengths and weaknesses, needs, interests, values, and priorities.

§5.29A Making People the Problem (New)

One very important, general principle of negotiation is that people should not be presented as the problem. R. Fisher & W. Ury, *Getting to Yes, Negotiating Agreement Without Giving In* (1981). This is one of the core rules of Fisher and Ury. Once people are identified as the problem, they tend to become defensive, seek to save face, or react with personal counter-attacks. All of those reactions can create serious impediments to productive negotiations. By articulating objective, impersonal issues, the dangers of those reactions are avoided. Furthermore, unless it is realistic to think that the persons who are viewed as all or part of the problem will change through negotiation, making them the focus of the problem is useless.

Change can come about in two ways. First, transfer, reassignment of duties, promotion, or demotion of the negotiator or one or more employees of the other party may eliminate the problem in cases where a present or future ongoing relationship is the subject of the negotiation. Second, personal behavior may be altered in response to the negotiation, thereby eliminating the problem behavior. Either type of change is difficult, if not impossible, to create because of personal traits, psychology, inter-corporate relationships, alliances, and managerial bureaucracy. There-fore, in many situations, it is unrealistic to negotiate an issue of specific people.

However, an important exception exists where such change is more feasible, or the problem cannot be solved without a change in the people involved. Examples of the latter are:

1. A negotiator whose highly antagonistic style or lack of understand-ing makes progress impossible after all realistic alternative tactics have been exhausted

2. In a contract for a present or future ongoing relationship, an employee or attorney of the other party whose personal style, behavior, or incompetence creates very significant problems that are (a) necessary to solve and (b) cannot be solved by alternative tactics.

In these limited circumstances and despite the inherent serious risks, one cannot effectively negotiate unless fingers are pointed, thereby commenc-ing a very subjective disagreement. Of course, this is a tactic of last resort, to be used as diplomatically and sensitively as possible. Face-saving should be used, whenever possible, in combination with this tactic. *See* §5.19.

§5.30   Combinations of Tactics

Page 182, text, add at end of section:

Loan Negotiations

Some of the most advantageous deals with lenders have been obtained through difficult and extremely aggressive negotiation behavior. Pulliam, *Corporate Borrowers Bankers Love to Hate*, Corp Fin, Aug 1989, at 34-39. According to Pulliam, those negotiators have been described as:

1. Being perceived as determined "to get what they want no matter what"

2. Shopping around for other deals and demanding 5 to 10 basis points below market rates

3. Being patient with "determination" and "months of haggling" (*see* §5.25)

4. Using "a competitive talk-off" with announcements of the price-to-beat combined with listening to possible modifications in the structure of the deal (*see* §5.15)

5. Employing "sheer intimidation . . . even throwing a chair or two to make his point . . . faking a phone call with a competitor" combined with "some smart shopping" among firms

6. Knowing the market: "how to find that razor-thin edge between not leaving a nickel on the table and yet not having a disaster of a deal on his hands . . . always knows where to get the best borrowing costs . . ."

7. Being "a mercurial negotiator who is constantly changing his strategy"

Id.

However, this level of aggression is dangerous. It can lead to being disliked, feared, and being without a loyal, cooperative lender when one is badly needed. *Id.* This especially is a concern when an ongoing relationship with a lender is needed, but should be balanced against the desirability of the loan(s) to lenders generally (i.e., the market).

Example 5-56

In a sale of corporate stock involving real estate as well as other property, a problem arose when the purchaser's lender suddenly demanded certain environmental protections from the title insurance two days before the scheduled closing. Due to this timing, those demands were impossible to satisfy without a delay in the closing.

Such a delay was unacceptable to both the sellers and the purchaser. However, the purchaser also could not obtain alternative financing without delaying the closing.

The sellers and the purchaser met with their respective attorneys and devised the following plan. First, an emergency meeting was scheduled for the following afternoon with the president of the bank and the involved bank officers.

The purchaser had a personal relationship from past transactions with some bank officials at the vice-president level who were not involved in this matter. The second part of the plan was that the purchaser would meet separately with each of those officials the following morning and make the following points:

1. The lender could have raised the title insurance issue at least one month earlier, but had not done so

2. The timing of the lender's demand made it impossible to satisfy without an unacceptable delay in the closing

3. If the purchaser were unable to close on time because of its lender, the purchaser would be in default and at risk for a loss of substantial earnest money

4. If the lender persisted in its position and thereby jeopardized the deal for the purchaser, the story of the difficulties created by the lender would be circulated in ways that would discourage other commercial purchasers from using this lender (*see* §6.06)

5. If the purchaser was defaulted by the sellers, it would sue the lender (see §7.02 regarding the tactic of litigation)

These points were made so that they would be communicated to the bank's president before the afternoon emergency meeting. This made it unnecessary to directly communicate these threats to the bank president, who might feel constrained to refuse to modify his position because of a personality and/or an organizational based need to save face. (See §5.19 regarding face-saving.)

The third part of the plan involved one of the sellers' attorneys, who was known for his litigation and trial work by the chief counsel for the bank. The parties decided that the attorney should attend the meeting with the bank president as an implied threat. (This was done with a written waiver of any conflict and the expressed ability of that attorney to represent the sellers against the purchaser in the future if necessary.)

After initial greetings, as the meeting opened, the bank's counsel spoke to the attorney.

BANK COUNSEL: I'm surprised to see you here.

ATTORNEY: The title insurance issue brought me.

BANK COUNSEL: Who are you here for?

ATTORNEY: At the moment, sellers and the purchaser.

BANK COUNSEL: What do you intend to do?

ATTORNEY: At this meeting, only to determine whether I need to do anything or whether this will be resolved now.

As part of the pre-arranged plan, after 10 minutes, the attorney leaned over to the purchaser, whispered just loudly enough to be heard, "Everything's ready," and left. His young associate remained with instructions to look grim, write down everything that was said, and not to engage in substantive discussions.

The meeting ended with the bank substantially altering its position so that the closing could proceed on schedule.

For real estate negotiations, several key points should be emphasized. Both buyer and seller must prepare by thoroughly researching the market value for comparable property in the relevant geographic area, including recent sales. The buyer's initial offer generally should be on the low side, since the buyer can go up, but cannot come down. Both should act as though they are not under any time pressure to make a deal, in order to avoid disclosing weakness. Each should try to learn facts about the other party, in order to discover ways to create or utilize power. *Negotiation Has a Motto: Be Prepared*, Chicago Trib, Oct 1, 1989, §16, at 1.

Tactics Involving Other Parties

6

§6.03   Negotiating Teams

Page 197, text, add after third full paragraph:

Whether a high degree of interest in the negotiation should be indicated is one factor in deciding whether to have a negotiating team meet with the other side. Another factor is the size of the team. Having a larger number of negotiators demonstrates a higher level of interest in the negotiation. Revealing a higher level of interest can increase the other party's expectation of the value of whatever it holds, but if a high level of interest is conveyed prior to negotiations, the size of the team need not be a consideration. On the other hand, if concealing or minimizing one's interest is important, one should determine whether having a team of negotiators is more advantageous than hiding one's true level of interest.

§6.04   Judicial Settlement Conferences

Page 202, note 18, add:

However, the Seventh Circuit has held that a court has inherent authority to require the parties themselves, not just the attorneys, to appear for a judicial settlement conference. G Heilman Brewing Co v Joseph Oat Corp, 871 F2d 648 (7th Cir 1989). That case upheld sanctions for costs and attorneys' fees imposed when attorneys appeared for a settlement conference without an official from their corporate client in violation of the order setting the conference. Although there is no express authority for a court to issue such an order in Rule 16 of the Fed R Civ P, the Seventh Circuit held that a court inherently has such authority and that this is consistent with Rule 16's purpose of promoting settlements.

Page 202, text, add after third full paragraph:

Properly performed, mediation is quite different from the usual pretrial settlement conference in court systems (*see* §6.07). A mediator should elicit positions, values, interests, goals and priorities, then seek to determine a potential range of agreement using creative solutions as needed. Shuttle diplomacy is utilized to encourage more open disclosures. Often, however, pretrial settlement conferences instead rely on informal information disclosure combined with the judge's expertise in order to lead to an informal judicial evaluation of "what the case is worth." This frequently culminates in not-too-subtle pressure on the parties to move into the range which the judge feels is appropriate. It also can create a psychological adverse effect on a party who defies the judge's opinion and refuses to settle.

Page 203, text, add at end of section:

Recently, 379 judges and 799 attorneys responded to a survey regarding 20 techniques that judges might use in judicial settlement conferences. Rude & Wall, *Judicial Involvement in Settlement: How Judges and Lawyers View It,* 72 Judicature 175 (1988). The judges were asked whether they would use those methods and the lawyers were asked whether they would want judges to use those methods. *Id* 176-77. The results of the survey, from most popular to least popular methods, were as follows:

1. Exercise discretion to order a settlement conference (62% judges) (67% lawyers)

2. Talk about settlements in similar cases (61% judges) (61% lawyers)

3. Focus on the areas where agreement is most likely (58% judges) (61% lawyers)

4. Suggest a new proposal not previously considered (53% judges) (63% lawyers)

5. Ask for a compromise (56% judges) (46% lawyers)

6. "Argue logically for concessions" (47% judges) (52% lawyers)

7. After listening to counsel, recommend a settlement amount (42% judges) (47% lawyers)

8. Speak to counsel separately (26% judges) (42% lawyers)

9. Refer to the high risk of a trial (39% judges) (18% lawyers)

10. Label a particular amount as "reasonable" (29% judges) (27% lawyers)

11. Require the parties to attend the conference (29% judges) (27% lawyers)

12. Set a firm date for trial (29% judges) (24% lawyers)

13. Note the advantages of settlement to the parties (20% judges) (27% lawyers)

14. "Analyze the case for the lawyer" (23% judges) (16% lawyers)

15. "Pressure" a lawyer who is poorly prepared (15% judges) (22% lawyers)

16. Tell the parties the strengths and weaknesses of their case (13% judges) (24% lawyers)

17. Advise an attorney (7% judges) (10% lawyers)

18. "Downgrade the merits of the stronger case and/or the demerits of the weaker" (8% judges) (6% lawyers)

19. Suggest a settlement amount to the parties (5% judges) (8% lawyers)

20. Try to directly "persuade" the parties to accept a settlement (4% judges) (5% lawyers)

Id 177.

That only 29 per cent of the judges indicated that they utilized absolutely firm trial dates as a method of promoting settlement seems surprisingly low given its effectiveness. It is not clear whether that figure was lessened because some of the judges surveyed could not set firm trial dates. Judges involved in settlement conferences might not be able to set definite trial dates because they lack sufficient control over their calendars or the case has only been assigned to them for pretrial purposes.

It is surprising that only a few of the tactics received the support of the majority of both judges and attorneys in the survey, and none of the tactics received overwhelming support from either group.

Katz, *The L'Ambiance Plaza Mediation: A Case Study in Judicial Settlement of Mass Torts*, 5 Ohio St J Dispute Resolution 277 (1990), examines the successful judicial mediation and settlement of the tort and commercial claims which arose when a building collapsed, killing 44 people and injuring 14 others. In addition to those plaintiffs, the interested parties included more than 50 contractors, several insurance companies, and the Occupational Safety and Health Administration (OSHA). An overall settlement of all claims was reached within 19 months. The judicial mediators tried to deflate unrealistically high aspirations by:

1. Stressing the risks of not settling to each side in order to increase the parties' willingness to compromise to avoid those risks

2. Emphasizing the monetary litigation costs

3. Emphasizing the emotional litigation costs

4. Stressing the estimated 7 to 10 years of litigation that would occur without settlement

In stressing the risks of not settling, the defendants were told of the tendency of jurors to sympathize with plaintiffs. The plaintiffs were told of potential appeals and the real possibility of collecting no more than insurance coverage, as many defendants might go out of business or file bankruptcy because of large verdicts.

In addition to suggesting potential compromises, the judicial mediators tried to create new opportunities for compromise by bringing the commercial claims into the negotiation, despite the resulting increase in complexity, in order to increase the potential for tradeoffs among issues. Thus, the mediators employed the tactic of injecting new issues.

In addition to the usual aspects of case management, L'Ambiance Plaza mediators also acted to facilitate the negotiations and to oversee the process by requiring the attendance of clients and nonparty decisionmakers and stressing the morality of providing relief to the victims' families.

Under certain unusual circumstances, settlement may involve the parties and the court agreeing to alter the judge's role from that of a mediator back to deciding a particular issue or issues. Such a change may be appropriate where the potential settlement deals with multiple issues, and the parties are deadlocked on one issue or a few issues, but have agreed as to all of the other issues. Under these circumstances, the parties might choose to agree to submit the remaining issue(s) to the judge for the judge to make a binding decision in order to break the deadlock. Thus, they would agree to the settlement with the final provision to be determined by the court. For example, in a nuisance suit for money damages arising out of a neighbor's pollution, the parties might have agreed on money, non-disclosure, and various other non-monetary provisions, but be deadlocked over the defendant's insistence that the settlement package include the defendant receiving a right of first refusal to purchase the plaintiff's property, should the plaintiff decide to sell its property in the future. Rather than not settling and going through a full trial, the parties, with the judge's approval, might decide to settle with the proviso that the judge will decide whether or not the defendant receives the right of first refusal as part of the settlement. This might involve holding a limited evidentiary hearing and/or the submission of briefs on that issue. If such a settlement procedure is utilized, it is important to clearly establish, whether formally or informally, how much latitude the judge has in deciding the deadlocked issue, whether final offer arbitration is to be used, or whether the judge may compromise or modify one of the parties' proposals. (*See* §6.07.) To the extent that the judge is being asked to be an arbitrator rather than follow formal rules of civil procedure, one must be careful that doing so is permissible in that particular jurisdiction.

§6.05   Allies

Page 205, text, add after Example 6-6:

An Indiana business created a barrier to being taken over and enhanced its own growth by having three large companies, with which it had business relationships, become minority shareholders. *Stock Purchase Deal May Prevent Engine Manufacturer's Takeover*, Chicago Trib, July 16, 1990, §1, at 4, cols 6-8. Using the tactic of creating allies, Cummings Engine Company negotiated with Ford Motor Company, Tenneco, and Kubota Corporation to have those companies purchase a total of 25 per cent of Cummings' stock. Ford and Tenneco each received the right to designate a representative on Cummings' board of directors. The agreement also included joint ventures with Kubota and Tenneco.

§6.06 Media or Community Pressure

Page 207, text, add at end of section:

In negotiations between a community group and governmental or private officials, it is crucial to identify the power that each side has prior to negotiations. *Organizing Training Materials* (Midwest Academy, Chicago, Ill 1987). This issue should be considered during planning regardless of whether the negotiator represents the community group or the officials. *Id.*

Professional sports negotiations often involve public posturing to create media and community pressure on one side or the other. In professional football, the collective bargaining is complicated by minority veto power among owners. *Owners vs. Union: The Game Within the Game*, Chicago Trib, Sept 23, 1990, §3, at 9, cols 6-8. Out of 28 teams in the National Football League, important decisions on many collective bargaining issues require a three-fourths majority vote. It remains to be seen whether that factor will create leverage for the owners and allow more extreme pro-owner positions to prevail, or block agreement and cause a strike or further litigation. The Players Association is wary of future negotiations, in part because a minority of hardline owners can prevent an agreement. Union director, Gene Upshaw, conveyed this attitude when he told the press "[t]here are two rooms, the bargaining room and the settlement room. We will not go into the bargaining room." *Id.*

The apparent meaning is that, understandably, the union does not want to engage in useless bargaining if management's position is well outside any reasonable zone of agreement due to the influence of a hardline minority of owners. The union sought to create media and public pressure on the owners to commence negotiations with lesser demands than the hardline owners wanted.

With the political and numerical decline of labor unions from representing one-fourth to one-sixth of workers, the settlement of the bitter 11-month United Mine Union-Pittston Co. strike demonstrates the power of the media and community pressure tactic. Broder, *For Union Labor, a Glimmer of New Hope*, Chicago Trib, Sept 2, 1990, §4, at 3, cols 4-6.

After a deadlock in negotiations, the company cancelled its contribution to an industry health plan which supposedly guaranteed benefits for active—as well as disabled and retired—workers and their families. *Id.* The union used the high emotions created to galvanize churches, community leaders, and even some other businesses. *Id.* The resulting church meetings, large demonstrations, and boycotts added to the strikers' feelings of unity. *Id.* Simultaneously, well-conceived, rational ads were used to generate pro-union national opinion. *Id.* Workers remained on strike in the face of fines and arrests for illegal picketing, as well as some acts of violence. *Id.* Finally, Secretary of Labor Elizabeth Dole intervened, despite the federal government's prior refusals to intervene in other major labor disputes. *Id.* The end result, announced by Secretary Dole, was a settlement in which all health benefits were restored, while the company achieved some of the work-rule changes it had demanded.

§6.07   Alternative Dispute Resolution

Page 208, text, add after third paragraph:

Alternative dispute resolution sometimes may be able to bridge the gap between parties who cannot agree on substantive terms, but who can agree on the *procedure* to determine substantive terms. For instance, in negotiating the buy-out of a minority shareholder in a close corporation, although all of the shareholders wanted the buy-out to proceed, the two sides could not agree on a fair market value price for the minority shares. A deadlock was broken by agreeing to submit the issue of fair market price to binding arbitration, and by agreeing to the procedures for selecting the arbitrator and conducting the arbitration.

An indication of the continuing growth in the utilization of alternative dispute resolution is the recent recognition by the American Institute for Certified Public Accountants (AICPA) that accountants may include work in the course of alternative dispute resolution in their engagement letters, although once the alternative dispute resolution begins the accounting firm may no longer be deemed to be independent of its client. *Alternative Dispute Resolution: ADR and the World Around Us*, Chicago Daily L Bull, Nov 19, 1993, at 19, col 4.

Alternative dispute resolution also has been used to facilitate negotiating structured settlements. *Alternative Dispute Resolution in Structured Settlements*, Chicago Daily L Bull, Nov 19, 1993, at 19, col 1. (*See* §7.03.)

Page 211, note 54, add:

Mediation involves interdisciplinary skills such as interpersonal communications and group dynamics. Nolan-Haley & Volpe, *Teaching Mediation as a Lawyering Role*, 39 J Legal Educ 571, 575 (1989). At one law school, for instance, a course on mediation is taught by an attorney and a sociologist. *Id.*

Page 212, text, add after second Item 2:

In addition to matrimonial litigation, mediation is also useful in commercial disputes (Rieders, *Mediation: Pros and Cons*, 26 Trial 60 (Oct 1990)) and has been successfully utilized in cases involving personal injuries, products liability, medical malpractice, real estate, construction, wrongful discharge, and disputes within close corporations. Gillie, *Voluntary Mediation: Tool to Assess Risks and Speed Settlements*, 26 Trial 58 (Oct 1990). One mediator has described mediation as "basically an assessment of risks, and risks are present in virtually every case." *Id.* Among a number of useful situations for considering mediation, three in particular are:

1. When one party to litigation is engaged in unnecessary discovery or procedural motions.

2. One or both [or all] parties have many similar cases.

3. The parties have a dispute, but also have continuing business relationships which are being, or in the future, may become impaired.

Id 61.

Page 212, text, add at end of subsection "Mediation":

Business dispute mediators have claimed an 80 per cent success rate. Ehrman, *Why Business Lawyers Should Use Mediation*, 75 ABA J 73 (June 1989). Ehrman asserts that "in fact, neither side has anything to lose in mediation." *Id.* On the contrary, time, expense, information and concessions otherwise available through further negotiations can be lost in an unsuccessful mediation.

The International Association of Defense Counsel supports pretrial-mediation to "help unclog the overburdened civil system." Under this concept, there is limited discovery, the mediation hearing is held within 90 days of a request by the claimant, and the defendant pays 75 per cent of the mediator's fee up to $1,000. *Mediation Finds Unlikely Ally*, Chicago Daily L Bull, Jan 7, 1991, at 3.

United States District Court Judge Marvin Aspen selectively utilizes mediation in about six to ten cases per year. The cases must fulfill the following criteria:

1. Settlement attempts have failed

2. The parties agree to mediation

3. The parties know the important facts and issues

4. The additional expense of a mediator is justifiable in view of the complexity of the case and the length of a projected trial

5. A mediator will provide either technical expertise or time and flexibility for intensive sessions, which a judge cannot provide

Mediation Catching on—Slowly, Chicago Daily L Bull, Jan 28, 1991, at 1.

In June, 1992, the Illinois Court Mediation Conference heard the following from speakers regarding Florida's judicial mediation program:

1. An hour of mediation saves almost two days of trial

2. Most cases were settled within an hour of mediation

3. The longest mediation sessions were no more than three hours

4. Mediation tends to be more effective when it is conducted relatively early in the process, before the expert costs are incurred, and before the stress and cost of pretrial preparation

5. Mediation does not cause delay or additional costs

6. Requiring the parties to attend the mediation helps to educate the parties about the realities of the case

7. Cooperation by insurance companies in mediating early results in savings to all parties

8. Even if mediation fails to result in settlement, the process tends to clarify the issues and result in better and shorter trial presentations

Demetrio, *Alternative Dispute Resolution: There Are No Losers*, CBA Rec 9 (Nov 1992).

Limited mediation programs of court cases in Cook County, Illinois have resulted in settlement rates of as high as 65 per cent in small claims cases, 85 per cent in eviction cases, and 53 per cent in civil cases involving more than $15,000. *Id.*

The 53 per cent success rate remained the same when used in civil cases involving more than $30,000 in Cook County, Illinois. *Mediation Clears Courts' Clogged Arteries*, Chicago Daily L Bull, Oct 28, 1994, at 1, cols 2-3. This has been a voluntary mediation program. *Id.* As a result of this and voluntary test programs in other Illinois counties, a committee of the Illinois Judicial Conference has proposed that a mandatory court-ordered mediation program be established. *Id.*

The National Institute For Dispute Resolution estimates that there are 250 to 300 mediation centers nationally, providing free services for neighbor and family disputes, and public policy issues concerning governmental services, as well as for smaller monetary disputes. In this way, litigation is often avoided. *In Sue-Happy Society, Mediators Lighten Court Load*, Chicago Trib, Dec 16, 1991, §1, at 3.

Thirty-three states now require mediation in custody and visitation matters. Fourteen reports have found sex bias in the court mediation process, specifically that women have less bargaining power in the process. Eight of those reports were by state task forces, including one in California. The studies suggest mediators often tend to take men more seriously, and view women as "unladylike" or "vindictive" for refusing to concede. Other factors cited were that men exploit their generally greater economic resources as well as business and legal experience, and, at times, their ability to physically intimidate. Attempts are being made to reform the process, although it is unclear at this point whether those attempts will be successful. *Task Forces Studying Courts Find Mediation Biased Against Women*, Chicago Daily L Bull, Aug 4, 1992, at 3.

It has been suggested that voluntary mediation may be particularly useful in employment litigation. Fitzpatrick, *Nonbinding Mediation of Employment Disputes*, 30 Trial 40 (June 1994). Fitzpatrick recommends that voluntary mediation be entered into through a written agreement which includes provisions that provide for:

1. A stay of discovery during the mediation process

2. Complete confidentiality of everything said or done in the mediation process

3. A schedule with a deadline for completion

4. A page limit for position statements to be submitted to the mediator

5. An allocation of the mediator's fees

6. A hold harmless clause for the mediator.

Id 42. The first, and possibly the second, of these elements will also require the agreement of the court.

Fitzgerald states that the decision to mediate is voluntary because "finding a consensus in favor of mediation is part of the conciliation process." *Id* 42. We note that if such a consensus is achieved, it would seem to naturally follow that there will be a higher rate of settlements reached because the parties will be more predisposed to settle, rather than forced to participate in mediation. However, that leaves the question of whether the success rate of a mandatory mediation program for all parties would be sufficiently high, so that overall, more cases are still resolved by settlement than through a voluntary program with fewer participants. This is a question which needs to be answered through empirical data comparing mandatory and voluntary mediation programs in which the same types of cases are being mediated.

Fitzgerald indicates that attorneys need to possess "mediation advocacy skills," as compared with trial advocacy skills. For example, at trial, one may not care how the other side reacts to one's presentation, whereas this is obviously important in the mediation process. However, the latter is true throughout the negotiation process.

Fitzgerald believes that the lawyers should play the role of problem solvers. This would not always seem to be true, particularly where only dollars are at issue. Whether to be a true problem solver in a mediation should be analyzed in the same way counsel decides whether that is the most effective approach in any stage of the negotiation. In other words, a strategy of high, realistic expectations with small systematic concessions may achieve better results in a particular mediation than a true problem solving strategy. *See* Chapter 3. Of course, to the extent that win/win solutions can be found, they should always be utilized. *See* §5.06.

Fitzgerald feels that if a settlement is reached, the agreement be written, whether by computer, typewriter, or by hand, and signed before the parties leave. While it is true that apparent agreements sometimes encounter difficulties, or even dissolve into disagreements in the drafting stage, rushing to have something written and signed before the clients leave for the day may or may not be a solution. There are cases where careful drafting and redrafting is necessary in order to fully cover both sides' needs and concerns. On the other hand, counsel obviously want to try to deal with all issues during the mediation and ensure that everyone has the same understanding of the parties' apparent agreement, as well as to prevent a party from changing his or her mind.

The continuing growth of complex litigation in the federal courts has had a corresponding growth in complex discovery disputes and settlement negotiations. Some federal courts are increasing utilization of special masters for these matters, pursuant to Rule 16 of the Fed R Civ P. The special masters may serve as mediators for either discovery or settlement, or may, in effect, arbitrate the discovery dispute. *Special Master's Role Increasing in Complex Cases*, Chicago Daily L Bull, Aug 3, 1992, at 5.

Page 212, note 62, add:

There has been a clear trend in the United States Supreme Court in favor of arbitration. In 1985, the Court held that agreements to arbitrate federal antitrust claims could be enforced. Mitsubishi Motors Corp v Soler Chrysler-Plymouth, 473 US 614 (1985). In 1987, the Court upheld agreements to arbitrate federal securities claims under the 1934 Securities Exchange Act and RICO (Racketeer Influenced and Corrupt Organizations Act) claims. Shearson/Am Express, Inc v McMahon, 482 US 220 (1987). (*See* 15 USC §77b *et seq* and 18 USC §1961 *et seq.*)

In 1989, that trend continued as the United State Supreme Court decided two arbitration cases. The Court held that the parties' contractual choice of state law provision governs an arbitration and the Federal Arbitration Act does not preempt the state arbitration act. Volt Information Sciences, Inc v Board of Trustees, 489 US 468 (1989). (*See* 9 USC §1 *et seq.*) Two months later, the Supreme Court overruled a 1953 precedent, holding that predispute agreements to arbitrate claims based on §12(2) of the 1933 Securities Act are enforceable. Rodriguez de Quijas v Shearson/Am Express, Inc, 490 US 477 (1989) (overruling Wilco v

Swan, 346 US 427 (1953)). (*See* 15 USC §771(2).) The Court cited, inter alia, the Federal Arbitration Act, which states that arbitration agreements are enforceable except on grounds which could be the basis to rescind any contract, such as fraud or duress. (*See* 9 USC §1 *et seq.*)

The trend in the United States Supreme Court in favor of arbitration continued in 1991. In Gilmer v Interstate/Johnson Lane Corp, 111 S Ct 1647 (1991), the Court held that a stockbroker's Age Discrimination Employment Act (ADEA) claim was subject to the mandatory arbitration rules of New York Stock Exchange (NYSE) where those rules required arbitration of all employment disputes. The *Gilmer* court distinguished prior holdings in Alexander v Gardner-Denver Co, 415 US 36 (1974); Barrentine v Arkansas-Bit Freight Sys, 450 US 728 (1981); and McDonald v City of West Branch, 466 US 284 (1984) that arbitration clauses in collective bargaining agreements do not bar federal statutory discrimination suits. The Federal Arbitration Act, 9 USC §1 *et seq*, exempts "contracts of employment of seamen, railroad employees, or any other class of workers engaged in foreign or interstate commerce" from arbitration. In *Gilmer*, the Supreme Court held that provision to be inapplicable and, therefore, the Court did not decide whether an arbitration requirement in an employee contract, as distinct from an industry rule, would preclude a discrimination suit. However, the arbitration requirement did not preclude the employee from making an age discrimination claim with the Equal Employment Opportunity Commission (EEOC), or preclude the EEOC initiating a case on its own. The *Gilmer* court specifically noted that "arbitration agreements will not preclude the EEOC from bringing actions seeking classwide and equitable relief." (111 S Ct at 1655.)

A majority of jurisdictions have adopted the Uniform Arbitration Act. These jurisdictions are: Alaska (Alaska Stat §09.43.010 *et seq)*; Arizona (Ariz Rev Stat Ann §12-1501 *et seq)*; Arkansas (Ark Code Ann §6-108-201 *et seq*); Colorado (Colo Rev Stat Ann §13-22-201 *et seq)*; Delaware (Del Code Ann tit 10, §5701 *et seq)*; Dist. of Columbia (DC Code Ann §16-4301 *et seq*); Florida (Fla Stat Ann §682.01 *et seq*); Idaho (Idaho Code §7-901 *et seq*); Illinois (710 Ill Comp Stat Ann §5/1 *et seq*); Indiana (Indiana Code Ann §34-4-2-1 *et seq*); Iowa (Iowa Code Ann §679A.1 *et seq*); Kansas (Kan Stat Ann §5-401 *et seq*); Kentucky (Ky Rev Stat Ann §417.045 *et seq*); Maine (Me Rev Stat Ann tit 10 §5927 *et seq*); Maryland (Code, Courts and Judicial Proceedings, §3-201 *et seq*); (Md Code Ann 251, §1 *et seq*); Michigan (Mich Comp Laws Ann §600.5001 *et seq*); Minnesota (Minn Stat Ann §572.08 *et seq*); Missouri (Mo Ann Stat §435.350 *et seq*); Montana (Mont Code Ann §27-5-111 *et seq*); Nebraska (Neb Rev Stat §25-2601 *et seq*); Nevada (Nev Rev Stat Ann §38.015 *et seq*); New Mexico (NM Stat Ann §44-7-1 *et seq* (1978)); North Carolina (NC Gen Stat §1-567.1 *et seq*); North Dakota (ND Cent Code §32-29.2-01 *et seq*); Oklahoma (Okla St Ann tit 15, §801 *et seq*); Pennsylvania (42 Pa Cons Stat Ann §7301 *et seq*); South Carolina (SC

Code Ann §15-48-10); South Dakota (SD Codified Laws Ann §21-25A-1 *et seq*); Tennessee (Tenn Code Ann §29-5-301 *et seq*); Texas (Tex Rev Civ Stat Ann arts 224 *et seq*); Utah (Utah Code Ann §78-31a-1 *et seq* (1953)); Vermont (Vt Stat Ann tit 12 §5651 *et seq*); Virginia (Va Code Ann §8.01-581.01 *et seq* (1950)); and Wyoming (Wyo Stat §1-36-101 *et seq* (1977)).

The Uniform Arbitration Act treats written arbitration agreements as "valid, enforceable and irrevocable save upon such grounds as exist in law or in equity for the revocation of any contract." (Section 1.) The arbitration agreement controls the method for choosing arbitrators. However, under the Act, if the agreement fails to provide for such a method "or if the agreed method fails or for any reason cannot be followed, or when an arbitrator appointed fails or is unable to act and his successor has not been duly appointed, the court on application of a party shall appoint one or more arbitrators." (Section 3.) Unless the arbitration agreement provides otherwise, the Act provides for an evidentiary hearing after which the written decision of a majority of the arbitrators is binding. (Sections 4, 5, and 8.) The parties have a right to be represented by counsel, and the arbitrators are empowered to issue subpoenas and to authorize deposition of witnesses who cannot be subpoenaed to the hearing or are unable to attend the hearing. (Sections 6 and 7.) Unless the arbitration agreement provides otherwise, the arbitrators determine who pays their fees and expenses, as well as any other expenses not categorized as attorney's fees. (Section 10.)

If there is a dispute as to whether there is a valid arbitration agreement, an application can be filed in court to compel or stay the arbitration. (Section 2.) After an award is made, an award can be confirmed in court, subject only to specified grounds for vacating, modifying, or correcting the award. (Section 11.) Judgment can then be entered on the confirmed, modified, or corrected award. (Section 14.)

Under the Act, the grounds for requesting the arbitrators to change an award are:

(1)   There was an evident miscalculation of figures or an evident mistake in the description of any person, thing or property referred to in the award;

(2)   The arbitrators have awarded upon a matter not submitted to them and the award may be corrected without affecting the merits of the decision upon the issues submitted;

(3)   The award is imperfect in form, not affecting the merits of the controversy; [or]

(4)   [F]or the purpose of clarifying the award. [Sections 9 and 13].

An application for such a change must be made within 20 days of the delivery of a copy of the award. (Section 9.)

Within 90 days of delivery of a copy of the award, a petition may be filed in court to modify or correct the award based on any of the first three grounds listed above for which the arbitrators can make changes. (Section 13.) Additionally, within the same time period, or within 90 days of when the applicant knew or should have known that the award was based on corruption, fraud, or other undue means, an application can be filed in court to vacate the award on the following grounds:

(1) The award was procured by corruption, fraud, or other undue means;

(2) There was evident partiality by an arbitrator appointed as a neutral or corruption in any one of the arbitrators or misconduct prejudicing the rights of any party;

(3) The arbitrators exceeded their powers;

(4) The arbitrators refused to postpone the hearing upon sufficient cause being shown therefor or refused to hear evidence material to the controversy or otherwise so conducted the hearing, contrary to the provisions of Section 5, as to prejudice substantially the rights of a party; or

(5) There was no arbitration agreement and the issue was not adversely determined in proceedings under Section 2 and the party did not participate in the arbitration hearing without raising the objection; but the fact that the relief was such that it could not or would not be granted by the circuit court is not ground for vacating or refusing to confirm the award [Section 12].

The Act is to be "construed as to effectuate its general purpose to make uniform the law of those states which enact it." (Section 21.)

Conspicuous by their absence is a provision for asking the arbitrators to change the award because of a mistake of fact or of law, or a provision by which the courts can vacate an arbitration award because it is against the manifest weight of the evidence or because of a mistake of law. Thus, in comparison to litigation, although binding arbitration limits costs and often shortens the time it takes to obtain a decision, it also sharply limits the opportunity for appeal.

Various states have modified various sections of the Act. Some of these modifications can have a critical impact. For instance, while the Uniform Act provides for court appointment of arbitrators if the agreement fails to designate a method, the Illinois statute omits this provision. 710 Ill Comp Stat Ann §5/3. Thus, in Illinois it would appear that the arbitration cannot proceed unless the agreement provides for the method by which the arbitrator(s) are to be chosen or the parties agree on the method. Accordingly, even if the Uniform Act has been adopted in a particular jurisdiction, counsel should check the specifics of the statute and should not assume that the Uniform Act has been adopted without any modifications.

Page 214, text, add after second full paragraph:

In designing an arbitration agreement, numerous issues should be considered. Blackford, *Arbitration Provisions for Business Contracts*, 48 Arb J 47 (Sept 1993). These questions include:

1.   What jurisdiction's law should control the arbitration and what, if any, arbitration statute does that jurisdiction have?

2.   Should good faith negotiations be a prerequisite to proceeding with the arbitration?

3.   Whether mediation should be a prerequisite to proceeding with the arbitration?

4.   Should all, or only some, disputes be subject to arbitration?

5.   What procedural rules should be followed in the arbitration?

6.   Where should the arbitration be held?

7.   How should the arbitrators be selected?

8.   How many arbitrators should be used?

9.   What qualifications should the arbitrator(s) have?

10.   Should disputed money or property be placed in escrow?

11.   What, if any, discovery should be permitted?

12.   If discovery is permitted, to what extent will the arbitrator(s) be able to rule on discovery questions or impose sanctions for failure to comply with discovery?

13.   Can equitable relief, such as specific performance, be awarded?

14.   Can punitive damages be awarded?

15.   Should there be a limit to the amount which can be awarded?

16.   How should the arbitrators be compensated?

17.   How should the cost of the arbitration be allocated between the parties?

18.   Should the arbitrator(s) be required to make written findings of fact and conclusions of law?

19.   Should there be a time limit within which to demand arbitration?

20.   Whether to have a time limit within which the arbitration award must be paid?

21.   Should attorney's fees be shifted in favor of the prevailing party or should attorney's fees be paid to the prevailing party if that party is required to take action to enforce or to collect the award?

One of the benefits of arbitration is the flexibility to tailor procedures to fit a particular situation. This may involve limiting the arbitration to written submissions where that provides the arbitrator(s) with an appropriate basis for deciding the issue(s), yet saves substantial costs in comparison to an evidentiary hearing with live testimony. On the other hand, it might involve deviating from the typical manner in which testimony is presented if it is believed that doing so will provide a clearer understanding of the issues. Groton, *Using ADR Methods to Solve the Dilemma When Experts Collide*, 47 Arb J 56 (Dec 1992). Groton describes an arbitration in which the parties and the arbitrator agreed to have simultaneous questioning of the opposing experts, as if the experts were sitting on a panel being interviewed together, in order to try to best determine the reasons for their conflicting conclusions. *Id.* This allowed the opposing experts to immediately respond to the point that the other expert had made. *Id.* In that particular case, it was felt that this procedure succeeded in highlighting the strengths and weaknesses of the opposing opinions. *Id.*

The effectiveness of mass arbitration programs is still being studied. In Cook County, Illinois, the Circuit Court has instituted a program for mandatory, nonbinding arbitration of personal injury cases where the damages involved are clearly less than $15,000 and judicial settlement conferences have not resulted in settlement. The arbitrators are a panel of three attorneys. In 1990, the first year for such arbitration in Cook County, 70 per cent of the arbitration awards were accepted. Keleher, *Mandatory Arbitration in Cook County, a Year of Progress*, CBA Rec 13 (Apr/May 1991). A substantial number of cases in which the arbitration award was rejected settled relatively soon after the arbitration.

Perhaps due to a lengthy backlog of these civil cases, primarily personal injury cases, the acceptance rate in Cook County is higher than the 60 per cent rate for most court systems. Other contributing factors may be the limited economic value of the cases and organized legal support for the program. Haldeman, *The Chicago Arbitration Program: An Independent Appraisal*, CBA Rec 16 (Apr/May 1991).

Court-ordered mandatory, nonbinding arbitration of smaller cases appears to have been a significant factor in reducing the backlog of civil cases involving more than $30,000 in Cook County, Illinois from seven years in 1989 to a little over four years in 1994. *Mediation Clears Courts' Clogged Arteries*, Chicago Daily L Bull, Oct 28, 1994, at 1, cols 2-3.

In contrast to the Illinois courts' arbitration system, private arbitration can allow the parties to select the arbitrators, and determine procedural and evidentiary rules. However, the grounds for appealing an arbitration award are quite narrow and limited in private arbitration. *See Moseley, Hallgarten, Estabrook & Weeden, Inc v Ellis*, 849 F2d 264, 267 (7th Cir 1988); Brown, *Differences Between Private Arbitration and Mandatory Court-Annexed Arbitration*, CBA Rec 20 (Apr/May 1991). The Cook County system uses what is, in fact, a brief, sometimes perfunctory, judicial mediation effort. The arbitration process is governed by State Supreme Court rules, with liberal evidentiary rules, including some use of affidavits. Ill Sup Ct Ruls 86-95. Any party can reject an award within 30 days by filing a written notice and paying a $200 fee. Ill Sup Ct Rul 93(a).

In Illinois, four other counties have similar mandatory arbitration programs. Relatively short hearings of about two hours are used. Arbitration has cut court backlogs. In one county, during a four-month period, parties rejected 450 of 1511 arbitration awards. *In Some Cases, Parties Prefer Arbitrating Instead of Litigating,* Chicago Trib, Dec 16, 1991, §2, at 3. However, only 181 of those cases actually proceeded to trial; the rest settled. *Id.* A four-year study of a federal district court in North Carolina has concluded that mandatory arbitration improves access to the civil system and reduces legal costs, but does not necessarily expedite the process. *Arbitration Reduces Costs: Study,* Chicago Daily L Bull, Sept 5, 1990, at 1, col 8. The Rand Corporation's Institute for Civil Justice studied the mandatory arbitration of contract and tort claims of $150,000 or less in the United States District Court for the Middle District of North Carolina. The study concluded that mandatory arbitration:

1. Encouraged litigants to pursue their cases, without necessarily increasing the number of cases filed
2. Was favored by litigants and attorneys
3. Lowered the parties' litigation costs by an average of more than $5,000, or 20 per cent
4. Did not appear to speed up the resolution of cases
5. Did not decrease the cost to the public of operating the court system

Id.

Page 214, text, add after third full paragraph:

Merely being eligible for arbitration has led to very high salary increases for baseball players. For example, in 1988, although the owners *won* almost 60 per cent of the arbitrations, the players who *lost* their arbitrations obtained a greater average salary increase than the players who *won* their arbitrations. O'Reilly, *Alternative Dispute Resolution Under the NLRA: Devaluation of the Strike,* 6 Lab Law 133, 141 (Winter 1990). That indicates that, in order to win a typical baseball arbitration, the owners had to offer a large salary increase. Some 76 per cent of baseball players who file for arbitration settle with the owner prior to arbitration. *Id* 142. In 1989, the average arbitration settlement brought a 67 per cent salary increase, while players who prevailed in arbitration obtained an average increase of 120 per cent. *Id.* That is a further, clear indication of the power players obtain by being eligible for arbitration in the baseball market. This also seems to be consistent with the general tendency of final offer arbitration to increase the desire to compromise and to decrease the difference in positions in order to maximize the possibility of having one's position chosen by the arbitrator. *Id* 139.

Unlike final offer arbitration, in most arbitrations, the arbitrator's discretion is not limited to picking one of two positions. In contrast to its use in settling labor disputes in the public sector, binding arbitration has not gained widespread acceptance in the private sector. *Id* 140. It has been suggested that the reasons for this are that: (1) arbitration can "inhibit meaningful collective bargaining;" (2) it may diminish the "incentive to find creative solutions" due to the tendency of many arbitrators to split the difference; (3) "neutral arbitrators are not accountable to the Board of Directors and are not generally familiar with the industry or with the employees' real concerns;" (4) labor-management relations may suffer due to provisions in the arbitration decision that are not acceptable to either side; and (5) "it may simply be a crutch for a weak union." *Id.* It has also been suggested that final offer arbitration eliminates most of those flaws. *Id.*

Baseball arbitration continues to lead to spiraling salaries. Arbitrators consider length of service and performance, but not the club's ability to pay. Many "fringe" players have leaped into the $700,000 range. *Players Can't Lose in Arbitration Game*, Chicago Trib, Feb 19, 1991, §4, at 9. Even players "losing" the arbitration still can triple their salaries, like Bobby Bonds. *Id.* Bonds' salary in 1989 was less than $400,000. Two straight "losing" arbitration years resulted in jumps to $850,000 and then $2,300,000. *The Press Box*, Chicago Trib, Feb 18, 1991, §3, at 3. Thus, while arbitration is an important methodology to consider, it is not a panacea.

In December, 1992, baseball owners sought to replace salary arbitration with increased revenue sharing and a cap on team salaries. *End to Salary Arbitration Urged*, Chicago Trib, Dec 15, 1992, §4, at 1. This demonstrates that arbitration is not always better than other negotiation alternatives.

Page 214, text, add to note 68:

See also Sander & Goldberg, *Making the Right Choice*, 79 ABA J 66 (Nov 1993).

Page 215, text, add at end of subsection "Arbitration":

Failure to know local arbitration rules can lead to legal malpractice claims. One firm was sued when it advised a personal injury plaintiff to ignore an arbitration hearing under the Circuit Court of Cook County, Illinois rules because the arbitration award limit was $15,000 and the lawyers believed that the case had a far greater value. However, the rules barred parties who failed to attend the arbitration from rejecting the award. After the arbitrators ruled for the defendant, the plaintiff learned that she could not reject the award. She then sued her attorneys for legal malpractice. *Firm in Arbitration Case Charged with Malpractice*, Chicago Daily L Bull, June 25, 1992, at 1.

Page 216, note 78, add:

Contrary to *Strandell*, other cases have concluded that summary jury trials can be compelled under Fed R Civ P 65. Arabian Am Oil Co v Scarface, 119 FRD 448 (MD Fla 1988); McKay v Ashland Oil, Inc, 120 FRD 43 (ED Ky 1988); Federal Reserve Bank v Carey-Canada, 123 FRD 603 (D Minn 1988). *See* Note, *The Catch-22 of Mandatory Summary Jury Trials*, 1990 J Dispute Resolution 135.

Page 216, text, after first full paragraph, add:

There is an inherent tension between not holding back in order to optimize one's chances of success in a summary jury trial, and disclosing and previewing nondiscoverable matters such as a line of cross-examination. Note, *The Catch-22 of Mandatory Summary Jury Trials*, 1990 J Dispute Resolution 135, 140. This is an issue of selective information disclosure in a different context. *See* §4.02.

An additional way in which a summary jury trial might help lead to settlement is by giving the parties their emotional "day in court." Note, *supra*, at 146; *McKay v Ashland Oil, Inc*, 120 FRD 43, 50 (ED Ky 1988); Metzloff, *How to Improve the Summary Jury Trial*, 30 Trial 22 (June 1994). Metzloff notes that the effectiveness of the summary jury trial in leading to settlements has been attributed to a number of different factors:

1. It provides a preview of a likely jury verdict
2. It enlightens clients regarding the strengths of the other side and/or has a cathartic effect by providing the client with his or her "day in court"
3. It forces a thorough review of the case in preparation for the summary jury trial
4. Some litigants may become more willing to settle due to a new perception of the uncertainties and expenses of the jury system

Id. However, while a summary jury trial may provide a preview of a likely jury verdict, a significantly different result might be reached at a real trial, either as a result of changes in trial strategies or tactics, or because of the change in the composition of the juries.

Some courts which utilize summary jury trials require that the jury make a finding regarding damages, even if it finds the defendant not guilty. Newman, *The Summary Jury Trial as a Method of Dispute Resolution in the Federal Courts*, 1990 U Ill L Rev 177, 197. The rationale for this procedure is that it provides a more complete basis for subsequent settlement discussions. *Id.*

Page 216, text, add after subsection "Mini-Trials":

Hybrid Methods of ADR

A key issue today is which alternative dispute resolution method should be chosen for any particular controversy. Ray, *Emerging Options in Dispute Resolution*, 75 ABA J 66 (June 1989). Hybrid methods include neutral fact-finding (possibly under Rule 706 of the Federal Rules of Evidence), or an ombudsman for complaints against institutions by constituents, clients, or employees. *Id.* The latter method is informal and nonbinding. *Id.*

Appropriateness and Criticisms of ADR

Mediation appears to usually be inappropriate in serious family disputes if there is substance or physical/emotional abuse, a significant disparity of power, or mental illness to the point of hospitalization. *Id* 68. In these situations, "agreements are difficult to forge and often broken." *Id.* On the other hand, mediation often is appropriate for other "people who know each other—neighbors, landlords and tenants, or business partners," and for money or other objective disputes "where an ongoing relationship underlies the dispute." *Id.*

One critical concern, in deciding to arbitrate, is whether the arbitrator, unless he or she is very competent, may be less careful than a judge because of the extremely limited scope of judicial review of arbitration. Goldberg, Green & Sander, *Litigation, Arbitration, Mediation: A Dialogue*, 75 ABA J 70 (June 1989). When arbitration is contemplated, the following factors also must be considered:

(1) increased privacy (confidentiality);

(2) generally much more relaxed rules for the admissibility of evidence;

(3) but far more limited discovery.

Id.

In a recent article, an administrative law judge and an attorney who represents government employees who are "whistle-blowers" articulate some of the strongest criticisms about alternative dispute resolution. Guill & Slavin, *Rush to Unfairness: The Downside of ADR*, 28 Judges J 8 (Summer 1989). Their major criticisms, in comparing ADR to the judicial system, are:

1. Loss of the right to a jury trial

2. Limited judicial review

3. Lack of general procedural fairness and public scrutiny in the selection and evaluation of prospective arbitrator-judges

4. Lack of judicial independence for arbitrator-judges

5. No general code of judicial-arbitrator ethics

6. Inferior qualifications and professionalism

7. Loss of public access to trials-arbitrations

For those considering ADR, the last of these criticisms raises a public policy and political issue for the general community. The other criticisms must be viewed against the specific judicial and ADR systems which could be utilized in a particular matter.

At times, the savings in time and costs intended to be achieved by an arbitration agreement are lost due to litigation over the applicability or validity of the arbitration agreement. Yeomans, *Counseling the Client on Commercial Arbitration Clauses*, 36 Practical Law 17, 25 (Jan 1990). In drafting arbitration provisions, it may be useful to provide disincentives for a party to refuse to cooperate with the arbitration. *Id.* Under the Federal Arbitration Act, if there are both arbitrable and nonarbitrable claims, the court should compel arbitration of the arbitrable claims regardless of whether that results in inefficient, multiple proceedings in separate forums. *Id; Dean Witter Reynolds v Bryd*, 470 US 213 (1985); 9 USC §§2-4.

Summary jury trials have been the subject of criticism for both their usefulness in resolving cases and their ethics. Metzloff, *How to Improve the Summary Jury Trial*, 30 Trial 22 (June 1994). *See* Posner, *The Summary Jury Trial and Other Methods of Alternative Dispute Resolution: Some Cautionary Observations*, 53 U Chi L Rev 366 (1986); Wiegand, *A New Light Bulb or the Work of the Devil*, 69 Or L Rev 87, 90 (1990). One of the drawbacks of the typical summary jury trial, in contrast to nonbinding arbitration, is that only the lawyers speak, not the witnesses themselves.

It has been suggested that summary jury trials could play a more effective role in alternative dispute resolution if they were employed on a voluntary, but binding, basis with the parties having latitude to decide on the procedures to be followed. Metzloff, *How to Improve the Summary Jury Trial*, 30 Trial 22, 26 (June 1994). Such procedures might include a high-low settlement agreement in order to minimize risks and some limited use of live testimony from witnesses. *Id. See* §7.03 (Supp).

§6.08   Class Actions

Page 217, note 92, add:

, *cert denied*, 444 US 870 (1979).

§6.09   Multiple Parties

Page 218, text, add at end of section:

Apparently successful negotiations can be undermined by unintended effects created by third parties. When the United States finally negotiated a reduction of quotas in Japan's domestic beef and citrus markets, American exports were expected to rise significantly. While wholesale prices dropped, Japan's middlemen, with control of distribution channels, refused to pass along the lower prices to consumers. Instead, they took higher profits. As a result, American exports of these products to Japan failed to increase as expected. *Japanese Beef about High Costs as Quotas Fall*, Chicago Trib, Mar 31, 1991, §7, at 3.

§6.09A   Intra-Organizational Negotiations (New)

Intra-organizational negotiations refer to negotiations between individuals or groups within the same organization. For purposes of analysis, labor union-management negotiations are excluded, since two distinct organizations are involved.

Within this definition of intra-organizational negotiations, the context of the negotiations often falls into two categories. First, the intra-organizational negotiation can be part of the process of an inter-organizational negotiation. For example, within a company, decision makers and those with input into the decisions may be negotiating how to set a bottom-line position. Thus, an inter-organizational negotiation also can involve two intra-organizational negotiations.

Figure 6-1

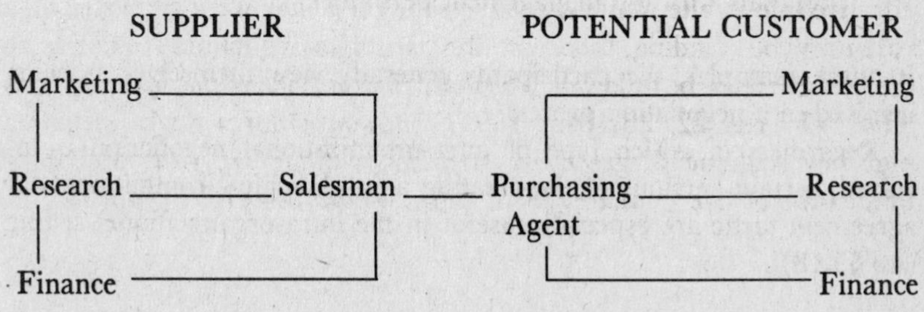

Each line represents a negotiation. Within each organization, each of these negotiations may be conducted separately, jointly, or both separately and jointly at different points.

The negotiation process also can be viewed as consisting of six levels:

Figure 6-2

	Within Seller	Between Seller & Buyer	Within Buyer
Entity's Interests	1	2	3
Individual's Interests	4	5	6

The importance of this model in analyzing the process is that it enhances one's ability to plan and effectively implement one's plans. Too often, the above intra-organizational negotiations are viewed only as discussions, policy setting, or as brainstorming. Such a limited perspective masks significant aspects of the interactions. Instead, what is occurring is a *negotiation*. Those participants who fail to view it as such miss the opportunity to increase their effectiveness through the planning and implementation process outlined in Chapters 8 and 9. Furthermore, by failing to perceive that the process involves a negotiation in both organizations, the negotiator cannot interact as effectively with his or her counterpart because the other negotiator's actions will be shaped by his or her own intra-organizational negotiations.

The second type of intra-organizational negotiation is one which does *not* involve negotiating with an outside party.

Example 6-13

Mr. Jones is negotiating a salary and compensation benefits package with Mrs. Louis.

Example 6-14

Corporate department heads are presenting and negotiating budget proposals with top management personnel.

In these examples, the participants generally view themselves as being involved in a negotiation process.

Regardless of which type of intra-organizational negotiation is involved, certain versions of the creating a psychological commitment for agreement tactic are especially useful in the intra-organizational setting (*see* §5.18):

1. Being liked
2. Creating dependence on one's self
3. Making others feel needed
4. At times, being feared

In intra-organizational negotiations, one management device to improve harmony is to create liaison responsibilities. Within each department, one capable individual is designated as the liaison to another specific department. Ideally under this system, if an organization has six departments, each department has five persons as liaisons, each responsible for one other department. A chart for each department would show:

Department 1

Person A	Dept. 2
Person B	Dept. 3
Person C	Dept. 4
Person D	Dept. 5
Person E	Dept. 6

The responsibility of the liaison is to treat that other department like a customer or client. The liaison is responsible for understanding the needs, interests, values, and priorities of the assigned other department, and to see that the other department remains a satisfied "customer."

The goal of this system is to minimize intra-organizational misunderstandings and friction by altering the focus and responsibilities within departments and the context of inter-departmental negotiations. Ideally, departments no longer directly negotiate with each other. Instead, a department communicates with the designated liaison in the appropriate other department, who is responsible for maintaining a satisfactory relationship between the departments. Each liaison then negotiates within his or her own department, often employing the problem solving strategy. This intra-department negotiation includes, if necessary, negotiating among the department's liaisons.

The liaison system alters the dynamics of the process. No longer are outsiders negotiating with each other, i.e., it is no longer department A versus department B. Instead, members of each department must work with each other to satisfy other departments as part of their personal responsibilities to satisfy the "customer." In many organizations, this system creates a direct responsibility for satisfying the other departments where no such system previously existed.

This liaison system should be considered for law firms, which have specialized departments, as well as for other types of organizations.

It has been suggested that in one's own intra-organizational negotiations, one should:

1. Be active "which includes building your own turf, building coalitions and having a long-range plan"

2. Avoid being ignored in meetings by repeating suggestions, directing comments to one person and forcing a response (in effect debating your position with one person in the meeting), and following up with a memo

3. If necessary, "postur[e]" so you look "calm and rather unimpressed" by "bullies." Kleinman, *Survival in Corporate Jungle—Workshop Teaches Self-Defense in Office Conflicts*, Chicago Trib, Nov 20, 1989, §4, at 1, 6 (reporting on a workshop by Andrea Medea of Chimera, Inc.)

These approaches utilize the negotiation concepts of planning, nonverbal communication, tone, allies, demanding responses to positions, debate, disclosing information, and fact creation.

Litigation Related Tactics

7

§7.02 Litigation

Page 224, text, add after fourth full paragraph:

Some commentators assert that forcing personal injury plaintiffs to trial does not necessarily deter claims. Citing aggressive defense strategies in the *Dalkon Shield* and *Rely Tampon* cases, these commentators contend that ignoring settlement possibilities and risks in an attempt to deter future claims is empirically unsound and may actually lead to more claims due to publicized adverse verdicts. Quinley & Khin, *We Love Settlements: An Insurer's Perspective*, 33 For the Def 26, 28 (Jan 1991).

Page 224, text, add at end of fifth full paragraph:

An analogous example occurred when, after repeated unsuccessful attempts to negotiate and 11 years of bloody fighting in El Salvador, the government and rebels finally agreed to a truce during which negotiations could be conducted. *Rebel Truce Proposal Offered at Salvadoran Talks*, Chicago Trib, Apr 5, 1991, §1, at 10. This led to an announced peace.

Page 226, note 12, add:

860 F2d 700 (1988).

Page 226, text, add at end of section:

One by-product of litigation can be adjusting or maintaining the parties' relationship. For example, in a series of lengthy (eight-year) concurrent lawsuits brought by Coca-Cola bottlers over their contract with Coca-Cola regarding the price of syrup, a significant issue has not been a formal part of the litigation. That issue is whether the bottlers, whose numbers have declined dramatically, will retain their historic "partner-ship" role. The litigation is being used, however, as a means to resolve that issue. Interestingly, as a separate example of tactics and strategy (regard-less of whether the following is accurate for the particular negotiation), the bottlers' chief attorney, Emmet J. Bondurant III, described Coca-Cola's negotiations: "Negotiating with the Coca-Cola Company is like negotiat-ing with the Russians: what's theirs is theirs and what's yours is negotiable." *Coca-Cola in Bitter Legal Fight over Cost of Sweetener*, Chicago Daily L Bull, May 22, 1989, at 3.

A hedge in monetary litigation is the high-low agreement in which the parties agree that no judgment higher than X dollars will have to be paid, and that at least Y dollars will be paid even if a lower judgment is entered. Sullivan, *The High-Low Agreement*, For the Defense, July, 1991, at 25. In some states, these are treated as *Mary Carter* agreements and may be either impermissible or required to be revealed to the jury. *Id. See* §7.07.

High-low agreements remain controversial. Some lawyers strongly oppose their use, but virtually everyone else agrees that, at best, they are appropriate only in limited circumstances. Berkman, *Controversial High-Low Deals Put Dollar Limits on PI Cases*, Chicago Lawyer 6 (June, 1970). A high-low agreement may be appropriate where the defense is likely to win at trial, but where a verdict for the plaintiff will be a high verdict. *Id.* An example of where a high-low agreement was used was a personal injury case involving burns, smoke inhalation, more than $50,000 in medical bills and an insurance policy limit of $300,000. *Id.* The case was triable, but a verdict for the defendant was likely. *Id.* Accordingly, the plaintiff's lawyer suggested to the insurer that they use a high-low agreement. In doing so, the plaintiff's lawyer stated: "Look, chances are I'm going to lose; but if I hit, I'm going to get you for $1,000,000. So I'll work out this deal with you." *Id.* The deal was that the insurance company would pay $200,000 if the verdict was for that much or more, $30,000 if the verdict was for the defendant or for $30,000 or less, and the amount of a verdict between $30,000 and $200,000. *Id.* An additional and important provision was that neither side would appeal. *Id.* The outcome of the case was that the jury found for the defendant and the plaintiff received the guaranteed "low" of $30,000. *Id.* To the extent that high-low agreements may be of interest, that interest may well peak at the time of trial, or even during jury deliberations.

In the continuing use of litigation to break deadlocked negotiations, a federal judge ruled that the National Football League has no exemption from the antitrust laws because the players' union has been decertified. This is part of the ongoing battle between the union and the NFL since the union's 24-day strike in 1987. *NFL Loses Antitrust Exemption*, Chicago Sun-Times, May 29, 1991, at 119. Even when another federal judge held that the NFL was liable for antitrust violations since the collective bargaining agreement expired in 1987 (a decision which conflicts with an Eighth Circuit opinion), the union refused to negotiate until after any appeals so that its court victory would be indisputable before any bargaining. The antitrust question focuses on the issue of how to handle player free agency.

§7.03 Structured Settlements

Page 226, note 13, add:

Some attorneys assert that structured settlements save insurance companies money, but usually fail to provide meaningful advantages for the plaintiff. *See* Fuchsberg, *Pitfalls in Structured Settlements*, 25 Trial 42 (Sept 1989). From the plaintiff's perspective, Fuchsberg criticizes structured settlements on the following grounds:

1. If much of the income is going to be spent on tax-deductible medical care, the "advantage" of tax-exempt structured payments is illusory because the investment interest earned from a lump-sum settlement can be offset by the large tax deduction of the medical expenses

2. Although structured payments are not taxable, a secure, long-term investment of a lump-sum settlement at approximately 10 per cent interest could produce as much or more income even after taxes

3. A yearly increase of three per cent per year in a structured settlement may not be sufficient to offset inflation nor be as good as investing a lump sum at ten per cent interest

4. Alternatively, investing a lump sum in tax-exempt bonds at approximately six per cent interest could produce as much or more income than structured payments

5. A lump-sum settlement may be invested, but the principal still belongs to the victim and can be inherited by the victim's family, whereas the principal invested to create structured payments belongs to an insurance company

6. A lump-sum settlement provides greater flexibility in the future if unexpected expenses occur

7. Depending on the rating of the insurance company and how well the State Guarantee Fund protects against insolvency of the insurance company, the structured settlement might not be completely secure

However, other plaintiffs' attorneys and commentators continue to believe that structured settlements can benefit many plaintiffs, provided they are analyzed and drafted with care. Mandel, *An Ounce of Prevention: Some Dos and Don'ts*, 24 Trial 32 (Dec 1988); Danninger & Palfin, *How to Evaluate Proposals; Avoid Fee Disputes*, 24 Trial 38 (Dec 1988). Mandel's "dos" and "don'ts" include:

1. Analyze the numbers, i.e., the present value, the injured person's life expectancy and the tax and investment consequences. (Danninger and Palfin assert that, although present value and the annuity's cost are theoretically identical, in reality, present-value figures may be higher due to the inclusion of "alleged tax or management-fee savings, which overstate the value of the settlement." Danninger & Palfin, *How to Evaluate Proposals; Avoid Fee Disputes,* 24 Trial 38, 39 (Dec 1988). Accordingly, they emphasize that plaintiff's counsel must deal with actual cost and not be satisfied with references to "present value" or "judgment value." *Id.*)

2. Do not rely just on the company issuing the annuity to fund the settlement. For more security, Mandel suggests that the defendant assign its liability to a gigantic, highly-rated insurance company which then purchases the annuity to fund the structured settlement from one of its affiliates. In that way, the plaintiff is not just relying on the affiliate which issued the annuity, but has a direct claim against the secure assignee. (Query: however, whether that is substantially more secure than having the gigantic, highly-rated insurance company issue the annuity itself?) Danninger and Palfin state that most structured settlements do use such assignments and that they can be beneficial to all parties if the assignee's financial stability is carefully analyzed. *Id* 39. (However, if the defendant itself is an extremely stable, major corporation, IBM for example, a plaintiff might prefer that there not be an assignment.)

3. Be sure that the settlement agreement and the assignment of liability, if one is used, are consistent.

4. Draft language that an assignee insurance company is likely to accept if that still provides the terms which the plaintiff needs for tax, estate, or other purposes.

5. If payments are guaranteed for a certain number of years even if the plaintiff dies, draft provisions which create a practical method of clearly identifying the beneficiaries. Avoid using probate language which may not clearly inform the annuity company who to pay. Instead, draft a contract provision which will readily allow the annuity company to know, with certainty, who to pay.

6. Provide in the assignment that the plaintiff can change the beneficiaries. Do not do so in the annuity contract because it will endanger the tax-exempt status.

Danninger and Palfin also emphasize that a structured settlement must clearly set forth the amounts and dates of future payments in order to avoid the possibility that the IRS would argue constructive receipt by the plaintiff which would destroy the tax-exempt status of the future payments.

Whether a structured settlement is in the best interests of the parties requires a case-by-case determination and opinions may differ.

Using Treasury bonds for structured settlement trusts avoids the risk that the insurance company from whom an annuity was bought may fail some time in the future. Halpern, *A Safe Alternative to Structured Settlements*, 30 Trial 34 (June 1994). Although the use of funding structured settlements through Treasury bonds has increased, that increase has been limited due to low interest rates. *Id.* As a result, in recent years, the use of structured settlements has declined. *Id.* One suggested nontraditional alternative is to place the settlement funds that would have been used to purchase an annuity into a "settlement fund management trust" for the purpose of providing professional financial management with trust provisions tailored to the plaintiff's particular needs. *Id.*

Page 227, note 17, add:

Most structured settlements have been funded through one annuity. Some structured settlements now involve splitting the funding between two life insurance companies. *Split Funded Structured Settlements*, Reed & Strattford's Structured Settlements-Technical Update (Dec 8, 1992). The potential benefits may include increasing the protection provided by the state insurance guaranty fund, reducing the risk of default by the insurance company, and possibly obtaining larger payments for the same cost, if more than one type of periodic payment is involved and one company offers more for one type of payment and the other offers more for the other type of payment. *Id.*

Often, in structured settlements, there is an assignment of the obligation to make periodic payments. In some cases where that occurs, the plaintiff can become a secured creditor with regard to the assignee, without losing the tax-free status of the structured payments. Winslow, *Security Interests in Structured Settlements*, 28 Trial 72 (May 1992). Whether this is truly desirable in a given case will depend on whether it increases the reliability that the plaintiff will receive the promised payments and any tradeoff in costs and benefits required by the structured settlement market in order to obtain such a security interest. *Id.*

For plaintiff's counsel negotiating a structured settlement using annuity products, one key factor is the strength of the life insurance company whose annuity is to be used. If the annuity is to provide adequate security, the life insurance company must be sound and not merely the one chosen by the defendant for the lowest cost. Plaintiff's counsel should check the Claims-Paying-Ability ("CPA") ratings of Duff & Phelps, Moody's, and Standard and Poor's. Jeffries, *Structured Settlement Security: Reality or Facade?*, 27 Trial 26, 28-29 (Aug 1991).

Recent history has shown that even billion-dollar companies, including insurance companies, can suffer an economic collapse. As of 1991, the largest insurance company to fail was Executive Life of First Executive Corporation, which had 15 billion dollars in stated assets. Loomis, *What*

Fred Carr's Fall Means to You, Fortune, May 6, 1991, at 60. First Executive had been among the leading companies in selling annuities for structured settlements. *Id.* Even beyond the normal plaintiff's consideration that the company from which the annuity is purchased should be highly rated, this suggests that, if possible, a contingency should be built into structured settlements in the event that the company paying the annuity fails. For example, in one structured settlement where the defendant was a municipality, one of the beneficiaries of an Executive Life annuity had an agreement that the municipality would make the agreed-upon payments if Executive Life failed to make them. *Id.* That agreement was made at a time when neither the municipality, nor plaintiff's counsel, had any suspicion that Executive Life would collapse. *Id.* It was simply a matter of good lawyering in which a possible contingency was accounted for and protection against it was built into the agreement. Thus, a settlement agreement involving a structured settlement might require that the original defendant, or its insurer, assume responsibility for the agreed upon payments if the annuity company fails to make them. Of course, such protection is only as good as the viability and resources of the defendant or its insurer. *See also* Jefferies, *Structured Settlement Security: Reality or Facade?*, 27 Trial 26 (Aug 1991).

Page 227, note 18, add:

It is essential that the structured settlement documents be drafted properly so that the "intent of the payer" is clear in order to preserve the payments as nontaxable. *Settlements Agreements: Keeping the IRS Away*, Reed & Strattford's Structured Settlements-Technical Update (Apr 7, 1992). One common problem is that language is used from various agreements, creating conflicts in the final document regarding the parties' rights and obligations which endangers the tax-exempt status of the payments. *Id.*

A recent change in the tax law has altered the status of a plaintiff with a structured settlement from a general creditor of the assignee to a secured creditor of the assignee. The Technical and Miscellaneous Revenue Act of 1988, amending 26 USC §130. *See* Winslow, *Drafting for Reliability and Favorable Tax Treatment*, 24 Trial 21 (Dec 1988); Fuchsberg, *Pitfalls in Structured Settlements*, 25 Trial 42 (Sept 1989).

Page 227, note 20, add:

In order to accurately evaluate all of the benefits and detriments of a proposed structured settlement, care must be taken to consider all of the tax implications. For example, a major benefit of structured settlements is generally considered to be that the payments are all nontaxable, whereas the money invested from a lump-sum settlement is taxable. However, as noted above, if much of that investment income is going to be spent for tax-deductible medical care, the true tax consequences of a lump-sum settlement may be substantially different than they first appeared. Fuchsberg, *Pitfalls in Structured Settlements*, 25 Trial 42 (Sept 1989).

Page 229, note 31, add:

See also Winslow, *Opportunities and Hazards in Structuring Attorneys' Fees*, 25 Trial 37 (Sept 1989), regarding the care which must be exercised to arrange and document a structured fee in order to obtain the tax benefits of deferring the fee.

Page 229, note 32, add at beginning:

The Board of Governors of the Association of Trial Lawyers of America has recommended that, unless the fee is also structured, "contingent fees on structured settlements should always be calculated on the cost or present value of the annuity, whichever is lower. . . ." Danninger & Palfin, *How to Evaluate Proposals; Avoid Fee Disputes*, 24 Trial 38 (Dec 1988). The attorneys' fees percentage should be based on actual cost, if possible, or on the present value of the structured settlement. Wyatt v United States, 783 F2d 45 (6th Cir 1986) (holding that the 25% maximum fee under the Federal Tort Claims Act must be calculated based on the actual cost of a structured settlement, not the higher purported present value). *Wyatt* demonstrates that present value can never properly be deemed to be higher than the actual cost of the annuity, at least for fee purposes.

Page 229, note 32, add:

Florida Bar v Gentry, 475 So 2d 678 (Fla 1985); *In re* Estate of Muccini, 118 Misc 2d 38, 460 NYS2d 680 (1983).

§7.05 The Policy Limits Letter

Page 231, text, add at end of section:

Policy limits letters are typically appropriate where there are excellent liability and damages which could exceed the policy limit. However, they are also appropriate if the potential verdict significantly exceeds the policy limits, even where liability is a jury question. *See* Fuchsberg, *Ten Commandments for Successful Evaluation and Settlement*, 27 Trial 16, 21 (Aug 1991).

§7.06 Loan Agreements

Page 233, note 41, add:

For example, loan agreements with setoffs can backfire. In Schoonover v International Harvester Co, 171 Ill App 3d 882, 525 NE2d 1041

(1988), *appeal denied*, 122 Ill 2d 594, 530 NE2d 264 (1989), two defendants settled with plaintiff for a joint $300,000 loan agreement, which was repayable solely from any recovery from the remaining defendant. Plaintiff won a $50,000 verdict against the remaining, third defendant. However, the third defendant moved to have the amount of the loan that did not have to be repaid, $250,000, set off against the $50,000 verdict, thereby reducing the verdict to zero. The *Schoonover* court held that, because the forgiven $250,000 of the loan agreement was to be treated as a normal settlement and a jury verdict is reduced by the amount of a prior settlement with another defendant, the verdict should be reduced to zero. The plaintiff was still obligated to repay the amount of the verdict, $50,000, to the settling defendants pursuant to the terms of the loan agreement. Thus, winning a $50,000 verdict actually cost plaintiff $50,000 (plus whatever expenses were wasted in obtaining this Pyrrhic victory). The *Schoonover* court had no problem with this outcome, commenting that: "There is nothing unfair in this result. Plaintiff retains $250,000, which is five times the value of his damages as determined by the jury, and to add thereto the $50,000 award would result in a double recovery as to that amount." *Id* at 886, 525 NE2d at 1044.

The recent case of *In re* Guardianship of Babb, ___ Ill ___ (Sept 29, 1994), is another example of how loan agreements can be viewed with disfavor and therefore not be given their intended effect. The Illinois contribution statute, 740 Ill Comp Stat Ann §100/2, bars claims for contribution by co-defendants against a defendant who has entered into a good faith settlement. In *Babb*, the Illinois Supreme Court held that loan agreements are not good faith settlements within the meaning of the statute, so that a defendant who enters into a loan agreement would not be protected from contribution claims by other defendants. The *Babb* court stated that, other than in *Babb* itself, its ruling would only be applied prospectively.

§7.07   "Mary Carter" Agreements

Page 235, note 49, add:

Indeed, all courts which have permitted "Mary Carter" agreements have held that they must be disclosed to the nonsettling codefendant and the court, and the American Bar Association has indicated that such disclosure is ethically required. Entman, *Mary Carter Agreements: Learn the Inside Deal*, 24 Tenn BJ 10, 13 (Jan/Feb 1988).

Certain states allow or require that "Mary Carter" agreements be revealed to the jury. Sullivan, *The High-Low Agreement*, For the Defense 25, 28 (July 1991).

Page 235, text, add at end of section:

For example, some States have banned "Mary Carter" agreements outright, eliminated their usefulness by setting off any guaranteed amount from a judgment against the nonsettling codefendant, or held that they are not good faith settlements and that the settling codefendant was, therefore, still subject to a contribution claim. Entman, *Mary Carter Agreements: Learn the Inside Deal*, 24 Tenn BJ 10, 13 (Jan/Feb 1988).

The Texas Supreme Court has ruled that "Mary Carter" agreements are void because they violate Texas public policy. *Elbaor v Smith*, 845 SW2d 240 (Tex 1992). The Court held that such agreements "allow plaintiffs to buy support for their case ... motivate more culpable defendants to make a good deal and thereby end up paying little or nothing in damages," even if the agreement is revealed to the jury. The dissent noted that Texas has chosen "a decidedly minority rule," since the majority approval permits "Mary Carter" agreements but allows full disclosure to the jury.

§7.09   Offers of Judgment

Page 239, note 68, add after 806 F2d 329 (1st Cir 1986):

, *cert denied*, 481 US 1029 (1987)

Systematic Planning: The First Stages

8

§8.01   Introduction

Page 249, text, add at end of paragraph after Example 8-1:

Highly publicized sports contract negotiations provide examples of "failed negotiations." For instance, it was widely reported that, when Chicago Cubs' star pitcher Gregg Maddux became a free agent, he rejected a five-year, $28-million offer from the Cubs, turned down a more lucrative offer from at least one other team, and ultimately signed with the Atlanta Braves for essentially the same terms that the Cubs had offered. This occurred even though he ultimately would have preferred to stay with the Cubs and accept their earlier offer that was no longer available. Assuming that the media reports were accurate, it appears that the negotiators failed to find the available, overlapping zone of agreement. Perhaps this was because of a failure to properly define the player's bottom line, a failure to close an acceptable deal, or perhaps the parties deadlocked on non-essential points. *See* **Examples 8-3** and **8-6**.

§8.04   —Step 2: Determining the Client's Goals

Page 259, text, add before first full paragraph:

The need to balance short-term and long-term interests is reflected by New York City labor negotiations with its employees. Unaffordable salary and benefit agreements would create short-term labor peace and long-term economic disaster. The disaster would not only affect the city as management, but almost inevitably cause service cuts with layoffs that would be counterproductive to labor's long-term goals. One negotiating plan scenario would be to tie present or deferred wage increases with avoiding or limiting layoffs, while allowing for some overall reduction in wage expenditures through a hiring freeze or restrictions. Rohatyn, *The Fall and Rise of New York*, 37 NY Rev Books, Nov 8, 1990, at 40, 41.

Page 259, text, add after fourth full paragraph:

Unless goals are clearly established, so that there is a standard by which to evaluate a proposed agreement, the following pitfalls may occur:

1. Negotiators may agree to terms that their constituents reject
2. Parties may concede too much
3. Negotiations may fail because parties never realize that they have obtained what they need
4. Parties may never reach an internal consensus on whether to accept or reject proposals

Folk-Williams, *The Use of Negotiated Agreements to Resolve Water Disputes Involving Indian Rights*, 28 Nat Resources J 63, 93-4 (1988). Note that the use of systematic planning avoids those pitfalls by determining client goal(s) (step 2) and setting the bottom line (step 9). Also note how the last potential problem underscores the need for effective intra-organizational negotiations. (See §6.09A of the Supplement regarding intra-organizational negotiations.)

§8.05   —Step 3: Identifying the Issues

Page 260, text, add after sixth paragraph:

So-called *procedural issues* can implicitly involve substantive issues. In December, 1991, Mideast peace talks were stymied by apparent procedural issues, such as whether Israel would negotiate with Palestinians except as part of joint a Palestinian-Jordanian delegation. *Mideast Peace Talks in D.C. near Collapse*, Chicago Trib, Dec 18, 1991, §1, at 2. Whether the Palestinians could negotiate as a separate delegation involved the substantive issue of whether Israel would implicitly recognize the Palestinians as a separate national entity. Similarly, in the internal South African constitutional negotiations to end apartheid, the Zulu-dominated Inkatha Party boycotted the talks because the king of the Zulu was not accorded status as a separate delegation, even though other politically allied groups were accorded separate status. The effect of this procedural issue was to prevent the Inkatha from having a strong ally in the negotiations. *Citing "Snub," ANC Rival to Boycott S. African Talks*, Chicago Trib, Dec 19, 1991, §1, at 14.

In legal and business negotiations, procedural issues can similarly affect substantive outcomes. For example, a substantive provision can be affected by the procedural issue of whether to negotiate a restructuring of current contractual terms to achieve an extension of the contract.

§8.06   —Step 4: Analyzing the Market and Customary Terms

Page 262, text, add after fourth full paragraph:

1990 economic trends appear to be leading to the decline of deals and the growth of reworked deals. *Debt Orchestrates '90's Theme: Deals Done Again*, Chicago Trib, Sept 16, 1990, §7, at 1, cols 7-8. While merger, acquisition, and takeover activity dramatically decreased, many overleveraged deals are ripe for being reworked to eliminate or greatly diminish debt. Some of this activity involves the Bankruptcy Courts (a growth area for lawyers) or informal workouts. The targets are otherwise good companies which failed to grow at unrealistically predicted rates, thereby leaving them financially distressed due to debt service and fiscally inappropriate capital structures in the current economic environment.

Page 263, text, add at end of "Negotiation Methods" subsection:

Knowing the market includes knowledge about the other party. For the plaintiff's personal injury attorney who handles relatively small to medium claims, this includes knowing which insurance companies seldom settle for a fair amount. This knowledge enables counsel to avoid lengthy but wasted settlement efforts in those cases where litigation will be needed. Rundlett III, *Negotiating a Small Personal Injury Claim*, 27 Trial 55 (Oct 1991).

§8.07   —Step 5: Assessing Strengths and Weaknesses

Page 270, text, add after first full paragraph:

In the context of discussing international crises, former National Security Council staffer Richard Haas stated that, "You're constantly trying to figure out what the other guy's objectives are, trying to put yourself in his shoes, trying to figure out his bottom line," while Dr. Jerrold Post, former director of the CIA's psychological profiling function said, "If you can't get into the head of an adversary on the eve of a major political-military confrontation, you are in deep trouble." *Ability to Psych Out Foes Crucial in Foreign Crisis*, Chicago Trib, Oct 23, 1994, §4, at 4, col 1. The same type of concerns apply in any negotiation. It is always helpful to be able to "get into the head" of the other negotiator or other party.

Systematic Planning: The Second Stages

9

§9.03 —Step 9: Setting the Bottom Line

Page 291, note 8, add:

In a strictly monetary, single-issue lawsuit, a typical model for formulating the bottom line is: the amount at stake times the chance of prevailing at trial, plus the future transaction costs. Katz, *The L'Ambiance Plaza Mediation: A Case Study in Judicial Settlement of Mass Torts*, 5 Ohio St J Dispute Resolution 277, 288 (1990). Though helpful, it should be noted that, in many cases such as personal injury, the amount at stake is a variable to be estimated and, more realistically, a range of the likely plaintiff's verdicts or an average of that range. Moreover, a far more elaborate model would be needed to try to reflect a multi-issue negotiation with possible tradeoffs between issues, or a problem-solving approach. *Id* 288-89. *See also* Stanley & Coursey, *Empirical Evidence on the Selection Hypothesis and the Decision to Litigate or Settle*, 19 J Legal Stud 145 (Jan 1990).

§9.07 —Step 12: The Agenda

Page 305, text, add after second full paragraph:

Negotiations also have been analyzed as often following three phases:

1. An initial informational phase for exchanging information
2. A competitive phase of offers and counteroffers
3. If the second phase resolves issues, a cooperative phase to create mutual gains.

Craver, *Negotiation Techniques*, 24 Trial 65 (June 1988). Craver suggests that those three phases are distinct and sequential. *Id*. However, an

64

effective negotiator will not be so rigid. Instead, one should use varied tactics to create the desired "phase" at various points during the negotiation.

§9.11   Implementation and Adjustment

Page 314, text, add at end of sixth paragraph:

As client counseling is a part of the planning process, repeating the planning process as needed during a negotiation may well involve repeated counseling of the client. (See §§8.04, 8.08, 9.02, and 9.03 regarding planning and client counseling.)

Effective Communication

10

§10.03 Sending Information—Only Deliberate Disclosures

Page 335, text, add at end of second paragraph:

Stating the facts in individual, humanistic terms, rather than generic terms, can be a subtle but persuasive method of presenting rationales. This allows the listener to realize the rationale on his or her own. Thus, in the context of representing a plaintiff in a personal injury case, "present your case from the perspective of the loss of enjoyment of life that your client has suffered rather than from the standpoint of a broken leg or lost wages." Erisman, *The Art of Negotiating a Settlement*, 25 Trial 26, 35 (Sept 1989). For example, a plaintiff's attorney might accurately tell an insurance claims representative that: "This is a broken leg case with specials of ten thousand dollars."

However, it would be more persuasive for the plaintiff's attorney to state that:

> Mrs. Smith suffered a compound fracture of her tibia which required her to undergo an operation and months of difficult physical therapy. She still walks with a limp and has daily pain. Before this happened, she was a very active, athletic person whose normal routine included running three miles a day. Mrs. Smith has not been able to resume that at all. This accident has drastically changed her life by stopping her from being on her feet for any protracted period of time. She can't even walk four blocks to the grocery store like she used to do. There are eight thousand dollars of medical bills and two thousand dollars of lost wages.

The same concept might also be applied to the consequences to the client from a breach of contract, a termination of employment, or whatever else has harmed the client.

Page 339, text, add after fifth full paragraph:

"Objective" criteria, such as appraisals, statistics, test results, and the like should be cited for persuasion whenever possible. Some negotiators have been taught that the negotiation result should be based on objective criteria. One of the cornerstones of Fisher and Ury's "principled nego-tiation" is that the negotiation result should be based on objective criteria. R. Fisher & W. Ury, *Getting to Yes, Negotiating Agreement Without Giving In* (1981). Therefore, for persuasion and to satisfy, as well as manipulate, the expectations of those negotiators, objective criteria should be built into rationales as much as possible. One important countermeasure is using other, more favorable, objective criteria of one's own. Other counter-measures include scrutinizing or questioning so-called *objective criteria* for bias and flawed methodology, challenging its general relevance or appli-cability, and resisting based on a subjective lack of importance for one's own needs, interests, or goals.

§10.04   Receiving Information

Careful Listening

Page 350, text, add after first full paragraph:

Sometimes, in order to accurately receive information, one must be aware of cultural differences in language and attitude. After Iraq invaded Kuwait, multinational negotiations began in an attempt to persuade Iraq to withdraw. Professor Cherif Bassiouni of DePaul's Law School ana-lyzed the cultural effects of language on the negotiation process. Professor Bassiouni explained that Iraq treated Kuwait's refusal to change its position on oil fields as an insulting act of aggression, which justified invasion as an alternative to the Arab's cultural concept of a loss of face from the insult. *Arab's Culture and Language Help Shape Crisis in Middle East*, Chicago Trib, Aug 19, 1990, §1, at 12, cols 6-8. In Arab countries, the invasion was termed "tadakhol," meaning intervention, instead of "oudwan," meaning aggression. *Id.* Bassiouni explained that the Arabic language's capacity for face-saving is enhanced since even "no" can mean that the speaker really just wants the other party to insist, such as for an offer of coffee or sweets. *Id.* He also analogized aspects of the international negotiation to bargaining in an Arab marketplace, referring to a seller who praises an item, while the buyer engages in the accepted practice of disagreeing by calling it junk. *Id.* However, if the buyer instead insults the seller by saying that the seller is lying, the situation explodes. *Id.* Bassiouni explained that example as demonstrating the Arab cultural difference in negotiations between pragmatic arguments and those of high principles. *Id.*

§10.06   Modes of Communication

Page 355, text, add at end of subsection "Meetings":

Claims adjusters are turning to "settlement days," when they negotiate face to face with claimants' attorneys, but without any third parties present. The face-to-face negotiations are often more productive than telephone negotiations, with proponents claiming 60 to 75 per cent settlement rates. The special days allow the adjusters, who may need to travel to various cities, to schedule as many negotiations per day as they wish. *Settlement Days Attract Interest*, National Underwriter, June 22, 1992, at 6.

Page 357, text, add at end of section:

Fax

The telecopier, or fax, provides an important mode of communication. Ducking telephone calls can be negated. Time pressure can be maintained. Instantly, the message can be delivered, regardless of geographic proximity. Furthermore, drafts and other documents can be circulated back and forth without a need for meetings and further delay.

However, with the proliferation of fax communications, there may, at times, be a backlog to transmit, receive, or move a fax to or from the telecopier to the intended recipient. For these reasons, overnight mail and messenger services still have a place in the market, even when the intended recipient has a fax machine.

Drafting

11

§11.02 The Initial Draft

Page 365, note 10, add:

If you may be considered the drafter, and not just the initial drafter, you may want to include a provision that the agreement was jointly drafted. The terms of the agreement then will not be construed against your client. Neubauer, *Settling Once and for All*, 27 Trial 31, 33 (Aug 1991).

§11.03 General Requirements

Page 368, text, add before Example 11-11:

The use of ambiguity in drafting agreements can be effective where the ambiguous terms constitute legally "magic words," such as a statutory phrase which, in fact, provides better legal protection to the client than any clarified version. "Material fact" under Rule 10-b(5) of the 1934 Securities Exchange Act is an example of such a term. Machlin & Prero, *When Words Don't Mean Too Much*, Chicago Bar Rec, Mar, 1991, at 35.

§11.04 Formal Agreements

Page 375, text, add at end of section:

Legal cultures differ in their approach to documentation. As American law firms flock to Brussels with its European Community officials, they have "buried" the officials with paper in legal cultures where "brevity is the rule." *Aggressiveness of U.S. Lawyers in Brussels Offends Members of Old World Bar*, Chicago Daily L Bull, May 14, 1991, at 3. In transactions, some European clients are shocked and uncomfortable with the expense and complicated provisions of the often much lengthier contracts drafted by American lawyers. *Id*; Baltz, *Chicago Firms Abroad*, 15 Chicago Law 1, 6 (Jan 1992). Japan is another culture where American legal formality and lengthy contracts are not the norm.

§11.05   —Standard versus Nonstandard Language

Page 376, text, add at end of section:

In drafting acquisition agreements, two critical portions are representations concerning the acquired company's financial condition and indemnification provisions. Walton, *Critical Issues in Drafting Acquisition Agreements (with Forms)*, 14 ALI-ABA Course Materials J 107 (Aug 1989). Both provide degrees of protection to the purchaser, depending on the continued solvency and worth of those potentially liable for a financial misrepresentation and to indemnify.

It is not uncommon for releases or other agreements to release all unknown claims. However, before agreeing to such language, care must be taken that there are not substantial possible, unknown claims. For instance, in the purchase of real estate where no environmental audit has been done and the history or the location of the property suggests even a remote possibility that there may be hazardous or toxic wastes on the property, releasing all unknown claims could lead to very substantial liability for cleanup costs. Neubauer, *Settling Once and for All*, 27 Trial 31, 32 (Aug 1991). It also is common for releases to release all of a corporate settlor's parent corporations, subsidiaries, affiliates, or divisions. Care must be taken to be aware of those corporate affiliations and any other, potential unrelated claims against such parent corporations, subsidiaries, affiliates, and the like before agreeing to such a release. *Id* 32.

The larger the agreed-upon lump-sum payment, the more important it is for the payee to have some time limit set within which the payment must be made, and to provide for interest if payment is not made in a timely manner. *See id*. If the settlement agreement merely contemplates that payment will not be made immediately, but will be within a reasonable, though unspecified time, the parties may well disagree on what constitutes payment within a reasonable time. *Id*. That situation can be avoided by specifying the payment schedule in the settlement documents. *Id*. Building in interest payments if the settlement payments are not made in a timely manner (as well as attorney's fees, costs, and even a higher amount) clearly gives the payor more incentive to comply with the payment schedule. However, even if there is no such provision for interest payments in the settlement documents, the applicable law may provide for prejudgment interest in such a situation. For example, in *In re Complaint of Rio Grande Transport, Inc*, 770 F2d 262 (2d Cir 1985), an admiralty case was settled and payment was to be made within a reasonable amount of time. The settlement agreement did not provide for interest if the payments were not made within a reasonable amount of time. When payment was not made in a timely manner, the plaintiff returned to court, had a judgment entered on the settlement, and sought prejudgment interest as compensation for the delay in payment. The Second Circuit held that prejudgment interest was available under admiralty law and that such interest was appropriate from the time that the delay in payment became unreasonable until the time that the payment was made. A statute which provides for prejudgment interest might also be used to obtain such a result. *See, e.g.*, 815 Ill Comp Stat Ann §205/2 (prejudgment interest can be awarded where money is withheld by an unreasonable and vexatious delay in payment).

§11.06 —Statutory Requirements and Case Law

Page 376, text, add at end of section:

When litigation is settled, there is frequently a concern regarding the means by which the settlement can be enforced, if enforcement becomes necessary. Although a settlement is a contract, a separate suit to enforce the settlement agreement or for damages for violation of the agreement can be burdensome. Therefore, where there is concern about the means for enforcement, there is usually a preference to have the court maintain jurisdiction to enforce the settlement. The Supreme Court has now ruled that federal courts do not maintain jurisdiction to enforce the settlement if the district court has simply entered a dismissal order with no other provisions. *Kokkonen v Guardian Life Insurance Co*, 114 S Ct 1673 (1994). However the *Kokkonen* court stated that jurisdiction would exist if there was either a provision in the order to retain jurisdiction to enforce the settlement agreement or if the terms of the settlement were incorporated into a court order. The Supreme Court stated that, under those circumstances, the district courts have ancillary jurisdiction to enforce settlements.

§11.07 Other Documents Evidencing Agreement

Letters of Intent

Page 377, text, add after first full paragraph:

Letters of intent are sometimes used by parties to set down basic, mutually acceptable terms before lawyers draft formal agreements. Depending on state law, this may be a dangerous practice for a party which either changes its mind or is unable to agree to terms demanded in the formal contract. Under legal principles like the duty of good faith and fair dealing, and if sufficient material terms appear in the letter of intent, some courts have ruled that a party is bound by its letter of intent, even if it does not agree to a formal contract. 17 Am Jur 2d *Contracts* §28 (1964).

An exception exists where closure is so important that a party is ready to be bound by the terms in the letter of intent, even without any other terms if no formal document ever is agreed on. Of course, in that situation, counsel should determine whether a formal agreement is needed at all or whether the letter should also be the agreement, instead of just the letter of intent.

§11.07A   Drafting Win/Win Proposals (New)

Careful drafting may allow one to create or effectuate win/win proposals. (*See* §5.06.) For instance, compensation for personal injury or loss of good will is not taxable. Neubauer, *Settling Once and for All*, 27 Trial 31, 33 (Aug 1991). Thus, if possible, the settlement documents should classify all, or as much as possible, of the settlement payment as compensation for such nontaxable compensation. *Id* 33. This may lead to a win/win solution when the settlement money, being nontaxable, leads to the plaintiff actually keeping more money, even though the defendant is paying a smaller amount of money to settle the case. "A creative lawyer who is smart about taxes can occasionally settle the 'unsettleable' case." *Id.* If possible, in order to maximize the amount which the plaintiff will actually keep, and thereby maximize the possibility of settlement, if there are both taxable and nontaxable claims, the proposed settlement agreement should allocate as much as is reasonable to the nontaxable claims. The courts, including the United States Tax Court as well as the Internal Revenue Service, have usually accepted the allocations made in settlement agreements. Isleib & Kahn, *Tax Strategies Can Increase the Value of Settlements*, 30 Trial 36, 38 (June 1994). However, the courts may examine whether the allocation is the result of good faith negotiations. *See McKay v Commissioner*, 102 TC 16 (1994) (accepting an allocation between a wrongful discharge tort claim and a breach of contract claim). The IRS also views court approval of a settlement as an additional factor in favor of the settlement's allocation between claims. *Id* (citing IRS Rev Rul 75-232, 1975-1 CB 94). Even nontax lawyers need to be aware of tax laws that create such opportunities in their areas of practice because taxes can be a key factor affecting how much the defendant has to pay in settlement and how much the plaintiff will actually receive from settlement. For instance, although it is common knowledge that personal injury awards are not taxable, it is not as well known that personal injury, for purposes of the tax code, has been held to mean more than just physical injury. *Rickel v Commissioner*, 900 F2d 655 (3d Cir 1990) (holding that the personal injury exclusion from income encompassed a settlement for employment discrimi-nation, even though the basis of the settlement appeared to be back pay); *Roemer v Commissioner*, 716 F2d 693 (9th Cir

1983) (holding that compensatory and punitive damages received in a defamation suit were excluded from gross income because defamation was considered to be a personal injury under California law). *But see Commissioner v Miller*, 914 F2d 586 (4th Cir 1990) (holding that the punitive damage portion of a defamation settlement was taxable income). (Furthermore, in considering whether *Roemer* is still applicable, it should be noted that since *Roemer* was decided, the Internal Revenue Code was amended in 1989 to provide that punitive damages are not excluded from taxation unless the case concerns physical injury or illness, though that can include psychological injury or illness). IRC §104(a)(2). Allocating the settlement proceeds may also be significant where pre-judgment or post-judgment interest is potentially involved, since some courts have held that such interest is taxable, even if the principle part of the judgment is not taxable. Isleib & Kahn, *Tax Strategies Can Increase the Value of Settlements*, 30 Trial 36, 38, n 12 (June 1994) (citing *Kovacs v Commissioner*, 100 TC 124 (1993)); *McShane v Commissioner*, 53 TCM (CCH) 409, 411 (1987).

To the extent that some or all of the settlement can be characterized as damages for personal injury or personal harm from a tort, money can be treated as compensation, rather than as taxable income. Edwards & Reiser, *Why Settle for Less? Factoring in Taxability*, ABA J 52 (Apr 1992). Readers of this article should note that it was written prior to the Supreme Court's decision in *Burke v Commissioner*, 112 S Ct 1867 (1992) which reversed *Burke v Commissioner*, 929 F2d 1119 (6th Cir 1991). Accordingly, the article's specific comments on the Sixth Circuit's decision in *Burke* and on employment discrimination settlements must be disregarded in light of the Supreme Court's subsequent decision.

The Sixth Circuit in *Burke*, like the Third Circuit in *Rickel v Commissioner*, 900 F2d 655 (3d Cir 1990), held that employment discrimination damages were damages for "personal injuries" within the meaning of the Internal Revenue Code and were, therefore, not taxable even though the measure of damages was backpay. (The Internal Revenue Code, IRC §104(a)(2), excludes damages for personal injury from income.) However, in *Burke*, the Supreme Court held that a backpay award in settlement of a Title VII claim was not nontaxable damages received for personal injuries. The Supreme Court's rationale was that the Internal Revenue Code exclusion was intended for traditional tort awards, and the Title VII action was not like a traditional tort claim because of the limited statutory remedies available.

The future significance of *Burke* is open to debate, however, because the Supreme Court was not considering Title VII in light of the 1991 amendments to the statute which expanded the available remedies. 112 S Ct at 1874 n 12. Thus, it would appear to be an open question as to whether damages in a Title VII case, in which the 1991 amendments apply, are or are not taxable income. Perhaps the answer will depend on which Title VII remedies actually apply in a particular case, or perhaps the issue will be decided in a broader manner so that all Title VII cases are treated alike with regard to this tax issue.

Employment rights is an area in which allocation may prove important, but it is also an area in which the law is developing. The IRS has issued a rule, Rev Rul 93-88, 1993-41 IRB 4, which treats the taxability of backpay differently, depending on the type of claim in which it arises. That Revenue Ruling states that damages for disparate sex and race discrimination claims under Title VII, 42 USC §2000(e) *et seq*, and damages for violations of the Americans with Disabilities Act, 42 USC §12101 *et seq*, including backpay awards, are excludable from gross income. However, it also states that backpay awards for disparate impact gender discrimination *are* taxable.

This discussion is meant to illustrate the potential for using tax law to facilitate settlement. However, it is not intended to be a comprehensive, substantive discussion given the complex and changing nature of the subject.

Ethics and Caveats

12

§12.02   Civil Matters

Page 384, note 10, add:

One commentator has concluded that "minimal truthfulness and fairness are functional ethical norms inherent in bargaining." Norton, *Bargaining and the Ethic of Process*, 64 NYU L Rev 493, 501 (1989). Puffing, bluffing, withholding certain types of information, and evading certain types of questions are considered to be ethical because they are the norm. *Id* 506, 526.

Page 384, text, add after carryover paragraph:

A "Doonesbury" Negotiation

"Doonesbury" has examined the ethics of negotiation. Gary Trudeau had a star television reporter seeking a raise suddenly sit down in a restaurant with "Fred," a high ranking executive of a rival network. "Fred" did not know or expect the reporter. From that position, the reporter said hello to a high ranking executive at his own network, "Russ." Fearing that the reporter was about to resign or be pirated away, "Russ" decided that he had better offer him a raise and maybe throw in a prime time show! *Doonesbury*, Chicago Trib, June 4, 1989, Sunday Comics, at 2.

This clever form of fact creation was successful; the issue is whether it is ethical. (See §4.03 regarding the creation of facts.) The reporter-negotiator did not make a misstatement of fact, either by word or omission. He merely allowed "Russ" to draw his own mistaken conclusion from the sight of the reporter with "Fred." Such misdirection does not constitute unethical conduct in the opinion of the authors, although it may be a dangerous form of bluff that can backfire, either if the bluff is discovered or "Russ" had reacted negatively to his perception that his reporter was willing to change networks.

Page 387, note 25, change "90 Or 127" to:

290 Or 127

Page 387, text, add at end of section:

The *Himmel* Case

In Illinois, "first of all, quite clearly, one cannot use the threat of reporting attorney misconduct as a bargaining tool in a negotiation. It seems reasonably obvious from the record in this case that one attorney agreed, in effect, to pay punitive damages in consideration of a promise of silence," i.e., for the now-suspended attorney's not reporting a disciplinary violation. Overton, *Strong Medicine from the Court*, CBA Rec 40 (Jan 1989). In *In re Himmel*, 125 Ill 2d 531, 533 NE2d 790 (1989), the Illinois Supreme Court suspended a lawyer for one year for failing to report fraudulent/dishonest conduct by another lawyer but, instead, settling the matter advantageously for the client without so reporting. The Illinois Supreme Court Rules require reporting "unprivileged knowledge" of such a violation. Ill Sup Ct Rul 1-103(a). The Illinois Supreme Court held that mandatory reporting requirements control, regardless of a client's directions. "A lawyer may not choose to circumvent the rules by simply asserting that his client asked him to do so." *Himmel*, 125 Ill 2d at 539, 533 NE2d at 793. The *Himmel* court cited similar requirements under the ABA Model Code of Professional Responsibility DR 1-103 (1979).

Single-Limit Insurance Policies

Single-limit insurance policies provide a single sum for both defense and indemnification. Shadoan, *Pressure Points in Settlement Negotiations*, 27 Trial 36, 38 (Aug 1991). This type of policy is most commonly seen in professional malpractice coverage. Since the amount of coverage available for settlement or paying a judgment is depleted by the costs of defense, defense attorneys must be careful of the potential for conflicts of interest inherent in such policies. *Id* 38. On the other hand, plaintiffs' attorneys should learn of the existence of this type of policy and the policy limits in discovery. If possible, the plaintiff's attorney should then seek to create pressure for a settlement with an appropriately reasoned demand letter and a specific request to the defendant's attorney that the demand letter be transmitted to the defendant, as well as the insurer.

§12.03   Criminal Matters

Page 388, text, add at end of section:

The United States Supreme Court has held that counsel cannot represent codefendants in a criminal case if there is a "serious potential" for a conflict of interest. *Wheat v United States*, 486 US 153 (1988). That case arose because the government opposed having the defense attorney represent an additional defendant. Kettlewell, *When Representing Co-Defendants*, 24 Trial 17 (Dec 1988). The federal government appears to be trying to disqualify defense attorneys from representing more than one codefendant, even where the defense attorney and the codefendants do not believe that there is a serious potential for conflict, with increasing frequency.

§12.04   Caveats

Page 390, text, add after second full paragraph:

Example 12-1A

The baseball players whose performances did not match their high salaries have been unconditionally released and replaced with rookies or other younger players with far lower salaries. *Rich Players Fat Targets for Ax-Wielding Owners*, Chicago Trib, Apr 4, 1991, §4, at 3. The Players Association contract prohibits the release of a player because of budgetary goals not in effect when the player was signed to his current contract. *Id.* Despite this provision, owners are apparently releasing some nonessential players they consider to be overpaid for budgetary reasons. *Id.* This reflects the difficulty of enforcing contractual provisions which become highly uneconomical.

Page 391, text, add at end of section:

Danger Signals

A negotiator should be aware of danger signals that emotional reactions are interfering with negotiating effectiveness. These danger signs include:

1. The negotiation seems unreal or mechanical at times
2. Anxiety, irritation or discomfort that does not relate to any specific problem or incident
3. Unduly emotional responses
4. Unreasoning strong dislikes or admiration

5. Difficulty focusing or concentrating
6. Repeated, unusually prolonged or unrewarding bickering or arguments
7. Feeling unusually defensive, sensitive or vulnerable
8. Significant misunderstandings regarding what has been said
9. Being unduly preoccupied with the negotiation

M. Schoenfield & B. Schoenfield, *Interviewing and Counseling* 23 (1981). If you recognize these danger signals, get back on track by adjourning, focusing on the process by yourself or with a colleague, and working through the planning steps again.

§12.04A   —Caveats for Particular Types of Negotiations (New)

Introduction

The caveats that follow are concepts and warnings, some in general and some for specific types of negotiations. Regarding the latter, since entire books are devoted to specific types of negotiation, the specific caveats are not intended to be all inclusive or make the reader a specialist in an area. Instead, they are important points to consider when negotiating in that area.

Sales and Marketing

Sales and marketing persons too often view negotiation as limited to sessions in which price and other terms are discussed. If price, for example, is set at one rate for everyone, even the price discussion may not be viewed as a negotiation by the participants.

Such a narrow view of negotiation, however, deprives those involved of many valuable lessons from negotiation theory and experience that can improve performance and results. Negotiation in sales and marketing is far more than bargaining on price and may not even involve that aspect. It is a dynamic process of exchanging and evaluating information to determine whether agreement is possible and, if so, the optimal agreement which can be achieved. Each contact with the current or potential customer or client is part of this process and must be viewed as such.

Sales are not always made because one has the best product in terms of goods or services. Whether an agreement results is a function of needs, interests and communication skills. As with any type of negotiation, one must discover the true needs and interests of the other side and persuasively disclose an ability to meet those needs and interests. While price can be a critical factor, persuasion to accept a higher price can require using negotiation tactics such as selective information disclosure, fact creation, win/win, creating a psychological commitment to agreement, and appeals to the negotiator's personal interests.

Negotiation concepts provide useful guidance for sales and marketing efforts. By viewing all customer contacts as part of the negotiation process, each contact can be focused on the ultimate goal—optimal agreement(s). In addition, the customer decisionmaking process may be analyzed in terms of a continuous negotiation among the owner(s), evaluator(s), and implementor(s) based on the different and sometimes conflicting needs and interests of each. Negotiation strategies and tactics can be used to guide one's behavior for each customer contact, and are not only limited to the tactic of bargaining. These points are explained below.

With regard to customer contacts, each contact is part of a process which is planned to lead to an optimal agreement. Any contact is not merely an isolated interaction. The goal is not just a sale or contract, but the most advantageous one possible at the time. Unless only a one-time agreement is planned, a long-term view, instead of just a short-term focus, is crucial. Every potential agreement should be evaluated on its own merits and as part of a long-term negotiation for future agreements, if that is a possibility.

Concerning the customer's decisionmaking process, the negotiation with another party often is influenced by the company's intra-organizational negotiation among various departments or centers (production, research and development, marketing and sales, purchasing, finance, training). These intra-organizational negotiations affect whether a sale is made and, if so, the terms. Each of these forces within the customer's structure has its own goals, needs, and agenda. The forces negotiate implicitly or explicitly with each other to determine sources, levels, and terms for purchases of goods or services. By recognizing the intra-organizational negotiations, a sales and marketing effort can more effectively decipher the customer's varied and, at times, conflicting internal needs and focus on which persons must be influenced.

Similarly, negotiation occurs in an intra-organizational context concerning corporate authorization for an acceptable sales or marketing position. Each employee and department has separate goals and concerns which can influence the process leading to the product and terms that can be offered. The most effective sales and marketing professionals recognize this and participate directly or through their company's hierarchy in the intra-organizational negotiations in order to have products and terms which are highly attractive to potential customers.

Negotiation strategies and tactics provide effective tools for sales and marketing. The role and influence of personality—whether one is liked, respected, credible, and so on—can be critical to a deal. Long-range goals must be balanced against short-range goals. Information gathering techniques and selective information disclosure are critical skills. Both competitive and cooperative approaches should be utilized, depending on the situational realities. There must be implementation of strategies and tactics such as:

1. Selective information disclosure
2. Development of personal relationships and otherwise creating psychological commitment to deal and appeals to personal interests
3. Use of allies
4. Problem solving
5. Face-saving
6. Focus on the process
7. Fact creation
8. Funnel approach
9. Win/win
10. Tone
11. Ability to achieve closure

Note that all of these tactics are used even if there is no bargaining on price and terms. Furthermore, systematic planning steps should be used to attain improved control and results.

Business Acquisitions

In acquiring a business, the potential purchaser must engage in careful information gathering and not rely on factual representations by the seller. The purchaser wants to buy a business, not a lawsuit for misrepresentation. For example, in acquiring an insurance company, the scrutiny must include:

1. The corporate organization, including the board of directors, corporate minutes, and shares of outstanding stock
2. At least three years of annual statements plus interim financial data since the last annual statement, and the reliability of the preparer, especially for any unaudited data
3. Regulatory matters
4. Employee and shareholder agreements and loans, including any stock options, pensions, profit-sharing, health, life and/or disability insurance, as well as noncompetition agreements
5. Reinsurance and insurance arrangements
6. Acquisitions and divestitures for at least five years
7. Pending and anticipated or threatened future litigation or claims

8. Past litigation or claims to the extent that future payments remain to be made, past payments-skewed financial data, or if a past injunction or ruling affects future operations

9. Tax consequences of different transactional structures

For various types of business acquisitions, expert tax advice can be critical. For example (at the time of publication):

1. The deductibility of "passive" investment losses may be increased by having the interest expense of a loan used for the investment structured as a loan against one's personal residence (Bernstein, *The Ernest & Young Tax Digest and Planner* (1990))

2. Tax deductions may not be allowed for some losses from sales or exchanges of property between certain related taxpayers. (*Id*)

3. Tax-free deferred corporate reorganizations can be structured (IRC §§355, 368(a)(1)(D))

While these examples may change with new tax laws or Internal Revenue Service rulings, the point is that expert tax advice can create gains for one's own side, win/win opportunities, and problem solving solutions, as well as avoid unnecessary adverse tax consequences.

In acquiring a business, decisions must be made whether to purchase a direct ownership interest (stock, partnership, etc.) or specific assets (including use of a name, etc.). Purchasing stock can involve buying liabilities as well as assets. Buying assets may necessitate filings and notices under state bulk transfer laws. Legal and tax expertise can be critical for a proper structuring of the transaction. This ties back to the use of letters of intent or even oral agreements by the parties on the basic structure of the deal which are to be followed by written contracts. One should not set the basic structure in place until legal and tax considerations indicate whether that structure is most advantageous or even acceptable.

Dissolution

When structuring entities, a general caveat is to consider alternatives to deadlock and statutory sales for dissolution. Some long-run agreements consist of establishing a new legal entity. It may be a corporation, partnership, or joint venture. Special concerns develop when the entity is to be owned by a very small group, because deadlock issues may arise.

The question, then, is whether traditional dissolution remedies would be effective and efficient, or whether an alternative arrangement should be structured into the agreement. The latter is generally preferable to a statutory sale of assets, which is often the normal procedure under traditional legal measures. The creative mechanisms can include an outside director to avoid deadlock, alternative dispute resolution procedures in the event of deadlock, and formulas for dividing the business assets, liabilities, and operations. Employment agreements, consulting contracts for owners, shareholder agreements, and ownership buyout agreements combined with covenants not to compete can also be used to establish the parties' relationships so that the entity functions as the parties originally intended. These decrease the chances of a deadlock as well. Again, tax advice is essential for such matters as whether stock buyout provisions should be structured as cross-purchases, rather than corporation redemptions. Sugar, *Cross-Purchase Agreements Are often More Beneficial than Redemption Agreements*, 44 Taxn For Accts 148 (1990).

Land and Buildings

If the purchase of any building is involved in the negotiation, an inspection of the structure and its mechanical elements is critical. While legal binding representations are important, the preacquisition examination is critical, since no buyer wants to purchase anything simply to bring a later lawsuit for a false contractual representation and latent (i.e., hidden) defects.

Fears of environmental hazards, especially when combined with uncertainty over the scope of liability for environmental cleanup, can complicate negotiations. In purchasing land or buildings, the issue of potential environmental dangers, such as toxic and hazardous waste or asbestos, must be explored. Before closing, if any possible question exists, an expert environmental inspection should be made as a part of information gathering. This is in addition to representations in the agreement and, if applicable, special title insurance protection.

There are many different types of businesses which use chemicals or materials with chemical components classified as toxic or hazardous. Even if the property never was a formal dumping ground or is not large, possible spills, permanent storage, or dumping by present or past commercial occupants must be considered. Since owners of property become responsible for any toxic or hazardous waste along with the generators of the waste, a purchaser does not want to unknowingly become liable for an environmental cleanup, large or small.

Both purchasers and sellers should consider creative financing when it may be advantageous. For example, in land development projects, equity participation loans can be used when a lender seeks or is convinced to share in the residual value of the real estate. Such loans can result in a higher rate of return to the lender than market interest, while the developer may be able to borrow a higher percentage of the project's acquisition and development costs at a lower interest factor. Financial pro formas are often a key to whether equity participation will be approved, since the projected residual value is critical. The analysis may be affected by the ADC (accounting for real estate acquisition, development or construction arrangements) decisions. For example, ADC can affect how the potential transaction is viewed with regard to its impact on calculations of regulated financial institutions' minimum capital requirements.

Sawaya, *Sometimes It Pays to Know More than Your Banker*, 1 Ernest & Young Real Est J 10, 10-13 (Spring 1990). See §5.30 of the Supplement.

In real estate negotiations, businesses must balance their needs for low-cost space with their need for flexibility. The latter refers to the length of real estate commitments in industries where unforeseen significant operational changes may be needed in six to twelve months. Periodic scrutiny and space and termination options are techniques for balancing the needs to maintain a competitive edge. *Corporate Real Estate: Learning Strategies*, Ernst & Young Real Est J 18-19 (Fall 1991).

Commercial Loans

When a bank negotiates a loan to fund a securities transaction, it must be diligent concerning the propriety of the transaction, so that it does not recklessly aid and abet a securities fraud. Such securities transactions are not limited to stock, but include limited partnerships and private placements for:

1. Office building financing
2. Loans to rehabilitate buildings
3. Oil or gas exploration financing
4. Loans for leasing equipment
5. Movie financing
6. Loans to start entrepreneurial enterprises

Feldman, *Bank Liability for Securities Fraud*, Banking LJ 100, 102 (Mar/Apr 1990). Those negotiating such loans may find increased scrutiny by banks concerned about potential securities fraud exposure. This should influence the borrower's planning for information disclosure tactics and the lender's planning for information gathering.

Lenders do have legitimate concerns over environmental hazards. Such hazards affect the value of the property and an appraisal may be grossly overstated if unknown contamination is present. The ability to foreclose may not be a sufficient or even viable remedy, if the lender then becomes liable for environmental violations. Such violations may involve significant costs, which will sometimes even far exceed the market value of the property. Borrowers must anticipate these concerns, and be prepared to respond effectively. See §5.30 of the Supplement.

Lock-Outs

In labor-management disputes, one tactical issue can be whether the employer will lock out the employees or the employees will strike. This is a form of power and deadlock. The 1990 major leagues baseball situation exemplified this. *Owners Move First with Lockout*, Chicago Trib, Feb 19, 1990, §3, at 4.

For the employer, a lock-out sets the timing of the disruption, rather than allowing the workers to set it by striking. Loss of wages places economic pressure on the workers. Conversely, a lock-out may limit replacements hired to a temporary status, while creating possible backpay awards to strikers. If the employer, on the other hand, awaits a strike, there may be greater current freedom to hire permanent replacements under some circumstances, but there also is a loss of control over the precise timing of the disruption of operations.

For employees, corresponding advantages and disadvantages exist. At times, a lock-out can solidify union members, at least initially. According to a former director of the Major League Baseball Players Association, unlike a strike where "constant effort" is required to keep union members informed and united, "when you have a lockout, all the work is done for you by the owners . . . . You have instant solidarity. There's no possibility of some players saying, well we're going back to work." *Old Strike Foes Still Disagree*, Chicago Trib, Feb 11, 1990, §3, at 14. These are examples of the factors to be weighed in deciding the use of the lock-out/strike tactic.

Sports Negotiations

Increasing numbers of attorneys negotiate contracts for professional athletes. from the perspective of Ted Phillips, chief negotiator for the Chicago Bears:

> . . . most of the work especially for a veteran, goes in before the negotiation begins . . . . Preparing your argument and understanding the market are the key. Understanding the agent, his personality, his traits, how he likes to approach contracts, the timing of approaching him . . . those are all very critical elements to getting the job done in as smooth a fashion as possible . . . . In most cases, I would be the first person to make an offer. It has happened in the past where agents will make the first offer. Typically, if they make the first offer, it will be a very high-ball offer with every incentive clause under the sun, especially if they haven't dealt with me before. All that usually does is drag out the process, so I usually try to make the first offer to set the tone.

Phillips Gearing Up for His "Season," Chicago Trib, June 9, 1991, §3, at 12. Thus, key elements to Phillips are planning, analyzing the market, assessing the strengths, weaknesses and personality of the other negotiator, and making the first offer to set the tone of the negotiation. *See* §§5.03, 5.09, 5.10, 5.14, 8.03, 8.06, and 8.07.

Sports negotiations, employment negotiations, and negotiations involving long-term working relationships ought to be viewed as a continual process, not simply as what happens when it is time to go to the bargaining table to renew a contract. Comments from publicized, unsuccessful sports negotiations illustrate that soured personal relationships and lost personal credibility can doom what should have been successful negotiations where the parties could have reached agreement on substantive terms.

Governmental Regulations

Under the Negotiated Rulemaking Act of 1990, 5 USC §581 *et seq*, some federal regulations are now developed through negotiations between the government and interested parties, rather than through the traditional rulemaking procedures. This process, which is known as "reg neg," can lead to regulations which are more palatable to all interested parties and avoid litigation challenging regulations. Lassila, *See You Later, Litigator*, Amicus J 5, 6 (Summer 1992). Although still utilized with regard to only a small number of regulations due, in part, to its "labor-intensive" nature, "reg neg" has proven to be useful in various areas, including that of environmental regulations. *Id.* William Becker, who has represented state and local air pollution control officials in several reg negs, has stated that the interaction of reg negs "often leads to dynamic solutions, that a regulatory agency might not come up with by itself." *Id* 6. In other words, despite conflicting interests, needs and goals, environmentalists, industry and government, through discussion and negotiation, can sometimes arrive at win/win solutions.

Bibliography

CASES

Alexander v Gardner-Denver Co, 415 US 36 (1974)

Arabian American Oil Co v Scarface, 119 FRD 448 (MD Fla 1988)

Barrentine v Arkansas-Bit Freight System, 450 US 728 (1981)

Burke v Commissioner, 112 S Ct 1867 (1992)

Charles, In re, 290 Or 127, 618 P2d 1281 (1980)

Commissioner v Miller, 914 F2d 586 (4th Cir 1990)

Complaint of Rio Grande Transport, Inc, In re, 770 F2d 262 (2d Cir 1985)

Crossman v Marcocio, 806 F2d 329 (1st Cir 1986), *cert denied*, 481 US 1029 (1987)

Daniziger v Pittsfield Shoe Co, 204 Ill 145, 68 NE 534 (1903)

Dean Witter Reynolds v Bryd, 470 US 213 (1985)

Elbaor v Smith, 845 SW2d 240 (Tex 1992)

Federal Reserve Bank v Carey-Canada, 123 FRD 603 (D Minn 1988)

Florida Bar v Gentry, 475 So 2d 678 (Fla 1985)

Ford v Citizens & Southern National Bank, 928 F2d 1118 (11th Cir 1991)

General Motors Engine Interchange Litigation, In re, 594 F2d 1106 (7th Cir), *cert denied*, 444 US 870 (1979)

G Heilman Brewing Co v Joseph Oat Corp, 871 F2d 648 (7th Cir 1989)

Gilmer v Interstate/Johnson Lane Corp, 111 S Ct 1647 (1991)

Guardianship of Babb, In re, ___ Ill ___ (Sept 29, 1994)

Himmel, In re, 125 Ill 2d 531, 533 NE2d 790 (1989)

Horn v City of Chicago, 860 F2d 700 (7th Cir 1988)

Humphreys v Chrysler Motors Corp, 399 SE2d 60 (W Va 1990)

Kazale v Flowers, 185 Ill App 3d 224, 541 NE2d 219 (1989)

King v King, 199 Ga App 496, 405 SE2d 319 (1991)

Kokkonen v Guardian Life Insurance Co, 114 S Ct 1673 (1994)

Kovaks v Commissioner, 100 TC 124 (1993)

McDonald v City of West Branch, 466 US 284 (1984)

McKay v Ashland Oil, Inc, 120 FRD 43 (ED Ky 1988)

McKay v Commissioner, 102 TC 16 (1994)

McShane v Commissioner, 53 TCM (CCH) 409 (1987)

Michaud v Michaud, 932 F2d 77 (1st Cir 1991)

Mitsubishi Motors Corp v Soler Chrysler-Plymouth, 473 US 614 (1985)

Moores v Greenberg, 834 F2d 1105 (1st Cir 1987)

Moseley, Hallgarten, Estabrook & Weeden, Inc v Ellis, 849 F2d 264 (7th Cir 1988)

Muccini, In re Estate of, 118 Misc 2d 38, 460 NYS2d 680 (1983)

Muhammad v Strassburger, McKenna, Messer, Shilobod & Gutnick, 526 Pa 541, 587 A2d 1346 (1991)

Patrick v Ronald Williams, PA, 402 SE2d 452 (NC Ct App 1991)

Rickel v Commissioner, 900 F2d 655 (3d Cir 1990)

Rodriguez de Quijas v Shearson/American Express, Inc, 490 US 477 (1989)

Roemer v Commissioner, 716 F2d 693 (9th Cir 1983)

Schoonover v International Harvester Co, 171 Ill App 3d 882, 525 NE2d 1041 (1988), *appeal denied*, 122 Ill 2d 594, 530 NE2d 264 (1989)

Shearson/American Express, Inc v McMahon, 482 US 220 (1987)

United States v Beebe, 180 US 343 (1901)

Volt Information Sciences, Inc v Board of Trustees, 489 US 468 (1989)

Wheat v United States, 486 US 153 (1988)

Wilco v Swan, 346 US 427 (1953)

STATUTES

Federal Arbitration Act
Federal Tort Claims Act
Negotiated Rulemaking Act of 1990
Public Laws
RICO (Racketeer Influenced and Corrupt Organizations Act)
Securities Act of 1933
Securities Exchange Act of 1934
Technical and Miscellaneous Revenue Act of 1988

United States Code

5 USC §581 *et seq*
9 USC §1 *et seq*
9 USC §§2-4
15 USC §77b *et seq*
15 USC §77l(2)
18 USC §1961 *et seq*
26 USC §104(a)(2)
26 USC §130
42 USC §2000(e) *et seq*
42 USC §12101 *et seq*

Federal Rules

Fed R Civ P 16
Fed R Civ P 65
Fed R Evid 706

State Statutes and Court Rules

Alaska Stat §09.43.010 *et seq*
Ariz Rev Stat Ann §12-1501 *et seq*
Ark Code Ann §6-108-201 *et seq*
Colo Rev Stat Ann §13-22-201 *et seq*
Del Code Ann tit 10, §5701 *et seq*
DC Code Ann §16-4301 *et seq*
Fla Stat Ann §682.01 *et seq*
Idaho Code §7-901 *et seq*
710 Ill Comp Stat Ann §5/1 *et seq*
740 Ill Comp Stat Ann §100/2
815 Ill Comp Stat Ann §205/2
Ill Sup Ct Rul 1-103(a)
Ill Sup Ct Ruls 86-95
Ill Sup Ct Rul 93(a)
Indiana Code Ann §34-4-2-1 *et seq*
Iowa Code Ann §679A.1 *et seq*
Kan Stat Ann §5-401 *et seq*
Ky Rev Stat Ann §417.045 *et seq*
Me Rev Stat Ann tit 10 §5927 *et seq*
Md Code Ann 251, §1 *et seq*
Mich Comp Laws Ann §600.5001 *et seq*
Minn Stat Ann §572.08 *et seq*
Mo Ann Stat §435.350 *et seq*
Mont Code Ann §27-5-111 *et seq*
Neb Rev Stat §25-2601 *et seq*
Nev Rev Stat Ann §38.015 *et seq*
NM Stat Ann §44-7-1 *et seq* (1978)
NC Gen Stat §1-567.1 *et seq*
ND Cent Code §32-29.2-01 *et seq*
Okla St Ann tit 15, §801 *et seq*
42 Pa Cons Stat Ann §7301 *et seq*
SC Code Ann §15-48-10
SD Codified Laws Ann §21-25A-1 *et seq*
Tenn Code Ann §29-5-301 *et seq*
Tex Rev Civ Stat Ann arts 224 *et seq*
Utah Code Ann §78-31a-1 *et seq* (1953)
Vt Stat Ann tit 12 §5651 *et seq*

Va Code Ann §8.01-581.01 *et seq* (1950)
Wyo Stat §1-36-101 *et seq* (1977)

Authorities

ABA Model Code of Professional Responsibility DR 1-103
ABA Model Rules of Professional Conduct Rule 1.2(a)
Ability to Psych Out Foes Crucial in Foreign Crisis, Chicago Trib, Oct 23, 1994, §4, at 4, col 1
Aggressiveness of U.S. Lawyers in Brussels Offends Members of Old World Bar, Chicago Daily L Bull, May 14, 1991, at 3
Alternative Dispute Resolution: ADR and the World Around Us, Chicago Daily L Bull, Nov 19, 1993, at 19, col 4
Arab's Culture and Language Help Shape Crisis in Middle East, Chicago Trib, Aug 19, 1990, §1, at 12, cols 6-8
Arbitration Reduces Costs: Study, Chicago Daily L Bull, Sept 5, 1990, at 1, col 8
Ash, *Germany Unbound*, 37 NY Rev Books, Nov 22, 1990, at 11
Behind Closed Doors: How Chicago Averted a Teachers Strike, Chicago Trib, Nov 24, 1991, §2, at 1
Berkman, *Disagreeing Without Being Disagreeable*, Chicago Law 1 (Jan 1993)
Bonn Walked into US Negotiating Trap, Chicago Trib, June 1, 1989, §1, at 2
Broder, *For Union Labor, a Glimmer of New Hope*, Chicago Trib, Sept 2, 1990, §4, at 3, cols 4-6
Burton, *Negotiating the Cleanup of Toxic Groundwater Contamination: Strategy and Legitimacy*, 28 Nat Resources J 105 (1988)
Carpenter & Kennedy, *The Denver Metropolitan Water Roundtable: A Case Study in Researching Agreements*, 28 Nat Resources J 21 (1988)
Citing "Snub," ANC Rival to Boycott S. African Talks, Chicago Trib, Dec 19, 1991, §1, at 14
Coca-Cola in Bitter Legal Fight over Cost of Sweetener, Chicago Daily L Bull, May 22, 1989, at 3
Conference with Reinsdorf Quieted Jordan, Chicago Trib, Nov 17, 1991, §1, at 1
Contract? Oh That Old Thing, Chicago Trib, Dec 11, 1988, §3, at 2
Cook County Arbitration Awards Accepted in 3 of 4 Cases, Chicago Daily L Bull, Sept 5, 1990, at 1, cols 3-8
Cooley & Stone, *Using Your Brain in Negotiation: Both Sides of It*, CBA Rec 24 (Feb 1988)
Corporate Real Estate: Learning Strategies, Ernst & Young Real Est J 18 (Fall 1991)
Craver, *Negotiation Techniques*, 24 Trial 65 (June 1988)
Danninger & Palfin, *How to Evaluate Proposals; Avoid Fee Disputes*, 24 Trial 38 (Dec 1988)

Debt Orchestrates '90's Theme: Deals Done Again, Chicago Trib, Sept 16, 1990, §7, at 1, cols 7-8

Demetrio, *Alternative Dispute Resolution: There Are No Losers*, CBA Rec 9 (Nov 1992)

Doonesbury, Chicago Trib, June 4, 1989, Sunday Comics, at 2

Edwards & Reiser, *Why Settle for Less? Factoring in Taxability*, ABA J 52 (Apr 1992)

Ehrman, *Why Business Lawyers Should Use Mediation*, 75 ABA J 73 (June 1989)

End to Salary Arbitration Urged, Chicago Trib, Dec 15, 1992, §4, at 1

Entman, *Mary Carter Agreements: Learn the Inside Deal*, 24 Tenn BJ 10 (Jan/Feb 1988)

Erisman, *The Art of Negotiating a Settlement*, 25 Trial 26 (Sept 1989)

Fallons, *The Great Japanese Misunderstanding*, 37 NY Rev Books, Nov 8, 1990, at 33

Feldman, *Bank Liability for Securities Fraud*, Banking LJ 100 (Mar/Apr 1990)

Firm in Arbitration Case Charged with Malpractice, Chicago Daily L Bull, June 25, 1992, at 1

R. Fisher & W. Ury, *Getting to Yes, Negotiating Agreement Without Giving In* (1981)

Fitzpatrick, *Nonbinding Mediation of Employment Disputes*, 30 Trial 40 (June 1994)

Folk-Williams, *The Use of Negotiated Agreements to Resolve Water Disputes Involving Indian Rights*, 28 Nat Resources J 63 (1988)

J. Freedman, *Crisis and Legitimacy* (1978)

Fuchsberg, *Pitfalls in Structured Settlements*, 25 Trial 42 (Sept 1989)

Fuchsberg, *Ten Commandments for Successful Evaluation and Settlement*, 27 Trial 16 (Aug 1991)

Gifford, *The Synthesis of Legal Counseling and Negotiation Models: Preserving Client Centered Advocacy in the Negotiation Context*, 34 UCLA L Rev 811 (1987)

Gillie, *Voluntary Mediation: Tool to Assess Risks and Speed Settlements*, 26 Trial 58 (Oct 1990)

Goldberg, Green & Sander, *Litigation, Arbitration Mediation: A Dialogue*, 75 ABA J 70 (June 1989)

Guill & Slavin, *Rush to Unfairness: The Downside of ADR*, 28 Judges J 8 (Summer 1989)

Haldeman, *The Chicago Arbitration Program: An Independent Appraisal*, CBA Rec 16 (May/Apr)

Halpern, *A Safe Alternative to Structured Settlements*, 30 Trial 34 (June 1994)

In Some Cases, Parties Prefer Arbitrating Instead of Litigating, Chicago Trib, Dec 16, 1991, §2, at 3

In Sue-Happy Society, Mediators Lighten Court Load, Chicago Trib, Dec 16, 1991, §1, at 3

Isleib & Kahn, *Tax Strategies Can Increase the Value of Settlements*, 30 Trial 36 (June 1994)

Japanese Beef about High Costs as Quotas Fall, Chicago Trib, Mar 31, 1991, §7, at 3

Japan Firms Behind 8 Ball, Chicago Trib, Nov 26, 1990, §4, at 1, cols 7-8

Japan Reneging on Trade Pledges 2 in Cabinet Say, Chicago Trib, Mar 3, 1989, §1, at 1

Jeffries, *Structured Settlement Security: Reality or Facade?*, 27 Trial 26 (Aug 1991)

Katz, *The L'Ambiance Plaza Mediation: A Case Study in Judicial Settlement of Mass Torts*, 5 Ohio St J Dispute Resolution 277 (1990)

Keleher, *Mandatory Arbitration in Cook County, A Year of Progress*, CBA Rec 13 (Apr/May 1991)

Kettlewell, *When Representing Co-Defendants*, 24 Trial 17 (Dec 1988)

Kleinman, *Survival in Corporate Jungle—Workshop Teaches Self-Defense in Office Conflicts*, Chicago Trib, Nov 20, 1989, §4, at 1 & 6

Lassila, *See You Later, Litigator*, Amicus J 5 (Summer 1992)

Lieberman, *Acquiring a Life Insurance Company*, Brief 39 (Winter 1989)

Loomis, *What Fred Carr's Fall Means to You*, Fortune, May 6, 1991, at 60

Machlin & Prero, *When Words Don't Mean Too Much*, CBA Rec 35 (Mar 1991)

Magladry & Macpherson, *Now Cut That Out! Extremes of Boorish Behavior*, 30 Trial 43 (July 1994)

Mandel, *An Ounce of Prevention: Some Dos and Don'ts*, 24 Trial 32 (Dec 1988)

McMichael May Sit out Season over Contract, Chicago Trib, Feb 21, 1990, §4, at 3, cols 4-7

Mediation Catching on—Slowly, Chicago Daily L Bull, Jan 28, 1991, at 1

Mediation Clears Courts' Clogged Arteries, Chicago Daily L Bull, Oct 28, 1994, at 1, cols 2-3

Mediation Finds Unlikely Ally, Chicago Daily L Bull, Jan 7, 1991, at 3

Metzloff, *How to Improve the Summary Jury Trial*, 30 Trial 22 (June 1994)

Mideast Peace Talks in D.C. near Collapse, Chicago Trib, Dec 18, 1991, §1, at 2

Money Talk, Chicago Trib, Oct 17, 1990, §4, at 7, cols 5-6

Neubauer, *Settling Once and for All*, 27 Trial 31 (Aug 1991)

Newman, *The Summary Jury Trial as a Method of Dispute Resolution in the Federal Courts*, 1990 U Ill L Rev 177 (1990)

NFL Loses Antitrust Exemption, Chicago Sun-Times, May 29, 1991, at 119

Nolan-Haley & Volpe, *Teaching Mediation as a Lawyering Role*, 39 J Legal Educ 571 (1989)

Norton, *Bargaining and the Ethic of Process*, 64 NYU L Rev 493 (1989)

Old Strike Foes Still Disagree, Chicago Trib, Feb 11, 1990, §3, at 14

O'Reilly, *Alternative Dispute Resolution under the NLRA: Devaluation of the Strike*, 6 Lab Law 133 (Winter 1990)

Organizing Training Materials (Midwest Academy, Chicago, Ill 1987)

Overton, *Strong Medicine from the Court*, CBA Rec 40 (Jan 1989)

Owners Move First with Lockout, Chicago Trib, Feb 19, 1990, §3, at 4

Owners vs. Union: The Game Within the Game, Chicago Trib, Sept 23, 1990, §3, at 9, cols 6-8

Pinckney, *Keeping the Faith*, 37 NY Rev Books, Nov 22, 1990, at 29

Players Can't Lose in Arbitration Game, Chicago Trib, Feb 19, 1991, §4, at 9

Playing Power Game at City Hall, Chicago Trib, July 3, 1991, §1, at 1

Politics Waylays Negotiations on Budget Deficit, Chicago Trib, July 31, 1990, §1, at 3

Posner, *The Summary Jury Trial and Other Methods of Alternative Dispute Resolution: Some Cautionary Observations*, 53 U Chi L Rev 366 (1986)

Pulliam, *Corporate Borrowers Bankers Love to Hate*, Corp Fin, Aug, 1989, at 34

Quinley & Khin, *We Love Settlements: An Insurer's Perspective*, 33 For The Defense 26 (Jan 1991)

Ray, *Emerging Options in Dispute Resolution*, 75 ABA J 66 (June 1989)

Rebel Truce Proposal Offered at Salvadoran Talks, Chicago Trib, Apr 5, 1991, §1, at 10

Recrafting America, Chicago Trib, Nov 6, 1991, §1, at 1

Rich Players Fat Targets for Ax-Wielding Owners, Chicago Trib, Apr 4, 1991, §4, at 3

Rieders, *Mediation: Pros and Cons*, 26 Trial 60 (Oct 1990)

Rohatyn, *The Fall and Rise of New York*, 37 NY Rev Books, Nov 8, 1990, at 40

Rude & Wall, *Judicial Involvement in Settlement: How Judges and Lawyers View It*, 72 Judicature 175 (1988)

Rundlett III, *Negotiating a Small Personal Injury Claim*, 27 Trial 55 (Oct 1991)

Sawaya, *Sometimes It Pays to Know More than Your Banker*, 1 Ernest & Young Real Est J 10 (Spring 1990)

M. Schoenfield & B. Schoenfield, *Interviewing and Counseling* 23 (1981)

Settlement Days Attract Interest, National Underwriter, June 22, 1992 at 6

Settlements Agreements: Keeping the IRS Away, Reed & Strattford's Structured Settlements-Technical Update (Apr 7, 1992)

Shadoan, *Pressure Points in Settlement Negotiations*, 27 Trial 36 (Aug 1991)

Shake Hands, Come out Bargaining, Chicago Trib, July 15, 1990, §7, at 1, cols 4-6

Soat Brown, *Differences Between Private Arbitration and Mandatory Court-Annexed Arbitration*, CBA Rec 20 (Apr/May 1991)

Special Master's Role Increasing in Complex Cases, Chicago Daily L Bull, Aug 3, 1992 at 5

Split Funded Structured Settlements, Reed & Strattford's Structured Settlements-Technical Update (Dec 8, 1992)

Stanley & Coursey, *Empirical Evidence on the Selection Hypothesis and the Decision to Litigate or Settle*, 19 J Legal Stud 145 (Jan 1990)

Still Far Apart on Auto Parts, Chicago Trib, Oct 6, 1991, §7, at 1

Stock Purchase Deal May Prevent Engine Manufacturer's Takeover, Chicago Trib, July 16, 1990, §1, at 4, cols 6-8

Sugar, *Cross-Purchase Agreements Are Often More Beneficial than Redemption Agreements*, 44 Taxn For Accts 148 (1990)

Sullivan, *The High-Low Agreement*, For the Defense 25 (July 1991)

Task Forces Studying Courts Find Mediation Biased Against Women, Chicago Daily L Bull, Aug 4, 1992, at 3

The Catch-22 of Mandatory Summary Jury Trials, 1990 J Dispute Resolution 135

The Press Box, Chicago Trib, Feb 18, 1991, §3, at 3

Twiggs, *Negotiating Claims with Insurance Adjusters*, 25 Trial 10 (May 1989)

Walton, *Critical Issues in Drafting Acquisition Agreements (with Forms)*, 14 ALI-ABA Course Materials J 107 (Aug 1989)

Where's the Info, Chicago Trib, Mar 31, 1991, §3, at 5

Wiegand, *A New Light Bulb or the Work of the Devil*, 69 Or L Rev 87 (1990)

Winslow, *Drafting for Reliability and Favorable Tax Treatment*, 24 Trial 21 (Dec 1988)

Winslow, *Security Interests in Structured Settlements*, 28 Trial 72 (May 1992)

Yeomans, *Counseling the Client on Commercial Arbitration Clauses*, 36 Practical Law 17 (Jan 1990)

Zmolek, *Art of Negotiation: Strategies and Tactics*, 27 Trial 22 (Aug 1991)

Index